JOHN WILLIS

SCREEN WORLD

1989

Volume 40

CROWN PUBLISHERS, INC.
201 East 50th Street
New York, New York 10022

Library of Congress Card No. 50–3023
ISBN 0-517-573326

TO

PAUL NEWMAN

whose athletic physique, handsome face, and exceptional talents as an actor, director, producer, political activist and philanthropist have deservedly kept him for 35 years among the top names on the world's popularity polls. In addition, whether by good judgment and/or good fortune, he has had the rare privilege of appearing in an impressive number of superior films.

LMS: The Silver Chalice (1954), the Rack/Somebody Up There Likes Me (1956), Until They Sail/The Helen Morgan Story/The Yard Run (TV/1957), Cat on a Hot Tin Roof (Oscar nomination)/Rally 'Round the Flag, Boys!/The Long Hot Summer/The ft-Handed Gun (1958), The Young Philadelphians (1959), From the Terrace/Exodus (1960), Paris Blues/The Hustler (Oscar mination)/1961), Hemingway's Adventures of a Young Man/Sweet Bird of Youth (1962), Hud (Oscar nomination)/A New nd of Love/The Prize (1963), What a Way to Go!/The Outrage (1964), Lady L (1965), Harper/Torn Curtain/Hombre (1966), ol Hand Luke (Oscar nomination)/The Secret War of Harry Frigg (1967), Winning/Butch Cassidy and the Sundance Kid 969), WUSA/King: A Filmed Record . . . Montgomery to Memphis (1970), Sometimes a Great Notion/Pocket Money (1971), e Life and Times of Judge Roy Bean (1972), The Sting/The Mackintosh Man (1973), The Towering Inferno (1974), The owning Pool (1975), Silent Movie/Buffalo Bill and the Indians (1976), Slap Shot (1977), Angel Death (narrator)/Quintet 979), When Time Ran Out (1980), Fort Apache the Bronx/Absence of Malice (1981), The Verdict (1982 Oscar nominated), rry and Son (1984), The Color of Money (1986 Oscar for Best Actor), Fat Man and Little Boy/Blaze/Mr. & Mrs. Bridge (1989)

RECTED: Rachel, Rachel (1968), Sometimes a Great Notion/Never Give an Inch (1971), The Effect of Gamma Rays on n-in-the-Moon Marigolds (1972), The Shadow Box (1980 TV), Harry and Son (1980), The Glass Menagerie (1987)

TOM CRUISE and DUSTIN HOFFMAN
in "Rain Man"
Academy Award for Best Picture
(United Artists)

CONTENTS

EDITOR: JOHN WILLIS
Assistant Editors: Barry Monush, Walter Willison

Staff: Marco Starr Boyajian, William Camp, Mark Cohen, Mark Gladstone, Doug Holmes, Miles Kreuger, Jerry Lacker, Tom Lynch, Stanley Reeves, Giovanni Romero, John Sala, Van Williams
Designer: Peggy Goddard

Acknowledgments: This volume would not be possible without the cooperation of Michelle Abbrecht, Michael Abeles, Ed Abosa, Barry Abrams, Ken Ausubel, Marina Bailey, Bill Banning, Regan Banderwerff, Nina Barron, John W. Beaman, Lewis Benavides, Marion Billings, Michael Blackwood, Rick Bowman, Ben Cammack, Diane Clinton, Elliot Chang, Guido Corso, Mickey Cottrell, Gale Daikoku, Joan Delaney, Mike Elliot, Zette Emmons, Jamie Geller, Jeffrey Godsick, Tom Grane, Aaron Griffith, Dan Harary, Stan Hayes, Peter Herzog, Jeffrey Hibert, Jeff Hill, Gayle Johnson, Terry Johnson, Amy Kimmelman, Margie Kitt, Lori Koonin, Zbigniew Kozlowski, Kim Langley, Pamela Lansberg, Wendy Lidell, Mark Lorber, Cathy Magill, Myrna Marcus, Jonathan Marder, Rikki Matthews, Michele Nasaway, Hap Passman, Brenda Perry, Robert Pleban, Heather Probert, Chris Regan, Patty Regan, Charles Rice, Mark E. Rosch, Lori Ruggiero, Tina Santanelli, Martin Schwartz, Richard Scott, Tajuana Sharpe, Jerilyn Shimandle, Stephen Soba, Richard T'Atille, Gwynne Thomas, Margaret Wass, Patty White, David Wright, Frank Wright

1. Tom Cruise
2. Eddie Murphy
3. Tom Hanks
4. Arnold Schwarzenegg
5. Paul Hogan
6. Danny De Vito
7. Bette Midler
8. Robin Williams
9. Tom Selleck
10. Dustin Hoffman
11. Cher
12. Michael Dougla
13. Sylvester Stallone
14. Michael J. Fox
15. John Candy
16. Bruce Willis

TOP 25 BOX OFFICE STARS OF 1988

(tabulated by Quigley Publications)

17. Mel Gibson

18. Glenn Close

19. Bill Murray

20. Sigourney Weaver

1988 RELEASES

January 1, through December 31, 1988

21. Harrison Ford

22. Clint Eastwood

23. Patrick Swayze

24. Meryl Streep

25. Steve Martin

Kevin Costner

Kathleen Turner

Michael Keaton

THE COUCH TRIP

(ORION) Producer, Lawrence Gordon; Director, Michael Ritchie; Screenplay, Steven Kampmann, Will Porter, Sean Stein; Based on a novel by Ken Kolb; Co-producer, Gordon A. Webb; Photography, Donald E. Thorin; Designer, Jimmie Bly; Editor, Richard A. Harris; Music, Michael Colombier; Music Performance, The Canadian Brass; Casting, Patricia Mock; Associate Producer, Tom Mack; Co-producer/ Production Manager, Gordon A. Webb; Assistant Directors, Tom Mack, Bruce Cohen; Production Supervisor, Pamela Easley; Set Decorator, Gary Fettis; Costume Supervisor, Eddie Marks; Costumers, Robin Borman, Stephen P. Shubin; Sound, Richard S. Church, James R. Alexander; Production Coordinator, Pamela Cederquist; Special Effects, Cliff Wenger; Stunts, Chuck Waters; Song: "*Fever*" by John Davenport, Eddie Cooley; DeLuxe Color; Rated R; 96 minutes; January release

CAST

John Burns .... Dan Aykroyd
Donald Becker .... Walter Matthau
George Maitlin .... Charles Grodin
Laura Rollins .... Donna Dixon
Harvey Michaels .... Richard Romanus
Vera Maitlin .... Mary Gross
Lawrence Baird .... David Clennon
Perry Kovin .... Arye Gross
Robin .... Victoria Jackson
Lopez .... Michael DeLorenzo
Watkins .... Mickey Jones
Unger .... J. E. Freeman
Dr. Smet .... David Wohl
Hendricks .... Michael Ensign
Mrs. Blair .... Carol Mansell
Night Watchman .... Robert Hirschfeld
TV Reporter .... Charles Levin
Klevin .... Scott Thomson
Condom Father .... Chevy Chase
Mrs. Guber .... Beverly Archer
Peterson .... Don Stark
and Kevin Rooney, Myrna White, Tony Rolon, Scott Weintraub, Donna Mitchell, Linda Rae Favila, David Grant Hayward, Jonathan Emerson, Gloria Dorson, Jerry Belson, Charles Sweigart, Susan Kellermann, Benbow Ritchie, Jack Ritchie, Jean Sterling, Susan Benn, Jan Cobler

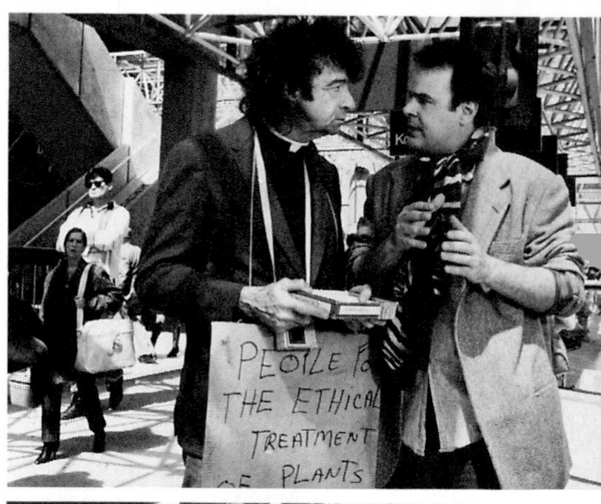

Right: Charles Grodin, Mary Gross, Richard Romanus, Scott Thomson Above: Donna Dixon, Walter Matthau, Dan Aykroyd Top: Walter Matthau, Dan Aykroyd *(Orion Pictures)*

Walter Matthau, Dan Aykroyd

Donna Dixon, Dan Aykroyd

Randall Batinkoff, Molly Ringwald (also top right)
Right: Miriam Flynn, Molly Ringwald, Kenneth Mars

FOR KEEPS?

'RI-STAR) Producers, Jerry Belson, Walter Coblenz; Director/ litor, John G. Avildsen; Screenplay, Tim Kazurinsky, Denise De- ue; Photography, James Crabe; Designer, William J. Cassidy; Cos- mes, Colleen Atwood; Music, Bill Conti; Casting, Caro Jones, Pat cCorkie; Production Manager, Jack Terry; Assistant Directors, Ron Wright, W. Kalaeloa Strode, Alice Blanchard; Associate Producers, illiam J. Cassidy, Douglas Seelig; Production Associate, Cindy erson; Set Decorator, Richard C. Goddard; Set Designer, Bernard itler; Assistant Editors, William Joseph Kruzykowski, Mitchel Stan- y, James H. Nau, Scott Arundale, Jerry C. Rogers; Sound, Kirk ancis, Neil Kaufman; Music Consultant, Stephen A. Hope; Special fects, Jerry D. Williams, Bob Stoker, Jr.; Production Coordinator, obin Hinz; Songs by various artists; From Tri-Star-ML Delphi Pre- ier Productions; Dolby Stereo; Technicolor; Rated PG-13; 98 inutes; January release

CAST

arcy .... Molly Ringwald
an .... Randall Batinkoff
r. Bobrucz .... Kenneth Mars
rs. Elliot .... Miriam Flynn
rs. Bobrucz .... Conchata Ferrell
la .... Sharon Brown
everend Kim .... Jack Ong
ee Willy .... Sean Frye
mbrosia .... Allison Roth
ce .... Trevor Edmond
esdemona .... Patricia Patts
rapper .... Brandon Douglas
aby Cakes .... Kimberly Bailey
on .... Darnell Rose
igh Flyer .... J. W. Fails
ngel .... Monika Khoury
rs. Sitwell .... Bonnie Hellman
eth .... Robin Morse
onald .... Steve Eckholdt
nastasia .... Annie Oringer
everly .... Pamela Harris
aby Thea .... Hailey Ellen Agnew
apt. O'Connell .... Tino Insana
gt. Blaine .... Steven Barr
hris .... John Zarchen
etro .... Pauly Shore
lichaela .... Michelle Downey
liss Giles .... Janet MacLachlan
ary Bobrucz .... Jaclyn Bernstein
ou Bobrucz .... Matthew Licht
larnie .... Renee Estevez
aine .... Darcy DeMoss
arlita .... Leslie Bega
r. Kolby .... John DiSanti

id Kelly McMahan, Candy Peak, Robert Ruth, Nancy Abramson, andra Jansen, Dr. Barry Herman, Jeff Marshall, Peggy Walton- 'alker, Larry Drake, Marty Zagon, Rae Worland, David Delange, oger Hampton, Patricia Barry, Helen Siff, Anne Curry, Robert Nad- r, Shane McCabe

Right Center: Molly Ringwald, Randall Batinkoff
(Tri-Star Pictures)

Janet MacLachlan, Molly Ringwald

5 CORNERS

(CINEPLEX ODEON) Producers, Forrest Murray, Tony Bill; Dire tor, Tony Bill; Screenplay, John Patrick Shanley; Casting, Doug Aib Editor, Andy Blumenthal; Music, James Newton Howard; Costume Peggy Farrell; Designer, Adrianne Lobel; Photography, Fred Murph Associate Producers, Michael McDonnell, John Patrick Shanley; Exe utive Producers, George Harrison, Denis O'Brien; Production Man ger, J. Boyce Harman, Jr., Assistant Directors, Joel Segal, Micha Ingber; Sound, Bill Daly; Set Decorator, Linda Ekstrand; Speci Effects, Bill Harison, Dan Kirshoff; Stunts, Jery Hewitt; Assista Editor, Claudia Hoover; Songs by various artists; Technicolor; minutes; Rated R; January release

CAST

Linda .... Jodie Fost
Harry .... Tim Robbi
James .... Todd Gr
Heniz .... John Turtur
Murray .... Michael R. Howa
George .... Pierre Epste
Mr. Glascow .... Jery Hew
Castro .... Rodney Harv
Willie .... Daniel Jenki
Melanie .... Elizabeth Berrid
Brita .... Cathryn De Prun
Sal .... Carl Capotor
Mrs. Fitzgerald .... Kathleen Chalfa
Sullivan .... John Se
Cop .... Anthony Powe
Desk Sergeant .... Jack McG
Mazola .... Gregory Rozak
Mrs. Sabantino .... Rose Grego
Bartender .... Mike St
Esther .... Kit Le Fev
Waitress .... Frances Fost
Samuel Kemp .... Eriq La Sa
Arthur .... Ray Aran
Plainclothesman .... David Brisb
and Jose Soto, Jr., Jerome Collamaore, Bill Cobbs, Robert Lempe Keith Reddin, Pepe Douglas, Dann Florek, Alex Kramarevsky, Thor as Kudlek, Mike Lisenco, Regis Mullavey, Frank Patton, James Rya Cambell Scott, Joel Segal, Victor Slezak, Richard Thomsen, Ma Small

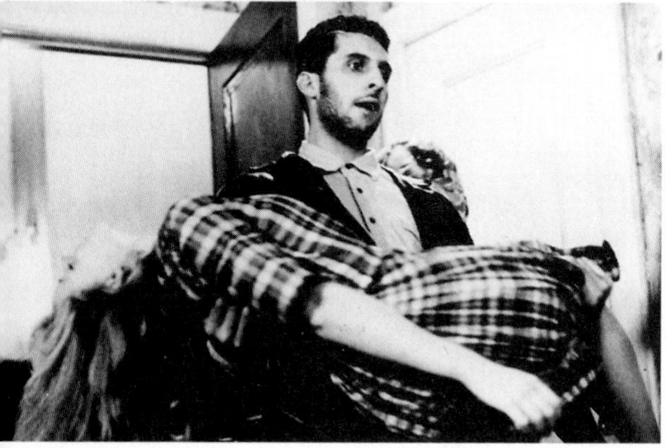

Left: John Turturro, Jodie Foster Above: Tim Robbins Top Left: Todd Graff, Jodie Foster *(Cineplex Odeon Films)*

John Turturro

Todd Graff

Chris Mulkey, John Jenkins, Karen Landry
Above: John Jenkins, Chris Mulkey Top Right: Chris Mulkey, John Jenkins Below: Chris Mulkey John Jenkins,

PATTI ROCKS

FILMDALLAS) Producers, Gwen Field, Greogry M. Cummins;)irector, David Burton Morris; Story/Screenplay, David Burton Moris, Chris Mulkey, John Jenkins, Karen Landry; Based on Characters 'reated by Victoria Wozniak; Executive Producer, Sam Grogg; Photo:raphy/Editor, Gregory M. Cummins; Art Director/Costumes, Charotte Whitaker; Music, Doug Maynard; Associate Producer, Brian John)iLorenzo; FilmDallas Executive, Marcus McWaters; Assistant Diectors, Kirby Dick, Daniel Gumnit, Derek Monroe; Casting, Laurie ;rossman; Special Effects, Gary Boham; Spiritual Advisor, John Mac;raw; Music Arranger, Doug Maynard; Music Producers, John Penny,)oug Maynard; Assistant Editor, Tonicka Janek; Sound, Matthew)uast; Color; 86 minutes; Rated R; January release

CAST

3illy .... Chris Mulkey
:ddie .... John Jenkins
'atti .... Karen Landry
3arge Worker .... David L. Turk
3artender .... Stephen Yoakam
)runken Couple .... Sally Tronnes, Ken Tronnes
)ld Drunk .... Ralph Estlie
'hicano Mechanic .... Joe Minjares
;as Station Attendant .... Brian Lambert
;teambeast .... Buffy Sedlachek
;teambeast's Daughter .... Joy Langer
)ld Lady .... Mae Mayhew

Chris Mulkey (Left)

Daniel Day-Lewis, Juliette Binoche
Top Right: Juliette Binoche, Daniel Day-Lewis
Right: Juliette Binoche, Daniel Day-Lewis

THE UNBEARABLE LIGHTNESS OF BEING

(ORION) Producer, Saul Zaentz; Director, Philip Kaufman; Screenplay, Jean-Claude Carriere, Philip Kaufman; Adapted from the Milan Kundera novel; Photography, Sven Nykvist; Supervising Editor, Walter Murch; Costumes, Ann Roth; Designer, Pierre Guffroy; Executive Producer, Bertil Ohlsson; Associate Producer, Paul Zaentz; Sabrina's Painting, Irena Dedicova; Casting, Dianne Crittenden, Margot Capelier, Sarah Koeppe; Special Consultant, Jan Nemec; Production Managers, Daniel Szuster, Jacques Bourdon; Assistant Directors, Charels Paviot, Eric Bartonio, Robert Kechichian, Vincent Bercholz; Production Coordinator, Judith Atwell; Sound, Chris Newman; Art Director Exteriors, Gerard Viard; Assistant Art Directors, Alain Guffroy, Albert Rajau, Anouk Markovits; Assistant Designers, Christian Ameri, Jamie Putnam; Special Effects, Trielli Bros.; Stunts, Remy Julienne; Music, Leos Janacek; Music Editor, Alan Splet; Original Music/Arrangements, Mark Adler; Dolby Stereo; DeLuxe Color; Rated R; 172 minutes; February release

CAST

Tomas .... Daniel Day Lewis
Tereza .... Juliette Binoche
Sabina .... Lena Olin
Franz .... Derek de Lint
The Ambassador .... Erland Josephson
Pavel .... Pavel Landovsky
Chief Sugeon .... Donald Moffat
Interior Ministry Official .... Daniel Olbrychski
The Engineer .... Stellan Skarsgard
Jiri .... Tomek Bork
Czech Editor .... Bruce Myers
Pavel's Nephew .... Pavel Slaby
Nurse Katya .... Pascale Kalensky
Swiss Restaurant manager .... Jacques Ciron
Swiss Photographer .... Anne Lonnberg
and Jacqueline Abraham-Vernier, Judith Atwell, Claudine Berg, Jean-Claude Bouillon, Miroslav Breuer, Niven Busch, Margot Capelier, Victor Chelkoff, Monica Constandache, Jean-Claude Dauphin, Dominique de Moncuit, Bernard Lepinaux, Josiane Leveque, Peter Majer, Laszlo Szabo, Vladimir Valenta, Clovis Covnillac, Leon Lissek, Consuelo de Haviland

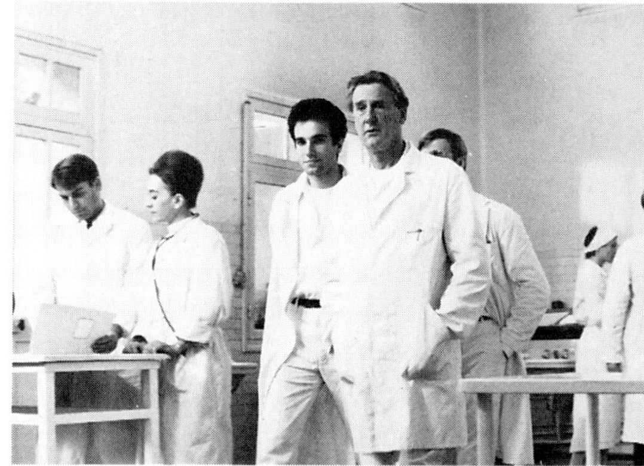

Right Center: Daniel Day-Lewis, Donald Moffat, Tomek Bork
(Orion Pictures)

Lena Olin, Daniel Day-Lewis

SHE'S HAVING A BABY

(PARAMOUNT) Producer/Director/Screenplay, John Hughes; Executive Producer, Ronald Colby; Photography, Don Peterman; Music, Stewart Copeland; Designer, John W. Corso; Editor, Alan Heim; Associate Producer, Bill Brown; Costumes, April Ferry; Casting, Janet Hirshenson, Jane Jenkins; Music Supervisor, Tarquin Gotch; Production Managers, Ronald Colby, James Herbert; Assistant Directors, Mark Radcliffe, James Giovanetti, Jr.; Set Decorator, Jennifer Polito; Stunts, Conrad E. Palmisano; Choreographer, Tony Stevens; Sound, James Alexander; Songs by various artists; Technicolor; Dolby Stereo; Rated PG-13; 106 minutes; February release

CAST

Jake Briggs .... Kevin Bacon
Kristy Briggs .... Elizabeth McGovern
Davis McDonald .... Alec Baldwin
Jim Briggs .... James Ray
Sarah Briggs .... Holland Taylor
Russ Bainbridge .... William Windom
Gayle Bainbridge .... Cathryn Damon
Grandmother .... Reba McKinney
Grandfather .... Bill Erwin
Howard .... Paul Gleason
Bill .... Dennis Dugan
Minister .... Anthony Mockus, Sr.
Ken .... John Ashton
Hank .... Larry Hankin
Lynn .... Edie McClurg
Cynthia .... Nancy Lenehan
Man with bike .... Steve Tannen
Young Jake .... Neal Bacon
Young Kristy .... Laure Aronica
Erin .... Valeri Breiman
Fantasy Girl .... Isabel Lorca
Photographer .... Al Leong
Girl at medical lab. .... Lili Taylor
Nurse at lab .... Sherry Narens
Nurse at hospital .... Kellye Nakahara
Receptionist .... Ellen Dweck
and Lis Neimi, Trudy Dochterman, Angela Alvarado (Models), Dr. Seth Yoser, M.D. (Doctor), Ruth F. Ekholm, Mimi Cagnetta, Susan Canestro, Bernadette Pelletier, Ingrid Ferring (Nurses), Patrick J. Salisbury (Groomsman), Gail O'Grady (Laura)

Right: Elizabeth McGovern, Kevin Bacon
Top: Alec Baldwin, Kevin Bacon *(Paramount Pictures)*

John Ashton, Kevin Bacon, Larry Hankin

Elizabeth McGovern, Nancy Lenehan, Edie McClurg

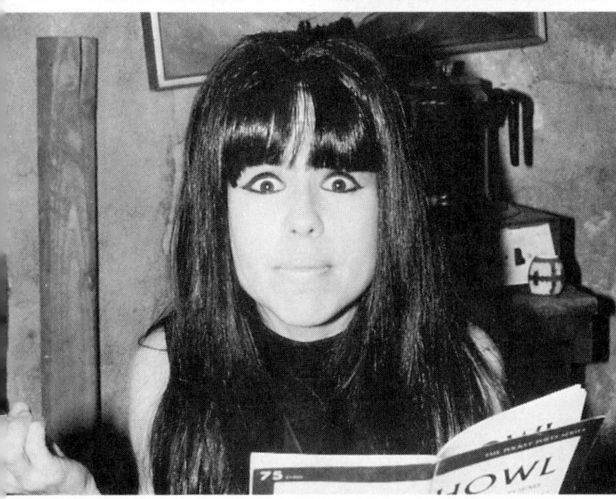

Pia Zadora

HAIRSPRAY

(NEW LINE CINEMA) Producer, Rachel Talalay; Director, Screenplay, John Waters; Executive Producers, Robert Shaye, Sar Risher; Co-Producers, Stanley F. Buchthal, John Waters; Line Producer, Robert Maier; Photography, David Insley; Editor, Janice Hampton; Hair Design, Christine Mason; Costume and Make-up Design, Va Smith; Art Director, Vincent Peranio; Casting, Mary Coquhoun, Pa Moran; Choreographer, Edward Love; Music Supervisor, Bonni Greenberg; Original Music, Kenny Vance; Production Manager, Pa Moran; Production Supervisor, Aron J. Warner; Assistant Directors Stephen Apicella, Julia Cort; Songs by various artists; Color; Ultra-Stereo; Rated PG; 90 minutes; February release

CAST

Franklin Von Tussle .... Sonny Bon
Motormouth Maybell .... Ruth Brow
Edna Turnblad/Arvin Hodgepile .... Divin
Amber Von Tussle .... Colleen Fitzpatric
Link Larkin .... Michael St. Gerar
Velma Von Tussle .... Debbie Harr
Tracy Turnblad .... Ricki Lak
Penny Pingleton .... Leslie Ann Power
Seaweed .... Clayton Princ
Wilbur Turnblad .... Jerry Stille
Tammy .... Mink Stol
Corny Collins .... Shawn Thompso
Beatnik Cat .... Ric Ocase
Beatnik Girl .... Pia Zador
Iggy .... Josh Charle
Bobby .... Jason Down
I. Q. .... Holter Ford Graha
Brad .... Dan Griffit
Pam .... Regina Hammon
Consuella .... Bridget Kimse
Dash .... Frankie Maldo
Lou Ann .... Brooke Mill
Fender .... Jon Orofin
Carmelita .... Kim Web
Shelly .... Debra Wirt
Nadine .... Dawn Hil
L'il Inez .... Cyrkle Milbourn
Mr. Pinky .... Alan Wend
Prudence Pingleton .... Jo Ann Havrill
Governor .... Leo Rocc
Dr. Fredrickson .... John Water
Himself .... Toussaint McCal
Gym Teacher .... Kathleen Wallac
Lead Lafayette .... Keith Dougla

Left: Colleen Fitzpatrick, Debbie Harry, Sonny Bono Above: Mink Stole, Shawn Thompson Top Left: Jerry Stiller, Ricki Lake, Divine *(New Line Cinema)*

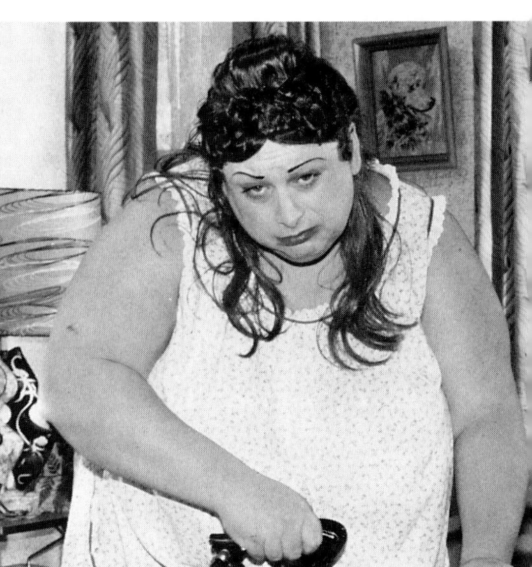

Divine

SHOOT TO KILL

(TOUCHSTONE) Producers, Ron Silverman, Daniel Petrie, Jr.; Director, Roger Spottiswoode; Screenplay, Harv Zimmel, Michael Burton, Daniel Petrie, Jr.; Story, Harv Zimmel; Executive Producer, Philip Rogers; Photography, Michael Chapman; Production Designer, Richard Sylbert; Editors, Garth Craven, George Bowers; Costumes, Richard Bruno; Music, John Scott; Casting, Penny Perry; Associate Producer, Fredda Weiss; Assistant Directors, Michael Steele, Julia Dastoor; Second Unit Director/Stunt Coordinator, Fred Waugh; Art Director, John Willett; Set Decorator, Jim Erickson; Special Effects Supervisor, John Thomas; Sound, Simon Kaye; Presented in association with Silver Screen Partners III; Distributed by Buena Vista; Alpha Cine color; Panavision; Dolby Stereo; Rated R; 106 minutes; February release

CAST

Warren Stantin .... Sidney Poitier
Jonathan Knox .... Tom Berenger
Sarah .... Kirstie Alley
Steve .... Clancy Brown
Norman .... Richard Masur
Harvey .... Andrew Robinson
Ben .... Kevin Scannell
Ralph .... Frederick Coffin
Fournier .... Michael MacRae
Minelli .... Robert Lesser
Mr. Berger .... Milton Selzer
Sheriff Arnett .... Les Lannom
Sam Baker .... Walter Marsh
Crilly .... Frank C. Turner
Inspector Hsu .... Samuel Hiona
Lawyer .... Michael Chapman
Mrs. Berger .... Janet Rotblatt
Denham .... Ken Camroux
Fisherman .... Howard Storey
Agent Owenby .... Fred Henderson
Maid .... Robyn Masumi Gildemeester
FBI Agents .... Jerry Wasserman, Gloria Lee
Computer Operator .... Freda Perry
San Francisco Policeman .... Kevin McNulty
Police Captain .... William Taylor
SWAT Sergeant .... Ric Reid
Mildred .... Claire Brown
Undercover Priest .... Blu Mankuma
Inspector .... Gary Hetherington
Sergeant .... Allan Lysall
Woman with stroller .... Michelle Goodger
Nuns .... Beatrice Boepple, Darcelle Chan
Couple .... Marynna Danguy, Craig Saunders
Woman with purse .... Carole Henshall
Purse Snatcher .... Andrew Rhodes
Washington State Patrolman .... Bill Croft

Left: Sidney Poitier, Tom Berenger (Also Above and Top) ***(Touchstone Pictures)***

Kirstie Alley, Tom Berenger

Sidney Poitier

Eric Stoltz *(New World Pictures)*

SISTER SISTER

(NEW WORLD) Producer, Walter Coblenz; Director, Bill Condc Screenplay, Bill Condon, Joel Cohen, Ginny Cerrella; Executive Pr ducers, Gabe Sumner, J. David Marks; Photography, Stephen M. Ka Editor, Marion Rothman; Music, Richard Einhorn; Production Exec tive, Joel Cohen; Costumes, Bruce Finlayson; Designer, Richa Sherman; Casting, Linda Francis; Associate Producers, Pegi Brotma Ira Trattner, Yvonne Ramond; Production Managers, Chuck Comisk Bill Wells; Assistant Directors, Phillip Christon, Suzanne Haas William A. Shea; Production Consultant, Gilles De Turenne; Art I rector, Philip Peters; Set Decorator, Cynthia Rebman; Producti Coordinator, Lisa Lunn Kearsley; Sound, David Lewis Yewdall, L Strosnider; Special Effects, Wayne Beauchamp, Paul Hickersc Stunts, Harry Wowchuk; Associate Editor, Virginia Katz; Orchest tions, Edgardo Simone; *"That Same Old Song"* by J. C. Phillips, B Boykin, and songs by various other artists; Presented in Associati with Odyssey Entertainment, Ltd.; Technicolor; Rated R; 91 minut February release

CAST

Matt Rutledge .... Eric Sto
Lucy Bonnard .... Jennifer Jason Lei
Charlotte Bonnard .... Judith Iv
Cleve Doucet .... Dennis Lipscor
Mrs. Bettleheim .... Anne Pitoni
Etienne LeViolette .... Benjamin Mout
Fran Steuben .... Natalia Noguli
Lenny Steuben .... Richard Minchenbe
Roger .... Bobby Pick
Jud Nevins .... Jason Sauc
Mr. Bonnard .... Jerry Legg
Mrs. Bonnard .... Fay Cc
Young Lucy .... Ashley McMu
Young Matt .... Ben Co
Young Etienne .... Casey Lev
Beau .... Ag

SCHOOL DAZE

(COLUMBIA) Producer/Director/Screenplay, Spike Lee; Co-Producers, Loretha C. Jones, Monty Ross; Executive Producer, Grace Blake; Photography, Ernest Dickerson; Editor, Barry Alexander Brown; Music, Bill Lee; Designer, Wynn Thomas; Choreographer, Otis Sallid; Casting, Robi Reed; Costumes, Ruthe Carter; Sound, Maurice Schell; Assistant Director, Randy Fletcher; Art Director, Allan Trumpler; Songs by various artists; a Forty Acres and a Mule Filmworks production; Dolby Stereo; Duart color/Deluxe color; Rated R; 114 minutes

CAST

Dap Dunlap .... Larry Fishburne
Julian Eaves .... Giancarlo Esposito
Jane Toussaint .... Tisha Campbell
Rachel Meadows .... Kyme
President McPherson .... Joe Seneca
Odrie McPherson .... Ellen Holly
Cedar Cloud .... Art Evans
Coach Odom .... Ossie Davis
Half-Pint .... Spike Lee
and Da Fellas: Bill Nunn (Grady), James Bond III (Monroe), Branford Marsalis (Jordan), Kadeem Hardison (Edge), Eric A. Payne (Booker T.); The Gammites: Anthony Thompkins (Doo-Doo Breath), Guy Killum (Double Rubber), Dominic Hoffman (Mustafa), Roger Smith (Yoda), Kirk Taylor (Sir Nose), Kevin Rock (Mussolini), Eric Dellums (Slim Daddy); Gamma Phi Gamma Big Brothers: Darryl M. Bell (X-Ray Vision), Rusty Cundieff (Chucky), Cylk Cozart (Dr. Feelgood), Tim Hutchinson (Lance), Leonard Thomas (Gen. George Patton); Jigaboos: Joie Lee (Lizzie Life), Alva Rogers (Doris Witherspoon), Delphine T. Mantz (Delphine), Terri Lynette Whitlow, Tanya Lynne Lee, Jacquelyn Bird, Traci Tracey, Sharon Ferrol, Laurnea Wilkerson, Stephanie Clark, Eartha Robinson; Gamma Rays: Angela Ali (Velda), Jhoe Breedlove (Kim), Paula Brown (Miriam); Tyra Ferrell (Tasha), Jasmine Guy (Dina), Karen Owens (Deidre), Michelle Whitney Morrison (Vivian), Greta Martin, Sharon Owens, Frances Morgan, Monique Mannen; Gregg Burge (Virgil Cloud), Cinque Lee (Buckwheat), Phyllis Hyman

Right Center: Giancarlo Esposito, Spike Lee *(Columbia Pictures)*

Tisha Campbell (Center)

FRANTIC

WARNER BROS.) Producers, Thom Mount, Tim Hampton; Director, Roman Polanski; Screenplay, Roman Polanski, Gerard Brach; Music/Orchestrations, Ennio Morricone; Editor, Sam O'Steen; Photography, Witold Sobocinski; Designer, Pierre Guffroy; Costumes, Anthony Powell; Casting, Margot Capelier, Bonnie Timmermann; Assistant Director, Michel Cheyko; Sound, Jean-Pierre Ruh; Production Manager, Daniel Szuster; Assistant Art Directors, Albert Rajau, Gerard Viard; Choreographer, Derf La Chapelle; Stunts, Daniel Breton; Music Coordinator, Enrico De Melis; *"I'm Gonna' Lose You"* by Mick Hucknall, and other songs by various artists; Soundtrack on Elektra Records; Dolby Stereo; Color; Rated R; 120 minutes; February release

CAST

ichard Walker .... Harrison Ford
ondra Walker .... Betty Buckley
Iichelle .... Emmanuelle Seigner
'axi Driver .... Djiby Soumare
esk Clerk .... Dominique Virton
aillard .... Gerard Klein
ellboys .... Stephane D'Audeville, Roch Leibovici, Alan Ladd
Iall Porter .... Laurent Spielvogel, Alain Doutey
Iotel Manager .... Jacques Ciron
ourist .... Louise Vinceni
Iotel Detective .... Patrice Melennec
estroom Attendant .... Ella Jaroszewicz
lorist .... Joelle Lagneau, Jean-Pierre Delage
'afe Owner .... Marc Dudicourt
Vaiter .... Artus De Penguern
Vino .... Dominique Pinon
esk Cop .... Richard Dieux
ıspector .... Yves Renier
.S. Security Officer .... Robert Ground
Iarine Guard .... Burce Johnson
.S. Embassy Clerk .... Michael Morris, Claude Doineau
Villiams .... John Mahoney
haap .... Jimmie Ray Weeks
Blue Parrot" Barman .... Andre "Quiqui"
astafarian .... Thomas M. Pollard
ede Martin .... Boll Boyer
WA Clerk .... Tina Sportolaro
eter .... David Huddleston
die .... Alexandra Stewart
win .... Robert Barr
he Kidnapper .... Yorgo Voyagis
he Bodyguard .... David Jalil
r. Metlaoui .... Raouf Ben Amor
nd Patrick Floersheim, Marcel Bluwal, Isabelle Noah, Fonky French amily, Jean-Claude Houbard

Right: Emmanuelle Seigner, Harrison Ford (Also Above) Top: Betty Buckley, Harrison Ford ***(Warner Bros.)***

Harrison Ford, Emmanuelle Seigner

Harrison Ford

THE SERPENT AND THE RAINBOW

(UNIVERSAL) Producers, David Ladd, Doug Claybourne; Director, Wes Craven; Screenplay, Richard Maxwell, A. R. Simoun; Inspired by the book by Wade Davis; Executive Producers, Rob Cohen, Keith Barish; Photography, John Lindley; Designer, David Nichols; Editor, Glenn Farr; Music, Brad Fiedel; Costumes, Peter Mitchell; Casting, Dianne Crittenden; Associate Producer, David B. Pauker; Assistant Directors, Bob Engelman, George P. Gregg; Production Executive, Curtis Burch; Sound Designer, Jay Boekelheide; Special Make-up Effects, Lance Anderson, David Anderson; Special Mechanical Effects, Image Engineering; Supervisor of Special Visual Effects, Gary Gutierrez; Special Choreography, Carmen De Lavallade; Art Director, David Brisbin; Set Designer, Dawn Snyder; Production Consultant, Ramiro Jaloma; Duart color; Dolby Stereo; Rated R; 98 minutes; February release

CAST

Dennis Alan .... Bill Pullman
Marielle Celine .... Cathy Tyson
Dargent Peytraud .... Zakes Mokae
Lucien Celine .... Paul Winfield
Mozart .... Brent Jennings
Christophe .... Conrad Roberts
Gaston .... Badja Djola
Simone .... Theresa Merritt
Schoonbacher .... Michael Gough
Andrew Cassedy .... Paul Guilfoyle
Mrs. Cassedy .... Dey Young
Celestine .... Aleta Mitchell
French Missionary Doctor .... William Newman
Julio .... Jaime Pina Gautier
Old Shaman .... Evencio Mosquera Slaco
Margrite .... Kimberleigh Burroughs
Priest .... Philogen Thomas
Mulatto Nurse .... Ana Rosa Smith Avila
American Doctor .... Francis Guinan
Nurse/Intern .... Sally-Anne Munn
Black Waiter .... Jean-Baptiste Rosvelt
Old Lame Peasant .... Robert De James
Possessed Dancer .... Jackson Delgado
Mozart's Whore .... Barbara Guillaume
Pretty Whore .... Betty Garcia Rodriguez
Kyle Cassedy .... Luis Tavare Pesquera
Old Crone .... Claudia Pimentel
Newscaster .... Michael Jackson

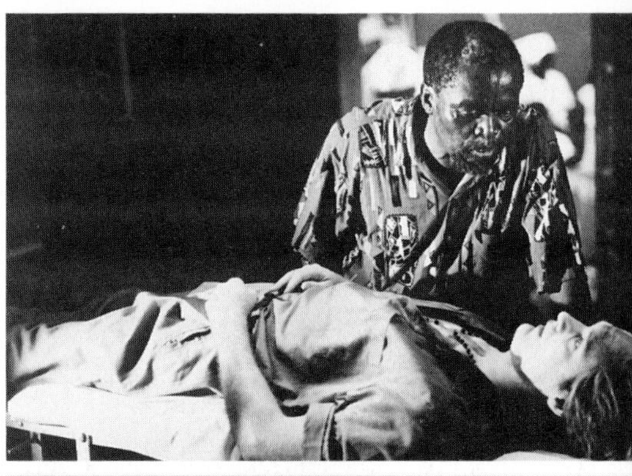

Right: Zakes Mokae, Bill Pullman, Badja Djola Above: Conrad Roberts Top: Zakes Mokae, Bill Pullman
(Universal Pictures)

Badja Djola, Cathy Tyson

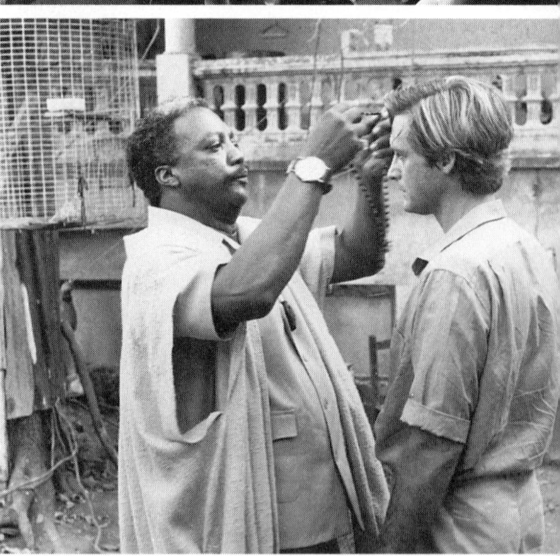

Paul Winfield, Bill Pullman

Burt Reynolds, Kathleen Turner Top Right: Christopher Reeve Right: Ned Beatty

SWITCHING CHANNELS

TRI-STAR) Producer, Martin Ransohoff; Director, Ted Kotcheff; Screenplay, Jonathan Reynolds; Based upon the play entitled *"The Front Page"* by Ben Hecht & Charles MacArthur; Executive Producer, Don Carmody; Photography, Francois Protat; Designer, Anne Pritchard; Editor, Thom Noble; Music, Michel Legrand; Casting, Lynn Stalmaster; Production Manager, Joyce Kozy King; Assistant Directors, Jim Kaufman, Kim Winther, Blair Roth; Theme Music, Michel Legrand, Neil Diamond; Production Coordinator, Deborah Zwicker; Art Director, Charles Dunlop; Set Decorators, Mark Freeborn, Rose Marie McSherry; Sound, David Lee, Special Effects, Rory Cutler; Costumes, Mary Mcleod; Assistant Costume Designer, Gail Filman; Stunts, Stuntco International; Color; Dolby Stereo; Rated PG; 108 minutes; March release

CAST

Christy Colleran .... Kathleen Turner
John L. Sullivan, IV .... Burt Reynolds
Blaine Bingham .... Christopher Reeve
Roy Ridnitz .... Ned Beatty
Ike Roscoe .... Henry Gibson
Siegenthaler .... George Newbern
Berger .... Al Waxman
Warden Terwilliger .... Ken James
Zaks .... Barry Flatman
Tillinger .... Ted Simonett
Carvalho .... Anthony Sherwood
Morosini .... Joe Silver
The Governor .... Charles Kimbrough
Jessica .... Monica Parker
Obregon .... Allan Royal
Pamela Farbrother .... Fiona Reid
Jesse .... Andre Mayers
Eric .... Bill Randolph
Governor's Aide .... Richard Comar
Crannock .... Grant Cowan
Bryce .... Wayne Fleming
Karen Ludlow .... Laura Robinson
Ridnitz's Sidekick .... Angelo Rizacos
Joker .... Tony Rosato
Abigail .... Jackie Richardson
Chaplain .... Jonathan Welsh
Jasper .... Russell Gordon
Yvonne .... Corrine Koslo
Nancy .... Noel Gray
"8" Cameraman .... Philip Malotte
Cop .... Chick Roberts
Rusty .... Bill Cotterell
Anchorman .... James Loxley
SNN Anchor Persons .... Cheryl S. Wilson, Ray Landry
Tattooee .... Peter Walachy
Aide .... John Davies
Butler .... Eric Fink
Emil, The Waiter .... Jack Duffy
and Laurie Paton, Warren Davis, Katya Ladan, Rex Hagon, Philip Akin, Patrick Patterson, Judah Katz, Jason Blicker, Diane Douglass, Ida Carnevali, Megan Smith, Jane Schoettle, John Dee, Robert Morel-, Arlene Mazerolle

Right Center: Kathleen Turner
(Tri-Star Pictures)

Christopher Reeve, Burt Reynolds, Kathleen Turner

STAND AND DELIVER

(WARNER BROS.) Producer, Rom Musca; Director, Ramo Menendez; Screenplay, Ramon Menendez, Tom Musca; Executiv Producer, Lindsay Law; Music, Craig Safan; Editor, Nanc Richardson; Photography, Tom Richmond; Associate Producer Production Manager, Iya Labunka; Art Director, Milo; Costumes Kathryn Morrison; Casting, Jaki Brown, Toni Livingston; Assistar Directors, Elliot Rosenblatt, John Scherer; Production Coordinator Vicki Rocco; Sound, Steve Halbert; Assistant Art Director A. Ja Vetter; Stunts, Perry Huseman; Assistant Editors, Christi Moore, Pau Wagner; *"Stand and Deliver"* by Richard Page, Steve George, Joh Lang/Performed by Mr. Mister; *"I Want You"* by Keith Clark Performed by Zander Schloss, Keith Clark, and songs by various othe artists; An American Playhouse Theatrical Film; A Menendez/Musca & Olmos Production; Technicolor; Rated PG; 103 minutes; March releas

CAST

Jaime Escalante .... Edward James Olmo
Raquel Ortega .... Virginia Par
Tito .... Mark Elic
Pancho .... Adelaida Alvare
Javier .... Patrick Bac
Lupe .... Ingrid Oli
Molina .... Carmen Argenzian
Joe Goddell .... Tyde Kierne
Fabiola Escalante .... Rosana De Sot
Fernando Escalante .... Bodie Olmo
Claudia .... Karla Montan
Ana .... Vanessa Marque
Chuco .... Danile Villarrea
Angel .... Lou Diamond Phillip
Coach .... Michael Goldfinge
Sanzaki .... Michael Yam
Rafaela .... Lydia Nicol
Craig .... Graham Gallowa
Angel's Grandma .... Betty Carvalh
Lupe's Mother .... Irene Olga Lope
Ana's Father .... James Victo
Claudia's Mother .... Yvette Cruis
Jaime Escalante, Jr. .... Victor Garro
Schloss .... Michael Adle
Proctor .... Barbara Ver
Ramirez .... Andy Garci
Pearson .... Rif Hutto

and Estelle Harris, Mark Phelan, Adelaida Alvarez, Richard Martinez Mart Everett, Aixa Clemente, Star Frohman, Jessica Seynos, Domini Lucero, Sonia Fuentes, David Brian Abalos, Irma Barrios, Henr Torres, Beatrie Giraldo, Richard Moreno, Phillip Elizalde

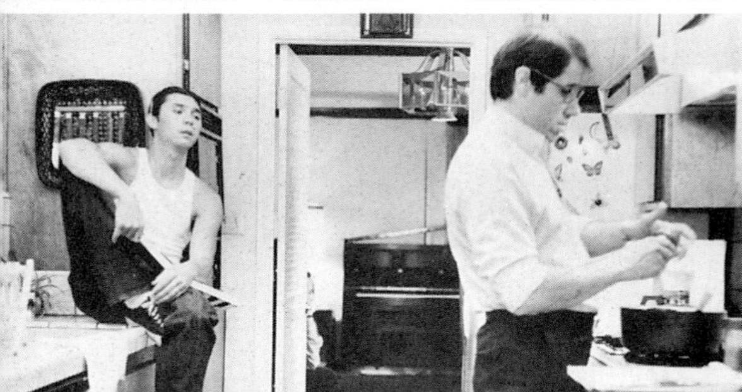

Left: Will Gotay, Victor Garron, Edward James Olmos, Bodie Olmos, Rosana DeSoto, Karla Monatana, Lou Diamond Phillips Above: Phillips, Olmos Top: Phillips, Mark Eliot, Olmos ***(Warner Bros.)***

Daniel Villarreal, Edward James Olmos

Edward James Olmos, Lou Diamond Phillips

Jeff Daniels, Kelly McGillis (Also Right), Top Right: Jessica Tandy

THE HOUSE ON CARROLL STREET

)RION) Producer/Director, Peter Yates; Co-Producer, Robert F. olesberry; Screenplay, Walter Bernstein; Executive Producers, rlene Donovan, Robert Benton; Music, Georges Delerue; Editor, Ray ovejoy; Photography, Michael Ballhaus; Designer, Stuart Wurtzel; ostumes, Rita Ryack; Art Director, W. Steven Graham; Set Decora-r, George DeTitta, Jr.; Casting, Howard Feuer; Associate Producer, ellie Nugiel; Production Manager, Thomas A. Razzano; Assistant irectors, Joseph Reidy, Amy Sayres; Sound, Tod Maitland; Deluxe olor; Rated PG; 101 minutes; March release

CAST

nily Crane .... Kelly McGillis
ochran .... Jeff Daniels
ay Salwen .... Mandy Patinkin
iss Venable .... Jessica Tandy
an .... Jonathan Hogan
enator Byington .... Remak Ramsay
ackett .... Ken Welsh
efan .... Christopher Rhode
lwen Aides .... Charles McCaughan, Randle Mell
enator .... Michael Flanagan
andolph Slote .... Paul Sparer
arren .... Brian Davies
aid .... Mary Diveny
eperson .... Bill Moor
oman in the house .... Patricia Falkenhain
BI Director .... Frederick Rolf
eneral Woman .... Anna Berger
cKay .... Cliff Cudney
ackadorf .... Alexis Yulin
eutenant Sloan .... Trey Wilson
BI Librarian .... William Duff-Griffin
onductor .... George Ede
ateman .... John Carpenter
orter .... Jamey Sheridan
arber .... P. J. Barry
urwitz .... Boris Leskin
strong .... Marat Yusim
ne Official .... James Rebhorn
oria .... Howard Sherman
gent Simpson .... John Randolph Jones
age Manager .... David Hart
rs. Byington .... Maeve McGuire
enator Byington's Daughter .... Suzanne Slade
enator Byington's Son .... Todd DeFreitas
d Charles McCaughan, Randle Mell, Patricia Falkenhain, Anna erger, John Carpenter, Jamey Sheridan, P. J. Barry, Gregory Jbara, olly O'Malley, Maureen Moore, Alice Drummond, Daniel Mills, Jim abchak

Center Right: Jonathan Hogan, Kelly McGillis

Mandy Patinkin (Right)
(Orion Pictures)

Meg Tilly, Rob Lowe (Also Top Right) Right:
Rob Lowe, Kim Cattrall

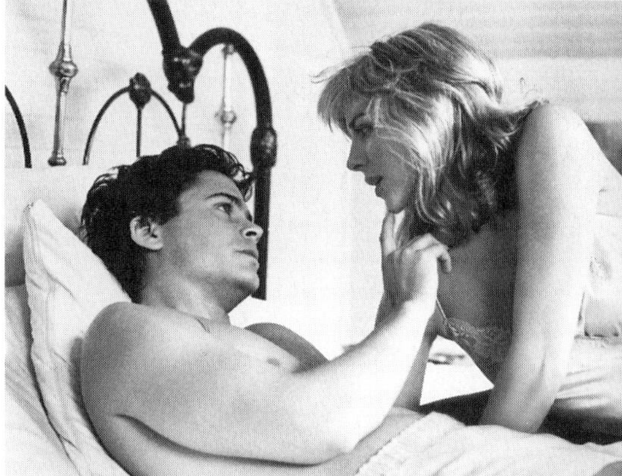

MASQUERADE

(MGM) Producer, Michael I. Levy; Director, Bob Swaim; Screenplay, Dick Wolf; Associate Producer, Kelliann Ladd; Music, John Barry; Photography, David Watkin; Production Designer, John Kasarda; Editor, Scott Conrad; Costumes, John Boxer; Casting, Wallis Nicita; Assistant Directors, Michael Tadross, Tony Adler; Art Director, Dan Davis; Set Decorator, Steve Jordan; Unit Production Manager, William C. Gerrity; Deluxe color; Dolby Stereo; Rated R; 91 minutes; March release

CAST

Tim Whalan .... Rob Lowe
Olivia Lawrence .... Meg Tilly
Brooke Morrison .... Kim Cattrall
Mike McGill .... Doug Savant
Tony Gateworth .... John Glover
Anne Briscoe .... Dana Delany
Chief of Police .... Erik Holland
Granger Morrison .... Brian Davies
Tommy McGill .... Barton Heyman
Harland Fitzgerald .... Bernie McInerney
Weyburn .... Bill Lopatto
Cantrell .... Pirie MacDonald
Aunt Eleanor .... Maeve McGuire
Uncles Charles .... Ira Wheeler
Sam .... Timothy Landfield
Holly .... Cristen Kauffman
Jillian .... Karen McLaughlin
Mrs. Chase .... Nada Rowland
Cousins .... Carl Tye Evans, Maryann Urbano
Mortician .... Edwin Bordo
Lt. Wacker .... Bruce Tuthill
Cops .... James Caulfield, John Henry Cox
Bridget .... Paddy Croft
Alberto .... Henry Ravelo
Tailor .... Peter Carew
Judge .... Lois Diane Hicks
Nun .... Dorothy Lancaster
Maid .... Marilyn Raphael
Morrison Maid .... Mary McTigue
Sedgewick .... Dick Wolf
Debutante .... Evan O'Neill
Store Manager .... James Raitt
Dock Man .... Robert D. Wilson, Sr.
Kid on dock .... Michael F. Tadross
French Boys .... Benjamin Lee Swaim, Christopher Thomas Swaim

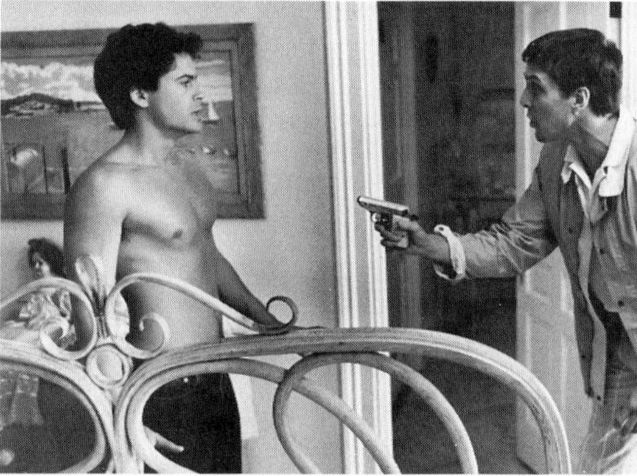

Right Center: Rob Lowe, John Glover
(Metro-Goldwyn-Mayer Pictures)

Meg Tilly, Doug Savant

Meg Ryan, Dennis Quaid
(Touchstone Pictures)

VICE VERSA

:OLUMBIA) Producers/Screenplay, Dick Clement, Ian La Frenais; rector, Brian Gilbert; Executive Producer, Alan Ladd, Jr.; Photogra- ıy, King Baggot; Designer, Jim Schoppe; Editor, David Garfield; ısting, Penny Perry; Music, David Shire; Associate Producer/ oduction Manager, Dean O'Brien; Assistant Directors, Jerry L. Bal- w, Steve Danton; Art Director, Eva Anna Bohn; Set Decorator, Karen Hara; Costumes, Jay Hurley; Sound, Scott D. Smith; Special 'fects, Dennis Sion; *"Vice Versa"* by Mick Zane, Mark Behn, Paul ıbu/*"Crazy in the Night"* by Mick Zane, Mark Behn, James Neal, and ngs by various other artists; Vocals, Malice and others; Dolby Stereo; eLuxe Color; Rated PG; 97 minutes; March release

CAST

ıarshall ... Judge Reinhold
harlie ... Fred Savage
ım ... Corinne Bohrer
na ... Swoosie Kurtz
obyn ... Jane Kaczmarek
ırk ... David Proval
very ... William Prince
ıarcie ... Gloria Gifford
rs. Luttrell ... Beverly Archer
ırry ... Harry Murphy
rad ... Kevin O'Rourke
oyd ... Richard Kind
liff ... Chip Lucia
ale ... Ajay Naidu
ooley ... Raymond Rosario
erschner ... Elya Baskin
wo ... James Hong
s. Lindstrom ... Jane Lynch
ori ... Danielle Kohl
ric ... Jason Late
ıdd ... Tom Crawford
lipper ... Christian Fitzpatrick
r. Ferriera ... Joe Gustaferro
rincipal's Secretary ... Peggy Roeder
eacher ... Paul Greatbatch
lusic Salesman ... Robert Bundy
ockey Coach ... P. J. Brown
uru ... Harry Yorku
and Singer ... Albert Fields
ıd Anuwat Tiernate, Surasri Klangsuwan, Penjit Prembudd, Ram 'aratum, Sulaleewan Suwanatat, Tuantone Kammesri, Martyn St. avid, Jeff Kahn, Robert Petkoff, Alan Shearman, Michelle Philpot, like Bacarella, Bettina Wendt, Bernie Landis, Ralph Foody, Steve ssad, Dany Goldring

Right Center: Fred Savage, Judge Reinhold
(Columbia Pictures)

D.O.A.

(TOUCHSTONE) Producers, Ian Sander, Laura Ziskin; Directors, Rocky Morton, Annabel Jankel; Screenplay, Charles Edward Pogue; Story, Charles Edward Pogue, Russle Rouse, Clarence Greene; Co-Producers, Cathleen Summers, Andrew J. Kuehn; Photography, Yuri Neyman; Designer, Richard Amend; Editor, Michael R. Miller; Casting, Nancy Foy; Music, Chaz Jankel; Production Manager, Jeanne M. Van Cott; Assistant Directors, Louis D'Esposito, Richard Patrick; Thomas Brandau; Set Decorator, Michael O'Sullivan; Costumes, Nancy Cone; Special Effects, Jack Bennett; Stunts, Randy "Fife"; Dolby Stereo; CFI Color/Black & White; Rated R; 100 minutes; March release

CAST

Dexter Cornell ... Dennis Quaid
Sydney Fuller ... Meg Ryan
Mrs. Fitzwaring ... Charlotte Rampling
Hal Petersham ... Daniel Stern
Gail Cornell ... Jane Kaczmarek
Bernard ... Christopher Neame
Cookie Fitzwaring ... Robin Johnson
Nicholas Lang ... Rob Knepper
Graham Corey ... Jay Patterson
Detective Ulmer ... Brion James
Detective Brockton ... Jack Kehoe
Elaine Wells ... Elizabeth Arlen
Jane Corey ... Karen Radcliffe
Chief Resident ... William Forward
Mr. Fitzwaring ... Lee Gideon
Nick Lang, Sr. ... Bill Bolende
Corey's daughter ... Hillary Hoffman
Sloane ... John Hawkes
College President ... Michael Costello
Desk Sergeant ... William Johnson
Metcalf ... Brent Anderson
Barb ... Wendye Clarendon
Cabbie ... Marco Perella
Survey Girl ... Joye Swan
English Professor ... Charles Beecham
Frat Jocks ... Gabriel Folse, Matt Thompson
Timbuk 3 ... Barbara MacDonald, Pat MacDonald

Judge Reinhold (Left)

Ann-Margret, John Shea Top Left: Alan Alda
Left: Alan Alda, Veronica Hamel

A NEW LIFE

(PARAMOUNT) Producer, Martin Bregman; Director/Screenplay Alan Alda; Executive Producer, Louis A. Stroller; Photography, Kel vin Pike; Editor, William Reynolds; Music, Joseph Turrin; Casting Mary Colquhoun, Stuart Aikens; Associate Producers, Barbara Kelly Michael Scott Bregman; Production Manager, Barbara Kelly, Assistan Directors, Yudi Bennett, Wendy Ross; Designer, Barbara Dunphy Costumes, Mary McLeod; Sound, Bruce Carwardine; Art Director Lucinda Zak; Set Decorator, Anthony Greco; Orchestrations, Josep Turrin; Production Coordinator, Janet Damp; *"Under Pressure"* by Michael Watson, Michael Jay/Performed by Phillip Ingram, and song by various other artists; Technicolor; Rated PG-13; 104 minutes; Marc release

CAST

Steve .... Alan Ald
Mel Arons .... Hal Linde
Jackie .... Ann-Margre
Kay Hutton .... Veronica Hame
Doc .... John She
Donna .... Mary Kay Plac
Judy .... Beatrice Ald
Billy .... David Eisne
Audrey .... Victoria Snov
Phil .... John Koza
Steve's Lawyer .... Alan Jorda
Maurice .... Tim Koettin
Student .... Catherine Dishe
Sybil .... Alec Map
Suitors .... Malcolm Stewart, Barry Flatman, Vince Metcalf
Tina .... Cynthia Bellivea
Sherry .... Michelle Duque
Waiter .... C. David Johnso
Dr. Dave Salisman .... Michael Kirb
Eleanor .... Celia Westo
Barry .... Paul Hech
E.R. Nurse .... Deanne Degruijte
Eric .... Bill Irwi
Teacher .... Janet Bailey
Sylvia .... Fiona Rei
Mara .... Jackie Samud
Ultrasound Doctor .... Stephen Hunte
Lamaze Instructor .... Jennifer Dea
O.B. Nurse .... Mary Ann Cole
Jackie's Lawyer .... Eve Crawfor
Gondolier .... John Madoni
Judge .... Ed McGibbo
Phil's Wife .... Lynn Vog
Shirley .... Deborah Theake
Obstetrician .... Barbara Cruikshank
Janet .... Laura Dickso

Left Center: Ann-Margret, Alan Alda, Beatrice Alda
(Paramount Pictures)

John Kozak, Hal Linden, Paul Hecht, Alan Alda

BEETLEJUICE

(WARNER BROS.) Producers, Michael Bender, Larry Wilson, Richard Hashimoto; Director, Tim Burton; Story, Michael McDowell, Larry Wilson; Screenplay, Michael McDowell, Warren Skaaren; Photography, Thomas Ackerman; Designer, Bo Welch; Editor, Jane Kurson; Music, Danny Elfman; Costumes, Aggie Guerard Rodgers; Casting, Jane Jenkins, Janet Hirschenson; Production Supervisor, Eric Angelson; Associate Producer, June Petersen; Production Manager, Don Heitzer; Assistant Directors, Bill Scott, K. C. Colwell, Jerry Beck; Art Director, Tom Duffield; Set Decorator, Catherine Mann; Set Designers, John Warnke, Dick McKenzie; Sound, David Ronne; Stunts, Fred Lerner; Choreographer, Chrissy Bocchino; Special Effects, Chuck Gaspar; Visual Effects, Alan Munro, Rick Heinrichs, Peter Kuran; Creature & Makeup Effects, Robert Short; Presented by the Geffen Company; Orchestrations, Steve Bartek; *"Day-O"* by Lord Burgess, William Attaway, and songs by various other artists; Vocals, Harry Belafonte; Dolby Stereo; Technicolor; Rated PG; 90 minutes; March release

CAST

Adam .... Alec Baldwin
Barbara .... Geena Davis
Jane Butterfield .... Annie McEnroe
Ernie .... Maurice Page
Old Bill .... Hugo Stanger
Betelgeuse .... Michael Keaton
Little Jane .... Rachel Mittelman
Delia .... Catherine O'Hara
Moving Men .... J. Jay Saunders, Mark Ettlinger
Charles .... Jeffrey Jones
Lydia .... Winona Ryder
Otho .... Glenn Shadix
Receptionist .... Patrice Martinez
-Fingered Typist .... Cynthia Daly
Char Man .... Douglas Turner
Messenger .... Carmen Filpi
Janitor .... Simmy Bow
Juno .... Sylvia Sidney
Maxie Dean .... Robert Goulet
Bernard .... Dick Cavett
Grace .... Susan Kellermann
Beryl .... Adelle Lutz
Dumb Football Players .... Gary Jochimsen, Bob Pettersen
Very Dumb Football Player .... Duane Davis
Sarah Dean .... Marie Cheatham
Preacher .... Tony Cox
Voice of Preacher .... Jack Angel
Old Bill #2 .... Harold Goodman

Right: Winona Ryder Above: Michael Keaton, Geena Davis, Alec Baldwin Top: Michael Keaton, Winona Ryder
(Geffen Films Co.)

Michael Keaton

Glenn Shadix, Catherine O'Hara, Jeffrey Jones

Winner 1988 Academy Award for Best Make-Up

THE MILAGRO BEANFIELD WAR

(UNIVERSAL) Producers, Robert Redford, Moctesuma Esparza; Director, Robert Redford; Screenplay, David Ward, John Nichols; Based on the Novel by John Nichols; Executive Producer, Gary J. Hendler; Photography, Robbie Greenberg; Art Director, Joe Aubel; Editor, Dede Allen, Jim Miller; Co-Producer, Charles Mulvehill; Music, Dave Grusin; Costumes, Bernie Pollack; Casting, Nancy Foy; Production Manager, David Wisnievitz; Assistant Directors, Myers, Tom Snyder; Sound, Jim Webb, Kay Rose; Associate Editors, Eric Beason, Nancy Frazen; Visual Consultant, Peter Jamison; Set Decorator, Tom Roysden; Set Designers, Antoinette Gordon, Dick McKenzie, Roy Barnes; Additional Editor, Stan Frazen; Special Effects, Tom Ward; Dolby Stereo; MGM Color; Rated R; 117 minutes; March release

CAST

Sheriff Bernabe Montoya .... Ruben Blades
Ladd Devine .... Richard Bradford
Ruby Archuleta .... Sonia Braga
Nancy Mondragon .... Julie Carmen
Horsethief Shorty .... James Gammon
Flossie Devine .... Melanie Griffith
Charlie Bloom .... John Heard
Amarante Cordova .... Carlos Riquelme
Herbie Platt .... Daniel Stern
Joe Mondragon .... Chick Vennera
Kyril Montana .... Christopher Walken
Mayor Sammy Cantu .... Freddy Fender
Nick Rael .... Tony Genaro
Emerson Capps .... Jerry Hardin
Jerry G .... Ronald G. Joseph
Carl .... Mario Arrambide
Coyote Angel .... Roberto Carricart
The Governor .... M. Emmet Walsh

and Alberto Morin, Frederico Roberto, Pablo Trujillo, Natividad Vacio, Eloy Vigil, Trinidad Silva, Consuelo Luz, Mike Gomez, Olga Merediz, Leandro Cordova, Eva Cantu, Astrea Romero, Donald Salazar, Reynaldo Cantu, Alfredo Romero, Arnold Burns, Cipriano Vigil, Rudy Fernandez, Victoria Plata, Frederick Lopez, Cletus Tafoya, Marcos L. Martinez, Waldo Cantu, Eddie G. Baros, Ishmael A. Avila, Douglas Yanez, Jimmy Martinez, Bonnie Apodaca, Ruby Marchant, Adelita Sandoval

Right: Christopher Walken Above: Chick Vennera, Ruben Blades Top: Sonia Braga, John Heard
(Universal City Studios)

Carlos Riquelme

Ruben Blades

Winner of 1988 Academy Award for Best Original Score

DOMINICK AND EUGENE

RION) Producers, Marvin Minoff, Mike Farrell; Director, Robert Young; Screenplay, Alvin Sargent, Corey Blechman; Story, Danny rfirio; Photography, Curtis Clark; Designer, Doug Kraner; Editor, thur Coburn; Associate Producer, Lee R. Mayes; Music/Conductor, evor Jones; Casting, Julie Hughes, Barry Moss; Costumes, Hilary senfeld; Production Manager, Lee. R. Mayes; Assistant Directors, ristopher Griffin, Lynn Wegenka; Sound, David E. Kirschner; Set corator, Derek R. Hill; Assistant Editor, Lauren Schaffer; Production Coordinator, Mary Lou Devlin; Choreographer, Lenora Nemetz; alogue Coach, Don Wadsworth; Production Supervisor, Pamela intenkamp; *"Game of Love"* by Mike Piccirillo, Gary Goetzman/ rformed by Christin Day, and songs by various other artists; Dolby ereo; DeLuxe Color; Rated PG-13; 111 minutes; March release

CAST

gene Luciano .... Ray Liotta
minick Luciano .... Tom Hulce
nnifer Reston .... Jamie Lee Curtis
. Levinson .... Robert Levine
rry Higgins .... Todd Graff
sse Johnson .... Bill Cobbs
rs. Gianelli .... Mimi Cecchini
ickey Chernak .... Tommy Snelsire
eresa Chernak .... Mary Joan Negro
ther T .... Tom Signorelli
oir Director .... John Romeri
levision Announcer .... David Perry
ido .... Joe Maruzzo
e .... R. Scott Peck
on .... Charles Susan
ens .... Jack Boslet, Matthew J. Ravenstahl, Shawn Ebbert
rs. Vinson .... Jaqueline Knapp
artin Chernak .... David Strathairn
nce .... Vincent Cinese
ny .... Joe Marmo
w .... Daniel Krell
rry .... Thomas Rocco
e .... Bingo O'Malley
ey .... Amanda Picciafoco & Megan Picciafoco, Lindsay Harms & Lauren Harms
ighbor boy .... John Naples, Jr.
. Gage .... Mel Winkler
oman's Voice .... Victoria Dym
porter .... Raymond Laine
ed (the dog) .... O'Malley

Right: Tom Hulce, Ray Liotta (Also Top)
Above: Jamie Lee Curtis, Liotta, Hulce
(Orion Pictures)

Ray Liotta, Tom Hulce

Jamie Lee Curtis, Ray Liotta

BILOXI BLUES

(UNIVERSAL) Producer, Ray Stark; Director, Mike Nichols; Screen play, Neil Simon; Based on the stage play by Neil Simon; Executiv Produces, Joseph M. Caracciolo, Marykay Powell; Photography, Bi Butler; Designer, Paul Sylbert; Costumes, Ann Roth; Editor, Sa O'Steen; Music, Georges Delerue; Casting, Juliet Taylor; Productio Manager, Joseph M. Caracciolo; Assistant Directors, Michael Haley James Skotchdopole; Associate Editor, Richard Nord; Sound, Alla Byer; Set Decorator, John Alan Hicks; Special Effects, Daniel Ottese Kevin Brink, John Ottesen; Stunts, Whitey Hughes, Rick LeFevou Songs by various artists; Dolby Stereo; Color; Super-35 Widescree Rated PG-13; 106 minutes; March release

CAST

Eugene Morris Jerome .... Matthew Broderic
Sgt. Toomey .... Christopher Walke
Joseph Wykowski .... Matt Mulher
Arnold Epstein .... Corey Parke
Roy Selridge .... Markus Flanaga
Don Carney .... Casey Siemaszk
James Hennesy .... Michael Dola
Daisy Hannigan .... Penelope Ann Mille
Rowena .... Park Overa
Peek .... Alan Pottinge
Pinelli .... Mark Evan Jacob
Corporal .... Dave Kienzl
Spitting Cook .... Matthew Kimbroug
Diggers .... Kirby Mitchell, Allen Turner, Tom Kag
Mess Hall Corporal .... Jeff Baile
Rifle Instructor .... Bill Russe
Girl at Dance .... Natalie Canerda
Private Roddey .... A. Collin Rodde
Corporal Ginnaven .... Christopher Ginnave
Corporal Mead .... Morris Mea
Tower Officer .... David Whitma
Newsreel Announcer .... Norman Ros
Corporal Haley .... Michael Hale
Private Lindstrom .... Ben Hynun
Corporal Wigington .... Andy Wigingto
Private Phelps .... Christopher Phelp
Private Sudbury .... Scott Sudbur

Left: Penelope Ann Miller, Matthew Broderick Top: Christopher Walken, Broderick
(Universal City Studios)

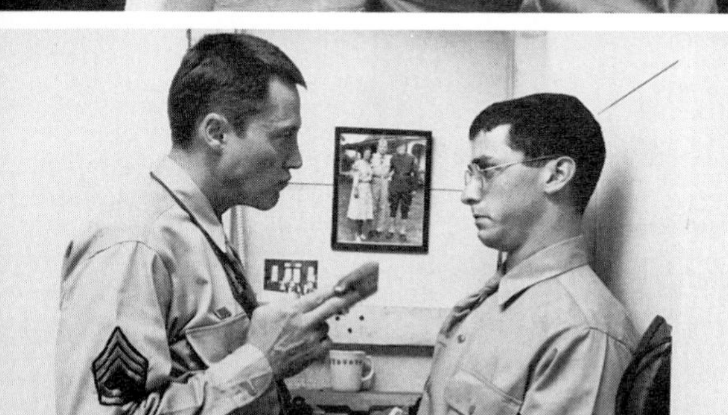

Christopher Walken Above: Walken, Corey Parker

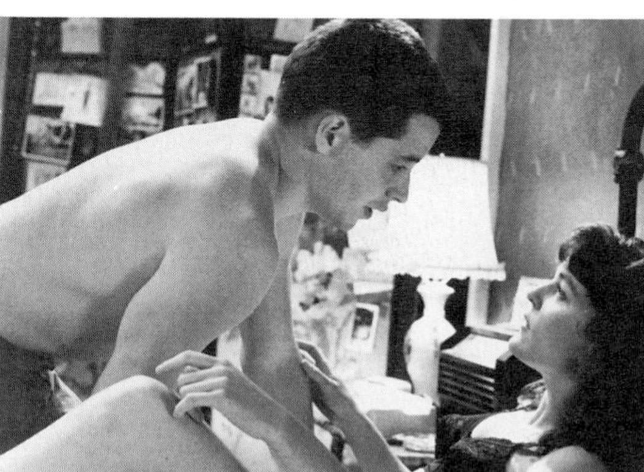

Matthew Broderick, Casey Siemaszko Above: Broderick, Park Overall

Kiefer Sutherland, Phoebe Cates, Michael J. Fox Left: Sutherland, Fox Top: Fox, Dianne Wiest

Swoosie Kurtz, Michael J. Fox

BRIGHT LIGHTS, BIG CITY

(UNITED ARTISTS) Producers, Mark Rosenberg, Sydney Pollack; Director, James Bridges; Screenplay, Jay McInerney, based on his novel; Executive Producer, Gerald R. Molen; Photography, Gordon Willis; Production Designer, Santo Loquasto; Editor, John Bloom; Music, Donald Fagen, Robert Mounsey; Executive Music Producer, Joel Sill; Costumes, Bernie Pollack; Associate Producer, Jack Larson; Casting, Mary Colquhoun; Unit Production Manager, Gerald R. Molen; Assistant Directors, David McGiffert, Stephen Wertimer; Art Director, Thomas C. Warren; Set Decorator, George Detitta; Songs by various artists; Sound, Les Lazarowitz; Coma baby created by Chris Walas, Inc.; a Mirage production; from MGM/UA Communications; Technicolor; Dolby Stereo; Rated R; 110 minutes; April release

CAST

Jamie Conway .... Michael J. Fox
Tad Allagash .... Kiefer Sutherland
Amanda .... Phoebe Cates
Megan .... Swoosie Kurtz
Clara Tillinghast .... Frances Sternhagen
Vicky .... Tracy Pollan
Mr. Vogel .... John Houseman
Michael Conway .... Charlie Schlatter
Alex Hardy .... Jason Robards
Rittenhouse .... David Warrilow
Mother .... Dianne Wiest
Yasu Wade .... Alec Mapa
Ferret man .... William Hickey
Kathy .... Gina Belafonte
Rich Vanier .... Sam Robards
Stevie .... Zette
Bald girl .... Marika Blossfeldt
Theresa .... Jessica Lundy
Elaine .... Kelly Lynch
Maitre D' .... Peter Boyden
Barbara .... Annabelle Gurwitch
Walter Tyler .... Russell Horton
Waiter .... Peter Maloney
Pony Tail girl .... Maria Pitillo
Leather lady .... Susan Traylor
Mannequin craftsman .... Michael Fischetti
Policeman .... Mike Badalucco

and Marika Blossfeldt, Peter Maloney, Maria Pitillo, Susan Traylor, Michael Fischetti, Mike Badalucco, David Hyde Pierce, Jim Babchak, Peg Murray, Barbara Rucker, Pat Santino, Mike Bacarella, Josie Bell, Anne Bezamat, Alva Chinn, Dianne DeWitt, Nathalie Gabrielli, Jennifer Houser, Lynn Howland, Sheila Johnson, Melanie Landestoy

Left Center: Jason Robards
(United Artists Pictures)

18 AGAIN!

(NEW WORLD) Producer, Walter Coblenz; Director, Paul Flaherty; Screenplay, Josh Goldstein, Jonathan Prince; Executive Producers, Irving Fein, Michael Jaffe; Associate Producers, Arthur Schaefer, Yvonne Ramond; Music, Billy Goldenberg; Photography, Stephen M. Katz; Editor, Danford B. Greene; Casting, Melissa Skoff; Designer, Dena Roth; Production Manager, Arthur Schaefer; Assistant Director, Stephen McEveety, Randall Badger; Costumes, John Buehler; Production Coordinator, Robin Hinz; Sound, Russell Williams; Set Decorator, John Myhre; Special Effects, Howard Jensen; Stunts, Charlie Croughwell; Choreographer, Larry S. Blum; *"I Wish I Was 18 Again"* by Sonny Throckmorton/Vocal, George Burns, and songs by various other artists; Technicolor; Rated PG; 100 minutes; April release

CAST

Jack Watson .... George Burns
David Watson .... Charlie Schlatter
Arnold .... Tony Roberts
Madelyn .... Anita Morris
Betty .... Miriam Flynn
Robin .... Jennifer Runyon
Charlie .... Red Buttons
Coach .... George DiCenzo
Horton .... Bernard Fox
Professor Swivet .... Kenneth Tigar
Russ .... Anthony Starke
Barrett .... Pauly Shore
Art Teacher .... Emory Bass
J. P. .... Joshua Devane
Red .... Benny Baker
Irv .... Hal Smith
Mikey .... Lance Slaughter
Robin's Dad .... Earl Boen
Robin's Mom .... Toni Sawyer
Robin's Sister .... Stephanie Baldwin
and Nancy Fox, Leeza Vinnichenko, Kimberlin Brown, Kevin Haley, Mark K. Kamiyama, Karl Wiedergott, Mark Kramer, Edwina Moore, Kate Benton, Pat Crawford Brown, Nicholas Cascone, Darren Powell, Michael J. Shea, Freddie Dawson, Jim Jackman, Michael Rider, Parker Whitman, Connie Gauthier, Cathy Scott, Michael Fallon

Right: Red Buttons, Charlie Schlatter
Top: Charlie Schlatter, George Burns
(New World Pictures)

Anita Morris, George Burns Above: Charlie Schlatter, Jennifer Runyon

Charlie Schlatter, George Burns Above: Tony Roberts

A TIME OF DESTINY

(COLUMBIA) Producer, Anna Thomas; Director, Gregory Nava; Screenplay, Gregory Nava, Anna Thomas; Executive Producers, Carolyn Pfeiffer, Shep Gordon; Designer, Henry Bumstead; Photography, James Glennon; Music, Ennio Morricone; Editor, Betsy Blankett; Costumes, Durinda Wood; Casting, Wally Nicita; Production Executive, Sue Baden-Powell; Assistant Director, Stephen Buck; Art Director, Les Gobruegge; Set Decorator, Anne Kuljian; Sound, Stephan Von Hase-Mihalik; Visual Effects, Fantasy II Film Effects; Special Effects, Gene Warren, Jr.; Stunts, Eddie Stacey; Dolby Stereo; DeLuxe Color; Rated PG-13; 118 minutes; April release

CAST

Martin .... William Hurt
Jack .... Timothy Hutton
Josie .... Melissa Leo
Jorge .... Francisco Rabal
Sebastiana .... Concha Hidalgo
Margaret .... Stockard Channing
Irene .... Megan Follows
Ed .... Frederick Coffin
Policeman .... Peter Palmer
Young Josie .... Kelly Pacheco
Father Basil .... John O'Leary
Young Martin .... Justin Cocke
Young George .... John Thatcher
Nelson .... David Gilliam
Bernotsky .... Mark Burton
Kentucky .... Rolf Saxon
Eppie .... Francisco Senosiain
Gabby .... Art Koustik
Bonifacio .... Mike Robelo
Father Tony .... Alan Tilvern
Young Sebastiana .... Nicolasa Calvo
Young Jorge .... Felix Arcarazo
and Allan Chambers, Darin Willis, Charmaine Glennon, Harriet Robinson, Sam Vlahos, Julie Philips, Erik Holland, Jeff Harding, Nancy Gair

Left: Stockard Channing (2nd from L), Concha Hidalgo, William Hurt, Melissa Leo, Megan Follows Top: Leo, Timothy Hutton ***(Columbia Pictures)***

SOUTH OF RENO

:ASTLE HILL) Producer, Robert Tinnell; Co-producer, Joanna ainton; Executive Producers, Victor Markowicz, Joanna Stainton; rector, Mark Rezyka; Screenplay, Mark Rezyka, T. L. Lankford; otography, Bernard Auroux; Editor, Marc Grossman; Music, Nigel olton, Clive Wright; Designer, Phillip Duffin; Art Director, Elizabeth oore; Sound, Rob Janiger; Associate Producer, Eric Liekefet; Cast-g, Barbara Remsen & Associates/Anne Remsen; CFI Color; Not ted; 94 minutes; April release

CAST

artin .... Jeffrey Osterhage
nette .... Lisa Blount
ector .... Joe Phelan
'illard .... Lewis Van Bergen
ısan .... Julia Montgomery
renda .... Brandis Kemp
ouise .... Danitza Kingsley
anager of motel .... Mary Grace Canfield
oward Stone .... Bert Remsen

Right Center: Jeffrey Osterhage, Bert Remsen ***(Castle Hill Productions)***

Lisa Blount, Jeffrey Osterhage

Keith Carradine Right: Carradine, Linda Fiorentino, Genevieve Bujold Top: John Lone, Geraldine Chaplin

THE MODERNS

(ALIVE FILMS) Producers, Carolyn Pfeiffer, David Blocker; Director, Alan Rudolph; Screenplay, Alan Rudolph, Jon Bradshaw; Executive Producer, Shep Gordon; Photography, Toyomichi Kurita; Designer, Steven Legler; Music, Mark Isham; Songs performed by Charlelie Couture; Associate Producer, Stuart Besser: Casting, Stuart Besser; Pam Dixon; Costumes, Renee April; Editors, Debra T. Smith, Scott Brock; Variations on Matisse, Cezanne & Modigliani by David Stein; Photography, Jan Kiesser; Production Executive, Dana Mayer; Production Consultant, Michael Wilson; Production Manager, Barbara Shrier; Assistant Directors, Michael Williams, Madeleine Henrie; Sound, Ron Judkins, Robert Jackson, Richard Portman; Set Decorator, Jean-Jean Baptiste Tard; Assistant Editor, Joan Alexander; Special Effects, Jacques Godbout, Yves Charbonneau; Songs, Jean Lenoir, CharlElie Couture, and various other artists; Stunts, Greg Walker; In Association with Nelson Entertainment; CFI Color; Not rated; 126 minutes; April release

CAST

Nick Hart .... Keith Carradine
Rachel Stone .... Linda Fiorentino
Oiseau .... Wallace Shawn
Libby Valentin .... Genevieve Bujold
Nathalie de Ville .... Geraldine Chaplin
Hemingway .... Kevin J. O'Connor
Bertram Stone .... John Lone
L'Evidence .... CharlElie Couture
Gertrude Stein .... Elsa Raven
Alice B. Toklas .... Ali Giron
New York Critic .... Gailard Sartain
Surrealist Poet .... Michael Wilson
Blackie .... Robert Gould
Babette .... Antonia Dauphin
Laurett .... Veronique Bellegarde
Armand .... Isabel Serra
Art critics .... David Stein, Hubert Loiselle
Francis .... Meegan Lee Ochs
Abigail .... Brooke Smith
Rose Selavy .... Marthe Turgeon
Bodyguards .... Pierre Chagnon, Eric Gaudry, Timothy Webber
Stone's Business Associate .... Mance Edmond
Butler Laloux .... Norman Brathwaite
Buffy .... Michael Rudder
Alexandre .... Paul Buissoneau
Femme de Lettres .... Lenie Scofie
Chapelle .... Reynald Bouchard
Pia Delarue .... Flora Balzano
Eve .... Beverly Murray
Chanteuse .... Renee Lee
Charlie the Bass Player .... Charlie Biddle
Saxophonist .... Glenn Bradley
Priest .... Didier Hoffmann
Hart's Conceirge .... Jean-Jacques Desjardins
Ada Fuoco .... Ada Fuoco
Mr. Brown .... Harry Hill
Filles de Nuit .... Danielle Schneider, Stephanie Biddle
Referee .... Louis Pharand
Natalie's Chauffeur .... Marcel Girard
M. Raymond .... Daniel Bloch
Cafe Modern Waiter .... Julien Carletti

Wallace Shawn, Kevin J. O'Connor, Keith Carradine

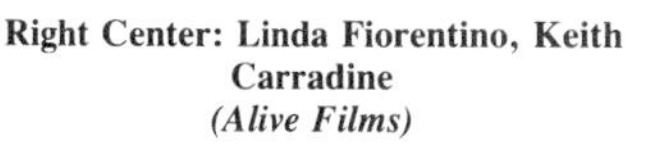

Right Center: Linda Fiorentino, Keith Carradine
(Alive Films)

SUNSET

'RI-STAR) Produce, Tony Adams; Director, Blake Edwards; :reenplay, Blake Edwards; Story, Rod Amateau; Associate Producer, :ish Caroselli; Photography, Anthony B. Richmond; Designer, Rod-·r Maus; Editor, Robert Pergament; Costumes, Patricia Norris; Mu-c, Henry Mancini; Casting, Nancy Klopper; Production Manager, lan Levine; Assistant Directors, Mickey McCardle, David Kelley, largaret Nelson; Art Director, Richard Y. Haman; Set Decorator, larvin March; Sound, Jerry Jost; Special Effects, Dany Cangemi; horeographers, Miranda Garrison, Miriam Nelson; Dolby Stereo; ınavision; Technicolor; Rated R; 107 minutes; April release

CAST

ɔm Mix .... Bruce Willis
'yatt Earp .... James Garner
lfie Alperin .... Malcolm McDowell
ıeryl King .... Mariel Hemingway
ancy Shoemaker .... Kathleen Quinlan
ictoria Alperin .... Jennifer Edwards
ıristina Alperin .... Patricia Hodge
aptain Blackworth .... Richard Bradford
ıief Dibner .... M. Emmet Walsh
ıtch Kieffer .... Joe Dellesandro
rthur .... Andreas Katsulas
larty Goldberg .... Dann Florek
al Flynn .... Bill Marcus
looch .... Michael C. Gwynne
lichael Alperin .... Dermot Mulroney
ɔanish Dancer .... Miranda Garrison
ɔsa .... Liz Torres
ıncho .... Castulo Guerra
'illiam Singer .... Dakin Matthews
ustralian Houseman .... Vernon Wells
ıul .... Dennis Rucker
ı .... John Dennis Johnston
owboy Fred .... Kenny Call
owboy Henry .... Jack Garner
eo Vogel .... Jerry Tullos
onductor .... Steem Tanney
·ank Coe .... Peter Jason
oscoe Arbuckle .... Glenn Shadix
lix Butler .... Arnold Johnson
lperin Butler .... Eric Harrison
lfie's 1st Wife .... Amy Michelson
ouglas Fairbanks .... Rod McCary
ɔhn Gilbert .... John Fountain
suncion Maria Romero .... Irene Oolga Lopez
ıd Richard Fancy, Lisa Alpert, Sonia Zimmer, Marina Palmier, Tessa aylor, John Van Ness, Randy Bowers, Maureen Teefy, James O'Con-ɔll

Right: Malcolm McDowell Above: Mariel Hemingway, Bruce Willis Top: James Garner, Bruce Willis
(Tri-Star Pictures)

M. Emmet Walsh, James Garner, Bruce Willis

Jennifer Edwards (Right)

Sean Penn, Maria Conchita Alonso
Above: Sy Richardson, Penn, Robert Duvall

COLORS

(ORION) Producer, Robert H. Solo; Director, Dennis Hopper Screenplay, Michael Schiffer; Story, Michael Schiffer, Richard Di Lello; Music, Herbie Hancock; Co-Producer, Paul Lewis; Photogra phy, Haskell Wexler; Production Designer, Ron Foreman; Art Direct or, Chas. Butcher; Set Decorator, Ernie Bishop; Supervising Film Editor, Robert Estrin; Casting, Lauren Lloyd; Assistant Directors, Eli Cohn, Willie E. Simmons, Jr.; Stunt Coordinator, Chuck Waters Sound, Jim Webb; Additional Score, Ice-T & Afrika Islam, Jeff Bova Bob Musso, Charlie Drayton, Tony Meilandt; Songs performed b various artists; Title song by Ice-T & Afrika Islam; DeLuxe color Dolby Stereo; Rated R; 120 minutes; April release

CAST

Danny McGavin .... Sean Pen
Bob Hodges .... Robert Duval
Louisa Gomez .... Maria Conchita Alons
Ron Delaney .... Randy Brook
Larry Sylvester .... Grand Bus
Rocket .... Don Cheadl
Bird .... Gerardo Maji
High Top .... Glenn Plumme
Melindez .... Rudy Ramo
Bailey .... Sy Richardso
Frog .... Trinidad Silv
Reed .... Charles Walke
T-Bone .... Damon Wayan
Cook .... Fred Asparagu
Officer Porter .... Sherman Augustu
Spanky .... Bruce Beatt
Tommie Hodges .... Brandon Bluhr
C.R.A.S.H. Secretary .... Verda Bridge
Rusty Baines .... R. D. Ca
Sullivan .... Steven Camarill
Diaz .... Seymour Cass
Officer Young .... Carlos Cervante
Phil .... Lawrence Coo
Preacher .... Nick Corell
Robert Craig .... Troy Curvey, J
Felipe .... Brian Davi
Rita Galegos .... Romeo De La
Flacco .... Marianne Diaz-Parto
Fabian Escobed
Sheriff Foster .... Virgil Fry
Whitey .... Courtney Gaine
Phillip .... Tomas Goro
Oso .... C. E. Grime
Lee .... Clark Johnso
Maria .... Keni
Killer-Bee .... Leon Robinso
Mrs. Craig .... Tina Lifor
Willie Wright .... Shawn McLemor
Angie .... Peggy Medin
Joan Hodges .... Micole Mercuri
Snakedance .... Nigel Migue
Locita .... Karla Montan
Shooter .... Allan Moor
Officer Samuels .... Jack Nanc
J. C. .... David Rayr
Homeboy .... Ray Orie
Dr. Feelgood .... Tee Rodger
Lewis .... Geoffrey Thorn
Sharon Robbins .... Ara Thorp
Veterano .... Peter Mark Vasque
Dog-Man .... Jeffrey Washingto
Spooky .... Dion William
Officer Rutley .... John Zend
and Paula Bellamy, Mark Booker, Ron Boyd, Eugene Collier, Greg G. Dandridge, Nay K. Dorsey, Dennis "Chicago" Fanning, Trys Jefferson

Top Left: Robert Duvall, Sean Penn Below: Romeo De Lan, Bruce Beatty, Trinidad Silva, Grand Bush, Gerardo Mejia, Courtney Gains (Far Right)
(Orion Pictures)

DA

(FILMDALLAS) Producer, Julie Corman; Director, Matt Clark; Screenplay, Hugh Leonard; From the play *"Da"* and the book *"Home Before Night"* by Hugh Leonard; Executive Producers, William R. Greenblatt, Martin Sheen, Sam Grogg; Production Executive, Marcus McWaters; Photography, Alar Kivilo; Editor, Nancy Nuttal Beyda; Music, Elmer Bernstein; Associate Executive Producer, Jeffrey Auerbach; Assistant Directors, Martin O'Malley, Robert Dwyer-Joyce, Rosemary Morton; Casting, Nuala Moiselle; Production Coordinator, Naimh Nolan; Associate Director, Jason Clark; Sound, Kieran Horgan; Designer, Frank Conway; Art Director, Frank Hallinan-Flood; Set Decorator, Josie MacAvin; Costumes, Carol Betera, Jill Spalding; Special Effects, Maurice Foley; Stunts, Dominick Hewitt, Seth Clark; Color; Rated PG; 102 minutes; April release

CAST

Da .... Barnard Hughes
Charlie .... Martin Sheen
Drumm .... William Hickey
Young Charlie .... Karl Hayden
Mother .... Doreen Hepburn
Boy Charlie .... Hugh O'Conor
Polly .... Ingrid Craigie
Mrs. Prynne .... Joan O'Hara
Mary, "The Yellow Peril" .... Jill Doule
Young Oliver .... Peter Hanly
Older Oliver .... Mauriece O'Donoghue
Danielle .... Aimee Clark
"Cat" McDonald .... Frank McDonald
Nurse .... Marie Conmee
Taxi Driver .... Ronan Wilmot
Sara .... Kathy Greenblatt
Barman .... Martin Dempsey
Priest .... Marcus Colley
Blackie, The Dog .... Fly
Mourners .... Jim Keogh, John Murphy, Eric Erskine, Mairin O'Sullivan, Julie Hamilton
Pallbearer .... Hugh Leonard

Left: Martin Sheen, Ingrid Craigie (Right)
Top Left: Martin Sheen, Barnard Hughes
(FilmDallas Pictures)

Hugh O'Conor, Barnard Hughes

Barnard Hughes, Doreen Hepburn

LADY IN WHITE

(NEW CENTURY/VISTA) Producers, Andrew G. La Marca, Frank Laloggia; Director/Screenplay/Music, Frank Laloggia; Executive Producers, Charles M. Laloggia, Cliff Payne; Photography, Russell Carpenter; Editor, Steve Mann; Designer, Richard K. Hummel; Costumes, Jacqueline Saint Anne; Casting, Lynn Stalmaster, Mali Finn; Visual Effects, Ernest D. Farino, Gene Warren, Jr.; Associate Producer, Carl Reynolds; Music Supervision/Conductor, John Massari; Production Manager, Kelly Van Horn; Assistant Directors, Betsy Pollock, Heidi Gutman; Production Coordinators, Jane Bartelme, Lorie Zerweck; Additional Editor, Bette Cohen; Stunts, Rawn Hutchinson; Sound, Robert Anderson, Jr.; Art Directors, Howard Kling, Kenneth Wolf, Jr.; Set Decorator, Sarah Burdick; Special Effects, Peter Chesney, Jarn Heil, Emmet Kane, Jim Kundig; *"Guaglione"* by G. Fanciulli & Nisa/Performance, Enzo Gagliardi, and songs by various other artists; Presented by New Sky Productions; Dolby Stereo; DeLuxe Color; Rated PG-13; 112 minutes; April release

CAST

Frankie Scarlatti .... Lukas Haas
Phil .... Len Cariou
Angelo .... Alex Rocco
Amanda .... Katherine Helmond
Geno .... Jason Presson
Mama Assunta .... Renata Vanni
Papa Charlie .... Angelo Bertolini
Melissa .... Joelle Jacobi
Donald .... Jared Rushton
Louie .... Gregory Levinson
Miss La Della .... Lucy Lee Flippen
Sheriff Saunders .... Tom Bower
Tony .... Jack Andreozzi
Mr. Lowry .... Sydney Lassick
Mrs. Cilak .... Rita Zohar
Mr. Cilak .... Hal Bokar
Matty Williams .... Rose Weaver
Harold Williams .... Henry Harris
Cabbie .... Bruce Kirby
Marianna .... Emily Tracy
Lady in White .... Karen Powell
Mary Ellen .... Lisa Taylor
Father Brennan .... Jack Holland
Reporter .... Daniel Rojo
Cameraman .... Gregory L. Everage

Top Right: Jason Pressman, Lukas Haas Below: Renata Vanni, Alex Rocco, Jason Pressman, Lukas Haas
(New Sky Communications)

ZELLY AND ME

(COLUMBIA) Producers, Sue Jett, Tony Mark; Director/Screenpla Tina Rathborne; Executive Producers, Tina Rathborne, Elliott Lewi Photography, Mikael Salomon; Editor, Cindy Kaplan Rooney; Musi Pino Donaggio; Conductor, Natale Massara; Casting, Barbara Shapir Associate Producer, Helena M. Consuegra; Hair/Makeup Desig Hiram Ortiz; Costumes, Kathleen Detoro; Designer, David Moror Production Manager, Eva Fyer; Assistant Directors, Dick Feury, Chi Mojtabai; Production Coordinator, Anne Nevin; Sound, Scott Breind Art Director, Dianna Freas; A Cypress Films and Mark/Jett Productic songs, Leo Trombetta, Edward Mann, Michael Trombetta, Jeremi Clarke; Soundtrack on Varese-Sarabande Records; DeLuxe Col Rated PG; 97 minutes; April release

CAST

Phoebe .... Alexandra John
Mademoiselle .... Isabella Rosselli
Co-Co .... Glynis Joh
Nora .... Kaiulani L
Willie .... David Lyn
Earl .... Joe Mort
Dora .... Courtney Vicke
Kitty .... Lindsay Dick
Alexander .... Jason McC
David .... Aaron Boo
Elegant Gentleman .... Lee Live
Bus Driver .... John Rayn
Waitress .... Lynne Hallow
Taxi Driver .... Michael Stanton Kenne
Policeman .... Rick Warn
Maid .... Julia Beale Williar
Chauffeur .... Terrance Afer-Anders
Joan of Arc Record Narration .... Lee Live
and Jason Allen, Haley Curvin, Justin Grant, Andy Grimes, Jennif Lee Harvey, Melissa Klein, Matt Laffler, Stephanie Malara, Shar May, Katie McGinty, Kris Monson, David Norris, Abby Parker, Eri Riter, Woody Sullender, Curtis Worth, Amy Young

(Columbia Pictures)

Alexandra Johnes, Isabella Rossellini

Helen Slater, Melanie Mayron

STICKY FINGERS

(SPECTRA FILM) Producers/Screenplay, Catlin Adams, Melanie Mayron; Director, Catlin Adams; Co-Producer, Carl Clifford; Executive Producer, Jonathan Olsberg; Associate Producer, Sam Irvin; Photography, Gary Thieltges; Editor, Bob Reitano; Designer, Jessica Scott-Justice; Music, Gary Chang; Costumes, David Norbury, Cynthia Shumacher; *"Sticky Fingers"* by Lisa Harlo, Jim Dyke, Ish/Vocal, Company B; Production Manager, Carl Clifford; Casting, Deborah Aquila; Assistant Director, Lewis H. Gould; Art Director, Susan Beeson; Sound, John "Sal" Sutton III; Choreographer, David Hurwith; Songs by various artists; A Hightop Films Production; Duart Color: Rated PG-13; 97 minutes; May release

CAST

Hattie .... Helen Slater
Lolly .... Melanie Mayron
Jean-Marc .... Adam Shaw
Evanston .... Danitra Vance
Reeba .... Shirley Stoler
Stella .... Eileen Brennan
Kitty .... Carol Kane
Diane .... Loretta Devine
Eddie .... Stephen McHattie
Sam .... Christopher Guest
Marcie .... Gwen Welles
Nancy .... Elizabeth Kemp
Jake .... Pierre Gautreau
Leslie .... Katherine Cortez
Ray .... Paul Brown
Michael .... Paul Hipp
Moura .... Erin Flannery
Ike .... Philip Moon
Hippie .... Stuart Rudin
Tina .... Mung Ling
Joey .... Henry Yuk
Speed .... Paul Calderon
Poo Powell .... Mimi Friedman
Diamond Johnny .... Edward Bianchi
Smokestack Sid .... Jim Bearden
Tortellini Tony .... David Walden
Gertie .... Sylvia Kauders
Frances .... Francine Beers

and George Buza, Jeff Braunstin, Zachary Bennett, T. J. Shimizu, Aaron Greenway, Bob Lem, Wendy Lum, Gy Mirano, Chad Burton, Jow Maruzzo, Matt Carlson, Hannah Cox, Bo Rucke, Fred Sphraim, Richard Blackburn, Stephane-Antorine Comtois, David Hurwith, Bill James

Left: Stephen McHattie, Loretta Devine
Above: Melanie Mayron, Christopher Guest
Top Left: Helen Slater, Melanie Mayron
(Spectrafilm)

Helen Slater

Jean Marsh

WILLOW

(MGM) Producer, Nigel Wooll; Director, Ron Howard; Screenpl
Bob Dolman; Story/Executive Producer, George Lucas; Music, Jam
Horner; Photography, Adrian Biddle; Designer, Allan Cameron;
Directors, Tim Hutchinson, Tony Reading, Malcolm Stone; Associ
Producer, Joe Johnston; Visual Effects, Industrial Light and Mag
Dennis Muren, Michael McAlister, Phil Tippett; Special Effects, Jo
Richardson; Costumes, Barbara Lane; Editors, Daniel Hanley, Mich
Hill; Casting, David & Zimmerman, Jane Jenkins, Janet Hirshens
Assistant Director, Ken Baker; Production Co-ordinator, Kathy Syk
Make-up/Creature Designer, Nick Dudman; Stunts, Gerry Crampt
Sound, Ivan Sharrock; A Lucasfilm Ltd. production in association w
Imagine Entertainment; DeLuxe Color; Panavision; Dolby Stere
Rated PG; 125 minutes; May release

CAST

Madmartigan .... Val Kilm
Sorsha .... Joanne Whal
Willow Ufgood .... Warwick Da
Queen Bavmorda .... Jean Ma
Raziel .... Patricia Ha
High Aldwin .... Billy Ba
General Kael .... Pat Roa
Airk .... Gavan O'Herli
Meegosh .... David Steinbe
Vohnkar .... Phil Fondaca
Vohnkar Warriors .... Tony Cox, Robert Gillibra
Burglekutt .... Mark Northo
Rool .... Kevin Poll
Franjean .... Rick Overt
Cherlindrea .... Maria Holv
Kiaya .... Julie Pete
Ranon .... Mark Vande Bra
Mims .... Dawn Dowli
Druid .... Michael Cotte
Ethna .... Zulema De
Barmaid .... Joanna Dicke
The Wench .... Jennifer G
Llug .... Ron T
Mother .... Sallyanne L
Elora Danan .... Ruth and Kate Greenfie

Left: Billy Barty Above: Joanne Whalley, Val Kilmer Top Left: Warwick Davis (R) *(Lucasfilm Ltd.)*

Joanne Whalley, Val Kilmer Above: Gavin O'Herlihy (Center)

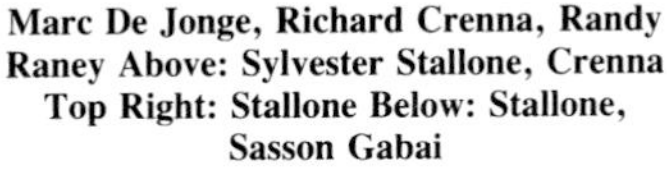

Marc De Jonge, Richard Crenna, Randy Raney Above: Sylvester Stallone, Crenna Top Right: Stallone Below: Stallone, Sasson Gabai

RAMBO III

TRI-STAR) Producer, Buzz Feitshans; Director, Peter MacDonald; creenplay, Sylvester Stallone, Sheldon Lettich; Based on characters reated by David Morrell; Executive Producers, Mario Kassar, Andrew 'ajna; Photography, John Stanier; Designer, Bill Kenney; Editors, ames Symons, Andrew London, O. Nicholas Brown, Edward A. Varschilka; Music, Jerry Goldsmith; Casting, Joy Todd; Production Manager, Charles Murray; Sound, William B. Kaplan, Eli Yarkoni; Assistant Directors, Terry Needham, Andrew Stone; Stunt Coordinaor, Vic Armstrong; Special Effects, Thomas L. Fisher, William Mesa; Associate Producer, Tony Munafo; A Carolco production; Technicolor; -D-C Widescreen; Dolby Stereo; Rated R; 104 minutes; May release

CAST

ohn Rambo .... Sylvester Stallone
Col. Trautman .... Richard Crenna
Zaysen .... Marc de Jonge
Griggs .... Kurtwood Smith
Masoud .... Spiros Focas
Mousa .... Sasson Gabai
Hamid .... Doudi Shoua
Kourov .... Randy Raney
Tomask .... Marcus Gilbert
Nissem .... Alon Abutbul
Rahim .... Mahmoud Assadollahi
Khalid .... Yosef Shiloah
Uri .... Shaby Ben-Aroya
and Harold Diamond, Seri Mati, Hany Said El Deen, Marciano Shorhi, and Sadiq Tawfiq, Julian Patrice, Tal Kastoriano, Benny Bruchim, Tikva Aziz, Milo Rafi

(Tri-Star Pictures)

Sylvester Stallone Above: Richard Crenna, Stallone

FUNNY FARM

(WARNER BROS.) Producer, Robert L. Crawford; Director, George Roy Hill; Screenplay, Jeffrey Boam; Based on the book by Jay Cronley; Executive Producers, Patrick Kelley, Bruce Bodner; Photography, Miroslav Ondricek; Designer, Henry Bumstead; Editor, Alan Heim; Music, Elmer Bernstein; Costumes, Ann Roth; Casting, Marion Bougherty; Production Manager, George Goodman; Assistant Director, Jim Van Wyck; Set Designer, Judy Cammer; Sound, Clark King; Special Effects, Peter Albiez; Dolby Stereo; Technicolor; Rated PG; 101 minutes; June release

CAST

Andy .... Chevy Chase
Elizabeth .... Madolyn Smith
Sheriff Ledbetter .... Kevin O'Morrison
Michael Sinclair .... Joseph Maher
Bud Culbetson .... Jack Gilpin
Betsy Culertson .... Caris Corfman
Newspaper Editor .... William Severs
Crocker .... Mike Starr
Mickey .... Glenn Plummer
Marion Corey, Jr. .... Dakin Matthews
Gus Lotterhand .... William Newman
Mrs. Dinges .... Alice Drummond
Brock .... Brad Sullivan
Hank .... Nesbitt Blaisdell
Peterbrook .... George Buck
Ivy .... Audrie J. Neenan
Mayor Barclay .... MacIntyre Dixon
Lon Criterion .... Bill Fagerbakke
Dirk Criterion .... Nicholas Wyman
Oates .... Raynor Scheine
Ike .... David Woodberry
Ewell .... Kevin Murphy
Marcus .... David Williams
Driving Instructor .... Steve Jonas
Councilman .... Russell Bletzer
and William Duell, Helen Lloyd Breed, Kit Le Fevre, Peter Boyden, Reg E. Cathey, Dan Desmond, Don Plumley, Brett Miller, Jamie Meyer, Dennis Barr, Barbara Baker, Evelyn McLean, Steven John, Robert Conner, Judson Duncan, Alison Hannas, Robert Ingram, Mary Johnson, Kristin Kellom, Paul Link

Right: Chevy Chase
Top Right: Chevy Chase, Madolyn Smith
(Warner Bros.)

The Bustros Family

BEIRUT: THE LAST HOME MOVIE

(CIRCLE RELEASING CORP.) Producer/Director/Co-Writer, Jennifer Fox; Editor/Co-Writer, John Mullen; Photography, Alex Nepomniaschy; Sound, Jeff Brown; Music, Lanny Myers; Lebanese Music Ziad Rahbani; Sound Editors, Francoise Bumoulin, Jonathan Lie[illegible] Documentary; Color; 120 minutes; June release

(Circle Releasing Corp.)

THE PRESIDIO

(PARAMOUNT) Producer, D. Constantine Conte; Director/ Photography, Peter Hyams; Screenplay, Larry Feguson; Executive Producer, Jonathan A. Zimbert; Designer, Albert Brenner; Art Director, Kiandy Stern; Editor, James Mitchell; Co-Producer, Fred Caruso; Music, Bruce Broughton; Casting, Janet Hirshenson, Jane Jenkins; Assistant Director, Alan B. Curtiss; Sound, Gene S. Cantamessa; Special Effects, Philip C. Cory, Al Broussard; Stunts, Glenn Wilder; Dolby Stereo; Technicolor; Panavision; Rated R; 99 minutes; June release

CAST

Lt. Col. Alan Caldwell .... Sean Connery
Jay Austin .... Mark Harmon
Donna Caldwell .... Meg Ryan
Sgt. Mjr. Ross Maclure .... Jack Warden
Arthur Peale .... Mark Blum
Col. Paul Lawrence .... Dana Gladstone
Patti Jean Lynch .... Jeanette Goldstein
Zeke .... Marvin J. McIntyre
Howard Buckley .... Don Calfa
Sgt. Marvin Powell .... John DiSanti
Lt. Mueller .... Robert Lesser
George Spota .... James Hooks Reynolds
Lt. Garfield .... Curtis W. Sims
Secretary .... Rosalyn Marshall
Julius .... Chuckie Davis
Clark .... Patrick Kilpatrick
Commander .... John Allen Vick
Capt. Gordon .... Michael Fosberg
Gloria .... Susan Saiger
Teacher .... Ruth DeSosa
Schmidt .... Peter Fitzsimmons
Dotson .... Pete Antico
Leroy .... Dean Miller
Officer .... Peter Kwong
Lieutenant .... Bob Delegall
Chef .... Richard Kwong
and Rick Zumwalt, Jessie Lawrence Ferguson, Larry Flash Jenkins, Jesse D. Goins, Kim Robillard, Michael Strasser, Ron Cummins, Joe Hart, Clay Wilcox, Bob Rochelle, Tracy Tanen, Jophery Brown, Justin DeRosa, Allan Graf, Frank Orsatti

Right: Sean Connery Top Right: Meg Ryan, Mark Harmon
(Paramount Pictures)

Sean Connery, Mark Harmon

Sean Connery, Jack Warden

BIG

(20th CENTURY FOX) Producers, James L. Brooks, Rob Greenhut; Director, Penny Marshall; Screenplay, Gary Ross, A Spielberg; Photography, Barry Sonnenfeld; Designer, Santo Loquas Editor, Barry Malkin; Costumes, Judianna Makovsky; Music, How Shore; Casting, Juliet Taylor, Paula Herald; Co-Producers, Anne Sp berg, Gary Ross; Production Manager, Robert Grenhut; Assistant rector, Thomas Reilly; Production Executive, Richard Sakai; Art rectors, Tom Warren, Speed Hopkins; Set Decorators, George DeTi Susan Bode; Choreographer, Patricia Birch; Sound, Les Lazarow Orchestrations, Homer Denison; *"It's In Everyone of Us"* by Da Pomeranz, and songs by various other artists; Dolby Stereo; DeL Color; Rated PG; 102 minutes; June release

CAST

Josh Baskin .... Tom Ha
Susan .... Elizabeth Perk
MacMillan .... Robert Log
Paul .... John He
Billy .... Jared Rush
Young Josh .... David Mosc
Scotty Brennen .... Jon Lo
Mrs. Baskin .... Mercedes Ru
Mr. Baskin .... Josh Cl
Cynthia Benson .... Kimberlee M. Da
Freddie Benson .... Oliver Bl
Derek .... Mark Bal
Miss Patterson .... Debra Jo Ru
Karen .... Susan Wil
Phil .... John Rothn
Adam .... Judd Trich

and Erika Katz, Allan Wasserman, Gary Klar, Alec Von Somm Chris Dowden, Rockets Redglare, Jaime Tirelli, Paul Herman, Na Giles, Jordan Thaler, Dana Kaminski, Harvey Miller, Tracy Rein James Eckhouse, Linda Gillen, Mildred R. Vandever, Bert Goldste Kevin Meaney, Peter McRobbie, Paul J. Q. Lee, Keith W. Redd Lela Ivey

Left: Tom Hanks, Elizabeth Perkins, Robert Loggia, John Heard Top Left: Loggia, Hanks
(20th Century Fox)

Tom Hanks, Elizabeth Perkins (Also Above)

Jared Rushton, Tom Hanks Above: David Moscow

Eddie Murphy, Arsenio Hall (Also Right)
Top Right: Murphy, James Earl Jones

COMING TO AMERICA

(PARAMOUNT) Producers, Robert D. Wachs, George Folsey, Jr.; Director, John Landis; Executive Producers, Leslie Belzberg, Mark Lipsky; Screenplay, David Sheffield, Bary W. Blaustein; Story, Eddie Murphy; Music, Nile Rodgers; Photography, Woody Omens; Designer, Richard MacDonald; Editors, Malcolm Campbell, George Folsey, Jr.; Special Make-up, Rick Baker; Costumes, Deborah Nadoolman; Associate Producer, David Sosna; Casting, Jackie Burch; Production Managers, William Watkins, Michael Tadross; Assistant Directors, David Sosna, Richard Patrick; Choreographer, Paula Abdul; Visual Effects, Syd Dutton, Bill Taylor; Art Director, Richard B. Lewis; Sound, William B. Kaplan; Technicolor; Dolby Stereo; Rated R; 116 minutes; June release

CAST

Prince Akeem/Clarence/Saul
Randy Watson .... Eddie Murphy
Semmi/Morris/Extremely Ugly Girl
Reverend Brown .... Arsenio Hall
Oha .... Paul Bates
King Jaffe Joffer .... James Earl Jones
Queen Aoleon .... Madge Sinclair
Colonel Izzi .... Calvin Lockhart
Iman Izzi .... Vanessa Bell
Cab Driver .... Jake Steinfeld
Sweets .... Clint Smith
Landlord .... Frank Faison
Stu .... Uncle Ray Murphy
Soul Glo Woman .... Paulette Banoza
Soul Glo Man .... Clyde R. Jones
Devil Woman .... Patricia Matthews
Fresh Peaches .... Janette Colon
Sugar Cube .... Vanessa Colon
Cleo McDowell .... John Amos
Patrice McDowell .... Allison Dean
Lisa McDowell .... Shari Headley
Darryl Jenks .... Eriq La Salle
Maurice .... Louie Anderson
Mr. Jenks .... Arthur Adams
Mrs. Jenks .... Loni Kaye Harkless
Grandma Jenks .... Montrose Hagins
Mortimer Duke .... Don Ameche
Randolph Duke .... Ralph Bellamy
Face on Cutting Room Floor .... Jim Abrahams
and Garcella Beauvais, Feather, Stephanie Simon, Victoria Dillard, Felicia Taylor, Michele Watley, Sheila Johnson, Raymond D. Turner, Billi Gordon, Cuba Gooding, Jr., Ruben Hudson, Mary Bond Davis, Zara Young, Carla Earle, Karen Renee Owens, Sharon Renee Owens

Right Center: Eddie Murphy , Clint Smith
(Paramount Pictures)

Allison Dean, John Amos, Shari Headley

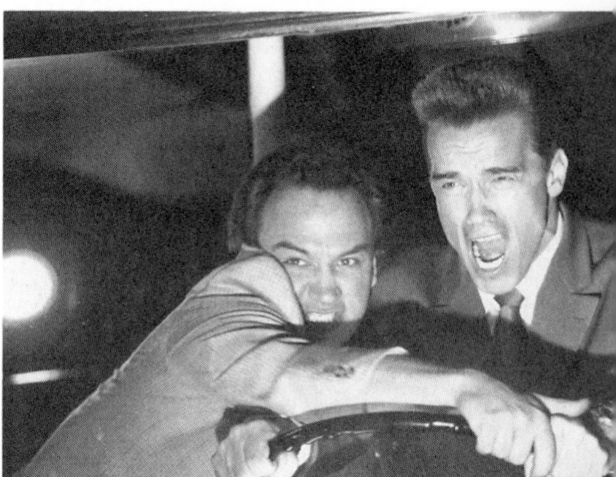

Ed O'Ross Right: Gina Gershon, Arnold Schwarzenegger Top Right: James Belushi, Schwarzenegger

RED HEAT

(TRI-STAR) Producers, Walter Hill, Gordon Carroll; Director/Story, Walter Hill; Screenplay, Harry Kleiner, Walter Hill, Troy Kennedy Martin; Executive Producers, Mario Kassar, Andrew Vajna; Associate Producer, Mae Woods; Photography, Matthew F. Leonetti; Designer, John Vallone; Art Director, Michael Corenblith; Set Decorator, Ernie Bishop; Editors, Freeman Davies, Carmel Davies, Donn Aron; Music, James Horner; Casting, Jackie Burch; Production Manager, Dirk Petersmann; Assistant Directors, James R. Dyer, Barry Thomas; Stunts, Bennie Dobbins; Sound, Richard Bryce Goodman; A Carolco/Lone Wolf/Oak production; Technicolor; Dolby Stereo; Rated R; 106 minutes; June release

CAST

Ivan Danko .... Arnold Schwarzenegger
Art Ridzik .... James Belushi
Lou Donnelly .... Peter Boyle
Viktor Rostavili .... Ed O'Ross
Lt. Stobbs .... Larry Fishburne
Cat Manzetti .... Gina Gershon
Sgt. Gallagher .... Richard Bright
Salim .... J. W. Smith
Abdul Elijah .... Brent Jennings
Hooker .... Gretchen Palmer
Night Clerk .... Pruitt Taylor Vince
Pat Nunn .... Michael Hagerty
Streak .... Brion James
Intern .... Gloria Delaney
TV Announcer .... Peter Jason
Yuri Ogarkov .... Oleg Vidov
Gregor Moussorsky .... Savely Kramarov
Consul Stepanovich .... Gene Scherer
Josip Baroda .... Tengiz Borisoff
Pytor Tatomovich .... Roger Callard
Vagran Rostavili .... Gabor Koncz
Col. Kulikov .... Geza Balkay
Lt. Redetsky .... Zsolt Kortvelyessy
Officer .... Janos Ban
Mongol Hippy .... Masanori Toguchi
Nikolai .... Sven-Ole Thorsen
Sacha .... Norbert Novenyi
Yegor .... Istvan Etlenyi
Piano player .... George Gati
Waiter .... Peter Marikovsky
Gangsters .... Gabor Nemeth, Istvan Vajas, Peter Kis, Atilla Fasi
Ali .... Eric Mansker
Jamal .... Lew Hopson
Nelligan .... Jason Ronard
Audrey .... Gigi Vorgan
Prison Guard .... Allan Graf
Detectives .... Kurt Fuller, Bruno Acalinas
Cop in hospital .... Christopher Mankiewicz
Newsie .... Bob O'Donnell
Waitress .... Marjorie Ransfield
Lupo .... Luis Contreras
Hooligan .... Christopher Anthony Young
Police photographers .... William McConnell, Ed Defusco
Man in phone booth .... Joey D. Vieira
Railroad engineer .... Mike Adams

James Belushi (2nd from L), Richard Bright, Larry Fishburne

Right Center: Richard Bright, Arnold Schwarzenegger, Peter Boyle *(Tri-Star Pictures)*

BIG BUSINESS

OUCHSTONE/BUENA VISTA) Producers, Steve Tisch, Michael yser; Director, Jim Abrahams; Screenplay, Dori Pierson, Marc ıbel; Photography, Dean Cuney; Designer, William Sandell; Editor, ırry Keramidas; Costumes, Michael Kaplan; Music, Lee Holdridge; ısting, Howard Feuer; Production Manager, William S. Beasley; sistant Director, Bruce A. Humphrey; Associate Producer, Bonnie uckheimer-Martell; Musical Supervision/Vocal Arrangements/ ontage Music, Marc Shaiman; Set Decorator, Richard C. Goddard; t Designers, James E. Tocci, Martha Johnston; Sound, Thomas ausey; Production Coordinator, Mauri Syd Gayton; Orchestrations, Hearshen; Stunts, Frank Ferrara, William Erickson; Visual Effects, ic Brevig; Special Visual Effects, Dream Quest Images; In Associa- n with Silver Screen Partners III; From Buena Vista Distribution, .; Dolby Stereo; Rated PG; 97 minutes; June release

CAST

die Shelton .... Bette Midler
se Shelton .... Lily Tomplin
die Ratliff .... Bette Midler
se Ratliff .... Lily Tomlin
one Dimmick .... Fred Ward
aham Sherbourne .... Edward Herrmann
bio Alberici .... Michele Placido
uck .... Daniel Gerroll
chael .... Barry Primus
. Jay Marshall .... Michael Gross
nky Shelton .... Deborah Rush
int Shelton .... Nicolas Coster
ıa Ratliff .... Patricia Gaul
rth Ratliff .... J. C. Quinn
nny Lewis .... Norma MacMillan
der Harlan .... John Hancock
dy .... Mary Gross
on .... Seth Green
enona .... Lucky Webb
. Parker .... Roy Brocksmith
. Stokes .... Lewis Arquette
oung Harlan .... Eddie Junior
ayor Bill Finker .... Ritch Brinkley
da .... Maureen McVerry
il Levon .... Nicholas Rutherford
tey .... Hunter Von Leer
ke .... Andrew Epper
die's Secretary .... Andi Chapman
orts Announcer .... Chick Hearn
ink Ratliff .... Troy Damien
erle Ratliff .... Ryan Francis
MCA Desk Clerk .... Judy Armstrong
b Driver .... Tom La Grua
ıfus .... Matthew James Carlson
d Joe Grifasi, John Vickery, Leo Burmester, Tony Mockus, Carmen genziano, Freddie Parnes, Dan Chambers, Lois De Banzie, Al ancini, Melanie Doctors, Maureen McVerry, Louis Rukeyser, mberly Goldman

Right: Edward Herrmann, Daniel Gerroll
Above: Lily Tomlin, Bette Midler (Also Top)
(Touchstone Pictures)

Lily Tomlin, Fred Ward

Michele Placido, Bette Midler

Dan Aykroyd, John Candy

THE GREAT OUTDOORS

(UNIVERSAL) Producer, Arne L. Schmidt; Director, Howar Deutch; Screenplay/Executive Producer, John Hughes; Photography Ric Waite; Designer, John W. Corso; Editors, Tom Rolf, Willia Gordean, Seth Flaum; Costumes, Marilyn Vance-Straker; Music, Thc mas Newman; Casting, Judith Weiner; Assistant Director, Stephe Lim; Associate Producers, Stephen Lim, Elena Spiotta; Speci Effects, John Frazier; Sound, Darin Knight; Dolby Stereo; CFI colo Rated PG; 92 minutes; June release

CAST

Roman .... Dan Aykroy
Chet .... John Cand
Connie .... Stephanie Farac
Kate .... Annette Benin
Buck .... Chris Youn
Ben .... Ian Giat
Cara .... Hilary Gordo
Mara .... Rebecca Gordo
Wally .... Robert Prosk
Juanita .... Zoaunne LeRo
Cammie .... Lucy Deakin
Waitress .... Nancy Leneha
Jimbo .... John Bloor
Herm .... Lewis Arquett
Reg .... Britt Leac
Boat Yard Owner .... Cliff Bemi
Hot Dog Vendor .... Paul Hanse
and Debra Lee Ortega (Dancing Biker Girl), Sierra Somerville (Girl i arcade), Christine Spiotta, Chris Bass, Shirley Harris, Christophe Kinsman, Andy Prosky, Raleigh Bond, Barry Thompson, Brian Heal

(Universal City Studios)

THE DECLINE OF WESTERN CIVILIZATION PART II: THE METAL YEARS

(NEW LINE CINEMA) Producers, Jonathan Dayton, Valerie Faris; Director, Penelope Spheeris; Executive Producers, Miles Copeland III, Paul Colichman; Production Executive, Daniel Raskov; Editor, Earl Ghaffari; Sound, Mark Hanes; Music Supervisor, Seth Kaplan; Photography, Jeff Zimmerman; Associate Producer, Guy Louthan; Additional Photography, Julio Macat; Additional Music, Simon Steele; Songs by various artists; Soundtrack on Capitol Records; Documentary: Ultra-Stereo; Fotokem Color; Rated R; 90 minutes; June release

CAST

Aerosmith .... Joe Perry, Steven Tyler
Alice Cooper
Kiss .... Gene Simmons, Paul Stanley
Motorhead .... Lemmy
Ozzy Osbourne
Poison .... C. C. DeVille, Bobby Dall, Bret Michaels, Rikki Rockett
Bill Gazzarri
Chris Holmes
Tawn Mastrey
Darlyne Pettinicchio
Lizzy Borden .... Lizzy Borden, Gene Allen, Michael Davis, J. Holmes, Joey Scott
Faster Pussycat .... Taime Downe, Mark Michals, Brent Muscat, Eric Stacy, Greg Steele
Seduce .... Mark Burns, Chuck Andrews, David Black
Odin .... Randy O., Jeff Duncan, Shawn Duncan, Aaron Samson
London .... Nadir D'Priest, Lizzie Grey, Frankie Jones, Brian West, Shea Darek
Megadeth .... Dave Mustaine, Dave Ellefson, Jeff Young, Chuck Beehler

Right Center: Megadeth
(New Line Cinema)

Poison

Kevin Costner, Susan Sarandon

Kevin Costner Left and Top: Susan Sarandon, Kevin Costner

BULL DURHAM

(ORION) Producers, Thom Mount, Mark Burg; Director/Screenplay, Ron Shelton; Executive Producer/Production Manager, David V. Lester; Photography, Bobby Byrne; Editors, Robert Leighton, Adam Weiss; Designer, Armin Ganz; Music, Michael Convertino; Costumes, Louise Frogley; Casting, Bonnie Timmerman; Music Supervisor, Danny Bramson; Associate Producer, Charles Hirschhorn; Assistant Director, Richard J. Kidney; Art Director, David Lubin; Set Decorators, Kris Boxell, David Brace; Production Coordinator, Janice F. Sperling; Sound, Kirk Francis; Special Effects, Vern Hyde, Jeff Hyde; Stunts, Webster Whinery; Sound, Michael Boudry; *"Goin' To The Show"* by Bennie Wallace, Mac "Dr. John" Rabennack, and songs by various other artists; Dolby Stereo; DeLuxe Color; Rated R; 108 minutes; June release

CAST

Crash Davis .... Kevin Costner
Annie Savoy .... Susan Sarandon
Ebby Calvin "Nuke" LaLoosh .... Tim Robbins
Skip .... Trey Wilson
Larry .... Robert Wuhl
Jimmy .... William O'Leary
Bobby .... David Neidorf
Deke .... Danny Gans
Tony .... Tom Silardi
Mickey .... Lloyd Williams
Jose .... Rick Marzan
Nuke's Father .... George Buck
Millie .... Jenny Robertson
Doc .... Greg Avelone
Teddy .... Carey "Garland" Bunting
Whitey .... Robert Dickman
Ed .... Timothy Kirk
Scared Batter .... Don Davis
Abused Umpire .... Stephen Ware
Bat Boy .... Tobi Eshelman
Mayor .... C. K. Bibby
Sandy .... Henry G. Sanders
Ball Park Announcer .... Antoinette Forsyth
Cocktail Waitress .... Shirley Anne Ritter
Minister .... Pete Bock
Chu Chu .... Alan Mejia
Max Patkin .... Max Patkin

Left Center: Susan Sarandon, Tim Robbins
(Orion Pictures)

Jessica Rabbit, Bob Hoskins, Stubby Kaye
Above: Baby Herman, Hoskins

WHO FRAMED ROGER RABBIT

(TOUCHSTONE/BUENA VISTA) Producers, Robert Watts, Fra Marshall; Director, Robert Zemeckis; Screenplay, Jeffrey Price, Pe S. Seaman; Based on the book *"Who Censored Roger Rabbit?"* by G. K. Wolf; Executive Producers, Steven Spielberg, Kathleen Kenne Photography, Dean Cundey; Editor, Arthur Schmidt; Animation rector, Richard Williams; Designers, Elliot Scott, Roger Cain; Mus Alan Silvestri; Visual Effects, Ken Ralston; Mechanical Effec George Gibbs; Costumes, Joanna Johnston; Associate Producers, D Hahn, Steve Starkey; Casting, Priscilla John, Reuben Cannon; Prod tion Manager, Patricia Carr, Jack Frost Sanders; Assistant Directo Michael Murray, David McGiffert; Production Coordinators, Ca Regan, Deborah Hakim; Sound, Tony Dawe, Michael Evje; Art Dir tor, Stephen Scott, William McAllister; Set Decorators, Peter How Robert R. Benton; Special Effects, Peter Biggs, Set Designers, R Barnes, Lunn-Ann Christopher, Brian Morrison, Roer Nichols, Da Watson, Brian Lince, Tony Dunsterville, Brian Warner, Bob Wies ger, Michael Lantieri, Clayton Pinney, Robert Spurlock; Chief P peteer, David Alan Barclay; Associate Editors, Peter Lonsdale, Co Wilson; Choreography, Quinny Sacks, David Toguri; Supervising A imators, Andreas Deja, Russell Hall, Phil Nibbelink, Simon We Animation Effects, Christopher Knott; Special Visual Effects, dustrial Light & Magic; Stunts, Peter Diamond; Dolby Stereo; Ra Color/Metrocolor/DeLuxe Color; Rated PG; 103 minutes; June rele

CAST

Eddie Valiant	Bob Hosk
Judge Doom	Christopher Llo
Dolores	Joanna Cass
Roger Rabbit	Charles Fleisc
Marvin Acme	Stubby Ka
R. K. Maroon	Alan Tilv
Lt. Santino	Richard Le Parmen
Baby Herman	Lou Hir
Benny the Cab	Charles Fleisc
Jessica's Performance Model	Betsy Brant
Raoul (Director)	Joel Sil
Augie	Paul Sprin
Angelo	Richard Ridi
Arthritic Cowboy	Edwin Cr
Soldier	Lindsay Holi
Midget	Mike Edmo
Editor	Morgan De
Kids	Danny Capri, Christopher Hollo John-Paul Si
Blonde Starlet	Laura Fran
Forensics	Joel Cuttrara, Billy J. Mitc
Mailman	Eric B. Sin
Newscaster	Ed Herl
Conductor	James O'Conr
Teddy Valiant	Eugene Guirter
Mrs. Heman	April Winc
Gorilla	Morgan De
Betty Boop	Mae Que
Daffy Duck/Tweety Bird/Sylvester/Porky Pig/Bugs Bunny	Mel Bl
Donald Duck	Tony Ansel
Hippo	Mary T. Radf
Yosemite Sam	Joe Alas
Smart Ass	David Lan
Greasy/Psycho	Charles Fleisc
Stupid	Fred Newn
Wheezy	June Fo
Birds	Russi Tay
Toad	Les Perk
Droopy	Richard Willia
Lena Hyena	June Fo
Mickey Mouse	Wayne Allw
Bullets	Pat Buttram, Jim Cummings, Jim Gall
Singing Sword	Frank Sin
Minnie Mouse/Birds	Russi Tay
Goofy/Wolf	Tony P
Pinocchio	Peter We
Woody Woodpecker	Cherry Da
Jessica Rabbit	Kathleen Tur
Jessica's Singing Voice	Amy Irv

Top Left: Roger Rabbit, Bob Hoskins
Below: Roger, Christopher Lloyd
(Touchstone Pictures)

1988 Academy Award Winner for Best Film Editing, Visual Effects, Sound Effects Editing,

Tom Cruise, Elisabeth Shue

COCKTAIL

(TOUCHSTONE) Producers, Ted Field, Robert W. Cort; Director, Roger Donaldson; Screenplay, Heywood Gould, based on his book; Photography, Dean Semler; Designer, Mel Bourne; Editor, Neil Travis; Costumes, Carole Childs; Music, J. Peter Robinson; Casting, Donna Isaacson, John Lyons; Assistant Director, Rob Cowan; Art Director, Dan Davis; Sound, Richard Lightstone; Songs by various artists; presented in association with Silver Screen Partners III, an Interscope Communications production; Distributed by Buena Vista Pictures; Dolby Stereo; Color; Rated R; 103 minutes; July release

CAST

Brian Flanagan .... Tom Cruise
Doug Coughlin .... Bryan Brown
Jordan Mooney .... Elisabeth Shue
Bonnie .... Lisa Banes
Mr. Mooney .... Laurence Luckinbill
Kerry Coughlin .... Kelly Lynch
Coral .... Gina Gershon
Uncle Pat .... Ron Dean
Eddie .... Robert Donley
Eleanor .... Ellen Foley
Dulcy .... Andrea Morse

and Chris Owens, Justin Louis, John Graham, Richard Thorn (Soldiers), Robert Greenberg, Harvey Alperin, Sandra Will Carradine, Allan Wasserman, E. Hampton Beagle, Parker Whitman, Rick Livingston, Bill Bateman, Jean Pflieger, Rosalyn Marshall, Jeff Silverman, Rich Crater, Marykate Harris, Lew Saunders (Job Interviewers), Jack Newman (Economics Teacher), Paul Benedict (Finance Teacher), Diane Douglass (Mrs. Rivkin), George Sperdakos (English Teacher), David Chant (Chinese Porter), Dianne Heatherington, Arlene Mazerole (Waitresses), Paul Abbott (Snotty Customer), Ellen Maguire, Joseph Zaccone (Bar Patrons), Larry Block (Bar Owner), Kelly Connell (Yuppie Poet), Gerry Bamman, James Eckhouse, Reathel Bean, Peter Boyden (Tourists), Luther Hansraj (Ambulance Attendant), Leroy Gibbons (Singer), Rupert "Ojiji" Harvey, Eric "Babyface" Walsh, Hal "Saint" Duggan, Walter "Crash" Morgan, Charles "Tower" Sinclair, Haile Yeates (Messenjah Band Members). Ken McGregor (Sculptor), Liisa Repo-Martell, Adam Furfaro (Young Couple in deli), Kim Nelles (Female artist), David L. Crowley (Doorman)

Left: Elisabeth Shue, Tom Cruise
Top: Cruise, Bryan Brown
(Touchstone Pictures)

Tom Cruise

Dudley Moore, Liza Minnelli

ARTHUR 2 ON THE ROCKS

(WARNER BROS.) Producer, Robert Shapiro; Director, Bud Yorkin; Screenplay, Andy Breckman; Executive Producer, Dudley Moore; Photography, Stephen H. Burum; Designer, Gene Callahan; Editor, Michael Kahn; Music, Burt Bacharach; Costumes, Anna Hill Johnston; Casting, Mike Fenton, Jane Feinberg, Valorie Massalas; Production Manager, Phil Rawlins; Assistant Director, Bob Girolami; Art Director, Hub Braden; Set Designer, P. Michael Johnstone; Set Decorator, Lee Poll; Sound, Jim Tannenbaum; *"Love Is My Decision (Theme from Arthur 2 On the Rocks)"* by Burt Bacharach, Carole Bayer Sager, Chris De Burgh/Vocal, Chris De Burgh, and songs by various other artists; Dolby Stereo; Soundtrack on A&M Records; Technicolor; Rated PG; 113 minutes; July release

CAST

Arthur Bach .... Dudley Moore
Linda Marolla Bach .... Liza Minnelli
Hobson .... John Gielgud
Martha Bach .... Geraldine Fitzgerald
Burt Johnson .... Stephen Elliott
Fairchild .... Paul Benedict
Susan Johnson .... Cynthia Sikes
Mrs. Canby .... Kathy Bates
Mr. Butterworth .... Jack Gilford
Bitterman .... Ted Ross
Ralph Marolla .... Barney Martin
Stanford Bach .... Thomas Barbour
Millionaire .... David O'Brien
Ship Steward .... P.J. Benjamin
Troy .... Daniel Greene
Greta .... Molly McClure
Cindy .... Brogan Lane
Hank .... Joseph Leon
Hardware Store Customers .... Kenneth Magee, Cameron Johann
and Ron Canada, John Vennema, John Zee, Marcia Wolf, Aileen Fitzpatrick, Frederikke Borge, John O'Neill, Mary Betten, Carl Bressler, Lynet Morrow, Linda Borgeson, Don Stark, J. Christopher Sullivan, Nick Demauro, Kenneth Magee, Cameron Johann

(Warner Bros.)

IT TAKES TWO

(UNITED ARTISTS) Producer, Robert Lawrence; Director, David Beaird; Screenplay, Richard Christian Matheson, Thomas Szollosi; Executive Producer, Steve Nicolaides; Designer, Richard Hoover; Photography, Peter Deming; Editor, David Garfield; Music Supervisor, Peter Afterman; Music, Carter Burwell; Costumes, Reve Richards; Casting, Paul Bengston, David Cohn; Production Manager, Steve Nicolaides; Assistant Director, Christopher Griffin; Production Executive, Anthony Amatullo; Production Coordinator, Linda Allan-Folsom; Art Directors, Mark Billerman, Gregory Wm. Bolton, Michael Okowita; Set Decorator, Suzette Sheets; Special Photography, Arthur Krauss; Sound, Walter B. Martin, Jr.; Sets, P.S.S.-Ed Angel; Special Effects, Greg Hull, William Purcell; Choreography, Sarah Elgart; *"Zydeco Down Dallas Alley"* by Stanley Dural, Jr. & Ted Fox/Vocal, Buckwheat Zydeco; from MGM/UA Communications; Dolby Stereo; Rated PG-13; 81 minutes; July release

CAST

Travis Rogers .... George Newbern
Stephi Lawrence .... Leslie Hope
Jonni Tigersmith .... Kimberly Foster
George Lawrence .... Barry Corbin
Wheel .... Anthony Geary
Joyce Rogers .... Frances Lee McCain
Dee Dee .... Patrika Darbo
Dave Chapman .... Marco Perella
Judd Rogers .... Bill Bolender
Dolan .... Jerry Biggs
Barry .... Scott Fult
Walter .... Jim Holme
Preacher .... John Hussey
Bucholtz .... Mickey Jone
Bus Driver .... Bill Thurma
Jasmine .... Ann Walke
Frank .... Glenn Withrov
Wang .... Ralph Ah
Mr. Brill .... Brian Apthorp
Seamstress #1 .... Tricia Aver
Lisa .... Theresa Bel
Megan .... Megan Blak
Louise .... Cindy Brook
Tina .... Bobbi Candle
Ahmet .... Leland Crook
O.T. .... Joe Delan
Carlotta .... Cecelia Flore
Theo .... David Husse
Baker .... Dale Kasse
Spence .... Robert Knot
Bus Clerk .... Dennis Lett
Jo Jo .... Linwoo
Tammy .... Kathleen Rodge
Pedro .... Carl Schaeffe
Jake .... Jules Tenno
Elizabeth .... Sheila Wilso
and Cora Cordona, Wes Forshaw, Anthony Geary, Vernon Grote, John Hawkes, Ada Lynn, Jim Mason, Corrine Plieth, Matthew Posey, David Poynter, Paula Reano, Sheila Wilson, Andrea Parker, Deborah Sites, Tina Omassi, Mia Togo, Charlie Croughwell, Danny Moore

(United Artists Pictures)

George Newbern, Barry Corbin

Clint Eastwood (Also Left)

THE DEAD POOL

(WARNER BROS.) Producer/Production Manager, David Valdes; Director, Buddy Van Horn; Story, Steve Sharon, Durk Pearson, Sandy Shaw; Screenplay, Steve Sharon; Based on characters created by Harry Julian Fink & R. M. Fink; Photography, Jack N. Green; Designer, Edward C. Carfagno; Editor, Ron Spang; Music, Lalo Schifrin; Assistant Director, L. Dean Jones, Jr.; Casting, Phyllis Huffman; Set Decorator, Thomas L. Roysden; Sound, Richard S. Church; Special Effects, Chuck Gaspar, Joe Day, Thomas Mertz, Bruce Robles, Robert Finley; Stunts, Richard (Diamond) Farnsworth; *"Welcome To The Jungle"* by Slash, W. Acl Rose, Steven Adler, Izzy Stradlin, Duff Rose McKagen/Performance, Guns N' Roses; Dolby Stereo; Technicolor; Rated R; 91 minutes; July release

CAST

Harry Callahan .... Clint Eastwood
Samantha Walker .... Patricia Clarkson
Peter Swan .... Liam Neeson
Al Quan .... Evan C. Kim
Harlan Rock .... David Hunt
Captain Donnelly .... Michael Currie
Lt. Ackerman .... Michael Goodwin
Patrick Snow .... Darwin Gillett
Lou Janero .... Anthony Charnota
D. A. Thomas McSherry .... Christopher Beale
Lt. Ruskowski .... John Allen Vick
Johnny Squares .... James Carrey
Jeff Howser .... Nicholas Love
Vicky Owens .... Maureen McVerry
Suzanne Dayton .... Victoria Bastel
Molly Fisher .... Ronnie Claire Edwards
Detective Hindmark .... Glenn T. Wright
Minister .... Stu Klitsner
TV Associate Producer .... Karen Kahn
Chester Docksteder .... Shawn Elliott
Perry .... Ren Reynolds
Warden Hocking .... Edward Hocking
Butcher Hicks .... Diego Chairs
Pirate Captain .... Patrick Valentino
Detective Dacey .... Phil Dacey
Gus Wheeler .... Louis Giambalvo
Sgt. Holloway .... Peter Anthony Jacobs
Nolan Kennard .... Bill Wattenburg
Sgt. Waldman .... Lloyd Nelson
Jason .... Justin Whalin
Carl .... Kris LeFan
Dr. Friedman .... John Frederick Jones
and Jeff Richmond, Patrick Van Horn, Sigrid Wurschmidt, Deborah A. Bryan, John X. Heart, Kathleen Turco-Lyon, Michael Faqir, Wallace Choy, Kristopher Logan, Scott Vance, Ed Hodson, Calvin Jones

Left Center: Clint Eastwood, Patricia Clarkson
(Warner Bros.)

Clint Eastwood Above: Eastwood, Evan Kim

John Ashton, Charles Grodin, Robert De Niro

MIDNIGHT RUN

(UNIVERSAL) Producer/Director, Martin Brest; Screenplay, Geor Gallo; Executive Producer, William S. Gilmore; Associate Produce Dan York; Photography, Donald Thorin; Designer, Angelo Grahar Editors, Billy Weber, Chris Lebenzon, Michael Tronick; Music, Da ny Elfman; Costumes, Gloria Gresham; Casting, Michael Chinic Bonnie Timmermann; Production Managers, Larry Powell, Murr Schwartz; Assistant Directors, Bill Elvin, Jerry Ziesmer; Stunts, Gler H. Randall, Jr.; Set Decorator, George R. Nelson; Art Director, Jam J. Murakami; Sound, Jim Alexander; Production Coordinator, P Chapman; Set Designer, Peter J. Kelly; Special Effects, Roy Arboga Orchestrator, Steve Bartek; A City Light Films Production; Soundtra on MCA Records; Astro Color/Metrocolor; Rated R; 122 minutes; Ju release

CAST

Jack Walsh .... Robert De Ni
Jonathan Mardukas .... Charles Grod
Alonzo Mosely .... Yaphet Kot
Marvin Dorfler .... John Asht
Jimmy Serrano .... Dennis Fari
Eddie Moscone .... Joe Pantolia
Tony Darvo .... Richard Foron
Joey .... Robert Miran
Jerry Geisler .... Jack Keh
Gail .... Wendy Philli
Denise .... Danielle DuCl
Sidney .... Philip Baker Ha
Red Woods .... Thom McCleist
Bus Ticket Clerk .... Mary Gil
Monroe Bouchet .... John Toles-B
Sergeant Gooch .... Thomas J. Hageboe
Stanley .... Stanley Whi
Mrs. Nelson .... Lois Smi
Dana Mardukas .... Fran Br
Carmine .... Frank Pes
Jason .... Matt Jennin
Coffee Shop Waitress .... Rosemarie Murp
FBI Agent Perry .... Tom Irw
FBI Agent Tuttle .... Jimmy Ray Wee
and Scott McAfee, Linda Margules, Michael D. Gainsborough, Jo Hammil, Lou Felder, Cameron Milzer, Sonia M. Roberts, Sam San ers, Paul Joseph McKenna, Jack N. Young, Robert Coleman, Willia Robbins

Top Left: Robert De Niro, Charles Grodin Below: Grodin, De Niro
(Universal City Studios)

Richard Foronjy, Robert Miranda, Robert De Niro, Charles Grodin

DIE HARD

(20th CENTURY FOX) Producers, Lawrence Gordon, Joel Silver; Director, John McTiernan; Screenplay, Jeb Stuart, Steven E. de Souza; Based on the novel by Roderick Thorp; Executive Producer, Charles Gordon; Photography, Jan De Bont; Designer, Jackson DeGovia; Editors, Frank J. Urioste, John F. Link; Visual Effects, Richard Edlund; Costumes, Marilyn Vance-Straker; Casting, Jackie Burch; Music, Michael Kamen; Associate Producer/Production manager, Beau E. L. Marks; Assistant Director, Benjamin Rosenberg; Production Executives, Lloyd Levin, Riley Kathryn Ellis; Art Director, John R. Jensen; Set Decorator, Phil M. Leonard; Set Designers, E. C. Chen, Roland Hill; Sound, Al Overton; Stunts, Charles Picerni; Special Effects, Al Di Sarro, William Aldridge; Visual Effects, Brent Boates; Songs by various artists; Dolby Stereo; Panavision; DeLuxe Color; Rated R; 131 minutes; July release

CAST

John McClane .... Bruce Willis
Holly Gennaro McClane .... Bonnie Bedelia
Sgt. Al Powell .... Reginald Veljohnson
Dwayne T. Robinson .... Paul Gleason
Argyle .... De'Voreaux White
Thornburg .... William Atherton
Ellis .... Hart Bochner
Takagi .... James Shigeta
Hans Gruber .... Alan Rickman
Karl .... Alexander Godunov
Franco .... Bruno Doyon
Tony .... Andreas Wisniewski
Theo .... Clarence Gilyard, Jr.
Alexander .... Joey Plewa
Marco .... Lorenzo Caccialanza
Kristoff .... Gerard Bonn
Eddie .... Dennis Hayden
Uli .... Al Leong
Heinrich .... Gary Roberts
Fritz .... Hans Buhringer
James .... Wilhelm von Homburg
Big Johnson .... Robert Davi
Little Johnson .... Grand L. Bush
Rivers .... Carmine Zozzora
Ginny .... Dustyn Taylor
Hasseldorf .... George Christy
Young Cop .... Anthony Pecik
Harvey Johnson .... David Ursin
Gail Wallens .... Mary Ellen Trainor
Lucy McClane .... Taylor Fry
John Jr. .... Noah Land
Paulina .... Betty Carvalho

and Bill Marcus, Rick Ducoomun, Cheryl Baker, Richard Parker, Diana James, Shelley Pogoda, Selma Archerd, Scot Bennett, Rebecca Broussard, Kate Finlayson, Shanna Higgins, Kym Malin, Kip Waldo, Mark Goldstein

Left: Alexander Godunov Top: Bruce Willis
Below: Alan Rickman, Bonnie Bedelia
(20th Century Fox)

Reginald VelJohnson, Paul Gleason

Bruce Willis

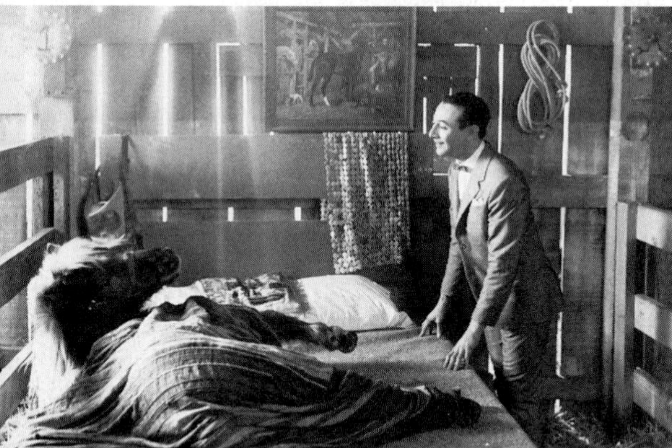

Valeria Golino, Pee-wee Herman Above: Herman

BIG TOP PEE-WEE

(PARAMOUNT) Producers, Paul Reubens, Debra Hill; Directo Randal Kleiser; Screenplay, Paul Reubens, George McGrath; Exec tive Producers, William McKuen, Richard Gilbert Abramson; Photo raphy, Steven Poster; Designer, Stephen Marsh; Editor, Jeff Gourso Visual Effects, Richard Edlund; Music, Danny Elfman; Casting, Vi toria Thomas; Costumes, Robert Turturice; Production Manager, Ki Neumann; Assistant Director, Roger Joseph Pugliese; Art Directo Beala B. Neel; Set Decorator, Anne D. McCulley; Set Designe Stephen Homsy, William J. Newmon II, Richard W. Pittman, C Aldana; Sound, Kirk Francis; Additional Editor, Dianne Ryd Rennolds; Orchestrators, Steve Bartek, William Ross, Steven Sc Smalley; Choreographer, Patsy Swayze; Animal Coordinator, Hub G. Wells, Animal Actors of Hollywood; Stunts, Bill Couch; Spec Effects, Matt Sweeney, Fred Tessaro; "*Barnyard Circus Parade*" "*The Girl on the Flying Trapeze*" by Danny Elfman "*Big Top Final* by Danny Elfman, Randal Kleiser, George McGrath, Paul Reuber and songs by other artists; Soundtrack on ARISTA Records; Dol Stereo; Technicolor; Rated PG; 86 minutes; July release

CAST

Pee-wee Herman .... Pee-wee Herm
Winnie .... Penelope Ann Mil
Mace Montana .... Kris Kristoffers
Gina Piccolapupula .... Valeria Goli
Voice of Vance the Pig .... Wayne Wh
Midge Montana .... Susan Tyrr
Mr. Ryan .... Albert Henders
Otis .... Jack Murdo
Deke .... David By
Mrs. Dill .... Mary Jacks
Mrs. Haynes .... Frances B
Joe the Blacksmith .... Leo V. Gord
Pearl .... Anne Seymo
Sheriff .... Kenneth Tob
Cook .... Ja Robins
Bunny .... Eve Smi
Paolo Piccolapupula .... Andrew Sha
Andy .... Mihaly "Michu" Meszar
Otto the Strongman .... Franco Collum
Snowball the Clown .... Terrence V. Ma
Clownie .... Vance Colv
Oscar the Liontamer .... Matthias Hu
Duke the Dog-Faced Boy .... Benicio Del To
Big John .... Kevin Peter H
Zelda the Bearded Lady .... Lynne Marie Stew
Dell the Human Cannonball .... John Sherr
Shim the Half Man/Half Woman .... Joey Ar
Ruth .... Helen Infield S
Dot .... Carol Infield Seno
Costume Woman .... Bunny Summe
Child-Mr. Ryan .... Kevin B. Kaplow
Child-Otis .... Jeffrey R. Sh
Child-Deke .... Dustin Diamo
Child-Mrs. Haynes .... Savanah Pr
Child-Mrs. Dill .... Lisa M. B
Child-Sheriff .... Shea Joach
Child-Pearl .... Marie Hawki
Honey .... Judy Rubenfe
Herman .... Milton Rubenfe
and Molly Ann Carter, Myka Peck, Dustin Berkovitz, Kit MacKenz Jered Aspenson, Shelly Rudolph, Cheryl Treibitz, Jenniffer Mill Diane C. Valentine, Gainer C. Johnson, Alison Logsden, Patricia Peters, Lynn Marie Polke, Lita Villacana, Stephanie Hodge

Top Left: Pee-wee Herman, Penelope Ann Miller Below: Pee-wee Herman, Kris Kristofferson
(Paramount Pictures)

Anthony Edwards, Lauren Bacall Right: Robert Mitchum Top Right: Virginia Madsen, Anthony Edwards

MR. NORTH

SAMUEL GOLDWYN) Producers, Steven Haft, Skip Steloff; Di-ector, Danny Huston; Executive Producer, John Huston; Co-Producer/'roduction Manager, Tom Shaw; Associate Producers, David R. ımes, Sandra Birnhak Ames; Screenplay, Janet Roach, John Huston, ames Costigan; Based on the novel *"Theophilus North"* by Thornton Vilder; Photography, Robin Vidgeon; Designer, Eugene Lee; Editor, ɭoberto Silvi; Music, David McHugh; Casting, Risa Bramon, Billy Iopkins; Costumes, Rita Riggs; Music Supervisor, Seth Kaplan; Pro-uction Supervisor, Eric Barrett; Production Executive, Al Ruban; Ken ɭeiner; Camera, Steven Shank; Assistant Director, Anthony J. Cer-one; Production Coordinator, Anne M. Shaw; Set Decorator, Sandra Nathanson; Sound, William Randall; Ultra-Stereo; Metrocolor; Rated 'G; 92 minutes; July release

CAST

heophilus North .... Anthony Edwards
ames McHenry Bosworth .... Robert Mitchum
Irs. Amelia Cranston .... Lauren Bacall
Ienry Simmons .... Harry Dean Stanton
'ersis Bosworth-Tennyson .... Anjelica Huston
Ilspeth Skeel .... Mary Stuart Masterson
ally Boffin .... Virginia Madsen
arah Baily-Lewis .... Tammy Grimes
Dr. Angus McPherson .... David Warner
Galloper Skeel .... Hunter Carson
YMCA Clerk .... Christopher Durang
George Harkness Skeel .... Mark Metcalf
Mary Skeel .... Katharine Houghton
udge .... Judge Thomas H. Needham
Willie .... Richard Woods
. Liselotte .... Harriet Rogers
Natalie Denby .... Layla Sommers
oseph Denby .... Lucas Hall
uther Denby .... Thomas-Lawrence Hand
Mrs. Denby .... Linda Peterson
Mr. Danforth .... Cleveland Amory
Michael Patrick Ennis III .... Christopher Lawford
Arresting Officer .... Albert H. Conti
Eloise .... Katherine Wiatt
ohnny .... Jason Adams
Claybourne Turhommounde .... Arthur Bowen
Amanda Venable .... Marieta Tree
Butler Venable .... Richard Kneeland
Miss Wetmore .... Allegra Huston
YMCA Visitors .... Barbara Blossom, Mara Clark, Belle McDonald, Bill L. McDonald, John Heeney McKay
Bartender .... William Lynch

(Samuel Goldwyn Co.)

Anjelica Huston, Anthony Edwards Above: Edwards

Lou Diamond Phillips, Kiefer Sutherland, Emilio Estevez, Casey Siemaszko, Charlie Sheen, Dermot Mulroney

YOUNG GUNS

(20th CENTURY FOX) Producers, Joe Roth, Christopher Cain; Director, Christopher Cain; Screenplay, John Fusco; Executive Producers, John Fusco, James G. Robinson; Co-Producers, Irby Smith, Paul Schiff; Photography, Dean Semler; Music, Anthony Marinelli, Brian Banks; Editor, Jack Hofstra; Designer, Jane Musky; Costumes, Richard Hornung; Casting, Penny Perry; Assistant Director, Myers; Sound, Mike Minkler, Wylie Stateman; Art Director, Harold Thrasher; Stunts, Everett Creach; Special Effects, Joe Quinlivan; a Morgan Creek Productions presentation; Dolby Stereo; Deluxe color; Rated R; 97 minutes; August release

CAST

William H. Bonney .... Emilio Estevez
Doc Scurlock .... Kiefer Sutherland
Chavez Y Chavez .... Lou Diamond Phillips
Dick Brewer .... Charlie Sheen
"Dirty Steve" Stephens .... Dermot Mulroney
Charley Bowdre .... Casey Siemaszko
John Tunstall .... Terence Stamp
L. G. Murphy .... Jack Palance
Alex McSween .... Terry O'Quinn
Susan McSween .... Sharon Thomas
J. McCloskey .... Geoffrey Blake
Yen Sun .... Alice Carter
Buckshot Roberts .... Brian Keith
Texas Joe Grant .... Tom Callaway
Pat Garrett .... Patrick Wayne
Mallory .... Lisa Banes
Morton .... Sam Gauny
Baker .... Cody Palance
Henry Hill .... Gadeek
Justice Wilson .... Victor Izay
John Kinney .... Allen Robert Keller
Peppin .... Craig M. Erikson
Dolan .... Jeremy H. Lepard
Sheriff Brady .... Daniel Kamin
and Richela Renkun (Bar Girl), Pat Lee (Janey), Gary Kanin (Colonel Dudley), Forrest Broadley (Rynerson), Jeff Prettyman (Judge Bristol), Randy Travis (Ring Member), Alan Tobin (Bartender), Joey Hanks (Hindman), Loyd Lee Brown (Soldier), Elena Parres (Manuela's Mother)

Top Right: Terence Stamp, Emilio Estevez Below: Jack Palance, Stamp
(Morgan Creek Productions)

Emilio Estevez, Terry O'Quinn, Sharon Thomas Above: Lou Diamond Phillips

CLEAN AND SOBER

'ARNER BROS.) Producers, Tony Ganz, Deborah Blum; Director, enn Gordon Caron; Screenplay, Tod Carroll; Executive Producer, n Howard; Photography, Jan Kiesser; Designer, Joel Schiller; Edi-, Richard Chew; Co-Producer, Jay Daniel; Music, Gabriel Yared; stumes, Robert Turturice; Casting, Marion Dougherty, Glenn niels; Production Manager, Robert Latham Brown; Assistant Direc-, James Simons; Art Director, Eric W. Orbom; Set Designer, Greg palia; Set Decorator, Don Remacle; Sound, Ron Judkins; Orchestra-n, Georges Rodi; Stunts, Chris Howell; Special Effects, Richard tliff; Songs by various artists; Dolby Stereo; Technicolor; Rated R; 4 minutes; August release

CAST

ryl Poynter .... Michael Keaton
arlie Standers .... Kathy Baker
aig .... Morgan Freeman
nald Towle .... Tate Donovan
vier .... Henry Judd Baker
s .... Claudia Christian
ler .... J. David Krassner
b .... Dakin Matthews
eryl Ann .... Mary Catherine Martin
e .... Pat Quinn
lmissions Counsellor .... Terri Hanauer
ctor .... David A. Kimball
ad Nurse (Detox) .... Veronica Redd
rses .... Sharie Doolittle, Sharon Medearis
ry "Ike Turner" .... Nick Savage
vier's Girlfriend .... Sandra Foster
chard Dirks .... M. Emmet Walsh
nny .... Luca Bercovici
e .... Pamela Dunlap
eila .... Leslie Neale
artin Laux .... Brian Benben
bbie Laux .... Anne Kerry Ford
amer .... Ben Piazza
ard Executives .... Michael Francis Clarke, Doug MacHugh
eaning Lady .... Claudia Robinson
lston Receptionist .... Harley Kozak
ren Peluso .... Serina Robinson
tective .... Al Pugliese
cket Agent .... Stephanie Menuez
eel Mill Foreman .... Michael Leopard
ark .... Douglas Roberts
a .... Jean Nash

Right: Tate Donovan, Michael Keaton
Top Right: Kathy Baker, Keaton
Below: Morgan Freeman, Keaton
(Warner Bros.)

Tate Donovan, Michael Keaton, Claudia Christian

Michael Keaton, M. Emmet Walsh

Matthew Modine, Michelle Pfeiffer

MARRIED TO THE MOB

(ORION) Producers, Kenneth Utt, Edward Saxon; Director, Jonath Demme; Screenplay, Barry Strugatz, Mark R. Burns; Executive Pr ducers, Joel Simon, Bill Todman, Jr.; Associate Producer, R Bozman; Editor, Craig McKay; Photography, Tak Fujimoto; Designe Kristi Zea; Music Supervision, Gary Goetzman, Sharon Boyle; Co tumes, Colleen Atwood; Music, David Byrne; Casting, Howard Feue Production Manager, Kenneth Utt; Assistant Director, Ron Bozma Art Director, Maher Ahman; Set Decorator, Nina Ramsey; Soun Christopher Newman, Michael Tromer, Arthur Bloom; Associate Ec tor, Bill Johnson; Stunts, Frank Ferrara, John Robotham; Speci Effects, EFEX Specialists, Inc.; Songs by Robert Merrill and vario other artists; A Mysterious Arts/Demme Production; Dolby Stere *"Mambo Italiano"* by Robert Merrill/Vocal, Rosemary Clooney, a songs by other artists: Soundtrack on Reprise Records; Dolby Stere Color; Rated R; 103 minutes; August release

CAST

Tommy .... Paul Laz
"Cucumber" Frank De Marco .... Alec Baldw
"The Fat Man" .... Captain Hagger
Mrs. "Fat Man" .... Marlene Willough
Angela De Marco .... Michelle Pfeiff
Rose .... Joan Cusa
Theresa .... Ellen Fol
Phyllis .... O-Lan Jon
Connie Russo .... Mercedes Rue
Tony Russo, Jr. .... Jason All
Joey De Marco .... Anthony J. Ni
Tara .... Tara Duckwor
"Lucky" De Marco .... Max the D
Mike Downey .... Matthew Modi
Ed Benitez .... Oliver Pl
Vinnie "The Slug" .... Frank Ferra
Nick "The Snake" .... Frank G
Al "The Worm" .... Gary Kl
Tony "The Tiger" Russo .... Dean Stockwe
The Guy At The Piano .... Gary Goetzma
Carlo Whispers .... Carlos Giovan
Karen Lutnick .... Nancy Trav
Johnny "King's Roost" King .... Warren Mill
"Stevarino" .... Steve Vigna
"Butch" .... James Reno Pellicc
Maitre d' .... Daniel Dass
Regional Director Franklin .... Trey Wils
Homicide Detective .... Colin Quir
"The Priest" .... David Johanse
Frank's Mom .... Maria Karnilo
Mr. Spoons .... Joseph L. "Mr. Spoons" Jon
Mr. Chicken Lickin' .... Tracey Walt
Rita "Hello Georgeous" Harcourt .... "Sister" Carol Ea
"The Clown" .... Chris Isa
Uncle Joe Russo .... Al Lew
The Gal At The Piano .... D. Stanton Miran
Jimmy "Fisheggs" Roe .... Ralph Cors
"The Ambassador" .... Bill Cart
The Face Of Justice .... Obba Babatun
Angie's First Customer! .... Roma Maff
Leonard "Tiptoes" Mazzilli .... Joe Spinne
Goodwill Hunk .... Patrick Phip
and Frank Acquilino, Charles Napier, Diana Puccerella, Suzanne Pu cerella, Dodie Demme, Gene Borkan, Wilma Dore, True Image, Le Jae, Alison Gordy, Pe De Boi, Buzz Kilman

Left Center: Dean Stockwell, Michelle Pfeiffer
Above: Mercedes Ruehl, Michelle Pfeiffer
Top Left: MIchelle Pfeiffer, Matthew Modine ***(Orion Pictures***

Kevin Dillon, Shawnee Smith (Also Right) Top Right: Michael Kenworthy, Smith

THE BLOB

TRI-STAR) Producers, Jack H. Harris, Elliott Kastner; Director, ;huck Russell; Screenplay, Chuck Russell, Frank Darabont; Line 'roducer, Rupert Harvey; Executive Producer, Andre Blay; Assistant)irector, Josh McLaglen; Assistant Director, J. Tom Archuleta; Pro-luction Managers, Gordon Wolf, Daryl Kass; Visual Effects, Hoyt (eatman, Dream Quest Images; Creature Effects/Blob Effects, Lyle ;onway; Make-Up Effects, Tony Gardner; Music, Michael Hoenig;)esigner, Craig Stearns; Casting, Johanna Ray; Editors, Terry Stokes, 'od Feuerman; Photography, Mark Irwin; Production Supervisor,)aryl Kass; Sound, Robert J. Anderson Jr.; Costumes, Joseph Porro; 'roduction Coordinator, Carl Kravetz; Art Director, Jeff Ginn; Set)ecorator, Anne Ahrens; Stunts, Gary Hymes, Steve Holladay; Set)esigners, Randy Moore, Gary Steele, Sally A. Thornton; Crystal 3lob/Meteor Effects, Diligent Dwarves Effects; Mechanical Effects, 'erry Frazee, Frazee & Frazee Inc.; Additional Creature Effects, Stuart Ziff; Blob Effects, Bill Corso, Trey Stokes; Makeup, Janeen Davis; *Prelude to Frenzy"* by Wayne Coster, "*Shattered*" by Mike Slamer, ınd songs by other artists; Ultra-Stereo; Technicolor; Rated R; 92 ninutes; August release

CAST

Aeg Penny .... Shawnee Smith
'aul Taylor .... Donovan Leitch
Scott Jeskey .... Ricky Paull Goldin
3rian Flagg .... Kevin Dillon
;an Man .... Billy Beck
Sheriff Herb Geller .... Jeffrey DeMunn
Fran Hewitt .... Candy Clark
Moss Woolsey .... Beau Billingslea
'harmacist/Mr. Penny .... Art La Fleur
Reverend Meeker .... Del Close
Kevin Penny .... Michael Kenworthy
Eddie Beckner .... Douglas Emerson
Mrs. Penny .... Sharon Spelman
Deputy Bill Briggs .... Paul McCrane
Vicki De Soto .... Erika Eleniak
Sally Jeffers .... Teddy Vincent
George Ruiz .... Clayton Landey
Dr. Meddows .... Joe Seneca
;ol. Hargis .... Jack Rader
Susie .... Judy McCullough
Lance .... Daryl Marsh
Anthony .... Jamison Newlander
Phil Hobbs—Projectionist .... Frank Collison
Theatre Manager .... Pons Maar
Eddie's Mother .... Judith Flanagan
Soldier Outside Town Hall .... Richard Crenna Jr.
Jennings .... Robert Axelrod
and Margaret Smith, Jack Nance, Charlene Fox, Don Brunner, Jacquelyn Masche, Wade Mayer, Charlie Spradling, Kristen Aldrich, M. James Arnett, Peter Crombie, Rick Avery, David Weininger, Moss Porter

(Tri-Star Pictures)

Shawnee Smith, Kevin Dillon (Also Above)

Barbara Hershey Top Left: Willem Dafoe

THE LAST TEMPTATION OF CHRIST

(UNIVERSAL) Producer, Barbara De Fina; Director, Martin Sco sese; Screenplay, Paul Schrader; Based on the novel by Nikos Kazan zakis; Executive Producer, Harry Ufland; Photography, Michael Ba lhaus; Music, Peter Gabriel; Editor, Thelma Schoonmaker; Designe John Beard; Costumes, Jean-Pierre Delifer; Casting, Cis Corman; Juli Alter; Production Manager, Laura Fattori; Assistant Director, Josep Reidy; Art Director, Andrew Sanders; Set Decorator, Giorgio Desider Sound, Amelio Verona; Special Effects, Dino Galliano, Iginio Fioren tini; Choreographer, Lachen Zinoune; Stunts, Franco Salamon; Pro duction Coordinator, Gabriella Toro; Dolby Stereo; Technicolor; Rate R; 164 minutes; August release

CAST

Jesus	Willem Dafo
Judas	Harvey Keite
Zealot	Paul Grec
Centurion	Steven Shi
Mary Mother of Jesus	Verna Bloor
Mary Magdalene	Barbara Hershe
Aged Master	Roberts Blossor
Jeroboam	Barry Mille
Andrew Apostle	Gary Basarab
Zebedee	Irvin Kershne
Peter Apostle	Victor Arg
John Apostle	Michael Bee
Phillip Apostle	Paul Herma
James Apostle	John Luri
Nathaniel Apostle	Leo Burmeste
John the Baptist	Andre Gregor
Martha Sister of Lazarus	Peggy Gormle
Mary Sister of Lazarus	Randy Danso
Lazarus	Tomas Aran
Thomas Apostle	Alan Rosenber
Money Changer	Del Russe
Rabbi	Nehemiah Persof
Saducee	Donald Hodso
Saul/Paul	Harry Dean Stanto
Beggar	Peter Berlin
Pontius Pilate	David Bowi
Girl Angel	Juliette Cato

and Russell Case, Mary Seller, Donna Marie, Mohamed Mabsou Ahmed Nacir, Mokhtar Salouf, Mahamed Ait Fdil Ahmen, Rober Spafford, Doris Von Thury, Penny Brown, Gabi Ford, Dale Wyatt Domenico Fiore, Tomas Arana, Ted Rusoff, Leo Damian, Rober Laconi

(Universal City Studios)

Willem Dafoe (Also Above)

STEALING HOME

VARNER BROS.) Producers, Thom Mount, Hank Moonjean; Di-ctor/Screenplay, Steven Kampmann, Will Aldis; Photography, Bob-· Byrne; Editor, Antony Gibbs; Music, David Foster; Associate ·oducer, Chana Ben-Dov; Designer, Vaughan Edwards; Costumes, ɔbert de Mora; Casting, Bonnie Timmermann; Production Manager, ıura J. Medina; Assistant Director, Betsy Pollock; Production Coordi-ıtor, Richard Liebegott; Sound, Gary Alper; Set Decorator, Robert ·anco; Special Effects, J. C. Brotherhood; A Mount Company Pro-ıction; *"And When She Danced (Love Theme from 'Stealing Home')"* ·/ David Foster, Linda Thompson-Jenner/Performance, Marilyn Mar-ı & David Foster, and songs by various other artists; Dolby Stereo; ·chnicolor; Rated PG-13; 98 minutes; August release

CAST

ılly Wyatt .... Mark Harmon
ınny Wyatt .... Blair Brown
·eenage Alan Appleby .... Jonathan Silverman
lan Appleby .... Harold Ramis
·eenage Billy Wyatt .... William McNamara
ank Chandler .... Richard Jenkins
ım Wyatt .... John Shea
atie Chandler .... Jodie Foster
race Chandler .... Christine Jones
ıeryl .... Jane Brucker
ıd Scott .... Ted Ross
oung Billy Wyatt .... Thacher Goodwin
oung Robin Parks .... Yvette Croskey
obin Parks .... Ollie Davidson
aura Appleby .... Judith Kahan
athan Appleby .... Samuel Chew, Jr.
Irs. Parks .... Miriam Flynn
ooker .... Dani Janssen
obin's Daughter .... Allison Hedges
·ank .... Peter Bucossi
aby Hope .... Katie Kampmann
pirits' Coach .... Richard Dauer
ıd Helen Hunt, Beth Broderick, James Talbot, Pat McDade, Brooke Iills

Right: William McNamara, Jodie Foster
Top Right: Jonathan Silverman, McNamara
(Warner Bros.)

Mark Harmon, Harold Ramis

John Shea, William McNamara Above: McNamara, Yvette Croskey

Christian Slater, Jeff Bridges, Joan Allen, Nina Siemaszko, Anders Johnson, Corky Nemec

TUCKER: THE MAN AND HIS DREAM

(PARAMOUNT) Producers, Fred Roos, Fred Fuchs; Director, Francis Ford Coppola; Screenplay, Arnold Schulman, David Seidler; Executive Producer, George Lucas; Photography, Vittorio Storaro; Designer, Dean Tavoularis; Costumes, Milena Canonero; Music, Joe Jackson; Editor, Priscilla Nedd; Sound, Richard Beggs; Associate Producer, Teri Fettis; Casting, Janet Hirshenson, Jane Jenkins; Art Director, Alex Tavoularis; Production Manager, Ian Bryce; Assistant Director, H. Gordon Boos; Set Decorator, Armin Ganz; Set Designers, Bob Goldstein, Jim Pohl; Production Coordinator, Marueen Murphy; Stunts, Buddy Joe Hooker; Sound, Michael Evje; Special Effects, David Pier, Bob Finley, Jr.; A Lucasfilm Ltd. Production; Additional Music, Carmine Coppola; Songs by various artists; Dolby Soundtrack on A&M Records; Dolby Stereo; Technovision; Technicolor; Rated PG; 111 minutes; August release

CAST

Preston Tucker	Jeff Bridges
Vera	Joan Allen
Abe	Martin Landau
Eddie	Frederic Forrest
Jimmy	Mako
Alex	Elias Koteas
Junior	Christian Slater
Marilyn Lee	Nina Siemaszko
Johnny	Anders Johnson
Noble	Corky Nemec
Frank	Marshall Bell
Kirby	Jay O. Saunders
Kerner	Peter Donat
Bennington	Dean Goodman
Ferguson's Agent	John X. Heart
Stan	Don Novello
Millie	Patti Austin
Stan's Assistant	Sandy Bull
Judge	Joseph Miksak
Floyd Cerf	Scott Beach
Oscar Beasley	Roland Scrivner
Howard Hughes	Dean Stockwell
Narrator	Bob Safford
Doc	Larry Menkin
Fritz	Ron Close
Dutch	Joe Flood
Gas Station Owner	Leonard Gardner
Garage Owner	Bill Bonham
Ferguson's Secretaries	Taylor Gilbert, Abigail Van Alyn
Board Member	Bill Reddick
Mayor	Ed Loerke
Head Engineer	Jay Jacobus
Bennington's Secretary	Anne Lawder
Tucker's Secretarys	Hope Alexander-Willis, Taylor Young
Police Sergeant	Jim Giovanni
Reporter at Trial	Joe Lerer
Ingram	Morgan Upton
SEC Agent	Ken Grantham
Blue	Mark Anger
Jury Foreman	Al Nalbandian
Senator Homer Ferguson	Lloyd Bridges

and David Booth, Jessie Nelson, Al Hart, Cab Covay, James Cranna, Jeanette Lana Sartain, Mary Buffett, Annie Stocking, Michael McShane, Dean Goodman

Left Center: Martin Landau, Jeff Bridges, Lloyd Bridges Above: Joan Allen, Jeff Bridges Top Left: Jeff Bridges
(Paramount Pictures)

Reizl Bozyk, Amy Irving, Sylvia Miles
Top Left: Peter Riegert, Irving
Left: Irving, Jeroen Krabbe

CROSSING DELANCEY

(WARNER BROS.) Producer/Production Manager, Michael Nozik; Director, Joan Micklin Silver; Executive Producer, Raphael Silver; Screenplay, Susan Sandler; Photography, Theo Van de Sande; Designer, Dan Leigh; Editor, Rick Shaine; Music, Paul Chihara, The Roches; Costumes, Rita Ryack; Casting, Meg Simon, Fran Kumin; Associate Producer, Nellie Nugiel; Assistant Director, Louis D'Esposito; Art Director, Leslie E. Rollins; Sound, Dany Michael; Stunts, Phil Neilson; *"Come Softly to Me"* by Gretchen Christopher, Barbara Ellis, Gary Troxel, *"Pounding"* by Terre and Suzzy Roch, *"Lucky" "Enchanted Evening"* by Terre & David Roche/Performances, The Roches, and songs *"Some Enchanted Evening"* by Richard Rodgers & Oscar Hammerstein II; Dolby Stereo; Duart color; Rated PG; 97 minutes; August release

CAST

Isabelle Grossman .... Amy Irving
Sam Posner .... Peter Riegert
Bubbie Kantor .... Reizl Bozyk
Anton Maes .... Jeroen Krabbe
Hannah Mandelbaum .... Sylvia Miles
Lionel .... George Martin
Nick .... John Bedford Lloyd
Cecilia Monk .... Claudia Silver
Mark .... David Pierce
Pauline Swift .... Rosemary Harris
Marilyn Cohen .... Suzzy Roche
Ricki .... Amy Wright
Candyce .... Faye Grant
Karen .... Deborah Offner
Myla Bondy .... Kathleen Wilhoite
Rabbi .... Moishe Rosenfeld
Diva .... Paula Laurence
Leslie .... Susan Blommaert
Aunt Miriam .... Delores Sutton
Mr. Kim .... Young Ho Kim
Book Peddler .... Tudor Sherrard
Mr. Grossman .... Bob Levine
Mrs. Grossman .... Mimi Bensinger
Mickey .... Michael Ornstein
Molly .... Susan Sandler
Sarah Jacobs .... Miriam Phillips
Pat Oleszko .... Pat Oleszko

and Christine Campbell, Reg E. Cathey, Sam Corsi, Vickilyn Reynolds, Myra Taylor, Jacob Harran, Arthur Rubin, Richard Frisch, Stan Page, Tony Perez, Arthur Tracey, Stan Rubin, Debra Johanna Cole, Brad O'Hare, Freda Foh Shen, Mina Bern, Ida Harnden, Ronnie Gilbert, Keith Reddin, John Patrick Shanley

Left Center: Amy Irving, Suzzy Roche
(Warner Bros.)

Sylvia Miles, Amy Irving, Peter Riegert, Reizl Bozyk

BETRAYED

(UNITED ARTISTS) Producer, Irwin Winkler; Director, Costa-Gavras; Screenplay, Joe Eszterhas; Executive Producers, Joe Eszterhas, Hal W. Polaire; Photography, Patrick Blossier; Designer, Patrizia Von Brandenstein; Editor, Joele Van Effenterre; Costumes, Joe I. Tompkins; Music, Bill Conti; Casting, Mary Goldberg; Production Supervisor, Michael Polaire; Production Manager, William Zborowsky; Assistant Director, Rob Cowan; Sound, Pierre Gamet; Art Director, Stephen Geaghan; Set Decorator, Jim Erickson; Special Effects, Ken Speed; Choreographers, Wayne & Doris Knight; "*The Race Is On*" by Don Rollins, and songs by various other artists; from MGM/UA Communications; Dolby Stereo; Alpha Cine & Astro Color; Rated R; 127 minutes; August release

CAST

Katie Phillips/Cathy Weaver .... Debra Winger
Gary Simmons .... Tom Berenger
Michael Carnes .... John Heard
Gladys Simmons .... Betsy Blair
Shorty .... John Mahoney
Wes .... Ted Levine
Flynn .... Jeffrey DeMunn
Al Sanders .... Albert Hall
Jack Carpenter .... David Clennon
Dean .... Robert Swan
Sam Kraus .... Richard Libertini
Rachel Simmons .... Maria Valdez
Joey Simmons .... Brian Bosak
Duffin .... Alan Wilder
Reverend Russell Johnson .... Clifford A. Pellow
Lyle .... Ralph Foody
Betty Jo .... Shawn Schepps
Toby .... Dolores Drake
Buster .... Stephen E. Miller
Ellie .... Suzie Payne
Gary's buddy .... Chris Kubasik
Jud/bartender .... Timothy Jerome
Del .... Jack Ackroyd
Hank .... Howard Siegel
Jeff: hunted man .... Kevin C. White
"Uncle Sam" .... Timothy Hutton

and Ruston Harker, Howard Storey, Bill Dow, Leslie Stolzenberger, Terry David Mulligan, Fred Keating, Dan Conway, Will Zahrn, Jefferson Wagner, Joel Daly, Bob Herron, Eric Geisreiter, Ed Johnson, Wayne Lawson, Reid Seibert, Vic Vogt, Frank Harmon, Wally Marsh, Leroy R. Horn, W. Wayne Arrants, Mimi Bensinger, Bill Corsair, Judith C. Jacobs, Joyce Leigh Bowden, Rodger Parsons, Mary Sharmat

Top Right: Debra Winger, Tom Berenger Below: Debra Winger
(United Artists Pictures)

Marianne Leone

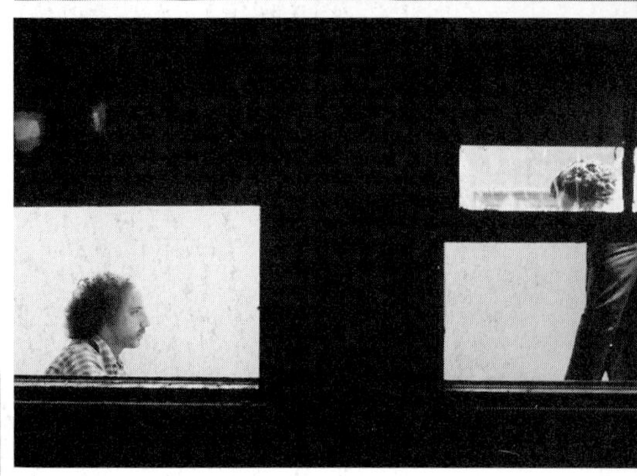

THE THIN BLUE LINE

(MIRAMAX FILMS) Producer, Mark Lipson; Director, Err Morris; Executive Producer, Lindsay Law; Photography, Stefan Czapsky, Robert Chappell; Associate Producer, Brad Fuller; Designer, Te Bafaloukos; Editor, Paul Barnes; Music, Philip Glass; Documentar Duart Color; not rated; 106 minutes; August release.

CAST

Randall Adams .... Adam Goldfir
David Harris .... Derek Hortc
Robert Wood .... Ron Thornhi
Teresa Turko .... Marianne Leor
Popcorn Lady .... Amanda Cap
Police Interrogator .... Michael Nicc

WITH: Randall Adams, David Haris, Gus Rose, Jackie Johnso Marshall Touchton, Dale Holt, Sam Kittrell, Hootie Nelson, Denn Johnson, Floyd Jackson, Edith James, Dennis White, Don Metcalf Emily Miller, R. L. Miller, Elba Carr, Michael Randell, Melvy Carson Bruder

Above: Adam Goldfine, Michael Nicoll
(Miramax Films/Mark Lipson)

HERO AND THE TERROR

(CANNON GROUP) Producer, Raymond Wagner; Director, William Tannen; Screenplay, Dennis Shryack, Michael Blodgett; Based upon the novel by Michael Blodgett; Executive Producers, Menahem Golan, Yoram Globus; Photography, Eric Van Haren Noman; Editor, Christian Adam Wagner; Costumes, Mary Ellen Winston; Designer, Holger Gross; Music, David Frank; Associate Producer/Production Manager, John Zane; Assistant Director, Frank Bueno; Art Directors, Douglas Dick, Mark Haskins; Production Executive, Marc S. Fischer; Casting, Caroline Zelder; Stunts, John Epstein; Fight Choreographer, Rick Prieto; Production Coordinator, Barbara Hall; Sound, Kim Ornitz; Set Decorator Kate Sullivan; Special Effects, John Eggett; *"Two Can Be One"* by David M. Frank, Robert Jason, Denise Osso/Performance, Joe Pizzulo, Stephanie Reach; Ultra-Stereo; TVC Color; Rated R; 97 minutes; August release

CAST

O'Brien .... Chuck Norris
Kay .... Brynn Thayer
Robinson .... Steve James
Simon Moon .... Jack O'Halloran
Dwight .... Jeffrey Kramer
Mayor .... Ron O'Neal
Betsy .... Heather Blodgett
Doheny .... Tony DiBenedetto
Dr. Highwater .... Billy Drago
Copelli .... Joe Guzalo
Chief Bridges .... Peter Miller
Ginger .... Karen Witter
Ginger's Manager .... Lorry Goldman
Doctor .... Christine Wagne
Interviewer .... Bill Harris
Victor .... Branscombe Richmond
Harriet .... Melanie Noble
Receptionist .... Shelley Pogoda
TV Announcer .... Tiiu Leek
Priest .... Dan Barrows
Wall .... Bob Wall
Gina .... Winifred Freedman
and Murphy Dunne, Francette Mace, Deborah Chesher, Saladin James, Michelle Michaels, Lucy Lee Flippin, Leona Mills, John Solari, Jamison Shea, Cynthia Wilde, John David Yarborough, William Tannen

Left: Chuck Norris, Jack O'Halloran Above: Jeff Kramer, Chuck Norris Top: Chuck Norris *(Cannon Films)*

Chuck Norris, Branscombe Richmond

Chuck Norris, Jack O'Halloran

John Sayles, Studs Terkel

Charlie Sheen Above: Christopher Lloyd, Richard Edson, Jim Desmond

EIGHT MEN OUT

(ORION) Producers, Sarah Pillsbury, Midge Sanford; Director Screenplay, John Sayles; Based on the book by Eliot Asinof; Co Producer, Peggy Rajski; Executive Producers, Barbara Boyle, Jerr Offsay; Music, Mason Daring; Photography, Robert Richardson; De signer, Nora Chavooshian; Editor, John Tintori; Costumes, Synthi Flynt; Casting, Barbara Shapiro, Carrie Frazier, Shani Ginsbert, Av Kaufman; Production Manager, Peggy Rajski; Assistant Director, Gar Marcus; Art Director, Dan Bishop; Sound, David Brownlow; Se Decorator, Lynn Wolverton; Production Supervisor, Mary Feldbaue Jansen; Production Coordinator, Heidi Vogel; Music Performances Billy Novick, Peter Ecklund, Butch Thompson, Art Baron, Roby Verdier, Bill Reynolds, Stu Gunn, Jim Mazzy; Arrangements, Bill Novick, Martin Brody; "*I Be Blue*" by John Sayles & Mason Daring Performance, Leigh Harris, and songs by other artists; Soundtrack o Varese Sarabande; Color; Rated PG; 120 minutes; September releas

CAST

Dickie Kerr	Jace Alexande
Buck Weaver	John Cusac
Ray Schalk	Gordan Clap
Swede Risberg	Don Harve
Eddie Collins	Bill Irwi
Fred McMullin	Perry Lan
Kid Gleason	John Mahone
Left Williams	James Rea
Chick Gandil	Michael Rooke
Hap Felsch	Charlie Shee
Eddi Cicotte	David Strathair
"Shoeless" Joe Jackson	D. B. Sweene
Smitty	Jim Desmon
Ring Lardner	John Sayle
Hugh Fullerton	Studs Terke
Billy Maharg	Richard Edso
Arnold Rothstein	Michael Lerne
Bill Burns	Christopher Lloy
Abe Attell	Michael Mante
Sport Sullivan	Kevin Tigh
Heydler	Eliot Asinc
Ban Johnson	Clyde Basse
Charles Comiskey	Clifton Jame
Rothstein's Lawyer	John D. Crai
Austrian	Michael Laski
Ahearn	Randle Me
D. A.	Robert Mo
Ben Short	Bill Raymon
Helen Weaver	Barbara Garric
Kate Jackson	Wendy Makken
Rose Cicotte	Maggie Ren
Lyria Williams	Nancy Travi
PeeWee	Brad Garre
Bucky	Tay Strathair
Scooter	Jesse Vince

and Jack George, Tom Surber, Tom Ledcke, David Carpenter, Be Hatch, Jerry Brent, Bruce Schumacher, Robert Walsh, Matthew Ha rington, Richard Lynch, Garry Williams, Michael Harris, Ken Berr David Rice, Tom Marshall, Merrill Holtzman, Josh Thompson, Leig Harris

Top Left: Michael Rooker, Perry Lang, Don Harvey, Charlie Sheen Below: John Cusack, D. B. Sweeney, Sheen
(Orion Pictures)

RUNNING ON EMPTY

ARNER BROS.) Producers, Amy Robinson, Griffin Dunne; Di-
tor, Sidney Lumet; Screenplay/Executive Producer, Naomi Foner; ecutive Producer, Burtt Harris; Photography, Gerry Fisher; De-ner, Philip Rosenberg; Costumes, Anna Hill Johnstone; Editor, drew Mondshein; Music, Tony Mottola; Casting, Todd M. Thaler; duction Manager, Joseph M. Caracciolo; Assistant Director, Burtt rris; Sound, James Sabat; Art Director, Robert Guerra; Set Decora-, Philip Smith; Songs by various artists; Lorimar Film Entertainment sents A Double Play Production; Metrocolor; Rated PG-13; 118 nutes; September release

CAST

nie Pope .... Christine Lahti
nny Pope .... River Phoenix
hur Pope .... Judd Hirsch
rry Pope .... Jonas Abry
na Phillips .... Martha Plimpton
. Phillips .... Ed Crowley
s Winant .... L. M. Kit Carson
. Patterson .... Steven Hill
s. Patterson .... Augusta Dabney
Jonah Reiff .... David Margulies
ntact at Eldridge St. .... Lynne Thigpen
ool Clerk .... Marcia Jean Kurtz
s. Phillips .... Sloane Shelton
rarian .... Justine Johnston
spital Clerk .... Herb Lovelle
me Ec Teacher .... Bobo Lewis
s. Taylor .... Ronnie Gilbert
id .... Leila Danette
ulding .... Michael Boatman
sic Girl .... Jenny Lumet
s. Powell .... Alice Drummond
glish Teacher .... Angela Pietropinto
iter .... Daniel Dassin
l William Foeller, Carol Cavallo, Joey Thrower, Donna Hanover, omas Fraioli, Burke Pearson, Elzbieta Czyzewska, Mick O'Rourke, a J. Harris

Right: River Phoenix, Judd Hirsch, Christine Lahti, Jonas Abry Above: Phoenix, Martha Plimpton Top Right: Abry, Lahti, Phoenix ***(Warner Bros.)***

ver Phoenix, Christine Lahti, Judd Hirsch, Jonas Abry

River Phoenix

PATTY HEARST

(ATLANTIC) Producer, Marvin Worth; Director, Paul Schrader; Screenplay, Nicholas Kazan; Based on the book *"Every Secret Thing"* by Patricia Campbell Hearst with Alvin Moscow; Executive Producers, Thomas Coleman, Michael Rosenblatt; Line Producer, James Brubaker; Photography, Bojan Bazelli; Designer, Jane Musky; Editor, Michael R. Miller; Associate Producer, Linda Reisman; Costumes, Richard Hornung; Music, Scott Johnson; Casting, Pamela Rack; Production Managers, Mark Allan, Gordon Wolf; Assistant Director, Stephen Dunn; Sound, Ed White; Art Director, Harold Thrasher; Stunts, Greg Walker, Rock Walker; Set Decorator, Jerie Kaelter; Also presented by Zeneith; Jerie Kaelter; Effects, Emmet Kane; *"Way Back Home"* by Wilton Felder/Performance, The Crusaders; Soundtrack on Nonesuch Records; DeLuxe Color; Rated R; 108 minutes; September release

CAST

Patricia Hearst .... Natasha Richardson
Teko .... William Forsythe
Cinque .... Ving Rhames
Yolanda .... Frances Fisher
Wendy Yoshimura .... Jodi Long
Fahizah .... Olivia Barash
Gelina .... Dana Delany
Zoya .... Marek Johnson
Gabi .... Kitty Swink
Cujo .... Pete Kowanko
Jim Browning .... Tom O'Rourke
Steven Weed .... Scott Kraft
Randolph A. Hearst .... Ermal Williamson
Catherine Hearst .... Elaine Revard
Charles Gould .... Marc Siegler
TV Announcer .... Toni Attell
F. Lee Bailey .... Gerald Gordon
Al Johnson .... John Achorn
Assistant D.A. .... Jeff Allin
Doctor .... Robert Dickman
Judge Carter .... Maurice Hill
Court Clerk .... Bill Feeney
Juror Wentz .... Anne Marie Gillis
Juror Wright .... Thomas Wagner
Construction Worker .... Joseph Hart
Student .... Dominic Hoffman

and Jeff Imada, Hawthorne James, Reggie Bruce, Stephannie Howard, Saba Shawel, Leilani Fields, Mayah McCoy, Carey Fox, Steven Avalos, James Lawrence Garfield, Christine Lund, James Kevin Ward, Erich Anderson, James Bershad, Bradford Bancroft, Valerie C. Robinson

Top Right: Olivia Barash, Ving Rhames, Natasha Richardson Below: Pete Kowanko, Richardson, Frances Fisher, Rhames, Barash, William Forsythe, Marek Johnson
(Atlantic Entertainment Group)

Burt Lancaster, Macaulay Culkin

ROCKET GIBRALTAR

(COLUMBIA) Producer, Jeff Weiss; Director, Daniel Petrie; Scree play, Amos Poe; Co-Producer/Production Manager, Marcus Visci Photography, Jost Vacano; Designer, Bill Groom; Editor, Melo London; Music, Andrew Powell; Casting, Donna Isaacson, Jo Lyons; Executive Produces, Michael Ulick, Geoffrey Mayo, Rob Fisher; Assistant Director, Matthew Carlisle; Costumes, Nord Hagg ty; Sound, Bill Daly; Set Decorator, Betsy Klompus; Associate C tume Designer, John Dunn; Special Effects, Steve Kirshoff; Songs various artists; Color; Rated PG; 100 minutes; September release

CAST

Levi Rockwell .... Burt Lancas
Aggie Rockwell .... Suzy An
Rose Black .... Patricia Clarks
Ruby Hanson .... Frances Conr
Amanda "Billi" Rockwell .... Sinead Cusa
Rolo Rockwell .... John Glov
Crow Black .... Bill Pullm
Dwayne Hanson .... Kevin Spac
Orson Rockwell .... John B
Max Hanson .... Nicky Brons
Kane Rockwell .... Dan Cork
Cy Blue Black .... Macaulay Culk
Dawn Black .... Angela Goeth
Flora Rockwell .... Sara Goeth
Emily Rockwell .... Emily P
Jessica Hanson .... Sara R
Dr. Bonacker .... George Mar
Mo Plumm .... Matt Norkl
Tony Joe Basta .... Robert Compo
Policeman .... James McDan
Monsieur Henri .... David Hyde Pie
Waitress .... Renee Colem

(Columbia Pictures)

MOON OVER PARADOR

(UNIVERSAL) Producer/Director, Paul Mazursky; Screenplay, Leon Capetanos, Paul Mazursky; Based on a story by Charles C. Booth; Co-Producers, Pato Guzman, Geoffrey Taylor; Photography, Donald McAlpine; Designer, Pao Guzman; Editor, Stuart Pappe; Costumes, Albert Wolsky; Music, Maurice Jarre; Associate Producers, Lindsay Flickinger, Gary Shusett; Casting, Ellen Chenoweth; Production Manager, John Broderick; Assistant Director, James W. Skotchdopole; Art Director, Markos Flaksman; Sound, Jim Webb; Set Decorator, Alexandre Meyer; Production Coordinator, Judi Rosner; Associate Costume Designer, Marillia Carneiro; Special Effects, Pat Domenico Alan Hill; Songs by various artists; Dolby Stereo; DeLuxe Color; Rated PG-13; 105 minutes; September release

CAST

Jack Noah .... Richard Dreyfuss
Roberto Strausmann .... Raul Julia
Madonna .... Sonia Braga
Ralph .... Jonathan Winters
Aljandro .... Fernando Rey
Himself .... Sammy Davis, Jr.
Clint .... Michael Greene
Midge .... Polly Holliday
Carlo .... Milton Goncalves
Madame Loop .... Charo
Magda .... Marianne Sagebrecht
Gunther .... Rene Kolldehoff
Dieter Lopez .... Richard Russell Ramos
Archbishop .... Jose Lewgoy
Toby .... Dann Florek
Desmond .... Roger Aaron Brown
Jenny .... Dana Delany
Himself .... Dick Cavett
Himself .... Ike Pappas
Himself .... Edward Asner
Momma .... "Carlotta Gerson" (Paul Mazursky)
1st Dictator .... Lorin Dreyfuss
Carmen .... Nika Bonfim
Director .... John C. Broderick
Edgar Low .... David Cale
Menachem Fein .... Reuven Bar-Yotam
Gordon Boyd .... Rod McCary
Alice .... Lora Milligan
Assistant Director .... Jill Mazursky
Casting Secretary .... Nina Fineman
Clara .... Regina Case
Tilde .... Bianca Rossini
Paulo .... Ariel Coelho
Forte .... Guilherme Karan
Nightclub Singer .... Vera Buono
Dante Guzman .... Flavio R. Tambellini
Antonio .... Antonio Negreiros
General Sinaldo .... Nelson Xavier
Umberto Solar .... Mario Guimaraes
Samuel .... Lutero Luiz
and Ursula Cantu, Guara, Giovanna Gold, Carlos Augusto Strasser, Betsy Mazursky, Rui Resende, Nildo Parente, Jorge Cherques

Top: Raul Julia, Richard Dreyfuss, Jose Lewgoy Below: Sonia Braga, Sammy Davis, Jr.
(Universal City Studios)

Fernando Rey, Charo Above: Richard Dreyfuss

Jonathan Winters, Richard Dreyfuss

Billy Mitchell, Michael Zelniker, Hubert Kelly, Forest Whitaker Right: Sam Wright, Whitaker Top: Whitaker, Diane Venora

BIRD

(WARNER BROS.) Producer/Director, Clint Eastwood; Screenplay, Joel Oliansky; Executive Producer/Production Manager, David Valdes; Photography, Jack N. Green; Designer, Edward C. Carfagno; Editor, Joel Cox; Music/Music Supervisor, Niehaus; Assistant Director, L. Dean Jones, Jr.; Casting, Phyllis Huffman; Set Decorator, Thomas L. Roysden; Sound, Willi D. Burton; Special Effects, Joe Day; Set Designer, Judy Cammer; A Malpaso Production; Songs by various artists; Soundtrack on CBS Records: Dolby Stereo; Technicolor; Rated R; 163 minutes; September release

CAST

Charlie "Bird" Parker .... Forest Whitaker
Chan Parker .... Diane Venora
Red Rodney .... Michael Zelniker
Dizzy .... Samuel E. Wright
Buster Franklin .... Keith David
Brewster .... Michael McGuire
Esteves .... James Handy
Young Bird .... Damon Whitaker
Kim .... Morgan Nagler
Dr. Heath .... Arlen Dean Snyder
Moscowitz .... Sam Robards
Dr. Caulfield .... Bill Cobbs
Mayor of 52nd Street .... Hamilton Camp
Gene .... Joey Green
Sid .... John Witherspoon
Frog .... Tony Todd
Mildred Berg .... Jo DeWinter
Ralph the Narc .... Richard Zavaglia
Audrey .... Anna Levine
Wilson .... Hubert Kelly
Prince .... Billy Mitchell
Stratton .... Karl Vincent
Benny Tate .... Jason Bernard
Pee Wee Marquette .... Tony Cox
Baroness Nica .... Diane Salinger
Grainge .... Slim Jim Phantom
Judge .... Matthew Faison
Bird's Lawyer .... Peter Cook
Nun .... Patricia Herd
Violet Welles .... Ann Weldon
Harris .... Tim Russ
Morello .... Richard Jeni
and Penelope Windust, Glenn T. Wright, George Orrison, Chris Bosley, George T. Bruce, Al Pugliese, Lou Cutell, Roger Etienne, Gretchen Oehler, Richard McKenzie, Johnny Adams, Natalia Silverwood, Duane Matthews, Alec Paul Rubinstein, Steve Zettler, Charley Lang, Don Starr, Richard Mawe

(Warner Bros.)

Damon Whitaker (L) Above: Forest Whitaker

1988 Academy Award Winner for Best Sound

SWEET HEARTS DANCE

(TRI-STAR) Producer, Jeffrey Lurie; Director/Executive Producer, Robert Greenwald; Screenplay, Ernest Thompson; Photography, Tak Fujimoto; Designer, James Allen; Editor, Robert Florio; Music/Adaptations, Richard Gibbs; Costumes, Bobbie Read; Associate Producer, Bruce Pustin; Casting, Lora Kennedy; Production Manager, Bruce S. Pustin; Assistant Director, Allan Nicholls; Co-Editor, Janet Bartels; Co-Executive Producers, Lauren Weissman, Gabrielle Mandelik; Set Decorator, R. Lynn Smartt; Scenic Supervisor, Anthony Baronelli; Orchestrations, Philip Giffin; Sound, Mark F. Ulano; Special Effects, Walter Wayne Walser, Layne Robinson; Stunts, Bobby Foxworth; A Chestnut Hill Production; Songs by various artists; Dolby Stereo; Technicolor; Rated R: 101 minutes; September release

CAST

Wiley Boon .... Don Johnson
Sandra Boon .... Susan Sarandon
Sam Manners .... Jeff Daniels
Adie Nims .... Elizabeth Perkins
Pearne Manners .... Kate Reid
Kyle Boon .... Justin Henry
Debs Boon .... Holly Marie Combs
BJ Boon .... Heather Coleman
Dick Merezini .... Matthew Wohl
Wayne Rodemeyer .... Stephen Stabler
Claire Noton .... Laurie Corbin
Darielle Johnson .... Lanie Conklin
Peter Barrett .... Jock MacDonald
Joe Canecki .... Frits Momsen
Bobby Canecki .... Stephen Robert Moorhead
Policeman .... Paul Schnabel
Ellen Becker .... Jerrilyn Miller
Sherry Rooney .... Heather Driscoll
Student .... Anna Groskin
Lois Clarent .... Mary Carol Maganzini
Mouse .... Meghan A. Brooks
Tom Sechrist .... Mark Brooks
Eunice Wimert .... Letitia Leahy
Buzzy Barker .... Henry Haselton
Rawson Mason .... Jack Hughes

Right: Jeff Daniels, Elizabeth Perkins, Don Johnson, Susan Sarandon Top: Perkins, Sarandon
(Tri-Star Pictures)

Justin Henry, Don Johnson Above: Jeff Daniels, Johnson

Jeff Daniels, Elizabeth Perkins Above: Don Johnson, Susan Sarandon

THE WIZARD OF LONELINESS

(SKOURAS) Producers, Philip Porcella, Thom Tyson; Direct Additional Material, Jenny Bowen; Executive Producer, Lindsay La Screenplay, Nancy Larson; Based on the novel by John Nichols; Ph tography, Richard Bowen; Editor, Lisa Day; Designer, Jeffrey B ecroft; Music, Michel Colombier; Costumes, Stephanie Maslansk Casting, Pat McCorkle; Co-Producer, David Batchhelder; Associa Producers, Mary Cooper, Shanly Heffelfinger; Production Manage Helen Pollak; Production Supervisor, Gary Gillingham; Assistant D rector, Chuck Alfred; Production Coordinator, Cynthia Jessen; Soun Doug Axtell; Art Director, Susan Beeson; Set Decorator, Steven Barnett; A Skouras Pictures, Inc., Virgin Vision, and American Pla house Theatrical Films Presentation; Color; Rated PG-13; 110 minute September release

CAST

Wendall ... Lukas Ha
Sybil ... Lea Thomps
Doc ... John Randol
Cornelia ... Anne Pitoni
Duffy ... Dylan Bak
John T. ... Lance Gue
Tom ... Jeremiah Warn
Fred ... Steve Hendricks
Singing Soldier ... Jeffrey Dreisba
Conductor ... Alan Wrig
Ercel ... Andrea Mathes
Irma ... Betty Mill
Dot Svenson ... Dorothy Yat
Marie Svenson ... Doris Yat
Jim ... Jerome Dempse
Jimmy Wiggen ... David Mosco
Monroe ... Jason Coc
Elaine Bergle ... Elizabeth Whi
Hank ... Barton Heyma
Joel Spende ... Ken Jenki
Chad Spender ... Michael Bu
Sheriff Flood ... Charles Whi
Willie Bayle ... Frank T. We
Carl Hatcher ... John Ree

Top Left: Lukas Haas Below Jeremiah Warner, Andrea Matheson, Lea Thompson, Anne Pitoniak
(Skouras Pictures)

THE PRINCE OF PENNSYLVANIA

(NEW LINE CINEMA) Producer, Joan Fishman; Director/Screenplay, Ron Nyswaner; Co-Producer, Kerry Orent; Executive Producers, Robert Shaye, Sara Risher; Production Executive, Rachel Talalay; Editor, William Scharf; Photography, Frank Prinzi; Music, Thomas Newman; Casting, Alan Amtzis; Costumes, Carol Wood; Designer, Toby Corbett; Production Manager, Mary McLaglen; Assistant Director, Mike Topoozian; Production Coordinator, Laura Greenlee; Color; Rated R; 90 minutes; September release

CAST

Gary Marshetta ... Fred Ward
Rupert Marshetta ... Keanu Reeves
Pam Marshetta ... Bonnie Bedelia
Carla Headlee ... Amy Madigan
Jack Sike ... Jeff Hayenga
Lois Sike ... Tracey Ellis
Roger Marshetta ... Joseph De Lisi
Trooper Joe ... Jay O. Sanders
Biker Girl ... Kari Keegan
Minister ... Demetria Mellot
Ed McLaglen ... Paul Palmer
Tommy Rutherford ... Jeff Monahan
Tony Minetta ... Don Brockett
Biker Boyfriend ... Jeff Forman
Prom Girl ... Julie Page
White Tux ... Todd Bryant
Leslie ... Lisa Mayer
Mr. Crane ... Milton E. Thompson, Jr.
Waitress ... Linda Carola
Marshal ... Bob Tracey
Lucky Bell White ... Pam Call
Chester ... G. Ross Berger
Deputy #1 ... David Early

(New Line Cinema)

Keanu Reeves, Bonnie Bedelia

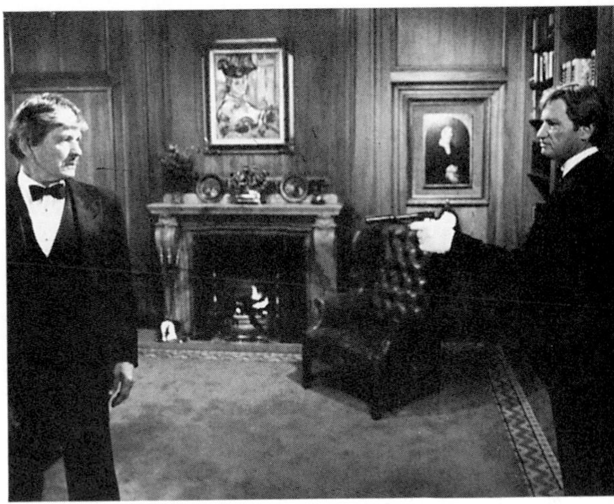

Charles Bronson Left: John Solari, Laurence Luckinbill, Daniel Benzali Top Left: Charles Bronson

Charles Bronson (R) Above: Jeff Corey, Bronson

MESSENGER OF DEATH

(CANNON GROUP) Producer, Pancho Kohner; Director, J. Lee Thompson; Screenplay, Paul Jarrico; Executive Producers, Menahem Golan, Yoram Globus; Photography, Gideon Porath; Art Director, W. Brooke Wheeler; Editor, Peter Lee Thompson; Costumes, Shelley Komarov; Music, Robert O. Ragland; Production Manager, Sheridan Dar Reid; Assistant Director, Robert C. Ortwin, Jr., Production Executive, Marc S. Fischer; Associate Producer, Patricia G. Payro; Casting, Perry Bullington; Additional Photography, Tom Neuwirth; Production Coordinator, M. Ginanne Carpenter; Sound, Craig Felburg; Set Decorator, Susan Carsello-Smith; Special Effects, Pioneer FX; Stunts, Ernie Orsatti; Color; Rated R; 92 minutes; September release

CAST

Garrett Smith .... Charles Bronson
Jastra Watson .... Trish Van Devere
Homer Foxx .... Laurence Luckinbill
Chief Barney Doyle .... Daniel Benzali
Josephine Fabrizio .... Marilyn Hassett
Orville Beecham .... Charles Dierkop
Willis Beecham .... Jeff Corey
Zenas Beecham .... John Ireland
Trudy Pike .... Penny Peyser
Saul .... Jon Cedar
Wiley .... Tom Everett
Lieutenant Scully .... Duncan Gamble
Sheriff Yates .... Bert Williams
Jimmy .... Jerome Thor
Sarah Beecham .... Sydna Scott
Magda Beecham .... Cheryl Waters
Rebecca Beecham .... Melanie Noble
Florinda Beecham .... Patricia Allison
Esther Beecham .... Maria Mayenzet
Ursula Beecham .... Sheila Gale Kandlbinder
Naomi Beecham .... Margaret Howell
Ruth Beecham .... Warner Loughlin
Piety Beecham .... Kimberly Beck
Mrs. Lucy Bigelow .... Beverly Thompson
Cyrus Pike .... Don Kennedy
Mrs. Doyle .... Susan Bjurman
Sgt. Purdue .... John F. McCarthy
Caleb Beecham .... Phil Zuckerman
Joshua, the Priest .... Jeffrey Concklin
Doc Turner .... William Edward Phipps
Elizabeth Beecham .... Tarrish Potter
Timothy Beecham .... Eric Fry
and Gene Davis, John Solari, David Cooper, Jim Bullock, Erez Yaoz, Saladin James, Enrica Gaspari, Joseph Darrell, Menash Benmoshe

(Cannon Group)

Sigourney Weaver, Bryan Brown Top: Sigourney Weaver (Also Left, Center)

Sigourney Weaver, Bryan Brown

GORILLAS IN THE MIST
The Adventure of Dian Fossey

(WARNER BROS./UNIVERSAL) Producers, Arnold Glimch Terence Clegg; Director, Michael Apted; Screenplay, Anna Hamilt Phelan; Story, Anna Hamilton Phelan, Tab Murphy; Based on the wo by Dian Fossey, and the article by Harold T. P. Hayes; Executi Producers, Peter Guber, Jon Peters; Photography, John Seale; D signer, John Graysmark; Editor, Stuart Baird; Music, Maurice Jar Co-Producers, Robert Nixon, Judy Kessler; Associate Producer, Ri Baker; Casting, Marion Dougherty, Mary Selway; Makeup Effec Rick Baker; Sound, Peter Handford; Costumes, Catherine Leterri Special Gorilla Photography, Alan Root; Special Effects, Rob Browne; Assistant Director, Patrick Clayton; Production Coordinato Pat Pennelegion, Leila Kirkpatrick; Art Director, Ken Court; Set Dec rator, Simon Wakefield; Songs by Harry Warren, Al Dubin, Peggy Le Dave Barbour, Maceo Pinkard, Sidney Mitchell, Edna Alexand Soundtrack on MCA Records; Technicolor; Rated PG-13; 125 minut September release

CAST

Dian Fossey .... Sigourney Weav
Bob Campbell .... Bryan Brow
Roz Carr .... Julie Har
Sembagare .... John Omirah Milu
Dr. Louis Leakey .... Iain Cuthberts
Van Vecten .... Constantin Alexandr
Mukara .... Waigwa Wachi
Brendan .... Iain Gle
Larry .... David Lansbu
Kim .... Maggie O'Ne
Rushemba .... Konga Mban
Howard Dowd .... Michael J. Reynol
Photographer .... Gordon Mast
Batwa Chief .... Peter Ndu
Mme. Van Vecten .... Helen Fras
and John Alexander, Peter Elliott, Denise Cheshire, Antonio Hoyo Jody St. Michael (Mime Artists)

Left Center: Sigourney Weaver
(Warner Bros./Universal City Studios)

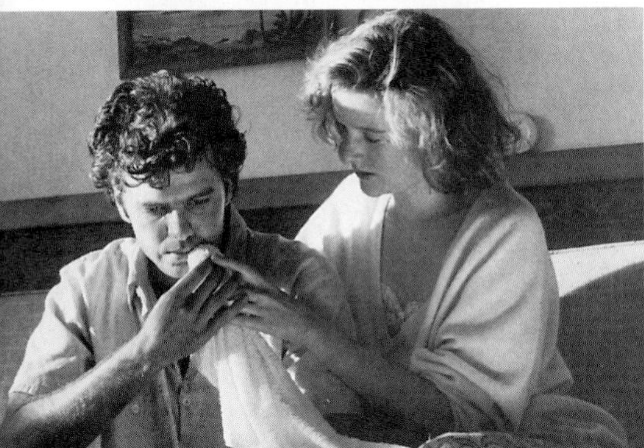

Kevin Anderson, Penelope Ann Miller

MILES FROM HOME

(CINECOM) Producers, Frederick Sollo, Paul Kurta; Director, Gary Sinise; Screenplay, Chris Gerolmo; Executive Producers, Amir J. Malin, Ira Deutchman; Associate Producers, Randy Finch, Russ Smith; Photography, Elliot Davis; Designer, David Gropman; Editor, Jane Schwartz Jaffe; Music, Robert Folk; Costumes, Shay Cunliffe; Casting, Bonnie Timmerman; Production Manager, Paul Kurta; Assistant Director, James A. Chory; Art Director, Nicholas Romanac; Set Decorator, Karen Schulz; Sound, Kim Ornitz; Production Coordinator, Cynthia Streit; Special Effects, Kevin Harris; Stunts, Jery Hewitt; Songs, Maggie Mayall, Duane Scisoqua, Jon Tiven, and other artists; Dolby Stereo; Color; Rated R; 113 minutes; September release

CAST

Frank Roberts .... Richard Gere
Terry Roberts .... Kevin Anderson
Frank Roberts, Sr. .... Brian Dennehy
Sally .... Penelope Ann Miller
Jennifer .... Helen Hunt
Frances .... Judith Ivey
Exotic Dancer .... Laurie Metcalf
Barry Maxwell .... John Malkovich
Young Frank .... Jason Campbill
Young Terry .... Austin Bamgarner
Nikita Krushev .... Larry Poling
Mark .... Terry Kinney
Tommy Malin .... Francis Guinan
Woman at sale .... Irma Boyle
Frank's Girl .... Moira Harris
Check-out Girl .... Mary Pat Hennagir
Trailer Park Neighbor .... Robert Otis
Sheriff .... Dennis Blome
Photographer .... Dean Tukano
Pick-up Owner .... Michael Talbott
Fairground Announcer .... James Clancy
Tom Castleman .... Robert Breuler
Farmer at fairground .... Eldon Trumm
Bankguard .... Beryl "Woody" Woodson
Miss Foster .... Megan Turner
Farmer Cox .... Randall Arney
Farmer's Wife .... Jo Anderson
Farmer's Son .... Jesse Coon
Man at Co-op .... Ralph Tranel
Trooper .... Martin Pratschel
and Robert Ayers, William B. Bicksler, Colter Wood, Zak Oval, Terrence Beasor, Walter Burr, Larry Moss, Jery Hewit, Bill Anagnos, Phil Nelson

Left: Richard Gere Above: Judith Ivey, Gere
Top Left: Gere, Kevin Anderson
(Cinecom)

Richard Gere, Helen Hunt

PUNCHLINE

(COLUMBIA) Producers, Daniel Melnick, Michael Rachmil; D rector/Screenplay, David Seltzer; Photography, Reynaldo Villalobo Designer, Jack DeGovia; Editor, Bruce Green; Casting, Jackie Burc Music, Charles Gross; Production Manager, Jerry Baerwitz; Assista Director, Jim Van Wyck; Associate Producers, Jerry Baerwitz, Jani Yarbrough, Jim Van Wyck; Art Director, John Jensen; Set Decorato Peg Cummings; Set Designers, Joe Hubbard, Pete Smith; Stunts, Har Madsen, Felix Mauras; Sound, Gene Cantamessa; A Fogwo Indieprod Production; *"Remember Tonight and Smile"* by Micha Pollock; Dolby Stereo; DeLuxe Color; Rated R; 128 minutes; Septen ber release

CAST

Lilah Krytsik	Sally Fiel
Steven Gold	Tom Hank
John Krytsick	John Goodma
Romeo	Mark Ryde
Madeline Urie	Kim Grei
Arnold	Paul Mazursk
Utica Blake	Pam Mattesc
Singing Nun	George Michael McGra
Albert Emperato	Taylor Negro
Krug	Barry Neikru
Rico	Angel Salaz
Percy	Damon Wayar
Joycee	Joycee Kat
Billy Lane	Mac Robbir
Mister Ball	Max Alexand
Jerry Petroviak	Paul Kozlows
Robyn Green	Barry Sob
Juggling Comic	Marty Polli
Eve	Katie Ric
Maitre d'	Charles David Richard
Ernie the Bartender	Casey Sande
Piano Player	Michael Polloc
Carrie	Candace Camero
Jenny	Laura Joacob
Heidi	Bianca Ros
Buffy	Robina Suwc
Murray	Robert Britto
Mark	Mark Goldstei
Mark's Wife	Melissa Tufel
Mrs. Ball	Dottie Archibal
Doctor Wishniak	Georeg D. Wallac

and Wanda Balay, Tiffany Terry, Christiane Eden, Renna Bogdanc wicz, Susan Michael, Kimberly Ryusaki, Consuela Nance, Barbar Collier, Darunee Doa Hale, Andrea Adams, Marcy Del Campos, Ro Ulstad, Howard Weller, Richard Parker, George Wallace, Andrev Parker, Randy Fechter

Left: Tom Hanks, Sally Field
Above: Mark Rydell, Tom Hanks
Top Left: Sally Field, Tom Hanks
(Columbia Pictures)

Sally Field, John Goodman

Sally Field, Tom Hanks

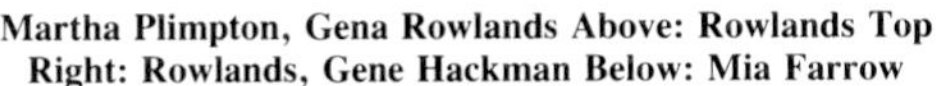

Martha Plimpton, Gena Rowlands Above: Rowlands Top Right: Rowlands, Gene Hackman Below: Mia Farrow

ANOTHER WOMAN

RION) Producer, Robert Greenhut; Director/Screenplay, Woody len; Executive Producers, Jack Rollins, Charles H. Joffe; Photogray, Sven Nykvist; Designer, Santo Loquasto; Editor, Susan E. Morse; stumes, Jeffrey Kurland; Casting, Juliet Taylor; Associate Produrs, Thomas Reilly, Helen Robin; Production Manager, Joseph Hartck; Assistant Director, Thomas Reilly; Production Coordinator, len Robin; Art Director, Speed Hopkins; Set Decorator, George Titta Jr.; Sound, James Sabat; Songs by various artists; Dolby ereo; Duart Color; Rated PG; 88 minutes; October release

CAST

arion .... Gena Rowlands
pe .... Mia Farrow
n .... Ian Holm
dia .... Blythe Danner
rry .... Gene Hackman
thy .... Betty Buckley
ura .... Martha Plimpton
arion's Father .... John Houseman
aire .... Sandy Dennis
ung Marion's Father .... David Ogden Stiers
m .... Philip Bosco
ul .... Harris Yulin
nn .... Frances Conroy
tient's Voice .... Fred Melamed
nald .... Kenneth Welsh
ark .... Bruce Jay Friedman
ano Player .... Bernie Leighton
d Jack Gelber, Paul Sills, John Schenck, Noel Behn, Gretchen ahm, Janet Frank, Dana Ivey, Fred Melamed, Alice Spivak

(Orion Pictures)

Gena Rowlands, Mia Farrow Above: Sandy Dennis, Ian Holm

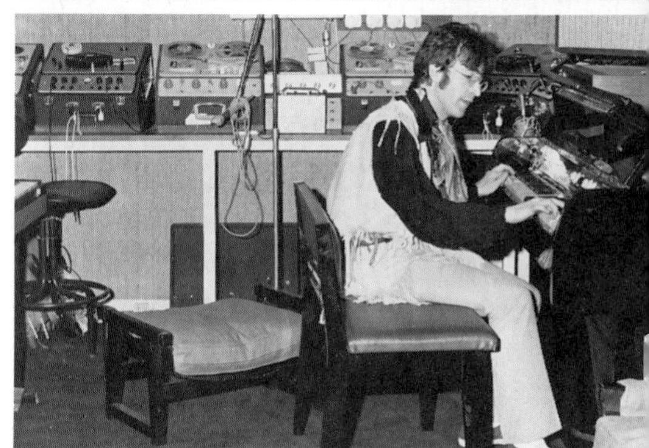

John Lennon (Also Above and Top Left)

Yoko Ono, John Lennon Above: John Lennon, Sean Lennon

IMAGINE: JOHN LENNON

(WARNER BROS.) Producers, David L. Wolper, Andrew Sol Director, Andrew Solt; Screenplay, Sam Egan, Andrew Solt; Co Producer, Sam Egan; Photography, Nestor Almendros; Associate Pro ducers, Bud Friedgen, Kevin Miller; Editor, Bert Lovitt; Narrator, Joh Lennon; Production Executive, Rachelle Katz; Production Manage Ted Kurdyla; Assistant Director, Lewis Gould; Sound, Midge Costin John Bolz; Set Decorator, Sarah Knowles; Songs, John Lennon, Pau McCartney, Yoko Ono, and other artists; Lennon songs remixed by Ro Stevens; Soundtrack on Capitol Beatles songs remixed by Georg Martin/John Lennon songs remixed by Rob Stevens; Color; Rated R 103 minutes; October release. Documentary, featuring interviews wit Yoko Ono, Julian Lennon, Sean Lennon, and Cynthia Lennon.

(Warner Bros.)

CLARA'S HEART

ARNER BROS.) Producer, Martin Elfand; Director, Robert Mul- n; Screenplay, Mark Medoff; Based on the novel by Joseph Olshan; ecutive Producer, Marianne Moloney; Photography, Freddie ncis; Music, Dave Grusin; Editor, Sidney Levin; Designer, Jeffrey ward; Associate Producers, Albert J. Salzer, Daniel T. Franklin, vid McGiffert; Costumes, Bambi Breakstone; Casting, Ken Carlson; duction Managers, Albert J. Salzer, Daniel T. Franklin; Assistant ector, David McGiffert; Art Director, Stephen Walker; Set Decora- Anne H. Ahrens; Sound, Bill Nelson; An MTM Production; *"God s Smiled on Me"* by Isaiah Jones Jr., *"See What the Lord Has Done"* Luther Barnes, and songs by various other artists: Dolby Stereo; hnicolor; Rated PG-13; 108 minutes; October release

CAST

ra Mayfield .... Whoopi Goldberg
Hart .... Michael Ontkean
na Hart .... Kethleen Quinlan
vid Hart .... Neil Patrick Harris
er Epstein .... Spalding Gray
a .... Beverly Todd
nche Loudon .... Hattie Winston
n Lipsky .... Jason Downs
este .... Caitlin Thompson
cia .... Maria Broom
ia .... Wanda Christine
s .... Maryce Carter
a .... Angel Harper
dy .... Fred Strother
ner Joe .... Father Joseph Muth
.... Warren Long
com Woman .... Dorthy Cunningham
le Girl .... Alaine Laughton
ng .... Randy Meeks
na .... Kathyrn Dowling
Stevens .... Mark Medoff
dley Laffety .... Tatum Adaire Gauthier
y Nurse .... Joy Green
sica .... Tania Gauthier
ch Stillson .... Forry Buckingham
m Team Members .... Dan Griffith, Jason Schuyler, Kevin Colborn

Right: Kathleen Quinlan, Neil Patrick Harris, Whoopi Goldberg Above: Whoopi Goldberg, Hattie Winston Top Right: Whoopi Goldberg, Neil Patrick Harris
(Warner Bros.)

Beverly Todd, Neil Patrick Harris, Whoopi Goldberg

Neil Patrick Harris, Kathleen Quinlan, Spalding Gray

Steve Antin, Woody Brown, Jodie Foster

THE ACCUSED

(PARAMOUNT) Producers, Stanley R. Jaffe, Sherry Lansing; I rector, Jonathan Kaplan; Screenplay, Tom Topor; Photography, R Bode; Designer, Richard Kent Wilcox; Editors, Jerry Greenberg, Nicholas Brown; Design Consultant, Mel Bourne; Music, Brad Fied Casting, Julie Selzer, Sally Dennison; Associate Producer, Jack Rc Production Manager, Warren Carr; Assistant Director, David W. Ros Art Director, Sheila Haley; Set Decorator, Barry W. Brolly; Costume Trish Keating; Sound, Rob Young; Stunts, Kerrie Cullen; Spec Effects, Gary Paller; Production Coordinator, Tammy S. Oates; "*I Talking Love*" by Brad Fiedel & Ross Levinson/Vocal, Vanessa A derson, and songs by various other artists; Dolby Stereo; Technicol Rated R; 115 minutes; October release

CAST

Kathryn Murphy .... Kelly McGi
Sarah Tobias .... Jodie Fos
Ken Joyce .... Bernie Couls
Cliff "Scorpion" Albrect .... Leo Ro
Sally Fraser .... Ann Hea
D. A. Paul Rudolph .... Carmen Argenzia
Bob Joiner .... Steve An
Larry .... Tom O'Bri
Attorney Paulsen .... Peter Van Nord
Lieutenant Duncan .... Terry David Mullig
Danny .... Woody Brov
Attorney Wainwright .... Scott Pau
Kurt .... Kim Kondrash
Polito .... Stephen E. Mil
Bartender Jesse .... Tom Heat
Defendant Matt Haines .... Andrew Kavad
Defendant Stu Holloway .... Tom McBe
Nurse .... Rose Weav
Assistant D. A. Massi .... Allan Lys
Plea Bargain Lawyers .... Antony Holland, Kevin McNul
Jerry Wasserm
Trial Judge .... Barney O'Sulliv
Angela .... Christianne H
Mrs. Albrect .... Frances Flanag
TV Commentators .... Marsha Andrews, Mike Winla
Pamela Mar
Bail Hearing Judge .... Wally Mar
Court Officer .... Deryl Hay
Court Reporter .... E. Andrea Kla
Bailiff .... Bryan Johns
Jury Foreman .... Dana S
Sarah's Mother on phone .... Denalda Willia
Woman Lawyer .... Babs Chu
911 Operator .... Rebecca Tool
Sally's Daughter .... Kirsten Kea
Sally's Son .... David Sherid
Record Store Clerk .... Scott Wald
and Peter Bibby, Stephen Dimopoulos, Laurie O'Byrne, Freda Per John H. Cox, Jim Bedard, Gary Chalk, Garwin Sanford, Gloria Le Stephen Brent Lambert, Matt LaFleur, Michele Goodger

Left : Jodie Foster, Bernie Coulson
Above: Tom O'Brien, Foster
Top: Foster, Kelly McGillis
(Paramount Pictures)

Jodie Foster received an Academy Award for Best Actres of 1988

Mandy Patinkin, James Caan (Also Top Left) Left: Leslie Bevis, Caan

ALIEN NATION

(20th CENTURY FOX) Producers, Gale Anne Hurd, Richard Kobritz; Director, Graham Baker; Screenplay, Rockne S. O'Bannon; Photography, Adam Greenberg; Designer, Jack T. Collis; Editor, Kent Beyda; Music, Curt Sobel; Casting, Karen Rea; Production Manager, Joan Bradshaw; Assistant Directors, Herb Adelman, Newton D. Arnold; Alien Creation, Alec Gillis, Shane Mahan, John Rosengrant, Tom Woodruff, Jr., Shannon Shea; Alien Makeup, Zoltan, John Elliott; Stunts, Conrad E. Palmisano; Sound, David MacMillan, Charles Wilborn; Special Effects, Stan Amborn; Songs by various artists; Dolby Stereo; Deluxe color; System 35 widescreen; Rated R; 96 minutes; October release

CAST

Matthew Sykes .... James Caan
Sam Francisco .... Mandy Patinkin
William Harcourt .... Terence Stamp
Kipling .... Kevyn Major Howard
Cassandra .... Leslie Bevis
Fedorchuk .... Peter Jason
Quint .... George Jenesky
Josh Strader .... Jeff Kobert
Bill Tuggle .... Roger Aaron Brown
Wiltey .... Tony Simotes
Human Dealer .... Michael David Simms
Alien Dealer .... Ed Krieger
Alterez .... Tony Perez
Trent Porter .... Brian Thompson
Capt. Warner .... Frank McCarthy
Winter .... Keone Young
Maffet .... Don Hood
Duncan Crais .... Earl Boen
Minkler .... Edgar Small
O'Neal .... Thomas Wagner
Mayor .... Abraham Alvarez
Ortiz .... Diana James
Bentner .... Frank Collison
Detective .... Tom DeFranco
Kristin Sykes .... Angela O'Neill
Mrs. Francisco .... Kendall Conrad
and Brian Lando (George Jr.), Tom Morga (Raincoat), Reggie Parton (Mr. Porter), Jessica James (Mrs. Porter), Tom Finnegan, Doug MacHugh, William E. Dearth, Robert Starr, Bobby Sargent, Bebe Drake-Massey, Seth Marten, Lawrence Kopp, Alec Gillis

Left Center: James Caan, Mandy Patinkin
(20th Century Fox)

Jeff Kober, Terence Stamp

Clayton Rohner, Danny Glover Above: Gene Hackman
Top Right: David Marshall Grant Below: Hackman (R)

BAT 21

(TRI-STAR) Producers, David Fisher, Gary A. Neill, Michael Balson; Director, Peter Markle; Screenplay, William C. Anderson, George Gordon; Based on the book "*Bat 21*" by William C. Angerson; Executive Producer, Jerry Reed; Line Producer, Evzen W. Kolar; Photography, Mark Irwin; Editor, Stephen E. Rivkin; Designer, Vincent Cresciman; Co-Producers, David Saunders, Mark Damon; Music, Christopher Young; Casting, Nancy Banks; Assistant Director, Craig Huston; Production Manager, Robert Waters; Art Directors, Art Riddle, Terry Weldon; Sound, Itzhak Ike Magal; Special Effects, Richard E. Johnson; Costumes, Audrey Bansmer; Stunts, Everett Creach; Production Coordinator, Cindy Hochman; Special Effects, Gene Warren, Jr.; Dolby Stereo; DeLuxe Color; Rated R; 105 minutes; October release

CAST

Lt. Colonel Iceal Hambleton .... Gene Hackman
Captain Bartholomew Clark .... Danny Glover
Colonel George Walker .... Jerry Reed
Ross Carver .... David Marshall Grant
Sgt. Harley Rumbaugh .... Clayton Rohner
Major Jake Scott .... Erich Anderson
Colonel Douglass .... Joe Dorsey
Vietnamese Man .... Rev. Michael Ng
Boy on Bridge .... Theodore Chan Woei-Shyong
and Don Ruffin, Scott Howell, Michael Raden, Timothy Fitzgerald, Stuart Hagen, Jeff Baxter, Alan King, Bonnie Yong, Willie Lai, Martin Yong, Jim Aman, Freddie Chin, Dennis Chong, Liow Hui Chun, Fung Yun Khiong, Henry Lee, Michael Lee, Jeffrey Liew, Fredolin Leong, Benedict Lojingkau, Walter Lojingkau, Johnny Michael

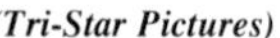

(Tri-Star Pictures)

Danny Glover Above: Gene Hackman (L)

THINGS CHANGE

OLUMBIA) Producer/Production Manager, Michael Hausman; ·ector, David Mamet; Screenplay, David Mamet, Shel Silverstein; otography, Juan Ruiz Anchia; Designer, Michael Merritt; Editor, ·dy Ship; Music, Alaric Jans; Costumes, Nan Cibula; Associate ·ducer/Assistant Director, Ned Dowd; Casting, Cyrene Hausman; A mhaus Production; DeLuxe Color; Rated PG; 105 minutes; October ·ease

CAST

ɪo .... Don Ameche
ry .... Joe Mantegna
·eph Vincent .... Robert Prosky
·nkie .... J. J. Johnston
. Silve .... Ricky Jay
. Green .... Mike Nussbaum
pair Shop Owner .... Jack Wallace
tler .... Dan Conway
ss Bathes .... Willo Varsi Hausman
usemaid .... Gail Silver
mone .... Len Hodera
llenza .... Josh Conescu
ırcotti .... Adam Biterman
Pals .... Merrill Holtzman
llie .... William Novelli
arface .... Chuck Stransky
ly Drake .... W. H. Macy
ndy .... Steven Goldstein
kie Shore .... Jonathan Katz
erry .... Sarah Eckhardt
ace .... Karen Koulhaas
nny .... Vincent Gustaferro
rry .... Christopher Kaldor
na .... Natalia Nogulich
d Kenny Lilliebridge, J. T. Walsh, Jordan Lage, Sarah Potok, Robert lla, Robert Ostrovsky, Melissa Bruder, Patrick O'Neill, Lionel ith, Scott Zigler, Felicity Huffman, Mary Bernadette McCann, ricia Wolff, G. Roy Levin, Andy Potok, Theo Cohan, Allen Soule

Right: Joe Mantegna, Don Ameche Above: Robert Prosky, Don Ameche Top Right: Don Ameche
(Columbia Pictures)

Joe Mantegna, Don Ameche

Don Ameche, Joe Mantegna, W. H. Macy, Jr.

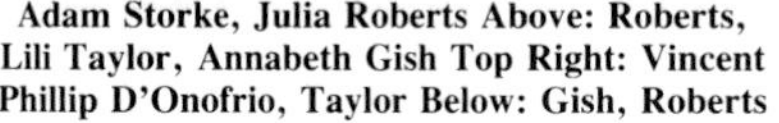
Adam Storke, Julia Roberts Above: Roberts, Lili Taylor, Annabeth Gish Top Right: Vincent Phillip D'Onofrio, Taylor Below: Gish, Roberts

MYSTIC PIZZA

(SAMUEL GOLDWYN) Producers, Mark Levinson, Scott Rosenfelt; Director, Donald Petrie; Screenplay, Amy Jones, Perry Howze, Randy Howze, Alfred Uhry; Story, Amy Jones; Production Manager, Scott Rosenfelt; Line Producer, Susan Vogelfang; Assistant Director, Mark Radcliffe; Production Coordinator, Cha Cha Jago; Photography, Tim Suhrdtedt; Sound, Russell Fager; Designer, David Chapman; Art Director/Set Decorator, Mark Haack; Casting, Jane Jenkins; Costumes, Jennifer Von Mayrhauser; Special Effects, Ken Levin; Ultra-Stereo; Duart Color; Rated R; 104 minutes; October release

CAST

Daisy Araujo .... Julia Roberts
Kat Araujo .... Annabeth Gish
Jojo Barboza .... Lili Taylor
Bill Montijo .... Vincent Phillip D'Onofrio
Tim Travers .... William R. Moses
Charles Gordon Winsor .... Adam Storke
Leona Valsouano .... Conchata Ferrell
Phoebe .... Porscha Radcliffe
Margaret .... Joanna Merlin
Manny .... Arthur Walsh
Jake .... John Fiore
Ed Barboza .... Gene Amoroso
Nicole .... Janet Zarish
Mitch .... Ray Zuppa
Everyday Gourmet .... Louis Turenne
Newscaster .... Wiley Moore
Polly .... Ann Flood
Aunt Tweedy .... Suzanne Sheperd
Teresa .... Jody Raymond
Steamer .... Matt Damon
Flower Girl .... Marrisa Carey

(Samuel Goldwyn Co.)

Annabeth Gish, Lili Taylor, Julia Roberts Above: William R. Moses, Gish

THEY LIVE

(UNIVERSAL) Producer, Larry Franco; Director, John Carpenter; Screenplay, Frank Armitage; Based upon the short story *"Eight O'Clock in the Morning"* by Ray Nelson; Photography, Gary B. Kibbe; Art Directors, William J. Durrell Jr., Daniel Lomino; Editors, Gib Jaffe, Frank E. Jimenez; Executive Producers, Shep Gordon, Andre Blay; Associate Producer, Sandy King; Music, John Carpenter, Alan Howarth; Production Managers, Stratton Leopold, Alan Levine; Assistant Director, Larry Franco; Sound, Ron Judkins; Set Decorator, Marvin March; Special Effects, Roy Arbogast; Stunts, Jeff Imada; Photographic Effects, Denali Prods. Effects Associates/Jim Danforth; Dolby Stereo; Presented by Alive Films; Dolby Stereo; Panavision; DeLuxe Color; Rated R; 93 minutes; November release

CAST

Nada .... Roddy Piper
Frank .... Keith David
Holly .... Meg Foster
Drifter .... George "Buck" Blower
Gilbert .... Peter Jason
Street Preacher .... Raymond St. Jacques
Family Man .... Jason Robards III
Bearded Man .... John Lawrence
Brown Haired Woman .... Susan Barnes
Black Revolutionary .... Sy Richardson
Family Man's Daughter .... Wendy Brainard
Female Interviewer .... Lucille Meredith
Ingenue .... Susan Blanchard
Foreman .... Norman Alden
Black Junkie .... Dana Bratton
Well Dressed Customer .... John F. Goff
Vendor .... Norm Wilson
Rich Lady .... Thelma Lee
Depressed Human .... Stratton Leopold
Arab Clerk .... Rezza Shan
Blonde Haired Cop .... Norman Howell
Neighbor .... Larry Franco
Biker .... Tom Searle
Scruffy Blonde Man .... Robert Grasmere
Passageway Guards .... Vince Inneo
Manager .... Bob Hudson
New Anchors .... Jon Paul Jones
Young Female Executive .... Dennis Michael, Nancy Gee
Woman on Phone .... Claudia Stanlee
Pregnant Secretary .... Christine Baur
Security Guards .... Gregory Barnett, Jim Nickerson
2nd Unit Guard .... Kenny Rossall
Naked Lady .... Cibby Danyla
Ghouls .... Jeff Imada, Michelle Costello

Left: Roddy Piper, Keith David Top Left: Roddy Piper Below: Aliens
(Universal City Studios)

Roddy Piper, Meg Foster

Keith David, Roddy Piper

Jason Robards, Diane Keaton

THE GOOD MOTHER

(TOUCHSTONE/BUENA VISTA) Producer, Arnold Glimcher; D rector, Leonard Nimoy; Screenplay, Michael Bortman; Based upon t novel by Sue Miller; Photography, David Watkin; Designer, St Jolley; Editor, Peter Berger; Costumes, Susan Becker; Casting, Ba bara Shapiro; Music, Elmer Bernstein; Production Manager, Dav Coatsworth; Assistant Directors, Tony Lucibello, Daniel Jason He ner; Art Directors, Richard Harrison, Hilton Rosemarin; Set Deco tors, Dan Wladyka, Don McQueen, Tracey Doyle; Production Coor nators, Mara McSweeny, Sharon O'Dwyer; Sound, Richard Lig stone, David Lee; Special Effects, Cinetrix; In association with Silv Screen Partners IV; Dolby Stereo; Metrocolor; Rated R; 104 minut November release

CAST

Anna .... Diane Keat
Leo .... Liam Nees
Muth .... Jason Robar
Grandfather .... Ralph Bellan
Grandmother .... Teresa Wrig
Brian .... James Naught
Molly .... Asia Viei
Frank Williams .... Joe Mort
Ursula .... Katey Sag
Aunt Rain .... Margaret Ba
Anna's Mother .... Nancy Bea
Anna's Father .... Barry Belchamb
Young Anna .... Mairon Benn
Young Bobby .... Zachary Benn
Eric .... Scott Bru
Arch .... Eugene A. Cla
Celia .... Beverley Coop
Uncle Rain .... Philip Eckm
Garrett .... Greg Ellwa
Alex .... Adan Furfa
Judge .... David Gardn
Bobby's Wife .... Gloria Giffo
Nanny .... Diane Gord
Muth's Secretary .... Joyce Gord
Babe .... Tracy Griff
Eddie .... Howard Jeror
Bobby (older) .... Marvin Kar
Jonathan .... Robert Kep
Uncle Orrie .... Charles Kimbrou
Catherine's Husband .... Tim L
Catherine .... Nina Lind
Dr. Payne .... Fred Melam
Mrs. Harkessian .... Monique Moji
Longshoreman .... Paul MacCallu
Buch McClendon .... Butch McClend
Aunt Weezie .... Maureen McR
Orrie's Wife .... Patricia Philli
William .... Karl Prun
Babe's '64 Boyfriend .... Branko Rac
Uncle Weezie .... Terrence Slat
Court Clerk .... Heather Smi
Jocelyn .... Tina Tegg
Babe's Boyfriend .... Rod Wils
Mark .... Brian You
and Elizabeth Clarke, Sheila Ferrini, Donna Galligan, Teal Gennar Tammy Heaberlin, Daniel J. Howard, Silas Jr., Richard LeBran Brian Mason, Gary Reidt, Cliff Woolner

Left Center: Ralph Bellamy, Teresa Wright Above: Liam Neeson, Asia Vieira, Diane Keaton Top Left: Diane Keaton, Asia Vieira ***(Touchstone Pictures)***

FULL MOON IN BLUE WATER

RANS WORLD ENTERTAINMENT) Producers, Lawrence Tur-an, David Foster, John Turman; Director, Peter Masterson; Screen-ay, Bill Bozzone; Photography, Fred Murphy; Editor, Jill Savitt; xecutive Producers, Moshe Diamant, Eduard Sarlui; Associate Pro-icer, Dennis Murphy; Production Executives, Paul Mason, Helen arlui-Tucker; Music, Phil Marshall; Casting, Ed Mitchell, Ed John-on; Production Manager, Mel A. Bishop, Dennis Murphy; Assistant irector, Robert Engelman; Costumes, Rondi Davis; Set Director, anette Scott; Sound, Doug Axtell; Stunts, Spiro Razatos, Phil Culot-; Production Coordinator, Tina Brawner; *"I Know I Belong To You"* & *Not a Tooth in Her Head (But Man Could She Beat a Drum)"* by John umke/Vocals, Billy Donahue & The Bayou City Beats, *"Survivor of ove"* & *"Soft Way of Talking"* by Phil Marshall/Performance, The lersh Bros. Band; Technicolor; Rated R; 94 minutes; November lease

CAST

oyd .... Gene Hackman
ouise .... Teri Garr
he General .... Burgess Meredith
mmy .... Elias Koteas
harlie .... Kevin Cooney
irgil .... David Doty
aytch .... Gil Glasgow
orothy .... Becky Gelke
ois .... Marietta Marich
nnie .... Lexie Masterson
ack Hill .... William Larsen
larone .... Mitchell Gossett
ohnny Gorman .... Mark Walters
oy .... Lawrence Elkins
igby .... Ben Jones
ocalist .... Billy Donahue
nd Ed Geldart, Tiny Skaggs, Bill Johnson, Elizabeth Williams, Sha-n Bunn, Brandon Smith, Sandra Zimmer, Billy Donahue

Right: Gene Hackman Top: Hackman, Teri Garr
(Trans World Entertainment)

Teri Garr, Elias Koteas Above: Gene Hackman

Elias Koteas, Burgess Meredith Above: Meredith, Gene Hackman, Teri Garr

U2 RATTLE AND HUM

(PARAMOUNT) Producer, Michael Hamlyn; Director/Editor, Phil Joanou; Executive Producer, Paul McGuinness; Associate Producer, Gregg Fienberg; Photography, Jordan Cronenweth, Robert Brinkmann; Music Producer, Jimmy Iovine; Production Manager/Assistant Director, Gregg Fienberg; Production Supervisor, Tom Seid; Special Consultant, John Sykes; Production Coordinator, Fiona Dent; Production Executives, Iain Brown, Juliet Naylor; Associate Editor, Tom Seid; Sound, William F. MacPherson; U2 Wardrobe, Lola Cashman, Fintan Fitzgerald; A Midnight Films Production; Songs by Brian Eno, U2, The Edge, John Lennon & Paul McCartney; and other artists; Soundtrack on Island Records; Documentary; Dolby Stereo; DeLuxe Color/Black & White; Rated PG-13; 99 minutes; November release

CAST

Vocals/Guitar/Harmonica .... Bono
Guitar/Keyboards/Vocals .... The Edge
Bass Guitar .... Adam Clayton
Drums .... Larry Mullen, Jr.
Graceland Tour Guide .... Stacey Sheppard
Press Conference Interviewer .... Gayle Murphy
and B. B. King, *New Voices of Freedom:* George Pendergrass, Dorothy Terrell, Dennis Bell, Sterling Magee, Adam Gussow, *The Memphis Horns:* Wayne Jackson, Andrew Love, Jack Hale, Jim Horn, Joseph M. Miskulin

Right: Bono Top Right: Larry Mullen, Jr., Adam Clayton, The Edge, Bono
(Paramount Pictures)

Tess Harper, Ann Wedgeworth Above: Jessica Lange

Donald Moffat, Charles Durning

FAR NORTH

(ALIVE ENTERPRISES) Producers, Carolyn Pfeiffer, Malcolm Harding; Director/Screenplay, Sam Shepard; Executive Producer, Shep Gordon; Photography, Robbie Greenberg; Editor, Bill Yahraus; Music, The Red Clay Ramblers; Designer, Peter Jamison; Costumes, Rita Salazar; Associate Producer, James Kelley; An Alive Films Production with Nelson Entertainment in Association with Circle JS Productions; Color; Rated PG-13; 90 minutes; November release

CAST

Kate .... Jessica Lange
Bertrum .... Charles Durning
Rita .... Tess Harper
Uncle Dane .... Donald Moffat
Amy .... Ann Wedgeworth
Jilly .... Patricia Arquette
Gramma .... Nina Draxten

(Alive Films)

COCOON: THE RETURN

(20th CENTURY FOX) Producers, Richard D. Zanuck, David Brown, Lili Fini Zanuck; Director, Daniel Petrie; Screenplay, Stephen McPherson; Story, Stephen McPherson, Elizabeth Bradley; Photography, Tak Fujimoto; Designer, Lawrence G. Paull; Editor, Mark Roy Warner; Music, James Horner; Based on characters created by David Saperstein; Casting, Beverly McDermott; Costumes, Jay Hurley; Associate Producer/Production Manager, Gary Daigler; Assistant Director, Katterli Frauenfelder; Cocoons by Robert Short; Set Decorators, Frederick C. Weiler, Jim Poynter; Sound, Hank Garfield; Special Effects, J. B. Jones, Richard Jones; Production Coordinator, Cynthia Streit; Stunts, Artie Malesci; Orchestrations, Grieg McRitchie, Billy May; Sound, Gary Rydstrom; Visual Effects, Scott Farrar; Alien Creatures/ Effects, Greg Cannom; Soundtrack on Varese Sarabande; Dolby Stereo; DeLuxe Color; Rated PG; 116 minutes; November release

CAST

Art Selwyn .... Don Ameche
Ben Luckett .... Wilfod Brimley
Sara .... Courteney Cox
Joe Finley .... Hume Cronyn
Bernie Lefkowitz .... Jack Gilford
Jack Bonner .... Steve Guttenberg
David .... Barret Oliver
Mary Luckett .... Maureen Stapleton
Ruby .... Elaine Stritch
Alma Finley .... Jessica Tandy
Bess McCarthy .... Gwen Verdon
Kitty .... Tahnee Welch
Susan .... Linda Harrison
Pillsbury .... Tyrone Power, Jr.
Doc .... Mike Nomad
Phil/Antareans .... Wendy Cooke
Rose .... Herta Ware
Dr. Barton .... Brian C. Smith
Alma's Doctor .... Fred Buch
Dr. Erwin .... Harold Bergman
Bess' Doctor .... Glenn Scherer
Doug .... Tom Kouchaloakos
Mrs. Cashman .... Iris Acker
General Jefferds .... Will Marchetti
Rebecca .... Shelley Spurlock
Janet .... Rachel Renick
Mr. Szydlo .... Glenn L. Robbins
Walter .... Brian Dennehy
and Alan R. Jordan, Fritz Dominique, Ted Milford, Chris Fuxa, Bill Wohrman, Jay Smith, Tony Vila, Jr., Brian Jay Andrews, David Easton, Matt Ford, Jack McDermott, Darcy Shean, Barrie Mizerski, Madeline Lee, Mal Jones, Patricia Rainier, Richard Jasen, Patricia Winters

Top: Barret Oliver, Wilford Brimley
Below: Don Ameche, Hume Cronyn, Brimley
(20th Century Fox)

Jessica Tandy, Gwen Verdon, Maureen Stapleton
Above: Hume Cronyn, Jack Gilford, Wilford Brimley, Don Ameche

Mike Nomad, Steve Guttenberg, Tahnee Welch, Tyrone Power, Jr.

EVERYBODY'S ALL-AMERICAN

(WARNER BROS.) Producers, Taylor Hackford, Laura Ziskin, I; Sander; Director, Taylor Hackford; Screenplay, Tom Rickman; Bas on the book by Frank Deford; Executive Producer, Stuart Benjami Co-Producer, Alan C. Blomquist; Photography, Stephen Goldbla Designer, Joe Alves; Editor, Don Zimmerman; Music, James Newt Howard; Costumes, Theadora Van Runkle; Casting, Nancy Kloppe Production Manager, Alan C. Blomquist; Assistant Director, Jer Ballew; Special Makeup, Dick Smith; Art Director, George Jenson; S Decorator, Rosemary Brandenbug; Set Designer, Sig Tingloff; Orche trators, Mark McKenzie, Brad Dechter; Sound, Jeff Wexler; Stunt Gary Davis; Special Effects, Greg Landerer, Bill Purcell; Songs b various artists; Soundtrack on Capitol Records; Dolby Stereo; Tec nicolor; Rated R; 127 minutes; November release

CAST

Babs .... Jessica Lan
Gavin .... Dennis Qua
Donnie "Cake" .... Timothy Hutt
Lawrence .... John Goodm
Narvel Blue .... Carl Lumb
Bolling Kiely .... Ray Bak
Darlene Kiely .... Savannah Smith Bouch
Leslie Stone .... Patricia Clarks
Pep Leader .... Joseph Mey
Roommate .... J. Kevin Bru
Fraternity Pisser .... Wayne Knig
Junie .... Roy B. Stewart, S
Willy Mae .... Pat Pierre Perki
Pageant M.C. .... Allen McCar
Baby Sitter .... Jerri Lauridse
1981 Cindy .... Melissa Mass
1981 Larry .... Sherrod Au
Retirement Banquet M.C. .... Dan Bor
Young Tommy .... Jeb Qua
Cheerleader #1 .... Barbara Har
and Aaron Neville, Shawn Burks, David Sheltraw, A. J. Duhe, Mi Fisher, Jeff Wickersham, J. C. Sealy, Neva Gage, Chuck Hicks, Fra Deford, Lyla Hay Owen, Sheri Tyrrell Brogdon, Kellee Kenned Bethlyn Weidler, Clarence Davis, Tom Mullen, Tom Rickman, Clau File, Tody Bernard, Philip Carter, Lewis A. Erber, Jr., Terren Beasor, John Erwin, Mitch Carter, Bob Neill

Right: Jessica Lange Above: Lange, Dennis Quaid
(Warner Bros.)

Dennis Quaid, John Goodman Above: Timothy Hutton, Quaid

Timothy Hutton, Jessica Lange Above: Dennis Quaid, Carl Lumbly

Cera, Littlefoot Left: Spike, Petrie, Ducky.
Littlefoot Top Left: Littlefoot and Family

Littlefoot, Petrie, Cera, Ducky, Spike

THE LAND BEFORE TIME

(UNIVERSAL) Producers, Don Bluth, Gary Goldman, John Pomeroy; Director/Designer, Don Bluth; Executive Producers, Steven Spielberg, George Lucas; Producer, Sullivan Bluth Studios; Co-Executive Producers, Frank Marshall, Kathleen Kennedy; Music, James Horner; "*If We Hold On Together*" by James Horner & Will Jennings/Vocals, Diana Ross; Screenplay, Stu Krieger; Story, Judy Freudberg, Tony Geiss; Supervising Executive, Morris F. Sullivan; Production Manager, Thad Weinlein; Production Supervisor, Cathy J. Carr; Editors, Dan Molina, John K. Carr; Assistant Directors, Russell Boland, G. Sue Shakespeare, David Steinberg; Layout Supervisor, David Goetz; Backgrounds, Don Moore; Special Effects, Dorse A. Lanpher; Character Key Supervisor, Vera Lanpher; Optical Effects, Jim Mann; Casting, Nancy Nayor; Associate Producer, Deborah Jelin Newmyer; Orchestrations, Greig McRitchie; Production Coordinator, Ken Cromar; Soundtrack on MCA Records; Dolby Stereo; Technicolor; Rated G; 73 minutes; November release

VOICE CAST

Narrator .... Pat Hingle
Littlefoot's Mother .... Helen Shaver
Littlefoot .... Gabriel Damon
Cera .... Candice Houston
Daddy Topps .... Burke Barnes
Rooter .... Pat Hingle
Ducky .... Judith Barsi
Petrie .... Will Ryan

(Universal City Studios)

CHILD'S PLAY

(UNITED ARTISTS) Producer, David Kirschner; Director, Tom Holland; Screenplay, Don Mancini, John Lafia, Tom Holland; Story, Don Mancini; Executive Producer, Barrie M. Osborne; Photography, Bill Butler; Designer, Daniel A. Lomino; Editors, Edward Warschilka, Roy E. Peterson; Music, Joe Renzetti; Costumes, April Ferry; Associate Producer, Laura Moskowitz; Casting, Richard Pagano, Sharon Bialy; Production Managers, Robert Latham Brown, Carl Olsen; Assistant Director, Michael Green; "Chucky" Doll Creator, David Kirschner/Designer-Executor, Kevin Yagher; Visual Effects, Peter Donen; Set Decorator, Cloudia; Set Designers, James E. Tocci, William David Arnold, Gary Baugh; Sound, James E. Webb, Jr.; Special Effects, Richard O. Helmer, James D. Schwalm; Orchestrations, Arlon Ober; "*Chucky's Animated Theme*" by Mike Piccirillo, and songs by B. Boyle, R. Bell & M. Lanning, R. Rome & R. Faith, D. Kitay & D. Darling/Performances, Mike Piccirillo, D. B. Night, Michael Lanning, African Suite, David Darling; Co-Executive Producer, Elliot Geisinger; Dolby Stereo; Stunts, Bud Davis, Joie Chitwood; from MGM/UA Communications; Technicolor; Rated R; 87 minutes; November release

CAST

Karen Barclay .... Catherine Hicks
Mike Norris .... Chris Sarandon
Andy Barclay .... Alex Vinent
Charles Lee Ray .... Brad Dourif
Maggie Peterson .... Dinah Manoff
Jack Santos .... Tommy Swerdlow
Dr. Ardmore .... Jack Colvin
Eddie Caputo .... Neil Giuntoli
Peddler .... Juan Ramirez
Mr. Criswell .... Alan Wilder
Dr. Death .... Raymond Oliver
Mona .... Tyler Hard
George .... Ted Liss
Lucy .... Roslyn Alexander
and Richard Baird, Aaron Osborne, Robert Kane, Leila Hee Olsen, Ed Gale, Lena Sack, Tommy Gerard, Michael Chavez, Jamie Gray, Erin Munz, Jana Twomey, Suaundra Black, Edan Gross, John Franklin, Michael Patrick Coster

Right: Alan Wilder, Dinah Manoff, Catherine Hicks Top: Alex Vincent, Chucky
(United Artists)

Alex Vincent, Catherine Hicks

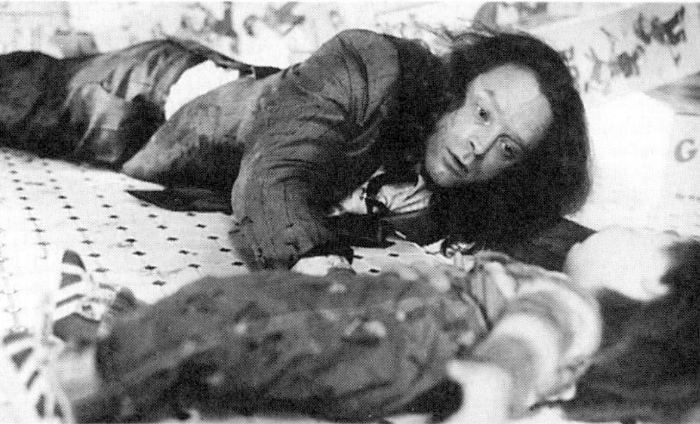

Brad Dourif, Chucky Above: Chris Sarandon, Alex Vincent, Catherine Hicks

Jim Varney Right: Buddy Douglas, Patty Maloney, Varney Top Right: Varney, Oliver Clark

ERNEST SAVES CHRISTMAS

OUCHSTONE/BUENA VISTA) Producers, Stacy Williams, oug Claybourne; Director, John Cherry; Screenplay, B. Kline, Ed urner; Story, Ed Turner; Executive Producers, Martin Erlichmabn, oseph L. Akerman, Jr.; Photography, Peter Stein; Editor, Sharyn L. oss; Art Director, Ian Thomas; Co-Producers, Justis Greene, Coke ams; Costumes, Peter Mitchell; Music, Mark Snow; Casting, Kathen Letterie; Visual Effects, Tim McHugh; Production Managers, stis Greene, Carol Sue Byron; Assistant Director, Patrice Leung; Set ecorator, Chris August; Sound, Rich Schirmer, Douglas Murray; pecial Effects, Mike Weesner; Production Coordinators, Loolee Deeon, Barbara Lange; Stunts, Jerry Gatlin, Chuck Waters; Dolby tereo; Metrocolor; Rated PG; 89 minutes; November release

CAST

rnest P. Worrell .... Jim Varney
anta .... Douglas Seale
e Carruthers .... Oliver Clark
armony .... Noelle Parker
huck .... Gailard Sartain
ary Morrissey .... Billie Bird
obby .... Bill Byrge
arty .... Robert Lesser
yramus .... Buddy Douglas
hisbe .... Patty Maloney
gent Skippy .... Beecher Martin
r. Dillis .... George Kaplan
atsy .... Lindsey Alley
acy .... Phran Gauci
arl .... Bill Cordell
rad .... Larry Francer
olice Chief Spenks .... Bob Norris
d Key Howard, Jack Swanson, Barry Brazell, Bill Christie, Joe andelora, Danny Dillon, Jackie Welch, Daniel Butler, Antonio Fabzzio, Tony Shepherd, Carmen Alexander, Miriam P. Saunders

Right Center: Noelle Parker, Douglas Seale
(Touchstone Pictures)

Noelle Parker, Billie Bird, Oliver Clark, Douglas Seale, Jim Varney, Patty Maloney, Buddy Douglas

Anne DeSalvo, Ernest Borgnine, Geraldine Smith

Sasha Mitchell, Maria Pitillo Left: Mitchell, Ernest Borgnine Top Left: Mitchell, Talisa Soto

SPIKE OF BENSONHURST

(FILMDALLAS) Producers, David Weisman, Nelson Lyon; D rector/Story, Paul Morrissey; Screenplay, Alan Bowne, Paul Morri sey; Executive Producer, Sam Grogg; Co-Producer, Mark Silverma Editor, Stan Salfas; Photography, Steven Fierberg; Production Execu tive, Marcus McWaters; Music, Coati Mundi; Casting, Leonard Finge Costumes, Barbara Dente; Designer, Stephen McCabe; Associate Pr ducers, Jane Holzer, Michael Maiello; Production Manager, Kevi Dowd; Assistant Director, Evan Dunsky; Sound, Danny Michael; A Director, Jocelyne Beaudoin; Set Decorator, Sonja Roth; Boxin Choreographers, Danny Aiello III, Roberto Compono, Jeff War Stunts, Jery Hewitt; Choreographer, Michele Assaf; Associate Edito Sandra Kaufman; Songs by various artists; Color; Rated R; 10 minutes; November release

CAST

Spike Fumo	Sasha Mitche
Baldo Cacetti	Ernest Borgnin
Sylvia Cacetti	Anne DeSalv
Congresswoman	Sylvia Mile
Helen Fumo	Geraldine Smit
Bandana's Mother	Antonia Re
Bandana	Rick Avile
Angel	Maria Pitill
Blondie	Karen Shall
Carmine	Chris Anthony Youn
Tortorella	Mario Todisc
Frankie	Rodney Harve
India	Talisa Sot
Vinaca	Frank Adon
Pete Fumo	Frankie Gi
Chicago Boxer	Robert Compon
Mafia Boss	Tony Goodston
Justin	Justin Lazar
Grandmother	Ida Bernadi
Spike's Brother	Michael Acciarit
Dealer	Steve Bak
Spike Jr.	Rutger G

and Carol Jean Lewis, Tommy Citera, Paul Dillon, Mark Tenor Angel David, Ron Maccone, Mary Lou Rosato, Patrick Indri, Tomm Clark, Ray Iannicelli, John Capodice, Arline Aiyazaki, Sal Vivian Anthony Bishop, Robert Mantana, Ralph Monaco, Tony La Fortezz Gene Amoroso

Left Center: Sasha Mitchell
(FilmDallas Pictures)

OLIVER & COMPANY

UENA VISTA) Director, George Scribner; Screenplay, Jim Cox, nothy J. Disney, James Mangold; Story, Vance Gerry, Mike Gab-l, Roger Allers, Joe Ranft, Gary Trousdale, Jim Mitchell, Kevin na, Chris Bailey, Michael Cedeno, Kirk Wise, Pete Young, Dave chener, Leon Joosen; Inspired by Charles Dickens' *"Oliver Twist"*; isic, J. A. C. Redford; Songs, Barry Mann & Howard Ashman, Tom ow & Dean Pitchford, Ron Rocha & Robert Minkoff, Dan Hartman Charlie Midnight, Barry Manilow, Jack Feldman & Bruce Sussman, cky Pedilla, Michael Eckhart & Jon St. James, Ruben Blaces; pervising Animators, Mike Gabriel, Hendel Burtoy, Glen Keane, irk Henn, Ruben A. Aquino, Doug Krohn; Art Director, Dan nsen; Character Design, Mike Gabriel, Andreas Deja, Glen Keane; ylist, Guy Deel; Production Manager, Kathleen Gavin; Assistant rector, Tim O'Donnell; Consultant, Walt Stanchfield; Casting, Mary Buck, Susan Edelman; Additional Story Material, Gerrit Graham, muel Graham & Chris Hubbell, Steve Hulett, Danny Mann; Editors, 1 Melton, Mark Hester; Sound, Sandy Berman; Orchestrator, Thom-Pasatieri; Presented by Walt Disney Pictures; Produced in Associa-n with Silver Screen Partners III; Animated; Dolby Stereo; Metroco-; Rated G; 72 minutes; November release

VOICE CAST

ver .... Joey Lawrence
dger .... Billy Joel
o .... Cheech Marin
nstein .... Richard Mulligan
ancis .... Roscoe Lee Browne
a .... Sheryl Lee Ralph
gin .... Dom DeLuise
scoe .... Taurean Blacque
soto .... Carl Weintraub
kes .... Robert Loggia
nny .... Natalie Gregory
nston .... William Glover
orgette .... Bette Midler

Right: Oliver, Fagin Top Right: Oliver, Dodger
(The Walt Disney Company)

Oliver, Francis, Tito, Einstein, Dodger, Rita Above: Tito, Georgette

Dodger, Oliver Above: Dodger, Jenny, Oliver

Bill Murray, Carol Kane

SCROOGED

(PARAMOUNT) Producers, Richard Donner, Art Linson, in associ tion with Mirage Productions; Director, Richard Donner; Screenpla Mitch Glazer, Michael O'Donoghue; Suggested by *"A Christm Carol"* by Charles Dickens; Photography, Michael Chapman; D signer, J. Michael Riva; Editors, Fredric Steinkamp, William Stein amp; Co-Producer/Production Manager, Ray Hartwick; Associate Pr ducer, Jennie Lew-Tugend; Costumes, Wayne Finkelman; Musi Danny Elfman; Casting, David Rubin; Assistant Director, Chris Sold Consultant, Stuart Baird; Set Decorator, Linda DeScenna; Art Direct Virginia L. Randolph; Sound, Willie Burton; Makeup Effects, Thom R. Burman, Bari Dreiband-Burman; Special Effects, Allen L. Ha Albert Delgado; Stunts, Mic Rodgers; Choreography, Lester Wilsc Jillian Hessel; Visual Effects, Dream Quest Images/Eric Brevig; Son by various artists; Soundtrack on A&M Records; Dolby Stereo; Tec nicolor; Rated PG-13; 101 minutes; November release

CAST

Frank Cross .... Bill Murr
Claire Phillips .... Karen All
Lew Hayward .... John Forsyt
Brice Cummings .... John Glov
Eliot Loudermilk .... Bobcat Goldthw
Ghost of Christmas Past .... David Johans
Ghost of Christmas Present .... Carol Ka
Preston Rhinelander .... Robert Mitchu
Calvin Cooley .... Nicholas Philli
Herman .... Michael J. Polla
Grace Cooley .... Alfie Wooda
Gramma .... Mabel Ki
James Cross .... John Murr
Jacob Marley .... Jamie Fa
Himself .... Robert Gou
Scrooge .... Buddy Hack
Himself .... John Housem
Himself .... Lee Majo
Ghost of Christmas Present (TV) .... Pat McCormi
Earl Cross .... Brian Doyle Murr
Herself .... Mary Lou Rett
Santa Claus .... Al "Red Dog" Web
Mrs. Claus .... Jean Speegle Howa
June Cleaver .... June Chandl
Wally Cleaver .... Michael Eida
Ted .... Mary Ellen Train
Wayne .... Bruce Jarcho
Archibishop .... Peter Bromilo
Steven Cooley .... Damon Hin
Shasta Cooley .... Tamika McCollu
Randee Cooley .... Koren McCollu
Lanell Cooley .... Reina Ki
Doris Cross .... Lisa Men
Frank as Child .... Ryan To
Tina .... Rebeca Arth
Mrs. Claus at Party .... Selma Arche
Foo-Ling .... Jennie Lew Tuge
Mike the Mailman .... Roy Brocksm
Belle .... Sachi Park
Hazel .... Delores H
Wendie Cross .... Wendie Mali
Ghost of Christmas Future (TV) .... Chaz Conner,
Mrs. Rhinelander .... Maria Ri
Marvin .... Winifred Tennis
and Sanford Jensen, Jeffrey Joseph, Dick Blasucci, Bill Marcus, C Gibson, Paul Tuerpe, Lester Wilson, Ronald Strang, Kate McGreg Stewart, Jack McGee, Bill Hart, Kathy Kinney, Ralph Gervais, Alv Hammer, Tony Steedman, Jay Byron, Harvey Fisher, C. Ransc Walrod, James R. Miller, Shawn Michaels, Stella Hal, Anne & Log Ramsey, Sydna Scott, Joel Murray, Mitch Glazer

Left Center: Bill Murray, Alfre Woodard, Bobcat Goldthwait Above: John Forsythe Top Left: David Johansen, Bill Murray
(Paramount Pictures)

Arnold Schwarzenegger, Danny DeVito Right: Kelly Preston, Schwarzenegger Top Right: Tom McCleister, DeVito, David Efron

TWINS

NIVERSAL) Producer/Director, Ivan Reitman; Screenplay, Wilm Davies, William Osborne, Timothy Harris, Herschel Weingrod; ecutive Producers, Joe Medjuck, Michael C. Gross; Photography, idrzej Bartkowiak; Designer, James D. Bissell; Editor, Sheldon ihn, Donn Cambern; Music, Georges DeLerue, Randy Edelman; stumes, Gloria Gresham; Casting, Michael Chinich; Associate Procers, Sheldon Kahn, Gordon Webb; Production Manager, Gordon ebb; Assistant Director; Peter Giuliano; Art Director, Chris Burianohr; Set Designers, Nancy Patton, William James Teegarden, Edrd S. Verreaux; Set Decorator, John T. Walker; Sound, Gene Cannessa, Steve Cantamessa; Production Coordinators, Pam Cedequist, mela Easley; Choreographer, Paula Tracy Smuin; Special Effects, chael Lantieri; Visual Effects, Boss Film Corp.; Soundtrack on TG Records; Dolby Stereo; DeLuxe Color; Rated PG; 115 minutes; cember release

CAST

ius Benedict .... Arnold Schwarzenegger
ncent Benedict .... Danny DeVito
arnie Mason .... Kelly Preston
nda Mason .... Chloe Webb
ary Ann Benedict .... Bonnie Bartlett
ebster .... Marshall Bell
etroot McKinley .... Trey Wilson
Greco .... David Caruso
anger .... Hugh O'Brien
erner .... Tony Jay
tchell Traven .... Nehemiah Persoff
rt Klane .... Maury Chaykin
b Klane .... Tom McCleister
orris Klane .... David Efron
er Garfield .... Peter Dvorsky
bert Larsen .... Robert Harper
ss Busby .... Rosemary Dunamore
ewardess .... Lora Milligan
stodian .... Richard De Faut
other Superior .... Frances Bay
Kinley's Man .... Marvin J. McIntyre
m Klane .... Sven-Ole Thorsen
ve Klane .... Gus Rethwisch
l Richard Portnov, S. A. Griffin, Billy D. Lucas, Lew Hopson, ry-Hiroyuki Tagawa, Wayne Grace, Thomas Wagner, Jay Arlen es, Tyrone Granderson Jones, Elizabeth Kaitan, Tom Platz, Roger llard, Catherine Reitman, Jason Reitman, Dendrie Taylor, Linda ter, Bruce McBroom, Joseph Medjuck, Frank Davis, John Michael lger, Steve Reevis, Jeff Beck, Nicolette Larson, Jill Avery, Tony mas, Terry Bozio

Right Center: Danny DeVito, Chloe Webb
(Universal City Studios)

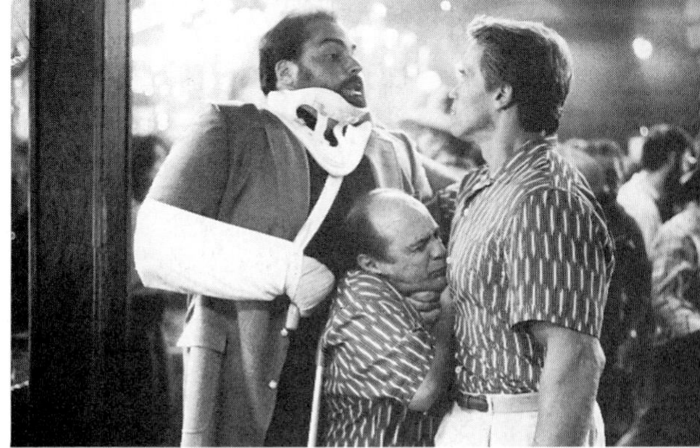

David Efron, Danny DeVito, Arnold Schwarzenegger

Leslie Nielsen, Priscilla Presley Top Right: Nielsen
Right: Nielsen, Jeannette Charles

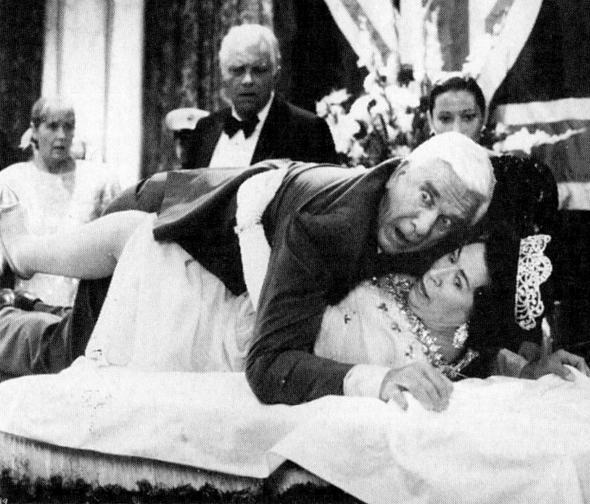

THE NAKED GUN
From the Files of Police Squad!

(PARAMOUNT) Producer, Robert K. Weiss; Director, David Zucker; Screenplay, Jerry Zucker, Jim Abrahams, David Zucker, Pat Proft; Executive Producers, Jerry Zucker, Jim Abrahams, David Zucker; Photography, Robert Stevens; Designer, John J. Lloyd; Editor, Michael Jablow; Costumes, Mary E. Vogt; Music, Ira Newborn; Associate Producers, John D. Schofield, Kevin M. Marcy; Casting, Fern Champion, Pamela Basker; Production Manager, John D. Schofield; Assistant Director, John T. Kretchmer; Set Decorator, Rick T. Gentz; Art Director, Donald B. Woodruff; Sound, Thomas D. Causey, Ronald Judkins; Orchestrators, Don Nemitz, Alf Clausen, Ira Newborn; Special Effects, Cliff Wenger; Stunts, Conrad E. Palmisano; *"I'm Into Something Good"* by Gerry Goffin & Carole King/Performance, Peter None, and songs by other artists; Technicolor; Rated PG-13; 90 minutes; December release

CAST
PEOPLE WHO ACTED IN THE MOVIE

Frank Drebin .... Leslie Nielsen
Jane Spence .... Priscilla Presley
Vincent Ludwig .... Ricardo Montalban
Ed Hocken .... George Kennedy
Nordberg .... O. J. Simpson
Mrs. Nordberg .... Susan Beaubian
Mayor .... Nancy Marchand
Pahpshmir .... Raye Birk
Queen Elizabeth II .... Jeannette Charles
Ted Olsen .... Ed Williams
Al .... Tiny Ron
"Weird Al" .... "Weird Al" Yankovic
"Weird Leslie" .... Leslie Maier
Stephie .... Winnifred Freedman
Foreman .... Joe Grifasi
Enrico Pallazzo .... Tony Brafa
Woman on Ledge .... Lorali Hart
Dominique .... Charlotte Zucker
Photographer .... Burton Zucker
Arafat .... David Katz
Khadafi .... Robert Lujane
Khomeini .... Charles Gherard
Idi Amin .... Prince Hughes
Gorbachev .... David Lloyd Austin
Ken & .... Ken Minyard
Bob .... Bob Arthur
Man & Woman Deleted from Fireworks Scene Greg & Sharon Breslau and Nicholas Worth, Ronald G. Joseph, Doris Hess, Larry Pines, Tom Dugan, Reggie Jackson, Michael J. Montes, Chuck Fick, Lawrence Tierney, Hank Robinson, Joe West, Jay Johnstone, Randy Harvey, Brett Bartlett, Dennis Packer, Dick Vitale, Dick Enberg, Jim Palmer, Mel Allen, Curt Gowdy, Tim McCarver, Dr. Joyce Brothers

(Paramount Pictures)

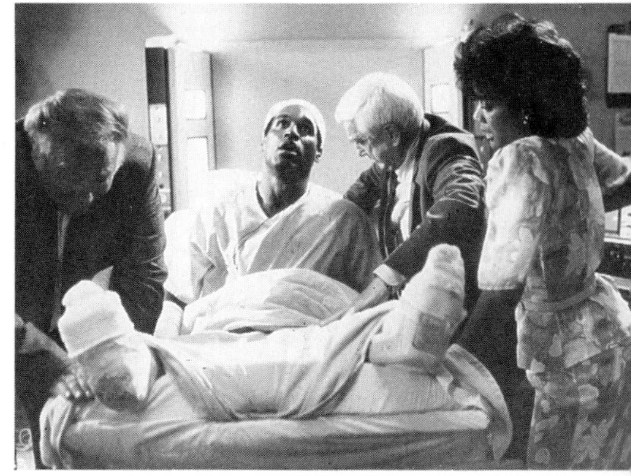

George Kennedy, O. J. Simpson, Leslie Nielsen, Susan Beaubian Above: Ricardo Montalban, Priscilla Presley

William Hurt, Geena Davis, Edward Right: Hurt, Edward Top Right: Hurt, Kathleen Turner

THE ACCIDENTAL TOURIST

ARNER BROS.) Producers, Lawrence Kasdan, Charles Okun, ichael Grillo; Director, Lawrence Kasdan; Screenplay, Frank Galati, wrence Kasdan; Based on the book by Anne Tyler; Executive Producers, Phyllis Carlyle, John Malkovich; Photography, John Bailey; esigner, Bo Welch; Editor, Carol Littleton; Music, John Williams; stumes, Ruth Myers; Casting, Wallis Nicita; Production Manager, harles Okun; Assistant Director, Michael Grillo; Art Director, Tom uffield; Set Decorator, Cricket Rowland; Orchestration, Herb encer; Sound, David MacMillan; Special Effects, Joe Mercurio; Set esigners, Paul Sonski, Nick Navarro, Ann Harris; Visual Effects, dustrial Light & Magic; *"I'm Gonna Lasso Santa Claus"* by Frankie dams & Wilbur Jones; Soundtrack on Warner Bros. Records; Dolby ereo; Technicolor; Panavision; Rated PG; 122 minutes; December lease

CAST

acon .... William Hurt
rah .... Kathleen Turner
uriel .... Geena Davis
se .... Amy Wright
rter .... David Ogden Stiers
harles .... Ed Begley, Jr.
lian .... Bill Pullman
exander .... Robert Gorman
r. Loomis .... Bradley Mott
han .... Seth Granger
ebbie .... Amanda Houck
rrie .... Caroline Houck
aroline .... London Nelson
rs. Barrett .... Peggy Converse
ura Canfield .... Maureen Kerrigan
ott Canfield .... Jacob Kasdan
lward the Dog .... Bud
d Gregory Gouyer, W. H. Brown, Donald Neal, Paul Williamson, alter Sparrow, Todd Adelman, Meg Kasdan, David Combs, nathan Kasdan, Thomas Paolucci, Neana N. Collins, Roland Riallot, one Narr, Audrey R. Rapoport

(Warner Bros.)

Geena Davis Received the Academy Award for Best Supporting Actress of 1988

Geena Davis, William Hurt, Robert Gorman Above: David Ogden Stiers, Amy Wright, Hurt, Ed Begley, Jr.

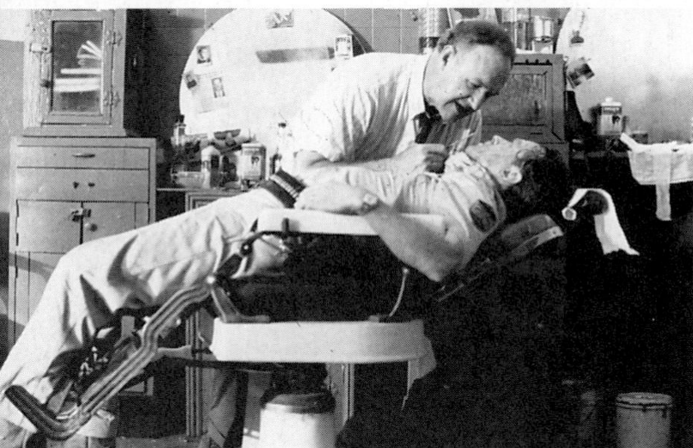

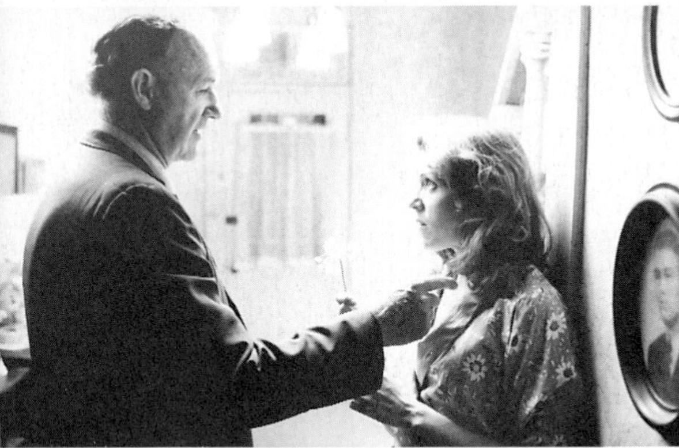

Darius McCrary, Ralnardo Davis, Willem Dafoe, Gene Hackman

MISSISSIPPI BURNING

(ORION) Producers, Frederick Zollo, Robert F. Colesberry; Directo Alan Parker; Screenplay, Chris Gerolmo; Photography, Peter Bizio Designers, Philip Harrison, Geoffrey Kirkland; Editor, Gerry Har bling; Costumes, Aude Bronson Howard; Music, Trevor Jones; Cas ing, Howard Howard Feuer, Juliet Taylor; Production Manager, Thor as A. Razzano; Assistant Director, Aldric La'Auli Porter; Art Directo John Willett; Set Decorator, Jim Erickson; Sound, Danny Micha Stunts, John Robotham; Special Effects, Stan Parks; Songs by vario artists; Dolby Stereo; DeLuxe Color; Rated R; 127 minutes: Decemb release

CAST

Anderson .... Gene Hackm
Ward .... Willem Daf
Mrs. Pell .... Frances McDorma
Deputy Pell .... Brad Dou
Mayor Tilman .... R. Lee Erm
Sheriff Stuckey .... Gailard Sarta
Townley .... Stephen Tobolows
Frank Bailey .... Michael Rook
Lester Cowens .... Pruitt Tylor Vin
Agent Monk .... Badja Djc
Agent Bird .... Kevin Du
Eulogist .... Frankie Fais
Judge .... Tom Mas
Goatee .... Geoffrey Nauf
Hattie .... Gladys Gre
Mose .... Jake Gips
Hollis .... Stanley W. Colli
Fennis .... Daniel Winfo
Floyd Swilley .... Marc Cleme
Earl Cooke .... Larry Shu
Wesley Cooke .... Stephen Wesley Bridgewa
Curtis Foy .... Bob Pen
Connie .... Park Over
Choctaw Man .... Barry Davis Jim, S
Television Commentator .... Dan Desmo
Aaron Williams .... Daruis McCra
Vertis Williams .... Lou Wal
Mrs. Williams .... Billie Jean You
Obie Walker .... Simeon Teag
Mrs. Walter .... Tonea Stew
Willie .... Ralnardo Da
Agent Stokes .... Tobin B
Agent MacMillan .... Daniel Chapm
Agent Brodsky .... Rick Washbu
Agent Nash .... Bob Glaud
Agent Reilly .... Kenneth MaG
Agent Tubbs .... E. A. Thr
Mrs. Cowens .... Brenda Dunl
and Rick Zieff, Christopher White, Dianne Lancaster, James F. Moo Georgia F. Wise, Lois Allen, Alisa R. Patrick, Barbara Gibson, F Funderburk, Dawn Boyd, Dwight Boyd, Linda Fuller, George Isbe Ethel L. Mayes, James Arnold Mayes, George Mason, Charles Fra zen, Harry Franklin, Virginia Bennett, James Lloyd, Jesse Me Speaks

Left Center: Gene Hackman, Frances McDormand Above: Gene Hackman, Brad Dourif Top Left: Simeon Teague, Willem Dafoe
(Orion Pictures)

Winner 1988 Academy Award for Best Cinematograph

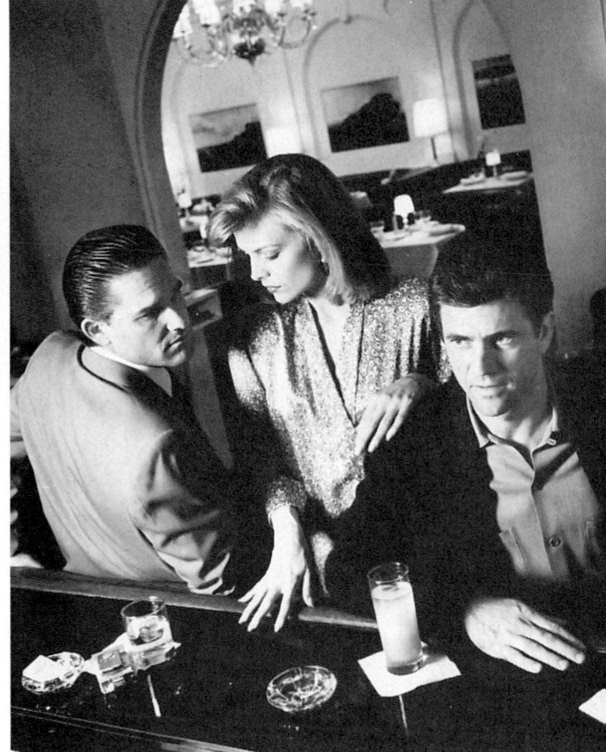

Kurt Rossell, Michelle Pfeiffer Right: Kurt Russell, Michelle Pfeiffer, Mel Gibson

TEQUILA SUNRISE

'ARNER BROS.) Producer, Thom Mount; Director/Screenplay, ›bert Towne; Executive Producer/Production Manager, Tom Shaw; otography, Conrad L. Hall; Designer, Richard Sylbert; Editor, aire Simpson; Music, Dave Grusin; Music Supervisor, Danny amson; Costumes, Julie Weiss; Casting, Bonnie Timmerman; Proction Assistant Directors, David Anderson, Albert Shapiro; Art rector, Peter Lansdown Smith; Set Decorator, Rick Simpson; Sound, uce Bisenz; Costumes, Carol Kunz, Nancy McArdle; Stunts, Bobby ss, Dave Cass; Special Effects, Jerry D. Williams, Chuck Stewart; t Designer, Judy Cammer; A Mount Company Production; *"Surren- to Me" (Love Theme)* by Richard Marx & Ross Vanelli/ rformance, Ann Wilson & Robin Zander, and songs by other artists; undtrack on Capitol Records; Dolby Stereo; DeLuxe Color; Rated R; 6 minutes; December release

CAST

:Kussic .... Mel Gibson
Ann .... Michelle Pfeiffer
scia .... Kurt Russell
rlos/Escalante .... Raul Julia
guire .... J. T. Walsh
ndroff .... Arliss Howard
dy Leonard .... Ayre Gross
dy McKussic .... Gabriel Damon
turo .... Garret Pearson
ttorio .... Eric Thiele
land .... Tom Nolan
s Sisters .... Dawn Martel, Lala
dge Nizetitch .... Budd Boetticher
aleen .... Ann Magnuson
ody .... Kenneth C. Moore
agician .... Jason Randal
lph Spudder .... Bob Swain
p .... Jim Bentley
eve .... Eric Waterhouse
pe .... Daniel Addes
d Geno Silva, Efrain Figueroa, Tomas Goros, Austin Hawk, Scott rms, Sarah Davis, John D. Steele, David Rees, Oscar Abadia, Jim dd, Tom Schnabel

(Warner Bros.)

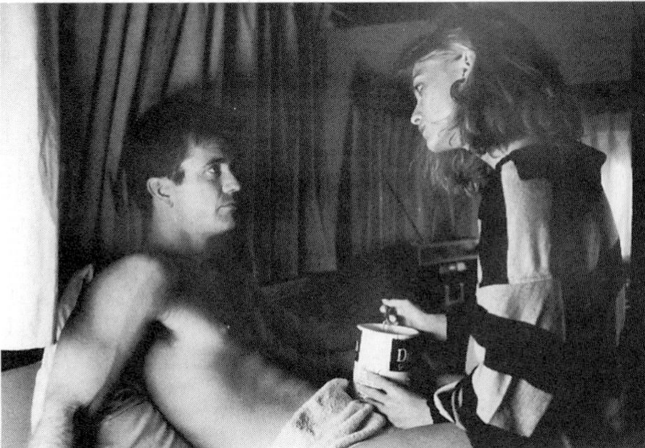

Mel Gibson, Michelle Pfeiffer Above: Gibson, Kurt Russell

DIRTY ROTTEN SCOUNDRELS

(ORION) Producer, Bernard Williams; Director, Frank Oz; Screenplay, Dale Launder, Stanley Shapiro, Paul Henning; Executive Producers, Dale Launder, Charles Hirschhorn; Music, Miles Goodman; Photography, Michael Balhaus; Designer, Roy Walker; Editors, Stephen A. Rotter, William Scharf; Costumes, Marit Allen; Casting, Donna Isaacson, John Lyons; Production Manager, Bernard Mazauric; Assistant Directors, Bernard Williams, David Tringham; Production Coordinator, Michelle Wright-Warnick; Art Directors, Steve Spence, Damien Lanfranchi; Set Decorator, Rosalind Shingleton; Sound, Ivan Sharrock; Orchestrators, Thomas Pasatieri, Oscar Castro-Neves; Violinist, Jerry Goodman; Songs by various artists; Dolby Stereo; DeLuxe Color; Rated PG; 110 minutes; December release

CAST

Freddy Benson	Steve Martin
Lawrence Jamieson	Michael Caine
Janet Colgate	Glenne Headly
Inspector Andre	Anton Rodgers
Fanny Eubanks	Barbara Harris
Arthur	Ian McDiarmid
Mrs. Reed	Dana Ivey
Lady from Oklahoma	Meagen Fay
Lady from Palm Beach	Frances Conroy
Lady in Dining Car	Nicole Calfan
Miss Krista Knudsen	Aina Walle
Lady with Pearls	Cheryl Pay
Marion	Nathalie Auffret
Lady in Rolls Royce	Lolly Susi
English Sailors	Rupert Holliday Evans, Hepburn Graham
Hotel Bellboy	Xavier Maly
Waiter on the Train	Andre Penvern
Greek Millionaire	Louis Zorich
Assistant Hotel Manager	Georges Gerrard Baffos
Pretty Beach Girl	Valerie Beaufils

Right: Michael Caine, Steve Martin (Also Top)
(Orion Pictures)

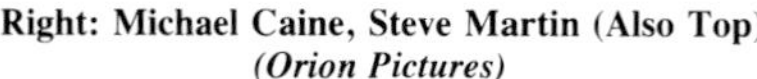

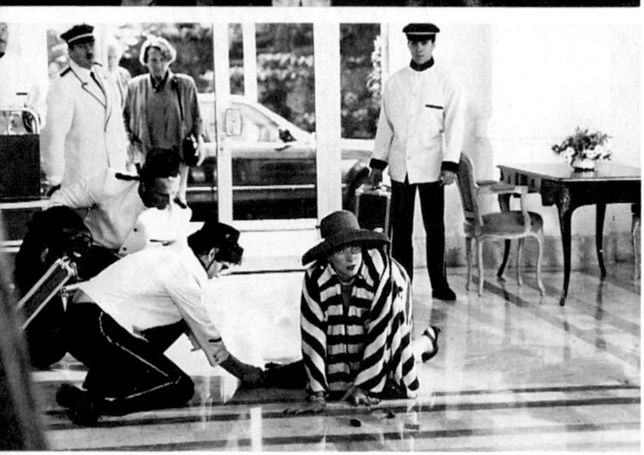

Glenne Headly Above: Michael Caine, Headly, Steve Martin

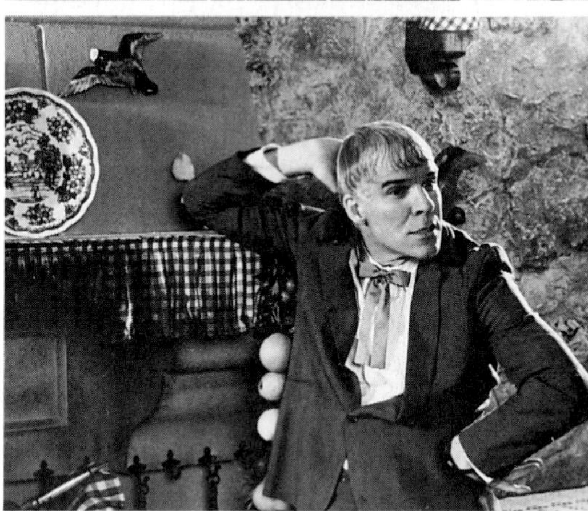

Steve Martin, Frances Conroy, Above: Martin

Melanie Griffith Right: Griffith, Harrison Ford
Top Right: Griffith, Ford, Sigourney Weaver

WORKING GIRL

0th CENTURY FOX) Producer, Douglas Wick; Director, Mike ichols; Screenplay, Kevin Wade; Executive Producers, Robert eenhut, Laurence Mark; Photography, Michel Ballhaus; Designer, trizia Von Brandenstein; Editor, Sam O'Steen; Costumes, Ann Roth; asting, Juliet Taylor, Ellen Lewis; Music, Carly Simon; Scoring, Rob ounsey; Production Manager, Robert Greenhut; Assistant Director, ike Haley; Production Supervisor, Todd Arnow; Art Director, Doug aner; Set Decorator, George DeTitta; Production Coordinator, Ingrid hanson; Sound, Les Lazarowitz; Stunts, Frank Ferrara, Jim Dunn; ng: *"Let the River Run,"* written and performed by Carly Simon; ngs by various artists; Dolby Stereo; DeLuxe Color; Rated R; 113 nutes; December release

CAST

ck Trainer .... Harrison Ford
atharine Parker .... Sigourney Weaver
ss McGill .... Melanie Griffith
ick Dugan .... Alec Baldwin
yn .... Joan Cusack
en Trask .... Philip Bosco
nny .... Nora Dunn
itz .... Oliver Platt
rkel .... James Lally
ob Speck .... Kevin Spacey
mbrister .... Robert Easton
rsonnell Director .... Olympia Dukakis
m Rourke .... Jeffrey Nordling
oreen DiMucci .... Elizabeth Whitcraft
. Executive .... Jim Babchak
n .... Zach Grenier
hn Romano .... Lee Dalton
yllis Trask .... Barbara Garrick
arbara Trask .... Madolin B. Archer
itsy .... Marceline A. Hugot
m Draper .... Tim Carhart
axter .... Amy Aquino
d Maggie Wagner, Lou DiMaggio, David Duchovny, Georgienne illen, Caroline Aaron, Nancy Giles, Judy Milstein, Nicole Chevance, athleen Gray, Jane B. Harris, Sondra Hollander, Samantha Shane, lie Silverman

(20th Century Fox)

1988 Academy Award for Best Original Song ("Let the River Run")

Harrison Ford, Melanie Griffith, Sigourney Weaver
Above: Nora Dunn, Joan Cusack

Anne Bancroft, Harvey Fierstein Left: Eddie Castrodad, Anne Bancroft Top Left: Matthew Broderick

Harvey Fierstein, Matthew Broderick
Above: Brian Kerwin, Karen Young

TORCH SONG TRILOGY

(NEW LINE CINEMA) Producer, Howard Gottfried; Director, Pa Bogart; Screenplay, Harvey Fierstein; Based on the play by Harve Fierstein; Photography, Mikael Salomon; Designer, Richard Hoove Editor, Nicholas C. Smith; Executive Producer, Ronald K. Fierstei Associate Producer/Production Manager, Marie Cantin; Music, Pete Matz; Costumes, Colleen Atwood; Choreography, Scott Salmon; Cas ing, Gail Levin, Lauren Lloyd; Assistant Directors, Dennis MaGuire Peter Bogart; Production Coordinator, Karen Altman Morgenstern; A Directors, Okowita, Marcie Dale; Set Decorator, Michael Warg Sound, Steve Nelson; Production Supervisor, Deborah Moore; Torc Songs by various artists; Soundtrack on Polydor Records; Dolby Stere Metrocolor; Rated R; 122 minutes; December release

CAST

Ma .... Anne Bancro
Alan .... Matthew Brodeic
Arnold .... Harvey Fierste
Ed .... Brian Kerw
Laurel .... Karen Youn
David .... Eddie Castroda
Murray .... Ken Pag
Bertha Venation .... Charles Pierc
Marina Del Rey .... Axel Ve
Young Arnold .... Benji Schulma
Chorus Boys .... Nick Montgomery, Robert Near
Phil Beckoff .... Lorry Goldma
Arnold's Father .... Edgar Sma
Gregory .... Byron Dee
Roz .... Bob Minc
Hustler .... Gregory Gilbe
and Kim Clark, Stephanie Penn, Geoffrey Harding, Michael Bonc Michael Warga, Phil Sky, Harriet C. Leider, Paul Joynt, Mitch Davi Carter, John Beckman, Rabbi Elliott T. Spar, Alva Chinn, John Nor man, Mark Zeisler, Peter MacKenzie, Peter Nevargic, Ted Hook, Nia Gartlan, Catherine Blue, John Branagan, Tracy Bogart, Frits de Kneg

(New Line Cinema)

DANGEROUS LIAISONS

VARNER BROS.) Producers, Norma Heyman, Hank Moonjean; rector, Stephen Frears; Screenplay/Co-Producer, Christopher Hampn; Based on the Play by Christopher Hampton; Adapted from the ovel *"Les Liaisons Dangereuses"* by Choderlos DeLaclos; Photogray, Philippe Rousselot; Designer, Stuart Craig; Editor, Mick Audsley; usic, George Fenton; Costumes, James Acheson; Production Supersor, Suzanne Wiensenfeld; Casting, Juliet Taylor, Howard Feuer; oduction Manager, Patrick Gordon; Assistant Director, Bernard itz; Sound, Peter Handford; Art Directors, Gerard Viard, Gavin ocquet; Set Decorator, Gerard James; Wigs, Peter Owen; Hair, Pierre ade, Malou Rossignol; Stunts, William Hobbs; Opera Staging, Pierre mans; Soundtrack on Virgin An NFM Limited Production from rimar Soundtrack on Virgin Movie Music Records; Dolby Stereo; olor; Rated R; 120 minutes; December release

CAST

arquise de Merteuil .... Glenn Close
icomte de Valmont .... John Malkovich
adame de Tourvel .... Michelle Pfeiffer
adame de Volanges .... Swoosie Kurtz
hevalier Danceny .... Keanu Reeves
adame de Rosemonde .... Mildred Natwick
ecile de Volanges .... Uma Thurman
zolan .... Peter Capaldi
eorges .... Joe Sheridan
lie .... Valerie Cogan
milie .... Laura Benson
dele .... Joanna Pavlis
ajordomo .... Nicholas Hawtrey
astrato .... Paulo Abel Do Nascimento
ure .... Francois Lalande
elleroche .... Francois Montagut
rmand .... Harry Jones
ailiff .... Christian Erickson
pera Singer .... Catherine Cauwet

Top Right: Glenn Close, John Malkovich
Below: John Malkovich, Michelle Pfeiffer
(Warner Bros.)

1988 Academy Awards for Best Adapted Screenplay, Best Costume Design, Best Art Direction

Uma Thurman, Glenn Close, John Malkovich, Mildred Natwick, Swoosie Kurtz

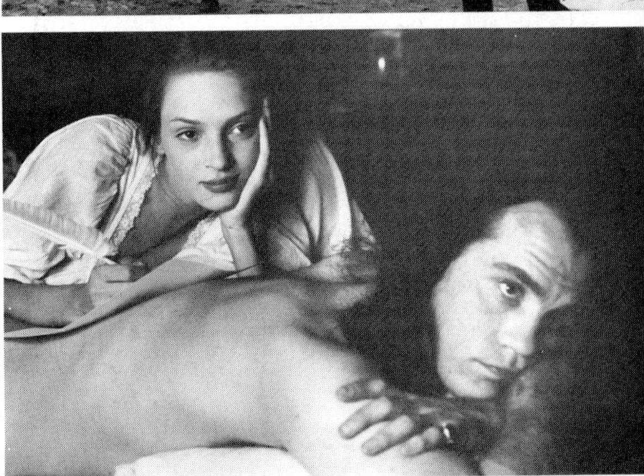

Uma Thurman, John Malkovich Above: Keanu Reeves, Malkovich

John Heard, Bette Midler, Barbara Hershey
Top Right: Midler Right: Lainie Kazan, Mayim Bialik, Marcie Leeds

BEACHES

(TOUCHSTONE/BUENA VISTA) Producers, Bonnie Bruckheimer-Martell, Bette Midler, Margaret Jennings South; Director, Garry Marshall; Screenplay, Mary Agnes Donoghue; Based on the novel by Iris Rainer Dart; Executive Producer, Teri Schwartz; Photography, Dante Spinotti; Designer, Albert Brenner; Editor, Richard Halsey; Co-Producer, Nick Abdo; Costumes, Robert de Mora; Music, Georges DeLerue; Casting, Mike Fenton, June Taylor, Lynda Gordon; Production Manager, William S. Beasley; Assistant Director, Benjamin Rosenberg; Song Producer, Arif Mardin; Choreographer, Dee Dee Wood; Art Director, Frank Richwood; Set Decorator, Garrett Lewis; Sound, Jim Webb; Special Effects, Alan E. Lorimer; Stunts, Bill Erickson; Production Coordinator, Christie Johnston; Theatrical Lighting, Chip Largman; Set Designer, Harold L. Fuhrman; In Association with Silver Screen partners IV of the Bruckheimer/South-All Girl Production; Dolby Stereo; Metrocolor; Rated PG-13; 123 minutes; December release

CAST

CC Bloom .... Bette Midler
Hillary Whitney Essex .... Barbara Hershey
John Pierce .... John Heard
Dr. Richard Milstein .... Spalding Gray
Leona Bloom .... Lainie Kazan
Michael Essex .... James Read
Victoria Essex .... Grace Johnston
CC (age 11) .... Mayim Bialik
Hillary (age 11) .... Marcie Leeds
Aunt Vesta .... Carol Williard
Mr. Melman .... Allan Kent
Sammy Pinkers .... Phil Leeds
Mrs. Myandowski .... Lynda Goodfriend
Miss Valdez .... Anne Betancourt
Cowboy Actor .... Ken Gibbel
Phillipe De Brassiere .... Steven Majewicz
Iris Myandowski .... Nikki Plant
Harry .... Robert Ball
Marjorie .... Diane Frazen
T. Kuhn .... Patrick Richwood
Maura .... Doris Hess
Michael's Mistress .... Lisa Savage
The Movie Director .... Harvey Alan Miller
Justice of the Peace .... Hector Elizondo
Otto Titsling .... Joe Grifasi

and Michael French, Frank Campanella, Michel Elias, Tracy Reiner, Zachary Weintraub, Nicky Blair, Joshua Levinson, Lori Marshall, Jenifer Jeanette Lewis, Charlotte Crossley, Julie Burrows, Kimberly Morgan, Andrea Paris, Adrienne Parker, Melissa Bremner, Laura Fremont, Charles McGowan, Todd Niles, Caitlin McLean, Ken Miller, Bill Bohl

(Touchstone Pictures)

Barbara Hershey, Bette Midler (Also Above)

Eric Bogosian, Alec Baldwin Right: John C. McGinley Top Right: Bogosian

TALK RADIO

NIVERSAL) Producers, Edward R. Pressman, A. Kitman Ho; irector, Oliver Stone; Screenplay, Eric Bogosian, Oliver Stone; ased on the play *"Talk Radio"* created by Eric Bogosian & Tad avinar, written by Eric Gogosian, and the Book *"Talked to Death: The fe and Murder of Alan Berg"* by Stephen Singular; Photography, obert Richardson; Designer, Bruno Rubeo; Costumes, Ellen Miroj-ck; Editor, David Brenner; Music, Stewart Copeland; Executive oducers, Greg Strangis, Sam Strangis; Casting, Risa Bramon, Billy opkins; Production Manager, Clayton Townsend; Assistant Director, seph Reidy; Production Executive, Michael Flynn; Production Coor-nator, Leeann Stonebreaker; Sound, Tod A. Maitland; Art Director, ilo; Set Decorator, Derek R. Hill; *"Bad to the Bone"* by George horogood/Performance, Michael Wetherwax, and songs by other tists; A Cineplex Odeon Films presentation in association with Ten our Prods.; Dolby Stereo; DeLuxe Color; Rated R; 110 minutes; ecember release

CAST

arry Champlain .... Eric Bogosian
len .... Ellen Greene
aura .... Leslie Hope
u .... John C. McGinley
an .... Alec Baldwin
etz .... John Pankow
ent .... Michael Wincott
eila Fleming .... Linda Atkinson
ffrey Fisher .... Robert Trebor
d Greenberg .... Zach Grenier
ino .... Tony Frank
oach Armstrong .... Harlan Jordan
ans .... Bill Johnson, Kevin Howard
oman at Basketball Game .... Anna Levine
ony .... Bruno Rubeo
dge Willard .... Pirie MacDonald
ince .... Allan Corduner
irls .... Mimi Cochran, Teresa Bell
iller .... Rockets Redglare
ngineers .... Angus G. Wynne III, David Pynter
nnouncer .... Chip Moody
d *VOICES:* Peter Zapp (Josh), Robert Trebor (Francine), Allan orduner (Morris), Carl Kissin (Glen), Michael Wincott (Michael), ark Overall (Debbie), Michele Mariana (Rhonda), Earl Hindman Chet), John Seitz, Anna Levine, Rockets Redglare, Kyle McClaran, ee Pyland, Daniel Escobar, Bill DeAcutis, Frederica Meister, Luis arajas

Right Center: Michael Wincott (Cineplex Odeon)

Leslie Hope, Eric Bogosian

Burt Reynolds, Liza Minnelli in "Rent-a-Cop" *(Kings Road)*

Burgess Meredith, Molly Ringwald in "King Lear" *(Cannon)*

RENT-A-COP (Kings Road Entertainment) Producer, Raymond Wagner; Director, Jerry London; Screenplay, Dennis Shryack, Michael Blodgett; Associate Producer, John D. Schofield; Photography, Giuseppe Rotunno; Designer, Tony Masters; Visual Effects Consultant, Kit West; Editor, Robert Lawrence; Music, Jerry Goldsmith; Costumes, Moss Mabry; Casting, Judith Holstra, Marcia Ross; Stunts, Bill Ferguson, Sergio Mioni; Production Managers, Enrico Pini R., Marco Valerio Pugine R., Michael Kowalski; Assistant Directors, Tony Brandt, Ken Flisak, Glen Trotiner, Paolo Percaus; Production Managers, Rita Grant-Miller, Laura Fattori; Additional Photography, William E. Hedenberg; Sound, Amelio Verona; Art Directors, Aurelio Crugnola, Maher Ahmed; Set Decorator, Franco Fumagalli; Assistant Costume Designer, Mary-Anne Aston; Special Effects, Kit West, Yves de Bono, Sherwin Tarnoff; Casting, Francesco Dinieri; Music Supervisor, Budd Carr; Orchestration, Arthur Morton, Nancy Beach; "*Dance the Night Away*" by Randy & Liz Jackson/"*Night Stick*" by Lenny Macaluso & Marcia Woods/and Songs by various other artists; Soundtrack on INTRADA records; Dolby Stereo; 96 minutes; Rated R; January release. CAST: Burt Reynolds (Church), Liza Minnelli (Della), James Remar (Dancer), Richard Masur (Roger), Dionne Warwick (Beth), Bernie Casey (Lemar), Robby Benson (Pitts), John Stanton (Alexander), John P. Ryan (Wieser), Larry Dolgin (Capt. James), Roslyn Alexander (Miss Barley), Cyrus Elias (Victor), Jo Be Cerny, Joe V. Greco (Hotel Clerks), Ned Schmidtke (Lindy), Rick LeFevour (Young Cop), Mary Ann Thebus (Mercedes Woman), John Shannon (Lenny), Micky Knox (Frank), Martin Dansky (Trick), Dennis Cockrum (Man at El), Barbara Houston (Mother), Matthew Libman (Little Roland), Michael Rooker (Joe), Lamar Jackson (Monster), John Drury (TV Announcer), Richard Wilkie (Shoplifter), Vince Viverito (John #1), Stephan Schulberg (Freak), John Scott Ament (Transvestite), Percy Hogan (Buyer), Dal Russel (Seller), Bruce McGuire (Cop #2), Paul Raci (Waiter), Jason Gero (Reporter)

RETURN OF THE LIVING DEAD PART II (Lorimar) Producer, Tom Fox; Director/Screenplay, Ken Wiederhorn; Co-Producer, William S. Gilmore; Executive Producer, Eugene C. Cashman; Photography, Robert Elswit; Editor, Charles Bornstein; Music, J. Peter Robinson; Visual Consultant, Raymond G. Storey; Special Makeup, Kenny Myers; Casting, Shari Rhodes; Assistant Directors, Bill Elvin, Rodney Allen Hooks; Stunts, Gary Davis; Art Director, Dale Allan Pelton; a Greenfox Production; Ultra-Stereo; Metrocolor; Rated R; 89 minutes; January release. CAST: Michael Kenworthy (Jesse Wilson), Thor Van Lingen (Billy), Jason Hogan (Johnny), James Karen (Ed), Thom Mathews (Joey), Suzanne Snyder (Brenda), Marsha Dietlei (Lucy Wilson), Suzan Stadner (Aerobics Instructor), Jonathon Terr (Colonel), Dana Ashbrook (Tom Essex), Sally Smythe (Billy's Mom), Allan Trautman (Tarman), Don Maxwell (Billy's dad), Reynold Cir drich (Soldier), Philip Bruns (Doc Mandel), Mitch Pileggi (Sarge), Arturo Bonilla (Les), Terrence Riggins (Frank), James McIntire (Officer), Forrest Ackerman, Douglas Benson, David Eby, Nicholas Hernandez, Derek Loughran, Annie Marshall, Richard Moore, Stev Neuvenheim, Brian Peck (Zombies)

KING LEAR (Cannon Group, Inc.) Producers, Menham Golar Yoram Globus; Director/Screenplay, Jean-Luc Godard; Based on th play by William Shakespeare; Associate Producer, Tom Luddy; Colo 91 minutes; Rated PG; January release. CAST: Peter Sellars (Wm Shakespeare Jr. the Fifth), Burgess Meredith (Don Learo), Moll Ringwald (Cordelia), Norman Mailer (Himself), Kate Mailer (Herself), Jean-Luc Godard (Professor), Woody Allen (Film Editor)

BRADDOCK: MISSING IN ACTION III (Cannon) Producers Menahem Golan, Yoram Globus; Director, Aaron Norris, Screenplay James Bruner, Chuck Norris; Based on characters created by Arthu Silver, Larry Levinson, Steve Bing; Photography, Joao Fernandes Editor, Michael J. Duthie; Production Designer, Ladislav Wilheim Associate Producers, Michael Hartman, Michael R. Sloan; Music, Ja Chattaway; Assistant Directors, Gerry Walsh, Chris Newman, Joe Wein; Casting, Perry Bullington, Michael Olton; Color; Ultra-stereo Rated R; 102 minutes; January release. CAST: Chuck Norris (Col James Braddock), Aki Aleong (General Quoc), Roland Harrah, II (Van Tan Cang), Miki Kim (Lin Tan Cang), Yehuda Efroni (Reveren Polanski), Ron Barker (Mik), Floyd Levine (General Duncan), Jac Rader (Littlejohn), Melinda Betron (Thuy), Richard Pietro, Jan Schult (C.I.A. agents), Keith David (Embassy gate captain), Robert Jocchier (Embassy guard), Thuy Lin Samora (Embassy secretary), Pita Libor (Lin's friend), Jeff Habberstad, Howard Jackson (U.S. helicopte pilots)

SPOOKIES (Sony) Producers, Eugenie Joseph, Thomas Doran Brendan Faulkner, Frank M. Farel; Directors, Eugenie Joseph, Thoma Doran, Brendan Faulkner; Screenplay, Thomas Doran, Brendan Faulkner, Frank M. Farel; Additional Material, Joseph Burgund; Photography, Robert Chappell, Ken Kelsch; Editor, Eugenie Joseph; Music Kenneth Higgins, James Calabrese; a Twisted Souls production fro

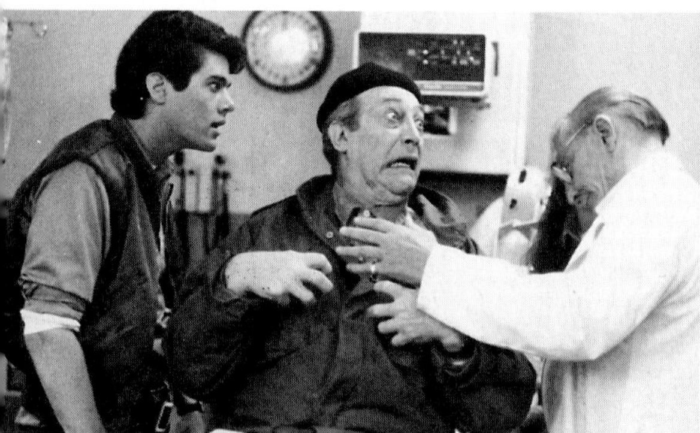

Dana Ashbrook, James Karen, Philip Burns in "Return of the Living Dead Part II" *(Lorimar Pictures)*

Chuck Norris in "Braddock: Missing in Action III" *(Cannon)*

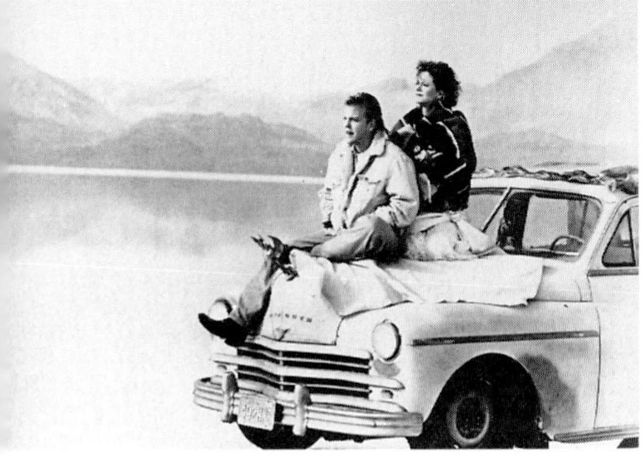

Kiefer Sutherland, Meg Ryan in "Promised Land" ***(Vestron Pictures)***

Lu Leonard, David Packer in "You Can't Hurry Love" ***(Lightning Pictures)***

'ir films; Precision color; Rated R; 84 minutes; January release. .ST: Felix Ward (Kreon), Dan Scott (Kreon's servant), Alec Nemser lly), Maria Pechukas (Isabelle)

OMISED LAND (Vestron) Producer, Rick Stevenson; Executive oducers, Robert Redford, Andrew Meyer; Director/Screenplay, chael Hoffman; Designer, Eugenio Zanetti; Music, James Newton ward; Casting, Risa Bramon, Billy Hopkins, Lora Kennedy; Associ- Producer/Production Manager, Dennis Bishop; Production Ex- tives, Mitchell Canold, Steven Reuther; Associate Producers, Mark ntley, Andy Paterson; Costumes, Victoria; Editor, David Spiers; otography, Ueli Steiger, Alexander Gruszynski; Costumes, Victoria lloway; Music, James Newton Howard; Production Executives, tchell Cannold, Steven Reuther; Associate Producers, Mark Bent- , Andy Paterson; Casting, Risa Bramon, Billy Hopkins, Lora Ken- dy; Associate Producer/Production Manager, Dennis Bishop; In ociation with Great American Films Ltd. Partnership; Dolby Stereo;) minutes; Rated R; January release. CAST: Jason Gedrick (Han- ck), Kiefer Sutherland (Danny), Meg Ryan (Bev), Tracy Pollan ary), Googy Gress (Baines), Deborah Richter (Pammie), Oscar wland (Mr. Rivers), Sondra Seacat (Mrs. Rivers), Jay Underwood ircle K Clerk), Herta Ware (Mrs. Higgins)

IE SISTERHOOD (Concorde) Producer/Director, Cirio H. San- go; Screenplay, Thomas McKelvey Cleaver; Photography, Ricardo mias; Editor, Edgar Viner; Sound, Vicente Dona, Do Bolutano; oduction Designer, Joe Mari Avellana; Assistant Director, Jose Tor- ; a Santa Fe Production; Color; Rated R; 76 minutes; January release. AST: Rebecca Holden (Alee), Chuck Wagner (Mikal), Lynn-Holly nson (Marya), Barbara Hooper (Vera), Henry Strzalkowski (Jon), bert Dryer (Lord Barah), David Light, Jim Moss, Anthony East, m McNeeley

AN OUTSIDE (Virgin Vision) Producers, Mark Stouffer, Robert Yoss; Director/Screenplay, Mark Stouffer; Executive Producers, m Earnhart, Ross Barrows; Photography, William Wages; Music, hn McEuen; Editor, Tony Lombardo; A Stouffer Enterprise Film rtners Production; Color; Rated PG-13; 109 minutes; January re- se. CAST: Robert Logan (Jack Avery), Kathleen Quinlan (Grace eemont), Bradford Dillman (Frank Simmons), Levon Helm (Sheriff and Laughlin)

YOU CAN'T HURRY LOVE (Lightning Pictures/Vestron) Producer, Jonathan D. Krane; Co-Producer, Simon R. Lewis; Director/ Screenplay, Richard Martini; Photography, Peter Lyons Collister, John Schwartzman; Associate Producer, Anthony Santa Croce; Executive Producers, Lawrence Kasanoff, Ellen Steloff, William J. Rouhana, Jr.; Music, Bob Esty; Editor, Richard Candib; Assistant Directors, Jan Ervin, Tony To, Edward M. Grant; Costumes, Colby Bart; Art Director, Douglas A. Mowat; Duart color; Dolby Stereo; Rated R; 92 minutes; January release. CAST: David Leisure (Newcomb), Scott McGinnis (Skip), Anthony Geary (Tony), Bridget Fonda (Peggy), Frank Bonner (Chuck Hayes), Lu Leonard (Miss Friggett), Merete Van Kamp (Monique), David Packer (Eddie), Charles Grodin (Mr. Glerman), Sally Kellerman (Kelly Bones), Kristy McNichol (Rhonda), Luana Anders (Macie Hayes), Jake Steinfeld (Sparky), Judy Balduzzi (Glenda), Danitza Kingsley (Tracey), Rudolph Laubscher (Bus driver), Diz McNally (Cab driver), Dan Golden (Photographer), Jean Poremba (Model in black), Theresa Burrell (Newcomb's secretary), Richard Perry (Bruce), Harry Perry (Himself), Tim Ryan (Tim), Kimber Sissions (Brenda), Jennifer Karr (Girl from Ohio), Kimberly Foster (Girl reading book), Jean McNally (Girl on pier), William Woff (Delivery man), Catherine Lacy (Sonya), Kari Peyton (Girl in elevator), Nancy Davis, Winnie Freedman, Jeanette Schwaba (Sample videotapes), James Hoyt Kelley (Sam), Michael Peppe (Performance artist), Michael Sorich (Drug dealer), Simon R. Lewis (Waiter), Francesca Brenner (Betty Newcomb)

GALACTIC GIGOLO (Urban Classics) Producers, Gorman Bechard, Kris Covello; Director/Photography, Gorman Bechard; Screenplay, Gorman Bechard, Carmine Capobianco; Editor, Joe Keiser; Music, Lettuce Prey; Sound, Shaun Cashman; Set Design, Shaun Cashman, George Bernota; Assistant Director, Kris Covello; Associate Producers, Carmine Capobianco, Shaun Cashman; From Titan Productions and Generic Films; Foto-Kem color; Rated R; 82 minutes; January release. CAST: Carmine Capobianco (Eoj), Debi Thibeault (Hildy Johnson), Ruth Collins (Dr. Pepper), Angela Nicholas (Peggy Sue Peggy), Frank Stewart (Waldo), Michael Citriniti (Sonny Corleone), Tony Kruk (Carmine), David Coughlin (Tony), Donna Davidge, Will Rokos, Todd Grant Kimsey, Barry Finkel, Bill Gillogly, J. E. L. Gitter, Lee Anne Baker, Toni Whyte, Lisa Schmidt, Jenny Bassett

Jason Gedrick, Tracy Pollan in "Promised Land" ***(Vestron Pictures)***

David Packer, Charles Grodin in "You Can't Hurry Love" ***(Lightning Pictures)***

James Woods in "Cop"
(Atlantic Entertainment)

Whoopi Goldberg
in "The Telephone" ***(New World)***

SORORITY BABES IN THE SLIMEBALL BOWL-O-RAMA (Urban Classics) Producers, David DeCoteau, John Schouweiler; Director, David DeCoteau; Screenplay, Sergei Hasenecz; Photography, Stephen Ashley Blake; Editors, Barry Zetlin, Tom Meshelski; Music, Guy Moon; Special Makeup/Creature Effects, Craig Caton; Assistant Director, Will Clark; a Titan production; Foto-Kem color; Rated R; 78 minutes; January release. CAST: Linnea Quigley (Spider), Michelle Bauer (Lisa), Andras Jones (Calvin), Robin Rochelle (Babs), Brinke Stevens (Taffy), Kathi Obrecht (Rhonda), Carla Baron (Frankie), Hal Havins (Jimmie), John Stuart Wildman (Keith), George "Buck" Flower (Janitor)

OUTLAW FORCE (Trans World) Producers, David Heavener, Ronnie Hadar; Director/Screenplay, David Heavener; Executive Producers, Sid Caplan, Tom Jenssen; Photography, David Huey, James Mathers; Editor, Peter Miller; Music, Donald Hulette; Songs by David Heavener; Casting, Jacov Bresler; Sound, Hamond Kouh, John Lifavi; Assistant Director, Jonathan Tzachor; a TBJ Films presentation of an Outlaw Film production; Ultra-Stereo; Foto-Kem color; Rated R; 95 minutes; January release. CAST: David Heavener (Billy Ray Dalton), Paul Smith (Inspector Wainwright), Frank Stallone (Grady), Robert Bjorklund (Washington), Devin Dunsworth (Jesse), Stephanie Cicero (Holly Dalton), Warren Berlinger (Capt. Morgan), Cecilea Xavier (Billy's Wife), Mickey Morton, John Reistetter, Steve Keeley, Mark Richardson, Arvid Homberg, Jeff D. Patterson, Francesca Wilde

THE LAWLESS LAND (Concorde) Producers, Tony Cinciripini, Larry Leahy; Director, Jon Hess; Executive Producers, Roger Corman, Juan Forch; Screenplay, Tony Cinciripini, Larry Leahy; Production Manager, Mara Sanchez; Assistant Directors, Pedro Pablo Celedon, Jose Vergara; Production Associates, Roberto Sancho, Freddy Ramsey; Art Director, Roberto Di Girolamo; Costumes, Pia Dominguez; Sound, Felipe Zabala; Additional Editors, Stephen Mark, Jose Vergara, Carolina Sprohnle; Foto-Kem Color; 87 minutes; Rated R; January release. CAST: Nick Corri (Falco), Leon (Road Kill), Xander Bekeley (Ez Andy), Amanda Peterson (Diana), Walter Kliche (Chairman), Alejandro Heinrich (Billy Boy), Ann-Marie Peterson (Venus), Patricio Bunster (Don Enrique), Luis Mora Del Solar (Priest), Gloria Laso (Battered Woman), Roberto Poblete (Battered Man), Oscar Vigoroux (Pit Owner), Teresa Ramos (Gasoline Attendant), Marcos Madrid (Gamina Boy), Joshua Sweek (Child Falco), Patricia Rivadeneira (Snake Woman), Rafael Sanudo (Marty), Joe Sharp (R Neck), Javier Maldonado (Warden), Lucas Roth (Sick Boy), Sanc Larenas (Driver), Douglas Hubner (Butler), Sebastian Rojas, Christi Roessner (Escorts), Melania Rojas (Church Woman), Los Gnom (Musicians), Maria Pia Salas (Girlfriend), Raimundo Calvo (Mut Felipe Dominguez (Torturer), Roberto Avendano, Victor G (Bartenders), Cecilia Godoy (Dancer), Isabel Caravajal, Gisela D gunsky (Pit Girls)

Lesley Ann Warren, Charles Durning
in "Cop" ***(Atlantic Entertainment)***

BORN TO RACE (United Artists) Producers, Andrew Bullians, Je Bullians; Director, James Fargo; Screenplay, Dennis McGee, Ma Janeway Bullians; Story, Mary Janeway Bullians; Photography, B nard Salzmann; Editors, Tony Lombardo, Thomas Stanford; Mus Ross Vannelli; Associate Producer, Nicholas Longhurst; Producti Designer, Katherine G. Vallin; Assistant Director, Dennis White; Romax Production from MGM/UA; Ultra-Stereo; Color; Rated R; minutes; January release. CAST: Joseph Bottoms (Al Pagura), M Singer (Kenny Landruff), George Kennedy (Vincent Duplain), Ma Heasley (Andrea Lombardo), Antonio Sabato (Enrico Lombard Robert F. Logan (Theo Jennings), Dirk Blocker (Bud), Mich McGrady (Walt), LaGena Hart (Jenny)

COP, aka *Blood on the Moon* (Atlantic) Producers, James B. Harr James Woods; Executive Producers, Thomas Coleman, Mich Rosenblatt; Director/Screenplay, James B. Harris; Based on the No *"Blood on the Moon"* by James Ellroy; Photography, Steve Dub Editor, Anthony Spano; Music, Michel Colombier; Designer, Ge Rudolf; Costumes, Gale Parker Smith; Assistant Director, Rich Wells; Casting, Pamela Rack; Associate Producer/Production Ma ger, Ann Gindberg; Color; Rated R; 110 minutes; January relea CAST: James Woods (Lloyd Hopkins), Lesley Ann Warren (Kathle McCarthy), Charles Durning (Dutch Peltz), Charles Haid (Whi Haines), Raymond J. Barry (Fred Gaffney), Randi Brooks (Joa Pratt), Steve Lambert (Bobby Franco), Annie McEnroe (Amy Cra field), Vicki Wauchope (Penny Hopkins), Christopher Wynne (Ja Gibbs), Jan McGill (Jen Hopkins), Melinda Lynch (Sarah), Jo Petievich (Deputy), Dennis Stewart (Birdman), Randi Pelish (E ployee), Rick Marotta (Wilson), Michael V. Allen (Harry), Helen Pa Camp (Estelle), Scott Sandler (Detective), Matt Almond, Christop Blane (Punks), Banks Harper (Teddy Bailey), Jim Wilkey (Wat man), Jimmy Woodward (Robber's voice)

THE TELEPHONE (New World) Producers, Robert Katz, Mocte ma Esparza; Director, Rip Torn; Screenplay, Harry Nilsson, Te Southern; Editor, Sandra Adair; Photography, David Claessen; Vis Consultant, David Myers; Music Adapted by Christopher You Associate Producer, Joel Glickman; Art Director, Jim Pohl; Set De rator, Antonia Vincent; Assistant Directors, Lope Yap, Jr., Ka Ochoa; an Odyssey Entertainment, Ltd. presentation of an Espar Katx production in association with Hawkeye Entertainment, In Technicolor; Rated R; 82 minutes; January release. CAST: Who Goldberg (Vashti Blue), Severn Darden (Max), Amy Wright (Hor Boxe/Irate neighbor/Jennifer's voice), Elliott Gould (Rodney), Jo Heard (Telephone man), Ronald J. Stallings (Saxophone player), Jo Hattan, Lina Chu (Sidewalk vendors), Don Blakely, James Vict Robin Menken, Herve Villechaize (Voices on the freeway), Da Torn (Voice of crying woman/Midge's voice), Don Blakely (Larr voice), James Victor (Big Ray's voice)

THE NEST (Concorde) Producer, Julie Corman; Director, Tere Winkless; Screenplay, Robert King; Based on the novel by Eli Can Associate Producer, Lynn Whitney; Photography, Ricardo Jacq Gale; Editors, James A. Stewart, Stephen Mark; Music, Rick Conr

Luciano Pavarotti in "Distant Harmony" ***(Circle Films)***

Vince Mazzilli, Richard Habersham in "Lou, Pat & Joe D" ***(Marshall)***

:t Director, Carol Bosselman; Set Decorator, Craig Sulli; Sound, Chat ınter; Casting, Linda Shayne; Special Effects, Cary Howe; Color; ıted R; 88 minutes; January release. CAST: Robert Lansing (Elias hnson), Lisa Langlois (Elizabeth Johnson), Franc Luz (Richard Tar-ll), Terri Treas (Dr. Morgan Hubbard), Stephen Davies (Homer), ana Bellamy (Mrs. Pennington), Jack Collins (Shakey Jake), Nancy organ (Lillian), Jeff Winkless (Church), Steve Tannen (Mr. Perkins), eidi Helmer (Jenny), Karen Smyth (Diner)

ELL COMES TO FROGTOWN (New World) Producers/Story, onald G. Jackson, Randall Frakes; Directors, R. J. Kizer, Donald G. ckson; Screenplay, Randall Frakes; Line Producer, William W. lwards; Photography, Donald G. Jackson, Enrico Picard; Editors, R. Kizer, James Matheny; Music, David Shapiro; Sound, Robert niger; Production Designer, Dins Danielsen; Art Director/Set Deco-tor, Suzette Sheets; Special Makeup Effects, Steve Wang; Assistant irector, Gary M. Bettman; Stunt Coordinator, Bobby Bragg; Casting, ındy Stone Associates, Shana Landsburg; Technicolor; Rated R; 86 inutes; January release. CAST: Roddy Piper (Sam Hell), Sandahl ergman (Spangle), Cec Verrell (Centinella), William Smith (Capt. evlin/Count Sodom), Rory Calhoun (Looney Tunes), Nicholas Worth ull), Kristi Somers (Arabella)

CAVENGERS (Triax Entertainment Group) Producers, Chris ıvies, David Barrett; Director/Screenplay, Duncan McLachlan; Edi-r, Patti Regan; Photography, Johan Van Der Veer, Nic Heroldt; Art irector, Jay Avery; Music, Nick Picard; Sound, Dale Ray; Casting, ariah Cunningham; Costumes, Ele Parker; Associate Producer, Har-t Ephraim; J. T. Avanti color; Rated PG-13; 94 minutes; January ease. CAST: Kenneth Gilman (Tom Reed), Brenda Bakke (Kimber-Blake), Crispin De Nys (Col. Chenko), Cocky "Two Bull" hothalemaj (February)

NE MINUTE TO MIDNIGHT (Curtin International Pro-ıctions) Producer, Dara Murphy; Director/Photography, Robert ichael Ingria; Screenplay/Executive Producer, Lawrence Curtin; Edi-rs, Lawrence Curtin, Dana Murphy; Sound, Paul Speck; Assistant irector/Production Manager/Casting, Dana Murphy; Continental col-; Not rated; 103 minutes; January release. CAST: Lawrence Curtin avid Lawrence), Diane Coyne (Bo), Rob Fuller (Brock), Nelson ungart (Mike), Sydney Messett (First wife)

ISTANT HARMONY: Pavarotti in China (Circle Films) Produc-s, John Goberman, Dewitt Sage, Daniel Wigutow; Director, Dewitt ge; Executive Producer, R. Scott Asen; Photography, Miroslav ıdricek; Cameraman, Richard Gordon; Sound, Andrew Wiskes, ıniel Gleich; Supervising Editor, Victor Kanefsky; Editors, Oreet es, Coco Houwer, Sam Pollard; Production Manager, Eva Fyer; ocumentary; Dolby Stereo; Color; Not rated: 85 minutes; February ease. CAST: Luciano Pavarotti and others

OXSEY: QUACKS WHO CURE CANCER? (Realidad Pro-ıctions) Producer/Writer/Director, Ken Ausubel; Producer/ lditional Direction, Catherine Salveson, R.N., M.S.; Editor, Ernest Shinagawa; Music, Peter Rowan, Jeff Nelson; Music Producers, ird Banner, Jeff Nelson; Medical Advisor, Hugh Riordan, M.D.; sociate Producers, David Brownlow, Ray Hemenez, Diana Sottler, urel Hargarten, Andrea Nasher, Murray Van Dyke; Production sociates, Luke Gatto, Alan Marks, Joshua Mailman, Richard J. oss, John Ross; Photography, Alton Walpole, Ernest T. Shinagawa, urray Van Dyke; Sound, David Brownlow, Ernest T. Shinagawa; oduction Manager, Murray Van Dyke; Assistant Editors, Sarah Gart-r, Wendy Johnson; Documentary; Not rated; 100 minutes; February release. WITH: Max Gail (Narrator), Mildred Nelson, Harry Hoxsey, Dr. Morris Fishbein, Oliver Field, William Grigg, James Wakefield Burke, Jimmy "Trombone" Martin, Robert L. Heath, Dr. Harry M. Spence, Peter Barry Chowka, James Duke, PhD, Dr. Bernie Siegel, Paul Lee, PhD, Robert DeBragga and others

LOU, PAT & JOE D (Marshall Entertainment Group) Producer, Nicholas Furris; Director/Screenplay, Stephen Vittoria; Co-Producer, Michelle Materre; Photography, Tom Denove; Editor, Leland Thomas; Music, Daryll Dobson; Production Designer, J. C. Svec; Associate Producers, Michael Peluso, Todd Shane; Assistant Directors, Roderick Giles, Tyrone Henderson; Costumes, Anna Torres; a Vittoria/Furris production; In black and white; Not rated; 104 minutes. CAST: Nick Furris (Pat Corelli), Kim Delgado (Jacob Branch), Frank Vincent (Pop), Eddie R. White (General Craig), Jerry Marino (Ben), Ben Vittoria (Pat—older), Vince Mazzilli (Pat—younger), Richard Habersham (Jacob—younger), Glen Venezio (Ooloose), Michael Peluso (Peterhawk), Martha Crane (Marie), Mary Lou Clark (Stephie), Lynn Lorfine (Rosanne), Joe Dickenson (Sgt. Muldoun), Charles Mitchell (Pvt. Jerry Sullivan), Joe Bodek (Pvt. Buzz Healy), Chris Innvar (Pvt. Kent-Erik Sundtrom), Bill Kearney (Col. Jarcovic), Rose Kebabjian (Ma), Tino Elice (Joe Fats), Ed McAveney (Tony Bo), Chris Virginio (Abedosh), Janice Cauwels (Mrs. Olshinski), Michael Collins (Det. O'Reilly), Leo Diano (Det. Goldberg), Tony Roland (Bus boy), Vincent Gerrard (Referee)

GOING BANANAS (Cannon) Producers, Menahem Golan, Yoram Globus; Director, Boaz Davidson; Screenplay, Menahem Golan; Based on the "Kofiko" books by Tamar Borenstein; Executive Producers, Avi Lerner, David Dortort; Music, Pino Donaggio; Editors, Natan Zahavi, Bruria Davidson; Photography, Joseph Wain; Art Director, John Rosewarne; Casting, Robert McDonald; Executive in Charge of Production, Rony Yacov; Assistant Directors, Zvi Shisel, Sharon Shamir, Mark West; TVC Color; Ultra-stereo; Rated PG; 93 minutes; February release. CAST: Dom DeLuise (Big Bad Joe), Jimmie Walker (Mozambo), David Mendenhall (Ben), Deep Roy (Bonzo), Warren Berlinger (Palermo), Herbert Lom (Mackintosh), Len Sparrowhawk (Ship's captain), Peter Elliott (First mate), Fats Dibeco (Sergeant Abdul), Graham Armitage (Cake waiter), Mike Westcott (American ambassador), Phillip Van Der Byl, Peter Elliott, Bobby Porter (Clowns), Irene Frangs (Nurse), Simpson Correra (Dentist), Gertrude Chifamba, Andrew Whaley, Zvi Shisel, Fidelis Cheza, Koos Strauss

David Mendenhall, Jimmie Walker, Dom DeLuise in "Going Bananas" ***(Cannon)***

Donovan Leitch, Joe Pantoliano, Jennifer Runyon in "The In Crowd" *(Orion Pictures)*

Ann-Margret, C. Thomas Howell in "A Tiger's Tale" *(Atlantic)*

THE IN CROWD (Orion) Producers, Keith Rubinstein, Lawrence Konner; Executive Producers, John F. Roach, Jeff Franklin; Director, Mark Rosenthal; Screenplay, Mark Rosenthal, Lawrence Konner; Co-Producers, Karen Essex, Jeffrey Hornaday; Photography, Anthony Richmond; Production Designer, Joseph T. Garrity; Editor, Jeffrey Wolf; Original Score, Mark Snow; Choreographer, Jerry Evans; Costumes, Peter Mitchell; Casting, Lynn Stalmaster & Associates, David Rubin; Associate Producers, Ken Golden, Patricia A. Whitcher; Assistant Directors, Fred Baron, Cathy Gesualdo; Art Director, Patrick E. Tagliaferro; Songs by various artists; a Force Ten production; DeLuxe Color; Dolby Stereo; Rated PG; 96 minutes; February release. CAST: Donovan Leitch (Del Green), Joe Pantoliano (Perry Parker), Jennifer Runyon (Vicky), Wendy Gazelle (Gail Goren), Sean Gregory Sullivan (Popeye), Charlotte D'Amboise (Ina), Bruce Kirby (Norris), Freddie Ganno (Orson), Page Hannah (Lydia), Richard Schave (Tucker), Matthew Nasatir (Bernstein), John Russell (Ming), Elliott Alexander (Jack Goren), Katherine Conklin (Norma Goren), Wayne Armstrong (Connie Green), Diane Cribbs (Ros Green), Nicholas Van Strander (Shelly Green), Concrete Cowboy (Tiny), Kelly Grant (Dorothy), Mark Soper (Station manager), Andrew Bloch (Director #2), Casey Nye (Julie), John Allen (Studio technician), Tommy Carrano, Gavin Danker, Lionel Douglass, Randi Pareira, Jeff Levy, Peter Pryor, Loren Kaufman, Don Auspitz, William T. Darling

ACTION JACKSON (Lorimar) Producer, Joel Silver; Director, Craig R. Baxley; Screenplay, Robert Reneau; Associate Producer/Production Manager, Steve Perry; Photography, Matthew F. Leonetti; Art Director, Virginia Randolph; Editor, Mark Helfrich; Costumes, Marilyn Vance-Straker; Casting, Karen Rea; Music, Herbie Hancock with Michael Kamen; Assistant Directors, Benjamin Rosenberg, Terry Miller, Jr.; Production Executive, Riley Katherine Ellis; Set Decorator, Phil M. Leonard; Sound, Jim Webb; Choreographer, Paula Abdul; Assistant Choreographer, Aurorah Allain; Stunts, Jophery Brown; Special Effects, Al Di Sarro, Jim Camomile; Music Supervisor, Jackie Krost; Assistant Editor, Theresa M. Friedrich; Associate Editor, Frank E. Jimenez; songs *"Action Jackson"* Song by Bernadette Cooper/Performed by Madame X, and Songs by various other artists; Soundtrack on Lorimar Records; Dolby Stereo; Metrocolor; Rated R; 95 minutes; February release. CAST: Carl Weathers ("Action" Jackson), Craig T. Nelson (Peter Dellaplane), Vanity (Sydney Ash), Sharon Stone (Patrice Dellaplane), Thomas F. Wilson (Officer Kornblau), Bill Duke (Capt. Armbruster), Robert Davi (Tony Moretti), Jack Thibe (Det. Kotterwell), Roger Aaron Brown (Officer Jack), Stan Fos (Albert), Mary Ellen Trainor (Secretary), Ed O'Ross (Stringer), B Minor (Gamble), David Glen Eisley (Thaw), Dennis Hayden (Shake Brian Libby (Marlin), David Efron (Birch), Armelia McQueen (De Sonny Landham (Mr. Quick), Alonzo Brown, Diana James, M Landers, Thomas Wagner, Deidre Conrad, Bill Burton, Sr., Pres Hanson, Ivor Barry

A TIGER'S TALE (Atlantic) Producer/Director, Peter Dougl Screenplay, Peter Douglas; Based on the Book *"Love and Other N ural Disasters"* by Allen Hannay II; Photography, Tony Pier Roberts; Music, Lee Holdridge; Designer, Shay Austin; Costum Elizabeth Palmer; Casting, Patricia Mock; Associate Produc Production Manager, Don Goldman; Assistant Directors, Alan Curtiss, B. Thomas Seidman; Sound, John Glascock; Production Co dinator, Susan Becton; Choreographer, Glen Hunsucker; Music Co dinator, Frank Capp; Stunts, Greg Gault, Monty Cox; Color; Rated 97 minutes; February release. CAST: Ann-Margret (Rose Butts), Thomas Howell (Bubber Drumm), Charles Durning (Charlie Drumr Kelly Preston (Shirley Butts), Ann Wedgeworth (Claudine), Willi Zabka (Randy), Tim Thomerson (Lonny), Steven Kampmann (Shorts), Traci Lin (Penny), Angel Tompkins (La Vonne), James No (Sinclair), Linda Rae Favila (Kiki Walker), Steve Farrell (Dr. Fran David Denny (Tyronne), Jo Perkins (Lucy), Scott Fults, Sean Flane Jimmy Pickens (Buddies), Mike Marich (Bob), Nik Hagler (D Dozel), Diane Perella (Samantha), Barbara Collins (Nurse), Charlc Stanton (Counselor), Shannon Collins (Clinic Girl), James Cole (R nie), Leigh Lombardi (Marcia), Paul Menzel (Husband), Sharon M zel (Wife), Amanda Goyen (Girl with dog), Ed Geldart (Gamekeepe Michael Bartula, Sumter Bruton, Jim Colegrove, Jim Milan, Johr Reno, Craig Simecheck (The Juke Jumpers), Valentino (Himself)

SATISFACTION (20th Century Fox) Producers, Aaron Spelli Alan Greisman; Director, Joan Freeman; Screenplay, Charles Purpu Executive Producers, Rob Alden, Armyan Bernstein; Photograp Thomas Del Ruth; Designer, Lynda Paradise; Editor, Joel Goodm Music, Michel Colombier; Music Producer, Steve Cropper; Mu Supervision, Peter Afterman; Casting, Johanna Ray; Associate P ducer, Ilene Chaiken; Executive Production Manager, Norman Her Production Executive, Joseph Dervin, Jr.; Production Managers,

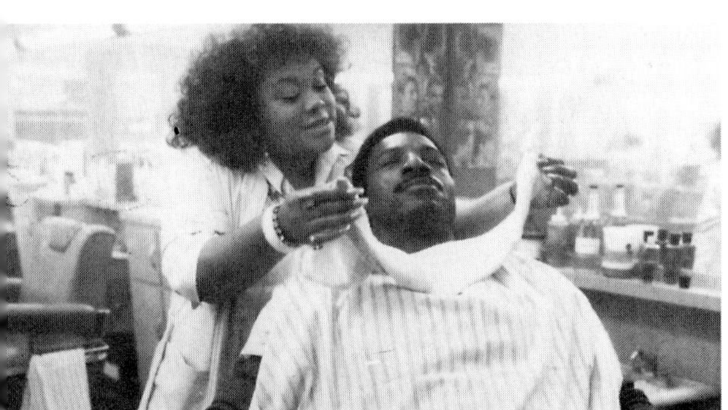

Armelia McQueen, Carl Weathers in "Action Jackson" *(Lorimar)*

Trini Alvarado, Britta Phillips, Justine Bateman, Scott Coffey, Julia Roberts in "Satisfaction" *(20th Century Fox)*

Yuji Okumoto, Warren Fabro, Blaine Kia, Scott Nakagawa, Don Michael Paul, Chris Makepeace in "Aloha Summer" ***(Spectrafilm)***

River Phoenix, Matthew Perry in "A Night in the Life of Jimmy Reardon" ***(20th Century Fox)***

aus, James Westman; Assistant Directors, Jerry Ketcham, Bruce hen; Set Decorator, Ernie Bishop; Costumes, Eugenie Bafaloukos; stume Supervisor, Dana Lyman; Sound, Willy Burton; Presented by 3C Productions; Songs by various artists; Soundtrack on AJK Music; rastereo; DeLuxe Color; Rated PG-13; 96 minutes; February re-se. CAST: Justine Bateman (Jennie Lee), Liam Neeson (Martin lcon), Trini Alvarado (May "Mooch" Stark), Scott Coffey (Nickie ngo), Britta Phillips (Billy Swan), Julia Roberts (Daryle Shane), bbie Harry (Tina), Chris Nash (Frankie Malloy), Michael De-renzo (Bunny Slotz), Tom O'Brien (Hubba Lee), Kevin Haley sh), Peter Craig (Mig Lee), Steve Cropper (Sal), Alan Greisman ob Elden), Sheryl Ann Martin (Sylvia), Lia Romaine (Lexie), Wyatt ngle, Greg Roszyk, "The Killer Whales"

.OHA SUMMER (Spectrafilm) Producer/Story, Mike Greco; Di-tor, Tommy Lee Wallace; Screenplay, Mike Greco, Bob Benedetto; ecutive Producer, Warren Chaney; Photography, Steven Poster; isic, Jesse Frederick, Bennett Salvay; Editors, James Coblentz, Jack fstra, Jay Cassidy; Art Director, Donald Harris; Casting, Caro Jones; oduction Manager, Jack Grossburg; Assistant Directors, Brian inkish, Harry Hogan, Harry Bring, Gary Law; Stunt Coordinators, eve Lambert, John Meier; Songs by various artists; a Hanauma Bay oduction; CFI color; Rated PG; 97 minutes; February release. CAST: ris Makepeace (Mike Tognetti), Yuji Okumoto (Kenzo Konishi), n Michael Paul (Chuck Granville), Tia Carrere (Lani Kepoo), Sho sugi (Yukinaga Konishi), Lorie Griffin (Amanda), Blaine Kia (Jerry hani), Warren Fabro (Kilarney Kahani), Andy Bumatai (Kimo), ott Nakagawa (Scott), Ric Mancini (Angelo Tognetti), Caron Abel-a (Linda), Marina Ferrier (Pat Tognetti), Robert Ito (Ted Tanaka), ri Ann Lynn (Mary Jean), Jerry Harper (Burton Granville), Jillian kamoto (Jean Tanaka), Fay Myers (Livy Granville), Tina Machado dy), Lisa Miller (Cindy), Del Courtney (Del), Jennifer Davis (Gail), nelle Kono (Ioi), Joyce Harumi Nakama (Mrs. Konishi), Vic Leon nger), Tina Littlewood (Monica), Henry Ahnee, Warren Chaney, aurice Char, Mary Ann Chow, Caryl Cochran, Chris Duque, Caro nes, Danny Kamekona, Arnold Kidder, Frank Lucketti, Denise cCloskey, Norman Tang

NIGHT IN THE LIFE OF JIMMY REARDON (20th Century x) Producer, Russell Schwartz; Director/Screenplay, William chert; Based upon the novel *"Aren't You Even Gonna Kiss Me Goodbye"* by William Richert; Executive Producers, Mel Klein, Noel Marshall; Co-producer, Richard H. Prince; Photography, John J. Connor; Designer, Norman Newberry; Editor, Suzanne Fenn; Costumes, Bob De Mora; Music, Bill Conti; Associate Producer, Lauren Graybow; Casting, Elisabeth Leustig; Production manager, Robert Kresmer; Assistant Directors, Craig Huston, Bruce A. Humphrey, Kevin Barry Howe; Associate Producer, Susan Kaufer; Art Director, John R. Jensen; Assistant Art Director, William Arnold; Production Coordinator, Terri Clemens; Assistant Editor, Clement Barclay; Production Associate, Nancy E. Kelley; Sound, Scott Smith; Set Decorator, Hilton Rosemarin; Assistant Set Decorator, Blair Conaghan; Assistant Costume Designer, John Glaser; Choreographer, Bobby Wells; Special Effects, Curtiss Smith; Stunts, Rick Lefevour; Presented by Island Pictures; DeLuxe Color; Dolby Stereo; DeLuxe Color; Rated R; 93 minutes; February release. CAST: River Phoenix (Jimmy Reardon), Ann Magnuson (Joyce Fickett), Meredith Salenger (Lisa Bentwright), Ione Skye (Denise Hunter), Louanne (Suzie Middleberg), Mathew L. Perry (Fred Roberts), Paul Koslo (Al Reardon), Jane Hallaren (Faye Reardon), Jason Court (Mathew Hollander), James Deuter (Mr. Spaulding), Marji Banks (Emma Spaulding), Margaret Moore (Mrs. Bentwright), Anastasia Fielding (Elaine), Kamie Harper (Rosie Reardon), Johnny Galecki (Toby Reardon), Melva Williams (Maid), Regan Andreas (Sailor Cap), E. J. Murray (Alice), Mark Winsten (Red Blazer), Jack McLaughlin-Gray (Carnation), Craig Wright Huston (Waiter), Kristin Weithas, Lisa Stodder, Kurt Bjorling, Alan Goldsher

PICASSO TRIGGER (Malibu Bay Films) Producer, Arlene Sidaris; Director/Screenplay, Andy Sidaris; Executive Producer, Michael Donohew; Photography, Howard Wexler; Editor, Michael Haight; Music, Gary Stockdale; Production Designer, Peter Munneke; Costumes, Fionn; Assistant Directors, M. M. Freedman, Christian Drew Sidaris; Casting, Tom Stockfisch; Sound, Neil Wolfson; United color; Rated R; 99 minutes; February release. CAST: Steve Bond (Travis Abilene), Dona Speir (Donna), Hope Marie Carlton (Taryn), Harold Diamond (Jade), John Aprea (Picasso Trigger), Roberta Vasquez (Agent Pantera), Guich Koock (L. G. Abilene), Bruce Penhall (Hondo), Rodrigo Obregon, Cynthia Brimhall, Dennis Alexio, John Brown, Kym Malin, Patty Dufek, Liv Lindeland, Wolf Larson, Rustam Branaman, Richard LePore

River Phoenix, Paul Koslo in "Jimmy Reardon" ***(20th Century Fox)***

Steve Bond in "Picasso Trigger" ***(Malibu Bay Films)***

Robert Locke, Terra Vandergaw in " '68" *(New World Pictures)*

Tamara Hyler, Ty Miller, Hope Marie Carlton in "Slaughterhouse Rock" *(Taurus)*

'68 (New World) Producers, Dale Djerassi, Isabel Maxwell, Steven Kovacs; Director/Screenplay, Steven Kovacs; Associate Producer, Eli Zaffaroni; Music, John Cipollina, Shony Alex Braun; Editor, Cari Coughlin; Photography, Daniel Lacombre; Stunt Coordinator, Rocky Capella; Production Manager, Kathy Witte; Assistant Directors, Karen McCabe, B. C. Cameron, Kerry Peterson; Art Director, Joshua Koral; Set Decorator, Kris Boxell; Casting, Shanda Sawyer; Sound, Anne Evans; Songs by various artists; Color; Rated R; 99 minutes; February release. CAST: Eric Larson (Peter Szabo), Robert Locke (Sandy Szabo), Sandor Tecsi (Zoltan Szabo), Anna Dukasz (Zsuzsa Szabo), Miran Kwun (Alana Chan), Terra Vandergaw (Vera Kardos), Neil Young (Westy), Shony Alex Braun (Tibor Kardos), Donna Pecora (Piroska Kardos), Elizabeth De Charay (Gizi Horvath), Jan Nemec (Dezso Horvath), Rusdi Lane (Bela Csontos), Nike Doukas (Beatrice), Sandy Bull (Gang leader), Anya Lem (Isadora), Maureen McVerry (Rusty), John Cipollina (Rock band leader), Richard Butterfield (Editor), Lee Carrau (Professor), Roger Hart (Percy Millard), Jim Russell, John Kovacs, Taylor Phelps, Cary Jay Silberman, Max Proudfoot, Paul Pedroli, Michael Sullivan, Ngaio Bealum, Darrell Williams, Tom Owens, Joel Parker, Frank X. Mur, Robert Boeckman, Genevieve Kovacs

MERCENARY FIGHTERS (Cannon) Producers, Menahem Golan, Yoram Globus; Director, Riki Shelach; Screenplay, Bud Schaetzle, Dean Tschetter, Andrew Deutsch; Story, Bud Schaetzle, Dean Tschetter; Executive Producer, Avi Lerner; Photography, Daniel Schneor; Editors, Michael Goodhill, Dean Goodhill; Production Manager, Michael Games; Assistant Directors, Raymond Bark, Mark West, Terry Asbury; Music, Harold Morgan; Casting, Pat Orseth; Additional Dialogue, Terry Asbury; Aerial Photography, Dave Dunn-Yarker; Sound, John Bergman; Production Designer, Leonard Coen Cagli; Art Director, Yahuda Ako; Stunt Coordinator, B. J. Davis; Costumes, Robyn Smith; Second Unit Director, D. Bruce McFarlane; Irene color; Rated R; 91 minutes; February release. CAST: Peter Fonda (Virelli), Reb Brown (T. J. Christian), Ron O'Neal (Cliff), James Mitchum (Wilson Jeffords), Robert Doqui (Kyemba), Jerry Biggs (Mac Jeffords), Joanna Weinberg (Ruth), Henry Cele (Jaunde), Laurens Cilliers (Sanchez), Graham Clarke (Wichinski), Robert Whitehead (Pardoux), Jonathan Rands (Deke Johannsen), Vusi Dibakwane (Kyemba's 21C), Allen Booi (Sgt. Obote), Sydney Chama (Sgt. Tala), Leslie Mongezi (President Lumbala), Winston Gama (Sgt. Thabu), Godfrey Moloi, Fanyana Sidumo (Kyemba's aides), Sorrel Touyz, Brumilda Van Rens burg, Wanda Majozi, Glory Legodi, Sonto Mazibuko, Thandi Vilika (Prostitutes), Joe Mafela, Ian Steadman, Martin Le Maitre, Mit Booysen, Janine Denison, Pexley Shabangu, Phillip Wolfhardt, Ben ley Mkononde, Martin Majola, Morake Bukolane, Polite Dhlamini

Robert Doqui, Rob Brown, Peter Fonda in "Mercenary Fighters" *(Cannon)*

SLAUGHTERHOUSE ROCK (Tarus Entertainment Company Producer, Louis George; Director/Story, Dimitri Logothetis; Executiv Producers, Nick Celozzi, Sr., Joseph Medawar; Associate Producer Orlando Vestuto, Maurice Ettleson, Daniel Somrack; Line Produce Charles P. Bernuth; Screenplay, Ted Landon; Written by Sandra Wi lard, Nora Goodman; Music, Mark Mothersbaugh, Gerald V. Casal Music Performance, Devo; Designer, Peter Paul Raubetas; Visu Effects, Ernest D. Farino; Editor, Daniel Gross; Photography, Nichol Von Sternberg; Assistant Directors, Richard Hench, Gerry Peter Production Coordinator, Jennifer West; Stunts, J. Hawk, John Stewa Set Decorator, Miranda Amador; Special Effects, Kevin McCarth Special Effects makeup, Wof-N-Bar Productions; Color; Rated R; 9 minutes; February release. CAST: Toni Basil (Sammy Mitchell Nicholas Celozzi (Alex Gardner), Tom Reilly (Richard Gardner), Do na Denton (Carolyn Harding), Hope Marie Carlton (Krista Halpern Tamara Hyler (Jan Squires), Steven Brian Smith (Jack), Ty Mill (Marty), Al Fleming (Commandant), Michael J. Scherlis (Tour Guide Danny Somback (Dead Guard), Lenka Novak, Julie Rhodes (Com mandant's Ladis), Richard Hench (Biff), Nathan Holland (Scooter Charles P. Bernuth (Skip), Denise Ferell, Jeff Speakman, Gera Dinardi, Lorraine Watson, Muna Deriane, Mindy Miller, Ma Daniels, Ron E. Dickenson, Ted Landon

THE DRIFTER (Concorde) Executive Producer, Roger Corma Co-Producer, Matt Leipzig; Producer, Ken Stein; Director/Screenpla Larry Brand; Production Manager, Susan Stremple; Assistant Dire tors, David Cobb, Randy Pope, Michael Becker; Production Coordin tor, Lisa Sloan; Casting, Al Guarino, Kerry Barden; Set Decorato Cara Haycak; Sound, David Kelson; Costumes, Daryl Binder; Add tional Editing, James Coblentz; Stunts, Patrick Statham; Color; Rate R; 90 minutes; February release. CAST: Kim Delany (Julia), Timoth Bottoms (Arthur), Al Shannon (Kriger), Miles O'Keefe (Trey), Ann Gray Garduno (Matty), Loren Haines (Willie Munroe), Larry Bran (Morrison), Thomas Wagner (Capt. Edwards), Ernest Alexander (E gene), Joanne Willette (Carrie), Gil Christner (Gas Attendant), A Guarino (Joe Santini), George Derby (Jawbone), Bob McVicke (Bodacious), Rebecca Reynolds (Biker Chick), Charles Zuckl (Jerome), Patrick McCord (Mr. Skank), Ken Stein (Shopper), Myva wy Jenn (Bathroom Woman), Bruce Vilanch (Cook), Kerry Barde (Hitchhiker)

STAR SLAMMER, formerly *Prison Ship* (Vidmark) Producers, Jac H. Harris, Fred Olen Ray; Director, Fred Olen Ray; Screenpla Michael D. Sonye; Photography, Paul Elliott; Editor, Miriam L. Prei sel; Music, Anthony Harris; Sound, Robert Janiger; Designer Michael Novotny, Wayne Springfield; Assistant Director, Tony Brew ster; Special Effects, Brett Mixon; Stunts, John Stewart; A Vikin Films International Production; Ultra-Stereo; Fujicolor; Rated R; 8 minutes; February release. CAST: Ross Hagen (Banter), Sandy Brook (Taura), Susan Stokey (Mike), John Carradine (The Justice), Aldo Ra (Torturer), Dawn Wildsmith (Muffin), Marya Gant (Warden Exene Michael D. Sonye (Krago), Richard Hench, Lindy Skyles, Johnn Legend, Bobbie Bresee, Jade Barrett

BLOODSPORT (Cannon International) Producer, Mark DiSall Director, Newt Arnold; Screenplay, Cheldon Lettich, Christoph

Bolo Yeung, Jean Claude Van Damme in "Bloodsport" ***(Cannon)***

Rebecca Ferratti in "Gor" ***(Cannon)***

osby, Mel Freidman; Story, Sheldon Lettich; Photography, David orth; Editor, Carl Kress; Designer, David Searl; Music, Paul Hertg; Production Manager, Barty Bluestein; Assistant Directors, O. J. n, Ken Siu; Production Executive, Ronny Yacov; Production Contant, Charles Wang; Casting, Michael Olton; Sound, George Weis; ssistant Art Director, Jonathan Cheung; Costumes, Wei Sau Ling; ints, Steve Lee Ka Ding; Fights, Frank Dux; Special Effects, John ian, Leung Kit; Production Supervisors, Michael Alden, Alain Jakuwicz; Production Coordinator, Omneya "Nini" Mazen; Assistant litor, Jeffrey Kress, Charles Woo, Tommy Cheung; Music Supersor, Paula Erickson; Music Coordinator, Stephanie Lee; *"Fight to rvive", "On My Own—Alone"* by Shandi & Paul Hertzog/*"Steal the ght"* by Michael Bishop; Music Performances, Stan Bush, Michael shop; RVC Color; Rated R; 97 minutes; February release. CAST: an Claude Van Damme (Frank), Donald Gibb (Jackson), Leah Ayres inice), Norman Burton (Helmer), Forest Whitaker (Rawlins), Roy iiao (Tanaka), Philip Chan (Capt. Chen), Pierre Rafini (Young ank), Bolo Yeung (Chong Li), Kenneth Siu (Victor), Kimo Lai Kwok (Hiro), Bernard Mariano (Hossein), Bill Yuen Ping Kuen (Oshima), ly Leung (Mrs. Tanaka), Joshua Schroeder (Chuck), Keith Davey ddie), Sean Ward (Shingo), Johnny Lai (Desk Clerk), Henry Ho, enry Kot, Thomas Lam, Simon Lai (Officials), A. P. George (Referee/Judge), Charles Wang (Chinese Doctor), John Foster (Gustafson), hn Cheung (Toon), Dennis Chiu (Chuan), Michelle Quissi (Parades), ithan Chkueke (Parades' Opponent), Geoff Brown (Parades' Friend), avid Ho (Pumola), Eric Neff (Morra), Michael Chan (Yasuda), Rick ikson (Cotard), John Law (Luu), Samson Li (Prang), Paulo Tocha aco), Greg Richardson (Aussie)

OR (Cannon International) Producers, Harry Alan Towers, Avi rner; Director, Fritz Kiersch; Screenplay, Rick Marx, Peter elbeck; Based on the novel *"Tarnsman of Gor"* by John Norman; otography, Hans Khule; Editors, Max Lemon, Ken Bornstein; Degner, Hans Nol; Production Supervisor, John Stodel; Assistant Dictors, Cedrid Sundstrom, Marc Roper; Production Executive, Ronny acov; Casting, Don Pemrick; Choreographer, Neil McKay; Stunts, o Ruiters; Sound, Peter Poole; Production Coordinator, Charmaine olhuter; Visual Effects, Rick Kerrigan; Special Effects, Noel Henry, anny Ferreira; Assistant Editors, Sherril Schlesinger, Allyson oucher, Patty Farah; Additional Editor, Ken Bornstein; Color; Rated G; 94 minutes; February release. CAST: Urbano Barberini (Cabot), ebecca Ferratti (Talena), Jack Palance (Xenos), Paul L. Smith (Surs), Oliver Reed (Sarm), Larry Taylor (Marlenus), Graham Clarke rusus), Janine Denison (Brandy), Donna Denton (Lara), Jennifer tmann (Tara), Martina Brockschmidt (Dorna), Ann Power (Bever-), Arnold Vosloo (Norman), Chris Du Plessis (Sarsam), Ivan Kruger arm's Rider), Joe Ribeiro (Auctioneer), Visser Du Plessis (Guard), ilip Van Der Byl (Whipman), George Magnussen, Fred Potgieter

LIEN FROM L.A. (Cannon) Producers, Menahem Golan, Yoram obus; Director, Albert Pyun; Screenplay, Debra Ricci, Regina avis, Albert Pyun; Line Producer, Tom Karnowski; Production Degner, Pamela Warner; Photography, Tom Fraser; Editor, Daniel ewenthal; Music, Drock; Executive Producer, Avi Lerner; Producn Manager, Michael Games; Assistant Directors, Scott Cameron, lly Ann Caro, Clive Pollick; Costumes, Birgitta Bjerke; Casting, cola van der Walt, Julie Pyken, Nancy Lara, Lindy Blythe; Art rectors, Francis Darvall, Drew Ogier; TVC Color; Ultra-Stereo; ited PG; 87 minutes. CAST: Kathy Ireland (Wanda Saknussemm), illiam R. Moses (Guten "Gus" Edway), Richard Haines (Professor knussemm), Don Michael Paul (Robbie), Thom Mathews (Charn'), Janie du Plessis (General Rykov/Shank/Claims officer), Simon Poland (Consul Triton Crassus/Mailman), Linda Kerridge (Roryis Freki/Auntie Pearl), Kristen Trucksess (Stacy), Lochner de Kock (Prof. Ovid Galba. Paddy Mahoney), Deep Roy (Mambino), Albert Maritz (Mago/Maintenance worker/Evangelist/Pack Slag Jack), Russell Savadier (Loki), Denis Smith (Anchorman), James Lithgow (Donaldson/Wrestling announcer/Emcee), Christian Andrews (Brick Bardo), Drummond Marais (Belli the bookie/Belguy the busybody/Maintenance chief), Fats Bookholane (Lord Over/Diner cook/Bartender), Paul Jacobs, Jeff Weston, Tony Epper, Greg Latter, Linda Marshall, Pixley Shabangu, Solly Ndlovu, Sydney Radebe, Sonto Ndlovu, Don Frost, Jacques McDuffy, Johanna Corrander, Gillian Hull

CHERRY 2000 (Orion) Producers, Edward R. Pressman, Caldecot Chubb; Director, Steve de Jarnatt; Screenplay, Michael Almereyda; Story/Executive Producer, Lloyd Fonvielle; Photography, Jacques Haitkin; Production Designer, John J. Moore; Costumes, Julie Wass; Editors, Edward Abroms, Duwayne Dunham; Casting, Jane Jenkins; Music, Basil Poledouris; Co-Producer/Production Manager, Elliot Schick; Assistant Director, Jerry G. Grandley; an ERP Production; Deluxe color; Rated PG-13; 93 minutes; February release. CAST: Melanie Griffith (E. Johnson), David Andrews (Sam Treadwell), Ben Johnson (Six Finger Jake), Tim Thomerson (Lester), Brion James (Stacy), Pamela Gidley (Cherry), Harry Carey Jr. (Snappy Tom), Cameron Milzer (Ginger), Michael C. Gwynne (Slim), Jennifer Mayo (Randa), Marshall Bell (Bill), Jeff Levine (Marty), Howard Swaim (Skeet)

PULSE (Columbia) Producer, Patricia Stallone; Director/Screenplay, Paul Golding; Executive Producer, William E. McEuen; Music, Jay Ferguson; Photography, Peter Lyons Collister; Editor, Gib Jaffe; Production Designer, Holger Gross; Associate Producer, Robert C. Edwards; Casting, Meg Liberman, Irene Cagen; Production Manager, Charlie Skouras; Assistant Directors, Mike Topoozian, Joe Camp III, Ken Brewer; Art Director, Maxine Shepard; Costumes, Jacqueline Saint Anne; Stunt Coordinator, Mike Cassidy; "Sidewalk/Street Talk" performed by The Boomers; an Aspen Film Society production; DeLuxe color; Dolby Stereo; Rated PG-13; 95 minutes; March release. CAST: Cliff De Young (Bill), Roxanne Hart (Ellen), Joey Lawrence (David), Matthew Lawrence (Stevie), Charles Tyner (Old Man), Dennis Redfield (Pete), Robert Romanus (Paul), Myron D. Healey (Howard), Michael Rider (Foreman), Jean Sincere (Ruby), Terry Beaver, Greg Norberg, Tim Russ

William Moses, Kathy Ireland in "Alien From L.A." ***(Cannon)***

Joan Cusack, Daniel Day-Lewis in "Stars and Bars" ***(Columbia)***

STARS AND BARS (Columbia) Producer, Sandy Lieberson; Director, Pat O'Connor; Screenplay, William Boyd, from his Novel; Co-Producer, Susan Richards; Photography, Jerzy Zielinski; Designers, Leslie Dilley, Stuart Craig; Costumes, Ann Roth; Associate Producer/Production Manager, Jack Cummins; Executive Producer, Sheldon Schrager; Editor, Michael Bradsell; Music, Stanley Myers; Casting, Risa Bramon, Billy Hopkins; Assistant Directors, Ned Dowd, Cheryl-anne Martin; Production Supervisor, Bonnie Arnold; Production Coordinator, Theresa Yarbrough; Sound, John Pritchett; Art Director, Becky Block; Set Decorator, Anne Kuljian; Stunts, Lonnie Smith; Songs by various artists; DuArt Color; Rated R; 98 minutes; March release. CAST: Daniel Day Lewis (Henderson), Harry Dean Stanton (Loomis Gage), Kent Broadhurst (Sereno), Maury Chaykin (Freeborn), Matthew Cowles (Beckman), Joan Cusack (Irene), Keith David (Teagarden), Spalding Gray (Rev. Cardew), Glenne Headly (Cora), Laurie Metcalf (Melissa), Bill Moor (Beeby), Deirdre O'Connell (Shanda), Will Patton (Duane), Martha Plimpton (Bryant), Rockets Redglare (Gint), Celia Weston (Monika), Beatrice Winde (Alma-May), Steven Wright (Pruitt), David Strathairn (Charlie), Bruce C. Taylor (General), Raynor Scheine (Drunk), Bob Bost (Auctioneer), Lit Conah, J. J. Johnston, Peter Cherevas, Tim Ware, Jeff Lewis, Matt Hoffman

EVIL LAUGH (Cinevest) Producers/Screenplay, Steven Baio, Dominick Brascia; Director, Dominick Brascia; Executive Producers, Arthur Schweitzer, Krisha Shah; Photography, Stephen Sealy; Editors, Brian McIntosh, Michael Scott; Music, David Shapiro; Casting, Johnny Venocur; Art Director, Jeffrey Diamond; Special Makeup Effects, David Cohen; a Wildfire Production; Color; Rated R; 87 minutes; March release. CAST: Steven Baio (Johnny), Kim McKamy (Connie), Tony Griffin (Sammy), Jody Gibson (Tina), Johnny Venocur (Freddy), Jerold Pearson (Barney), Myles O'Brien, Susan Grant, Howard Weiss, Karyn O'Bryan, Gary Hays

THE INVISIBLE KID (Taurus Entertainment) Producer, Philip J. Spinelli; Director/Screenplay, Avery Crounse; Executive Producers, Avery Crounse, Philip J. Spinelli; Co-Producers, Nancy Nickerson, Thomas Rolapp; Photography, Michael Barnard; Editor, Gabrielle Gilbert; Music, Steve Hunter, Jan King; Art Director, Charles Tomlinson; Mechanical Effects, Tassilo Baur; Costumes, Bernadette O'Brien; Casting, Reuben Cannon, Carol Dudley; Production Manager, Nancy Nickerson; Assistant Directors, Thomas Rolapp, Eric Dawson; Production Coordinator, Hamp Simmons; Sound, Jan Brodin, Jerry Wolfe; Set Decorator, Clarie Bowin; Special Effects, Lou Carlucci, Charlie Belardinelli; Visual Effects, Ernie Farino; Stunts, Joh Stewart; Color; Rated PG; 96 minutes; March release. CAST: Ja Underwood (Grover Dunn), Wally Ward (Milton McClane), Chynr Phillips (Cindy Moore), Mike Geneovese (Officer Chuck Malone Nicolas De Toth (Donny Zanders), Thomas Cross (Officer Terrell John Madden Towey (Principal Baxter), John Miranda (Carl the Janitor), Brother Theodore (Dr. Theodore), Karen Black (Mom), Evere Lamar (Avery), David Katims (Mr. Christeau), Michael Goyak (Max Jan King, Karina Utter, Che Zuro, Lauren Grace Bell (Puss 'n' Boots Lou Felder (Mr. Moore), Florence Peters (Mrs. Moore), Ellen Crawford (Teacher), Randy Baughman (Bears Coach), Corie Henning (Gung Ho Cheerleader), Shawna Thomas (Debby the Cheerleader John O'Brien (O'Brien)

Jay Underwood, Wally Ward in "The Invisible Kid" ***(Taurus)***

"Pound Puppies: The Legend of Big Paw" ***(Tri-Star)***

POUND PUPPIES AND THE LEGEND OF BIG PAW (Tri-Star Producers, Donald Kushner, Peter Locke; Director, Pierre DeCelle Screenplay, Jim Carlson, Terrence McDonnell; Executive Producers Edd Griles, Ray Volpe; Editor, John Blizek; Music, Steve Tyrel Richard Kosinski, Sam Winans, Bill Reichenbach; Original Songs b Steve Tyrell, Stephanie Tyrell, Ashley Hall; Sound, A/K-L Soun Design; Co-Producers, Diana Dru Botsford, Beth Broday; Assista Director, Chiou Wen Shian; a Family Home Entertainment and Tonk Corp. presentation of an Atlantic/Kushner-Locke Production with th Maltese Cos.; Color; Rated G; 76 minutes; March release. An animate feature with the voices of George Rose (McNasty), B. J. Ward (Whopper), Ruth Buzzi (Nose Marie), Brennan Howard (Cooler), Cath Cadavini (Collette), Nancy Cartwright (Bright Eyes)

PRISON (Empire) Producer/Original Story, Irwin Yablans; Director Renny Harlin; Screenplay, C. Courtney Joyner; Executive Producer Charles Band; Music, Richard Band; Special Effects, Eddie Surkin Mechanical and Make-up Imageries, Inc; Executive in Charge of Production, Frank Hildebrand; Assistant Directors, Matthew Carlisle Shiho Ito, Bill Barvin; Photography, Mac Ahlberg; Art Director, Phillip Duffin; Stunt Coordinator, Kane Hodder; Casting, Anthony Barnac Sound, Jan Brodin; Ultra-Stereo; Color; Rated R; 102 minutes; Marc release. CAST: Lane Smith (Sharpe), Viggo Mortensen (Burke) Chelsea Field (Katherine), Andre De Shields (Sandor), Lincoln Kilpatrick (Cresus), Ivan Kane (Lasagna), Steven Little (Rhino), Micke Yablans (Brian Young), Tom "Tiny" Lister, Jr. (Big Sam), Tor Everett (Rabbitt), Larry Flash Jenkins (Hershey), Arlen Dean Snyde (Horton), Hal Landon, Jr. (Wallace), Matt Kanen (Johnson), Jeff Dies (Kramer), Rod Lockman (Gateguard), Kane Hodder (Forsythe/Ga Mask Guard), George D. Wallace (Joe Reese), Luciana Capozzo (Collins), Duke Spencer (Scully), Rob Brox (Pervis), Larry Moor (Reptile Guard), John Hoke (Old Warden)

AND GOD CREATED WOMAN (Vestron) Producers, George G Braunstein, Ron Hamady; Supervising Producer, Patrick McCormick Director, Roger Vadim; Screenplay, R. J. Stewart; Executive Producers, Steven Reuther, Michell Cannold, Ruth Vitale; Co-Executive Producers, Emilia and Robert Crow; Music, Thomas Chase, Stev Rucker; Casting, Amanda Mackey; Designer, Victor Kempster; Photography, Stephen M. Katz; Editor, Suzanne Pettit; Production Manager, Lenny Vullo; Assistant Directors, Peter Giuliano, Nathalie Vadim Costumes, Sharon Boyle; Presented in Association with Crow productions; Deluxe color; Dolby Stereo; Songs by various artists; Rated R 94 minutes; March release. CAST: Rebecca De Mornay (Robin Shay) Vincent Spano (Billy Moran), Frank Langella (James Tiernan), Donovan Leitch (Peter Moran), Benjamin Mouton (Blue), Judith Chapma (Alexandra Tiernan), Jaime McEnnan (Timmy Moran), David Shelle

Vincent Spano, Rebecca DeMornay in "And God Created Woman" ***(Vestron)***

River Phoenix, Sidney Poitier in "Little Nikita" ***(Columbia)***

David), Einstein Brown (Einstein), David Lopez (Hawk), Thelma Houston (Prison Singer), Gail Boggs (Denise), Dorian Sanchez (Alice), Maria Duval (Maxine), Lee Ann Martin (Shirley), Pat Lee (Inmate), Connie Moore Kranz (Warden), Elle Collier, Gilbert Anthony Silva, Danny S. Martin, Helen S. Pacheco, Nancy B. Kenney (Guards), Gary Goetzman (Al Lawrence), Lenny Vullo (Lenny), Kenny Ortega (Mike), Christopher Murray (Harold), Gary Grubbs (Rupert Willis), Allison Davies (Tiernan's secretary), J. D. Lincoln (Governor Miller)

LURKERS (Crown International) Producer/Music, Walter E. Sear; Director/Photography, Roberta Findlay; Screenplay, Ed Kelleher, Harriette Vidal; Editors, Walter E. Sear, Roberta Findlay; Lurker Prosthetics and Make-up Effects, Ed French; Sound, William Titus; Casting, Roberta Findlay, James M. Cirile; Assistant Cameraman, Richard Giliano; a Reeltime Distributing Corporation production; Studio Film Labs Color; Rated R; 90 minutes; March release. CAST: Christine Moore (Cathy), Gary Warner (Bob), Marina Taylor (Monica), Roy MacArthur (Desmond), Peter Oliver-Norman (Steve), Nancy Groff (Rita), Carissa Channing (Sally), Thomas Billett (Leo "The Hammer"), Dana Nardelli (Young Cathy), Lauren Ruane (Ghost Child), C. C. Banks (Agnes), Gil Newsom (Phil), Eva Baumann (Guardian Angel), Ruth Collins (Jane), Anne Grindlay (Lulu), Jeffrey Wallach (Salesman), Wayne Burcham (John—father), Jodi Armstrong (Rita's friend), Walter Sear (Engineer), William Titus (Assistant Engineer), Gregory Sullivan, Timothy Rule, Jeanette Smith, Steve Villalobos, Lynne Nonenmacher, Bonnie Sterner (Lurkers), Elka Shapiro, Dayna Shapiro, Janeen Rossi, Danielle Leonard, Tara Lyn Catanzaro, Deanna Rossi, Christina Rossi (Jump rope girls)

LITTLE NIKITA (Columbia) Producer, Harry Gittes; Director, Richard Benjamin; Screenplay, John Hill, Bo Goldman; Story, Tom Musca, Terry Schwartz; Photography, Laszlo Kovacs; Designer, Gene Callahan; Co-Producer/Production Manager, Art Levinson; Costumes, Patricia Norris; Music, Marvin Hamlisch; Casting, David Rubin; Editor, Jacqueline Cambas; Associate Producer, Gail Nutrux; Assistant Directors, Dennis Maguire, Robin Oliver; Art Director, Hub Braden; Set Decorator, Lee Poll; Set Designer, Ann Harris; Sound, Jerry Jost; Orchestrations, Jack Hayes; Special Effects, Michael Edmonson; Stunts, Conrad Palmisano; *"Sleeping Beauty Ballet"* Sequence Choreography, Sir Kenneth MacMillan/Set & Costumes, Nicholas Georgiadis/Lig, Thomas R. Skelton; Additional Music, Joe Curiale; *"Til the Next Time"* by Charlie Mitchell, and songs by various other artists; Dolby Stereo; DeLuxe Color; Rated PG; 98 minutes; March release. CAST: Sidney Poitier (Roy Parmenter), River Phoenix (Jeff Grant), Richard Jenkins (Richard Grant), Caroline Kava (Elizabeth Grant), Richard Bradford (Konstantin Karpov), Richard Lynch (Scuba), Loretta Devine (Verna McLaughlin), Lucy Deakins (Barbara Kerry), Jerry Hardin (Brewer), Albert Fortell (Bunin), Ronald Guttman (Spassky), Jacob Vargas (Miguel), Roberto Jimenez (Joaquin), Robb Madrid (Sgt. Leathers), Chez Lister (Tom), Bill Stevenson (Tony), Tom Zak (Brett), Newell Alexander (Drill Sgt.), Ingrid Rhoads (Corp. Hogan), Richard Holden (Russian Diplomat), Vojo Goric (Joe), Kim Strange (DMV Clerk), David M. Paynter (Spike), Biff Wiff (Bucky), Lisa McCullough, Lou Hancock, Tasha Stewart, John Spafford, Jonathan McMurtry, Charles T. Salter, Jr., Rick L. Nahera, Jim Parrott, Arlin L. Miller, Julio Medina, *"Sleeping Beauty" Ballet:* Martine van Hamel (Princess Aurora), Robert Hill (Prince Desire), Michael Owen (Fairy Carabosse), Christine Dunham (Lilac Fairy)

HOLLYWOOD CHAINSAW HOOKERS (Camp Motion Pictures) Producer/Director, Fred Olen Ray; Executive Producers, Salvatore Richichi, James Golff, Nick Marino; Screenplay, Fred Olen Ray, T. L. Lankford; Photography, Scott Ressler; Editor, William Shaffer; Sound, Dennis Fuller; Costumes, Jill Conner; Music, Michael Perilstein; Associate Producers, Nancy Paloian, Gary J. Levinson; Production Designer, Corey Kaplan; A Savage Cinema production released in association with American-Independent Productions; United color; Not rated; 74 minutes; March release. CAST: Gunnar Hansen (Cult Leader), Linnea Quigley (Samantha Kelso), Jay Richardson (Jack Chandler), Michelle Bauer (Mercedes), Dawn Wildsmith (Laurie), Dennis Mooney, Jerry Fox, Esther Alyse, Tricia Burns, Michael D. Sonye, Jimmy Williams

PASS THE AMMO (New Century/Vista) Producers, Herb Jaffe, Mort Engelberg; Director, David Beaird; Screenplay, Neil Cohen, Joel Cohen; Line Producer, David Strait; Photography, Mark Irwin; Editor, Bill Yahraus; Music, Carter Burwell; Production Designer, Dean Tschetter; Art Director, Mayling Cheng; Set Decorator, Michele Starbuck; Costumes, Reve Richards; Sound, Walt Martin; Associate Producer, Bill Yahraus; Casting, Nina Axelrod; Special Effects Coordinator, Rick Josephson; a Vista Organization Production; Deluxe Color; Ultra-Stereo; Rated R; 97 minutes; March release. CAST: Bill Paxton (Jesse), Linda Kozlowski (Claire), Tim Curry (Reverend Ray Porter), Annie Potts (Darla Porter), Dennis Burkley (Big Joe), Glenn Withrow (Arnold), Anthony Geary (Stonewall)

Carissa Channing, Gary Warner in "Lurkers" ***(Crown International)***

Annie Potts, Bill Paxton in "Pass the Ammo" (New Century/Vista)

Matt McCoy, Janet Jones, Marion Ramsey, Tab Thacker in "Police Academy 5" (Warner Bros.)

Lori Laughlin, Keanu Reeves in "The Night Before" ***(Kings Road)***

POLICE ACADEMY 5: ASSIGNMENT MIAMI BEACH (Warner Bros.) Producer, Paul Maslansky; Director, Alan Myerson; Screenplay, Stephen J. Curwick; Based on characters created by Neal Israel, Pat Proft; Photography, James Pergola; Production Designer, Trevor Williams; Editor, Hubert C. De La Bouillerie; Co-Producer, Donald West; Music, Robert Folk; Casting, Fern Champion, Pamela Basker; Assistant Directors, Bill Baker, Marty Ewing, Carla Breitner, Jodi Ehrlich, Cary Gordon; Set Decorator, Don Ivey; Sound, Howard Warren; Costumes, Robert Musco; Stunt Coordinator, Gary Hymes; Technicolor; Rated PG; 90 minutes; March release. CAST: Bubba Smith (Hightower), David Graf (Tackleberry), Michael Winslow (Jones), Leslie Easterbrook (Callahan), Marion Ramsey (Hooks), Janet Jones (Kate), Lance Kinsey (Proctor), Matt McCoy (Nick), G. W. Bailey (Harris), George Gaynes (Lassard), Rene Auberjonois (Tony), George R. Robertson (Hurst), Tab Thacker (House), Archie Hahn (Mouse), James Hampton (Mayor of Miami), Jerry Lazarus (Sugar), Dan Barrows (Bob the Janitor), Dana Mark (Graduating Policewoman), Richard Jasen (Kid with toy plane), Ruth Farley (Airport Information), Kathryn Graf, Via Van Ness (Stewardesses), A. L. Meat (Cigar Smoker), Dan Fitzgerald (Commissioner Murdock), Arthur Edwards (Thief in drag), Jeff Gillen (Thief's victim), Susan Hatfield (Mayor's wife), Ed Kovens (Dempsey), Tom Kouchalakos (Manny), Ruben Rabasa (Julio), Angelo Reno (Pete), Scott Weinger (Shark Attack Kid), Pam Bogart (Harris' Pick-up), Toni Crabtree (Activities Announcer), Nelson Oramas (Crowd Control Cop), Julio Oscar Mechoso (Shooting Range Cop), Joni Siani (TV Interviewer), Jeff Breslauer (News Photographer)

OFF LIMITS (20th Century Fox) Producer, Alan Barnette; Director, Christopher Crowe; Screenplay, Christopher Crowe, Jack Thibeau: Photography, David Gribble; Designer, Dennis Washington; Editor, Douglas Ibold; Associate Producer/Production Manager, Michael S. Glick; Casting, Mike Fenton, Jane Feinberg, June Taylor; Music, James Newton Howard; Assistant Directors, Doug Metzger, Linda Brachman; Art Director, Scott Ritenour; Set Decorator, Crispian Sallis; Production Coordinator, Michelle Wright; Special Effects, Joe Digaetano; Costume Supervisor, Peter V. Saldutti; Sound, David Lee; Stunts, Buddy Van Horn, Richard Ziker, Tawan Mahathavorn; Orchestrations, Brad Dechter; Dolby Stereo; DeLuxe Color; Rated R; 102 minutes; March release. CAST: Willem Dafoe (Buck McGriff), Gregory Hines (Albaby Perkins), Fred Ward (Dix), Amanda Pays (Nicole), Kay Tong Lim (Lime Green), Scott Glenn (Col. Armstrong), David Alan Grier (Rogers), Keith David (Maurice), Raymond O'Connor (Flowers), Richard Brooks (Preacher), Thuy Ann Luu (Lanh), Richard Lee Reed (Col. Sparks), Woody Brown (Copilot), Ken Siu (Plowboy), Viladda Vanaduronogwan (Sister Agnes), Nguyen Kim Hoa (Sapper's Mother), Norah Elizabeth Cazaux (Mother Superior), Piathip Kumwong (Dragonlady), Tongaow Taveprungsenukul (Aborigine), Pra Petchompoo (Francine), Jim Kinnon (Top), Louis Roth (Captain), Kanya Wongsawasdi (Nguyen), Kamsine Spinob (Gen. Vin), Elizabeth LeCompte (Nurse), Father Buncha (Bishop), Greg Elam (Batman)

Gregory Hines, Willem Dafoe in "Off Limits" ***(20th Century Fox)***

CHAIN LETTERS (First Run Features) Producers, Mark Rappaport, Harvey Wildman; Director/Screenplay, Mark Rappaport; Photography, Martin Schafer; Editors, Mark Rappaport, Anthony Szuk Sound, Barbara Zahm; Art Director, John Arnone; Music, Robert Previte; Color; Not rated; 96 minutes; March release. CAST: Mark Arnott, Reed Birney, David Brisbin; Randy Danson, Daniel Davis Marilyn Jones, Ellen McElduff, Joan MacIntosh

NIGHT WARS (SVS Films) Producer, Fritz Matthews; Director Screenplay, David A. Prior; Story, David A. Prior, Ted Prior, William Zipp; Executive Producers, David Winters, Marc Winters; Photography, Stephen Ashley Blake; Editor, Reinhard Schreiner; Sound, Ken Segar; Art Director, Ted Prior; Music, Tim James, Steve McClintock Mark Mancina; Assistant Director, Richard Wright; Special Effects Chuck Whitton; Stunt Coordinator, Bob Ivy; Casting, William Zipp Associate Producer, Bruce Lewin; an Action Intl. Pictures production United color; Rated R; 88 minutes; March release. CAST: Brian O'Connor (Sgt. Trent Matthews), Dan Haggerty (Dr. Campbell) Cameron Smith (Jim), Steve Horton (McGregor), Chet Hood (Johnny) Jill Foor (Susan), Mike Hickam, David Ott, Kimberley Casey

THE NIGHT BEFORE (Kings Road Entertainment) Producer Martin Hornstein; Director, Thom Eberhardt; Story, Gregory Scherick Photography, Ron Garcia; Designer, Michel Levesque; Casting Reuben Cannon, Monica Swann; Production Manager/Assistant Director, Steven Pomeroy; Assistant Director, Eric Heffron; Production Coordinator, William Chapman; Art Director, Jon Rothschild; Set Decorator, Cecilia Rodarte; Special Effects, Greg Landerer, Eric Rylander; Sound, Kim Ornitz; Choreographer, Randall Thomas; Songs by various artists; Technicolor; Rated PG-13; 85 minutes; March release. CAST: Keanu Reeves (Winston Connelly), Lori Loughlin (Tara Mitchell), Theresa Saldana (Rhonda), Trinidad Silva (Tito), Suzanne Snyder (Lisa), Morgan Lofting (Mom), Morgan Lofting (Mom), Gwil Richards (Dad), Chris Hebert (Brother), Michael Greene (Capt. Mitchell), Pamela Gordon (Burly Waitress), David Sherrill (Dannya Boy), Larry Mintz (Cueball), Bobby McGee (Willis), Wren Brown (Harold), Lucille Bliss (Gal Baby), Lorrie Marlow (Whore), Israel Jurabe, Charels Gruber, Michael Strasser, Ned Bellamy, Tom "Tiny" Lister, Kim Ornitz, Dan Halleck, Sydney Goldsmith

JOHNNY BE GOOD (Orion) Producer, Adam Fields; Director, Bud Smith; Screenplay/Executive Producers, Steve Zacharias, Jeff Buhai David Obst; Photography, Robert D. Yeoman; Designer, Gregg Fonseca; Editor, Scott Smith; Co-producer/Production Manager, Jeffrey Chernov; Music Supervisor, Dick Rudolph; Music, Jay Ferguson; Associate Producer, Karen Penhale; Casting, Gary M. Zuckerbrod; Assistant Director, Paul Moen, Vicki Rhodes; Costumes, Susie DeSanto; Sound, Luigi Phonica; Art Director, Sharon Seymour; Set Decorator, Doree Cooper; Jon G. Belyeu; Stunts, Russell Towery; Songs by various artists; Soundtrack on Atlantic Records; DeLuxe Color; Rated PG-13; 84 minutes; March release. CAST: Anthony Michael Hall (Johnny Walker), Robert Downey, Jr. (Leo Wiggins), Paul Gleason (Wayne Hisler), Uma Thurman (Georgia Elkans), Steve James (Coach

Anthony Michael Hall, Robert Downey, Jr. (front) in "Johnny Be Good" ***(Orion)***

Richard Pryor, Dana Carvey in "Moving" ***(Warner Bros.)***

ıders), Seymour Cassel (Wallace Gibson), Michael Greene (Tex ade), Marshall Bell (Chief Elkans), Deborah May (Mrs. Walker), chael Alldredge (Vinny Kroll), Jennifer Tilly (Connie Hisler), Jon ıfford (Bad Breath), Pete Koch (Pete Andropolous), Howard Cosell imself), Jim McMahon (Himself), George Hall (Grandpa Walker), cianne Buchanan (Lawanda Wade), Tony Frank (Joe Bob), David nny (Benny Figg), Chris Dunn (Flick Weaver), John Deluna (Jose pupu), Adam Faraizl (Randy Walker), Megan Morris (Raylene Wal-), Jack Gould (Priest), Dennis Letts (General), Craig Tonelson (Pete ovolone), John F. Cunningham (Substitute), Denise Thorson (Eunice kans), Hayley Ladner (Joanie Dorfman), Robert Downey, Sr. CAA Investigator), Tim Rossovich, Larry Wolf, Michael Colyar, e Ritchey, Linwood Phillip Walker, Ted Dawson, Holly Harrington, ilisha Sanders

OVING (Warner Bros.) Producer, Stuart Cornfeld; Director, Alan etter; Screenplay, Andy Breckman; Photography, Donald McAlpine; signer, David L. Snyder; Editor, Alan Balsam; Music, Howard ore; Costumes, Deborah L. Scott; Associate Producer/Production anager, Kim Kurumada; Casting, Marion Dougherty; Assistant Di-tors, Marty Ewing, Artist Robinson; Art Director, Joe Wood; Set corator, Linda DeScenna; Sound, Jim Tanenbaum; Stunts, David lis, Mickey Gilbert; Special Effects, Michael Lantieri; Orchestrator, mer Denison; *"Moving"* by Ollie E. Brown; Dolby Stereo; Tech-olor; Rated R; 89 minutes; March release. CAST: Richard Pryor rlo Pear), Beverly Todd (Monica Pear), Stacey Dash (Casey Pear), phael Harris (Marshall Pear), Ishmael Harris (Randy Pear), Randy aid (Frank/Cornell Crawford), Clair Malis (Helen Fredericks), John esley (Roy Hendersen), Traci Lin (Natalie), Don Franklin (Kevin), rdon Jump (Simon Eberhart), Dave Thomas (Gary Marcus), Julius rry III (Coach Wilcox), Paul Willson (Mr. Seeger), Lynne Stewart rs. Seeger), Dorothy Meyer (Grandma), Al Fann (Grandpa), Alan ppenheimer (Mr. Cadell), Dana Carvey (Brad Williams), Brooke derson (Mrs. Cadell), Ji Tu Cumbuka (Edwards), Robert LaSardo erry), Darrah Meeley (Mrs. Davenport), Bill Wiley (Arnold Butter-rth), Bibi Osterwald (Crystal Butterworth), Morris Day (Rudy), ng Kong Bundy (Gorgo), Shirley Brown (Mr. Messina), Jacque nn Colton (Mrs. Griffin), Joe Praml (Ted Barnett), Roger Reid (Bob laney), Lisa Moncure (Nina Franklin), Dian Kobayashi (Anchor-an), Rae Allen (Dr. Phyllis Ames), Rodney Dangerfield (Banker)

RIA (Miramax) Producer, Don Boyd; Segments: *"I Paliacci"* by oncavallo/Director, Bill Bryden; *"Un Ballo In Maschera"* by Verdi/irector, Nicolas Roeg; *"La Forza Del Destino"* by Verdi/Director, harles Sturridge; *"Armide"* by Lully/Director, Jean-Luc Godard; *igoletto"* by Verdi/Director, Julian Temple; *"Die Totestadt"* by orngold/Director, Bruce Beresford; *"Les Boreades"* by Rameau/irector, Robert Altman; *"Tristan Und Isolde"* by Franc Roddam; *urandot"* by Puccini/Director, Ken Russell; *"Louise"* by Charpen-r/Director, Derek Jarman; Executive Producers, Jim Mervis, Light-ar Entertainment, Tom Kuhn, Charles Mitchell; Co-producers, Al ark, Mike Watts; Co-ordinating Associate Producers, David Barber, ichael Hamlyn; Co-ordinating Editors, Marie Therese Boiche, Mike ragg; Assistant Co-ordinating Editor, Paul Naissbit; Color; Rated R; minutes; March release. CAST: *Actors:* John Hurt, Teresa Russell, icola Swain, Jack Kayle, Marion Peterson, Valerie Allain, Buck enry, Anita Morris, Beverly D'Angelo, Elizabeth Hurley, Peter irch, Julie Hagerty, Genevieve Page, Bridget Fonda, James Mathers, nzi Drew, Tilda Swinton, Spencer Leigh, Amy Johnson. *Singers:* Enrico Caruso, Leontyne Price, Carlo Bergonzi, Robert Merrill, Shirley Verrett, Peri Grist, Giorgio Tozzi, Ezio Flagello, Rachel Yakar, Anna Moffo, Alfredo Krauss, Anna de Stasio, Carole Neblett, Rene Kollo, Jennifer Smith, Anne-Marie Rodde, Philip Langridge, Leontyne Price, Brigit Nilsson, Renata Tebaldi, Jussi Bjoerling

FRANKENSTEIN GENERAL HOSPITAL (New Star Entertainment) Producer, Dimitri Villard; Director, Deborah Roberts; Screenplay, Michael Kelly, Robert Deel; Based on the novel "Frankenstein" by Mary Shelley; Executive Producer, Robby Wald; Photography, Tom Fraser; Editor, Ed Lotter; Music, John Ross; Sound, Izak Ben-Meir; Production Designer, Don Day; Assistant Director, Michael Grossman; Make-up Effects, Doug White; Stunt Coordinator, Bud Graves; Casting, Kevin Alber; Color and black & white; Rated R; 92 minutes; March release. CAST: Mark Blankfield (Dr. Bob Frankenstein), Leslie Jordan (Iggy), Jonathan Farwell (Dr. Frank Reutger), Kathy Shower (Dr. Alice Singleton), Irwin Keyes (Monster), Hamilton Mitchell (Dr. Andrew Dixon), Lou Cutell (Dr. Saperstein), Katie Caple (Nurse Verna), Dorothy Patterson, Bobby "Boris" Pickett

MADE IN USA (Tri-Star) Producer, Charles Roven; Director, Ken Friedman; Screenplay, Zbigniew Kempinski; Story, Zbigniew Kempinski, Nick Wechsler; Associate Producer/Production Manager, Mark Allan; Production Executive, Graham Henderson; Photography, Curtis Clark; Editor, Curtiss Clayton; Visual Consultant, James William Newport; Assistant Directors, William Corcoran, Phillip Christon; Art Director, Tom Southwell; Set Decorator, Cynthia Rebman; Costumes, Kathryn Morrison; Special Effects Makeup, Scott Redwine; Sound, David Brownlow; Casting, Saly Dennison, Julie Selzer; Music, Sonic Youth; *Sonic Youth:* Kim Gordon, Thurston Moore, Lee Ranaldo, Steve Shelley; Songs by various artists; Stunts, Harry Wowchuk; A Hemdale Film Corp. presentation; Color; Rated R; 87 minutes; March release. CAST: Christopher Penn (Tuck), Lori Singer (Annie), Adrian Pasdar (Dar), Judy Baldwin (Dorie), Marji Martin (Ma Frazier), Tiny Wells (Pa Frazier), Jacqueline Murphy (Cora), Frank Beddor (Bud), Katherine Kelly Land (Kelly), Anthony Duran (Lonny), Dean Paul Martin (Cowboy), Marie Antoinette Bresadola, Mark Carlton, Scott Casey, Pete Concha, Lionel Croll, Cindi Dietrich, AntLoren Elmer, Emil Faithe, Ira Flitter, Dinah Leavitt, Steven Lippman, Dean Paul Tom McCarthy, Mac McClure, Robert Noble, Rosemarie Pasdar, Rob Pivonka, James Purcell, Thomas Rosales, Jr., Rick Seaman, Ben Zeller, Jessica Zeller

Lori Singer, Adrian Pasdar, Christopher Penn in "Made in USA" ***(Tri-Star)***

Keanu Reeves, Michelle Meyrink, Alan Boyce in "Permanent Record" ***(Paramount)***

Dave Thomas, Stuart Pankin, Audrie J. Neenan, Bud Cort in "Love at Stake" ***(Tri-Star/Hemdale)***

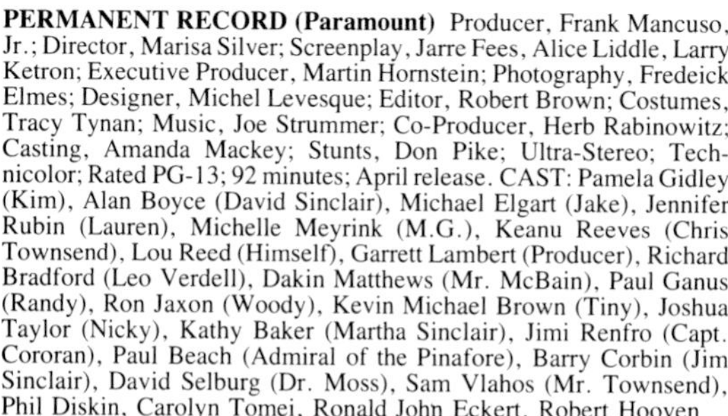

PERMANENT RECORD (Paramount) Producer, Frank Mancuso, Jr.; Director, Marisa Silver; Screenplay, Jarre Fees, Alice Liddle, Larry Ketron; Executive Producer, Martin Hornstein; Photography, Fredeick Elmes; Designer, Michel Levesque; Editor, Robert Brown; Costumes, Tracy Tynan; Music, Joe Strummer; Co-Producer, Herb Rabinowitz; Casting, Amanda Mackey; Stunts, Don Pike; Ultra-Stereo; Technicolor; Rated PG-13; 92 minutes; April release. CAST: Pamela Gidley (Kim), Alan Boyce (David Sinclair), Michael Elgart (Jake), Jennifer Rubin (Lauren), Michelle Meyrink (M.G.), Keanu Reeves (Chris Townsend), Lou Reed (Himself), Garrett Lambert (Producer), Richard Bradford (Leo Verdell), Dakin Matthews (Mr. McBain), Paul Ganus (Randy), Ron Jaxon (Woody), Kevin Michael Brown (Tiny), Joshua Taylor (Nicky), Kathy Baker (Martha Sinclair), Jimi Renfro (Capt. Cororan), Paul Beach (Admiral of the Pinafore), Barry Corbin (Jim Sinclair), David Selburg (Dr. Moss), Sam Vlahos (Mr. Townsend), Phil Diskin, Carolyn Tomei, Ronald John Eckert, Robert Hooven

ABOVE THE LAW (Warner Bros.) Producers/Story, Steven Seagal, Andrew Davis; Director, Andrew Davis; Screenplay, Steven Pressfield, Ronald Shusett, Andrew Davis; Executive Producer, Robert Solo; Co-Producer, John Wilson; Photography, Robert Steadman; Designer, Maher Ahmad; Editor, Michael Brown; Music, David M. Frank; Casting, Richard Kordos, Nan Charbonneau, Billy Damota; Production Manager, John G. Wilson; Assistant Directors, Peter Giuliano, Robert J. Wilson; Set Decorator, Bill Arnold; Sound, Scott Smith; Aikido Choreography, Steven Seagal; Special Effects, Art Brewer, Leo Solis; Dolby Stereo; Technicolor; Rated R; 99 minutes; April release. CAST: Steven Seagal (Nico Tosacani), Pam Grier (Delores Jackson), Henry Silva (Zagon), Ron Dean (Lukich), Daniel Faraldo (Salvano), Sharon Stone (Sara Toscani), Micuel Nino (Chi Chi), Nicholas Kusenko (Neeley), Joe V. Greco (Father Gennaro), Chelcie Ross (Nelson Fox), Gregory Alan-Williams (Halloran), Jack Wallace (Uncle Branca), Metta Davis (Rosa Toscani), Joseph Kosala (Lt. Strozah), Ronnie Barron (CIA Bartender), Joe D. Lauck (Sen. Harrison), Henry Godinez (Father Tomasino), Danny Goldring (Zagon's Aide), Thalamus Rasulala (Dep. Supt. Crowder), Gene Barge (Det. Henderson), Mike James (Officer O'Hara), India Cooper (Nun), Michelle Hoard (Lucy), Christopher Peditto (Pimp), Rafael Gonzalez (Abandano), Cheryl Hamada (Watanabe), Vince Viverito (Giuseppe), Alex Ross (Luigi), Toni Fleming (Grandma Zingaro), John Drummond (TV Reporter), Clare Peck (Judge Alspaugh), Nydia Rodriguez-Terracina, Ralph Foody, Gene Hartline, Tom Milanovich

LOVE AT STAKE (Tri-Star/Hemdale) Producer, Michael Gru koff; Director, John Moffitt; Executive Producers, John Daly, Der Gibson; Screenplay, Terry Sweeny, Lanier Laney; Co-Produc Armand Speca; Editor, Danford B. Greene; Music, Charles Fox; Pr duction managers, Donald C. Klune; Assistant Directors, Jerram Swartz, Jeff Authors, Tom Quinn; Production Coordinator, Bet Filwood; Art Director, Gordon White; Set Decorator, Brendan Smi Sound, Peter Shewchuk; Orchestrations, Thomas Pasatieri; Dan Coordinator, Joanne Divito; Special Effects, Cliff Wenger, Mich Kavanaugh; Stunts, Ted Hanlan; A Hemdale Film Corporation Pr sentation; Color; 83 minutes; Rated R; April release. CAST: Patri Cassidy (Miles Campbell), Kelly Preston (Sara Lee), Georgia Brov (Widow Chastity), Barbara Carrera (Faith Stewart), Bud Cort (Pars Babcock), Annie Golden (Abigail), David Graf (Nathaniel), Audrie Neenan (Mrs. Babcock), Sutart Pankin (Judge John), Dave Thom (Mayor Upton), Anne Ramsey (Old Witch), Mary Hawkins (Prisci Upton), Jackie Mahon (Belinda Upton), Norma MacMillan (Au Deliverance Jones), Dr. Joyce Brothers (Herself), Colleen Karn (Adultress), Juul Haalmeyer (Executioner), Julien Richings (Tov Crier), Danny Higham (Newsboy), Marshall Perlmutter (Mr. Ne berry), Anna Ferguson (Mrs. Newberry), Cathy Gallant (Constanc Elaine Wood (Mrs. Ogelthorps), Nick Ramus (Chief Wannatoka Michael Horse (Medicine Man), Kay Hawtrey (Mrs. Johnson), Ja Jessop (Jury Foreman), Jayne Eastwood (Annabelle Foster), Pa Lyons (Deputy), Ron Richards (Church Idiot), Peter Blaise, An Pellet, Helen Corscallen

THE FURTHER ADVENTURES OF TENNESSEE BUCK (Tra World Entertainment) Producer, Gideon Amir; Director, Dav Keith; Executive Producer, Moshe Diamant; Coproducer, Peter She ard; Screenplay, Barry Jacobs, Stuart Jacobs; Story, Paul Maso Photography, Avraham Karpick; Editor, Anthony Redman; Designe Erroll Kelly; Stunts, Gregg Brazzel; Sound, Jacob Goldstein; Spec Effects, Adams Calvert; Makeup, Camille Calvet; Color; Rated R; minutes; April release. CAST: David Keith (Buck Malone), Kat Shower (Barbara Manchester), Brant Van Hoffman (Ken Manchester Sillaiyoor Selvarajan (Sinaga), Tiziana Stella (Che), Patrizia Zane (Monique), Sumith Mudanayaka (Chief), Pearl Vesudeva (Chief Mother), Somi Ratanayaka (Witch Doctor), Solomon Hapte-Selass (Tui), Steve Davis (Argo)

Steven Seagal (R) in "Above the Law" ***(Warner Bros.)***

David Keith, Kathy Shower in "Further Adventures of Tennessee Buck" ***(Trans World)***

Adam Ant, Bruce Dern in "World Gone Wild" ***(Apollo/Lorimar)***

"Powaqqatsi" ***(Cannon)***

ORLD GONE WILD (Lorimar) Producer, Robert L. Rosen; irector, Lee H. Katzin; Screenplay, Jorge Zamacona; Photography, on Burgess; Designer, Donald L. Harris; Editor, Gary A. Griffen; ostumes, Dona Granata; Music, Laurence Juber; Casting, Al Onoro, Jerold Franks; Associate Producer/Production Manager, Donald C. lune; Assistant Directors, Jerram Swartz, Warren Glen Chidester, 'aggie Parker; Set Decorators, Andrew Bernard, Christian W. Ruson; Production Coordinator, Gillian P. Glen; Sound, Stephan von ase; *"A World Gone Wild"* by Michael Des Barres, Steve Jones, aurence Juber/Performance, Chequered Past; Stunts, Mic Rodgers; oto-Kem Color; Rated R; 94 minutes; April release. CAST: Bruce ern (Ethan), Michael Pare (George Landon), Catherine Mary Stewart angie), Adam Ant (Derek Abernathy), Anthony James (Ten Watt), ick Podell (Exline), Julius J. Carry III (Nitro), Alan Autry (Hank), 'indy McEnnan (Kate), Bryan J. Thompson (Matthew), David oersch (Daniel), Peppi Sanders (Mina), Fred Nelson (Paul), Henry lax Kendrick (Leland), Larry Stuckey (Eric), Richard Israel (Lance), ugh Burritt (Joel), Earl Smith (Roy), Deborah Shore (Lilli Lyric), Mic odgers (Challenger #9211), Ron Campbell, Will Hannah, Larry etchum, Norman Stone, Steve Hastings, Karen Newhouse, Nancy oward, Charles Julian, Marie Grafanakis, Marlon Darton

ACK'S BACK (Palisades Entertainment) Producers, Tim Moore, assian Elwes; Director/Screenplay, Rowdy Herrington; Photography, nelly Johnson; Editor, Harry B. Miller III; Casting, Kimba Hills; esigner, Piers Plowden; Production Manager, Mary McLaglen; ssistant Directors, Ellen Rauch, Richard Abramitis; Costumes, Susie e Santo; Production Coordinator, Laura Greenlee; Sound, Robert J. nderson, Jr.; Set Decorator, Deborah Evans; Effects Makeup, John 'aulin; Stunts, Jerry Spier; Color; Rated R; 97 minutes; April release. AST: James Spader (John/Rick Wesford), Gynthia Gibb (Christine loscari), Rod Loomis (Dr. Sidney Tannerson), Rex Ryon (Jack Pendr), Robert Picardo (Dr. Carlos Battera), Jim Haynie (Sgt. Gabriel), 'endell Wright (Capt. Walter Prentis), Chris Mulkey (Scott Moroky), John Wesley (Sam Hilliard), Bobby Hosea (Tom Dellerton), nne Betancourt (Mary), Sis Greenspoon (Martha), Danitza Kingsley Denise Johnson), Graham Timbes (Surgeon), Diane Erikson (Andrea anks), Mario Machado (Anchorman), Paul Dupratt (Collin Marsh), aniela Petr (Sister), Rana Ford (Emily Miller), Shawne Rowe Ielen), Kevin Glover (Neil Finchley), Cassian Elwes, Spencer Clarke 'imps), Leonard Termo (Chooch), Anna Navaro (Irene), Fats Bender 'at Man), Pola Del Mar (Mrs. Battera), Cindy Guyer (Neighbor), Jeremy Spicer, Jeff Jensen, Richard Parker, Kathryn O'Reilly, Francis Fleming

POWAQQATSI (Cannon Group) Producers, Mel Lawrence, Godfrey Reggio, Lawrence Taub; Director, Godfrey Reggio; Music, Philip Glass; Executive Producers, Menahem Golan, Yoram Globus; Music/Soundtrack Producer, Kurt Munkacsi; Conductor, Michael Riesman; Photography, Graham Berry, Leonidas Zourdoumis; Editors, Iris Cahn, Alton Walpole; Associate Editor, Miroslav Janek; Screenplay, Godfrey Reggio, Ken Richards; Unit Directors, Marcel Kahn, Alton Walpole; Associate Producers, Marcel Kahn, Tom Luddy; Project Coordinator, Sharon Fentiman; Associate Cinematographer, Bill Rosser; Sound, Bob Bielecki, Connie Kieltyka; Lyrics, Bernardo Palombo; A Francis Ford Coppola and George Lucas Presentation; Dolby Stereo; Soundtrack on Elektra/Nonesuch Records; Dolby Stereo; Rated G; 97 minutes; April release

DESTROYER aka *Shadow of Death* (TMS Pictures) Producers/Screenplay, Peter Garrity, Rex Hauck; Director, Robert Kirk; Executive Producer, Joseph Ignat; Photography, Chuy Elizondo; Editor, Mark Rosenbaum; Designer, Paul Staheli; Music, Patrick O'Hearn; Casting, Cecily Adams; Art Director, Randy Holland; Costumes, Julie West Staheli; Production manager, Rex Hauck; Assistant Directors, Robert King, Greg Babcock; Sound, Robert Abbott; Set Decorators, Keith Kalohelani, Barbara Coon; Production Coordinator, Michele Vignieri; *"Kiss My Stinky White Ass"* by Jim Turner, Tom Nelson, Greg McVerry, Jim Hyden/Performance, Boomer, *"Never Say You'll Fall in Love"* by Henry Vars, George R. Brown; Ultra-Stereo; Color; Rated R; 94 minutes; April release. CAST: Deborah Foreman (Susan Malone), Clayton Rohner (David Harris), Lyle Alzado (Ivan Moser), Anthony Perkins (Robert Edwards), Toias Andersen (Russell), Lannie Garrett (Sharon Fox), Jim Turner (Rewire), Pat Mahoney (Warden Karsh), David Kristin (Fingers), Vanessa Townsell (Bea), Stanley Kirk (Cabbie), Bernie Welch (Officer Callahan), Robert Himber (Len), Eric Meyer (Foley), Kurt Hubler (Tommy), Jacqui Clay (Mac), Tim Drnec (Boomer), Margaret Sjoberg (Wardrobe Lady), Michael Ford (Actor), Steve Kelley (TV Host), Gary Owens (TV Announcer), Cathy Eberhard (Susan Starr), Chuck Henry (Newscaster), Laura Dewild (TV Hostess), Charles Hutchinson, Craig McNeil, Chris Lotz, Dutch Shindler, David Clemens, A. G. Gilliam, John Larsen, Damien Veatch, Joseph Wilkins, Patricia A. Dodd

James Spader (R) in "Jack's Back" ***(Palisades)***

Deborah Foreman, Clayton Rohner in "Destroyer" ***(TMS Pictures)***

Yutaka Tadokoro, Carrie Hamilton in "Tokyo Pop" *(Spectrafilm)*

Ann Magnuson in "Mondo New York" *(Island/4th & Broadway)*

TOKYO POP (Spectrafilm) Producers, Kaz Kuzui, Joel Tuber; Director/Story, Fran Rubel Kuzui; Executive Producers, Jonathan Olsberg, Kaz Kuzui; Screenplay, Fran Rubel Juzui, Lynn Grossman; Associate Producers, Akira Morishiga, Nancy Tuber; Photography, James Hayman; Music, Alan Brewer; Editor, Camilla Toniolo; Costumes, Asako Kobayashi; Lighting, Toshiaki Yoneyama; Designer, Terumi Hosoishi; Sound, Yutaka Tsurumaki; Production Executives, David Lubell, Hajime Yuki; Casting, Ellen Lewis, Julie Alter, Yoshikuni Matsunaga; Co-Production Executives, Com Planning Corp., Noriaki Nakagawa; Assistant Directors, Yoshikuni Matsunaga, Shinichiro Makata; Production Manager, Hiroshi Mukuju; Songs, Takehiki Yagura, Carrie Hamilton, Tadokoro, Alan Brewer, Papaya Paranoia, Katogawa Rin, Carl Lee Perkins, Gerry Gofin, Carole King, John Sebastian, Jon Kisk, The Junkyard Band, Mute Seat, The Spiders; Music Performances, Red Warriors, Yutaka Tadokoro, Carrie Hamilton, Michael Cerveris, Papaya Paranoiz, Katogawa Rin, The Be Bops, Jon Kisk, The Junkyard Band, Mute Seat, The Spiders, Zoo N. Boo, Red Warriors, Adams; Music Producer, Alan Brewer; TVC Color; Rated R; 99 minutes; April release. CAST: Carrie Hamilton (Wendy Reed), Yutaka Tadokoro (Hiro Yamaguchi), Taiji Tonoyoma (Grandfather), Tetsuro Tanba (Dota), Masumi Harukawa (Mother), Toki Shiozawa (Mama-san), Hiroshi Mikami (Seki), Mike Cerveris (Mike), Gina Belefonte (Holly), Daisuke Oyama (Yoji), Hiroshi Kobayash (Kaz), Hiroshi Sugita (Taro), Satoshi Kanai (Shun), Rikiya Yasuoka (Club Ume Manager), Senri Yamazaki (Ava), Hirofumi Hamada (Misoru), Kazuo Ishigaki (Chief Waiter), Makoto Fukuda (Father), Yuko Kimoto (Sister), Shun Shioya (Mickey House Manager), Tommy Bell (John), Michael Waters (Yogi), Catherine Bird (Riva)

CASUAL SEX? (Universal) Producers, Ilona Herzberg, Sheldon Kahn; Director, Genevieve Robert; Screenplay, Wendy Goldman, Judy Toll; Based on the play *"Casual Sex"* with Book & Lyrics by Wendy Goldman, Judy Toll/Music, Alan Axelrod; Executive Producer, Ivan Reitman; Photography, Rolf Kestermann; Designer, Randy Ser; Editors, Sheldon Kahn, Donn Cambern; Music, Van Dyke Parks; Casting, Stanzi Stokes, Glenis Gross; Associate Producer, Kool Marder; Art Director, Phil Dagort; Assistant Directors, Betsy Magruder, Terry Edwards; Sound, David Brownlow; Set Decorator, Julie Kaye Towery; Costumes, Grania Preston; Stunts, Eddie Paul; Choreographer, Susie Inouye; Orchestration, Todd Hayen; *"(No More) Casual Sex"* by August Darnell, Stoney Browder, Jr., and songs by various artist; CF Color; Rated R; 90 minutes; April release. CAST: Lea Thompso (Stacy), Victoria Jackson (Melissa) Stephen Shellen (Nick), Jerr Levine (Jamie), Andrew Dice Clay (Vinny), Mary Gross (Ilene), Vale Breiman (Megan), Peter Dvorsky (Matthew), David Sargent (Frankie) Cynthia Phillips (Ann), Don Woodard (Gary), Danny Breen (Dr Goodman), Bruce Abbott (Keith), Susan Ann Connor (Dierdre), Da Woren (Clerk), Dale Midkiff (Attractive Stranger), John Edwar Coburn, Sheri Stoner, Scott Thomson

Victoria Jackson, Jerry Levine in "Casual Sex" *(Universal)*

SOMEONE TO LOVE (Castle Hill) Producer, M. H. Simonsons Director/Screenplay, Henry Jaglom; Associate Producer, Judit Wolinsky; Photography, Hanania Baer; Sound, Sunny Meyer; Assistant Editor, Ruth Wald; *"Someone to Love"* by Diane Bulgarelli/Voca Andrea Marcovicci, *"Looking for the Right One"* by Stephen Bishop *"Listen Here"* by Dave Frishberg, and songs by Jerome Kern & Ir Gershwin; An International Rainbow Picture; Color; Not rated; 11 minutes; April release. CAST: Orson Welles (Danny's Friend), Henr Jaglom (Danny Sapir), Andrea Marcovicci (Helen Eugene), Michae Emil (Mickey Sapir), Sally Kellerman (Edith Helm), Oja Kodar (Yelena), Stephen Bishop (Blue), Dave Frishberg (Harry), Geraldine Baron Ronee Blakely, Barbara Flood, Pamela Goldblum, Robert Hallak Kathryn Harrold, Monte Hellman, Jeremy Kagan, Michael Kaye Miles Kreuger, Amnon Meskin, Sunny Meyer, Ora Rubens, Katherin Wallach

MONDO NEW YORK (Island Pictures/Fourth & Broadwa Films) Producer, Stuart S. Shapiro; Director, Harvey Keith; Screenplay, David Silver, Harvey Keith; Photography, Leonard Wong; Editor, Richard Friedman; Music, Johnny Pacheco, Luis Perico Ortiz Designer, Jacquiline Jacobsen; Executive Producer, Dorian Hendrix Associate Producers, John Paige, Steven Menkin; Production Consultant, Alan Douglas; Documentary; Color; Not rated; 83 minutes; Apr release. WITH: Joey Arias, Rick Aviles, Charlie Barnett, Joe Coleman Emilio Cubiero, Karen Finley, Dean Johnson, Phoebe Legere, Lydi Lunch, Ann Magnuson, Frank Moore, John Sex, Shannah Lameiste

SHE MUST BE SEEING THINGS (McLaughlin) Producer Director/Screenplay, Sheila McLaughlin; Photography, Mark Daniels Heinz Emigholz; Music, John Zorn; Editor, Ila Von Hasperg; Color Not rated; 90 minutes; April release. CAST: Sheila Dabney (Agatha) Lois Weaver (Jo), Kyle Decamp (Catalina), John Erdman (Eric)

BRAIN DAMAGE (Palisades Entertainment) Producer, Edga Ievins; Director/Screenplay, Frank Henenlotter; Executive Producers Andre Blay, Al Eicher; Photography, Bruce Torbet; Associate Producers, Charles Bennett, Ray Sundlin; Music, Gus Russo, Clutch Reiser Production Manager, Ed Walloga; Sound, Joe Warda; Editors, James Y. Kwei, Frank Henenlotter; Special Make-up Effects, Gabe Bartalos Special Visual Effects, Al Magliochetti; Assistant Director, Gregory Lamberson; Art Director/Wardrobe, Ivy Rosovsky; Casting, Frank Calo; "Elmer" created by Gabe Bartalos, David Kindlon; an Ievins Henenlotter production; TVC color; Rated R; 95 minutes; April release CAST: Rick Herbst (Brian), Gordon MacDonald (Mike), Jennife Lowry (Barbara), Theo Barnes (Morris), Lucille Saint-Peter (Martha), Vicki Darnell (Blonde in Hell), Joe Gonzales (Guy in shower), Bradle Rhodes (Night Watchman), Michael Bishop (Toilet Victim), Beverly Bonner (Neighbor), Ari Roussimoff (Biker), Michael Rubenstein (Bum in alley), Angel Figueroa (Junkie), John Reichert, Don Henenlotte (Police), Kennith Packard, Artemis Pizarro (Subway Riders), Slam Wedgehouse (Mohawked Punk), Kevin Van Hentenryck (Man with basket)

Sherilyn Fenn, Richard Tyson in "Two Moon Junction" ***(Lorimar)***

Demi Moore in "*Seventh Sign*" ***(Tri-Star)***

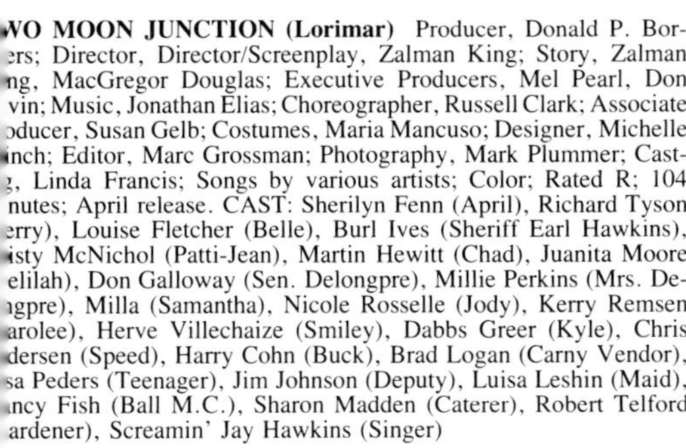

WO MOON JUNCTION (Lorimar) Producer, Donald P. Bor-ers; Director, Director/Screenplay, Zalman King; Story, Zalman ng, MacGregor Douglas; Executive Producers, Mel Pearl, Don vin; Music, Jonathan Elias; Choreographer, Russell Clark; Associate oducer, Susan Gelb; Costumes, Maria Mancuso; Designer, Michelle inch; Editor, Marc Grossman; Photography, Mark Plummer; Cast-, Linda Francis; Songs by various artists; Color; Rated R; 104 nutes; April release. CAST: Sherilyn Fenn (April), Richard Tyson erry), Louise Fletcher (Belle), Burl Ives (Sheriff Earl Hawkins), isty McNichol (Patti-Jean), Martin Hewitt (Chad), Juanita Moore elilah), Don Galloway (Sen. Delongpre), Millie Perkins (Mrs. De-ngpre), Milla (Samantha), Nicole Rosselle (Jody), Kerry Remsen arolee), Herve Villechaize (Smiley), Dabbs Greer (Kyle), Chris dersen (Speed), Harry Cohn (Buck), Brad Logan (Carny Vendor), sa Peders (Teenager), Jim Johnson (Deputy), Luisa Leshin (Maid), ancy Fish (Ball M.C.), Sharon Madden (Caterer), Robert Telford ardener), Screamin' Jay Hawkins (Singer)

AIN CLOTHES (Paramount) Producers, Richard Wechsler, chael Manheim; Director, Martha Coolidge; Screenplay, A. Scott ank; Story, A. Scott Frank, Dan Vining; Executive Producer, Steven-arles Jaffe; Photography, Daniel Hainey; Designer, Michel vesque; Editor, Patrick Kennedy, Edward Abroms; Music, Scott ilk; Costumes, Tracy Tynan; Casting, Jackie Burch; Associate Pro-cer/Production Manager, Don Goldman; Assistant Directors, Peter ies, Frank Capra III; Set Decorator, Marya Delia Javier; Sound, Dan eich; Art Director, William Apperson; Set Designer, Lach Loud; chestrations, James Campbell; "*You're Rich*" by Sarah Taylor, Billy amy, Robert Haimer/Vocal, Sarah Taylor, and songs by various her artists; Stunts, Edward J. Ulrich; Ultra-Stereo; Technicolor; ted PG; April release. CAST: Arliss Howard (Nick Dunbar), Suzy nis (Robin Torrence), George Wendt (Chet Butler), Diane Ladd ne Melway), Seymour Cassel (Ed Malmburg), Larry Pine (Dave echtor) Jackie Gayle (Coach Zeffer), Abe Vigoda (Mr. Wiseman), bert Stack (Mr. Gardner), Alexandra Powers (Daun-Marie Zeffer), ter Dobson (Kyle Kerns), Harry Shearer (Simon Feck), Loren Dean latt Dunbar), Reginald Veljohnson (Capt. Graff), Max Perlich (Car-), James D. Parker, Jr. (Deaf Jeff), Tee Dennard (Sal), Brenda Hayes amille), Jennifer Krug (Terez), Michael Watson, Landon Wine, thony D. Pancho, Kimberly Pistone, Bernhard Pock, Kitty Murray

THE SEVENTH SIGN (Tri-Star) Producers, Ted Field, Robert W. Cort; Director, Carl Schultz; Screenplay, W. W. Wicket, George Kaplan; Executive Producer, Paul R. Gurian; Photography, Juan Ruiz Anchia; Designer, Stephen Marsh; Editor, Caroline Biggerstaff; Costumes, Burinda Rice Wood; Music, Jack Nitzsche; Co-producer, Kathleen Hallberg; Casting, Pennie du Pont; Production Manager, Pieter Jan Brugge; Assistant Directors, Chris Soldo, Robert Yannetti; Visual Effects, Michael L. Fink; Special Makeup Effects, Craig Reardon; Special Effects, Philip Cory, Ray Svedin, Hans Metz; Special Visual Effects, Craig Newman/Dream Quest Images; Art Director, Francesca Bartoccini; Set Decorator, Cricket Rowland; Sound, Peter Hliddal; Stunts, Gary Hymes; "*Jenae*" by David Kurtz; Soundtrack on CINE-DISC; Dolby Stereo; Panavision; Technicolor; Rated R; 97 minutes; April release. CAST: Demi Moore (Abby Quinn), Michael Biehn (Russell Quinn), Jurgen Prochnow (The Border), Peter Friedman (Lucci), Manny Jacobs (Avi), John Taylor (Jimmy), Lee Garlington (Dr. Inness), Akosua Busia (Penny), John Heard (Reverend), Harry W. Basil, Arnold Johnson, John Walcutt, Michael Laskin, Hugo L. Stanger, Patricia Allison, Ian Buchanan, Glenn Edwards, Robin Groth, Dick Spangler

BAD DREAMS (20th Century Fox) Producer, Gale Anne Hurd; Director, Andrew Fleming; Screenplay, Andrew Fleming, Steven E. de Souza; Based on a story by Andrew Fleming, Michael Dick, Yuri Zeltser, P. J. Pettiette; Photography, Alexander Gruszynski; Designer, Ivo Cristante; Editor, Jeff Freeman; Associate Producer, Ginny Nugent; Casting, Mindy Marin; Costumes, Deborah Everton; Music, Jay Ferguson; Production Manager, Charles Skouras III; Assistant Directors, John Woodward, Robin Oliver; Production Coordinator, Jennifer Eden Zolten; Sound, Joseph Geisinger; Art Director, A. Rosalind Crew; Costumes, Deena Appel Caplow; Special Makeup Design, Michele Burke; Special Effects, Roger George, Lise Romanoff; Stunts, Tony Cecere; John Pospisil; Dolby Stereo; DeLuxe Color; Rated R; 84 minutes; April release. CAST: Jennifer Rubin (Cynthia), Bruce Abbott (Dr. Alex Karmen), Richard Lynch (Harris), Dean Cameron (Ralph), Harris Yulin (Dr. Berrisford), Susan Barnes (Connie), John Scott Clough (Victor), E. G. Daily (Lana), Damita Jo Freeman (Gilda), Louis Giambalv (Ed), Susan Ruttan (Miriam), Sy Richardson (Det. Wasserman), Missy Francis (Young Cynthia), Sheila Scott Wilkinson (Hettie), Ben Kronen (Edgar), Charles Fleischer (Ron the Pharmacist), Brian Katkin (Physica (Physical Therapist), Stephen Anderson, Ellaraino, Alba Francesca, Maria Melendez, Chip Johnson, Diane Zolten Wiltse

Arliss Howard, Alexandra Powers in "Plain Clothes" ***(Paramount)***

Jennifer Rubin, Bruce Abbott in "Bad Dreams" ***(20th Century Fox)***

Dylan McDermott, Jessica Harper in "Blue Iguana" ***(Paramount)***

THE BLUE IGUANA (Paramount) Producers, Steven Golin, Sigurjon Sighvatsson; Director/Screenplay, John Lafia; Executive Producers, Michael Kuhn, Nigel Sinclair; Photography, Rodolfo Sanchez; Editor, Scott Chestnut; Designer, Cynthia Sowder; Associate Producer, Winnie Fredriksz; Costumes, Isis Mussenden; Music, Ethan James; Co-Producers, Othon Roffield, Angel Flores-Marini; Casting, Jeff Gerrard; Line Producer, Alejandra Hernandez Esquivel; Assistant Directors, David Householter, Miguel Lima Martinez; Production Coordinators, Merrick Wolfe, Luz Maria Reyes Gil; Art Director, Jesus Buenrostro; Set Decorators, Sergio Nicolau, Heidy Gomez; Sound, Bob Dreebin; Stunts, John Escobar; Special Effects, Jorge Farfan; Choreographer, Felix Greco; *"Blue Iguana"* by Kurtis Blow, Michael Green, and songs by various other artists; Color; Rated R; 90 minutes; April release. CAST: Dylan McDermott (Vince Holloway), Jessica Harper (Cora), James Russo (Reno), Pamela Gidley (Dakota), Yano Anaya (Yano), Flea (Floyd), Michele Seipp (Zoe "The Bartender"), Tovah Feldshuh (Det. Vera Quinn), Dean Stockwell (Det. Carl Strick), Katia Schkolnik (Mona), John Durbin (Louie Sparks), Eliett (Veronica), Don Pedro Colley (Boat Captain), Pedro Altamirano (Rubberhead), Benny Corral (Roy), Alejandro Bracho (Hotel Clerk), Honorato Matgaloni (Smuggler), Enrique Garcia (Drunken Man), Arturo R. Doring, Siro, Alberto Colin, Jorge Luis Corzo, Amelia Zapata (Gangsters), Raul Araiza, Alvaro Carcano (Teenagers), Jonathan Kano (Solo), Carlos Romano (Banker)

CRITTERS 2: THE MAIN COURSE (New Line Cinema) Producer, Barry Opper; Director, Mick Garris; Executive Producer, Robert Shaye; Screenplay, D. T. Twohy, Mick Garris; Photography, Russell Carpenter; Designer, Philip Dean Foreman; Editor, Charles Bornstein; Music, Nicholas Pike; Casting, Robin Lippin; Costumes, Lesley Lynn Nicholson; Critters by Chiodo Brothers productions; Special Effects/Phyrotechnics, Marty Bresin; Stunts, Dan Bradley; A New Line Cinema/Sho Films production; DeLuxe Color; Ultra-stereo; Rated PG-13; 87 minutes; April release. CAST: Scott Grimes (Brad Brown), Diane Curtis (Megan Morgan), Don Opper (Charlie McFadden), Barry Corbin (Harv), Tom Hodges (Wesley), Sam Anderson (Mr. Morgan), Lindsay Parker (Cindy Morgan), Herta Ware (Nana), Lin Shaye (Sal Roos), Terrence Mann (Ug), Roxanne Kernohan (Lee), Doug Rowe (Quigley), Frank Birney (Rev. Fisher), David Ursin (Sheriff Pritchett), Al Stevenson (Bus driver), Eddie Deezen (Geek)

Scott Grimes in "Critters 2: Main Course" ***(New Line)***

Ian Hutton, Anthony Starke, George Clooney, Rock Peace in "Return of the Killer Tomatoes" ***(New World Pictures)***

RETURN OF THE KILLER TOMATOES (New World) Produc J. Stephen Peace; Director, John De Bello; Screenplay, Constanti Dillon, J. Stephen Peace, John De Bello; Line Producer, Lowell Blank; Photography, Stephen Kent Welch; Designer, Constantine D lon; Editor, Stephen F. Aldrich, John De Bello; Music, Rick Patters Neal Fox; Casting, Samuel Warren; Assistant Directors, Thom Owens, Maura McCoy; Sound, Paul Fabbrini; Set Decorator, Melir Ritz; Art Director, Roger Ambrose; Stunts, Sam Alma Kuoha; P sented with Four Square Productions; *"Big Breasted Girls Go To T Beach and Take Off Their Tops"* & *"Love Theme from Return of Killer Tomatoes"* by Rick Patterson & Neal Fox/*"Who Did It"* by R Walz, Neal Fox, Rick Patterson; Stupendo-Sound; Filmed in Lamb ama; Color; Rated PG; 99 minutes; April release. CAST: Mike Vil (Bob Downs), Harvey Weber (Sid), John Astin (Prof. Gangree Karen Mistal (Tara), "Rock" Peace (Wilbur Finnletter), Antho Starke (Chad Finnletter), John De Bello (Charles White/Directo George Clooney (Matt Stevens), Gordon Howard (Pizza Custome Rick Rockwell (Jim Richardson), Alice Easy Squeezin' (Larry Snake), Steve Lundquist (Igor), "FT" (Himself), C. J. "Clark" Dill (Prison Guard), (Prison Guard/Man/SAG Representative/Custom Reporter), Mark Wenzel (Mime), Spike Sorrentino (Store Owne Rick Rockwell (Tomato Dealer), Devlin (Shopper), John Ara Mar (Waiter), D. J. Sullivan (Mrs. Williams), Debbie Gates (Parking L Woman), Frank Davis (Sam Smith), Charlie Jones (Charlie Jone Mike Lambert (Al Schwartz), Dave Adams (Mad Scientist), T Weigel (Matt's Playmate), Debie Fares (Matt's Tomato), Ian Hutt (Greg Colburn), Deirdre Andrews, Ron Trim (Reporters), Ka' I Kuoha (Little Girl), Bruce Binkowski (Daddy)

NO HARD FEELINGS (Triax Entertainment Group, Inc.) P ducers, Chris Davies, Lionel A. Ephraim; Director/Screenplay, Dire tor, Charles Norton; Screenplay, Charles Norton; Executive Produce David Barrett, Don Parker; Photography, Hanro Mohr; Editor, Sim Grimley; Color; Rated R; April release. CAST: Kevin Bernhardt (D Potter), Holaday Mason (Eve), Tim Wallace (Craig Merkel), Anton Caprari (Red), Leslie Monezi (Alfred), Saul Bamberger (Gary), J Stewardson (John Campo), Shaun Naidoo (Jazz Pianist), Gerry Mar (College Pres.), Paul Ditchfield (Disco MC), Terry Norton (Jear Debbi Pretorius (Linda), Sidney Hart (Jeff), Joseph Motsani (Benn Tyrone Deche (Nick), Steffan Erikh (Chuck), Guy Pringle (Shogu Jim Renwick (Danny), Laurence Michael (Marv), Daryl Riekh (Theo), Martin Dewee (Willie), Vincent M. Meni (Dennis), Dav Nelson (Det. Varnado), Polite Dlamini (Officer Kendall), Gret Brazeolle (Donna), David Armitt (Ed), Derek Shirley (Max), Allis Currell (Nancy), Gerry Ford (Pres. Harrison), Joe McNeill (Coa Dobbins), David Sherwood (Regent), Myra Chason (TV Reporte Willy Lock (Al Greenblatt), Fanyana Sidumo (Janitor), Paul Hlor wane (Scrap Iron), Pippa Dyer (Mrs. Anderson), Carolyn Barkhuize Tom Aigner, Allan Tait, Greg Caines, Liam Cundill, Ivan Kruger

NIGHTFALL (Concorde) Producer, Julie Corman; Direct Screenplay, Paul Mayersberg; Story, Isaac Asimov; Associate Pr ducer, Lynn Whitney; Photography, Dariusz Wolski; Editor, Bre Schoenfeld; Art Director, Carol Bosselman; Designer, Craig Hodge Music, Frank Serafine; Production Manager, Reid Shane; Assista Directors, Richard Strickland, Jonathan Winfrey; Sound, Craig F burg; Costumes, Stephen Chudej; Production Coordinator, Janet Els ser; Casting, Al Guarino; Stunts/Pyrotechnician, Brad Fletcher; Col Rated PG-13; 82 minutes; April release. CAST: David Birney (Ato Sarah Douglas (Roa), Alexis Kanner (Sor), Andra Millian (Ana), St Andreeff (Bet), Charles Hayward (Kin), Jonathan Emers (Architect), Susie Lindeman (Boffin), Russell Wiggins (Zol)

Ben Cross in "The Unholy"
(Vestron)

John Laughlin, Faye Dunaway
in "Midnight Crossing" ***(Vestron)***

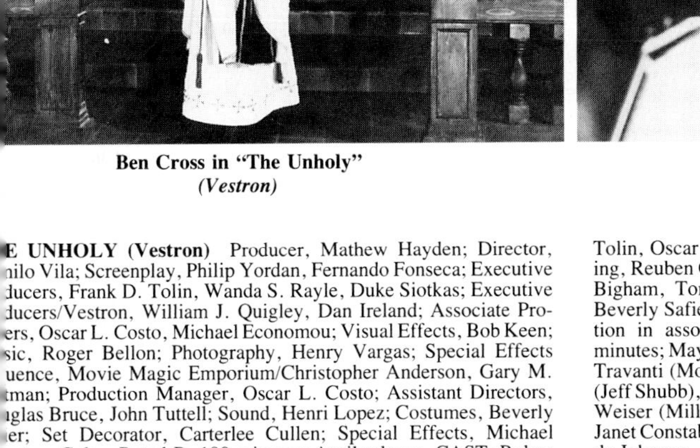

E UNHOLY (Vestron) Producer, Mathew Hayden; Director, nilo Vila; Screenplay, Philip Yordan, Fernando Fonseca; Executive ducers, Frank D. Tolin, Wanda S. Rayle, Duke Siotkas; Executive ducers/Vestron, William J. Quigley, Dan Ireland; Associate Pro- ers, Oscar L. Costo, Michael Economou; Visual Effects, Bob Keen; sic, Roger Bellon; Photography, Henry Vargas; Special Effects uence, Movie Magic Emporium/Christopher Anderson, Gary M. tman; Production Manager, Oscar L. Costo; Assistant Directors, aglas Bruce, John Tuttell; Sound, Henri Lopez; Costumes, Beverly ier; Set Decorator, Carterlee Cullen; Special Effects, Michael votny; Color; Rated R; 100 minutes; April release. CAST: Ruben asa (Father Dennis), Nicole Fortier (Demon), Peter Frechette aude), Phil Becker (Doctor) Ned Beatty (Lt. Stern), Susan Bearden tel Manager), Xavier Barquet (Bell Boy), Lari White (House- per), Jeff D'Onofrio (Paramedic), Ben Cross (Father Michael), Hal brook (Archbishop Mosely), Trevor Howard (Father Silva), Martha ster (Young Nun), John Boyland (Dr. Valerio), Claudia Robinson resa), Norma Donaldson (Abby), William Russ (Luke), Earleen ey (Lucille), Jill Carroll (Millie), Anthony Deans, Jr. (Manolo), ra Pivacco (Lorna), Alan Warhaftig (Intern), Sandy Queen (Nurse), n Cody (Old Woman), Frank Barnes, Selma Jones, Willemina ey, Steven Hadley, Anthony Deans, Joshua Sussman, David San- son

LLETPROOF (CineTel Films) Producer, Paul Hertzberg; Direc- Steve Carver; Executive Producer, Lisa M. Hansen; Associate ducer, Fred Olen Ray; Co-Producer, Neil C. Lundell; Screenplay, L. Lankford, B. J. Goldman; Story, T. L. Lankford, Fred Olen Ray; sic, Tom Chase, Steve Rucker; Editor, Jeff Freeman; Casting, bara Claman, Margaret McSharry; Photography, Francis mman; Designer, Adrian H. Gorton; United Color; Rated R; 96 utes; May release. CAST: Gary Busey (Bulletproof McBain), Darl- e Fluegel (Lt. Devon Shepard), Henry Silva (Col. Kartiff), Juan nandez (Pantaro), Rene Enriquez (Gen. Brogado), L. Q. Jones, lmus Rasulala, Bill Smith, R. G. Armstrong

DNIGHT CROSSING (Vestron) Producer, Mathew Hayden; Producer, Doug Weiser; Director/Story, Roger Holzberg; Screen- y, Roger Holzberg, Doug Weiser; Executive Producers, Dan Ire- d, Gary Barber, Gregory Cascante, Wanda Rayle; Editor, Earl tson; Music, Paul Buckmaster, Al Gorgoni; Music Supervisor, ve Tyrell; Photography, Henry Vargas; Associate Producers, Frank Tolin, Oscar Costo, Duke Siotkas; Line Producer, Jack Lorenz; Casting, Reuben Cannon & Assoc., Carol Dudley; Assistant Directors, Jim Bigham, Tommy Barone, John Tuttle, Jim Van Voris; Costumes, Beverly Safier; Art Director, CaterLee Cullen; A Team Effort production in association with Limelight Studios; Color; Rated R; 104 minutes; May release. CAST: Faye Dunaway (Helen Barton), Daniel J. Travanti (Morley Barton), Kim Cattrall (Lexa Shubb), John Laughlin (Jeff Shubb), Ned Beatty (Ellis), Pedro de Pool (Capt. Mendoza), Doug Weiser (Miller), Vincent Fall, Michael Thompson, Chick Bernhardt, Janet Constable, Mara Goodman, Pat Selts, Armando Gonzales, Rhonda Johnson, Lynn Syvante, Dana Mark, Lori Bivins, Tonda Weeder, Kami Grigsby, Debra Schuster

JUDGMENT IN BERLIN (New Line Cinema) Producers, Joshua Sinclair, Ingrid Windisch; Director, Leo Penn; Executive Producers, Martin Sheen, William R. Greenblatt, Jeffrey Auerbach; Screenplay, Joshua Sinclair, Leo Penn; Based on the book *"Judgment in Berlin"* by Herbert J. Stern; Photography, Gabor Pogany; Art Directors, Jan Schlubach, Peter Alteneder; Costumes, Ingrid Zore; Sound, Karl Laabs; Editor, Teddy Darvas; Casting, Horst D. Scheel, Joyce Gaollie; Camera, Luciano Tonti; Art Directors, Jan Schluback, Peter Alteneder; Costumes, Ingrid Zore; Music, Peter Goldfoot; Assistant Director, Eva M. Schoenecker; Eastmancolor; Rated PG; 92 minutes; May release. CAST: Martin Sheen (Herbert J. Stern), Sam Wanamaker (Bernard Hellring), Max Gail (Judah Best), Juergen Heinrich (Uri Andreyev), Heinz Hoenig (Helmut Thiele), Carl Lumbly (Edwin Palmer), Max Volkert Martens (Hans Schuster), Cristine Rose (Marsha Stern), Marie-Louise Sinclair (Kim Becker), Joshua Sinclair (Alan Sherman), Jutta Speidel (Sigrid Radke), Harris Yulin (Bruno Ristau), Sean Penn (Guenther X), Burt Nelson (Col. Heller), Malgoscha Gebel (Beata Levandovska), Ed Bishop (Dyson Wilde), Peter Kybart (Capt. Wiszevski), Horst D. Scheel (Pavel Gavlik), Helga Sloop (Jury Foreman), Martina Treger (Maria X), Eileen Ryan (Gerta X), Rolf Marnitz (Chauffeur), Piero Von Arnim (Laeufer), Gerhard Lenz (Newscaster), Ted Herold (Rock Singer), Dagmar Cassens (Court Reporter), R. D. Call (Stephen N. Rabourn), Peter Dolle (Col. Martins), Nora Chmiel (Marina Radke), Deirdre E. Fitzpatrick (Andreyev's Assistant), Helmut Ellfeldt (Aleksandrovitch), Mario Zettel (Son X), Jan Boettcher, Christian Mueller (Helmut's sons), Herbert Chwoika (Stranger), Annie Bataillard, Ian-Lloyd Graham, Jim Pearcy, Jeanette Patterson-Pollock (Reporters)

Gary Busey, Darlanne Fluegel
in "Bulletproof" ***(CineTel)***

Sean Penn, Sam Wanamaker
in "Judgment in Berlin" ***(New Line)***

Joe Piscopo, Treat Williams in "Dead Heat" ***(New World)***

Doug Cooyate in "Mala Noche" ***(Gus Van Sant)***

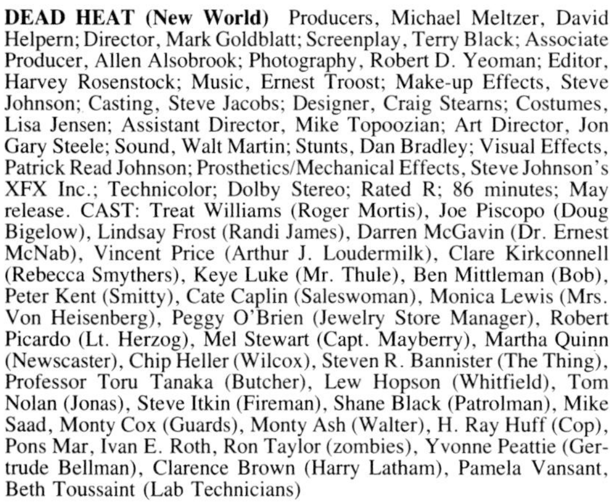

DEAD HEAT (New World) Producers, Michael Meltzer, David Helpern; Director, Mark Goldblatt; Screenplay, Terry Black; Associate Producer, Allen Alsobrook; Photography, Robert D. Yeoman; Editor, Harvey Rosenstock; Music, Ernest Troost; Make-up Effects, Steve Johnson; Casting, Steve Jacobs; Designer, Craig Stearns; Costumes, Lisa Jensen; Assistant Director, Mike Topoozian; Art Director, Jon Gary Steele; Sound, Walt Martin; Stunts, Dan Bradley; Visual Effects, Patrick Read Johnson; Prosthetics/Mechanical Effects, Steve Johnson's XFX Inc.; Technicolor; Dolby Stereo; Rated R; 86 minutes; May release. CAST: Treat Williams (Roger Mortis), Joe Piscopo (Doug Bigelow), Lindsay Frost (Randi James), Darren McGavin (Dr. Ernest McNab), Vincent Price (Arthur J. Loudermilk), Clare Kirkconnell (Rebecca Smythers), Keye Luke (Mr. Thule), Ben Mittleman (Bob), Peter Kent (Smitty), Cate Caplin (Saleswoman), Monica Lewis (Mrs. Von Heisenberg), Peggy O'Brien (Jewelry Store Manager), Robert Picardo (Lt. Herzog), Mel Stewart (Capt. Mayberry), Martha Quinn (Newscaster), Chip Heller (Wilcox), Steven R. Bannister (The Thing), Professor Toru Tanaka (Butcher), Lew Hopson (Whitfield), Tom Nolan (Jonas), Steve Itkin (Fireman), Shane Black (Patrolman), Mike Saad, Monty Cox (Guards), Monty Ash (Walter), H. Ray Huff (Cop), Pons Mar, Ivan E. Roth, Ron Taylor (zombies), Yvonne Peattie (Gertrude Bellman), Clarence Brown (Harry Latham), Pamela Vansant, Beth Toussaint (Lab Technicians)

IN A SHALLOW GRAVE (Skouras) Producers, Kenneth Bowser, Barry Jossen; Director/Screenplay, Kenneth Bowser; Based on the novel by James Purdy; Photography, Jerzy Zielinski; Editor, Nicholas C. Smith; Music, Jonathan Sheffer; Designer, David Wasco; Executive Producers, Lindsay Law, Marilyn G. Haft; Line Producer, Ron Wolotzky; Coproducer, Sandra Mosbacher; Art Director, Sharon Seymour; Set Decorator, Sandy Reynolds Wasco; Costumes, Molly Maginnis; Sound, Russell C. Fager; Makeup, Michele Burke; Associate Producer, Ron Tippe; Assistant Director, Elliot Lewis Rosenblatt; Casting, Pam Dixon; An American Playhouse Theatrical Film, presented in association with Lorimar Home Video, Film Trustees Ltd. and John Wolstenholme; Foto-Kem color; Rated R; 92 minutes; May release. CAST: Michael Biehn (Garnet Monrose), Maureen Mueller (Georgina Rance), Michael Beach (Quintas Pearch), Patrick Dempsey (Potter Daventry), Thomas Boyd Mason (Edgar Doust), Mike Pettinger (Milkman), Prentias Rowe (Postman)

MALA NOCHE (Gus Van Sant) Producer/Director/Screenplay, G Van Sant; From the story by Walt Curtis; Photography, John Campbe Sound, Pat Baum; Music, Creighton Lindsay; A Northern Film C production; Black & White; Not rated; 78 minutes; May release. CAS Tim Streeter (Walt), Doug Cooyate (Johnny), Ray Monge (Pepper Nyla McCarthy (Betty)

SALSA (Cannon) Producers, Menahem Golan, Yoram Globus; D rector, Boaz Davidson; Screenplay, Boaz Davidson, Tomas Benite Shepard Goldman; Story, Boaz Davidson, Eli Tabor; Associate Pr ducer/Choreographer, Kenny Ortega; Photography, David Gurfink Editor, Alain Jakubowicz; Designer, Mark Haskins; Costumes, Car Hooper; Production Managers, John Zane, Daniel Schneider; Assista Directors, Elie Cohn, Michael Kennedy, Jeffrey Stacey; Casting, Na cy Lara; Marc S. Fischer; Stunts, Al Jones; Music Supervisors, Ja Fishman, Michael Linn; Sound, Peter Bentley, Kim Ornitz; Songs b various artists; TVC color; Ultra-Stereo; Rated PG; 97 minutes; M release. CAST: Robby Rosa (Rico), Rodney Harvey (Ken), Mag Alvarado (Rita), Miranda Garrison (Luna), Moon Orona (Lola), A gela Alvarado (Vicki), Loyda Ramos (Mother), Valente Rodrigu (Chuey), Daniel Rojo (Orlando), Humberto Ortiz (Beto), Roxan Flor (Nena), Robert Gould (Boss), Deborah Chester (Sister), Debra Orteg Renee Victor (Aunts), Joanne Garcia (Waitress), Leroy Anderso Bobby Caldwell, Chain Reaction, Willie Colon, Celia Cruz, Ma Vegas Davis, The Edwin Hawkins Singers, Marisela Esqueda, Gru Latino, La Dimencion, Mongo Santamaria, Kenny Ortega, Ti Puente, Michael Sembello, H. Wilkins, Mari Winsor, James Woo bury

ASSAULT OF THE KILLER BIMBOS (Empire Pictures) Produ ers, David DeCoteau, John Schouweiler; Executive Producer, Deb Dion; Director, Anita Rosenberg; Screenplay, Ted Nicolaou; Stor Anita Rosenberg, Patti Astor, Ted Nicolaou; Photography, Thom Calloway; Editor, Barry Zetlin; Music Supervisor, Jonathan Sc Bogner; Music, Fred Lapides, Marc Ellis; Sound, D. J. Ritchie; D signer, Susan Rosenberg; Stunts, John Stewart; Coproducer, Thom A. Keith; Production Manager, Ellen Cabot; Assistant Director, W Clark; A Titan Production; Color; Rated R; 81 minutes; May releas CAST: Christina Whitaker (Peaches), Elizabeth Kaitan (LuLu), Ta mara Souza (Darlene), Nick Cassavetes (Wayne-O), Griffin O'Ne (Troy), Jamie Bozian (Billy), Mike Muscat (Vinnie), Patti Astor (Po dles), David Marsh (Shifty Joe)

Patrick Dempsey, Maureen Mueller in "In a Shallow Grave" ***(Skouras)***

Peter Weller, Sam Elliott in "Shakedown" ***(Universal)***

Robby Rosa, Angela Alvarado in "Salsa" ***(Cannon)***

Mariel Hemingway, Lenny Henry in "Suicide Club" ***(Angelika)***

ANIAC COP (Shapiro Glickenhaus Entertainment) Producer/ eenplay, Larry Cohen; Director, William Lustig; Co-Producer, Jef hard; Executive Producer, James Glickenhaus; Photography, Vin- t J. Rabe; Art Director, Jonathon Hodges; Editor, David Kern; sic, Jay Chattaway; Sound, Craig Felburg; Assistant Director/ duction Manager, Sanford Hampton; Casting, Geno Havens; dallion color; Ultra-Stereo; Rated R; 92 minutes; May release. ST: Tom Atkins (Det. Frank McCrae), Bruce Campbell (Jack For-), Laurene Landon (Teresa Mallory), Richard Roundtree (Com- ssioner Pike), William Smith (Capt. Ripley), Sheree North (Sally land), Robert Z'Dar (Matthew Cordell)

AKEDOWN (Universal) Producer, J. Boyce Harman, Jr.; Di- tor/Screenplay, James Glickenhaus; Executive Producers, Leonard apiro, Alan Solomon; Photography, John Lindley; Designer, Charles nnett; Costumes, Peggy Farrell Salten; Editor, Paul Fried; Music, athan Elias; Sound, William Daly; Casting, Donna DeSeta; Produc- n Manager, Gerrit Van Der Meer; Assistant Director, Joel B. Segal; nts, Alan Gibbs, Jack Gill; Special Effects, Michael Wood; Set corator, Guido DeCurtis; Special Effects, James K. Fredburg; *oking for Love"* by Jonathan Elias & John Waite, and songs by other sts; Dolby Stereo; Color; Rated R; 100 minutes; May release. CAST: er Weller (Roland Dalton), Sam Elliott (Richie Marks), Richard ooks (Michael Jones), Jude Ciccolella (Patrick O'Leary), George ros (Varelli), Tom Waites (Kelly), Daryl Edwards (Dr. Watson), Jos niado (Ruben), Blanche Baker (Gail Feinberger), John McGinley an Phillips), Patricia Charbonneau (Susan Cantrell), Shirley Stoler na), Walter Bobbie (Dean Howland), Judd Henry Baker (Big oy), Andrew Johns (Billy), Roy Milton Davis (Preacher), Kathryn ssetter (Mrs. O'Leary), Larry Joshua (Rydel), Michael Medeiros impers), Bill Cwikowski (Collins), Everett Mendes III (Stevie), ry Beth Lee (Mary), Julia Mueller (Nancy), Antonio Fargas (Nicky r), Roy Thomas (Leon), James Eckhouse (Steve Rosen), David val (Larry), Harold Perrineau, Jr. (Tommie), Rockets Redglare), Lisa Ann Poggi (Suzi), Augusta Dabney (Judge Maynard), Wil- n Prince (Mr. Feinberger), Anthony Crivello (Julio), Richard Epper ade), Ronald Macone (Mastrangelo), Marie Marshall (Muffy), rya D. Dornya (Mrs. Feinberger), Walter Flanagan, James Kruk, n Plumridge, Stacey Heinz, Kevin Ruskin, Vondie Curtis Hall, Karl ylor

LL ME (Vestron) Producers, John E. Quill, Kenneth F. Martel; ector, Sollace Mitchell; Screenplay, Karyn Kay; Story, Karyn Kay, llace Mitchell; Associate Producers, Karyn Kay, Kenneth Berg; otography, Zoltan David; Editor, Paul Fried; Music, David Frank; duction Designer, Stephen McCabe; Production Executive, Alan abelsky; Line Producers, Richard Gelfand, Mary Kane; Sound, Tom lson; Assistant Director, Gary Marcus; Casting, Lynn Kressel; A rtel Media Enterprises production presented in association with eat American Films Ltd. Partnership; DuArt Color; Dolby Stereo; ted R; 96 minutes; May release. CAST: Patricia Charbonneau nna), Patti D'Arbanville (Cori), Sam Freed (Alex), Boyd Gaines ll), Stephen McHattie (Jelly Bean), Steve Buscemi (Switchblade), n Seitz (Pressure), David Strathairn (Sam), Ernest Aruba (Boss), ek Krupa (Henryk), George Gerdes (Fred), Pi Douglas (Nikki), vin Harris (Dude), Gy Mirano (Waitress)

IE SUICIDE CLUB (Angelika Films) Producer/Director, James uce; Executive Producer, Steve Crisman; Screenplay, Susan uguell, Carl Capotorto; Based on a short story by Robert Louis venson; Co-Producers, Paula Herold, Mariel Hemingway. Sam ksal; Dialogue, Mathew Gaddis; Music, J. Aaron Diamond; Pho- raphy, Frank Prinzi; Sound, Paul Cote; Designer, Stephen McCabe; stumes, Natasha Landau; Editors, James Bruce, Keith W. Rouse; Associate Producers, Keith W. Rouse, Ferle Bramson; Production Manager, Keith W. Rouse; Assistant Directors, Mary Beth Hagner, Janice Wilde; Color; Rated R; 90 minutes; May release. CAST: Mariel Hemingway (Sasha), Robert Joy (Michael), Lenny Henry (Cam), Madeleine Potter (Nancy), Michael O'Donoghue (Mervin), Anne Lange (Catherine), Sullivan Brown (Brian), Keith Berger, Tom Cayler (Attendants), Leta McCarthy (Cowgirl), Alice Drummond (Maltha), Alisabetta Ramella (Fausta), Anne Carlisle (Felicity), Eleni Kelakos (Ahmi), Christopher Lawford, James Gillis, Michael Mosolino, Stephane Palay, Noel Beck, Daryl Delvin, Tony Liford, Annabelle Gurwitch, Freddy Deane

MY BEST FRIEND IS A VAMPIRE (Kings Road Entertainment) Producer, Dennis Murphy; Director, Jimmy Huston; Screenplay/ Associate Producer, Tab Murphy; Photography, James Bartle; Editors, Janice Hampton, Gail Yasunaga; Designer, Michael Molly; Music, Steve Dorff; Casting, Pennie du Pont; Production Manager, Tina Brawner; Assistant Director, Sanford Hampton; Sound, Art Names, Tim Himes; Costumes, Rona Lamont; Sets, Richard Huston; Set Decorator, Jeanette Scott; Stunts, Spiro Razatos; Orchestration, Larry Herbstritt; Songs by various artists; Technicolor Rated PG; 90 minutes; May release. CAST: Robert Sean Leonard (Jeremy Capello), Lee Anne Locken (Candy Andrews), Cheryl Pollak (Darla Blake), Cecilia Peck (Nora), Fannie Flagg (Mrs. Capello), Kenneth Kimmins (Mr. Capello), Evan Mirand (Ralph), Michelle La Vigne (Flo), Harvey Christiansen (George), David Warner (Prof. McCarthy), Paul Willson (Grimsdyke), Rene Auberjonois (Modoc), Erica Zeitlin (Gloria), Gary Chason (Instructor), Kathy D. Bates (Helen Blake), John Chappell (Buddy Blake), Jill Bianchini, J. P. Conroy, Mimi Kincaide, Marianne Simpson, Staness Caroll, Ronald P. Rondell, Chris Wycliff, Coy Sevier

BLACK EAGLE (Taurus Entertainment) Producer, Shimon Arama; Director, Eric Karson; Screenplay, A. E. Peters, Michael Gonzales; Story, Shimon Arama; Photography, George Koblasa; Music, Terry Plumeri; Editor, Michael Kelly; Casting, Penny Perry; Assistant Director, Sharon Shamir; Sound, Shlomo Freiman; a Rotecon/Magus Prods. presentation of a Shah/Arama production; Rank color; Rated R; 94 minutes; May release. CAST: Sho Kosugi (Ken Tani), Jean-Claude Van Damme (Andrei), Doran Clark (Patricia Parker), Bruce French (Father Joseph Bedelia), Vladimir Skontarovsky (Vladimir Klimenko), William H. Bassett (Dean Richert), Kane Kosugi (Brian Tani), Shane Kosugi (Denny Tani)

Boyd Gaines, Patricia Charbonneau in "Call Me" ***(Vestron)***

Kane Hodder, Susan Blu, Terry Kiser in "Friday the 13th" ***(Paramount)***

Franklin Ajaye, Richard Lewis, Richard Belzer, Louie Anderson in "Wrong Guys" ***(New World)***

FRIDAY THE 13TH PART VII—THE NEW BLOOD (Paramount) Producer, Ian Paterson; Director, John Carl Buechler; Screenplay, Daryl Haney, Manuel Fidello; Music, Harry Manfedini, Fred Mollin; Photography, Paul Elliott; Editors, Barry Zetlin, Maureen O'Connell, Martin Jay Sadoff; Designer, Richard Lawrence; Costumes, Jacqueline Johnson; Sound, Jan Brodin; Stunts, Kane Hodder; Associate Producer, Barbara Sachs; Assistant Director, Francis R. "Sam" Mahony; Casting, Anthony Barnao; Special Mechanical Effects, Image Engineering, Inc.; Special Makeup Effects, Magical Media Industries; a Friday Four, Inc. production; Technicolor; Ultrastereo; Rated R; 90 minutes; May release. CAST: Lar Park Lincoln (Tina), Kevin Blair (Nick), Susan Blu (Mrs. Shepard), Terry Kiser (Dr. Crews), Kane Hodder (Jason), Heidi Kozak (Sandra), Jennifer Sullivan (Melissa), Jeff Bennett (Eddie), Jon Renfield (David), Elizabeth Kaitan (Robin), Diana Barrows (Maddy), Larry Cox (Russell), Craig Thomas (Ben), Diane Almedia (Kate), John Otrin (Mr. Shepard), William Clarke Butler (Michael), Staci Greason (Jane), Jennifer Banko (Young Tina), Michael Schroeder, Debora Kessler

KISS DADDY GOODNIGHT (Upfront Films) Producers, Maureen O'Brien, William Ripka; Director/Story, Peter Ily Huemer; Screenplay, Peter Ily Huemer, Michael Gabrieli; Photography, Bobby Bukowski; Editor, Ila von Hasperg; Sound, Michael Lazar; Music, Don King, Duncan Lindsay; Associate Producer, Ica Mueller; Assistant Director, Matthias Leutzendorff; Casting, Maureen Fremont; A Beast of Eden presentation; Color; Rated R; 80 minutes; May release. CAST: Uma Thurman (Laura), Paul Dillon (Sid), Paul Richards (William B. Tilden), Steve Buscemi (Johnny), Annabelle Gurwitch (Sue), David Brisbin (Nelson Blitz)

THE PENITENT (Cineworld) Producer, Michael Fitzgerald; Director/Screenplay, Cliff Osmond; Photography, Robin Vidgeon; Editor, Peter Taylor; Music, Alex North; Sound, Grieve Smith; Assistant Director, Ruben Gonzalez; A Vista Organization/Michael & Kathy Fitzgerald presentation of an Ithaca-Cinevest production; Technicolor; Rated PG-13; 94 minutes; May release. CAST: Raul Julia (Ramon Guerola), Armand Assante (Juan Mateo), Rona Freed (Celia Guerola), Julie Carmen (Corina), Lucy Reina (Margarita), Eduardo Lopez Rojas (Mayor), Juana Molinero (Ramon's Mother)

THE WRONG GUYS (New World) Producers, Chuck Gordc Ronald E. Frazier; Director, Danny Bilson; Screenplay, Paul De Me Danny Bilson; Co-Producer, Paul De Meo; Executive Producer, La rence Gordon; Music, Joseph Conlan; Photography, Frank Byers; D signer, George Costello; Costumes, Jill Ohanneson; Casting, N Dutton; Editor, Frank J. Jimenez; Associate Producer, Lloyd Lev Assistant Directors, Mary Ellen Woods, Chip Vucelich; Stunt, Al Gibbs; CFI Color; Rated PG; 86 minutes; May release. CAST: Lou Anderson (Louie), Richard Lewis (Richard), Richard Belzer (Bel Franklyn Ajaye (Franklyn), Tim Thomerson (Tim), Brion James (Gl Grunski), Biff Manard (Mark Grunski), John Goodman (Duke Earl Ernie Hudson (Dawson), Timothy Van Patten (J.T.), Bunny Summe (Louie's mom), Carol Ita White (Ginger Grunski), Garth Winsor (Marsha Grunski), Dion Zamora (Kid Louie), Joshua Horowitz (K Richard), Josh Saviano (Kid Belz), Garland Spencer (Kid Franklyn Danny Thomason (Kid Mark), Parker Jacobs (Kid Glen), Bridg Walsh (Louie's sister), Lindsay Parker (Tim's sister), Rita Rudr (Pam), Susan Issacs (Dresser), Ely Pouget (Nicole), Jonathan Schmo (Hatchet), Deborah Falconer (Wendy), Suzanne Courtney (Sandra Galyn Gorg (Carla), Lenny Clarke (Cab driver), Jan Stango, K Wiedergott, Zoanunne Le Roy, Lori Dunford, Art La Fleur, Isa A derson, Shirley Brown, Eileen Conn, Cynthia Szgeti, Blanche Lew Kathleen Freeman, John Calvin, Jimmy Weldon, Ketchum

NOT OF THIS EARTH (Concorde) Producers, Jim Wynorsk Murray Miller; Director, Jim Wynorski; Screenplay, R. J. Robertso Jim Wynorski; Based on a screenplay by Charles B. Griffith & Ma Hanna; Photography, Zoran Hochstatter; Art Director, Hayden Yate Production Manager/Assistant Director, Murray Miller; Producti Coordinator, Christina Anderson; Sound, Al Ramirez; Costumes, Li by Jacobs; Stunts, Patrick Statham; Special Effects/Designers, J Stewart, Linda Obalil; Foto-Ken color; Rated R; 80 minutes; M release. CAST: Traci Lords (Nadine Story), Arthur Roberts (Alien Lenny Juliano (Jeremy), Roger Lodge (Harry), Ace Mask (Dr. R chelle), Rebecca Perle (Davanna Woman), Michael Delano (Vacuu Cleaner Salesman), Becky LeBeau (Stripper), Monique Gabrielle (B Lady), Roxanne Hernohan, Ava Cadell, Cynthia Thompson (Hookers Kelli Maroney (Nurse Osford), Belinda Grant, Zoran Hochstatter, Morgan, Murray Miller, John Dresden, Shawn Klugman, Paul Shave R. J. Robertson, John Branagan, Parick Statham

Armand Assante, Raul Julia in "The Penitent" ***(CineWorld)***

"Killer Klowns from Outer Space" ***(Trans World)***

Kathy Baker in "A Killing Affair" (Hemdale)

VISTED NIGHTMARE (United Film Makers) Producer, Sandy rowitz; Director/Screenplay, Paul Hunt; Executive Producer, T. auclerc Rogers 4th; Photography, Paul Hunt, Gary Graver; Editor, en Persselin; Special Effects, Cleve Hall; Associate Producers, ederic Leslie, Robert Goldman; Pathe Color; Rated R; 94 minutes; ay release. CAST: Rhonda Gray (Laura), Cleve Hall, Brad Bartrum, bert Padillo, Heather Sullivan, Scott King, Juliet Martin

LLER KLOWNS FROM OUTER SPACE (Trans World tertainment) Producers, Edward Chiodo, Stephen Chiodo, Charles iodo; Director, Stephen Chiodo; Screenplay, Charles Chiodo, ephen Chiodo; Executive Producers, Paul Mason, Helen Sarlui-cker; Photography, Alfred Taylor; Visual Effects, Fantasy II Film fects; Music, John Massari; Editor, Chris Roth; Sound, Patrick oriarity; Designer, Charles Chiodo; Art Director, Philip Dean Fore-an; Costumes, Darcee Olson; Assistant Director, Fred Wardell; own Design, Charles Chiodo; A Sarlui/Diamant Presentation; Dolby reo; Color; Rated PG-13; 90 minutes; May release. CAST: Suzanne yder (Debbie), Grant Cramer (Mike), John Allen Nelson (Dave), ve Hanson (Officer Mooney), Royal Dano (Farmer Green), John rnon (Officer Mooney), Michael Siegel (Rich), Peter Licassi (Paul)

RFECT MATCH (Sandstar Releasing) Producers, Mark Deimel, bert Torrance; Director, Mark Deimel; Screenplay, Nick Duretta, vid A. Burr, Mark Deimel; Photography, Robert Torrance; Music, n Torrance; Editor, Craig A. Colton; Designer, Maxine Shepard; und, Rob Janiger; Associate Producers, Daniel Carlson, George ughan; An Airtight Production from Manson International; Color; ted PG; 92 minutes; May release. CAST: Marc McClure (Tim ainwright), Jennifer Edwards (Nancy Bryant), Diane Stilwell icki), Rob Paulsen (John Wainwright), Jeane Byron (Mother), Karen itter

IPER (Fries Distribution) Producer/Director, Peter Maris; Screen-ay, Frank Kerr; Photography, Gerald Wolfe; Editor, Jack Tucker; usic, Scott Roewe; Sound, Bill Robbins; Stunts, Peter Horak; Assis-nt Director, Jeff Mallians; Associate Producer, Sunny Vest; Assistant oducer, Bradley Chambers; Casting, Valerie McCaffrey; United olor; Rated R; 94 minutes; May release. CAST: Linda Purl (Laura cCalla), James Tolkan (Col. Tanzer), Jeff Kober (Richard Gelb), en Foree (Harley Trueblood), Chris Robinson (Jim McCalla), David . Sterling (Powell), Charles Hoyes (Broadnax)

KILLING AFFAIR (Hemdale) Producers, Michael Rauch, Peter McIntosh; Director/Screenplay, David Saperstein; Based on the vel *"Monday, Tuesday, Wednesday"* by Robert Houston; Executive oducers, John Backe, Myron A. Hyman; Photography, Dominique apuis; Costumes, Elisabeth Ann Seley; Casting, Pat McCorkle; esigner, John J. Moore; Music, John Barry; Editor, Patrick cMahon; Set Decoration, Lynn Wolverton; Sound, Tom Braden; ssistant Director, Alex Hapsas; Technicolor; Rated R; 100 minutes; ay release. CAST: Peter Weller (Baston Morris), Kathy Baker (Mag-e Gresham), John Glover (Sheb Sheppard), Bill Smitrovich (Pink esham), Rhetta Hughes (Vinia), Amy Fields (Bessie Gresham), chard Westrick (Warren Gresham), Trevor Jackson (Eldridge), Susie ll (Blanche), Sandi Branon (Sara), Bob Hannah (Stillwell), Joel mon, Edward Potter Haggard (Men at Mill), Curt Walters (Parrish eriff), Mert Hatfield (Oakman Sheriff), Stuart Culpepper (Mr. Shep-rd), Nicole Anderson-Ellis (Young Maggie), George H. Hammett, (Young Sheb), Victoria Loving (Morris' Wife), Danny Nelson ara's Father), Lana Sloniger (Anna Sheppard), Wallace Wilkinson 929 Judge), Bill Fleet (1929 Sheriff), John Bradley (1929 Deputy)

ILLEGALLY YOURS (United Artists) Producer/Director, Peter Bogdanovich; Screenplay, M. A. Stewart, Max Dickens; Executive Producers, Peggy Robertson, William Peiffer; Photography, Dante Spinotti; Editors, Richard Fields, Ronald Krehel; Music, Phil Marshall; Songs, Johnny Cash, Peter Bogdanovich, Vocals, Johnny Cash; Sound, Art Rochester; Designer, Jane Musky; Stunts, Greg Walker; Associate Producer, Steve Foley; Co-Producer, George Morfogen; Casting, Jane Jenkins, Janet Hirshenson; A De Laurentiis Entertainment Group presentation of a Crescent Moon production; Technicolor; Rated PG; 102 minutes; May release. CAST: Rob Lowe (Richard Dice), Colleen Camp (Molly Gilbert), Kenneth Mars (Hal Keeler), Harry Carey Jr. (Wally), Kim Myers (Suzanne Keeler), Marshall Colt (Donald Cleary), Linda MacEwen (Ruth), Rick Jason (Freddie Bone-flecker), Jessica James (Mrs. Dice), Andrew Heiden (Andrew Dice), George Morfogen (Judge), Tony Longo (Konrat), Howard Hirdler (Harry), L. B. Straten (Sharon)

SLIME CITY (Slime City Co.) Producers, Gregory Lamberson, Peter Clark, Marc Makowski; Director/Screenplay, Gregory Lamberson; Photography, Peter Clark; Editors, Gregory Lamberson, Britton Petrucelly; Designer, Bonnie Brinkley; Make-up Effects, J. Scott Coulter; Music, Robert Tomaro; Assistant Director, Ed Walloga; Color; Not rated; 85 minutes; May release. CAST: Robert C. Sabin (Alex), Mary Huner (Lori/Nicole), T. J. Merrick (Jerry), Dick Biel (Irish), Jane Reibel (Lizzy), Bunny Levine (Ruby), Dennis Embry (Roman), Marilyn Oran (Selina)

MORTUARY ACADEMY (Taurus Entertainment) Producers, Dennis Winfrey, Chip Miller; Director, Michael Schroeder; Screenplay, William Kelman; Photography, Roy H. Wagner; Executive Producer, Kim Jorgensen; Editor, Ellen Keneshea; Music, David Spear, Brian Mann; Sound, Trevor Black; Designer, Jon Rothschild; Art Director, Gary New; a Landmark Films production; Monaco & FotoKem color; Ultra-Stereo; Rated R; 85 minutes; May release. CAST: Paul Bartel (Dr. Paul Truscott), Mary Woronov (Mary Purcell), Perry Lang (Sam Grimm), Tracey Walter (Dickson), Christopher Atkins (Max Grimm), Lynn Danielson (Valerie), Stoney Jackson (James Dandridge), Anthony James (Abbott Smith), Wolfman Jack (Bernie Berkowitz), Cesar Romero (Captain), Cheryl Starbuck (Corpse)

Marc McClure in "Perfect Match" *(Sandstar)*

Rob Lowe, Colleen Camp in "Illegally Yours" *(United Artists)*

Billy McNamara, John Savage in "The Beat" *(Vestron)*

"Rights and Reactions—" *(Tapestry)*

GIRL TALK (Double Helix Films) Producer/Director, Kate Davis; Photography/Associate Director, Alyson Denny; Additional Photography, Richard Leacock; Editors, Kate Davis, Alyson Denny; Associate Producer, Pat Gross; Assistant Editor, Eliza Gagnon; Documentary; Color; 85 minutes; May release. CAST: Pinky, Mars, Martha

BEACH BALLS (Concorde) Producer, Matt Leipzig; Director, Joe Ritter; Screenplay, David Rocklin; Photography, Anthony Cobbs; Designer, Stephen Greenberg; Editor, Carol Oblath; Music, Mark Governor; Sound, David Kelson; Assistant Director, Randy Pope; Casting, Al Guarino; A New Classics presentation; Foto-Kem color; Rated R; 77 minutes; May release. CAST: Phillip Paley (Charlie Harrison), Heidi Helmer (Wendy), Amanda Goodwin (Toni), Steven Tash (Scully), Tod Bryant (Doug), Douglas R. Starr (Keith), Leslie Danon (Kathleen), Morgan Englund (Dick), Charles Gilleran (Babcock), Tami Smith (Gina)

THE BEAT (Vestron) Producers, Julia Phillips, Jon Kilik, Nick Wechsler; Director/Screenplay, Paul Mones; Executive Producers, Ruth Vitale, Lawrence Kasanoff; Photography, Thomas DiCillo; Editor, Elizabeth Kling; Music, Carter Burwell; Color; Rated R; 98 minutes; June release. CAST: David Jacobson (Rex Voorhs Ormine), William McNamara (Billy), Kara Glover (Kate), Atuart Alexander (Doug), Marcus Flanagan (Vis), David McCarthy (Dirt), Reggie Bythewood (Danny), Tony Moundroukas (Auggie), Paul Dillon (Lon), Richard Eigen (Ian), Lisa Richards (Amy), John Savage (Frank Ellsworth)

POLTERGEIST III (MGM) Producer, Barry Bernardi; Director/Executive Producer, Gary Sherman; Screenplay, Gary Sherman, Brian Taggert; Photography, Alex Nepomniaschy; Designer, Paul Eads; Music, Joe Renzetti; Special Effects Make-up, Dick Smith; Special Make-up Design, John Caglione, Jr., Doug Drexler; Visual Effects Design, Gary Sherman; Casting, Jane Alderman, Shelley Andreas; Editor, Ross Albert; Stunts, Ben R. Scott; Technicolor; Dolby Stereo; Rated PG-13; 97 minutes; June release. CAST: Tom Skerritt (Bruce Gardner), Nancy Allen (Patricia Gardner), Heather O'Rourke (Carol Anne), Zelda Rubinstein (Tangina Barrons), Lara Flynn Boyle (Donna Gardner), Kip Wentz (Scott), Richard Fire (Dr. Seaton), Nathan Davis (Kane), Roger May (Burt), Paul Graham (Martin), Meg Weldon (Sandy), Stacy Gilchrist (Melissa), Joey Garfield (Jeff), Chris Murphy (Dusty), Roy Hytower (Nathan), Meg Thalken (Deborah), Dean Tokuno (Takamitsu), Catherine Gatz (Marcie), Paty Lombard (Helen), E. Murray (Mary), Sherry Narens (Mrs. Seaton), Phil Locker (Bill Maureen Steindler (Old Woman), Alan Wilder, Brent Shaphren, Mi dy Bell, Conrad Allan, Maureen Mueller, John Rusk, Sam Sander Laurie V. Logan, Jerry Birn, Jane Alderman

DADDY'S BOYS (Concorde Pictures) Producer, Roger Corma Director, Joe Minion; Screenplay, Daryl Haney; Photography, Dav G. Stump; Music, Sasha Matson; Designer, Gabrielle Petrissans; Editor, Norman Hollyn, Sound, Steve Hawk; Stunts, Mike Ryan; Associate Producer, Anna Roth; Assistant Director, Melitta Fitzer; Foto-Ke Color; Rated R; 85 minutes; June release. CAST: Daryl Haney (Jimmy), Laura Burkett (Christie), Raymond J. Barry (Daddy), Dan Sh (Hawk), Christian Clemenson (Otis), Ellen Gerstein (Madame Wang Robert V. Barron (Axelrod), Paul Linke (Traveling Salesman)

RIGHTS AND REACTIONS: Lesbian and Gay Rights on Tri (Tapestry International) Producers, Phil Zwickler, Jane Lippma Director, Phil Zwickler; Screenplay/Editor, Jane Lippman; Associa Producers, Conrad Johnson, Maria Maggenti; Music, James Ferrera Photography, Geoffrey O'Connor; On-line Editor, Jim Burgess; A Directors, Richard Kuhn, Susan Wilcox; Additional Photograph WNYC Foundations, Bettye Lane, Gay Cable Network, Kim Hanso Abigail Norman/Heramedia, Inc.; Executives Producers, Paul Fishe Nancy Walzog, Phil Zwickler; A Realis Pictures and Syzygy Med Production; Documentary; Color; Not rated; 60 minutes; June releas

PUSS IN BOOTS (Cannon) Producers, Menahem Golan, Yora Globus; Director, Eugene Marner; Screenplay, Carole Lucia Satrin Based on the fairy tale by Charles Perrault; Photography, Avi Karpic Editors, Carole Lucia Satrina, Eugene Marner; Music, Rafi Kadishso Songs, Michael Abbott, Anne Croswell; Sound, Eli Yarkoni; Designe Marek Dobrowolski; Costumes, Ora Strikovsky; Dolby Stereo; Ran color; Rated G; 96 minutes; June release. CAST: Christopher Walke (Puss), Jason Connery (Corin), Carmela Marner (Vera), Yossi Grab (King), Elki Jacobs (Lady Clara), Amnon Meskin (Ogre)

PARAMEDICS (Vestron) Producer, Leslie Greif; Director, Stua Margolin; Screenplay, Barry Bardo, Richard Kriegsman; Photograph Mic Watkins; Editor, Allan A. Moore; Music, Murray MacLeo Music Producer/Supervisor, Jim Messina; Art Director, Jack Mart

Nancy Allen, Tom Skerritt in "Poltergeist III" *(MGM)*

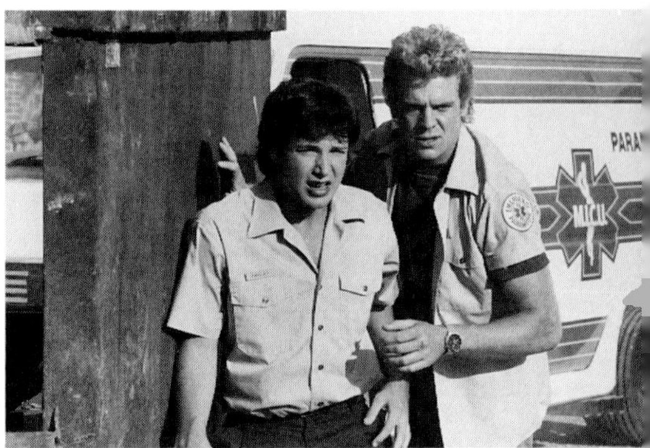

George Newbern, Chris MacDonald in "Paramedics" *(Vestron)*

David Warner in "Waxwork"
(Vestron Pictures)

Corey Haim, Heather Graham, Corey Feldman in "License to Drive" *(20th Century Fox)*

sociate Producer, Dennis Bishop; Casting, Shari Rhodes; Production anager, Kathleen Caton; Assistant Directors, Ron Wright, Cliff Cole-n; Production Executive, Alan Grabelsky; Line Producer, Alan P. rowitz; Costumes, Elizabeth Pine; Production Coordinator, Diane verson; Sound, Skip Frazee; Color; Rated PG-13; 91 minutes; June ease. CAST: George Newbern (Uptown), Christopher McDonald (ad Mike), John P. Ryan (Capt. Prescott), James Noble (Chief ilkens), John Pleshette (Doctor Lido), Elaine Wilkes (Savannah), die Denier (Liette), Javier Grajeda (Bennie), Lawrence-Hilton cobs (Blade Runner), Karen Witter (Danger Girl), Ray Walston eart Attack Victim), Leigh Hamilton (Dispatcher), Sally Kellerman ispatcher's Voice), Robert DoQui (Moses), Bill Johnson (Big esar), Cliff Stephens (Little Caesar), Peter Isacksen (Breedlove), ic Boardman (White), Mark St. Amant (Mouse), Helaine Lembeck t. Holcomb), Wmilio Ruiz (Bus Boy), Charlie Seybert (Wino), Lisa plewhite (Nurse Helms), Creighton Weir, Jerry Cotton (Tennis ayers), Ben H. Hogan (Sports Car Victim), Gary Carter (Cart Intern), arner Roberts (Receptionist), C. Jack Robinson (Bleeding Man), oug Jackson (Dr. Salt)

AXWORK (Vestron) Producer, Staffan Ahrenberg; Director/ reenplay, Anthony Hickox; Executive Producers, Mario Sotela, Wil-m J. Quigley, Dan Ireland; Line Producer, William W. Edwards; otography, Gerry Lively; Designer, Gianni Quaranta; Editor, Chris-pher Cibelli; Makeup Effects, Bob Keen; Music, Roger Bellon; usic Supervisor, Jimmy Ienner; Costumes, Leonard Pollack: Art rector, Peter Marangoni; Associate Producer, Eyal Rimmon; Cast-g, Caro Jones; Production Consultant, Mark Burg; Dolby Stereo; to-Kem Color; Rated R; 97 minutes; June release. CAST: Zach lligan (Mark), Jennifer Bassey (Mrs. Loftmore), Joe Baker (Jenk-s), Deborah Foreman (Sarah), Michelle Johnson (China), David arner (Mr. Lincoln), Eric Brown (James), Clare Carey (Gemma), ckley Norris (Lecturer), Dana Ashbrook (Tony), Micha Grant hnathan), Mihaly "Michu" Mesza (Hans), Jack David Warner (Ju-or), John Rhys-Davies (Anton Weber), Nelson Welch (Elderly Man), iles O'Keefe (Count Dracula), Christopher Bradley (Stephen), omas Mac Greevey (Charles), Irene Olga Lopez (Maid), Charles cCaughn (Insp. Roberts), Julian Forbes (Police Driver), Edward shley (Prof. Sutherland), Kendall Conrad (Pyramid Girl), Patrick acnee (Sir Wilfred), J. Kenneth Campbell (Marquis De Sade), An-ony Kickox (English Prince), Staffan Ahrenberg (French Guard), briella Dufwa (Courtesan)

OVER-UP: BEHIND THE IRAN-CONTRA AFFAIR mpowerment Project) Producers, Barbara Trent, Gary Meyer, avid Kasper; Director, Barbara Trent; Screenplay, Eve Goldberg; arrator, Elizabeth Montgomery; Photography, Gary Meyer; Music, chard Elliott; Editors, David Kasper, Eve Goldberg; an MPI release an Empowerment Project production; Documentary; Color; Not ted; 76 minutes; June release.

AMPIRE AT MIDNIGHT (Skouras Pictures) Producers/Story, son Williams, Tom Friedman; Director, Gregory McClatchy; Screen-ay, Dulhany Ross Clements; Photography, Daniel Yarussi; Editor, aye Davis; Art Director, Beau Peterson; Assistant Director, Darcy own; Music, Robert Etoll; Makeup Effects, Mecki Heussen; Color; ted R; 93 minutes; June release. CAST: Jason Williams (Det. Roger tter), Gustav Vintas (Victor Radkoff), Lesley Milne (Jenny Carlon), anie Moore (Amalia), Esther Alise (Lucia), Ted Hamaguchi (Capt. kato), Robert Random (Childress), Jonny Solomon (Lee), Barbara ammond, Eddie Jr., Christina Whitaker

LICENSE TO DRIVE (20th Century Fox) Producers, Jeffrey A. Mueller, Andrew Licht; Director, Greg Beeman; Screenplay, Neil Tolkin; Executive Producer, John Davis; Photography, Bruce Surtees; Designer, Lawrence G. Paull; Editor, Wendy Green Bricmont; Casting, Penny Perry; Music, Jay Ferguson; Associate Producer/Production Manager, Mack Bing; Assistant Director, Mike Kusley; Set Decorator, Jeff Haley; Sound, Art Rochester; Production Coordinators, Wanda Mull, David Russell; Special Effects, Stan Parks, Kevin Quibell; Costumes, Hilary Wright; Stunts, Joe Dunne; Songs by various artists; Soundtrack on MCA Records; Dolby Stereo; DeLuxe Color; Rated PG-13; 90 minutes; July release. CAST: Corey Haim (Les), Corey Feldman (Dean), Carol Kane (Mom), Richard Masur (Dad), Heather Graham (Mercedes), Michael Manasseri (Charles), Harvey Miller (Professor), M. A. Nickles (Paolo), Nina Siemaszko (Natalie), Grant Goodeve (Mr. Nice Guy), James Avery (DMV Examiner), Grant Heslov (Karl), Michael Ensign (Teacher/Bus Driver), Helen Hanft (Miss Hellberg), Hames Avery (Mr. Kelly), Christopher Buton (Rudy), Jill Jaress (Dean's Mom), Kimberly Hope (Dean's Sister), Parley Baer (Grandpa), Christina Chocek (Anchorwoman) Bernie Polk, Jon Pochron, Daniel W. Barringer, Jerry Tullos, Kelly Ames

PHANTASM II (Universal) Producer, Roberto A. Quezada; Director/ Screenplay, Don Coscarelli; Executive Producer, Dac Coscarelli; Photography, Daryn Okada; Editor, Peter Teschner; Music, Fred Myrow, Christopher L. Stone, Malcolm Seagrave; Designer, Philip J. C. Duffin; Associate Producer/Production Manager, Robert Del Valle; Assistant Director, Alan Brent Connell; Special Makeup, Mark Shostrom; Casting, Elizabeth Miller Fels; Production Coordinators, John Stolfi, Eddie Salmon; Art Director, Byrnadette di Santo; Set Decorator, Dominic Wymark; Costumes, Carla Gibbons; Special Effects, Wayne Beauchamp; Visual Effects, Justin Klarenbeck/Dream Quest Images; Sound, Izak Ben-Meir, Alan Howarth; Dolby Stereo; Foto-Kem color; Rated; 100 minutes; July release. CAST: James Le Gros (Mike), Reggie Bannister (Reggie), Angus Scrimm (The Tall Man), Paula Irvine (Liz), Samantha Phillips (Alchemy), Kenneth Tigar (Father Meyers), Ruth C. Engel (Grandma), Mark Anthony Major (Mortician), Rubin Kushner (Grandpa), Stacey Travis (Jeri), J. Patrick McNamara (Psychologist), Amanda Gray, Elizabeth Quezada, Lauren Gray, June Jordan, Megan Gibbons, Craig Murkey, Amanda Gibbons, Troy Fromin, Georgeanna Valdez, Guy Alford, Irene Korman, Ricky Murkey, Katie Carlin, Delia Ortega, Lee Craig, Ramona Ortega, Richard F. Berry, Patrick W. Allen

Paula Irvine, Angus Scrimm in "Phantasm II" *(Universal)*

Jack Weston in "Short Circuit 2"
(Tri-Star)

Seth Barrish in "Home Remedy"
(Kino International)

SHORT CIRCUIT 2 (Tri-Star) Producers, David Foster, Lawrence Turman, Gary Foster; Director, Kenneth Johnson; Screenplay, S. S. Wilson, Brent Maddock; Executive Producer, Michael MacDonald; Photography, John McPherson; Designer, Bill Brodie; Editor, Conrad Buff; Associate Producer, Eric Allard; Music, Charles Fox; Casting, Stuart Aikins, Stuart Howard, Kathy Rowe; Production Managers, Michael MacDonald, Lacia Kornylo; Assistant Directors, Donald Eaton, Tony Lucibello; Art Director, Alicia Keywan; Set Decorator, Steve Shewchuk; Sound, Douglas Ganton; #5 Voice Design, Frank Serafine; Special Effects, Jeff Jarvis, Mike Edmonson; Costumes, Larry Wells; Robot Supervisor, Eric Allard; Visual Effects, Michael Bigelow/Dream Quest Images; Production Supervisor, Craig Newman, Keith Shartle; Songs by various artists; Stunts, Ken Bates; Dolby Stereo; Technicolor; Rated PG; 112 minutes; July release. CAST: Fisher Stevens (Ben Jahrvi), Michael McKean (Fred Ritter), Cynthia Gibb (Sandy Banatoni), Jack Weston (Oscar Baldwin), Dee McCafferty (Saunders), David Hemblen (Jones), Tim Blaney (Voice of Johnny Five), Don Lake (Manic Mike), Damon D'Oliveira (Bones), Tito Nunez (Zorro), Jason Kuriloff (Lil Man), Robert LaSardo (Spooky), Lili Francks (Officer Mendez), Wayne Best (Officer O'Malley), Gerry Parkes (Priest), Adam Ludwig (Hans de Ruyter), Rex Hagon (Dartmoor), Richard Comar (Mr. Slater), Jeremy Ratchford (Bill), Kurt Reis (Mr. Arnold), Gary Robbins (Francis), Robert Mills, Gordon Robertson, Trish Leeper, Michael Sorensen, Rummy Bishop, Tony DeSantis, Eric Keenleyside, Phil Jarrett, Ric Sarabia, Barry Flatman, Jane Schoettle, Carlton Watson, Eve Crawford, Craig Gardner, Micki Moore, Sam Moses, Norwich Duff, Claudette Roach, Frank Adamson, Chris Barker, Peter Shanne, James Killeen, Parick Greenwood

CADDYSHACK II (Warner Bros.) Producers, Neil Canton, Jon Peters, Peter Guber; Director, Allan Arkush; Screenplay, Harold Ramis, Peter Torokvei; Based on Characters Created by Brian Doyle-Murray, & Harold Ramis & Douglas Kenney; Photography, Harry Stradling; Designer, William F. Matthews; Editor, Bernard Gribble; Music, Ira Newborn; Costumes, May Routh; Casting, Glenn Daniels; Production Manager, Michael S. Glick; Assistant Director, Marty P. Ewing; Visual Effects, Michael Owens; Art Director, Joseph P. Lucky; Set Decorator, Catherine Mann; Set Designers, Carroll B. Johnston, Dawn Snyder; Sound, Gene S. Cantamessa; Special Effects, Michael Lantieri, Donald Elliott; Stunts, James M. Halty; Choreography, Jaime Rogers; Orchestration, Don Nemitz; Songs by various artists; Soundtrack on CBS Records; Dolby Stereo; Technicolor; Rated PG; 9 minutes; July release. CAST: Jackie Mason (Jack Hartounian), Robe Stack (Chandler Young), Dyan Cannon (Elizabeth Pearce), Dina Me rill (Cynthia Young), Jonathan Silverman (Harry), Brian McNama (Todd Young), Marsha Warfield (Rayette Tyler), Paul Bartel (Jam son), Jessica Lundy (Kate Hartounian), Chynna Phillips (Mif Young), Randy Quaid (Peter Blunt), Chevy Chase (Ty Webb), Da Aykroyd (Capt. Tom Everett), Tony Mockus (Pierpont), Pepe Serr (Carlos), Michael J. Howard (Tim), Bibi Osterwald (Mrs. Pierpont Don Draper (Club Manager), Ted Hartley (Club Member) Ria Guilia (Martha), Frank Welker (Gopher Vocals), Andre "Rosey Brown, Ca los Cervantes, Dennis Bowen, Mark Christopher Lawrence, Kenn D'Aguila (Construction Workers), Sid Conrad, Ben Hartigan, Joh MacBride (Naked Men), Diana James, Trish Ramish, Mary Stavi Tamara Steffan (Bar Girls)

HOME REMEDY (Kino International) Producer, Kathie Hersc Director/Screenplay, Maggie Greenwald; Executive Producer, Rog L. Fidler; Music, Steve Katz; Photography, Thomas H. Jewett; Edito Pamela Scott Arnold; Designer, Robert P. Kracik; Costumes, Rebecc Collins; Sound Editors, Beth Sterner, Julie Hall, Randle Akerso Color; Not rated; 91 minutes; July release. CAST: Seth Barrish (Rich Rosenbaum), Maxine Albert (Nancy Smith), Richard Kidney (F Smith), David Feinman (Moshe), John Tsakonas (Donnie), Ale (Mary), Cynde Kahn (Bambi)

RENTED LIPS (Cineworld) Producer, Mort Engelberg; Executi Producer, Martin Mull; Line Producer, Mel Howard; Director, Robe Downey; Screenplay, Martin Mull; Photography, Robert D. Yeoma Editors, Christopher Greenbury, Brian Berdan, Jay Ignaszewski; De signer, George Costello; Costumes, Lisa Jensen; Sound, David Browr low; Assistant Director, Anthony Brand; Associate Producer, Chris opher Greenbury; Casting, Nina Axelrod; A Vista Organization pre sentation; Ultra-Stereo; Color; Rated R; 80 minutes; July release CAST: Martin Mull (Archie Powell), Dick Shawn (Charlie Slater Jennifer Tilly (Mona Lisa), Edy Williams (Heather Darling), Robe Downey Jr. (Wolf Dangler), June Lockhart (Archie's Mother), Ker neth Mars (Rev. Farrell), Shelley Berman (Bill Slotnik), Mel Welle (Milo), Jack Riley (Herb), Pat McCormick (Winky), Eileen Brenna (Hotel Desk Clerk), Michael Horse (Bobby Leaping Mouse), Tony Cc (Tyrell), Eric Bruskotter, Karl Bruskotter (Goons)

Chevy Chase, Jackie Mason, Dan Aykroyd in "Caddyshack II" ***(Warner Bros.)***

Martin Mull in "Rented Lips"
(CineWorld)

Jason Beghe with Ella in "Monkey Shines" *(Orion)*

Dick Van Patten, Tami Erin in "The New Adventures of Pippi Longstocking" *(Columbia)*

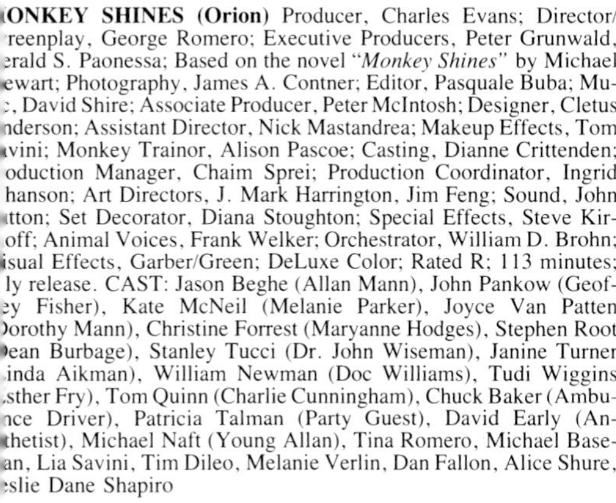

IONKEY SHINES (Orion) Producer, Charles Evans; Director/ reenplay, George Romero; Executive Producers, Peter Grunwald, erald S. Paonessa; Based on the novel *"Monkey Shines"* by Michael ewart; Photography, James A. Contner; Editor, Pasquale Buba; Mu- :, David Shire; Associate Producer, Peter McIntosh; Designer, Cletus nderson; Assistant Director, Nick Mastandrea; Makeup Effects, Tom ıvini; Monkey Trainor, Alison Pascoe; Casting, Dianne Crittenden; oduction Manager, Chaim Sprei; Production Coordinator, Ingrid hanson; Art Directors, J. Mark Harrington, Jim Feng; Sound, John ıtton; Set Decorator, Diana Stoughton; Special Effects, Steve Kir- off; Animal Voices, Frank Welker; Orchestrator, William D. Brohn; isual Effects, Garber/Green; DeLuxe Color; Rated R; 113 minutes; ly release. CAST: Jason Beghe (Allan Mann), John Pankow (Geof- ey Fisher), Kate McNeil (Melanie Parker), Joyce Van Patten)orothy Mann), Christine Forrest (Maryanne Hodges), Stephen Root)ean Burbage), Stanley Tucci (Dr. John Wiseman), Janine Turner .inda Aikman), William Newman (Doc Williams), Tudi Wiggins .sther Fry), Tom Quinn (Charlie Cunningham), Chuck Baker (Ambu- nce Driver), Patricia Talman (Party Guest), David Early (An- ıthetist), Michael Naft (Young Allan), Tina Romero, Michael Base- an, Lia Savini, Tim Dileo, Melanie Verlin, Dan Fallon, Alice Shure, eslie Dane Shapiro

HE REJUVENATOR, aka *Rejuvenatrix* (SVS Films) Producer, even Mackler; Director, Brian Thomas Jones; Screenplay, Simon uchtern, Brian Thomas Jones; Story, Simon Nuchtern; Line Pro- ıcer, Robert Zimmerman; Photography, James McCalmont; Editor, ian O'Hara; Music, Larry Juris; Sound, Pawel Wdowczak, Mark 'eingarten; Designer, Susan Bolles; Make-up Effects, Edward ench; Assistant Director, Denis Hann; Casting, Lisa Gladstone; A wel Production; Technicolor; Rated R; 86 minutes; July release. AST: Vivian Lanko (Elizabeth Warren/Monster), John MacKay (Dr. regory Ashton), James Hogue (Wilhelm), Katell Pleven (Dr. Stella one), Marcus Powell (Dr. Germaine), Jessica Dublin (Ruth Warren), oy MacArthur (Hunter), Louis F. Homyak (Tony), Poison Dollys hemselves)

HE NEW ADVENTURES OF PIPPI LONGSTOCKING :olumbia) Producers, Gary Mehlman, Walter Moshay; Director/ reenplay, Ken Annakin; Photography, Roland "Ozzie" Smith; De- gner, Jack Senter; Costumes, Jacqueline Saint Anne; Co-Producer, vensk Filmindustri; Executive Producer, Mishaal Kamal Adham; litor, Ken Zemke; Casting, Garrison True; Music, Misha Segal; ongs, Harriet Schock, Misha Segal; Co-Producer, Ken Annakin; ssociate Producer/Production Manager, Robin Clark; Assistant Di- ctors, Tom Connors, James Turley; Art Director, Stephen M. Berger; et Decorator, Frederick C. Weiler; Set Designer, Chris Senter; Sound, avid Kelson; Choreographer, Nancy Gergory; Special Effects, ichard Parker, Richard Huggins; Production Coordinator, Lorna eal; Stunts, Joe Gilbride; Dolby Stereo; Rated G; 100 minutes; July lease. CAST: Tami Erin (Pippi), David Seaman, Jr. (Tommy), Cory row (Annika), Eileen Brennan (Miss Bannister), Dennis Dugan (Mr. ettigren), Dianne Hull (Mrs. Settigren), George Di Cenzo (Mr. Black- ırt), J. D. Dickinson (Rype), Chub Bailly (Rancid), Dick Van Patten ilue Man), John Schuck (Capt. Efraim), Branscombe Richmond ridolf), Evan Adam (Freckled Face Boy), Fay Masterson (Head irl), Romy Mehlman (Lisa), Geoffrey Seaman (Billy), Bridget Ann rno (Chrissy), Christopher Broughton (Manuel), Carole Kean (Miss esserschmidt), Leila Hee Olsen (Miss Ward), Clark Neiderjohn ake), Louis Seeger Crume (Fire Chief), Joe Gilbride (Horseman), Jim rimshaw (Police Chief), Joseph John Kutzo, Jr. (Janitor), Russ 'heeler (Ice Cream Vendor), Gail Klicman (Townswoman)

THE EXPENDABLES (Concorde) Producers, Anna Roth, Christopher Santiago; Director, Cirio H. Santiago; Screenplay, Phillip Alderton; Photography, Ricardo Remias; Editor, Edgar Viner; a Premiere Prods. Intl. production; Color; Rated R; 95 minutes; July release. CAST: Anthony Finetti (Capt. Rosello), Peter Nelson (Sterling), Loren Haynes (Lord), Kevin Duffis (Jackson), William Steis (Col. Ridamann), Vic Diaz (Col. Tran Um Phi), David Light (Cabrini), Leah Navarro (Phu Ling), Janet Price, Jeff Griffith, Jim Moss

THE RESCUE (Touchstone/Buena Vista) Producer, Laura Ziskin; Director, Ferdinand Fairfax; Screenplay/Co-Producers, Jim Thomas, John Thomas; Photography, Russell Boyd; Designer, Maurice Cain; Editors, David Holden, Carroll Timothy O'Meara; Supervising Producers, Barrie M. Osborne, Barrie M. Melrose; Costumes, Mary Malin; Casting, Mary Gail Artz; Music, Bruce Broughton; Production Manager, Margaret Hilliard; Assistant Director, Mark Egerton; Art Directors, Robin Tarsnane, Dan Hennah; Set Decorator, Thomas L. Roysden; Orchestrator, Mark McKenzie; Sound, Graham Morris; Stunts, Bill Erickson, Peter Bell; Special Effects, Nick Allder, Terry Schubert; In association with Silver Screen Partners III; Dolby Stereo; Color; Rated PG; 98 minutes; August release. CAST: Kevin Dillon (J. J. Merrill), Christina Harnos (Adrian Phillips), Marc Price (Max Rothman), Ned Vaughn (Shawn Howard), Ian Giatti (Bobby Howard), Charles Haid (Commander Howard), Edward Albert (Commander Merrill), Timothy Carhart (Lt. Phillips), Michael Gates Phenicie (Wicks), Mel Wong (Kim Song), James Cromwell (Admiral Rothman), Ellen Barber (Virginia Phillips), Anne E. Curry (Sybil Howard), Joyce Reehling (Vella Rothman), Lorry Goldman (Secretary Gates), Leon Russom (Capt. Miller), Shim Sung Sool (Instructor), Commancer Tom Nelson (Capt. Stillman), Herbert Wong (Riverman), Rocky Wing Cheung Ho (Cell Guard), Ock Youn Chang (Commandant), Stephen Ng, Trevor Sai Loue, Pak Kun Tang, No Tran, Seong Hee Lee

SATURDAY THE 14TH STRIKES BACK (Concorde) Producer, Julie Corman; Director/Screenplay, Howard R. Cohen; Photography, Levie Isaacks; Music, Parmer Fuller; Editor, Bernard Caputo; Associate Producer, Lynn Whitney; Foto-Kem color; Rated PG; 78 minutes; August release. CAST: Jason Presson (Eddie Baxter), Ray Walston (Gramps), Avery Schreiber (Frank), Patty McCormack (Kate), Julianne McNamara (Linda), Rhonda Aldrich (Alice), Daniel Will-Harris (Bert), Pamela Stonebrook (Charlene), Joseph Ruskin, Leo V. Gordon, Michael Berryman, Phil Leeds, Tommy Hall

Ian Giatti, Marc Price, Shawn Howard, Christina Harnos in "The Rescue" *(Touchstone/Buena Vista)*

Jeff Goldblum, Peter Falk, Cyndi Lauper in "Vibes" ***(Columbia)***

Robert Englund, Tuesday Knight in "Nightmare 4. . . ." ***(New Line)***

VIBES (Columbia) Producers, Deborah Blum, Tony Ganz; Director, Ken Kwapis; Screenplay, Lowell Ganz, Babaloo Mandel; Story, Deborah Blum, Lowell Ganz, Babaloo Mandel; Executive Producer, Ron Howard; Photography, John Bailey; Designer, Richard Sawyer; Costumes, Ruth Myers; Editor, Carol Littleton; Visual Effects, Richard Edlund; Casting, Carrie Frazier, Shani Ginsburg; Co-Producer/Production Manager, Ray Hartwick; Associate Producers, Kate Long, David Wolff; Music, James Horner; Assistant Director, Alan Cutiss; Sound, Richard Bryce Goodman; Art Director, Gregory Pickrell; Set Decorator, George Nelson; Set Designer, David Klassen; Special Effects, Allen Hall, Gary Karas; Stunts, John Branagan; Choreographer, Miranda Garrison; Production Coordinator, Shari Leibowitz; Visual Effects, George Jenson; An Imagine Entertainment Production; *"I've Got a Hole in My Heart"* by Richard Orange/Vocal, Cyndi Lauper, and songs by various artists; Dolby Stereo; DeLuxe Color; Rated PG; 99 minutes; August release. CAST: Jeff Goldblum (Nick Deezy), Cyndi Lauper (Sylvia Pickel), Peter Falk (Harry Buscafusco), Karen Akers (Hilary), Bill McCutcheon (Mr. Van Der Meer), Julian Sands (Dr. Harrison Steele), Googy Gress (Ingo Swedlin), Ramon Bieri (Eli Diamond), Michael Lerner (Burt Wilder), Hecules Vilchez (Juan), Ray Stoddard (Dr. Scott), Harvey J. Goldenberg (Dr. Scott), Tom Henschel (Lyle), Susan Bugg (Dr. Silver), Rodney Kageyama (Dr. Harmon), Van Dyke Parks (Dr. Weiner), Steven Scott (Dr. Thompson), Joseph V. Perry (Dave), Park Overall (Jane), John Kapelos (Eugene), Bruce MacVittie (Tony), Don "Bubba" Bexley (Lou), Steve Buscemi (Fred), Jennifer Balgobin (Gloria), Ronald G. Joseph (Carl), Aharon Ipale (Alejandro De La Vivar), Elizabeth Pena (Consuela), Darryl Henriques (Ricardo)

MAC AND ME (Orion) Producer, R. J. Louis; Director, Stewart Raffill; Screenplay, Stewart Raffill, Steve Feke; Executive Producer, Mark Damon, William B. Kerr; Photography, Nick McLean; Designer, W. Stewart Campbell; Editor, Tom Walls; Music, Alan Silvestri; Casting, Caro Jones; Production Managers, Lester Wm. Berke, William B. Kerr; Assistant Director, Clifford C. Coleman; Alien EFX, Martin J. Becker; Associate Editor, John Rosenberg; Alien Designers, Ruben Aquino, Christopher Swift; Choreographer, Marla Blakey; Stunts, Fernando Celis; Sound, Darren Knight; Set Decorator, John Anderson; Special Effects, Dennis Dion, Chris Burton; Orchestrations, James Campbell; Production Coordinators, Joyce Warren, Penny Jo Davis; Visual Effects, Sid Dutton; Alien makeup, Margaret Beserra, Edouard Henriques III; *"Down to Earth"* by Allee Willis & Danny Sembello/Vocals, Ashford & Simpson, and songs by Larry Hart, Gre Allen, Jeff Barry, Marcy Levy, Marti Sharron, Glen Ballard, Ala Silvestri, Bobby Caldwell, and others; Color; Rated PG; 99 minutes August release. CAST: Christine Ebersole (Janet), Jonathan War (Michael), Katrina Caspary (Courtney), Lauren Stanley (Debbie), Jad Calegory (Eric), Vinnie Torrente (Mitford), Martin West (Wickett) Ivan Jorge Rado (Zimmerman), Danny Cooksey (Jack Jr.), Laur Waterbury (Linda), Jack Eiseman (Cab Driver), Barbara Allyne Bennet, Richard Bravo, Gary Brockette, Sherri Stone Butler, Joseph Chapman, Sheila Chambers, Alyce Coleman, John Curtin, Andrew Divoff James C. Duke, Bud Ekins, Buck Flower, Ray Forchion, Tom Fuccello, Ernie Fuentes, Michael Geary, Heather Green, J. D. Hall, Roge Hampton, Dixon Harding, Christopher Law, Mayah McCoy, Elen Moure, Buckley Norris, Jack Ong, J. Jay Saunders

A NIGHTMARE ON ELM STREET 4: THE DREAM MASTEI (New Line Cinema) Producers, Robert Shaye, Rachel Talalay; Director, Renny Harlin; Screenplay, Brian Helgeland, Scott Pierce; Story William Kotzwinkle, Brian Helgeland; Executive Producers, Sar Risher, Stephen Diener; Photography, Steven Fierberg; Designers Mick Strawn, C. J. Strawn; Editors, Michael N. Knue, Chuck Weiss Music, Craig Safan; Makeup Effects, Steve Johnson, Magical Medi Industries Inc., Screaming Mad George, R. Christopher Biggs; Fredd Krueger Makeup, Kevin Yagher; Mechanical Effects, Image Engineering; Visual Effects, Dream Quest Images; Casting, Annette Benson; Associate Producer/Production Manager, Karen Koch; Productio Executive, Michael DeLuca; Assistant Director, Mary Ellen Woods Art Director, Thomas A. O'Conor; Costumes, Audrey M. Bansmer Production Supervisor, Joe Fineman; Music Supervisor, Kevin Benson, Dolby Stereo; Metrocolor; Rated R; 93 minutes; August release CAST: Robert Englund (Freddy Krueger), Rodney Eastman (Joey) Danny Hassel (Danny), Andras Jones (Rick), Tuesday Knight (Kristen), Toy Newkirk (Sheila), Ken Sagoes (Kincaid), Brooke Theis (Debbie), Lisa Wilcox (Alice), Brooke Bundy (Mother), Jeff Levin (Paramedic), Nicolas Mele (Johnson), Hope Marie Carlton (Waterbe Bunny)

THE WASH (Skouras) Producer, Calvin Skaggs; Director, Michae Toshiyuki Uno; Screenplay, Philip Kan Gotanda; Photography, Wal Lloyd; Music, John Morris; Editor, Jay Freund; Designer, David Wasco; Art Director, Robert Bovill; Costumes, Lydia Tanji; Sound Agamennon Andrianos; Production Manager, Carl Clifford; Assistan

Lauren Stanley, Jade Calegory, Tina Caspary, Jonathan Ward in "Mac and Me" ***(Orion)***

Mako, Nobu McCarthy in "The Wash" ***(Skouras)***

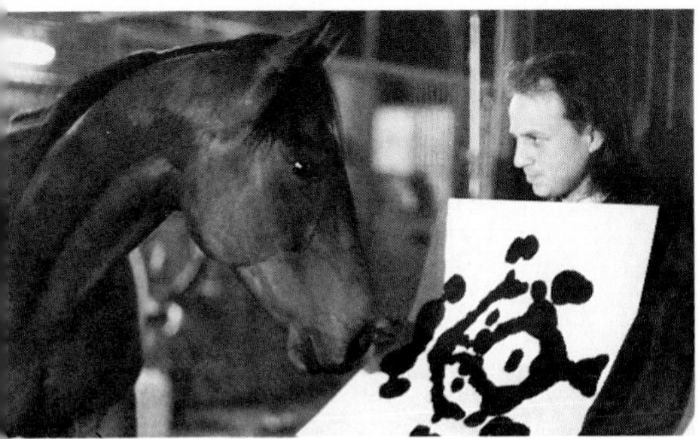

Don, Bon Goldthwait in "Hot to Trot" *(Warner Bros.)*

Sam Bottoms, Renee Coleman in "After School" *(Moviestore)*

rector, Michael Kitchens; Production Coordinator, Lisa Tesone; sting, Donna Newton, Judy Courtney, Emily Schweber, Debra tell; Set Decorator, Sandy Wasco; Color; Not rated; 93 minutes; gust release. CAST: Mako (Nobu), Nobu McCarthy (Masi), Patti sutake (Marsha), Marion Yue (Judy), Sab Shimono (Sadao), Shizu- Hoshi (Kiyoko), Danny Kamekona (Blackie), Takayo Fischer niyo), Ken Narasaki (Brad), Jim Hirobayashi (Gardener), Peter zsimmons (Jimmy), Clay McSwain/Jason Wong (Timothy), Dennis kamoto (Singing Businessman), Kayoko Kuchiishi (Piano Player), emasa Shimizu (Man in Bar), Rev. Akinori Imai (Rev. Hamanako)

)T TO TROT (Warner Bros.) Producer, Steve Tisch; Director, chael Dinner; Story, Stephen Neigher, Hugo Gilbert; Screenplay, phen Neigher, Hugo Gilbert, Charlie Peters; Photography, Victor mper; Designer, William Matthews; Editor, Frank Morriss; Co- ducer, Wendy Finerman; Music, Danny Elfman; Production Mana- r, Phil Rawlins; Assistant Director, Joseph Moore; Casting, Melissa off; Set Decorator, Mickey S. Michaels; Sound, Glen Anderson; nts, Mike McGaughy; Special Effects, Albert Delago; Orchestra- ns, Steve Bartek; Songs by various artists; Dolby Stereo; Tech- olor; Rated PG; 83 minutes; August release. CAST: Bob Goldthwait ed P. Chaney), Dabney Coleman (Walter Sawyer), John Candy oice of "Don"), Virginia Madsen (Allison Rowe), Cindy Pickett ictoria Peyton), Jim Metzler (Boyd Osborne), Tim Kazurinsky eonard), Santos Morales (Carlos), Barbara Whinnery (Denise), Gar- Kluger (Pomeroy), Mary Gross (Ms. French), Liz Torres (Bea), ko Marcellino (Marvin), Deana Oliver (Lorraine), Harry Caesar ideon Cole), Allen Williams (Ted Braithwaite), Lonny Price ank), Angel Salazar (Snake), Henry "Hank" Levy (Marv), John sbon Wood (Mike), Jack Whitaker (Himself), Tom Wolski (Michael urphy), Kevin Furlong (Dennis Riday), Don (Himself), Chino "Fats" lliams

AVESTARR (Taurus Entertainment) Producer, Lou Scheimer; rector, Tom Tataranowicz; Screenplay, Bob Forward, Steve Hayes; usic, Frank W. Becker; Camera Supervisor, F. T. Ziegler; Editor, dmilla Saskova; Art Director, John Grusd; Special Effects Anima- n, Brett Hisey; A Filmation Production; Animated; Dolby Stereo; I Color; Rated PG; 91 minutes; August release. VOICE CAST: arlie Adler, Susan Blu, Pat Fraley, Ed Gilbert, Alan Oppenheimer

.OODY POM POMS, aka *Cheerleader Camp* (Atlantic Releasing) oducers, Jeffrey Prettyman, John Quinn; Director, John Quinn; reenplay, David Lee Fein, R. L. O'Keefe; Photography, Bryan gland; Music, Murielle Hodler-Hamilton, Joel Hamilton; Editor, frey Reiner; Production Designer, Keith Barrett; Costumes, Gini amer; Assistant Director, Matt Hinkley; Casting, Geno Havers, arcia Karr; a Quinn/Prettyman production in association with Prism tertainment and Daiei Co. Ltd.; Foto-Kem color; Rated R; 88 nutes; August release. CAST: Betsy Russell (Alison Wentworth), if Garrett (Brent Hoover), Lucinda Dickey (Cory Foster), Lorie iffin (Bonnie Reed), Buck Flower (Pop), Travis McKenna (Timmy oser), Teri Weigel (Pam Bently), Rebecca Ferratti (Theresa Salazar), ckie Benson (Miss Tipton), Jeff Prettyman, Krista Pflanzer, Craig igian, William Johnson Sr., Kathryn Litton

FTER SCHOOL, aka *Private Tutor* (Moviestore Entertainment) oducer, Hugh Parks; Director, William Olsen; Co-Producer, William sen; Associate Producer, Joseph Tankersley; Screenplay, Hugh rks, John Linde, Rod McBrien, John Tankersley; Photography, istin McKinney; Editor, John David Allen; Music, David C. Wil- ms; Casting, Donna DeSeta; Production Manager, Jan Thompson; Art Director, David Meo; Assistant Director, Gus Holzer; Sound, Lee Strosnider; Costumes, Lucy Oleny; Stunts, Artie Malesci; Special Effects, Ray Bivens; Production Coordinator, Robin Rhyne: A Quest Studios Production; *"The Magic of Love"* / *"Somewhere in Your Heart"* / *"Embraced in a Dream"* by David C. Williams & Glen Reifsteck/ Vocals, Laura Martier; TVC Color; Rated R; 89 minutes; September release. CAST: Sam Bottoms (Father Michael McCarren), Renee Coleman (September Johnson), Edward Binns (Monsignor Frank Barrett), Dick Cavett (Himself), Page Hannah (Annie), Don Harvey (Nathan), Robert Lansing (C. A. Thomas), Holt McCallany (Jay), John Perkins (Cardinal Gurney), Carol Surface (Coach), Tom Nowicki, Phil Moore, Robert Jacoby (Basketball Players), Jill Miller (Bookstore Clerk), Virginia Light (Ice Cream Lady), Clair Jordan (Aerobics Coach), Wilbur Fitzgerald (Housekeeper), Tony Shepard (Guard), Stephen Rahn (Jeffrey); *Early Man Segment:* James Farkas, Catherine Williams, Jacqueline Rodriguez, Jon Jacobs, Pam West, Melanie Adams, Jennifer Helbraun, Tony Cucci, Alison Woodward, Leo Besstette, Michael Lassiter, Dale Greifenstein, Dale Greifenstein, Michael Lassiter, Joseph Tate, Tamara Griffith, Joye McQuerter, Reggie Jacobi, Grant Garcia, Michael Naishtut, Kelly Cecil, Sherrie Rose, Gayle Logan, Jack Malone, Bill Christie, Jim Thomas, Byron Radu, Jim Rios, Mimi Zatuchni, Jan Shea, Rae Dolores, Dee Ennis, Russtina Fell

THE BEAST (Columbia) Producer, John Fiedler; Director, Kevin Reynolds; Screenplay, William Mastrosimone; Based on the play *"Nanawatai"* by William Mastrosimone; Executive Producers, Gil Friesen, Dale Pollock; Photography, Douglas Milsome; Music, Mark Isham; Art Director, Richard James; Costumes, Rochelle Zaltzman; Casting, Ilene Starger; Associate Producer/Production Manager, Christopher Dalton; Assistant Director, Robert Roe; Designer, Kuli Sander; Set Decorators, Doron Efrat, Shimon Alon; Sound, David Crozier; Editor, Peter Boyle; Special Effects, Peter Hutchinson; An A&M Films Production; Stunts, Paul Weston; *"Streetcar Headed East"* by Victor Tsoi/Performance, Kino; Soundtrack on A&M Records; Dolby Stereo; Rated R; 109 minutes; September release. CAST: George Dzundza (Daskal), Jason Patric (Koverchenko), Steven Bauer (Taj), Stephen Baldwin (Golikov), Don Harvey (Kaminski), Kabir Bedi (Akbar), Erick Avari (Samad), Haim Gerafi (Moustafa), Shosh Marciano (Sherina), Itzhak Babi Ne'eman (Iskandar), Moshe Vapnik (Hasan), Claude Aviram (Sadique), Victor Ken (Ali), Avi Keedar (Noor), Avi Gil-Or (Khahzaman), Roberto Pollak (Shahzaman), Beni Baruchin (Afzal), David Sherrill, Osnat Mor, Ramy Heuberger

Steven Bauer, Jason Patric in "The Beast" **(Columbia)**

Andrew McCarthy, Matt Dillon in "Kansas" ***(Trans World)***

Cassandra Peterson in "Elvira . . ." ***(New World Pictures)***

KANSAS (Trans World Entertainment) Producer, George Litto; Director, David Stevens; Screenplay, Spencer Eastman; Music, Pino Donnagio; Conductor, Natale Massara; Photography, David Eggby; Editor, Robert Barrere; Executive Producers, Moshe Diamant, Chris Chesser; Associate Producer, Vic Ramos; Production Manager, Joseph M. Ellis; Mel A. Bishop; Assistant Directors, Michael Kusley, Herb Gains; Production Executives, Paul Mason, Helen Sarlui-Tucker; Sound, Jacob Goldstein; Costumes, Nancy G. Fox; Set Decorator, Stewart K. McGuire; Stunts, Wally Crowder; Special Effects, Tom Sindicich; Production Coordinator, Suzy Beugen; Songs by various artists; Panavision; Dolby Stereo; DeLuxe Color; Rated R; 106 minutes; September release. CAST: Matt Dillon (Doyle Kennedy), Andrew McCarthy (Wade Corey), Leslie Hope (Lori Bayles), Alan Toy (Nordquist), Andy Romano, (Fleener) Brent Jennings (Buckshot), Brynn Thayer (Connie), Kyra Sedgwick (Prostitute Drifter), Harry Northup (Governor), Clint Allen (Ted), Arlen Dean Snyder (George Bayles), Craig Benton (Casson), T. Max Graham (Mr. Kennedy), Mimi Wickliff (Mrs. Bayles), Ken Boehr (Ferson), Joseph R. Scrivo (Rodriguez), Brett Pearson (Alvin), Roger Richman (Ellwood), Rusty Howard (Swift), James Lovelett, Louis Giambalvo, James Lea Raupp, John Lansing, Gale Mayron, Annie Kellogg

BIG TIME (Island Visual Arts) Producer, Luc Roeg; Director, Chris Blum; Executive Producer, Chris Blackwell; Line Producer/Assistant Director, Lucy Phillips; Photography, Daniel Hainey; Editor, Glenn Schantlebury; Associate Producer, Ellen Smith; Co-Associate Producer, Catherine Peacock-Longo; Production Manager, Liz Gazzano; Production Coordinator, Connie Lemasson; Art Director, Sterling Storm; Costumes, Hank Ford; Concert/Documentary; Dolby Stereo; Color; Rated PG; 90 minutes; September release. CAST: Tom Waits, Michael Blair, Ralph Carney, Greg Cohen, Marc Ribot, Willy Schwarz

DAFFY DUCK'S QUACKBUSTERS (Warner Bros.) Producer, Steven S. Greene; Co-Producer, Kathleen Helppie-Shipley; Director/Story, Greg Ford, Terry Lennon; Sequence Directors, Chuck Jones, Friz Freleng, Robert McKimson; Photography, Nick Vasu Inc.; Music, Carl Stalling, Milt Franklyn, Bill Lava; Animators, Brenda Banks, Nancy Beiman, Daniel Haskett, Mark Kausler, Norm McCabe, Rebecca Rees, Darrell Van Citters, Frans Vischer; Designer, Robert Givens; Technicolor; Rated G; 80 minutes; September release. VOICE CAST: Mel Blanc, Mel Torme, Roy Firestone, B. J. Ward

Tom Waits in "Big Time" ***(Island Visual Arts)***

DARK BEFORE DAWN (PSM Entertainment) Producer, Ben Mi ler; Director, Robert Totten; Screenplay, Reparata Mazzola; Photogra phy, Steve M. McWilliams; Executive Producer, E. K. Gaylord 2d Editors, Ron Hanthaner, Tom Boutross; Music, Ken Sutherland; Asso ciate Producer, Rex Linn; Casting, Becky Grantham; An E. K. Gaylor 2d presentation of a Lazy "E" production in association with Kingp Prods.; Panavision; Color; Rated PG-13; 95 minutes; September re lease. CAST: Sonny Gibson (Jeff Parker), Doug McClure (Jame Kirkland), Reparata Mazzola (Jessica Stanton), Ben Johnson (Sheriff Billy Drago (Cabalistas Leader), Rance Howard (Glen Logan), Morga Woodward (J. B. Watson), Buck Henry (Charlie Stevens), Paul New som (Roger Crandall), Jeff Osterhage (Andy Peterson), Red Steaga (Hal Porter), John L. Martin (Sen. Henry Vance), Rex Linn (Dc Haleys)

DEFENSE PLAY (Trans World Entertainment) Producer, Wo Schmidt; Director, Monte Markham; Screenplay, Aubrey Solomor Steven Greenberg; Story, Wolf Schmidt, Stan Krantman; Photography Timothy Galfas; Editor/Associate Producer, James Ruxin; Music Arthur B. Rubinstein; Designer, Petko Kadiev; Sound, Peter Chaiki Special Effects, Pete Slagle; Assistant Director, Bradley M. Gros Casting, Carol Dudley; A Kodiak Films presentation; Ultra-Stere Foto-Kem color; Rated PG; 93 minutes; September release. CAST David Oliver (Scott Denton), Susan Ursitti (Karen Vandemeer), Mont Markham (Col. Mark Denton), Eric Gilliom (Starkey), William Frank father (Gen. Philips), Jamie McMurray (Norm Beltzer), Jack Esforme (Eddie Dietz), Tom Rosqui (Chief Gill), Milos Kirek (Anton), Patc Mackenzie (Ann Denton), Terrance Cooper (Prof. James Vandemeer) Rutanya Alda (Mrs. Vandemeer)

ELVIRA, MISTRESS OF THE DARK (New World) Producers Eric Gardner, Mark Pierson; Director, James Signorelli; Screenplay Sam Egan, John Paragon, Cassandra Peterson; Executive Produce Michael Rachmil; Supervising Producer, Joel Thurm; Music, Jame Campbell; Editor, Battle Davis; Costumes, Betsy Heimann; Designe John DeCuir, Jr.; Photography, Hanania Baer; Casting, Denni Erdman; Production Manager, Cleve Landsberg; Assistant Directo Paul Moen; Additional Photography, Matthew Leonettil; Productio Coordinator, Laura Hoffman; Sound, William Nelson; Set Decorato Bruce A. Gibeson; Set Designer, Beverli Eagan; Special Effects, Der nis Dion; Makeup Effects, Doug Beswick, Steve Laporte; Stunts Monty Cox; Choreographer, Dona Davis-Clarke; Also presented b NBC Productions; *"I Put a Spell On You"* by Jay Hawkins/ Vocal Joanna St. Claire, *"Elvira's Theme"* by Mark Whitney Pierson, an songs by various other artists; Dolby Stereo; CFI Color; Rated PG-13 96 minutes; September release. CAST: Elvira (Cassandra Peterson) Phil Rubenstein (Director), Larry Flash Jenkins (Technical Director) Damita Jo Freeman (Associate Producer), Tress Mac Neille (Ancho Woman), Edwina Morre (Hairdresser), Mario Celario (Rudy), Le McLaughlin (Earl Hooter), Bill Swearingen (Cameraman), Charle Woolf (Manny), William Dance (Messenger), William Cort (Lawye Game Show Host), Sharon Hays (Game Show Girl), Bill Cable (Cop) John Paragon (Gas Station Attendant), Joseph Arias (Hitchhiker), Edi McClurg (Chastity Pariah), Kris Kamm (Randy), Scott Morris (Sean) Ira Heiden (Bo), Bill Morey (Mr. Rivers), Pat Crawford Brown (Mrs Meeker), William Duell (Mr. Meeker), Ellen Dunning (Robin Meek er), Jeff Conaway (Travis), Frank Collison (Billy), Daniel Greene (Bo Redding), Susan Kellermann (Patty), Lynn Stewart (Bartender), Dery Carroll (Charlie), Marie Sullivan (Mrs. Morissey), W. Morgan Shep pard (Vincent Talbot), Jack Fletcher (Mr. Bigelow), Gonk (Himself) Robert Benedetti (Calvin Cobb), Kurt Fuller (Mr. Glotter), Kate Brow (Anita), Hugh Gillin (Sheriff), Eve Smith (Little Old Lady), Raleig Bond (Minister)

Alan King, Billy Crystal, JoBeth Williams in "Memories of Me" ***(MGM)***

Beau Bridges, Julianne Phillips, Ron Leibman in "Seven Hours to Judgment" ***(Trans World)***

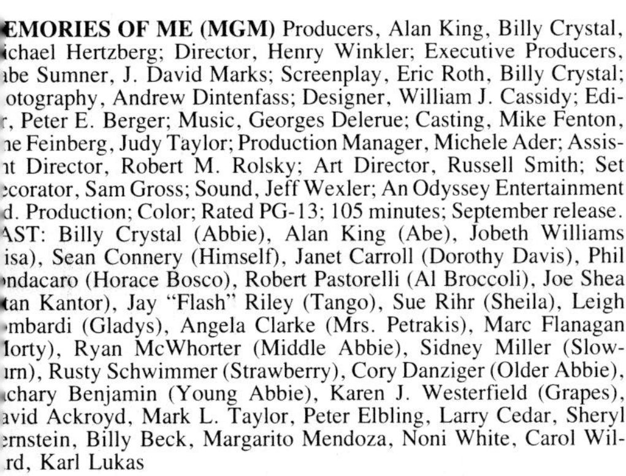

EMORIES OF ME (MGM) Producers, Alan King, Billy Crystal, ichael Hertzberg; Director, Henry Winkler; Executive Producers, ibe Sumner, J. David Marks; Screenplay, Eric Roth, Billy Crystal; otography, Andrew Dintenfass; Designer, William J. Cassidy; Edi-r, Peter E. Berger; Music, Georges Delerue; Casting, Mike Fenton, ne Feinberg, Judy Taylor; Production Manager, Michele Ader; Assis-nt Director, Robert M. Rolsky; Art Director, Russell Smith; Set ecorator, Sam Gross; Sound, Jeff Wexler; An Odyssey Entertainment d. Production; Color; Rated PG-13; 105 minutes; September release. AST: Billy Crystal (Abbie), Alan King (Abe), Jobeth Williams isa), Sean Connery (Himself), Janet Carroll (Dorothy Davis), Phil ndacaro (Horace Bosco), Robert Pastorelli (Al Broccoli), Joe Shea tan Kantor), Jay "Flash" Riley (Tango), Sue Rihr (Sheila), Leigh mbardi (Gladys), Angela Clarke (Mrs. Petrakis), Marc Flanagan lorty), Ryan McWhorter (Middle Abbie), Sidney Miller (Slow-irn), Rusty Schwimmer (Strawberry), Cory Danziger (Older Abbie), chary Benjamin (Young Abbie), Karen J. Westerfield (Grapes), avid Ackroyd, Mark L. Taylor, Peter Elbling, Larry Cedar, Sheryl ernstein, Billy Beck, Margarito Mendoza, Noni White, Carol Wil-rd, Karl Lukas

IGHT OF THE DEMONS (International Film Marketing) Pro-cer/Screenplay, Joe Augustyn; Director, Kevin Tenney; Executive oducer, Walter Josten; Supervising Producer, Jeff Geoffray; Associ-e Producers, Rene Torres, Patricia Bando Josten; Photography, David ewis; Art Director, Ken Aichele; Editor, Daniel Duncan; Effects akeup, Steve Johnson; Sound, Bo Harwood; Production Supervisor, ckson Harvey; Line Producer, Don Robinson; Production Coordina-r, Holly Crawford; Assistant Director, Kelly Schroeder; Set Decora-r, Sally Nicolau; Costumes, Donna Reynolds; Stunts, John Stewart; rotechnician, Roger George; Animator, Kathy Zielinski; Casting, edra Gabriel; A Meridian Pictures presentation of a Paragon Arts Intl. oduction; Ultra-Stereo; Color; Rated R; 89 minutes; September re-ase. CAST: Linnea Quigley (Suzanne), Cathy Podewell (Judy), Wil-im Gallo (Sal), Hal Havins (Stooge), Mimi Kinkade (Angela), Alvin lexis (Roger), Jill Terashita (Frannie), Helen Barron (Helen), Phillip inzini (Max), Lance Fenton (Jay), Harold Ayer (Old Man), Donnie ffcoat (Billy), Karen Ericson (Mother), Marie Denn (Wife)

EVEN HOURS TO JUDGEMENT (Trans World Entertainment) oducer, Mort Abrahams; Director, Beau Bridges; Screenplay, Walter avis, Elliot Stephens; Executive Producers, Paul Mason, Helen Sar-lui-Tucker; Associate Producer, Alana H. Lambros; Editor, Bill Butler; Designer, Phedon Papamichael; Photography, Hanania Baer; Casting, Alana H. Lambros; Music, John Debney; Production Manager, Mel Bishop; Assistant Director, Newt Arnold; Set Decorator, Geraldine Hofstatter; Production Supervisor, Lisa Yesko; Costumes, Larry Lefler; Production Coordinator, Vicki Wilson; Sound, Jim Pilcher; Stunts, Sandy Gimpel; Special Effects, Darrell D. Prichett; A Sarlui/Diamant Production; "*Whistle While You Work-Out*" by Tom Chase & Steve Rucker/"*March of the Killer Klowns*" by John Massari/"*Sensational Love*" by Douglas Fraser & S. A. Wylmz/Vocal, Victoria Hamilton; Ultra-Stereo; DeLuxe Color; Rated R; 96 minutes; September release. CAST: Beau Bridges (John Eden), Ron Leibman (David Reardon), Julianne Phillips (Lisa Eden), Tiny Ron (Ira), Al Freeman, Jr. (Danny Larwin), Reggie Johnson (Chino), Glen-Michael Jones (Doctor), Chris Garcia (Victor), Shawn Miller (Doowa), Albert Ybarra (Carlos), Tony Lee Troy (Kiki), Nick Granado (Jorges), Sandra Gimpel (Ellen Reardon), Johnny S. B. Willis (Officer Wilton), Harris Smith/Vaughn (Bailiff), John Billingsley (Eddie), Kurt Garfield (Kaplan), Jane Bray (TV Reporter), Katherine Mesney-Hetter (McKay), David Wasman, Laurel Anne White, Tom Hammond, Gayle Brellows, John Aylward, George Catalano

SOME GIRLS (MGM) Producer, Rick Stevenson; Director, Michael Hoffman; Screenplay, Rupert Walters; Executive Producer, Robert Redford; Music, James Newton Howard; Associate Producers, Andy Paterson, Mark Bentley; Editor, David Spiers; Photography, Ueli Steiger; Designer, Eugenio Zanetti; Casting, Lora Kennedy; Production Manager, Mark Bentley; Assistant Director, Andy Paterson; Production Coordinator, Lynn Mallay; Art Director, Peter Paul Raubertas; Set Decorator, Jean-Baptiste Tard; Sound, Patrick Rousseau; Costumes, Nicoletta Massone; Stunts, Jerome Thiberghien; Orchestrations, Brad Dechter; A Wildwood Enterprises Presentation of an Oxford Film Company Production; Songs, Hakan Bjorn & John Utter, Julia Fordham, Ziggy Marley; Dolby Stereo; Rated R; 94 minutes; September release. CAST: Patrick Dempsey (Michael), Jennifer Connelly (Gabriella), Sheila Kelley (Irenka), Lance Edwards (Nick), Lila Kedrova (Granny), Florinda Bolkan (Mrs. D'Arc), Andre Gregory (Mr. D'Arc), Ashley Greenfield (Simone), Jean-Louis Millette (Father Walter), Sanna Vraa (Young Granny), Cedric Noel, John Cuthbert (Porters), Harry Hill (Uncle Danny), Renee Girard (Lady Patient), Claude Prefontaine (Doctor), "Fanny" (Beowulf)

Mimi Kinkade in "Night of Demons"
(Paragon Arts)

Patrick Dempsey, Sheila Kelley, Jennifer Connelly, Ashley Greenfield in "Some Girls" ***(MGM)***

Darlanne Fluegel, James Russo in "Freeway" ***(New World)***

IN DANGEROUS COMPANY (Sandstar) Producers, Ruben Preuss, Robert Newell; Director, Ruben Preuss; Screenplay, Mitch Brown; Co-Producers, John Herman Shaner, Mitch Brown; Photography, James Carter; Editor, W. O. Garrett; Music, Berington Van Campen; Sound, Scott Smith; Designer, Mark Simon; Assistant Director, Matt Hinkley; A Preuss Entertainment Group presentation of a Zuban production; Foto-Kem color; Rated R; 96 minutes; September release. CAST: Cliff DeYoung (Blake), Tracy Scoggins (Evelyn), Steven Keats (Ryerson), Chris Mulkey (Chris), Henry Darrow (Alex Auilar), Catherine Ai (Peggy), Dana Lee (Troung), Michael Shaner (Richie)

FREEWAY (New World) Producers, Peter S. Davis, William Panzer; Director, Francis Delia; Screenplay, Darrell Fetty, Francis Delia; Based on the Novel *"Freeway"* by Deane Barkley; Designer, Douglas Metrov; Music, Joe Delia; Photography, Frank Byers; Editor, Philip J. Sgriccia; Casting, Janet Cunningham; Associate Producer/Production Manager, Steve Beswick; Assistant Directors, Tony Perez, Marty Schwartz; Production Coordinator, Eileen Fields; Art Director, Shane Nelson; Set Decorator, Archie D'Amico; Special Effects, Gary D'Amico; Sound, Brian Bidder; Costumes, B. J. Rogers; Stunts, Mario Roberts, Ron Burke; Color; Rated R; 91 minutes; September release. CAST: Darlanne Fluegel (Sarah "Sunny" Harper), James Russo (Frank Quinn), Billy Drago (Edward Anthony Heller), Richard Belzer (Dr. David Lazarus), Michael Callan (Lt. Boyle), Joey Palese (Det. Gomez), Steve Franken (Lawyer), Brian Kaiser (Morrie), Kenneth Tobey (Monsignor Kavanaugh), Julianne Dallara (Roseanna Rivera), Laurie Foshay (Laura), Gloria Edwards (Nurse Mary), Deem Bristow (TV Interviewer), Gyl Roland (TV Newscaster), Toby Anderson (Bud Clay), Kimberly Hall (Thelma Clay), Robert Lane (Joel Clay), Jesse Shapiro (Jaime Clay), Genevieve Anderson (Baby Clay), Richard Chavez (Ricardo), Ann Shala (Psychiatrist), Alice Ferris (Mrs. Harper), Jeff St. Joseph (Robert Harper), Clint Howard (Ronnie)

GROTESQUE (Concorde) Producers, Mike Lane, Chris Morrell; Director, Joe Tornatore; Screenplay, Mikel Angel; Based on characters and concept by Joe Tornatore; Executive Producers, Maurice Smith, Ray Sterling; Photography, Bill Dickson; Sound, Craig Felburg; Music, Bill Loose, Jack Cookerly; Effects Make-up, John Naulin; Assistant Director/Stunts, Eddie Donno; Associate Producers, Linda Blair, Lincoln Tate; A United Filmmakers Group production; Foto-Ke color; Rated R; 79 minutes; September release. CAST: Linda Bl (Lisa), Tab Hunter (Rod), Donna Wilkes (Kathy), Brad Wils (Scratch), Nels Van Patten (Gibbs), Guy Stockwell (Orville Kruge Sharon Hughes, Michelle Bensoussan, Charles Dierkop, Chuck Mc rell, Lincoln Tate, Luana Patten, Robert Zdar, Billy Frank, Bunki John Goff, Mikel Angel, Stacy Alden, Mike Lane

HEARTBREAK HOTEL (Touchstone/Buena Vista) Produce Lynda Obst, Debra Hill; Director/Screenplay, Chris Columbu Supervising Producer, Stephanie Austin; Photography, Steph Dobson; Designer, John Muto; Editor, Raja Gosnell; Costumes, Nc Haggerty; Music, Georges DeLerue; Casting, Todd M. Thaler; Exec tive Consultant, Jerry Schilling; Associate Producer, Stacey Sh Production Managers, Robin Clark, Timothy Silver; Assistant Dire tor, Mark Radcliffe; Choreographer, Monica Devereux; Art Directo Dan Webster; Set Decorator, Anne Kuljian; Stunts, Joe Gilbric Sound, Donald B. Summer; Special Effects, Randy E. Moore; Metr color; Rated PG-13; 90 minutes; September release. CAST: Dav Keith (Elvis Presley), Tuesday Weld (Marie Wolfe), Charlie Schlat (Johnny Wolfe), Angela Goethals (Pam Wolfe), Jacque Lynn Colt (Rosie Pantangellio), Chris Mulkey (Steve Ayres), Karen Land (Irene), Tudor Sherrard (Paul Quinine), Paul Harkins (Brian Gaste nick), Noel Derecki (Tony Vandelo), Dana Barron (Beth Devereux), Graham Grown (Jerry Schilling), Dennis Letts (Alan Fortas), Steph Lee Davis (George Klein), Blue Deckert (Jones), Michael Costello (D Charles Devereux), John L. Martin (Sheriff Abrams), John Hawk (M.C.), Jerry Haynes (Mr. Hansen), Ruth Sadlier (Aunt Anne), Mo ca Devereux (Monica), Debra Luijtjes (Cheryl), Christine M. Poc (Judy), Diane Robin (Donna), Clark Devereux (Teacher), Mil Mutchler, Cheryl Beckham, Al Dvorin, Hal Ketchum, Urban Kneu per, Joe Gilbride, Brad Gilbride, Tom Morga, Bobby Sargent

BORDER RADIO (International Film Marketing) Producer, Ma cus De Leon; Directors/Screenplay, Allison Anders, Dean Lent, Ku Voss; Additional Dialogue, The Cast; Photography, Dean Lent; Soun Nietzehka Keene; Music, Dave Alvin; Associate Producer, Robe Rosen; A Coyote Films presentation; Black & White; Rated R; 8 minutes; September release. CAST: Chris D. (Jeff), John Doe (Dean Luana Anders (Lu), Chris Shearer (Chris), Dave Alvin (Dave), I Berry (Scenester), Texacala Jones (Babysitter), Devon Anders (D von), Chuck Shepard (Expatriot), Craig Stark, Eddie Flowers, Seba tian Copeland (Thugs), Green On Red (Themselves)

DANGEROUS LOVE (Concorde) Producers, Brad Krevoy, Steve Stabler; Director/Screenplay, Marty Ollstein; Photography, Nichol von Sternberg; Editor, Tony Lanza; Sound, Clifford Glynn; Productic Designer, Michael Clousen; Casting, Lee Daniels; Assistant Directo Matt Hinkley; a Motion Picture Corp. of America production; Colo Rated R; 94 minutes; September release. CAST: Lawrence Monosc (Gabe), Brenda Bakke (Chris), Peter Marc (Jay), Elliott Gould (Rick Anthony Geary (Mickey), Sal Landi, Angelyne, Eloise Broady, Te Austin, Robin Klein, Bernie Pock

SPELLBINDER (MGM) Producers, Joe Wizan, Brian Russell; D rector, Janet Greek; Executive Producers, Howard Baldwin, Richa Cohen; Screenplay, Tracey Torme; Associate Producers, Bob Doubel Tracey Tormey; Photography, Adam Greenberg; Designer, Rodge Maus; Editor, Steve Mirkovich; Casting, Ellen Myer, Sally Stine Music, Basil Poledouris; Co-Producers, Todd Black, Kate Bentor Mickey Borofsky, Steve Berman; Production Manager, Bob Doude Assistant Director, Craig R. West; Set Decorator, Tom Bugenhage Set Designer, Roland Hill; Sound, Joe Kenworthy; Special Effect

Charlie Schlatter, David Keith in "Heartbreak Hotel" (Touchstone)

Rich Rossovich, Timothy Daly in "Spellbinder" ***(MGM)***

t Dalton, Pat Lee, William Klinger; Effects Makeup, Rick Stratton; ıts, Douglas Coleman; An MGM/Indian Neck Entertainment Pre- ation; A Wizan Film Properties, Inc. Production; Color; Rated R; minutes; September release. CAST: Timothy Daly (Jeff Mills), y Preston (Miranda Reed), Rick Rossovich (Derek Clayton), Audra dley (Mrs. White), Anthony Crivello (Aldys), Diana Bellamy ace Woods), Cary-Hiroyuki Tagawa (Lt. Lee), James Louis Wat- s (Tim Weatherly), Kyle Heffner (Herbie Green), M. C. Gainey ock), Sally Kemp (Marilyn DeWitt), Stefan Gierasch (Edgar De- t), Bob McCracken (Simmons), Karen Baldwin (Mona), Roderick k (Ed Kennerle), Cynthia Steele (Receptionist), Richard Fancy t. Barry), John Finnegan (George), Peter Schreiner (Barry), John Mita (Brad), Diane Racine (Coven Woman), Alexandra Morgan mela), Christopher Lawford (Phil), Dale Cummings (Frye), Harold mond (Man), Don Woodard (Steve)

ER WARSAW (Sony Pictures) Producer/Director, Amin Q. udhri; Screenplay, Roy London; Executive Producer, Navin Desai; tography, Robert Draper; Editor, Brian Smedley-Aston; Music, est Troost; Designer, Tom Targownik; Set Decorator, Chris Neal; Costumes, Sherila Kehoe; Sound, Abe Nejad; Assistant Di- or, Bob Hurrie; Associate Producers, Gay Mayer, Watson C. War- r Jr.; Casting, Deborah Aquila; A Continental Film Group pro- tion; Color; Rated R; 92 minutes; September release. CAST: Patrick ayze (Chuck "Tiger" Warsaw), Piper Laurie (Frances Warsaw), Lee hardson (Mitchell Warsaw), Mary McDonnell (Paula Warsaw), bara Williams (Karen), Bobby DiCicco (Tony), Jenny Chrisinger l), James Patrick Gillis (Roger), Michelle Glaven (Emily), Kevin er (Robin), Beeson Carroll (Uncle Gene), Sally-Jane Heit (Aunt bara), Kaye Ballard (Aunt Thelma), Thomas Mills Wood (Lt. tana), Cynthia Lammel (Secretary), Sloane Shelton (Patricia), Syl- Davis (Ms. Lily), Christopher Douglas (Young Chuck), Aimee ks (Young Paula), Socrates Kolitsos (Stan), Don Brockett (Carl), go Washington (Ernie), Tom Madden, Kenneth Clarke, Lisa Cloud, t Debor, David J. Graban, Charles Barletto, Linda Weaver, Nick ncuso

UGHER THAN LEATHER (New Line Cinema) Producer, Vin- t Giordano; Director, Rick Rubin; Screenplay, Ric Menello, Rick bin; Story, Bill Adler, Lyor Cohen, Ric Menello; Executive Pro- er, Russell Simmons, Rick Rubin; Editor, Steve Brown; Photogra- , Feliks Parnell; A DEF American Pictures Presentation; Color; ed R; 92 minutes; September release. CAST: Joseph Simmons n), Darryl McDaniels (DMC), Jason Mizell (Jam Master Jay), hard Edson (Bernie), Jenny Lumet (Pam), Rick Rubin (Vico), Lois er (Charlotte), George Godfrey (Nathan), Russell Simmons (Rus-), Ric Menello (Arthur), Raymond White (Runny Ray), Mickey bin (Marty), Francesca Hodge (Mrs. Walker), Daniel Simmons arden), Vic Noto (Steve), Nick D'Avolio (Jerry), Carl Jordan, Russ ehl, Larry Kase, Tim Summer, Will Rokos, Wayne Carisi, Stan wartz, Wendel Fite, Roy Sundance, Ricky Rhodes, Riff Thunder, n Christiansen, Scott Koenig, Steve Walker, Brian Pulido, Christo- r Jones, Steve Williams, David Noble, Mike Espindle, Peter ugherty, John Moscato, Con Kiernan, Buddy Mantia, Randy Pearl, nna Fiducia, Eddie Dixon, Greg Buttle, Mike Blake, Cey Adams, guel Santana, Douglas Hayes, Paradise Gray, Jeff Sutton, Glen E. edman, George Drakoulias, Vanya Edwards, Scott Gomez, Hugh more, Arthur Forte, Frank Santopadre, Simone Reyes, Lee Bullock

OMA'S WAR (Troma) Producers, Lloyd Kaufman, Michael z; Directors, Michael Herz, Samuel Weil; Story, Lloyd Kaufman; eenplay, Mitchell Dana, Lloyd Kaufman; Additional Material, Eric tler, Thomas Martinek; Photography, James London; Associate

Patrick Swayze in "Tiger Warsaw"
(Sony)

Producers, Jeffrey W. Sass, Ryan Richards; Production Manager, Jeffrey W. Sass; Stunts, Scott Leva; Weapons Choreographer/Stunts, Ryan Richards; Special Effects, Illiam Jennings, Pericles Lewnes; Makeup Effects, Stephen Patrie, Paul Pisoni; Designer, Alexis Grey; Assistant Director, Denis Hahn; Sound, David Pastecchi; Set Designer, Michael Reed; Songs by various artists; Color; Not rated; 99 minutes; September release. CAST: Carolyn Beauchamp (Lydia), Sean Bowen (Taylor), Michael Ryder (Parker), Patrick Weathers (Kirkland), Jessica Dublin (Dottie), Steven Crossley (Marshall), Lorayn Lane DeLuca (Maria), Charles Kay Hune (Hardwick), Ara Romanoff (Cooney), Brenda Brock (Kim), Lisbeth Kaufman (Jingoistic Baby), Lisa Patruno (Jennifer), Alex Cserhart (Sean), Aleida Harris (Nancy), Mary Yorio (Laurie), Susan Bachli (Susan), Dan Snow (Rev. Brown), Nora Hummel (Shelly Somers), James Galvin (Samson), David Louden (Sal Longo), Rick Collins (Col. Jennings), Ted Johnson (Capt. Schweinhart), Zenon Zelenich (Mjr. Asyolsky), Alexis Grey (Mjr. Ramirez), Burt Wright, Michael Lacascio (Siamese Twin), Paolo Frassanito (Senor Sida)

DOIN' TIME ON PLANET EARTH (Cannon) Producers, Menahem Golan, Yoram Globus; Director, Charles Matthau; Screenplay, Darren Star; Story, Darren Star, Andrew Licht, Jeffrey A. Mueller; Photography, Timothy Suhrstedt; Editors, Alan Balsam, Sharyn L. Ross; Music, Dana Kaproff; Sound, Ronald Judkins; Production Designer, Curtis A. Schnell; Costumes, Reve Richards; Visual Effects Designer, Bill Millar; Assistant Director, Frank Bueno; Associate Producer, Karen Koch; Casting, Don Pemrick, Paula Herold; Ultra-Stereo; TVC color; Rated PG; 85 minutes; September release. CAST: Nicholas Strouse (Ryan Richmond), Hugh Gillin (Fred Richmond), Gloria Henry (Mary Richmond), Hugh O'Brian (Richard Camalier), Martha Scott (Virginia Camalier), Timothy Patrick Murphy (Jeff Richmond), Isabelle Walker (Jenny Camalier), Paula Irvine (Marilyn Richmond), Andea Thompson (Lisa Winston), Adam West (Charles Pinsky), Candice Azzara (Edna Pinsky), Roddy McDowall (Minister), Maureen Stapleton (Harriett), Matt Adler (Dan Forrester), Susan Ursitti (Sharry), Linda Lutz (Nurse), Christian Hoff (Steve Bruckner), Diana Chesney (Mrs. Edelstein), Amy Lynne (Cute Girl), Kyra Stempel (Susie Hellman), Kellie Martin (Sheila), Dominick Brascia (Jock Student), Charles Matthau (Punk Student), Nathan Dyer (Hippy Student), Richard Connor (Eliot), Michael Allen Ryder ("Normal" Student), Kelly Mohre (Ponytail Donna)

Lois Ayer, Jason Mizell, Darryl McDaniels in "Tougher Than Leather" ***(New Line)***

Candice Azzara, Adam West, Nicholas Strouse in "Doin' Time . . ." (Cannon)

Mary Gross, Rebecca DeMornay
in "Feds" *(Warner Bros.)*

Donald Pleasence, Beau Starr
in "Halloween 4 . . ." *(Galaxy)*

AFTER THE RAIN, aka ***The Passage*** **(New Century/Vista)** Producer, Raul Carrera; Director, Harry Thompson; Executive Producer, Brandon Baade; Photography, Peter Stein; Editor, Peter Appleton; Music, Paul Loomis; A Spectrum/Carrera production; Eastmancolor; Rated PG; 105 minutes; September release. CAST: Alexandra Paul (Annie May Bonner), Ned Beatty (Matthew Bonner), Barbara Barrie (Rachel Bonner), Brian Keith (Byron Monroe), Dee Law

FEDS (Warner Bros.) Producers, Ilona Herzberg, Len Blum; Director, Dan Goldberg; Screenplay, Len Blum, Dan Goldberg; Executive Producer, Ivan Reitman; Photography, Timothy Suhrstedt; Editor, Don Cambern; Designer, Randy Ser; Music, Randy Edelman; Costumes, Isabella B. Van Soest; Associate Producers, Kool Marder, Robert E. Lee; Casting, Stanzi Stokes, Glenis Gross; Production Manager, David Marder; Assistant Director, Betsy Pollock; Art Director, Phil Dagort; Set Decorator, Julie Kaye Towery; Set Designer, Sally Thornton; Sound, David Brownlow; Stunts, Don Pike; Special Effects, Gregory C. Landerer; "*Special Kinda Lovin'* " by Roy Gaines & Barry Goldberg, and songs by other artists; Soundtrack on GNP Crescendo Records; Dolby Stereo; Technicolor; Rated PG-13; 98 minutes; October release. CAST: Rebecca DeMornay (DeWitt), Mary Gross (Zuckerman), Ken Marshall (Brent), Fred Dalton Thompson (Bilecki), Larry Cedar (Butz), Raymond Singer (Hupperman), James Luisi (Sperry), Rex Ryon (Parker), Norman Bernard (Bickerstaff), Don Stark (Willy), David Sherrill (Duane), Jon Cedar (Senior Agent), Tony Longo (Sailor), Bradley Weissman (Graham), Michael Chieffo (Louie), Jared Chandler, Charlie Phillips, Geoffrey Thorne, Wendy Cutler, Niles Brewster, Karl Anthony Smith, Webster Williams, Mitch Hara, Barbara C. Adsie, Annie Cerillo, Lee Arnone, Don Woodard, Gary Pike, Charlie Skeen, Rick Avery, Hal Burton

PARTY LINE (SVS Films) Producers, Tom Byrnes, Kurt Anderson, William Webb; Co-Producer, Monica Webb; Director, William Webb; Screenplay, Richard Brandes; Story, Tom Byrnes; Photography, John Huneck; Editor, Paul Koval; Music, Sam Winans; Sound, Glen Berkovitz; A Westwood production; Color; Rated R; 91 minutes; October release. CAST: Richard Hatch (Dan), Shawn Weatherly (Stacy), Leif Garrett (Seth), Greta Blackburn (Angelina), Richard Roundtree (Capt. Barnes), James O'Sullivan (Henry), Terrence McGovern (Simmons), Shelli Place (Mrs. Simmons), Tara Hutchins (Alice), Marty Dudek (Butch)

Joanna Pacula, Meredith Salenger
in "The Kiss" *(Tri-Star)*

HALLOWEEN 4: THE RETURN OF MICHAEL MYE (Galaxy International) Producer, Paul Freeman; Executive Produc Moustapha Akkad; Director, Dwight H. Little; Story, Dhani Lipsi Larry Rattner, Benjamin Ruffner, Alan B. McClroy; Screenplay, A. B. McElroy; Music, Alan Horwarth; "*Halloween Theme,*" John C penter; Associate Producer, M. Sanousi; A Trancas International Fil Production; Casting, David Cohn, Paul Bengston; Editor, Cu Clayton; Art Director, Roger S. Crandall; Photography, Peter Ly Collister; Production Manager, S. Michael Formica; Assistant Dir tor, Denis Stewart; Sound, Mark McNabb; Set Decorator, Nic Lauritzen; Costumes, Rosalie Wallace; Stunts, Fred Lerner; Spec Effects, Larry Fioritto; Ultra-Stereo; Color; Panavision; Rated R; minutes; October release. CAST: Donald Pleasence (Dr. Loomis), E Cornell (Rachel Carruthers), Danielle Harris (Jamie Lloyd), George Wilbur (Michael Myers), Michael Pataki (Dr. Hoffman), Beau St (Sheriff Meeker), Kathleen Kinmont (Kelly), Sasha Jenson (Brad, Gene Ross (Earl), Carmen Filpi (Jack Sayer), Jeff Olson (Rich Carruthers), Karen Alston (Darlene Carrusthers), Jordan Brad (Kyle), Richard Stay (Wade), Danny Ray (Tommy), Michael Fly (Deputy Pierce), George Sullivan (Logan), Morgan B. White (Justi Walt Logan Field (Unger), Michael Ruud (Big Al), Eric Hart (Orri Raymond O'Connor, Nancy Borgenicht, David Jensen, Rand Ke nedy, Don Glover, Robert Conder

THE KISS (Tri-Star) Producers, Pen Densham, John Watson; Dire tor, Pen Densham; Screenplay, Stephan Volk, Tom Ropelewski; Sto Stephan Volk; Executive Producer, Richard B. Lewis; Editor, St Cole; Makeup/Creature Effects, Chris Walas; Casting, Pennie DuPo Music, J. Peter Robinson; Designer, Roy Forge Smith; Photograph Francois Protat; Production Manager, Wendy Grean; Assistant Dire tor, Henry Bronchtein; Costumes, Renee April; Production Coordir tor, Lynn Mallay; Special Effects, Louis Craig; Art Director, Suzan Smith; Set Decorator, Gilles Aird; Stunts, Steve Davison; Songs, Peter Robinson, Tom Canning, Pen Densham, Richard B. Lewis, La Williams; Dolby Stereo; Bellevue Pathe Color; Rated R; 101 minut October release. CAST: Pamela Collyer (Hilary), Peter Dvors (Father Joe), Joanna Pacula (Felice), Meredith Salenger (Amy), Mi Kuzyk (Brenda), Nicholas Kilbertus (Jack), Sabrina Boudot (Heathe Shawn Levy (Terry), Jan Rubes (Tobin), Celine Lomez (Aunt Iren Dorian Joe Clark (T.C.), Richard Dumont (Abe), Priscilla Mouzakio (Young Felice), Talya Rubin (Young Hilary), Philip Pretten (Fathe Johanne Herelle, Shannon McDonough (Eileen), Vlasta Vra (Bishop), Johanne Herelle, Tyrone Benskin, Marty Finkelstein, Cla Rodger, Norris Domingue, Robin Bronfman, Nevin Densham, Andre Johnson

PURGATORY (New Star Entertainment) Producer/Director, A Artzi; Screenplay, Felix Kroll, Paul Aratow; Photography, Tom Frase Executive Producers, Dimitri Villard, Robby Wald; Editor, Ettie Fel man; Music, Julian Laxton; Sound, Philip Key; Stunts, Mark Myro Casting, Pat Cordes; Assistant Director, Howard Rennie; produced association with Intl. Media Exchange, Filmco and Kingsway Cor munications; Color; Rated R; 93 minutes; October release. CAS Tanya Roberts (Carly Arnold), Julie Pop (Melanie), Hal Orlandi (Bledsoe), Rufus Swart (Paul Cricks), Adrienne Pearce (Janine), Mar Human (Kirsten), David Sherwood (Stern), Clare Marshall (Ru Arnold), Hugh Rouse (Rivers), John Newland (Ambassador Whitne

PUMPKINHEAD (United Artists) Producers, Howard Smit Richard C. Weinman; Director, Stan Winston; Screenplay, Mark Pa rick Carducci, Gary Gerani; Story, Mark Patrick Carducci, Stan Wis ton, Richard C. Weinman; Inspired by a Poem by Ed Justin; Executi Producer, Alex De Benedetti; Photography, Bojan Bazelli; Productic

Lance Henriksen in "Pumpkinhead"
(DEG/DeLaurentiis Group)

Michael Dudikoff in "Platoon Leader"
(Cannon)

ager, Gordon Wolf; Assistant Director, Anderson G. House; Crea- Effects, Alec Gillis, Richard Landon, Shane Patrick Mahan, John engrant, Tom Woodruff, Jr.; Designer, Cynthia Kay Charette; or, Marcus Manton; Music, Richard Stone; Casting, Bob Morones; nd, Itzhak "Ike" Magal; Production Coordinator, Carol Kravetz; tumes, Leslie Peters Ballard; Set Decorator, Kurt Gauger; Stunts, hard Warlock; from MGM/UA Communications; Ultra-Stereo; hnicolor; Rated R; 86 minutes; October release. CAST: Lance riksen (Ed Harley), Jeff East (Chris), John DiAguino (Joel), berly Ross (Kim), Joel Hoffman (Steve), Cynthia Bain (Tracy), ry Remsen (Maggie), Florence Schauffler (Haggis), Brian Bremer nt), Buck Flower (Mr. Wallace), Matthew Hurley (Billy Harley), DeBroux (Tom Harley), Peggy Walton Walker (Ellie Harley), nce Oorbitt, Jr. (Eddie Harley), Richard Warlock (Clayton Heller), on Odessa (Hessie), Joseph Piro (Jimmy Joe), Mayim Bialik, Jandi nson (Wallace Kids), Robert Fredrickson (Ethan), Greg Michaels l Man), Madeleine Taylor Holmes (Old Hill Woman), Mary Boes- (Mountain Girl), Mushroom (Gypsy), Tom Woodruff, Jr. npkinhead)

ATOON LEADER (Cannon) Producer, Harry Alan Towers; Di- or, Aaron Norris; Executive Producer, Avi Lerner; Screenplay, Marx, Andrew Deutsch, David Walker; Adaptation, "Peter Wel- ", Harry Alan Towers; Based on the book by James R. McDon- h; Photography, Arthur Wooser; Editor, Michael J. Duthie; Music, Chattaway; Production Supervisors, Michael Games, Clive Challis; istant Directors, Miguel Gil, Steve Fillis; Stunts, Dean Ferrandini; Director, John Rosewarne; Casting, Perry Bullington; Stunts, Jan- Wienand, Jan Michael Schultz; Production Coordinator, Carol kson; Sound, Paul le Mare; Set Decorator, Emilia Roux; Costumes, y Dover; Special Effects, John Gant; A Breton Film Productions Production; Rank Color; Ultra-Stereo; Rank Color; Rated R; 100 utes; October release. CAST: Michael Dudikoff (Jeff Knight), ert F. Lyons (Michael McNamara), Michael De Lorenzo ymond Bacera), Jesse Dabson (Joshua Parker), Rick Fitts (Robert es), Tony Pierce (Jan Shultz), Daniel Demorest (Duffy), Brian oy (Roach), Michael Rider (Don Pike), William Smith (Major n), Al Karaki (Kemp), Evan J. Klisser (Larsen), Evan Barker inski), A. J. Smith (Lt. Riley), Dean Ferrandini, Bill Olmstead, mi Venturis, Joyce Long, Yasmin Jacobs

PEHEADS (Avenue Pictures) Producer, Peter McCarthy; Direc- Bill Fishman; Screenplay, Bill Fishman, Peter McCarthy; Story, Fishman, Peter McCarthy, Jim Herzfeld, Ryan Rowe; Executive ducer, Michael Nesmith; Associate Producers, Eric Barrett, An- v Z. Davis; Co-Producer, Robert Lecky; Music, Fishbone, David ne; Designer, Catherine Hardwicke; Editor, Mondo Jenkins; Pho- aphy, Bojan Bazeli; Casting, Victoria Thomas; Production Execu- , Esther Greif; Production Manager, Andrew Z. Davis; Assistant ector, Josh King; Costumes, Elizabeth McBride; Art Director, Don rs; Set Decorator, Carole Lee Davis; Sound, John Pritchett; Produc- Coordinator, Benjamin Allanoff; Choreographers, Cholly Atkins, ie Batos; Special Effects, Peter M. Chesney; Stunts, Rick Barker, istopher Doyle; Presented by Avenue Pictures, NBC Productions, hael Nesmith/A Front Films Production; Songs by various artists; a-Stereo; DeLuxe Color; Rated R; 97 minutes; October release. ST: John Cusack (Ivan Alexeev), Tim Robbins (Josh Tager), Mary sby (Samantha Gregory), Clu Gulager (Norman Mart), Katy Boyer inda Mart), Jessica Walter (Kay Mart), Sam Moore (Billy Di- nd), Junior Walker (Lester Diamond), Susan Tyrrell (Nikki Mor- , Doug McClure (Sid Tager), Connie Stevens (June Tager), King Cotton (Roscoe), Don Cornelius (Mo Fuzz), Ebbe Roe Smith (Mr. G), Keith Joe Dick (Mr. B), Lee Arenberg (Norton), Lyle Alzado (Thor Alexeev), Milton Selzer (Merlin Kinkle), Xander Berkeley (Ricky Fell), Stiv Bator (Dick Slammer), Jo Harvey Allen (Madame Olga), Jack Cheese (Don Druzel), Slavitza Jovan (Tish), John Lykes (Body Buddy), Jim Ward (Dutch Reagan), Joe Cosentino (Stu Beaumont), Jordan Lancer (Young Roscoe), Rocky Giordani, J.J., John Durbin, Zander Schloss, Sy Richardson, Coati Mundi, Patrick O'Neill, "Agent" Ava Hubbard, Martha C. Quinn, John Fleck, Bob Forrest

TWICE DEAD (Concorde) Producers, Guy J. Louthan, Robert McDonnell; Director, Bert Dragin; Screenplay, Bert Dragin, Robert McDonnell; Photography, Zoran Hochstatter; Casting, Kevin Alber; Music, David Bergeaud; Editor, Patrick Rand; Designer, Stephan Rice; Costumes, Claire Joseph; Stunts, John Branagan; Makeup Effects, Michael Burnett; Special Effects, Steve Galich; Production Coordinator, Diana Schmidt; Set Decorator, Anna Rita Raineri; Sound, William Fiege; *"Twice Dead"* by Christopher Burgard, James Steve Sharp, David Bergeaud/Performance; Poor Saint Christopher, and songs by various artists; Foto-Kem Color; Rated R; 85 minutes; October release. CAST: Tom Brezhahan (Scott), Jill Whitlow (Robin), Jonathan Chapin (Myrna/Crip/Tyler), Christopher Burgard (Silk), Sam Melville (Harry), Brooke Bundy (Sylvia), Todd Bridges (Petie), Shawn Player (Stony), Joleen Lutz (Candy), Raymond Garcia (Cheeta), Travis McKenna (Melvin), Charlie Spradling (Tina), Bob McLean (Harry Cates, Sr.), Richard Meadows (Potter), Lance Gordon (Calvin), Lance Wilson-White, Janice Ehrlich, Bud Anthony, Eric Fleeks, Steve Finley, Brett Garrison, Dean Alexander, Susie McDonnell, Barry Diamond

SLEEPAWAY CAMP 2: UNHAPPY CAMPERS (Double Helix Films) Producers, Jerry Silva, Michael A. Simpson; Director, Michael A. Simpson; Executive Producer, Stan Wakefield; Screenplay, Fritz Gordon; Story, Robert Hiltzik; Photography, Bill Mills; Editor, John David Allen; Music, James Oliverio; Sound, Mary Ellis; Assistant Director, Jerry Pece; Makeup Effects, Bill Johnson; Stunts, Lonnie Smith; Casting, Shay Griffin; Color; Rated R; 80 minutes; October release. CAST: Pamela Springsteen (Angela Baker), Brian Patrick Clarke (T.C.), Renee Estevez (Molly), Walter Gotell (Uncle John), Susan Marie Snyder (Mare), Heather Binion (Phoebe), Tony Higgins, Terry Hobbs, Kendall Bean, Valerie Hartman, Julie Murphy, Carol Chambers, Amy Fields

John Cusack, Tim Robbins
in "Tapeheads" ***(Avenue Pictures)***

Peter Elliott in "Missing Link"
(Universal)

Kay Lenz, Scott Schwartz in "Fear"
(CineTel)

MISSING LINK (Universal) Producer, Dennis B. Kane; Directors/Photography/Screenplay, David & Carol Hughes; Executive Producers, Peter Guber, John Peters; Makeup Effects, Rick Baker; Narrator, Michael Gambon; Editor, David Dickie; Music, Mike Trim, Sammy Hurden; Sound, David Hughes; Special Effects, Jane Owen, Robyn Paxton, Carole Roberts; Visual Design Consultant, James Gurney; Color: Rated PG; 91 minutes; November release. CAST: Peter Elliott (Man-ape)

THE CHOCOLATE WAR (Management Company Entertainment Group) Producer, Jonathan D. Krane; Director/Screenplay, Keith Gordon; Co-Producer, Simon Lewis; Associate Producer, Susan I. Spivak; Photography, Tom Richmond; Casting, Susan Dixon; Art Director, David Ensley; Costumes, Elizabeth Kaye; Editor, Jeff Wishengrad; Music, Yaz, Scott Cossu, Joan Armatrading, J. S. Bach, Kate Bush, Peter Gabriel, Emil Waldteufel; Line Producer, Ron Diamond; Production Coordinator, Virginia Bogert; Assistant Director, Michelle Solotar; Special Casting, Rachel Griffin; Sound, Mary Jo Devenney; Set Decorator, Melissa Matthies; Production Manager, Ron Diamond; Production Coordinator, Virginia Berta Bogert; Songs by various artists; Color; Rated R; 100 minutes; November release. CAST: John Glover (Brother Leon), Ilan Mitchell-Smith (Jerry), Wally Ward (Archie), Doug Hutchison (Obie), Corey Gunnestad (Goober), Brent Fraser (Emile Janza), Robert Davenport (Brian Cochran), Jenny Wright (Lisa), Bud Cort (Brother Jacques), Adam Baldwin (Carter), Ethan Sandler (Caroni), Kurt Bloom, Wyeth Orestes Johnson (Kids), Landon Wine (Frank Bollo), Matthew Burke (Porter), Douglas A. Forsyth (Johnson), Peter Boyack (McClosky), Sean K. Hagerty (Perkins), Colin Mitchell (Crane), Max Dixon (Coach), Rick May (Doctor), John Sudol (Priest), Roger Tompkins (Father), Elizabeth Yoffee (Mother), Robert Munns (Brother Eugene), Jason Hardlicka (Young Jerry)

FEAR (Cinetel Films) Producer, Lisa M. Hansen; Director/Story, Robert Ferretti; Executive Producer, Paul Hertzberg; Screenplay, Rick Scarry, Kathryn Connell; Photography, Dana Christiaansen; Editor, Albert Coleman, Michael Eliot; Music, Alfi Kabiljio; Art Director, Fernando Altschul; Set Decorator, Trevor Norris; Costumes, Jan Rowton; Sound, Thomas E. Allen Sr.; Assistant Director, Richard Oswald; Casting, Billy Damota; Foto-Kem Color; Rated R; 96 minutes; November release. CAST: Cliff DeYoung (Don Haden), Kay Lenz (Sharon Haden), Robert Factor (Jack Gracie), Scott Schwartz (Brian Haden), Geri Betzler (Jennifer Haden), Frank Stallone (Robert Ar tage), Charles Meshack (Cy Canelle), Michael Watson (Mitch B nett), Eddit Banker (Lenny)

FRESH HORSES (Weintraub Entertainment Group/Columb Producer, Dick Berg; Director, David Anspaugh; Executive Produc Allan Marcil; Associate Producer, John G. Wilson; Screenplay, La Ketron; Based on the Play by Larry Ketron; Photography, Fred Murp Designer, Paul Sylbert; Costumes, Colleen Atwood; Music, Da Foster, Patrick Williams; Casting, Amanda Mackey; Editor, Da Rosenbloom; Production Manager, John G. Wilson; Assistant Dir tor, Peter Giuliano; Production Coordinator, Jeannie Jeha; Sou Hank Garfield; Set Decorator, Ken Turek; Special Effects, S Barkan; Color; Rated PG-13; 105 minutes; November release. CA Molly Ringwald (Jewel), Andrew McCarthy (Larkin), Patti D'Arb ville (Jean), Ben Stiller (Tipton), Leon Russom (Larkin's Dad), Mc Hagan (Ellen), Viggo Mortensen (Green), Doug Hutchison (Sprol Chiara Peacock (Alice), Marita Geraghty (Maureen), Rachel Jo (Bobo), Welker White (Christy), Christy Budig (Laurel), Larry Ket (Roy), Ken Strunk (Dr. Lippincott), William Youmans (Gary), Rich Woods (Buddy), Kent Poole (Stephen), Dan Davis (Fletcher), Ba Williams (Fairgate), Carol Schneider (Jane), Joan MacIntosh (Larki Mother), Sheri Norton-Stearn (Mrs. Price), K. C. Jones (Dr. Pric Jacqueline Verdeyen (Jewel's Mother), Ann Johnson, Jessica Brow Jennifer P. Born, Peter Duchin

GHOST TOWN (Trans World Entertainment) Producer, Timo D. Tennant; Director, Richard Governor; Screenplay, Duke Sandef From a Story by David Schmoeller; Executive Producer, Charles Ba Photography, Mac Ahlberg; Editors, Peter Teschner, King Wild Music, Harvey R. Cohen; Sound, Bill Fiege, Margaret Duke; Design Don De Fina; Art Director, Rick Brown; Makeup Effects, MMI—Jc Carl Buechler; Assistant Director, Jim Avery; Production Manag Amanda DiGiulio; Stunts, Kane Hodder; Mechanical Effects, Ed Surkin; An Empire Pictures production; Ultra-Stereo; Foto-Kem Co Rated R; 85 minutes; November release. CAST: Franc Luz (Langle Catherine Hickland (Kate), Jimmie F. Skaggs (Devilin), Penel Windust (Grace), Bruce Glover (Dealer), Zitto Kazann (Blacksmi Blake Conway (Harper), Laura Schaefer (Etta), Michael Aldre (Bubba), Ken Kolb (Ned), Will Hannah (Billy)

Ilan Mitchell-Smith in "Chocolate War"
(Management Company)

Andrew McCarthy, Molly Ringwald in "Fresh Horses" *(Weintraub)*

"Ghost Town" *(New World)*

Daphne Zuniga, Tom Berenger in "Last Rites" *(MGM)*

AT AND SUNLIGHT (Snowball Prods.) Producers, Steve Burns, ly Burns; Director/Screenplay, Rob Nilsson; Photography, Tomas ker; Editor, Henk van Eaghen; Music, David Byrne, Brian Eno, n *"My Life in the Bush of Ghosts"*; Sound, Dan Gleich; co-produced h New Front Alliance Films; Black & White; Not rated; 92 minutes; ember release. CAST: Rob Nilsson (Mel), Consuelo Faust (Car-), Don Bajema (Mitch), Raven de la Croix

NNA'S WAR (Cannon Group) Producers, Menahem Golan, am Globus; Director, Menahem Golan; Screenplay, Menahem an, Stanley Mann; Based on the books *"The Diaries of Hanna esh"* by Hanna Senesh & *"A Great Wind Cometh"* by Yoel Palgi; tography, Elemer Ragalyi; Editor, Alain Jakubowicz; Music, Dov zer; Associate Producer, Carlos Gil; Costumes, John Mollo; Art ector, Tividar Bertalan; Assistant Director, Miguel Gil; Production ervisor, Zoli Ben Chorin; Production Executive, Rony Yacov; ting, Noel Davis, Jeremy Zimmerman; Production Coordinator, mi Mayberg; Sound, Cyril Collick; Set Decorator, Fred Carter; ociate Editor, Dory Lubliner; Special Effects, Ferenc Habetler, or Budahazy; Panavision; Ultra-Stereo; Color; Rated PG-13; 148 utes; November release. CAST: Ellen Burstyn (Katalin), Marus-a Detmers (Hanna), Anthony Andrews (McCormack), Donald Plea-ce (Rosza), David Warner (Capt. Simon), Vincenzo Ricotta (Yoel), istopher Fairbank (Ruven), Rob Jacks (Peretz), Serge El-Baz ny), Eli Gorenstein (Aba), Josef El-Dror (Yonah), Ingrid Pitt (Mar-, Jon Rumney (Uncle Egon), Magda Faluhely (Aunt Ella), Emma vis (Cousin Evi), Dorota Stalinska (Maritza), Russell Porter orge), Yehuda Efroni (Sandor), George Dillon (Milenko), Nigel tings (Jancsi), John Stride (Dr. Komoly), Patsy Byrne (Rosie), le Serbedzija (Capt. Ivan), Miodrag Krivokapic (Col. Illya), Agi rgitai (Prof. Ravas), Patrick Monckton (Kalosh), Istvan Hunyadkur- (Smuggler), Teri Tordai (Baroness Hatvany), Barry Langford dley), Jeff Gerner (Simmonds), Shimon Finkel (Ben Gurion), Rami uch (Enzo Sireni), Avi Koren (Eliyahu Golomb), Mordechai enbaum (Avigur), Peter Czajkowski (Andy), Tamas Philippovich dras), Terez Varhegyi (Marietta), Jozsef Lakky

ST RITES (MGM) Producers, Donald P. Bellisario, Patrick Cormick; Director/Screenplay, Donald P. Bellisario; Photography, David Watkin; Designer, Peter Larkin; Editor, Pembroke J. Herring; Designer, Joseph G. Aulisi; Casting, Joy Todd; Music, Bruce Broughton; Production Manager, Lenny Vullo; Assistant Director, Joe Napolitano; Art Director, Victor Kempster; Set Decorator, Steven Jordan; Sound, Les Lazarowitz, David Moshlak; Production Coordinator, Jill Sprecher; Special Effects, Conrad Brink; Stunts, Richard "Diamond" Farnsworth; Choreographer, Lee Ann Martin; *"All of My Life"* by Bruce Broughton & Deborah Pratt/Vocals, Deborah Pratt; Dolby Stereo; DeLuxe Color; Rated R; 103 minutes; November release. CAST: Tom Berenger (Michael), Daphne Zuniga (Angela), Chick Vennera (Nuzo), Anne Twomey (Zena Pace), Dane Clark (Carlo Pace), Paul Dooley (Father Freddie), Vassili Lambrinos (Tio), Adrian Paul (Tony), Deborah Pratt (Robin Dwyer), Tony Di Benedetto (Lt. Jericho), Christine Poor (Teri), Al Rodriguez (Luis De Vega), Jack Halett (Officer Reardon), Father Louis Gigante (Bishop Frascati), Ibi Kaufman (Theresa), Frank Patton (O'Bannon), Maurizio Benazzo (Vaneltino), Robert Corbo (Geno), Leslie Arnett (Casey), Damien Leake (Det. Brown), Ernesto Gonzalez, Mary Diveny

1969 (Atlantic Entertainment Group) Producers, Daniel Grodnik, Bill Badalato; Director/Screenplay, Ernest Thompson; Executive Producer, Thomas Coleman; Photography, Jules Brenner; Designer, Marcia Hinds; Editor, William Anderson; Associate Producer, Ariel Bagdadi; Costumes, Julie Weiss; Music, Michael Small, Robert Randles; Casting, Mike Fenton, Jane Feinberg, Valorie Massalas; Associate Editor, Armen Minasias; Production Executive, R. P. Sekon; Associate Producer/Production Manager, Sue Baden-Powell; Assistant Director, David Householter; Sound, Donald F. Johnson; Art Director, Bo Johnson; Set Decorator, Jan K. Bergstrom; Production Coordinator, Keith A. Baumgartner; Songs by various artists; Soundtrack on Polydor Records; Ultra-Stereo; CFI Color; Rated R; 90 minutes; November release. CAST: Robert Downey, Jr. (Ralph), Kiefer Sutherland (Scott), Bruce Dern (Cliff), Mariette Hartley (Jessie), Winona Ryder (Beth), Joanna Cassidy (Ev), Christopher Wynne (Alden), Keller Kuhn (Marsha), Steve Foster (Marshall), Mert Fatfield (Coach Heart), Welton Tootle (Junior Roberts), Don Devendorf (Rev. Hardy), Dr. Robert Louis Stevenson (Dean Bonner), Howard Kingkade (Matty), Carl Espy (Billy), Jason Summers, Scott Stevens, Michael Fowler, David Webster, Jennifer Rubin, John Garber, Paul Gillon, Alfred Cerullo, Mical Whitaker, Kara Zielke

Anthony Andrews (C), Maruschka Detmers(R) in "Hanna's War" *(Cannon)*

Winona Ryder, Kiefer Sutherland in "1969" *(Atlantic)*

Donna Dixon, Joe Alaskey in "Lucky Stiff" ***(New Line)***

Jennifer Rubin, Matt Lattanzi in "Blueberry Hill" ***(MGM)***

LUCKY STIFF (New Line Cinema) Producer, Gerald T. Olson; Director, Anthony Perkins; Line Producer, Deborah Moore; Executive Producer/Screenplay, Pat Proft; Executive Producers, Miles Copeland, Laurie Perlman, Derek Power; Photography, Jacques Haitkim; Editor, Michael Knue; Casting, Annette Benson; Designer, C. J. Strawn; Effects Makeup, Brian Moore; Special Effects, Mick Strawn; Color; Rated PG; 85 minutes; November release. CAST: Joe Alaskey (Ron Douglas), Donna Dixon (Cynthia Mitchell), Jeff Kober (Ike), Barbara Howard (Frances), W. Morgan Sheppard (Pa), Fran Ryan (Ma), Charles Frank (Durel), Steven & Philip Ross (Ike, Jr. & Ike III), Frank Birney (Priest), Hilary Shepard (Cissy), Andy Wood (Mr. Futteman), Leigh McCloskey (Erik), Joe Unger (Sheriff Kirby)

SPLIT DECISIONS (New Century/Vista) Producer, Joe Wizan; Director, David Drury; Screenplay, David Fallon; Co-Producers, Mickey Borofsky, Todd Black; Associate Producers, Jean Higgins, Rachel Singer; Music, Basil Poledouris; Editors, John W. Wheeler, Jeff Freeman, Thomas Stanford; Photography, Timothy Suhrsedt; Visual Consultant, Alfred Brenner; Casting, Lynn Stalmaster, Mali Finn; Production Manager, Jean Higgins; Assistant Director, Michael Davis; Art Director, Michael Z. Hanan; Set Decorator, Kathe Klopp; Costumes, Hilary Cochran; Fights, Paul Stader; Sound, Steve Nelson; Special Makeup, Matthew Mungle; Special Effects, Reel EFX, Eric Dressor; Production Coordinator, Carolyn Olman; *"The Spirt of Man"* by Chris DeBurgh; Ultra-Stereo; CFI Color; Rated R; 95 minutes; November release. CAST: Craig Sheffer (Eddie McGuinn), Jeff Fahey (Ray McGuinn), Gene Hackman (Dan McGuinn), John Mcliam (Pop McGuinn), Jennifer Beals (Barbara Uribe), Eddie Velez (Julian "Snake" Pedroza), Carmine Caridi (Lou Rubia), James Tolkan (Benny Pistone), DeVoreaux White (Coop), David Labiosa (Rudy), Harry Van Dyke (Douby), Anthony Trujillo (Angel), Victor Campos (Santiago), Tom Bower (Det. Walsh), Julius Harris (Tony Leone), Father Terry Sweeney (Priest), Herb Muller (Mr. "D"), John Thomas, Dean Webber, Oz Tortora, William Brent Kirkland, Cathleen A. Master, Lou Bonacki, Pat Cupo, Steve Vignari, Gregory Goosen, Carmine Iannaceone, Danny Valdivia, Geoff Witcher, Marty Denkin, Dirk Kooiman, Michael Garcia, Al Allen, Aaron Akins

SLIPPING INTO DARKNESS (MCEG) Producer, Jonathan D. Krane; Director/Screenplay, Eleanor Gaver; Executive Producer, William J. Rouhana, Jr.; Co-producers, Don Schain, Simon R. Lewis; Line Producer, Lydia Pilcher; Photography, Loren Bivens; Editor, Barbara Pokras; Music, Joey Rand; Sound, Dennis Carr; Production Design Patricia Woodbridge; Assistant Director, Heidi Gutman; Associ Producer, Judith Ann Friend; FotoKem Color; Rated R; 87 minut November release. CAST: Michelle Johnson (Carlyle), John DiAqui (Fritz), Neill Barry (Ebin), Anastasia Fielding (Genevieve), Cris Kauffman (Alex), Vyto Ruginis (Otis), David Sherrill, Terrence M kovich, Adam Roarke

BLUEBERRY HILL (MGM) Producer/Production Manager, M Michaels; Director, Strathford Hamilton; Screenplay, Lonon Smi Photography, David Lewis; Designer, John Sperry Wade; Editor, M cy Hamilton; Visual Consultant, Marlene Stewart; Costumes, She Wade; Music, Ira Ingber; Casting, Gary Zuckerbrod; Production Ex utive, Jeffrey Leach; Assistant Director, John Axness; Producti Supervisor, Suzanne Hostka; Production Coordinator, Jeffrey Zeit Sound, Ed Sommers; Set Decorator, Claire Bowen; Presented Mediacom Industries and Prism Entertainment in association w MVA-1 and Tricoast Production Partners, Inc.; Ultra-Stereo; Fo Kem Color; Rated R; 87 minutes; December release. CAST: Ca Snodgress (Becca Dane), Margaret Avery (Hattie Cale), Jennifer Ru (Ellie Dane), Matt Lattanzi (Denny Logan), Tommy Swerdlow (R Porter), Dendrie Allynn Taylor (Rachel), Ian Patrick Williams (Ow Shackelford), Richard Haines (Charlie Dane), David Shurtleff (Caru ers), Hal Havens (Gas Station Attendant), Katherine Atwood (Gi Cassandra Lee Hamilton (Baby Decker), Frank Strike (Voice of M Danny Mora (Other DJ's Voice), Ira Ingber, Jerry Jumonville, Stan Kipper, Larry Taylor

BREAK OF DAWN (Cinewest) Producer, Jude Pauline Eberha Director/Screenplay, Isaac Artenstein; Photography, Stephen Lighth Music, Mark Adler; Editor, John Nutt; Sound, Anne Evans; color; N rated; 105 minutes; December release. CAST: Oscar Chavez (Pedro González), Maria Rojo (Wife), Pepe Serna (Cousin), Tony Plana, Pe Henry Schroeder, Socorro Valdez, Kamala Lopez, Harry Woolf

THE BOOST (Hemdale) Producer, Daniel H. Blatt; Director, Har Becker; Screenplay, Darryl Ponicsan; Based on the book *"Ludes"* Benjamin Stein; Executive Producers, John Daly, Derek Gison; Ph tography, Howard Atherton; Music, Stanley Moss; Associate P ducer, Associate Producer/Assistant Director, Tom Mack; Product Managers, Terry Carr, Mel Howard; Assistant Production Coordinat Patricia Bischetti; Sound, Walter Hoylman; Costumes, Lisa Lova

Gene Hackman, John McLiam, Craig Sheffer in "Split Decisions" ***(New Century/Vista)***

John Kapelos, James Woods, Sean Young in "The Boost" ***(Hemdale)***

David Carradine in "Crime Zone"
(Concorde)

Isaac Hayes, Bernie Casey, Keenen Ivory Wayans, Jim Brown in "I'm Gonna Git You Sucka"
(United Artists)

akeup Effects, Bill Myer; Special Effects, Larry Fioretto; Set Decora-, Cindy Carr; Art Director, Ken Hardy; Associate Editor, Melvin apiro; Orchestrations, Stanley Myers, Randy Waldman; Stunts, Ed-rd J. Ulrich; Dolby Stereo; Color; Rated R; 95 minutes; December ease. CAST: James Woods (Lenny), Sean Young (Linda), John pelos (Joel), Steven Hill (Max), Kelle Kerr (Rochelle), John Roth-n (Ned), Amanda Blake (Barbara), Grace Zabriskie (Sheryl), Marc ppel (Mark), Fred McCarren (Tom), Suzanne Kent (Helen), Libby one (Delores), Greg Deason (Michael), Barry Jenner (Billy), David ess (Dr. Shapiro), David Bantly (Dr. Bishop), Virginia Morris ary), David Preston, June Chandler, Edith Fields, Bill Gratton, rker Whitman, Michael Strasser, Jim Staskel, Charles David chards, Austin Kelly, Stogie Harrison, Dan Moriarty, Scott McGin-, David Haskell, Lucky Butler, Christopher Carroll, Fernand Poi-s, Clement Von Franckenstein, Kate Zentall, Ricardo Gutierrez, dy Lambert, Jim Jansen, Dan Peters, Jack Sargent, Ron Poniewaz, na Bethune

RIME ZONE (Concorde) Producer/Director, Luis Llosa; Executive oducer, Roger Corman; Associate Producers, David Carradine, Gail nsen; Screenplay, Daryl Haney; Music, Rick Conrad; Editor, Wil-m Flicker; Photography, Cusi Barrio; Assistant Director, Jorge Gar-Bustamante; Casting, Al Guarino, Sandra Wiese; Sound, Edgar stanau; Costumes, Patricia MaGuill; Stunts, Jose Luy, Guillerm Pin, ver Ruiz; Special Effects, Fernando Vasquez De Velasco; Foto-Kem lor; Rated R; 93 minutes; December release. CAST: David Carradine son), Peter Nelson (Bone), Sherilyn Fenn (Helen), Michael Shaner reon), Orlando Sacha (Alexi), Don Manor (J.D.), Alfredo Calderon ruz), Jorge Bustamante (Hector), Claire Beresford, Diana Quijano, rlos Banvelos, Roy Morris, Brayton Lewis, Gerald Powell, Guido lanos, Tim Dallman, Raymond Waldrom, Andres Dasso, David lleby, Jeanne Cervantes, Erika Stockholm, Linda Vetze, Luis Orruti-r, Alfredo Salazar

AKOTA (Miramax) Producers, Darryl J. Kuntz, Frank J. Kuntz; sociate Producer, Lou Diamond Phillips; Director, Fred Holmes; reenplay, Lynn & Darryl Kuntz; Photography, Jim Wrenn; Editor, on Seith; Music, Chris Christian; Art Director, Pat O'Neal; Cos-mes, Rondi Hillstrom Davis; Sound, Darrell Henke; Assistant Direct-, John Colwell; Color; Rated PG; 96 minutes; December release. AST: Lou Diamond Phillips (Dakota), Herta Ware (Aunt Zard), eDee Norton (Molly), Jordan Burton (Casey), Eli Cummins (Walt), Steven Ruge (Bo), John Hawkes (Rooster), Tom Campitelli (Rob), Leslie Mullin (Cynthia), Lawrence Montaigne (Diamond), Susan Crippin (Alicia), Rodger Boyce (Sheriff), Robert Aloha (Mechanic), Connie Coit (Mrs. Diamond), Robert Lemus (Eric), Helena Humann (Gym Teacher), Derek Odom, Vernon Walker, Tammy Stevens, Daniel Massey, Nicholas Mezzls, Richard Weils (Aunt Zard's Kids)

I'M GONNA GIT YOU SUCKA (United Artists) Producers, Eric Barrett, Tamara Rawitt, Peter McCarthy, Carl Craig; Director/Screenplay, Keenen Ivory Wayans; Co-Producers, Eric Barrett, Tamara Rawitt; Executive Producers, Raymond Katz, Eric L. Gold; Photography, Tom Richmond; Designers, Melba Farquhar, Catherine Hardwicke; Editor, Michael R. Miller; Music, David Michael Frank; Costumes, Ruth E. Carter; Casting, Jaki Brown, Robi Reed; Production Manager, Andrew D. Given; Assistant Directors, Elliot Lewis Rosenblatt, Scott White; Set Decorator, Kathryn Peters-Hollingsworth; Sound, Oliver L. Moss; Production Coordinator, Belinda Ellis; Effects Makeup, Barbie Gotschall; Choreographer, Russell Clark; Special Effects, Fred J. Cramer; from MGM/UA Communications; In Association with Front Films; Title Song by Norman Whitfield & William Bryant II, and songs by various artists; Soundtrack on Arista Records; Ultra-Stereo; DeLuxe Color; Rated R; 87 minutes; December release. CAST: Keenen Ivory Wayans (Jack Spade), Bernie Casey (John Spade), Antonio Fargas (Flyguy), Steve James (Kung Fu Joe), Isaac Hayes (Hammer), Jim Brown (Slammer), Janet DuBois (Ma Bell), Dawnn Lewis (Cheryl), John Vernon (Mr. Big), Clu Gulager (Lt. Baker), Kadeem Hardison (Willie), Damon Wayans (Leonard), George James (Bruno), Marc Figueroa (Knuckles), Robert Colert (Farrell), Jester Hairston (Pop), Hawthorne James (One Eyed Sam), Anne Marie Johnson (Cherry), Eve Plumb (Kalinga's Wife), Clarence Williams III (Kalinga), Vickilyn Reynolds (Sadie), Paul Motley (Luther), Charles Cozart (Anchorman), Marilyn Coleman, Gary Owens, Michael Goldfinger, John Witherspoon, Homeselle Joy, Brian MaGuire, David Alan Grier, Ariana Richards

NOBODY LISTENED (Cuban Human Rights Film Project) Producers/Directors/Screenplay, Nestor Almendros, Jorge Ulla; Photography, Orson Ochoa; Editors, Gloria Pineyro, Esther Duran; Sound, Phil Pearle; Associate Producers, Marcelino Miyares, Jorge A. Rodriguez, Albert E. Jolis; color; Not rated; 117 minutes; December release. A documentary on Cuban human rights under the Castro regime, narrated by Geoffrey Carey and Sondra Lee

DeeDee Norton, Lou Diamond Phillips in "Dakota" ***(Miramax)***

Clarence Williams III, Eve Plumb, Keenen Ivory Wayans in "I'm Gonna Git You Sucka"
(United Artists)

Kim Basinger, Alyson Hannigan in "My Stepmother Is an Alien" ***(Weintraub)***

Mary Beth Hurt, Randy Quaid, Bryan Madorsky in "Parents" ***(Vestron Pictures)***

LANDLORD BLUES (L.L. Pictures) Producer/Director, Jacob Burckhardt; Co-Producer, Howard David Deutsch; Co-Director, William Gordy; Screenplay/Editors, Jacob Burckhardt, William Gordy; Story, George Schneeman; Photography, Carl Teitelbaum; Music, Roy Nathanson, Marc Ribot, Nona Hendryx, Oliver Lake; Kodak color; Not rated; 96 minutes; December release. CAST: Mark Boone Jr.

MY STEPMOTHER IS AN ALIEN (Weintraub Entertainment Group/Columbia) Producers, Franklin R. Levy, Ronald Parker; Director, Richard Benjamin; Executive Producers, Laurence Mark, Art Levinson; Screenplay, Jerico & Herschel Weingrod, Tomothy Harris, Jonathan Reynolds; Photography, Richard H. Kline; Designer, Charles Rosen; Costumes, Aggie Guerard Rodgers; Visual Effects, John Dykstra; Music, Alan Silvestri; Casting, Nancy Foy; Editor, Jacqueline Cambas; Production Manager, Art Levinson; Assistant Director, Alan Cutiss; Sound, Jerry Jost; Set Decorator, Don Remacle; Set Designer, Harold Fuhrman; Special Effects, Phil Cory, Ray Svedin, Hans Metz; Puppeteer, Pat Brymer; Stunts, Richard Ziker; Choreography, Don Correia; In Association with Catalina Production Group, Ltd.; Color; Rated PG-13; 108 minutes; December release. CAST: Dan Aykroyd (Dr. Steve Mills), Kim Basinger (Celeste), Jon Lovitz (Ron Mills), Alyson Hannigan (Jessie Mills), Joseph Maher (Dr. Lucas Budlong), Seth Green (Fred Glass), Wesley Mann (Grady), Ann Prentiss (Voice of Bag), Harry Shearer (Voice of Carl Sagan), Adrian Sparks (Dr. Morosini), Juliette Lewis (Lexie), Tany Fenmore (Ellen), Karen Haber (Kristy), Amy Kirkpatrick (Kimberly), Suzie Plakson (Tenley), Robyn Mundell (Kat), Kevin McDermott (Olaf), Barbara Sharma (Mrs. Glass), Michele Rogers (Skippy Budlong), Lisa Croisette (Winnek Wolfet), Dave the Dog (Peanut)

PARENTS (Vestron) Producer, Bonnie Palef; Director, Bob Balaban; Screenplay, Christopher Hawthorne; Executive Producers, Mitchell Cannold, Steven Reuther; Production Executives, Dori Berinstein Wasserman; Editor, Bill Pankow; Photography, Ernest Day, Robin Vidgeon; Art Director, Andris Hausmanis; Music, Angelo Badalamenti; Costumes, Arthur Rowsell; Casting, Risa Bramon, Billy Hopkins; In Association with Great American Films Ltd. Partnership; Production Manager, Suzanne Lore; Assistant Director, Gary Flanagan; Set Decorator, Michael Harris; Sound, Douglas Thane Stewart; Stunts, Rick Forsyth; Special Effects, Gord Smith; Associate Editor, Janice Keuhnelian; Dolby Stereo; Color; Rated R; 82 minutes; December release. CAST: Randy Quaid (Nick Laemle), Mary Beth Hurt (Lily Laemle), Sandy Dennis (Millie Dew), Bryan Madorsky (Micha Laemle), Juno Mills-Cockell (Sheila Zellner), Kathryn Grody (Mi Baxter), Deborah Rush (Mrs. Zellner), Graham Jarvis (Mr. Zellne Helen Carscallen (Grandmother), Warren Van Evera (Grandfathe Wayne Robson, Uriel Byfield, Mariah Balaban, Larry Palef, Richa Berube, Brent Meyer, Leslie Munro

PURPLE PEOPLE EATER (Concorde) Producers, Brad Krevc Steve Stabler; Director/Screenplay, Linda Shayne; Based on the so by Sheb Wooley; Photography, Peter Deming; Editor, Cari Ell Coughlin; Designer, Stephen Greenberg; Creative Consultant, Ji Wynorski; Assistant Director/Production Manager, Randy Pope; Pu peteer, Tim Lawrence; Choreographers, Ted Lin, Ben Lokey; Soun Ike Magal; A Motion Picture Corp. of American production; Foto-Ke Color; Rated PG; 92 minutes; December release. CAST: Ned Bea (Grandpa), Shelley Winters (Rita), Neil Harris (Billy Johnson), Peg Lipton (Mom), Chubby Checker (Himself), Little Richard (Mayo James Houghton (Dad), Thora Birch (Molly Johnson), John Brumfie (Mr. Noodle), Molly Cheek (Mrs. Orfus), Kimberly McCullou (Donna Orfus), Sheb Wooley (Harvey Skitters), Shonda Whipple (Al son), Lindsay Price (Kory Kamimoto), Katie Gonzales (Patty Kamim to), Dustin Diamond (Big Z), Cheri Hoppe (Heidi Johnson), Lau Bruneau (Coach Miller), Randy Pope (Coach Warzecka), Arnie Mil (Father of the Bride), Beverly Miller (Purple's Mom???), Jack Be (Dr. Rubin), Linda Shayne (Nurse Thompson), Mitsuru Yamaha Cecile Krevoy, Rita Tavill, Francis Buchsbaum, Marjorie Gough

SCREWBALL HOTEL (Universal) Producer, Maurice Smith; Exe utive Producers, Joe Garofolo, Robert Patterson, Jon Gansel Brew Director, Rafal Zielinski; Screenplay, B. K. Roderick, Phil Kuebe Charles Wiener, Nick Holeris; Assistant Director, James R. Van Vor Photography, Thomas F. Denove; Editor, Joseph Tornatore; Mus Nathan Wang; Sound, Tom Colucci, Michael Eric Fowler; Producti Designer, Naomi Shohan; Casting, Dennis Gallegos; Associate Pr ducers, Terrea Smith, Debi Davis; produced in association with Ava Film; Foto-Kem color; Ultra-Stereo; Rated R; 101 minutes; Decemb release. CAST: Michael C. Bendetti (Mike), Andrew Zeller (Herbi Jeff Greenman (Norman), Kelly Monteith (Mr. Ebbel), Corin Alphen (Cherry Amour), Charles Ballinger (Stoner), Laurah Guill (Miss Walsh), Lori Deann Pallet (Candy), Theresa Bell, Jack L. D lard, Tina Bayne, Richard Norton, Gianna Amore, Laura Lewis, Ren Shugart, Andi Bruce

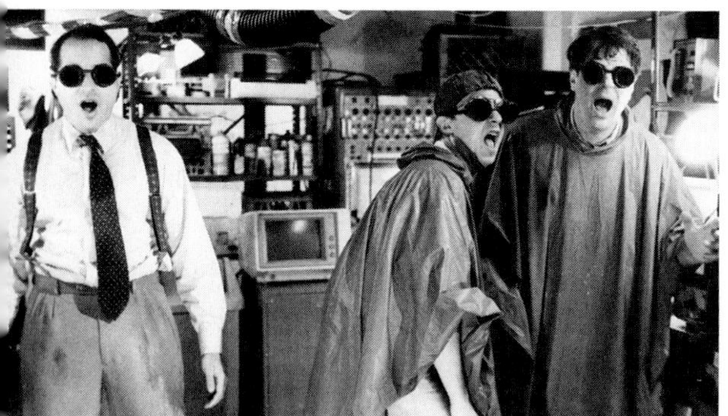

Jon Lovitz, Wesley Mann, Dan Aykroyd in "My Stepmother. . . ." ***(Columbia/Weintruab)***

Neil Patrick Harris and his band in "Purple People Eater" ***(Concorde)***

OUTSTANDING NEW ACTORS OF 1988

ROBERT DOWNEY, JR.

PENELOPE ANN MILLER

NATASHA RICHARDSON

TODD GRAFF

WILLIAM McNAMARA

JULIA ROBERTS

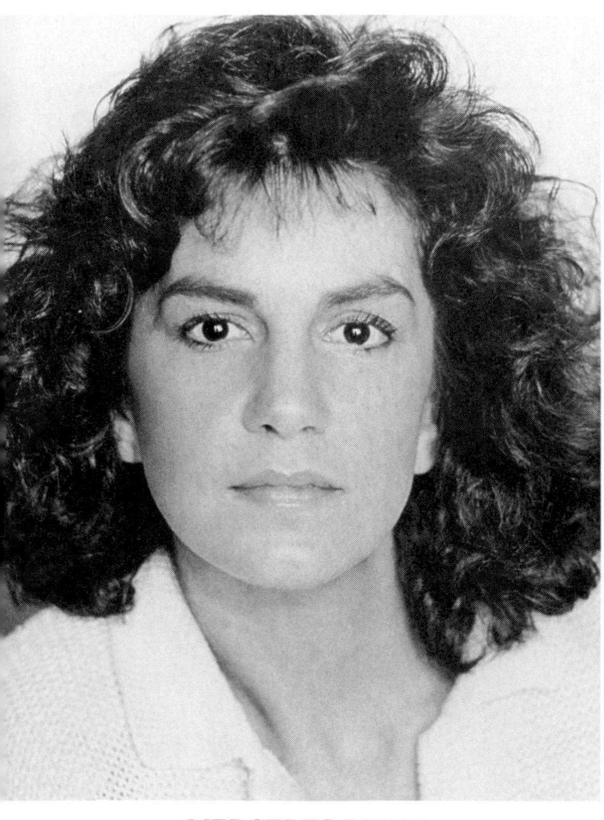

MERCEDES RUEHL

KEANU REEVES

CHRISTIAN SLATER

WINONA RYDER

KIEFER SUTHERLAND

UNA THURMAN

ACADEMY AWARDS FOR 1988

(Presented Wednesday, March 29, 1989 in Shrine Civic Auditorium, Los Angeles)

RAIN MAN

(UNITED ARTISTS) Producer, Mark Johnson; Director, Ba Levinson; Screenplay, Ronald Bass, Barry Morrow; Story, Ba Morrow; Executive Producers, Peter Gruber, Jon Peters; Photograpl John Seale; Designer, Ida Random; Editor, Stu Linder; Music, Ha Zimmer; Co-Producer, Gerald R. Molen; Associate Producers, G Mutrux, David McGiffert; Costumes, Bernie Pollack; Casting, Lo DiGiaimo; Production Manager, Gerald R. Molen; Assistant Direct David McGiffert; Art Director, William A. Elliott; Set Decorat Linda DeScenna; Additional Editor, Thomas R. Moore; Sou Richard Goodman, Richard Beggs; Special Effects, Don Myers; *"Wis ful Thinking"* by Jocko Marcellino & Randy Handley, *"Lovin' Ain't Hard"* by Jocko Marcellino/Performances, Jocko Marcellino, a songs by other artists; from MGM/UA Communications; Dolby Ster DeLuxe Color; Rated R; 132 minutes; December release

CAST

Raymond Babbitt .... Dustin Hoffm
Charlie Babbitt .... Tom Cru
Susanna .... Valeria Goli
Dr. Bruner .... Jerry Mol
John Mooney .... Jack Murdo
Vern .... Michael D. Robe
Lenny .... Ralph Seymo
Iris .... Lucinda Jenn
Sally Dibbs .... Bonnie Hu
Small Town Doctor .... Kim Robilla
Mother at farm house .... Beth Gra
Dr. Bruner's Secretary .... Loretta Wendt Jolive
Nurse .... Donna J. Dicks
Kelso .... Ray Bak
Psychiatrist .... Barry Levins
and Dolan Dougherty, Marshall Dougherty, Patrick Dougherty, Joh Michael Dougherty, Peter Dougherty, Andrew Dougherty, Donald Jones, Bryon P. Caunar, Earl Roat, William J. Montgomery J Elizabeth Lower, Michael C. Hall, Robert W. Heckel, W. Todd Ke ner, Kneeles Reeves, Jack W. Cope, Nick Mazzola, Ralph Tabak Isadore Figler, Ralph M. Cardinale, Sam Roth, Nanci M. Harve Kenneth E. Lowden, Jocko Marcellino, John Thorstensen, Kas Se

Left: Dustin Hoffman, Tom Cruise

Academy Awards for Best Picture, Director, Actor (Dustin Hoffman), Original Screenplay

Valeria Golino, Dustin Hoffman

Dustin Hoffman, Tom Cruise

Tom Cruise, Dustin Hoffman and also top left and below
Top Right: Valeria Golino, Tom Cruise

DUSTIN HOFFMAN
in "Rain Man"
© United Artists
1988 ACADEMY AWARD FOR BEST ACTOR

JODIE FOSTER
in "The Accused"
© *Paramount/Rob McEwan*
1988 ACADEMY AWARD FOR BEST ACTRESS

KEVIN KLINE
in "A Fish Called Wanda"
© MGM Pictures/David James
1988 ACADEMY AWARD FOR BEST SUPPORTING ACTOR

GEENA DAVIS
in "The Accidental Tourist"
© *Warner Brothers*
1988 ACADEMY AWARD FOR BEST SUPPORTING ACTRESS

PELLE THE CONQUEROR

(MIRAMAX) Producer, Per Holst; Director/Screenplay, Bille Augus Based on the novel by Martin Anderson Nexo; Photography, Jorge Persson; Editor, Janus Billeskov Jansen; Music, Stefan Nilsson; De signer, Anna Asp; Sound, Niels Arild Nielsen, Lars Lund; Costumes Kicki Ilander, Gitte Kolvig, Birthe Qualmann; 1988 Best Film Priz (Palme d'Or) at the Cannes Film Festival; Danish with subtitles; Colo Not rated; 150 minutes; December release

CAST

Lasse Karlsson .... Max von Sydo
Pelle Karlsson .... Pelle Hvenegaar
Manager .... Erik Paask
Anna .... Kristina Tornqvis
Trainee .... Morten Jorgense
Mr. Kongstrup .... Axel Stroby
Mrs. Kongstrup .... Astrid Villaum
Erik .... Bjorn Grana
The Sow .... Lena Pia Bernhardsso
Rud .... Troels Asmusse
Karna .... Anne Lise Hirsch Bjerru
Ole Koller .... Buster Larse
Mr. Fris (Teacher) .... John Witt
Henrik Bodker .... Benjamin Holck Henrikse
Nilen .... Thure Lindhar
Mrs. Olsen .... Karen Wegene
Miss Sine .... Anne Sofie Grab
The Preacher .... Nils Bank-Mikkelse

Top Left: Pelle Hvenegaard, Max von Sydow
Below: Max von Sydow, Pelle Hvenegaard

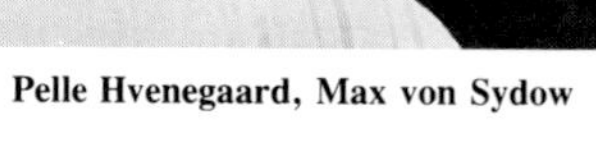
Pelle Hvenegaard, Max von Sydow

Max von Sydow

Klaus Barbie

HOTEL TERMINUS: THE LIFE AND TIMES OF KLAUS BARBIE

(SAMUEL GOLDWYN) Producer/Director, Marcel Ophuls; Chief Editors, Albert Jurgenson, Catherine Zins; Executive Producers, John S. Friedman, Hamilton Fish, Peter Kovler; Associate Producer, Bernard Farrell; Documentary; France; French with subtitles; Not rated; 267 minutes; October release

Top: Klaus Barbie (in front of pillar with translator on his right) and his defense lawyer, Jacques Verges, is in front of him wearing glasses.
© Samuel Goldwyn Company/Marc Riboud

Julie Andrews

George Chakiris

Greer Garson

Jack Lemmon

Joanne Woodward

James Stewart

PREVIOUS ACADEMY AWARD WINNERS

(1) Best Picture, (2) Actor, (3) Actress, (4) Supporting Actor, (5) Supporting Actress, (6) Director, (7) Special Award, (8) Best Foreign Language Film, (9) Best Feature Documentary

1927–28: (1) "Wings," (2) Emil Jannings in "The Way of All Flesh," (3) Janet Gaynor in "Seventh Heaven," (6) Frank Borzage for "Seventh Heaven," (7) Charles Chaplin.
1928–29: (1) "Broadway Melody," (2) Warner Baxter in "Old Arizona," (3) Mary Pickford in "Coquette," (6) Frank Lloyd for "The Divine Lady."
1929–30: (1) "All Quiet on the Western Front," (2) George Arliss in "Disraeli," (3) Norma Shearer in "The Divorcee," (6) Lewis Milestone for "All Quiet on the Western Front."
1930–31: (1) "Cimarron," (2) Lionel Barrymore in "A Free Soul," (3) Marie Dressler in "Min and Bill," (6) Norman Taurog for "Skippy."
1931–32: (1) "Grand Hotel," (2) Fredric March in "Dr. Jekyll and Mr. Hyde" tied with Wallace Beery in "The Champ," (3) Helen Hayes in "The Sin of Madelon Claudet," (6) Frank Borzage for "Bad Girl."
1932–33: (1) "Cavalcade," (2) Charles Laughton in "The Private Life of Henry VIII," (3) Katharine Hepburn in "Morning Glory," (6) Frank Lloyd for "Cavalcade."
1934: (1) "It Happened One Night," (2) Clark Gable in "It Happened One Night," (3) Claudette Colbert in "It Happened One Night," (6) Frank Capra for "It Happened One Night," (7) Shirley Temple.
1935: (1) "Mutiny on the Bounty," (2) Victor McLaglen in "The Informer," (3) Bette Davis in "Dangerous," (6) John Ford for "The Informer," (7) D. W. Griffith.
1936: (1) "The Great Ziegfeld," (2) Paul Muni in "The Story of Louis Pasteur," (3) Luise Rainer in "The Great Ziegfeld," (4) Walter Brennan in "Come and Get It," (5) Gale Sondergaard in "Anthony Adverse," (6) Frank Capra for "Mr. Deeds Goes to Town."
1937: (1)"The Life of Emile Zola," (2) Spencer Tracy in "Captains Courageous," (3) Luise Rainer in "The Good Earth," (4) Joseph Schildkraut in "The Life of Emile Zola," (5) Alice Brady in "In Old Chicago," (6) Leo McCarey for "The Awful Truth," (7) Mack Sennett, Edgar Bergen.
1938: (1) "You Can't Take It with You," (2) Spencer Tracy in "Boys' Town," (3) Bette Davis in "Jezebel," (4) Walter Brennan in "Kentucky," (5) Fay Bainter in "Jezebel," (6) Frank Capra for "You Can't Take It with You," (7) Deanna Durbin, Mickey Rooney, Harry M. Warner, Walt Disney.
1939: (1) "Gone with the Wind," (2) Robert Donat in "Goodbye, Mr. Chips," (3) Vivien Leigh in "Gone with the Wind," (4) Thomas Mitchell in "Stagecoach," (5) Hattie McDaniel in "Gone with the Wind," (6) Victor Fleming for "Gone with the Wind," (7) Douglas Fairbanks, Judy Garland.
1940: (1) "Rebecca," (2) James Stewart in "The Philadelphia Story," (3) Ginger Rogers in "Kitty Foyle," (4) Walter Brennan in "The Westerner," (5) Jane Darwell in "The Grapes of Wrath," (6) John Ford for "The Grapes of Wrath," (7) Bob Hope.
1941: (1) "How Green Was My Valley," (2) Gary Cooper in "Sergeant York," (3) Joan Fontaine in "Suspicion," (4) Donald Crisp in "How Green Was My Valley," (5) Mary Astor in "The Great Lie," (6) John Ford for "How Green Was My Valley," (7) Leopold Stokowski, Walt Disney.
1942: (1) "Mrs. Miniver," (2) James Cagney in "Yankee Doodle Dandy," (3) Greer Garson in "Mrs. Miniver," (4) Van Heflin in "Johnny Eager," (5) Teresa Wright in "Mrs. Miniver," (6) William Wyler for "Mrs. Miniver," (7) Charles Boyer, Noel Coward.
1943: (1) "Casablanca," (2) Paul Lukas in "Watch on the Rhine," (3) Jennifer Jones in "The Song of Bernadette," (4) Charles Coburn in "The More the Merrier," (5) Katina Paxinou in "For Whom the Bell Tolls," (6) Michael Curtiz for "Casablanca."
1944: (1) "Going My Way," (2) Bing Crosby in "Going My Way," (3) Ingrid Bergman in "Gaslight," (4) Barry Fitzgerald in "Going My Way," (5) Ethel Barrymore in "None but the Lonely Heart," (6) Leo McCarey for "Going My Way," (7) Margaret O'Brien, Bob Hope.
1945: (1) "The Lost Weekend," (2) Ray Milland in "The Lost Weekend," (3) Joan Crawford in "Mildred Pierce," (4) James Dunn in "A Tree Grows in Brooklyn," (5) Anne Revere in "National Velvet," (6) Billy Wilder for "The Lost Weekend," (7) Walter Wanger, Peggy Ann Garner.
1946: (1) "The Best Years of Our Lives," (2) Fredric March in "The Best Years of Our Lives," (3) Olivia de Havilland in "To Each His Own," (4) Harold Russell in "The Best Years of Our Lives," (5) Anne Baxter in "The Razor's Edge," (6) William Wyler for "The Best Years of Our Lives," (7) Laurence Olivier, Harold Russell, Ernst Lubitsch, Claude Jarman, Jr.
1947: (1) "Gentleman's Agreement," (2) Ronald Colman in "A Double Life," (3) Loretta Young in "The Farmer's Daughter," (4) Edmund Gwenn in "Miracle On 34th Street," (5) Celeste Holm in "Gentleman's Agreement," (6) Elia Kazan for "Gentleman's Agreement," (7) James Baskette, (8) "Shoe Shine," (Italy).
1948: (1) "Hamlet," (2) Laurence Olivier in "Hamlet," (3) Jane Wyman in "Johnny Belinda," (4) Walter Huston in "The Treasure of the Sierra Madre," (5) Claire Trevor in "Key Largo," (6) John Huston for "The Treasure of the Sierra Madre," (7) Ivan Jandl, Sid Grauman, Adolph Zukor, Walter Wanger, (8) "Monsieur Vincent," (France).
1949: (1) "All the King's Men," (2) Broderick Crawford in "All the King's Men," (3) Olivia de Havilland in "The Heiress," (4) Dean Jagger in "Twelve O'Clock High," (5) Mercedes McCambridge in "All the King's Men," (6) Joseph L. Mankiewicz for "A Letter to Three Wives," (7) Bobby Driscoll, Fred Astaire, Cecil B. DeMille, Jean Hersholt, (8) "The Bicycle Thief," (Italy).
1950: (1) "All about Eve," (2) Jose Ferrer in "Cyrano de Bergerac," (3) Judy Holliday in "Born Yesterday," (4) George Sanders in "All about Eve," (5) Josephine Hull in "Harvey," (6) Joseph L. Mankiewicz for "All about Eve," (7) George Murphy, Louis B. Mayer, (8) "The Walls of Malapaga," (France/Italy).
1951: (1) "An American in Paris," (2) Humphrey Bogart in "The African Queen," (3) Vivien Leigh in "A Streetcar Named Desire," (4) Karl Malden in "A Streetcar Named Desire," (5) Kim Hunter in "A Streetcar Named Desire," (6) George Stevens for "A Place in the Sun," (7) Gene Kelly, (8) "Rashomon," (Japan).
1952: (1) "The Greatest Show on Earth," (2) Gary Cooper in "High Noon," (3) Shirley Booth in "Come Back, Little Sheba," (4) Anthony Quinn in "Viva Zapata," (5) Gloria Grahame in "The Bad and the Beautiful," (6) John Ford for "The Quiet Man," (7) Joseph M. Schenck, Merian C. Cooper, Harold Lloyd, Bob Hope, George Alfred Mitchell, (8) "Forbidden Games," (France).
1953: (1) "From Here to Eternity," (2) William Holden in "Stalag 17," (3) Audrey Hepburn in "Roman Holiday," (4) Frank Sinatra in "From Here to Eternity," (5) Donna Reed in "From Here to Eternity," (6) Fred Zinnemann for "From Here to Eternity," (7) Pete Smith, Joseph Breen, (8) no award.
1954: (1) "On the Waterfront," (2) Marlon Brando in "On the Waterfront," (3) Grace Kelly in "The Country Girl," (4) Edmond O'Brien in "The Barefoot Contessa," (5) Eva Marie Saint in "On the Waterfront," (6) Elia Kazan for "On the Waterfront," (7) Greta Garbo, Danny Kaye, Jon Whitely, Vincent Winter, (8) "Gate of Hell," (Japan).

1955: (1) "Marty," (2) Ernest Borgnine in "Marty," (3) Anna Magnani in "The Rose Tattoo," (4) Jack Lemmon in "Mister Roberts," (5) Jo Van Fleet in "East of Eden," (6) Delbert Mann for "Marty," (8) "Samurai," (Japan).
1956: (1) "Around the World in 80 Days," (2) Yul Brynner in "The King and I," (3) Ingrid Bergman in "Anastasia," (4) Anthony Quinn in "Lust for Life," (5) Dorothy Malone in "Written on the Wind," (6) George Stevens for "Giant," (7) Eddie Cantor, (8) "La Strada," (Italy).
1957: (1) "The Bridge on the River Kwai," (2) Alec Guinness in "The Bridge on the River Kwai," (3) Joanne Woodward in "The Three Faces of Eve," (4) Red Buttons in "Sayonara," (5) Miyoshi Umeki in "Sayonara," (6) David Lean for "The Bridge on the River Kwai," (7) Charles Brackett, B. B. Kahane, Gilbert M. (Bronco Billy) Anderson, (8) "The Nights of Cabiria," (Italy).
1958: (1) "Gigi," (2) David Niven in "Separate Tables," (3) Susan Hayward in "I Want to Live," (4) Burl Ives in "The Big Country," (5) Wendy Hiller in "Separate Tables," (6) Vincente Minnelli for "Gigi," (7) Maurice Chevalier, (8) "My Uncle," (France).
1959: (1) "Ben-Hur," (2) Charlton Heston in "Ben-Hur," (3) Simone Signoret in "Room at the Top," (4) Hugh Griffith in "Ben-Hur," (5) Shelley Winters in "The Diary of Anne Frank," (6) William Wyler for "Ben-Hur," (7) Lee de Forest, Buster Keaton, (8) "Black Orpheus," (Brazil).
1960: (1) "The Apartment," (2) Burt Lancaster in "Elmer Gantry," (3) Elizabeth Taylor in "Butterfield 8," (4) Peter Ustinov in "Spartacus," (5) Shirley Jones in "Elmer Gantry," (6) Billy Wilder for "The Apartment," (7) Gary Cooper, Stan Laurel, Hayley Mills, (8) "The Virgin Spring," (Sweden).
1961: (1) "West Side Story," (2) Maximilian Schell in "Judgment at Nuremberg," (3) Sophia Loren in "Two Women," (4) George Chakiris in "West Side Story," (5) Rita Moreno in "West Side Story," (6) Robert Wise for "West Side Story," (7) Jerome Robbins, Fred L. Metzler, (8) "Through a Glass Darkly," (Sweden).
1962: (1) "Lawrence of Arabia," (2) Gregory Peck in "To Kill a Mockingbird," (3) Anne Bancroft in "The Miracle Worker," (4) Ed Begley in "Sweet Bird of Youth," (5) Patty Duke in "The Miracle Worker," (6) David Lean for "Lawrence of Arabia," (8) "Sundays and Cybele," (France).
1963: (1) "Tom Jones," (2) Sidney Poitier in "Lilies of the Field," (3) Patricia Neal in "Hud," (4) Melvyn Douglas in "Hud," (5) Margaret Rutherford in "The V.I.P's," (6) Tony Richardson for "Tom Jones," (8) "8½," (Italy).
1964: (1) "My Fair Lady," (2) Rex Harrison in "My Fair Lady," (3) Julie Andrews in "Mary Poppins," (4) Peter Ustinov in "Topkapi," (5) Lila Kedrova in "Zorba the Greek," (6) George Cukor for "My Fair Lady," (7) William Tuttle, (8) "Yesterday, Today and Tomorrow," (Italy).
1965: (1) "The Sound of Music," (2) Lee Marvin in "Cat Ballou," (3) Julie Christie in "Darling," (4) Martin Balsam in "A Thousand Clowns," (5) Shelley Winters in "A Patch of Blue," (6) Robert Wise for "The Sound of Music," (7) Bob Hope, (8) "The Shop on Main Street," (Czech).
1966: (1) "A Man for All Seasons," (2) Paul Scofield in "A Man for All Seasons," (3) Elizabeth Taylor in "Who's Afraid of Virginia Woolf?," (4) Walter Matthau in "The Fortune Cookie," (5) Sandy Dennis in "Who's Afraid of Virginia Woolf?," (6) Fred Zinnemann for "A Man for All Seasons," (8) "A Man and A Woman," (France).
1967: (1) "In the Heat of the Night," (2) Rod Steiger in "In the Heat of the Night," (3) Katharine Hepburn in "Guess Who's Coming to Dinner," (4) George Kennedy in "Cool Hand Luke," (5) Estelle Parsons in "Bonnie and Clyde," (6) Mike Nichols for "The Graduate," (8) "Closely Watched Trains," (Czech).
1968: (1) "Oliver!," (2) Cliff Robertson in "Charly," (3) Katharine Hepburn in "The Lion in Winter" tied with Barbra Streisand in "Funny Girl," (4) Jack Albertson in "The Subject Was Roses," (5) Ruth Gordon in "Rosemary's Baby," (6) Carol Reed for "Oliver!," (7) Onna White for "Oliver!" choreography, John Chambers for "Planet of the Apes" make-up, (8) "War and Peace," (USSR).
1969: (1) "Midnight Cowboy," (2) John Wayne in "True Grit," (3) Maggie Smith in "The Prime of Miss Jean Brodie," (4) Gig Young in "They Shoot Horses, Don't They?," (5) Goldie Hawn in "Cactus Flower," (6) John Schlesinger for "Midnight Cowboy," (7) Cary Grant, (8) "Z," (Algeria).
1970: (1) "Patton," (2) George C. Scott in "Patton," (3) Glenda Jackson in "Women in Love," (4) John Mills in "Ryan's Daughter," (5) Helen Hayes in "Airport," (6) Franklin J. Schaffner for "Patton," (7) Lillian Gish, Orson Welles, (8) "Investigation of a Citizen above Suspicion," (Italy).
1971: (1) "The French Connection," (2) Gene Hackman in "The French Connection," (3) Jane Fonda in "Klute," (4) Ben Johnson in "The Last Picture Show," (5) Cloris Leachman in "The Last Picture Show," (6) William Friedkin for "The French Connection," (7) Charles Chaplin, (8) "The Garden of the Finzi-Continis," (Italy).
1972: (1) "The Godfather," (2) Marlon Brando in "The Godfather," (3) Liza Minnelli in "Cabaret," (4) Joel Grey in "Cabaret," (5) Eileen Heckart in "Butterflies Are Free," (6) Bob Fosse for "Cabaret," (7) Edward G. Robinson, (8) "The Discreet Charm of the Bourgeoisie," (France).
1973: (1) "The Sting," (2) Jack Lemmon in "Save the Tiger," (3) Glenda Jackson in "A Touch of Class," (4) John Houseman in "The Paper Chase," (5) Tatum O'Neal in "Paper Moon," (6) George Roy Hill for "The Sting," (8) "Day for Night," (France).
1974: (1) "The Godfather Part II," (2) Art Carney in "Harry and Tonto," (3) Ellen Burstyn in "Alice Doesn't Live Here Anymore," (4) Robert DeNiro in "The Godfather Part II," (5) Ingrid Bergman in "Murder on the Orient Express," (6) Francis Ford Coppola for "The Godfather Part II," (7) Howard Hawks, Jean Renoir, (8) "Amarcord," (Italy).
1975: (1) "One Flew over the Cuckoo's Nest," (2) Jack Nicholson in "One Flew over the Cuckoo's Nest," (3) Louise Fletcher in "One Flew over the Cuckoo's Nest," (4) George Burns in "The Sunshine Boys," (5) Lee Grant in "Shampoo," (6) Milos Forman for "One Flew over the Cuckoo's Nest," (7) Mary Pickford, (8) "Dersu Uzala," (U.S.S.R.), (9) "The Man Who Skied Down Everest."
1976: (1) "Rocky," (2) Peter Finch in "Network," (3) Faye Dunaway in "Network," (4) Jason Robards in "All the President's Men," (5) Beatrice Straight in "Network," (6) John G. Avildsen for "Rocky," (8) "Black and White in Color" (Ivory Coast), (9) "Harlan County U.S.A."
1977: (1) "Annie Hall," (2) Richard Dreyfuss in "The Goodbye Girl," (3) Diane Keaton in "Annie Hall," (4) Jason Robards in "Julia," (5) Vanessa Redgrave in "Julia," (6) Woody Allen for "Annie Hall," (7) Maggie Booth (film editor), (8) "Madame Rosa" (France), (9) "Who Are the DeBolts?"
1978: (1) "The Deer Hunter," (2) Jon Voight in "Coming Home," (3) Jane Fonda in "Coming Home," (4) Christopher Walken in "The Deer Hunter," (5) Maggie Smith in "California Suite," (6) Michael Cimino for "The Deer Hunter," (7) Laurence Olivier, King Vidor, (8) "Get Out Your Handkerchiefs" (France), (9) "Sacred Straight."
1979: (1) "Kramer vs. Kramer," (2) Dustin Hoffman in "Kramer vs. Kramer," (3) Sally Field in "Norma Rae," (4) Melvyn Douglas in "Being There," (5) Meryl Streep in "Kramer vs. Kramer," (6) Robert Benton for "Kramer vs. Kramer," (7) Robert S. Benjamin, Hal Elias, Alec Guinness, (8) "The Tin Drum" (Germany), (9) "Best Boy."
1980: (1) "Ordinary People," (2) Robert DeNiro in "Raging Bull," (3) Sissy Spacek in "Coal Miner's Daughter," (4) Timothy Hutton in "Ordinary People," (5) Mary Steenburgen in "Melvin and Howard," (6) Robert Redford for "Ordinary People," (7) Henry Fonda, (8) "Moscow Does Not Believe in Tears" (Russia), (9) "From Mao to Mozart: Isaac Stern in China."
1981: (1) "Chariots of Fire," (2) Henry Fonda in "On Golden Pond," (3) Katharine Hepburn in "On Golden Pond," (4) John Gielgud in "Arthur," (5) Maureen Stapleton in "Reds," (6) Warren Beatty for "Reds," (7) Fuji Photo Film Co., Barbara Stanwyck, (8) "Mephisto" (Germany/Hungary), (9) "Genocide."
1982: (1) "Gandhi," (2) Ben Kingsley in "Gandhi," (3) Meryl Streep in "Sophie's Choice," (4) Louis Gossett, Jr. in "An Officer and a Gentleman," (5) Jessica Lange in "Tootsie," (6) Richard Attenborough for "Gandhi," (7) Mickey Rooney, (8) "Volver a Empezar" (To Begin Again) (Spain), (9) "Just Another Missing Kid."
1983: (1) "Terms of Endearment," (2) Robert Duvall in "Tender Mercies," (3) Shirley MacLaine in "Terms of Endearment," (4) Jack Nicholson in "Terms of Endearment," (5) Linda Hunt in "The Year of Living Dangerously," (6) James L. Brooks for "Terms of Endearment," (7) Hal Roach, (8) "Fanny and Alexander" (Sweden), (9) "He Makes Me Feel Like Dancin'."
1984: (1) "Amadeus," (2) F. Murray Abraham in "Amadeus," (3) Sally Field in "Places in the Heart," (4) Haing S. Ngor in "The Killing Fields," (5) Peggy Ashcroft in "A Passage to India," (6) Milos Forman for "Amadeus," (7) James Stewart, (8) "Dangerous Moves" (Switzerland), (9) "The Times of Harvey Milk."
1985: (1) "Out of Africa," (2) William Hurt in "Kiss of the Spider Woman," (3) Geraldine Page in "The Trip to Bountiful," (4) Don Ameche in "Cocoon," (5) Anjelica Huston in "Prizzi's Honor," (6) Sydney Pollack for "Out of Africa," (7) Paul Newman, Alex North, (8) "The Official Story" (Argentina), (9) "Broken Rainbow."
1986: (1) "Platoon," (2) Paul Newman in "The Color of Money," (3) Marlee Matlin for "Children of a Lesser God," (4) Michael Caine for "Hannah and Her Sisters," (5) Dianne Wiest for "Hannah and Her Sisters," (6) Oliver Stone for "Platoon," (7) Ralph Bellamy, (8) "The Assault" (Netherlands), (9) "Artie Shaw: Time Is All You've Got" tied with "Down and Out in America"
1987: (1) "The Last Emperor," (2) Michael Douglas in "Wall Street," (3) Cher in "Moonstruck," (4) Sean Connery in "The Untouchables," (5) Olympia Dukakis in "Moonstruck," (6) Bernardo Bertolucci for "The Last Emperor," (8) "Babette's Feast" (Denmark), (9) "The Ten-Year Lunch: The Wit and Legend of the Algonquin Round Table"

THE GRAND HIGHWAY (Le Grand Chemin)

(MIRAMAX FILMS) Producers, Pascal Hommais, Jean Francois Lepetit; Director/Screenplay, Jean-Loup Hubert; Photography, Claude Lecomte; Camera, Jean Paul Meurisse; Sound, Bernard Aubouy; Set Design, Thierry Flamand; Editor, Raymonde Guyot; Music, Georges Granier; Production Manager, Farid Chaouche; Executive Producer, Flach Films; Assistant Directors, Olivier Horlait, Martine Durand, Jean Charles Beleteau; Costumes, Annick Francois; French; Color; Not rated; 104 minutes; January release

CAST

Marcelle .... Anemone
Pelo .... Richard Bohringer
Louis .... Antoine Hubert
Martine .... Vanessa Guedj
Claire .... Christine Pascal
Priest .... Raoul Billerey
Yvonne .... Pascale Roberts
Solange .... Marie Matheron
Chauffeur .... Jean Francois Derec
Hippolyte .... Andre Lacombe
Mary the Frog .... Denise Peron
Le Gros .... Jean Cherlian
La Lubie .... Eugenie Charpentier
Doctor Gauthier .... Thierry Flamand
Chicken Pluckers .... Marcelle Lucas, Jeanne Allaire
Butchers .... Christine Aubert, Robert Averty
Client in butcher shop .... Marie Therese Allaire

Vanessa Guedj, Antoine Hubert
© *Miramax*

Gerulf Pannach, Fabienne Babe
© *Angelika Films*

WELCOME IN VIENNA

(ROXIE CINEMA) Director, Axel Corti; Screenplay, Georg Stefan Troller, Axel Corti; Photography, Gernot Roll; Decor & Mountings, Fritz Hollergschwandtner; Costumes, Uli Fessler; Make-up, Ellen Just, Adolf Uhrmacher; Editors, Ulrike Pahl, Claudia Rieneck; Sound, Rolf Schmidt-Gentner'; Music, Hans Georg Koch; Music, Franz Schubert; Production Director, Matija Barl; Production Manager, Hermann Wolf; Produced by Thalia Film Gesmbh, Vienna, commissioned by ORF in association with ZDF and SRG, sponsored by the Austrian Federal Ministry of Education, Arts, and Sports; German; Black & White; 121 minutes; January release

CAST

Freddy Wolff .... Gabriel Barylli
Sergeant Adler .... Nicolas Brieger
Claudia Schutte .... Claudia Messner
Captaion Karpeles .... Hubert Mann
The Russian Woman .... Liliana Nelska
Stodola .... Kurt Sowinetz
Treschensky .... Karlheinz Hackl
Lieutenant Binder .... Joachim Kemmer
Oberst Schutte .... Heinz Trixner

SINGING THE BLUES IN RED

(ANGELIKA FILMS) Producer, Ramond Day; Director, Ken Loa Screenplay Trevor Griffiths; Photography, Chris Menges; Execut Producer, Irving Teitelbaum; Co-Producer, Fritz Buttenstedt; Assc ate Producer/Production Manager, Ingrid Windisch; Designer, Ma Johnson; Costumes, Antje Petersen; Sound, Karl Laabs; Edit Jonathan Morris; England; German and English with subtitles; Co 110 minutes; Not rated; January release

CAST

Klaus Drittemann .... Gerulf Panna
Emma .... Fabienne B
Lucy Bernstein .... Cristine R
James Dryden .... Sigfrit Stei
Lawyer .... Robert D
Marita .... Heike Schro
Max .... Stephan Sam
Young Drittemann .... Thomas Oeh
Thomas .... Patrick Gil
Jurgen Kirsch .... Heinz Diesl
Rosa .... Eva Krut
Schiff .... Hans Peter Hallwa
Uwe .... Ronald Simor
American Official .... Marlowe Sh
Braun .... Jim Rak
Journalist .... Bernard Bl
Herr Herring .... Winifred Tro

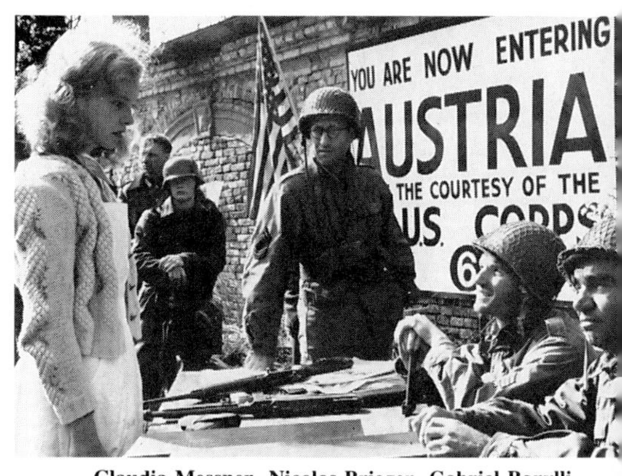

Claudia Messner, Nicolas Brieger, Gabriel Barylli, Joachim Kemmer © *Roxie Cinema*

HALF OF HEAVEN
(La Mitad del Cielo)

:KOURAS) Producer, Luis Megino; Screenplay, Manuel Gutierrez agon, Luis Megino; Director, Manuel Gutierrez Aragon; Music, lladoiro; Photography, Jose Luis Alcaine; Cameraman, Alfredo F. ıyo; Decorator/Costumes, Gerardo Vera; Editor, Jose Salcedo; sistant Director, Jose R. San Mateo; Sound, D. Goldstein, R. inberg; Casting, Carmen Zorrilla; Special Effects, Pablo Perez; bsidized by the Ministry of Culture, In collaboration with Televisio panola, S.A.; Spanish; Color; 127 minutes; Not Rated; January ease

CAST

sa .... Angela Molina
andmother .... Maragarita Lozano
ın .... Antonio V. Valero
lgado .... Nacho Martinex
ıtonio .... Santiago Ramos
miro .... Francisco Merino
ung Rosa .... Monica Molina
vido .... Carolina Silva
n Pedro .... Fernando Fernan-Gomrz
sa's Sisters .... Enriqueta Carballeira, Mercedes Lezcano
n Pedro's Sisters-in-Law .... Julia Martinez, Concha Leza
sa's Father .... Raul Frair
sa's Mother .... Concha Hidalgo
eese Vendor .... Pedro del Rio
lice Officers .... Ramon Reparaz, Marcelo G. Flores, Valentin Paredes
ıtonio's Friends .... Tino Diaz
oecleaner .... Sergio Lopez
lgado's Friend .... Santiago Alvarez
tcher .... Marisa Porcel
ifegrinder .... Francisco Catala
ocer .... Jose Segura
ok .... Francisco Torres
ıests .... Angel Acinas, Francisco Maestre
spectors .... Antonio Chamorro, Julio Gavilanes, Richardo Moya

Angela Molina, Francisco Merino
© ***Skouras Pictures***

Fanny Ardant, Phillipe Noiret in "The Family"
© ***Vestron Pictures/Bruno Bruni***

THREE STRANGE LOVES

ILM FORUM) Director, Ingmar Bergman; Screenplay, Herbert evenius; Based on a novel by Birgit Tengroth; Photography, Gunnar scher; A Janus Film released by Kino International in association with Swedish Information Service; Sweden; Swedish with subtitles; 84 ınutes; Not Rated; January release

CAST

ıt .... Eva Henning
rtil .... Birger Malmsten
ola .... Birgit Tengroth
. Rosengren .... Hasse Ekman
ılborg .... Mimi Nelson
ıoul, the Captain .... Bengt Eklund

No photos available

THE FAMILY

(VESTRON) Producer, Girogio Scotton; Director, Ettore Scola; Screenplay Adaptation, Ruggero Maccari, Furio Scarpelli, Ettore Scola; Assisted by Graziano Diana; Photography, Ricardo Aronovich; Designer, Luciano Ricceri; Costumes, Gabriella Pescucci, Tirelli Costumi; Music, Armando Trovaioli; Editor, Francesco Malvestito; Assistant Director, Paola Scola; A Co-production of Les Films Ariane-Cinemax-FR3 Films Production (France)/Massfilm S.R.L.-Cinecitta S.p.A-Rai Uno (Italy); Color; 127 minutes; Rated PG; January release

CAST

Carlo .... Emmanuele Lamaro, Andrea Occhipinti, Vittorio Gassman
Carlo's Grandfather .... Vittorio Gassman
Beatrice .... Cecilia Dazzi, Stefania Sandrelli
Adriana .... Jo Ciampa, Fanny Ardant
Giulio .... Ioska Versari, Alberto Gimignani, Massimo Dapporto, Carlo Dapporto
Adelina .... Consuelo Pascali, Ilaria Stuppia, Ottavia Piccolo
Aunt Margherita .... Athina Cenci
Aunt Luisa .... Alessandra Panelli
Aunt Ornella .... Monica Scattini
Aristide .... Meme Perlini
Susanna .... Hania Kochansky
Paolino .... Allesandro Pizzolato, Fabrizio Cerusico, Ricky Tognazzi
Maddalena .... Barbara Scoppa
Jean-Luc .... Philippe Noiret
Uncle Nicola .... Giampiero Gregori, Renzo Palmer
Carletto .... Marco Vivio, Sergio Castellitto
Enrico .... Maurizio Marsala, Riccardo Massimi, Giuseppe Cederna
Armando .... Massimo Venturiello
Marika .... Dagmar Lassande
Marina .... Andrea Livier Aronovich
Juliette I .... Silvana De Santis
Juliette II .... Paola Agosti
Carlo's Grandmother .... Francesca Balletta
Gardienne .... Raffaela Davi
Dr. Giordani .... Piriou Dit Peyrac Jacques
Uncle Michele .... Antonio De Leo
Uncle Michele's wife .... Alessandra Zoppi

EL SUR

(NEW YORKER) Producers, Elias Querejeta (Spain)/Chloe Productions (France); Director, Victor Erice; Screenplay, Jose Luis Lopez Linares; Based on a story by Adelaida Garcia Morales; Photography, Jose Luis Alcaine; editor, Pablo G. del Amo; Art Director, Antonio Belizon; Sound, Bernardo Fco. Menzo; Assistant Director, John Healey; Production Coordinator, Primitivo Alvaro; Wardrobe, Maiki Marin; Spain; Spanish with subtitles; Color; 94 minutes; Not Rated; January release

CAST

Agustin	Omero Antonutti
Estrella (age 8)	Sonsoles Aranguren
Estrella (age 15)	Iciar Bollan
Julia	Lola Cardona
Milagros	Rafaela Aparicio
Dona Rosario	Germaine Montero
Irene Rios/Laura	Aurora Clement
Irene Rios' co-star	Francisco Merino
Casilda	Maria Caro
Waiter	Jose Viivo
Chauffeur	Jose G. Murilla

Omero Antonutti, Lola Cardona, Sonsoles Arangures © *New Yorker Films*

Ugo Tognazzi (R)

THE LAST MINUTE

(SACIS) Producer, Antonio Avati; Director, Pupi Avati; Treatmen Screenplay, Pupi Avati, Antonio Avati, Italo Cucci; Photography Pasquale Rachini; Music, Riz Ortolani; Editor, Amedeo Salfa; Screer play, Giuseppe Pirotta; Costumes, Graziella Virgili; Sound, Raffae De Luca; A DUEA Film/D.M.V. Distribuzione production in associa tion with RAI Channel 1; presented by Cinema Italia—Roberto Rosse lini; Italy; Color; Not rated; 100 minutes; February release

CAST

Walter	Ugo Tognaz
Duccio	Diego Abatantuor
Boschi	Massimo Bone
Marta	Elena Sofia Ric
Egle	Giovanna Maldo
DiCarlo	Lino Capolicchi
Corti	Luigi Dibe
Nik	Nik Novecen
Paolo	Marco Leonar
Ornella	Cinzia De Pon
Lele	Cesare Barbe

A MONTH IN THE COUNTRY

(ORION CLASSICS) Producer, Kenith Trodd; Director, Pat O'Connor; Screenplay, Simon Gray; Based on the novel by J. L. Carr; Executive Producers, John Hambley, Johnny Goodman; Photography, Ken MacMillan; Camera Operator, Mike Frift; Associate Producer/ Production Supervisor, Dominic Fulford; Editor, John Victor Smith; Production Designer, Leo Austin; Art Director, Richard Elton; Music, Howard Blake; Assistant Director, Bill Craske; Set Decorator, Derek Nice; Sound, Tony Dawe; Costumes, Judy Moorcroft; Casting, Michelle Guish; a Euston Films production presented by Film Four International in association with PFH Limited; British; Color; Rated PG; 96 minutes; February release

CAST

Tom Birkin	Colin Firth
John Moon	Kenneth Branagh
Mrs. Keach	Miranda Richardson
Reverend Keach	Patrick Malahide
Douthwaite	Tony Haygarth
Ellerbeck	Jim Carter
Colonel Hebron	Richard Vernon
Kathy Ellerbeck	Vicky Arundale
Edgar Ellerbeck	Martin O'Neil
Emily Clough	Lis Taylor
Mossop	Tim Barker
Milburn	David Gillies
Mrs. Ellerbeck	Eileen O'Brien
Mrs. Sykes	Barbara Marten
Lucy Sykes	Elizabeth Anson
Mrs. Clough	Judy Gridley
Young Blind Man	Maurice D. Iley
Birkin—Much Older	David Garth
Mr. Sykes	Ken Kitson
Shop Assistant	Andrew Wilde
Old Man on train	John Atkinson
Shop Assistant	Mary Wray

Kenneth Branagh, Natasha Richardson, Colin Firth © *Orion Classics*

Harris Yulin (R)

CANDY MOUNTAIN

(INTERNATIONAL FILM EXCHANGE) Producer, Ruth Waldburger; Directors, Robert Frank, Rudy Wurlitzer; Screenplay, Rudy Wurlitzer; Photography, Pio Corradi; Sound, David Joliat; Art Directors, Brad Ricker, Keith Currie; Wardrobe/Styling, Carol Wood; Casting, Risa Braemon, Billy Hopkins, Heidi Lewitt, Gail Carr; Assistant Directors, Richard Garber, Alain Klarer, Lydie Mahias; Special Effects, Jacques Godbout; Les Film-Films Plain Chant-Films Vision 4 Inc.; Swiss-Canadian-French; Eastmancolor; Rated R; 91 minutes; February release

CAST

Julius ... Kevin J. O'Connor
Elmore ... Harris Yulin
Al Silk ... Tom Waits
Cornelia ... Bulle Ogier
Archie ... Roberts Blossom
Huey ... Leon Redbone
Henry ... Dr. John
Winnie ... Ria MacNeil
Mario ... Joe Strummer
Alice ... Laurie Metcalf
Lucille ... Jayne Eastwood
Koko ... Kazuko Oshima
Gunther ... Eric Mitchell
Couple ... Mary Joy, Bob Joy
Alston ... Arto Lindsay
Darlene ... Mary Margaret O'Hara
Keith ... David Johansen
Lawyer ... David Margulies
Musician ... Tony "Machine" Krasinski
Suzie ... Susan J. Kirschner
Lou Sultan ... Dee De Antonio
Musician's Son ... Jose Soto
Gas Station Attendant ... Bob Maroff
Van Driver ... Rockets Redglare
Maid ... Nancy Fish
Lola ... Liz Porrazzo
Gas Station Owner ... Harry Fox
Customs Officer ... Roy Maceachern
Buddy Burke ... Wayne Robson
Doctor ... Eric House, Rosalee Larade
Kids ... John Simon Beaton, Norman Rankin
School Bus Driver ... Stanley MacNeil
Annie ... Tantoo Cardinal
Molly ... Jo-Ann Rolls
Musician ... Ralph Dillon
and Joey Barron, Mark Bingham, Michael Blair, Ralph Carney, Crispin Cioe, Greg Cohen, Joe De Lia, Bob Funk, Tony Garnier, Arno Hecht, Brian Koonan, Arto Lindsay, Paul Litteral, Magic Dick, Steve Morrell, Parc Ribot, Fernando Saunders, John Saunders, John Scofield, Chris Spedding, Peter Stampfel, Kevin Tooley

ANGELE

TERAMA) Director/Screenplay, Marcel Pagnol; Based on a novel Jean Giono; Photography, Willy-Bricha; Assistant Cameraman, ger Ledru; Set Decorator, Marius Brouquier; Art Director, Arno rles Brun; Editors, Suzanne de Troye, Andre Robert; Music, Vint Scotto; France, 1934; French with subtitles; Black & White; 150 utes; February release

CAST

gel ... Orane Demazis
urnin ... Fernandel
rius ... Henri Poupon
lomene ... Anni Toinon
edee ... Edouard Delmont
in ... Jean Servais
is ... Andrex
in ... Charles Blavette
rence ... Blanche Poupon

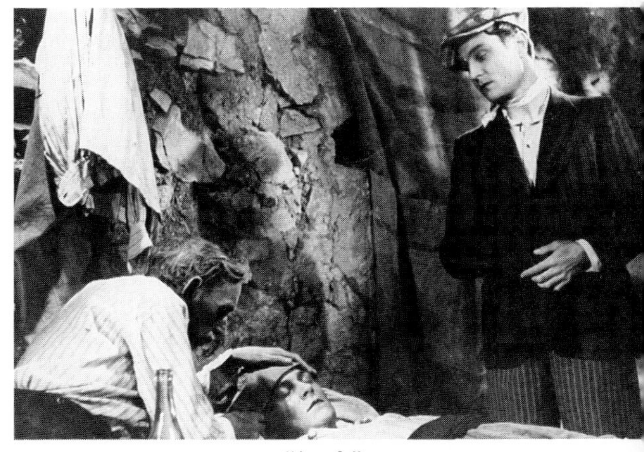

"Angele"

Ofelia Medina, Margarita Sanz
© *New Yorker Films*

FRIDA

(NEW YORKER FILMS) Producer, Manuel Barbachano Ponce; I rector, Paul Leduc; Screenplay, Jose Jaoquin Blanco, Paul Led Photography, Angel Goded, Jose Luis Esparza; Editor, Rafael C tanedo; Set Design, Alejandro Luna; Sound, Ernesto Estrada, Penelo Simpson; Executive Producer, Dulce Kuri; Docudrama; Mexic Spanish with subtitles; Not rated; 108 minutes; February release

CAST

Frida Kahlo .... Ofelia Md
Diego Rivera .... Juan Jose Gurr
Siqueiros .... Salvador Sanch
Leon Trotsky .... Max Kerl
Frida's Father .... Claudio Bro
Frida's Sister .... Cecilia Toussa
Frida Kahlo (as a child) .... Vanentina Led
Frida's Sister (as a child) .... Lolita Cor
Carpenter .... Juan Angel Martin
Photographer .... Francois Lartig
Friend .... Margarita Sa
Nurses .... Gina Morett, Agueda Inchausteg

TRAVELLING NORTH

(CINEPLEX ODEON) Producer, Ben Gannon; Director, Carl Schultz; Screenplay, David Williamson; Production Supervisor/ Casting, Sandra McKenzie; Production Manager, Julia Overton; Photography, Julian Penney; Sound, Syd Butterworth; Editor, Henry Danger; Designer, Owen Paterson; Costumes, Jennie Tate; Music Coordinator, Alan John; Production Assistant, Harriet McKern; Australian; Color; Rated PG-13; 98 minutes; February release

CAST

Frank .... Leo McKern
Francis .... Julia Blake
Freddie .... Graham Kennedy
Saul .... Henri Szeps
Helen .... Michele Fawdon
Sophie .... Diane Craig
Joan .... Andrea Moor
Martin .... Drew Forsythe
Jim .... John Gregg

Julia Blake, Leo McKern
© *Cineplex Odeon Films*

Kathleen Turner, Gabriel Byrne
© *Cinecom*

JULIA AND JULIA

(CINECOM) Executive Producers, Francesco Pinto, Gaetano Stucc Director, Peter Del Monte; Story, Silvia Napolitano, Peter Del Mon Screenplay, Silvia Napolitano, Sandro Petraglia, Peter Del Mon Dialogue, Joseph Minion; Photography, Giuseppe Rotunno; Edit Michael Chandler; Music, Maurice Jarre; Set Designer, Mario G buglia; Costumes, Danda Ortona; Produced by RAI-Radiotelevisio Italiana; Italy; Color; Rated R; 98 minutes; February release

CAST

Julia .... Kathleen Turr
Paolo .... Gabriel Byr
Daniel .... Sti
Paolo's Father .... Gabriele Ferze
Paolo's Mother .... Angela Goodw
Carla .... Lidia Broccoli
Marco .... Alexander Van W
Commissioner .... Renato Sca

APPRENTICE TO MURDER

EW WORLD) Producers, Howard K. Grossman; Director, R. L. ıomas; Screenplay, Alan Scott, Wesley Moore; Executive Producer, ichael Jay Rauch; Associate Producer, Michael R. Haley; Photogray, Kelvin Pike; Music, Charles Gorss; Editor, Patrick McMahon; ostumes, Elizabeth Ann Seley; Designer, Gregory Bolton; Casting, nn Kressel, Charkham Casting; Production Manager, Svein H. Tor-; Assistant Director, Torill Ek; Set Decorator, Pearly E. Grindvold; und, Jan Brodin; Special Effects, Derek Meddings, Mark Meddings, y Spencer; Orchestration, Gary Anderson; Stunts, Mark Boyle; orwegian; Color; Rated PG-13; 94 minutes; February release

CAST

hn Reese .... Donald Sutherland
lly Kelly .... Chad Lowe
ie Spangler .... Mia Sara
rs Hoeglin .... Knut Husebo
ma Kelly .... Rutanya Alda
m Kelly .... Eddie Jones
ay Myers .... Mark Burton
vin Myers .... Adrian Sparks
ıfus .... Tiger Haynes
ama Isobel .... Minnie Gentry
oreman .... Blain Fairman
eriff .... Mert Hatfield
op 1 .... Keith Edwards
tterson .... Chris Langham
puty .... Lars Hiller
r. Krieglander .... Ed Wiley
rs. Krieglander .... Agnette Haaland
ssica .... Irina Eidsvold
ctory Workers .... Bembo Davis, Tor Hansen
iler .... Michael R. Haley
d Woman .... Edel Eckblad

Right: Mia Sara, Chad Lowe
Top: Donald Sutherland
© New World Pictures

Dominic Guard Above: Dai Bradley
Richard Burton © *Trans World*

ABSOLUTION

(TRANS WORLD ENTERTAINMENT) Producers, Elliott Kastner, Danny O'Donovan; Director, Anthony Page; Screenplay, Anthony Shaffer; Photography, Herbert Smith; Executive Producers, George Pappas, Alan Cluer; Associate Producer, Denis Holt; Assistant Director, Richard Hoult; Sound, Peter Handford, Ken Barker; Casting, Celestia Fox; Assistant Art Director, Andrew Saunders; Costumes, Anne Gainsford; Assistant Editor, Teddy Mason; Banjo Music, Billy Connolly; British, 1979; Color; Rated R; 91 minutes; February release

CAST

Father Goddard .... Richard Burton
Benji .... Dominic Guard
Arthur .... Dai Bradley
Blakey .... Billy Connolly
Headmaster .... Andrew Kier
Brigadier Walsh .... Willoughby Gray
Father Hibbert .... Preston Lockwood
Father Mathews .... James Ottaway
Father Clarence .... Brook Williams
Father Piers .... Jon Plowman
Father Henryson .... Robin Soans
Mr. Gladstone .... Trevor Martin
Louella .... Sharon Duce
Policemen .... Brian Glover, Dan Meaden
Miss Froggatt .... Hilary Mason
Mrs. Haskins .... Hilda Fenemore
Cawley .... Robert Addie
Peterson .... Kevin Hart
Gregory .... Philip Leake
O'Dowd .... Michael Crompton
and Andrew Boxer, Richard Willis, Michael Parkhouse, Richard Kates, Martyn Hesford, Clive Gehle, Charles Rigby, Michael Bell, Martin Stringer, Francis Fry, Julian Firth, Tim Short

BEATRICE

(SAMUEL GOLDWYN COMPANY) Producer, Adolphe Vie; Director, Bertrand Tavernier; Screenplay, Colo Tavernier O'Hag Art Director, Guy Claude Francois; Photography, Bruno De Key Sound, Michel Desrois; Costumes, Jacqueline Moreau; Edit Armand Psenny; Music, Ron Carter; Assistant Directors, Olivier H lait, Philippe Berenger; Make-up, Paul Le Marinel; Special Effe Jacques Martin; A Co-Production of Clea Productions—A.M.L.F T.F. 1 Films Production—Les Films De La Tour—Little Bear—Sc Film Production (Rome); French-Italian; Color; Rated R; 128 minu March release

CAST

Francois .... Bernard Pierre Donnad
Beatrice .... Julie De
Arnaud .... Nils Taverr
Francois' Mother .... Monique Chaum
Raoul .... Robert Dh
Helene .... Michele Glei
Richard .... Maxime Lerc
Bertrand Lemartin .... Jean-Claude Ade
Maitre Blanche .... Jean-Louis Grinf
The Priest .... Claude Dune
The Nanny .... Isabelle Na
Jehan .... Jean-Luc Riv
Marie .... Roseline Villau
The Dark Woman .... Maite Ma
The Recluse .... Albane Gui
Marguerite .... Marie Pri
Francois (in prologue) .... Sebastien Koniecz
Francois' Father (in prologue) .... Vincent Saint Ou
Francois' Mother (in prologue) .... Tina Sportol
The Priest .... Francois Hadji Laz
The Lover .... Erick Bern
Pauline .... Nicole Sif
Mariette .... Myriam Thon
Jacques .... Christophe F
Thomas .... David Ordo
Joseph .... Jacques Rayna
Gildas .... Petrus Leo Cron
Blandine .... Beatrice Aba
and Jean-Claude De Brou, Stephane Bedrossian, Christophe Poir Yves Frexinos, Raymond Pazzaglia (Marauders), Marie Cosr (Nicolette), Sylvie Beyssen, Anne Bolon, Frederique Figuero, Ag Hick (Prostitutes)

Left: Jean-Claude Adelin, Julie Delpy
Above: Bernard Pierre Donnadieu, Nils Tavernier
Top: Julie Delpy, Donnadieu
© *Samuel Goldwyn Co.*

WHEN THE WIND BLOWS

(KINGS ROAD) Producer, John Coates; Director, Jimmy T. Murakami; Executive Producer, Iain Harvey; Screenplay, Raymond Briggs; Based on his novel; Art Director/Animation and Layout Design, Richard Fawdry; Art Director/Background and Color Design, Errol Bryant; Special Effects Planned and Animated by Stephen Weston; Music, Roger Waters; *"When the Wind Blows"* Lyrics/Performance, David Bowie, Music, David Bowie, Erdal Kiziicay, and songs by Roger Waters, Genesis, Paul Hardcastle, Glen Tilbrook, Pete Hammond; Animated; British; Color; Not rated; 81 minutes; March release

VOICE CAST

Hilda .... Dame Peggy Ashcroft
James .... Sir John Mills
and James Russell, David Dundas, Matt Irving

Jim and Hilda Bloggs
© ***International Video Entertainment***

THE TWO LIVES OF MATTIA PASCAL

ₗRAI/SACIS) Producers, Silvia D'Amico Bendico, Carlo Cucchi; irector, Mario Monicelli; Idea/Screenplay, Suso Cecchi D'Amicoi, nnio De Concini, Amazio Todini, Mario Monicelli; Photography, 'amillo Bazzoni; Music, Nicola Piovani; Editor, Ruggero Mastroianni; Coproduction of RAI Channel 1, Antenne 2, Telemunchen, TVE, hannel 4, RTSI, Cinecitta, Excelsior Cinematografica; Italy; Italian ith subtitles; Color; Not rated; 120 minutes; March release

CAST

lattia Pascal	Marcello Mastroianni
lara	Senta Berger
aleari	Bernard Blier
erenzio Papiano	Flavio Bucci
driana Paleari	Laura Morante
omilda	Laura Del Sol
lalagna	Nestor Garay
lino Pomino	Alessandro Haber
ellegrinotto	Carlo Bagno
eronique	Caroline Berg
liva	Clelia Rondinella
he Widow Pescatore	Rosalia Maggio
ilvia Caporale	Andrea Ferreol

Right: Marcello Mastroianni, Laura Morante
Top: Mastroianni, Caroline Berg
© *RAI/SACIS*

VINCENT:
The Life and Death of Vincent Van Gogh

(ROXIE RELEASING) Producer, Tony Llewellyn-Jones; Director/Scenario, Paul Cox; Words, Vincent Van Gogh; Music, Vivaldi, Rossini, Norman Kaye; Produced by Illumination Films; Documentary; Australian; color; Not rated; 105 minutes; March release. VOICE CAST: John Hurt

Left: Vincent Van Gogh's self portrait

THE GIRL FROM HUNAN

NEW YORKER FILMS) Producer, Dong Yaping, for the Beijing 'outh Film Studio; Directors, Xie Fei, U Lan; Screenplay, Zhang Hian; rom the Novel *"Xiao Xiao"* by Shen Congwen; Photography, Fu ngshen; Editor, Zhang Lanfang; Designer, Xing Zheng; People's epublic of China, 1986; Mandarin with subtitles; Color; Not rated; 99 inutes; March release

CAST

iao Xiao	Na Renhua
lua Gou (farmhand)	Deng Xiaotuang
'hun Guan (2-year-old boy-husband)	Zhang Yu
iao Xiao (Child)	Liu Qing
'hun Guan's Mother	Ni Meiling

Zhang Yu, Na Renhua
© *New Yorker Films*

Maxime Leroux (L), Richard Anconina (R)
© *Gaumont*

BELLMAN AND TRUE

(ISLAND PICTURES) Producers, Michael Wearing, Christopher Neame; Director, Richard Loncraine; Screenplay, Desmond Lowden, Richard Loncraine, Michael Wearing; Executive Producers, George Harrison, Denis O'Brien (Handmade Films)/John Hambley, Johnny Goodman (Euston Films); Music, Colin Towns; Associate Producers, Basil Rayburn, Malcolm R. Burgess; Photography, Ken Westbury; Camera, Mike Proudfoot; Designer, Jon Bunker; Editor, Paul Green; Sound, Tony Jackson; Casting, Irene Lamb; Production Coordinator, Monica Rogers; Art Director, John Ralph; Set Decorator, Ann Mollo; Assistant Directors, Ken Tuohy, Chris Thompson, Ian Cameron; Costumes, David Perry; Stunts, Terry Forestal; British; Color; Rated R; 112 minutes; April release

CAST

Hiller .... Bernard Hill
The Boy .... Kieran O'Brien
Salto .... Richard Hope
Anna .... Frances Tomelty
Guv'nor .... Derek Newark
Donkey .... John Kavanagh
Gort .... Ken Bones
Peterman .... Arthur Whybrow
Bellman .... Peter Howell
Wheelman .... Jim Dowdall
Man with walkman .... Richard Strange
Hotel Clerk .... William Sleigh
Shop Keeper .... Badi Uzzaman
Pauline .... Ann Carroll
Commuter .... Chris Sanders
Mo .... Kate McEnery
Commercial Traveller .... Stephen Churchett
Lorry Driver .... Roger McKern
Sergeant Security Guard .... Peter Jonfield
Driver Security Guard .... Richard Walsh
Young Security Guard .... Andrew Paul
Anna's Lover .... Camilla Nash
Check-in Girl .... Alisa Bosschaert
Immigration Officer .... Alan Cowner
Chief Steward .... Michael Bertenshaw

Right Center: Bernard Hill, and above with Kieran O'Brien, Ken Bones, Richard Hope © ***Island Pictures/Mark Green***

LEVY AND GOLIATH

(KINO INTERNATIONAL) Executive Producer, Alain Poire; Director, Gerard Oury; Screenplay, Gerard Oury, Daniele Thompson; Photography, Vladimir Ivanov, Andre Domage; Editor, Albert Jurgenson; Art Director, Theobald Meurisse; Sound, Alain Sempe; Music, Vladimir Cosma; A Grange Communications/Jerry Winters Presentation; France; French with subtitles; Not rated; 97 minutes; March release

CAST

Moses Levy .... Richard Anconina
Albert Levy .... Michel Boujenah
Bijou .... Jean-Claude Brialy
Goliath .... Maxime Leroux
Malika .... Souad Amidou
Brigitte Levy .... Sophie Barjac

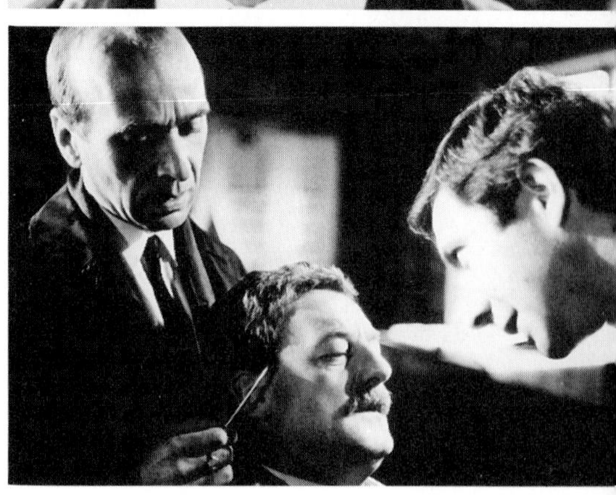

Peter Ustinov, Lauren Bacall
© *Cannon*

APPOINTMENT WITH DEATH

(CANNON GROUP) Producer/Director, Michael Winner; Screenplay, Anthony Schaffer, Peter Buckman, Michael Winner; Based on the novel by Agatha Christie; Executive Producers, Menahem Golan, Yoram Globus; Photography, David Gurfinkel; Designer, John Blezard; Editor, Arnold Crust; Costumes, John Bloomfield; music, Pino Donaggio; Associate Producer, Mati Raz; Production Supervisor, Itzik Kol; Production manager, Asher Gat; Assistant Directors, Christopher Carreras, Shaul Gorodetzki; Art Director, Avi Avavar; Set Decorator, Alan Cassie; Sound, Eli Yarkoni; Choreographer, Jakob Kalusky; British; Color; Rated PG; 102 minutes; April release

CAST

Hercule Poirot .... Peter Ustinov
Lady Westholme .... Lauren Bacall
Nadine Boynton .... Carrie Fisher
Colonel Carbury .... John Gielgud
Emily Boynton .... Piper Laurie
Miss Quinton .... Hayley Mills
Dr. Sarah King .... Jenny Seagrove
Jefferson Cope .... David Soul
Lennox Boynton .... John Terlesky
Ginevera Boynton .... Amber Bezer
Captain Rogers .... Douglas Sheldon
Healy .... Mike Sarne
Lord Peel .... Michael Craig
Hassan .... Mohammed Hirzalla
Tourist Guide .... Ruggero Comploy
Italian Policeman .... Danny Muggia
Boynton Driver .... Lutuf Nuayser
Arab Vendor .... Babi Neeman
British Officials .... Rupert Horrox, Hugh Brophy
Ship's Captain .... Marcel Solomon

RETURN TO SNOW RIVER PART II

ɜUENA VISTA) Producer/Director, Geoff Burrowes; Screenplay, ɔhn Dixon, Geoff Burrowes; Executive Producers, Dennis Wright, ɛnt Lovell, John Kearney; Production Supervisor, Bill Regan; Sound, ɛrry Rodman; Editor, Gary Woodyard; Music, Bruce Rowland; Phoɡraphy, Keith Wagstaff; Designer, Leslie Binns; Assistant Director, ɔhn Powditch; Art Director, Robert Leo; Set Decorators, Viv Wilson, ick Bell; Costumes, Jenny Arnott; Stunts, Chris Anderson; Master of orse, Charlie Lovick; Special Effects, Brian Pearce; Casting, Suzie laizels; Presented by Walt Disney Pictures; Australian; Dolby Stereo; olor; Panavision; Rated PG; 100 minutes; April release

CAST

m .... Tom Burlinson
ssica .... Sigrid Thornton
arrison .... Brian Dennehy
listair Patton .... Nicholas Eadie
ɜb .... Mark Hembrow
awker .... Bryan Marshall
atton, Snr .... Rhys McConnochie
ke .... Peter Cummins
Irs. Darcy .... Cornelia Frances
cko .... Tony Barry
riest .... Wynn Roberts
atton's Croney .... Alec Wilson
eilly .... Peter Browne
immons .... Alan Hopgood
ollins .... Mark Pennell
harlie .... Charlie Lovick
acko's son .... Wayne Lovick
ockey .... Greg Stroud
rank .... Geoff Beamish
amie McKay .... Gerald Egan
nd Nick Waters, Cae Rees, John Raaen, Bruce Clarkson, Peter Tulɔch, Christopher Stevenson, Charlie Lovick, Ken Connley, Clive lodges, Jim Campbell, John Harper, Noel Elliott, Greg Purcell, Dick orrest, Kevin Stower, Keith Nicholson, Max Scanlon, Wayne Anerson, Barry Stephen, Wayne Pinder, Gary Neil, Julien Welsh, John ird, Derek Scott, Graeme Stoney, Rusty Connley, Kevin Higgins, raeme Fry, Lloyd Parks, Tony Lovick, Robert Purcell, John Coombs, aul Purcell, Bruce McCormack, Basil Egan, Robert Gough, Curly IcCormack, Craig Edwards, Dennis Vickery, Tony Larkins, Steve larrison, John Lovick, Col Reynolds, Brendan Purcell, John Klingɔorn, Mark Arbuthnot, Graydon Marks, Chris Stoney, Peter Purcell, lax Jeffries, Martin Myors, Peter McElroy, Brendan Egan, John ohnston, Steve Arbuthnot

Right Center: Tom Burlinson, Sigrid Thornton
© *Burrowes Film Group*

Brian Dennehy, Sigrid Thornton

Bruno Ganz (also top), Otto Snader
Top Right and Below: Bruno Ganz,
Solvieg Dommartin

WINGS OF DESIRE

(ORION CLASSICS) Producers, Wim Wenders, Anatloe Dauman; Director, Wim Wenders; Screenplay, Wilm Wenders, Peter Handke; Photography, Henri Alekan; Camerman, Agnes Godard; Art Director, Heidi Ludi; Costumes, Monika Jacobs; Music, Jurgen Knieper; Editor, Peter Przygodda; Assistant Directors, Claire Denis, Knut Winkler; Associate Producer, Joachim Von Mengershausen; Film Consultant, Chris Sievernich; Executive Producer, Ingrid Windisch; A French/German co-production of Argros Films and Road Movies in association with Westdeutscher Rundfunk; In black and white and color; Rated PG-13; 130 minutes; April release

CAST

Damiel .... Bruno Ganz
Marion .... Solveig Dommartin
Cassiel .... Otto Sander
Homer .... Curt Bois
Peter Falk .... Peter Falk

Bruno Ganz, Peter Falk
Above: Bruno Ganz

A HUNGRY FEELING
The Life and Death of Brendan Behan

FIRST RUN FEATURES) Director/Producer, Allan Miller: Executive Producer, Walter Scheuer; Editor, Tom Haneke; Photography, on Lenzer; Production Manager/Assistant Editor, Donald Klocek; roduction Coordinator, Kathry Quinn; Narrator/Vocals, Liam Clancy; ocumentary; Not rated; 85 minutes; April release

Right: Brendan Behan
© First Run Features

Melanie Griffith, Sean Bean
Above: Sting

STORMY MONDAY

(ATLANTIC) Producer, Nigel Stafford-Clark; Director/Screenplay/Music, Mike Figgis; Photography, Roger Deakins; Production Designer, Andrew McAlpine; Editor, David Martin; Costumes, Sandy Powell; Associate Producer, Alan J. Wands; Assistant Director, John Watson; Stunt Coordinator, Denise Ryan; Casting, Mary Selway, Teresa Topolski; Sound, Tony Jackson; Art Director, Charmian Adams; released in association with British Screen and Film Four International, a Moving Picture Company production; British; Rank Agfa color; Dolby Stereo; Rated R; 93 minutes; April release

CAST

Kate .... Melanie Griffith
Cosmo .... Tommy Lee Jones
Finney .... Sting
Brendan .... Sean Bean
Tony .... James Cosmo
Patrick .... Mark Long
Jim .... Brian Lewis
First Heavy .... Ying Tong John
Pianist .... Mick Hamer
Man at Record Shop .... Ian Hinchcliffe
Andrej .... Andrzej Borkowski
Finney's Secretary .... Caroline Hutchinson
Customs Officer .... Les Wilde
Man in Airport Lounge .... Desmond Gill
Passport Officer .... Benny Graham
Bob .... Derek Hoxby
Cosmo's Secretary .... Catherine Chevalier
Airport Official .... Brendan Philip Healey
Cosmo's Bodyguard .... Clive Curtis
Peter Reed .... Heathcote Williams
Hotel Receptionist .... Fiona Sloman
Councillor Perry .... Roderic Leigh
Carol .... Dulice Liecier
Weegee's Manager .... Richard Hawley
Waitress .... Elizabeth Mason
Chef .... Tony Bluto
Don Weller .... Himself
Don Weller Band .... Andrew Cleyndert, Mark Taylor, Nick Pyne
Bouncers .... Nicholas Lumley, Cy Benson,
Barman .... Keith Edwards
Finney's Woman .... Louise Hobkinson
Mrs. Finney .... Prunella Gee
Mayor .... Alison Steadman
Chief Constable .... Peter Marshall
Christine .... Dorota Zienska
Radio DJ .... Al Matthews

and Ying Tong John, Mick Hamer, Ian Hinchcliffe, Les Wilde, Desmond Gill, Benny Graham, Brendan Philip Healey, Andrew Cleyndert, Mark Taylor, Nick Pyne, Nicholas Lumley, Cy Benson, Louise Hobkinson, Guy Manning, Czeslaw Grocholski, Denny Ferguson, Billy Fellowes, Charlie Hart, Paul Jolly, Terry Day, Mel Davis, Ed Deane, Davey Payne

Top Left: Melanie Griffith, Sean Bean
© Atlantic Releasing Corp.

MATADOR

(CINEVISTA/WORLD ARTISTS) Executive Producer, Andres Vicente Gomez; Director, Pedro Almodovar; Screenplay, Pedro Almodovar, Jesus Ferrero; Photography, Angel Luis Fernandez; Production Designers, Romano Arango, Jose Morales, Josep Rosell; Editor, Jose Salcedo; Music, Ernard Bonezzi; Production Manager, Miguel Gomez; Sound, Bernard Orthion; Costumes, Jose M. Cossio; Make-up, Juan Pedro Hernandez; Spanish; Color; Not rated; 107 minutes; April release

CAST

Maria Cadinal	Assumpta Serna
Angel	Antonio Banderas
Diego	Nacho Martinez
Eva	Eva Cobo
Berta	Julietta Serrano
Pilar	Chus Lampreave
Julia	Carmen Maura
Police Detective	Eusebio Poncela
Flower Seller	Bibi Andersen
Designer	Pedro Almodovar

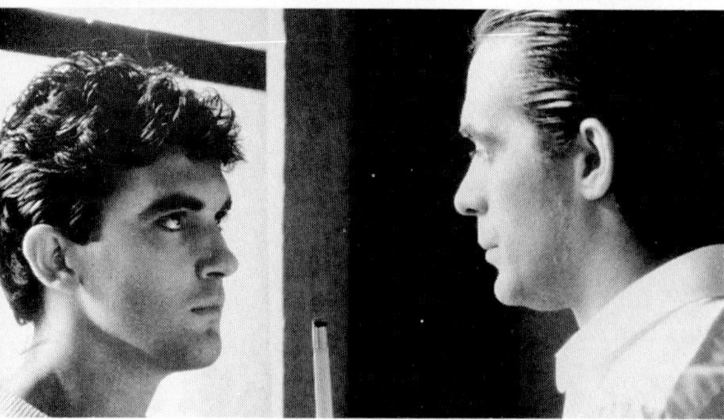

Antonio Banderas, Nacho Martinez

Assumpta Serna, Nacho Martinez
Left: Nacho Martinez, Assumpta Serna
Below: Nacho Martinez, Eva Cobo
© ***Cinevista/World Artists***

PLAYING AWAY

(ALIVE FILMS) Producers, Brian Skilton, Vijay Amarnani; Directo Horace Ove; Screenplay, Caryl Phillips; Associate Producer, Christo pher Sutton; Casting, Michael Barnes; Production Coordinator, De Hodgson; Assistant Directors, Simon Hinkly, Paul Frift, Carol Broc Sound, Christian Wangler; Editor, Graham Whitlock; Music Directo Simon Webb; Theme Song, Junior Giscombe; Art Director, Pip Gar ner; Costumes, Alyson Ritchie; British; Color; Not rated; 100 minute April release

CAST

Willie-Boy	Norman Beato
Godfrey	Robert Urquha
Marjorie	Helen Linds
Derek	Nicholas Farre
Stuart	Brian Bove
Errol	Gary Bead
Yvette	Suzette Llewelly
Jeff	Trevor Thom
Louis	Stefan Kalipl
Fredrick	Bruce Purcha
Robo	Joseph Marce
Viv	Sheila Rusk
Kevin	Mark Barra
Pat	Valerie Buchan
Boots	Jim Findle
Mick	Julian Grang
Wilf	Ram John Hold
The Colonel	Patrick Ho
Sandra	Elizabeth Ansc
Julie	Juliet Wale
Sony	Ross Kem
Tommy	Gareth Kirklan
Steadroy	Archie Po
Desert-Head	Errol Shak
Masie	Femi Taylo
John	Larry Dar
Ian	Neil Morrise
Constable	Charles Pemberto
Vicar	Roddy Maude-Roxb
Miss Rye	Zulema Den
David	Ian Cros
Tavern Barman	Jimmy Reddingto
Angie	Mary Tempe
Lady in Telephone Box	Lucita Lijertwoo

(No photos available)

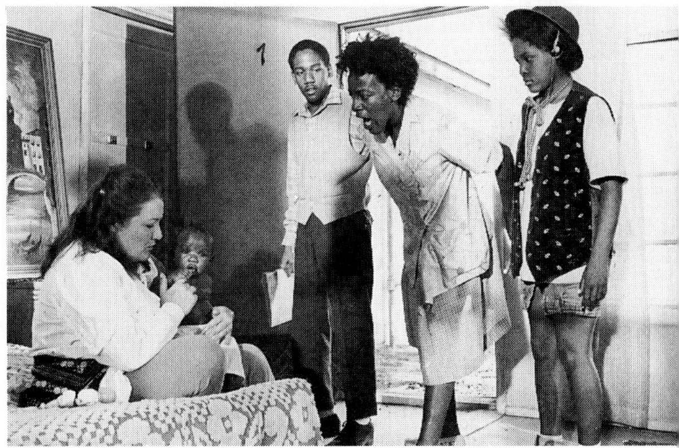

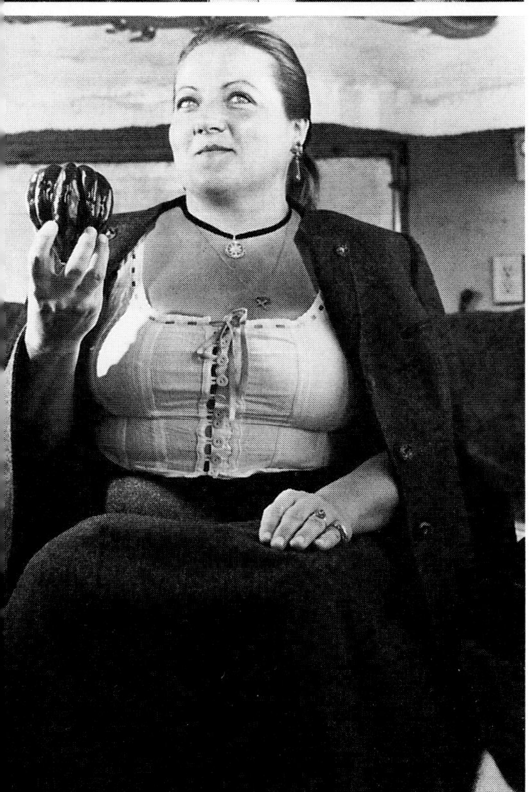

Marianne Sagebrecht

BAGDAD CAFE

(ISLAND PICTURES) Producer, Percy & Eleonore Adlon; Director/Story, Percy Adlon; Screenplay, Percy & Eleonore Adlon, Christopher Doherty; Line Producer, Eleonore Adlon; Production Executive, Dietrich V. Watzdorf; Photography, Bernd Heinl; Editor, Norbert Herzner; Music, Bob Telson; *"Calling You"* by Bob Telson/Vocals, Jevetta Steele, *"Brenda, Brenda"* by Lee Breuer & Bob Telson/Vocals, Jearlyn Steele-Battle & Tommy Joe White; Art Director, Bernt Amadeus Capra; Set Decorator, Byrnadette di Santo; Costumes, Elizabeth Warner, Regine Baetz; Sound, Heiko Hinderks; Casting, Al Onorato, Jerold Franks; Production manager, Llewellyn Wells; Assistant Directors, Helenka Hummel-Hinderks, Marc Pickett; Presented by Pelemele Film; German; Dolby Stereo; Color; Rated PG; 91 minutes; April release

CAST

Jasmin .... Marianne Sagebrecht
Brenda .... CCH Pounder
Rudi Cox .... Jack Palance
Debby .... Christine Kaufmann
Phyllis .... Monica Calhoun
Sal Jr. .... Darron Flagg
Cahuenga .... George Aguilar
Sal .... G. Smokey Campbell
Muenchstettner .... Hans Stadlbauer
Eric .... Alan S. Craig
Sheriff Arnie .... Apesanahkwat
Trucker Ron .... Ronald Lee Jarvis
Trucker Mark .... Mark Daneri
Trucker Ray .... Ray Young
Trucker Gary .... Gary Lee Davis

Top (L) Jack Palance (R) CCH Pounder, Marianne Sagebrecht Below: (L) Pounder, Sagebrecht (R) Sagebrecht, Flagg, Pounder, Calhoun
© Island Pictures

Geraldine Chaplin, Greta Scacchi
Right: Sarah Miles, Charles Dance
Below: Jacqueline Pearce, Sarah Miles, Murray Head

WHITE MISCHIEF

(COLUMBIA) Producer, Simon Perry; Director, Michael Radford; Screenplay, Michael Radford, Jonathan Gems; Derived from the book by James Fox; Executive Producer, Michael White; Costumes, Marit Allen; Production Designer, Roger Hall; Photography, Roger Deakins; Associate Producer, Simon Bosanquet; Editor, Tom Priestley; Sound, Tony Jackson; Casting, Mary Selway; Production Coordinator, Mary Richards; Art Director, Len Huntingford; Music, George Fenton; "The Alphabet Song" sung by Sarah Miles; Assistant Directors, Chris Rose, John Dodds, Lee Hilton; a Nelson Entertainment/Goldcrest presentation of a Michael White/Umbrella Films production in association with Power Tower Investments (Kenya) and the BBC; British; Color; Dolby Stereo; Rated R; 100 minutes; April release

CAST

Alice de Janze .... Sarah Miles
Sir "Jock" Delves Broughton .... Joss Ackland
Gilbert Colvile .... John Hurt
Diana Broughton .... Greta Scacchi
Josslyn Hay, 22nd Earl of Erroll .... Charles Dance
Gwladys Delamere .... Susan Fleetwood
Harragin .... Alan Dobie
Hugh Dickinson .... Hugh Grant
Lady Idina Gordon .... Jacqueline Pearce
June Carberry .... Catherine Neilson
Lizzie Lezard .... Murray Head
McPherson .... Gregor Fisher
Morris .... Ray McAnally
Nina Soames .... Geraldine Chaplin
Jack Soames .... Trevor Howard
Land Agent .... Tristram Jellinek
Raymond de Trafford .... Tim Myers
Gerald Portman .... Sean Mathias
Club Manager .... Ron Donachie
Kiptobe .... Douglas Chege
Sheridan .... Wensley Pithey
Carberry .... Stephen Chase
Muffin-Faced Woman .... Clare Travers-Deacon
Maasai Warriors .... Seipal Ngojine, Pilip Saitoti
Nancy Wirewater .... Amanda Farkin
Abdullah .... Louis Mahoney
African Policeman .... Ilario Bisi-Pedro
Poppy .... David Quilter
Baines .... John Rees
Kaplan .... Olivier Pierre
Fox .... Anthony Benson

and Clare Travers-Deacon, Seipal Ngojine, Pilip Saitoti, Ilario Bisi-Pedro, Nigel Le Vaillant, Basil Whybray, John Darrell, Billy Moody, Susannah Harker, Gary Beadle, Edwin Mahinda

Right Center: John Hurt, Greta Scacchi
© Columbia Pictures

Joss Ackland, Greta Scacchi, Trevor Howard

Stephen Kearney
Top: Stephen Kearney, Nina Landis
© *MGM/UA/United International*

RIKKY AND PETE

(UNITED ARTISTS) Producers, Nadia Tass, David Parker; Director, Nadia Tass; Screenplay/Photography, David Parker; Co-Producer, Timothy White; Executive Producer, Bryce Menzies; Production Manager, Lynda House; Assistant Director, Tony Mahood; Editor, Ken Sallows; Music, Eddie Rayner, with Brian Baker; Songs, Philip Judd; Designer, Josephine Ford; Production Coordinator, Sue Stephens; Sound, Lloyd Carrick; Art Director, Graeme Duesbury; Costumes, Phil Eagles, Anje Bos; Special Effects, Peter Stubbs; Stunts, Glen Ruehland; Sound, Roger Savage; With the Assistance of Film Victoria; from MGM/UA Communications; Music Producer, Chris Gough; Australian; Dolby Stereo; Rated R; 107 minutes; May release

CAST

Pete Menzies .... Stephen Kearney
Rikky Menzies .... Nina Landis
Flossie .... Tetchie Agbayani
Whitstead .... Bill Hunter
Sonny .... Bruno Lawrence
Ben .... Bruce Spence
Adam .... Lewis Fitz-Gerald
Mrs. Menzies .... Dorothy Alison
Mr. Menzies .... Don Reid
Delahunty .... Peter Cummins
George Pottinger .... Ralph Cotterill
Holy Joe .... Roderick Williams
Fingers .... Denis Lees
Winton Barman .... Richard Healy
Con Ionides .... Nicos Lathouris
Aunt .... Patti Perkins
Alistair .... Christopher Waters
Jack Donaldson .... Michael Brophy
Harris .... John Raaen
Gallery Stuffed Shirts .... Charles Dance, Peter Drake and Peter Hehir, Rob Baxter, Graham Rouse, Roger Cox, John Lee, Alan Hopgood, Burt Cooper, Denzil Howson, Lillian Frank, Rennie Ellis, Mark Williams, Peter Flett, Paula Langlands, Christopher Mayer, Don Bridges, Jack Bent, John Bishop, Beverley Ratcliff, Phillip Ross, John Barrett, Tony Serasina, Bill McCormack, Jayne Burns, Eddie McShortall, Greg McMahon, Russell Allen, Craig Alexander, Glen Robbins, Jaime Gough, Michael Den Elzen, Doug Beach, Louis McManus, Philip Judd, Noel Crombie, Nigel Griggs

SORCERESS

JROPEAN CLASSICS) Producers, Pamela Berger, Annie Leiboi, George Reinhart; Director, Suzanne Schiffman; Screenplay, nela Berger, Suzanne Schiffman; Story, Pamela Berger; Executive ducers, Vincent Malle, Martine Marignac; Photography, Patrick ssier; Sound, Jean-Paul Mugel, Dominique Hennequin; Art Direc- Bernard Vezat; Costumes, Mouchi Houblinne, Francoise Autran; tor, Martine Barraque; Music, Michel Portal; Production Managers, rtine Marignac, Michelle Cretel; Administrator, Hilda Smuk; Assoe Producer, Barbara Lucey; France; French with subtitles; Color; t rated; 97 minutes; April release

CAST

enne de Bourbon .... Tcheky Karyo
a .... Christine Boisson
e Cure .... Jean Carmet
neon .... Raoul Billerey
cile .... Catherine Frot
e Count .... Feodor Atkine
nes .... Maria de Medeiro
e Cure's Housekeeper .... Gilette Barbier
deleine .... Nicole Felix
ristophe .... Jean Daste
rtin .... Mathieu Schiffman
ung Etienne .... Michel Karyo
lage Woman .... Joelle Bernier

© *European Classics*

Jean Carmet, Tcheky Karyo, Christine Boisson

THE KITCHEN TOTO

(CANNON) Producer, Ann Skinner; Director/Screenplay, Ha Hook; Executive Producers, Menahem Golan, Yoram Globus; I signer, Jamie Leonard; Costumes, Barbara Kidd; Production Sup visor, Ted Morley; Photography, Roger Deakins; Editor, Tom Prie ley; Sound, Christian Wangler; Music, John Keane; Assistant Direct Guy Travers; Special Effects, Digby Milner; A Skreba Film present in association with British Screen and Film Four International; Briti Color; Rated PG-13; 96 minutes; May release

CAST

Mwangi	Edwin Mahir
John Graham	Bob Pe
Janet Graham	Phyllis Log
D. C. McKinnon	Robert Urquh
Mary	Kirsten Hugh
Dick Luis	Edward Ju
Mzee—Mwangi's Father	Nathan Dambuza Mdle
Mwangi's Mother	Ann Wanju
Kamau	Job Se
Sergeant Stephen	Leo Wring
Mugo the Houseboy	Nicholas Char
Edward Graham	Ronald Pi
Kamau's Henchman	Konga Mban
Gikuya the Cook	Abdullah Suna
Walimi the Nanny	Lidya Kiga
Muriuki the Gardener	Emmanuel Mng
Oath Administrator	Paul Onson
Samburu Askari	Lawi Lebo

Left: Bob Peck salutes Leo Wringer
Top: Edwin Mahinda, Ronald Pirie
© *Cannon*

SALOME'S LAST DANCE

(VESTRON) Producer, Penny Corke; Director./Screenplay, Ken Russell; Translated from the French by Vivian Russell; Co-Producer, Robert Littman; Executive Producers, William J. Quigley; Music, classical selections, conducted by Richard Cooke; Dan Ireland; Photography, Harvie Harison; Editor, Timothy Gee; Set Designer, Christopher Hobbs; Art Director, Michael Buchanan; Additional Designs, Michael Jeffery; Costumes, Michael Arrals; Choreography, Arlene Phillips; Assistant Choreographer, Wanda Rokicki; Casting, Rebecca Howard; Assistant Director, Mike Gowans; Production Coordinator, Winnie Wishart; Sound, Ray Beckett; British; Dolby Stereo; Technicolor; Rated R; 90 minutes; May release

CAST

Herodias/Lady Alice	Glenda Jackson
Herod/Alfred Taylor	Stratford Johns
Oscar Wilde	Nickolas Grace
John the Baptist/Bosie	Douglas Hodge
Salome/Rose	Imogen Millais-Scott
Tigellenus/Chilvers	Denis Ull
Pageboy	Russell Lee Nash
Cappadodem	Alfred Russell
A. Nabda	David Doyle
Young Syrian	Warren Saire
Soldiers	Kenny Ireland, Michel Van Wuk
Nazareans	Paul Clayton, Imogen Claire
Pharlose	Tim Potter
Saddocean	Matthew Taylor
Slaves	Linzi Drew, Tina Shaw, Caron Anne Kelly
Jews	Mike Edmonds, Willie Coppen, Anthony Georghiou
Nauman	Leon Herbert
Phoney Salome	Doug Howes
Police Sergeant	Lionel Taylor
Police Constables	Colin Hunt, David Addison
Black Maria Drivers	Robert Goodey
Hansom Cab Driver	Danny Godfrey
Photographer	Ken Russell

and Alison Cella, Frank Cella, Simon Gilbey, James Harte, Martino Lazzeri, Sinead Lightly, Sheree Murphy, Charles Richards (Children)

© *Vestron Pictures*

Douglas Hodge, Nickolas Grace
Above: Stratford Johns, Glenda Jackson

DARK HABITS

INEVISTA) Executive Producer, Luis Calvo; Director/Screenplay, dro Almodovar; Photography, Angel L. Fernandez; Designers, Pin orales, Roman Arango; Editor, Jose Salcedo; Production Manager, deo Villalba; Assistant Director, Terry Lenox; Sound, Martin Mul-, Armin Fausten; Makeup, Angel L. DeDiego; Costumes, Teresa eto; Spanish; Color; Not rated; 95 minutes; May release

CAST

landa .... Cristina S. Pascual
other Superior .... Julieta Serrano
ter Manure .... Marisa Paredes
ter Sin .... Carmen Maura
e Marquesa .... Mari Carillo
ter Snake .... Lina Canalejas
aplain .... Manuel Zarzo
ter Rat .... Chus Lampreave
other General .... Berta Riaza

Below Left: Yolanda (C) Below Right: Mari Carillo, Julieta Serrano Right: Carmen Maura
© *Cinevista*

Ric Young, Bhasker
© *New Yorker Films*

DRAGON CHOW

(NEW YORKER) Director, Jan Schutte; Screenplay, Jan Schutte, Thomas Strittmatter; Photography, Lutz Konermann; Art Director, Katharina Mayer-Woppermann; Sound, Ernst-Hermann Marell; Editor, Renate Merck; Music, Claus Bantzer; West German, 1987; In German, Mandarin, Urdu, and Sanskrit with subtitles; Black & White; Not rated; 75 minutes; May release

CAST

Shezad .... Bhasker
Xiao .... Ric Young
Rashid .... Buddy Uzzaman
Herde .... Wolf-Dieter Sprenge
Udo the cook .... Ulrich Wildgruber

CROCODILE DUNDEE II

(PARAMOUNT) Producers, John Cornell, Jane Scott; Director, John Cornell; Screenplay, Paul Hogan, Brett Hogan; Executive Producer, Paul Hogan; Associate Producer/Assistant Director, Mark Turnbull; Photography, Russell Boyd; Designer, Lawrence Eastwood; Costumes, Norma Moricwau; Editor, David Stiven; Music, Peter Best; Art Directors, Jeremy Conway, Rob Robinson; Set Decorator, Leslie Pope; Sound, Ron Brandau; Production Managers, Fiona McConaghy, Kelly Van Horn; Production Coordinator, Lesley Parker; Special Effects, Chris Murray, Steven Kirshoff; Stunts, Alan Gibbs, Spike Silver; Australian; Dolby Stereo; Duart Color; Panavision; Rated PG; 111 minutes; May release

CAST

Mick "Crocodile" Dundee .... Paul Hogan
Sue Charlton .... Linda Kozlowski
Walter Reilly .... John Mellon
Charlie .... Ernie Dingo
Donk .... Steve Rackman
Nugget .... Gerry Skilton
Frank .... Gus Mercurio
Erskine .... Jim Holt
Denning .... Alec Wilson
Ida .... Maggie Blinco
Teddy .... Bill Sandy
Diamond .... Mark Saunders
Meg .... Betty Bobbitt
Dorrigo Brothers .... Jim & Sam Cooper
Hotel Manager .... Fernando Segura
Rico .... Hechter Ubarry
Miguel .... Juan Fernandez
Leroy .... Charles Dutton
Brannigan .... Kenneth Welsh
DEA Agent .... Stephen Root
Bob Tanner .... Dennis Boutsikaris
Garcia .... Carlos Carrasco
Jose .... Luis Guzman
Doris .... Marilyn Sokol
and Gregory Jbara, Doug Skinner, Anthony Crivello, Susie Essman, Ron Yamamoto, Doug Yasuda, Tom Batten, Rhett Creighton, Edwin Maldonado, Angela Castle, Tatyana Ali, John Ramsey, Anthony Ruiz, Jace Alexander, Bryan Krivak, Mark Folger, Julio Rios, Alberto Vazquez, Luis Arriaga, Jose R. Andrews III, Roger Serbagi, Hannah Cox, Colin Quinn, Vincent Jerosa, Steven Arvanites, Rita Lane, Stacey Rockafellow, Maria Antoinette Rogers, Ahvi Spindell, Hisayo Asai, Al Cerullo Jr., Dianne Derfner, Homay Shams

Right: Charles Dutton, Paul Hogan
Above: John Meillon, Juan Fernandez, Hechter Ubarry Top: Linda Kozlowski, Paul Hogan, Dianne Deysner
© *Rimfire/Paramount/Eric Liebowitz, Peter Carrette*

Tsutomu Yamazaki

A TAXING WOMAN

(ORIGINAL CINEMA) Producers, Yasushi Tamaoki, Seigo Hos goe; (Itami Productions/New Century Producers)-Director/Screenpla Juzo Itami; Photography, Yonezo Maeda; Editor, Akira Suzuki; Mus Toshiyuki Honda; Japan; Japanese with English Subtitles; Color; N rated; 127 minutes; May release

CAST

Ryoko Itakura .... Nobuko Miyamo
Hideki Gondo .... Tsutomu Yamaza
Hanamura .... Masahiko Tsuga
Ishii .... Hideo Mur
Tsuyuguchi .... Shuji Ot
Taro Gondo .... Daisuke Yamash

© *Original Cinema*

·IE PROFOUND DESIRE OF THE GODS (Kamigami No Fukaki Yokubo)

.ST-WEST CLASSICS) Producer, Imamura Productions; Direc- Shohei Imamura; Screenplay, Shohei Imamura, Keiji Hasebe; ·tography, Masao Tochizawa; Art Director, Takeshi Omura; Music, hiro Mayuzumi; Editorial Restoration, Tom Bullock; Recipient of *Kinema Junpo* Best Film Award, 1968; Japan, 1968; Color; Nikkat- :ope; 170 minutes; May release

CAST

.ichi Futori .... Rentaro Mikuni
netaro Futori .... Choichiro Kawarazaki
iya the Engineer .... Kazuo Kitamura
·ko Futori .... Kazuko Okiyama
a Futori .... Yasuko Matsui
·gen Ryu .... Yoshi Kato
najiri .... Hosei Komatsu
.ndpa Futori .... Kanjuro Arashi
:. Higashi .... Chikako Hosokawa
:. Kariya .... Chikage Ogi
.uri the Balladeer .... Jun Hamamura

Right: Choichiro Kawarazaki, Hideko Okiyama
© *East-West Classics*

38:VIENNA BEFORE THE FALL

(EAST-WEST CLASSICS) Producer, Michael von Wolkenstein; Director/Screenplay, Wolfgang Gluck; Based on the novel *"Auch das war Wien" (What else Vienna was)* by Friedrich Torberg; Photography, Gerard Vandenberg; Art Director, Herwig Libowitzky; Costumes, Birgit Hutter; Music, Bert Editor, Heidi Handorf; Designer, Herwig Libowitzky; Grund; Production Manager, Otto-Boris Dworak, Herbert Reutterer; A Co-production by Satel-Film GmbH Vienna/Almaro Film GmbH Munich and Bavarian Broadcaster (Bayerischer Rundfunk); German; Color; Not rated; 96 minutes; May release

CAST

Martin .... Tobias Engel
Carola .... Sunnyi Melles
Toni .... Heinz Trixner
Mother .... Lotte Ledl
Frau Schostal .... Ingrid Burkhard
Sovary .... Romuald Pekny
Kemetter .... Josef Frohlich
Colonel Jovanovic .... David Cameron
Frau Pekarek .... Maria Singer
Ferry .... Miguel Herz-Kestranek
Hebenstein .... Michael Kehlmann
Sollnah .... Walter Starz
Andi Luttenfellner .... Ulf Dieter Kusdas
Taxidriver .... Lukas Resetarits

Top Left: Tobias Engel, Lukas Resetarits
© *East-West Classics*

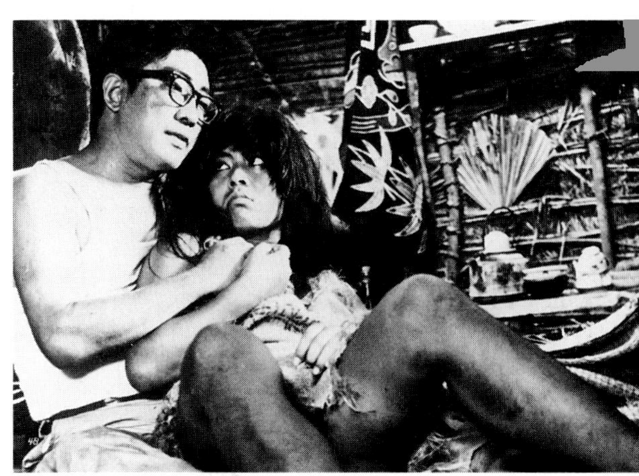

Nanni Moretti

THE MASS IS ENDED

(SACIS) Producer, Achille Manzotti; Director, Nanni Moretti; Idea/ Screenplay, Nanni Moretti, Sandro Petraglia; Photography, Franco Di Giacomo; Music, Nicola Piovani; Editor, Mirco Garrone; Italy; Italian with subtitles; Not rated; 94 minutes; May release

CAST

Don Giulio .... Nanni Moretti
Don Giulio's Father .... Ferruccio De Ceresa
Valentina .... Enrica Maria Modugno
Don Giulio's Mother .... Margarita Lozano
Saverio .... Marco Messeri
Cesare .... Roberto Vezzosi
Gianni .... Dario Cantarelli
Andrea .... Vincenzo Salemme
Antonio .... Eugenio Masciari
Lucia .... Luisa De Santis
Brother of the convent .... Pietro De Vico
The Lawyer .... Giovanni Buttafava
The Judge .... Luigi Moretti

© *RAI/SACIS*

SATURDAY NIGHT AT THE PALACE

(INTERNATIONAL FILM MARKETING) Producer/Director/Photography, Robert Davies; Screenplay, Paul Slabolepszy, Bill Flynn; Production, Carla Sandrock, Tony Stubbs; Sound, Humphrey Weale; Art Director, Wayne Attrill; Set Design, Sandy Attrill; Editors, Lena Farugia, Carla Sandrock; *"Third World Child"* by Johnny Clegg; South African; Color; Rated R; 87 minutes; May release

CAST

September .... John Kani
Vince .... Paul Slabolepszy
Forsie .... Bill Flynn
Dougie .... Arnold Vosloo
Van Vuuren .... Marius Weyers
Sally .... Joanna Weinberg
Shadrack .... Elias Madini
Pedro .... Nicky Rebello
Solomon .... Ramalao Makhene
Klaas .... Lawrence Zama Tshuma

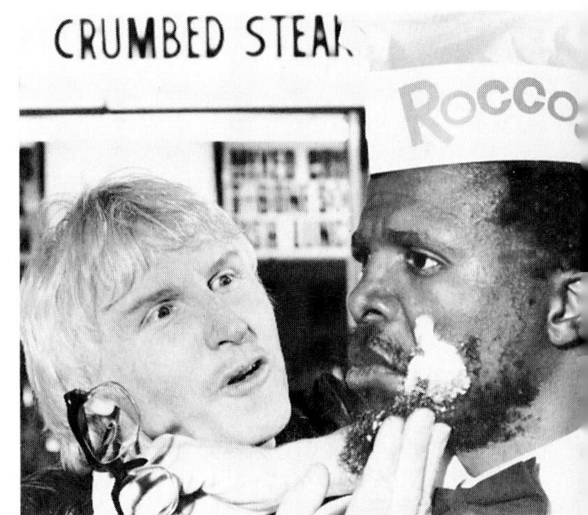

Barbara Hershey Above: with Tim Roth, Jodhi May

A WORLD APART

(ATLANTIC) Producer, Sarah Radclyffe; Director, Chris Meng Screenplay/Associate Producer, Shawn Solvo; Executive Produce Tim Bevan, Graham Bradstreet; Photography, Peter Biziou; Design Brian Morris; Music, Hans Zimmer; Costumes, Nic Ede; Casti Susie Figgis; Sound, Judy Freeman; Editor, Nicolas Gaster; Product Manager, Caroline Hewitt; Assistant Directors, Guy Travers, Cl Thompson, Rupert Ryle-Hodges, Isaac Madhikwa; Art Director, M Philips; a British Screen presentation of a Working Title production association with Film Four International; British; Metrocolor; Do Stereo; Rated PG; 112 minutes; June release

CAST

Diane Roth .... Barbara Hersh
Molly Roth .... Jodhi M
Gus Roth .... Jeroen Kra
Miriam Roth .... Carolyn Clayton-Cr
Jude Roth .... Merav Gr
Bertha .... Yvonne Brycel
Solomon .... Albee Leso
Elsie .... Linda Mv
Mrs. Harris .... Rosalie Crutch
Milius .... Mackay Tic
Harold .... Tim R
Le Roux .... Adrian Dun
Kruger .... Paul Free
Muller .... David Suc
June Abelson .... Kate Fitzpat
Gerald Abelson .... Toby Salan
Yvonne Abelson .... Nadine Chalm
Priest .... Jude Akuwi

Above: Tim Roth, Barbara Hershey
Left Center: Hershey, Jodhi May

A HANDFUL OF DUST

(NEW LINE CINEMA) Producer, Derek Granger; Director, Charles Sturridge; Screenplay, Tim Sullivan, Derek Granger, Charles Sturridge; Based on the novel by Evelyn Waugh; Executive Producers, Jeffrey Taylor, Kent Walwin; Associate Producer, David Wimbury; Music, George Fenton; Photography, Peter Hannan; Designer, Eileen Diss; Costumes, Jane Robinson; Sound, Peter Sutton; Editor, Peter Coulson; Casting, Celestia Fox; Production Manager, Matthew Binns; Assistant Director, Peter Kohn; Art Director, Chris Townsend; A Stagescreen production; British; Technicolor; Rated PG; 118 minutes; June release

CAST

Tony Last ..... James Wilby
Brenda Last ..... Kristin Scott Thomas
John Beaver ..... Rupert Graves
Mrs. Rattery ..... Anjelica Huston
Mrs. Beaver ..... Judi Dench
Mr. Todd ..... Alec Guinness
Marjorie ..... Beatie Edney
Jock ..... Pip Torrens
Dr. Messinger ..... Christopher Godwin
Mr. Graceful ..... Graham Crowden
John Andrew ..... Jackson Kyle
Ben ..... Richard Beale
Nanny ..... Jeanne Watts
Ambrose ..... Norman Lumsden
Maid ..... Peggy Aitcheson
MacDougal ..... Timothy Bateson
Maid ..... Maureen Bennett
Daisy ..... Annabel Brooks
Station Master ..... Geoffrey Cousins
Winnie ..... Alice Dawnay
Polly ..... Marsha Fitzalan
Mrs. Northcote ..... Moyra Fraser
Reggie ..... Stephen Fry
Millie ..... Cathryn Harrison
Porter ..... Alan Hay
Richard Last ..... Tristram Jellinek
Blenkinsop ..... John Junkin
Doctor ..... Richard Leech
Vicar ..... Roger Milner
Veronica ..... Tamsin Olivier
Miss Rippon ..... Kate Percival
Solicitor ..... John Quentin
Page ..... Matthew Ryan
Clerk ..... Hugh Simon

Left: Kristin Scott Thomas, Rupert Graves
Above: Kristin Scott Thomas, James Wilby
Top: Rupert Graves © *New Line Cinema/Murray Close*

James Wilby, Kristin Scott Thomas

Kristin Scott Thomas

HISTORY

(SACIS) Producer, Paolo Infascelli; Director, Luigi Comencini; Screenplay, Suso Cechi D'Amico, Cristina Comencini, Luigi Comencini; Based on the Novel by Elsa Morante; Photography, Franco Di Giacomo; Designer, Paola Comencini; Costumes, Carolina Ferrara; Music, Fiorenzo Carpi; Editor, Nino Bargagli; A Production for RAI Channel 2/Ypsilon Cinematografica in coproduction with Antenne 2/Maran Film/TVE S.A.; Color; Italian; Not rated; 146 minutes; June release

CAST

Ida .... Claudia Cardinale
Remo .... Francisco Rabal
Useppe .... Andrea Spada
Nino .... Antonio Degli Schiavi
Cucchiarelli .... Fiorenzo Fiorentini
Gunther .... Tobias Hoesl
Carlo Davide .... Lambert Wilson

Claudia Cardinale

WEDDING IN GALILEE

(KINO INTERNATIONAL) Director/Screenplay, Michel Khle Executive Producers, Jacqueline Louis, Bernard Lorain; Photograp Walther van der Ende; Camera, Yves Vandermeeren; Editor, Ma Castro Vasquez; Music, Jean-Marie Senia; Sound, Ricardo Cast Dick Bombey, Jean-Paul Loublier; Sound Effects, Jean-Pierre Lelo Makeup, Nancy Baudoux; Costumes, Anne Verhoeven; Sets, Y Brover, Rachid Michirawi; Production Companies, Marisa Films (B gium), LPA (France), Q.A Prod. (London), ZDF (West German with the assistance of the French Community, Belgium, and the CNC Belgium; FIPRESCI Award (Intl. Federation of Film Critics), Cann 1987; British; Hebrew & Arabic with subtitles; Color; Not rated; minutes; June release

CAST

The Mukhtar (Abu Adel) .... Ali M. El A
The Mother .... Bushra Karan
Military General .... Makram Kho
The Groom (Adel) .... Nazih Ak
The Bride (Samia) .... Anna Achd
The Daughter (Sumaya) .... Sonia An
Baccum .... Youssef Abou Wa
Hassan .... Eyad A
Ziad .... Wael Barcko
Officers .... Juliano Mer Khamis, Ilan Che
Female Soldier (Tali) .... Tali Do
The Grandfather .... Tawfik Khl
The Grandmother .... Oum Fayez Dei
Uncle Khamis .... Mohamed Dagha
Zouhaira .... Laila Warv

Left: Ali M. El Akili Above: Anna Achdian
© ***Kino International***

COMMISSAR

(INTERNATIONAL FILM EXCHANGE LTD.) Producer, Gorky Studio; Director/Screenplay, Alexander Askoldov; Based on the story *"A City of Berdish"* by Vasily Grossman; Photography, Valeri Ginzberg; Montage, V. Isaeva, N. Loginova, S. Lyashinshaya; Music, Alfred Schnittke; Sets, S. Serebrennikov; Sound, L. Benevlskaya, V. Shary, E. Bazanov; A Today Home Entertainment Film; Russian; Black and White; Not rated; 110 minutes; June release

CAST

Klavdia .... Nonna Mordukova
Yefim .... Rolan Bykov
Maria .... Raisa Nedaskovskaya
Commander .... Vasily Shukshin
and Ludmila Volynskaya, Lyuba Katz, Pavlik Levin, Dima Kleinman, Igor Fishman, Marta Bratkova, O. Koveridze, L. Reutov, V. Shakhov

© ***International Film Exchange***

Nonna Mordukova (R)

A FISH CALLED WANDA

IGM) Producer, Michael Shamberg; Director, Charles Crichton; ːecutive Producers, Steve Abbott, John Cleese; Screenplay, John eese; Story, John Cleese, Charles Crichton; Associate Producer, hn Comfort; Assistant Director, Jonathan Benson; Photography, an Hume; Designer, Roger Murray-Leach; Music, John Du Prez; litor, John Jympson; Costumes, Hazel Pethig; Casting, Priscilla John; ımera, Neil Binney; Sound, Chris Munro; Art Director, John Wood; t Decorator, Stephanie McMillan; Special Effects, George Gibbs, ave Watson; Production Co-Ordinator, Janine Lodge; Stunts, Romo orrara; British; Technicolor; Rated R; 108 minutes; July release

CAST

rchie Leach .... John Cleese
anda Gershwitz .... Jamie Lee Curtis
tto West .... Kevin Kline
en Pile .... Michael Palin
endy .... Maria Aitken
eorge .... Tom Georgeson
rs. Coady .... Patricia Hayes
dge .... Geoffrey Palmer
ortia .... Cynthia Caylor
ıstomer in Jeweller's Shop .... Mark Elwes
anager of Jeweller's Shop .... Neville Phillips
spector Marvin .... Peter Jonfield
artlett .... Ken Campbell
'arder .... Al Ashton
ocksmith .... Roger Hume
avidson .... Roger Brierley
r John .... Llewellyn Rees
ercival .... Michael Percival
agistrate .... Kate Lansbury
opper .... Robert Cavendish
ebedee .... Andrew MacLachlan
icar .... Roland MacLeod
r. Johnson .... Jeremy Child
rs. Johnson .... Pamela Miles
hild Johnson (13) .... Tom Piggot Smith
hild Johnson (10) .... Katherine John
hild Johnson (8) .... Sophie Johnstone
anny .... Kim Barclay
st Junior Barrister (Defense Counsel) .... Sharon Twomey
ınior Barrister (Prosecution Counsel) .... Tia Lee
olice Officer (Old Bailey) .... Robert Putt
st Prison Officer .... Waydon Croft
nd Prison Officer .... John Dixon
ate Driver .... Anthony Pedley
otel Clerk .... Robert McBain
irline Employee .... Clare McIntyre
dian Cleaner .... Charu Bala Chokshi
utchison .... Stephen Fry

Top: (L) Maria Aitken, Cynthia Caylor, Jamie Lee Curtis, John Cleese (R) Jamie Lee Curtis, Kevin Kline Below: John Cleese
© MGM/David James

Kevin Kline received an Academy Award for Best Supporting Actor of 1988

Kevin Kline, John Cleese

PASCALI'S ISLAND

(AVENUE PICTURES) Producer, Eric Fellner; Director/Screenplay, James Dearden; Executive Producer, Cary Brokaw; Co-Producer, Paul Raphael; Music, Loek Dikker; Photography, Roger Deakins; Editor, Edward Marnier; Designer, Pam Tait; Casting, Noel Davis, Jeremy Zimmerman; Production Supervisor, Yannis Petropoulakis; Production Manager, Angela Petropoulakis; Art Directors, Philip Elton, Petros Kapouralis; Set Decorator, Jennifer Williams; Sound, Ian Voigt; Assistant Director, Guy Travers; Special Effects, Universal LTD.; *"Der Hirt Auf Dem Felsen"* by Franz Schubert; British; Color; Rated PG-13; 101 minutes; July release

CAST

Basil Pascali .... Ben Kingsley
Anthony Bowles .... Charles Dance
Mardosian .... Kevork Malikyan
Herr Gesing .... George Murcell
Lydia Neuman .... Helen Mirren
Pasha .... Nadim Sawalha
Izzet Effendi .... Stefan Gryff
Pariente .... Vernon Dobtcheff
Mrs. Marchant .... Sheila Allen
Dr. Hogan .... T. P. McKenna
Mrs. Hogan .... Danielle Allan
Chaudan .... Nick Burnell
Greek Rebel .... George Ekonomou
Captain .... Alistair Campbell
Boy in Bath .... Ali Abatsis
Turkish Officer .... Brook Williams
Turkish Soldier .... Josh Losey

Right: Ben Kingsley (also above), Helen Mirren
© Avenue Pictures/Tom Collins

Charles Dance, Helen Mirren

Helen Mirren Above: Charles Dance, Ben Kingsley

THE COLOR OF DESTINY

(EMBRAFILME) Producer/Director, Jorge Duran; Screenplay, Ne son Natotti, Jorge Duran with the collaboration of Jose Joffily; Photog raphy, Jose Tadeu Ribeiro; Art Director, Clovis Bueno; Editor, Dom nique Paris; Music, David Tygel; Production, Nativa Filmes; Brazi Portugese with subtitles; 1986; Color; Not rated; 104 minutes; Ju release

CAST

Paulo .... Guilherme Fonte
Laura .... Norma Benge
Victor .... Franklin Caiced
Patricia .... Julia Lemmer
Helena .... Andrea Beltra
and Chico Diaz, Antonio Grassi

(No photos available)

LOOSE CONNECTIONS

)RION CLASSICS) Producer, Simon Perry; Director, Richard Eyre; :reenplay, Maggie Brooks; Photography, Clive Tickner; Music, ominic Muldowney, Andy Roberts; Editor, David Martin; Associate oducer, Paul Cowan; An Umbrella Greenpoint Films production in sociation with National Film Finance Corp. and Virgin Films; Brit-n, 1983; Color; Not rated; 90 minutes; July release

CAST

arry .... Stephen Rea
ılly .... Lindsay Duncan
xel .... Jan Niklas
aya .... Carole Harrison
evin .... Gary Olsen
ıurie .... Frances Low
ıpporter .... Ken Jones

Stephen Rea, Lindsay Duncan
© *Orion Classics*

A SUMMER STORY

(ATLANTIC) Producer, Danton Rissner; Director, Piers Haggard; Screenplay, Penelope Mortimer; Based on a story by John Galsworthy; Editor, Ralph Sheldon; Music, Georges Delerue; Casting, Celestia Fox; Photography, Kenneth MacMillan; Costumes, Jenny Beavan; Designer, Leo Austin; Production Executive, Dennis A. Brown; Production Supervisor, Christab Albery; Assistant Director, Chris Hall; Art Director, Diane Dancklefsen; Richard Elston; David Hildyard; Sound, John Pitt; Presented by ITC Entertainment Group; British; Color; Rated PG-13; 95 minutes; July release

CAST

Megan .... Imogen Stubbs
Ashton .... James Wilby
Jim .... Ken Colley
Stella .... Sophie Ward
Mrs. Narracombe .... Susannah York
Joe .... Jerome Flynn
Nick .... Lee Billett
Rick .... Oliver Perry
Garton .... Harry Burton
Halliday .... John Elmes
Sabina .... Camilla Power
Freda .... Juliette Fleming
Betsy .... Sukie Smith
Bank Clerk .... John Savident
Post Office Girl .... Rachel Joyce

Left: Imogen Stubbs, Susannah York
Above: Imogen Stubbs, James Wilby
© *Atlantic Entertainment Group*

BOYFRIENDS AND GIRLFRIENDS
(L'Ami De Mon Amie)

ORION CLASSICS) Producer, Margaret Menegoz; Director/ creenplay, Eric Rohmer; Photography, Bernard Lutic, Sabine Lan-elin; Editor, Luisa Garcia; Music, Jean-Louis Valero; Sound, Geroges 'rat, Pascal Ribier, Dominique Hennequin; France; French with sub-itles; Color; Rated PG; 102 minutes; July release

CAST

3lanche .... Emmanuelle Chaulet
.ea .... Sophie Renoir
Adrienne .... Anne-Laure Meury
'abien .... Eric Viellard
Alexandre .... Francois-Eric Gendron

© *Orion Pictures*

Emmanuelle Chaulet, Eric Viellard

SHAME

(SKOURAS) Producers, Damien Parer, Paul D. Barron; Director, Steve Jodrell; Screenplay, Beverly Blankenship, Michael Brindley; Photography, Joseph Pickering; Designer, Phil Peters; Music, Mario Millo; Editor, Kerry Regan; Associate Producer, Pru Donovan; Production Manager, Deb Copland; Assistant Director, Stuart Wood; Production Coordinator, Susie Campbell; Sound, David Glasser; Costumes, Noel Howell; Effects Makeup, Liddy Reynolds; Special Effects, Aldis Bernsteins, Sanjiva, Charles Staples; Stunts, Peter West; Australia; Color; Rated R; 90 minutes; July release

CAST

Asta Cadell .... Deborra-Lee Furness
Tim Curtis .... Tony Barry
Lizzie Curtis .... Simone Buchanan
Tina Farrel .... Gillian Jones
Sgt. Wal Cuddy .... Peter Aanensen
Norma Curtis .... Margaret Ford
Danny Fiske .... David Franklin
Ross .... Bill McClusky
Penny .... Allison Taylor
Gary .... Phil Dean
Bobby .... Graeme "Stig" Wemyss
Andrew .... Douglas Walker
Brian .... Matthew Quartermaine
Wayne .... Matt Hayden
Bruce .... Warren Jones
Dulcie .... Faith Clayton
Rita .... Mandy Henning
Fay .... Julie Hudspeth
Mrs. Rodolph .... Pat Skevington
Little Stevie .... Robert Luobikis
Stevie's Friends .... Jeremy Grove, Dean Daley, Darren Taylor
Beryl .... Libby Stone
Eileen .... Patricia Cote
Mrs. Hemmingway .... Tiffany Evans
Mr. Hemmingway .... Bob Faggetter
Mrs. Sullivan .... Eileen Colocott
Lorna .... Karen Hobson
Dave .... Dickon Oxenburgh
Melina .... Kerri Lemus
Mr. Fiske .... Colin McEwan
Mr. Morgan .... Leslie Wright
Betty .... Marian Rawlings
Constable Gavin .... Don Halbert
Meatworker .... Ann Goodale
Susie .... Sarissa White

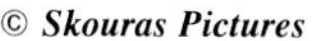

Deborra-Lee Furness (also above)

Patrick Bruel, Marie-Sophie L.

BANDITS

(GRANGE COMMUNICATIONS/JERRY WINTERS) Produce Director, Story, Claude Lelouch; Executive Producer, Tania Zaz linsky; Screenplay, Claude Lelouch, Pierre Uytterhoeven; Photogr phy, Jean-Yves Le Mener Berto, Olivier Bory; Sound, Harald Maur Gilles Ortion; Art Director, Jacques Bufnoir; Costumes, Charlot David; Editor, Hugue Darmois; Music, Francis Lai; Musical Directio Christian Gaubert; Production Manager, Tadek Zietara; Administr tors, Michelle Yvars, Jean-Marc Homand; Presented by Films 13 ar TFI Films Productions; France; French with subtitles; Color; Not rate 98 minutes; August release

CAST

Simon Verini, or "The Expert" .... Jean Yanr
Marie Sophie, or "The Princess" .... Marie-Sophie I
"Mozart" .... Patrick Bru
Charlot .... Charles Gera
Manouchka .... Corinne Marchar

THE YEAR MY VOICE BROKE

AVENUE PICTURES) Producers, Terry Hayes, Doug Mitchell, ieorge Miller; Director, John Duigan; Associate Producer, Barbara iibbs; Production Manager, Dixie Betts; Sound, Ross Linton; Editor, Jeil Thumpston; Designer, Roger Ford; Photography, Geoff Burton; icreenplay, John Duigan; Production Supervisors, Claire O'Brien, Iarcus D'Arcy; Casting, Alison Barrett; Production Coordinator, Julie 'lummer; Assistant Director, Tom Blacket; Set Decorator, Alethea)eane; Stunts, Guy Norris; Choreographer, Robyn Moase; Songs by arious artists; Australia; Color; Rated PG-13; 103 minutes; August elease

CAST

)anny .... Noah Taylor
'reya .... Loene Carmen
'revor .... Ben Mendelsohn
Jils Olson .... Graeme Blundell
Anne Olson .... Lynette Curran
Bruce Embling .... Malcolm Robertson
heila Embling .... Judi Farr
Bob Leishman .... Tim Robertson
onah .... Bruce Spence
'om Alcock .... Harold Hopkins
iail Olson .... Anja Coleby
Alison .... Kylie Ostara
Barry .... Kelly Dingwall
Ars. Beal .... Dorothy St. Heaps
iran Olson .... Colleen Clifford
Ieadmaster .... Vincent Ball
Ar. Keith .... Kevin Manser
.isa .... Emma Lyle
.yn .... Louise Bigan
Miss McCall .... Mary Regan
Aalseed .... Matthew Ross
Aartin .... Allan Penney
Ars. O'Neil .... Queenie Ashton
'ierdon .... Robert Carlton
gt. Pierce .... Nick Tate
'oliceman .... Gary Dale
Ros .... Brenda Burcul
ially .... Helen Lomas
'ony .... Michael Kent
ohnny .... Leigh Biolos
'arol .... Suzi Dougherty
'riend .... Andrew Jackson

Right: Noah Taylor, Loene Carmen
Above: Loene Carmen, Ben Mendelsohn
Top: Noah Taylor (R)
© *Avenue Pictures*

Kristyna Kohoutova

ALICE

(FIRST RUN FEATURES) Producer, Peter-Christian Fueter; Director/Designer/Editor, Jan Svankmajer; Photography, Svatopluk Maly; Animator, Bedrich Glaser; A Condor Features Production in association with Film Four International and Hessischer Runfunk; Live action & animation; Czechoslovak; In English; Color; Not rated; 84 minutes; August release

CAST

Alice .... Kristyna Kohoutova

© ***First Run Features***

THE DECEIVERS

(CINECOM) Producer, Ismail Merchant; Director, Nicholas Meyer; Co-Producer, Tim Van Rellim; Executive Producer, Michael White; Based on the novel by John Masters; Screenplay, Michael Hirst; Photography, Walter Lassally; Music, John Scott; Editor, Richard Trevorl; Designer, Ken Adam; Costumes, Jenny Beavan, John Bright; Associate Producer, Leon Falk; Production Supervisor, Anthony Waye; Production Manager, Deepak Nayar; Production Coordinators, Dena Vincent, Eleanor Chaudhuri; Assistant Directors, Chris Carreras, Shah Jehan; Choreographer, Denny Martin Flinn; Sound, Claude Hitchcock; Art Directors, Gianfranco Fumagalli, Ram Yedekar; Casting, Celestia Fox, Jennifer Jaffrey; Special Effects, Brian Smithies; Stunts, Gerry Crampton; A Merchant Ivory Prods./Michael White Production, in association with Cinecom and Film Four Inl.; British/Indian; Dolby Stereo; Technicolor; Rated PG-13; 112 minutes; September release

CAST

William Savage .... Pierce Brosnan
Hussein .... Saeed Jaffrey
Chandra Singh .... Shashi Kapoor
Sarah Wilson .... Helena Michell
Colonel Wilson .... Keith Michell
George Anglesmith .... David Robb
Feringeea .... Tario Yunis
Nawab .... Jalal Agha
Lieutenant Maunsell .... Gary Cady
Piroo .... Salim Ghouse
Widow .... Neena Gupta
Sepoy .... Nayeem Hafizka
Harlot .... Bijoya Jena
Nawab Servant .... H. N. Kalla
Official .... Kammo
Sher Dil .... Goga Kapoor
Old Rajput .... Manmohan Krishna
Sepoy .... Harish Magon
Ferryman .... Manmaujee
Captain Devril .... Giles Masters
Rajput's Son .... Ramesh Ranga
Sowar .... Dilip Singh Rathore
Chandra Singh's Maidservant .... Hilla Sethna
Prisoner .... R. P. Sondhj
Gopal .... Kanwaljit Singh
Hira Lai .... Shanmukha Srinivas
Daffadar Ganesha .... Dalip Tahil
Reverend Matthias .... Tim Van Rellim
Priest .... Rajesh Vivek
and Amin, Akbar Bakshj, Ramesh Goyal, Kaushel, Haroon Khan, Nilesh Malhotra

Right: Pierce Brosnan, Saeed Jaffrey
Top: Helena Michell, Pierce Brosnan

Rafaela Aparicio

MAMA TURNS 100

(INTERAMA) Producer, Elias Querejeta; Director/Screenplay, Carlo Saura; Assistant to Director, Francisco J. Querejeta; Production Manager, Primitivo Alvaro; Photography, Gregorio Hebrero; Camera, Te Escamilla; Editor, Pablo G. Del Amo; Assistant Editor, Juan Sanmateo Set Decorator, Antonio Belizon; Spanish with subtitles; Not rated; 10 minutes; September release

CAST

Ana .... Geraldine Chapli
Natalia .... Amparo Muno
Fernando .... Fernando Fernan Gome
Madre .... Rafaela Aparici
Antonio .... Norman Brinsk
Luchi .... Charo Sorian
Juan .... Jose Viv
Carlotta .... Angeles Torre
Victoria .... Elisa Nand
Solange .... Rita Maide
Anny .... Minique Ciro

DEAD RINGERS

(20th CENTURY FOX) Producers, David Cronenberg, Marc Boyman; Director, David Cronenberg; Screenplay, David Cronenberg, Norman Snider; Based on the Book *"Twins"* by Bari Wood & Jack Geasland; Associate Producer/Assistant Director, John Board; Executive Producers, Carol Baum, Sylvio Tabet; Photography, Peter Suschitzky; Music, Howard Shore; Designer, Carol Spier; Editor, Ronald Sanders; Costumes, Denise Cronenberg; Production Manager/Production Supervisor, Gabriella Martinelli; Art Directors, Alicia Keywan, James McAteer; Set Decorator, Elinor Rose Galbraith; Sound, Bryan Day; Associate Editor, Steve Weslak; Production Coordinator, Alice Ferrier; Orchestration, Homer Denison; Songs by various artists; A Mantle Cinic II Production; Canadian; Color; Rated R; 115 minutes; September release

CAST

Beverly Mantle/Elliot Mantle .... Jeremy Irons
Claire Niveau .... Genevieve Bujold
Cary .... Heidi Von Palleske
Danuta .... Barbara Gordon
Laura .... Shirley Douglas
Anders Woleck .... Stephen Lack
Leo .... Nick Nichols
Arlene .... Lynn Cormack
Birchall .... Damir Andrei
Mrs. Bookman .... Miriam Newhouse
Superintendent .... David Hughes
Dean of Medicine .... Richard Farrell
Anatomy Class Supervisor .... Warren Davis
Beverly, Age 9 .... Jonathan Haley
Elliot, Age 9 .... Nicholas Haley
Raffaella .... Marsha Moreau
Mr. Glaser .... Bob Bainborough
M. C. .... Nicholas Rice
Sean .... Joe Matheson
Mrs. Randall .... Nora Colpman
Soap Opera Characters .... Rena Polley, Madeleine Atkinson and Denis Akiyama, Dee McCafferty, Susan Markle, Murray Cruchley, Jane Luk, Tita Trevisan, Jacqueline Hennessy, Jillian Hennessy, David Walden, Liliane Stillwell, Denise McLeod, Hadley Kay, Cynthia Eastman

Left: Heidi Von Palleske, Jeremy Irons (also Top)
© 20th Century Fox/Attila Dory

Jeremy Irons, Genevieve Bujold (also above)

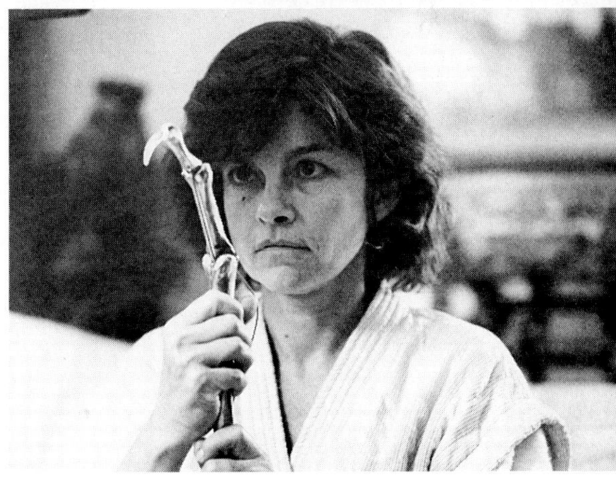

Genevieve Bujold
Above: Jeremy Irons

GROUND ZERO

(AVENUE ENTERTAINMENT) Producer, Michael Pattinson; Directors, Michael Pattinson, Bruce Myles; Screenplay, Mac Gudgeon, Jan Sardi; Executive Producers, Kent Lovell, John Kearney, Dennis Wright; Line Producer, Stuart Freeman; Designer, Brian Thomson; Music, Tom Bahler; Editor, David Pulbrook; Photography, Steve Dobson; Production Manager, Narelle Barsby; Assistant Director, Stuart Freeman; Camera, Ian Jones; Sound, Gary Wilkins; Art Director, Robert Dein; Production Coordinator, Christine Hart; Special Effects, Alan Maxwell, Brian Pearce, Peter Evans; Choreographer, Tony Bartuccio; Stunts, Glen Boswell; Australia; Color; Panavision; Rated PG-13; 100 minutes; September release

CAST

Harvey .... Colin Frields
Trebilcock .... Jack Thompson
Prosper .... Donald Pleasence
Pat .... Natalie Bate
Charlie .... Burnham Burnham
Commission President .... Simon Chilvers
Hocking .... Neil Fitzpatrick
Walamari .... Bob Maza
Vice Admiral Windsor .... Brian James
Freddy Tjapaljarri .... Steve Dodd
Carl Denton .... Peter Sardi
Mrs. Denton .... Marion Mackenzie
Domenic .... Cameron Kavanagh
3 year old Harvey .... Brodie Jackman
5 year old Harvey .... Aleisha Sardi
Mrs. Berkowitz .... Ruth Erlichman
and Beverley Dunn, Alan Hopgood, Peter Cummins, Bob Hornery, Alfred Austen, Maude Pepper, Beryl Brunette, Julius Szappanos, Greg Carroll, Dean Nottle, Kim Gyngell, Mark Mitchell, Stewart Faichney, David Le Page, Wayne Hirst, Kylie Belling, Peggy Nichols, Gerard Maguire, Peter Harvey-Wright, John Allan, John Murphy, Douglas Hedge, Fred Steele, Johnny Hallyday, Michael Bishop, Tommy Dysart, John Heywood, Janet Andrewartha, Michael Read, Alan Barrett, Roger Oakley, Gary Down, Glen Rhueland, Alana Clark

Colin Friels

© ***Avenue Pictures***

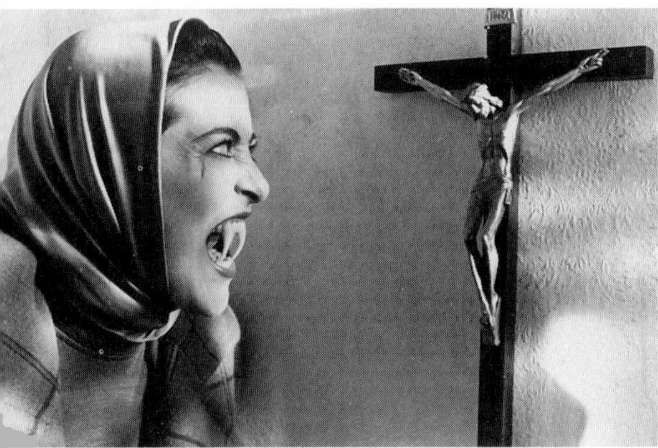

Amanda Donohoe

THE LAIR OF THE WHITE WORM

(VESTRON) Producer/Director/Screenplay, Ken Russell; Line Pro ducer, Ronaldo Vasconcellos; Executive Producers, William J. Quig ley, Dan Ireland; Photography, Dick Bush; Music, Stanislas Syrewicz Editor, Peter Davies; Sets, Anne Tilby; Costumes, Michael Jeffrey *"The D'Ampton Worm"* Arranged & Performed by Emilio Pere Machado, Stephan Powys/Violinist, Louise Newman; Bagpipe Music Ian Fleming; Harmonica Music, Harry Pitch; Casting, Gail Stevens Choreographer, Iogen Claire; Stunts, Stuart St. Paul; Production Exec utive, Jack Lorenz; Production Manager, Laura Julian; Productio Coordinator, Winnie Wishart; Assistant Director, Chris Hall; Sound Ray Beckett; Makeup/Creature Effects, Image Animation; British Color; Rated R; 94 minutes; October release

CAST

Lady Sylvia Marsh .... Amanda Donoho
Lord James D'Ampton .... Hugh Gran
Eve Trent .... Catherine Oxenber
Angus Flint .... Peter Capald
Marcy Trent .... Sammi Davi
Peters .... Stratford John
P.C. Erny .... Paul Brook
Dorothy Trent .... Imogen Clair
Kevin .... Chris Pi
Nurse Gladwell .... Gina McKe
Joe Grant .... Christopher Gabl
Jesus Christ .... Lloyd Peter
Snakewoman .... Jackie Russel
and Miranda Coe, Linzi Drew, Caron Anne Kelly, Fiona O'Conner Caroline Pope, Elisha Scott, Tina Shaw, Paul Easom, James Hicks David Kiernan, Matthew King, Ross King, Andy Norman, Bob Smith Chrissy Monk, Abbi Collins

Left Center: Hugh Grant, Catherine Oxenberg
© ***Vestron Pictures/Clive Coote***

The Dorrits leaving the Marshalsea/Alec Guinness

LITTLE DORRIT (Part 1: Nobody's Fault and Part 2: Little Dorrit's Story)

(CANNON GROUP) Producers, John Brabourne, Richard Goodwin; Director/Screenplay, Christine Edzard; Editors, Olivier Stockman, Fraser MacLean; Music, Giuseppe Verdi; Arranger, Michael Sanvoisin; Photography, Philippe Brun, Mick Mason, John Fletcher, David Hatter, Michaela Mason; Sound, Godfrey Kirby, Paul Carr; Casting, Elisabeth Woodthorpe, John Downes; Costumes, Barbara Sonnex & others; A Sands Film Production; British; Technicolor; Rated G; *Part 1:* 3 hours/*Part 2:* 3 hours; October release

CAST

Arthur Clennam .... Derek Jacobi
William Dorrit .... Alec Guinness
Pancks .... Roshan Seth
Little Dorrit .... Sarah Pickering
Flora .... Miriam Margolyes
Frederick Dorrit .... Cyril Cusack
Flintwinch .... Max Wall
Mrs. Merdle .... Eleanor Bron
Merdle .... Michael Elphick
Mrs. Clennam .... Joan Greenwood
Affery .... Patricia Hayes
Decimus Barnacle .... Robert Morley
Mr. Casby .... Bill Fraser
Fanny .... Amelda Brown
Tip .... Daniel Chatto
Maggy .... Pauline Quirke
Doyce .... Edward Burnaham
Meagles .... Roger Hammond
Captain Hopkins .... John McEnery
Minnie .... Sophie Ward
Tite Barnacle .... John Savident
Henry Gowan .... Pip Torrens
Clarence Barnacle .... Brian Pettifer
Sparkler .... Simon Dormandy
and Luke Duckett, Roshan Seth, Mollie Maureen, Diana Malin, Janice Cramer, Kathy Staff, Amanda Bellamy, Tracey Wilkinson, Julia Lang, Graham Seed, Beth Ellis, Ian Gelder, Lee Fox, Robert Mill, Morwenna Banks, Nadia Chambers, Dawn Charatan, Patricia Napier, Sophie Brew, John Harding, Alec Wallis, Michael Mears, Ken Morley, John Quarmby, Stuart Burge, Donald Pelmear, Arthur Nightingale, David Stoll, Donald Bisset, Christopher Birch, Harold Innocent, David Pugh, Terence Conoley, Richard Henry, Steve Ismay, Johnny Irving, David Doyle, Christopher Whittingham, Ruth Mitchell, Eric Francis, Anna, Eve, Harry & Nicholas Whittingham, Kate Williams, Ronnie Brody, Joan Dainty, Susan Field, Robert Demeger, Cordelia Ditton, David Thewlis, Gerald Campion, Rita Triesman, Betty Turner, Johnny Clatyon, Moya Brady, John Fahey, Joanna Maude, Iris Sadler, Joanna Brookes, Nat Pearn, Cyril Epstein, Alan Bungay, Mark Arnold, Howard Goorney, Liz Smith, Gwenda Hughes, Celia Banerman, Murray Melvin, Darlene Johnson, Bernard Padden, Dermot Crowley, Richard Cubison, Arthur Blake, John Scott Martin, David Trevena, David Bale, Anthony Benson, Ian Lindsay, Doug Roe, Tom McCabe, Ramon Martino, Joan Stafford, Terry Day, Cate Fowler, Carol Street, Siobhan Nicholas, Katherine Best, Yvonne D'Alpra, Robin Meredith, Marcel Steiner, Charles Reynolds, Tony Jay, Lizzie McKenzie, Harry Cross, Sarrina Caruthers, Susan Tanner, Sandra O'Rourke, Joanna Hurley, Ricky Cave, Zephyr & Sam Steer

Left Center: Susan Tanner, Alec Guinness
Top: Sarah Pickering, Derek Jacobi
© Cannon/Sands Film

Geoffrey Bayldon, Peggy Ashcroft, Shirley MacLaine, Navin Chowdhry, Twiggy
Right: Shirley MacLaine, Navin Chowdhry

MADAME SOUSATZKA

(UNIVERSAL) Producer, Robin Dalton; Director, John Schlesinger; Screenplay, Ruth Prawer Jhabvala, John Schlesinger; From the novel by Bernice Rubens; Associate Producer, Simon Bosanquet; Editor, Peter Honess; Photography, Nat Crosby; Music, Gerald Gouriet; Sound, Simon Kaye; Costumes, Amy Roberts; Designer, Luciana Arrighi; Casting, Noel Davis, Jeremy Zimmerman; Production Manager, Mary Richards; Assistant Director, Chris Rose; Art Directors, Ian Whittaker, Stephen Scott; Production Coordinator, Diane Chittell; Stunts, Colin Skeaping, Sadie Eden; *"Hiding From the "Feel the Motion"* & *"Hiding From the Eyes of Love"* by Charlie Skarbek, Tim Smit/Vocal, Twiggy; Classical Music by various composers; A Additional Material, Peter Morgan, Mark Wadlow; A Cineplex Odeon Films Presentation; British; Color; Rated PG-13; 122 minutes; October release

CAST

Madame Sousatzka .... Shirley MacLaine
Lady Emily .... Peggy Ashcroft
Jenny .... Twiggy
Sushila .... Shabana Azmi
Ronnie Blum .... Leigh Lawson
Cordle .... Geoffrey Bayldon
Vincent Pick .... Lee Montague
Lee Milev .... Robert Rietty
Manek Sen .... Navin Chowdhry
Edward .... Sam Howard
Woodford .... Jeremy Sinden
Lefranc .... Roger Hammond
Sunil .... Mohammed Ashig
Sousatzka's Mother .... Carol Gillies
Mrs. Ahuja .... Jamila Massey
Beechy .... Trevor Baxtor
and Roland Curram, Katherine Schlesinger, Elizabeth Hayes, Manuel Bagorro, Humphrey Burton, Vernon Dobtcheff, Ryan Ward, Peter Hugo Daly, Sue Robinson, Jean Anderson, Stephen Webber, Charu Bala Choksi, Usha Patel, Sam Beazley, Cheryl Miller, Matthew Hodson, Kieron O'Shea, Jane Bedford, Sebastian Taylor, David Doyle, Sam Smart, Susan Porrett, Keith Horsley, Sara Jane Mckechnie, Andrew St. Clair, Edward Kirby, Jonathan Poland, Benet Brandreth, Michelle Brown, Eamon Geoghegan, Greg Ellis, Gary Forbes, The Fairer Sax, Barry Douglas

Right Center: Navin Chowdhry, Twiggy
© *Cineplex Odeon Films/Simon Mein*

Leigh Lawson, Shirley MacLaine

WITHOUT A CLUE

)RION) Producer, Marc Stirdivant; Director, Thom Eberhardt; :creenplay, Gary Murphy, Larry Strawther; Music, Henry Mancini; hotography, Alan Hume; Designer, Brian Ackland-Snow; Editor, :ter Taner; Costumes, Judy Moorcroft; Casting, Noel Davis, Jeremy immerman, Nancy Foy; Production Executive, Dennis A. Brown; roduction Supervisor, Christable Albery; Designer, Martyn Hebert; ssociate Producers, Diana Buckhantz, Ben Moses; Assistant Direc-r, Don French; Production Coordinators, Harriet Fenner, Pamela ırker; Art Directors, Terry Ackland-Snow, Robin Tarsnane; Set Dec-:ators, Peter James, Ian Whittaker; Sound, David Hildyard; Special ffects, Ian Wingrove; An ITC Entertainment Presentation; Stunts, ıul Weston; British; CFI Color; Rated PG; 106 minutes; October lease

CAST

ıerlock Holmes .... Michael Caine
r. Watson .... Ben Kingsley
spector Lestrade .... Jeffrey Jones
ıke Leslie .... Lysette Anthony
:rof. Moriarty .... Paul Freeman
ord Smithwick .... Nigel Davenport
rs. Hudson .... Pat Keen
reenhough .... Peter Cook
:bastian .... Tim Killick
iggins .... Matthew Savage
:ter Giles .... John Warner
:eal Lesley .... Matthew Sim
ayor Johnson .... Harold Innoent
hn Clay .... George Sweeney
rchie .... Murray Ewan
hristabel .... Jennifer Guy
r. Andrews .... John Tordoff
rs. Andrews .... Alexandra Spencer
ındlady .... Elizabeth Kelly
ıe Duke .... Prince the Wonder Dog
ıd Stephen Tiller, Michael O'Hagan, Ivor Roberts, Martin Pallot, regor Fisher, Caroline Milmoe, Steven O'Donnell, James Bree, ırah Parr-Byrne, Clive Mantle, Dave Cooper, Richard Henry, Lesley aine, Sam Davies, Adam Kotz, John Surman, Les White, Chris ebb, Andy Bradford, Evan Rusell, Alan Bodenham

Right: MIchael Caine Above: Paul Freeman Top: Ben Kingsley, Michael Caine

"Gonza the Spearman"

GONZA THE SPEARMAN (Yari No Gonza)

(KINO INTERNATIONAL) Producers, Kiyoshi Iwashita, Tomiyuki Motomochi, Masatake Wakita; Director, Masahiro Shinoda; Screenplay, Tacko Tomioka; From a play by Monzaemon Chikamatsu; Photography, Kazuo Miyagawa; Editor, Sachiko Yamachi; Sound, Shotaro Yoshida; Music, Toru Takemitsu; Sets, Kiyoshi Awazu; Japan; Japanese with subtitles; Eastmancolor; Not rated; 121 minutes; October release

CAST

Gonza Sasano .... Hiromi Goh
Osai .... Shima Iwashita
Bannojo Kawazura .... Shohej Hino
Oyuki .... Misako Tanaka
Oyuki's Governess .... Haruko Kato
Ichinoshin Asaka .... Takashi Tsumura
Okiku .... Kaori Mizushima

RED SORGHUM

(NEW YORKER FILMS) Producers, Xi'An Film Studio, Wu Tianming; Director, Zhang Yimou; Screenplay, Chen Jianyu, Zhu Wei, Mo Yan; Story, Mo Mo Yan; Photography, Gu Changwei; Art Director, Yang Gang; Music, Zhao Jiping; Sound, Gu Changning; People's Republic of China, 1987; Mandarin with subtitles; Color; Cinemascope; Not rated; 91 minutes; October release

CAST

Grandmother, Nine .... Gong Li
Grandfather .... Jiang Wen
Father .... Liu Ji
Luohan .... Teng Ru-Jun
Sanpao .... Ji Cun Hua

Right: Jang Wen, Liu Ji
© *New Yorker Films*

Glenda Jackson, Cathy Tyson, Buki Armstrong
Above: Glenda Jackson (C)
© *Cannon*

BUSINESS AS USUAL

(CANNON GROUP) Producer, Sara Geater; Director/Screenplay Lezli-An Barrett; Executive Producers, Menahem Golan, Yora Globus; Associate Producer, Michael J. Kagan; Editor, Hen Richardson; Designer, Hildegard Bechtler; Photography, Ernie Vincz Costumes, Monica Howe; Production Manager, Laura Julian; Assista Director, Ray Corbett; Sound, Ken Weston; *"Cost of Loving"* by Pa Weller; Music, Andrew Scott, Paul Weller; In association with Fil Four International; British; Dolby Stereo; Color; Rated PG; 88 minute October release

CAST

Babs Flynn .... Glenda Jacksc
Kieran Flynn .... John Tha
Josie Patterson .... Cathy Tysc
Stevie Flynn .... Mark McGar
Mr. Barry .... Eamon Bolan
Mark .... James Hazeldir
Paula Douglas .... Buki Armstron
Terry Flynn .... Steve McGar
Tim Flynn .... Philip Fost
Rosa .... Natalie Duf
Brian Lewis .... Jack Ca
Joan Sankey .... Mel Mart
Jude .... Michelle Bya
Doug .... Robert Keega
Eddie .... Craig Charl
Mrs. Rummage .... Christine Moo
Mr. Dunlop .... Stephen Dillc
Rowena Freeman .... Lucy Shee
Trisha Lane .... Eithne Browr
Solicitor .... Roland Oliv
TV Producer .... Graham Call
P. C. Whitcombe .... John Flanag
and Christopher Quinn, Kathy Jamieson, Rachel Laurence, W Tacey, Barry Eaton, Mark Reader, Dean Williams, Tom Peppe Sharon Power, Lorraine Michaels, Ian Puleston Davis, Lesley Dain Margo Stanley, Cathy Williams, Joanne Ellis, Simon Barratt

THE LAST EMPEROR

(SOUTHERN FILMS) Director/Screenplay, Li Han Hsiang; Based on Li Shu Xian's *"Pu Yi and I," "Pu Yi's Latter Life,"* and *"Pu Yi's My Former Life";* A New Kwun Lun Film Production Co and China International Television Corp. coproduction; China; Mandarin with subtitles; Color; Not rated; 100 minutes; October release (no other credits provided)

CAST

Pu Yi (Liang Jia Heui) .... Tony Leung
Li Shu Xian .... Pan Hung
Empress Wan Jung (Margaret) .... Li Dien Lang
Li Yu Qin (Mary) .... Li Dien Xing

Pan Hung, Tony Leung
© *Southern Films*

SALAAM BOMBAY!

NECOM) Producer/Director, Mira Nair; Story, Mira Nair, Sooni aporevala; Screenplay, Sooni Taraporevala; Co-Producer, Mitch tein; Photography, Sandi Sissel; Editor, Barry Alexander Brown; igner, Mitch Epsteinl Music, L. Subramaniam; Executive Produ-s, Anil Tejani, Michael Nozik, Gabriel Auer; Co-Executive Pro-er, Cherie L. Rodgers; Associate Producer, Jane Balfour; Assistant ector, Hassan Kutty; Hindi Dialogue, Hriday Lani; Art Directors, ish Roy, Nitin Desai; Sound, Juan Rodriguez; Children's Workshop ector, Barry John; India; Indian with subtitles; Not rated; 113 utes; October release

CAST

shna/Chaipau .... Shafiq Syed
yla .... Sarfuddin Qurrassi
ra .... Raju Barnad
llum .... Raghubir Yadav
ha .... Aneeta Kanwar
a .... Nana Patekar
nju .... Hansa Vithal
m .... Mohanraj Babu
ngal .... Chandrashekhar Naidu
assal/Sweet Sixteen .... Chanda Sharma
dame .... Shaukat Azmi
si Bawa ji .... Dinshaw Daji
a Chor .... Alfred Anthony
rtaza .... Ramesh Deshavani
erintendent .... Anjan Srivastava

Right: Chanda Sharma
Top: Shafiq Syed, Chanda Sharma
© Cinecom Pictures

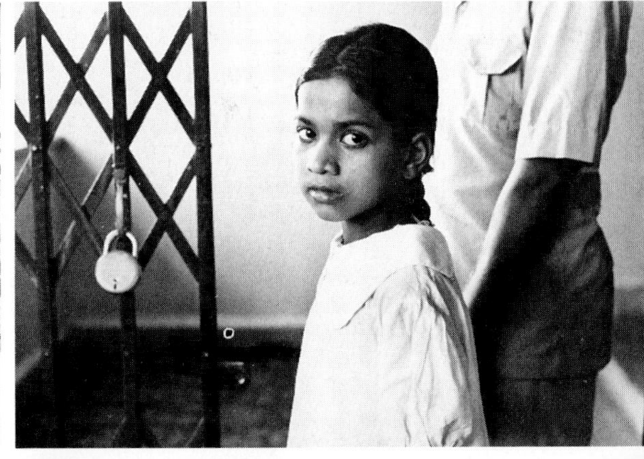

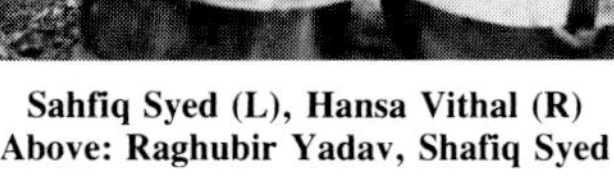

Sahfiq Syed (L), Hansa Vithal (R)
Above: Raghubir Yadav, Shafiq Syed

Shafiq Syed (C)
Above: Hansa Vithal

FILM ACTRESS

(R5/S8) Producers, Tomoyuki Tanaka, Kon Ichikawa; Director, Kon Ichikawa; Story, Kaneto Shindo; Screenplay, Kaneto Shindo, Shinya Hidaka, Kon Ichikawa; Planning, Kazuo Baba; Editors, Chizuko Osada, Junichiro Tanaka; Photography, Yukio Isohata; Art Director, Shinobu Muraki; Sound, Tetsuo Ohashi; Lighting, Kaoru Saito; Music, Kensaku Tanigawa; A Toho production; Japan; Japanese with subtitles; Color; Not rated; 130 minutes; October release

CAST

Kinuyo Tanaka .... Sayuri Yoshinaga
Yae, the mother .... Mitsuko Mori
Uncle Gentaro .... Fujio Tokita
Sister Tamayo .... Michiyo Yokoyama
Brother Haruji .... Minoru Toida
Brother Shozo .... Ryuzo Tanaka
Senkichi Nakama .... Mitsuru Hirata
Studio Head (Shiro Kido) .... Koji Ishizaka
(Hiroshi) Shimizu .... Toru Watanabe
Heinosuke Gosho .... Kiichi Nakai
Himself (in *Aizen Katsura*) .... Ken Uehara
The Landlady .... Kyoko Kishida
Isoya .... Hiroshi Igawa
Sakanashi .... Tomoko Jinbo
Himself .... Kokichi Takada
Seiko .... Yasuko Sawaguchi
Mizouchi (Kenji Mizoguchi) .... Bunta Sugawara

Right: Kiichi Nakai, Sayuri Yoshinaga
Above: Mitsuko Mori, Sayuri Yoshinaga

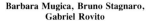

Barbara Mugica, Bruno Stagnaro, Gabriel Rovito

UNDER THE WORLD (Debajo Del Mundo)

(NEW WORLD) Producers, Jorge E. Estrada Mora, Leo Mehl; rector/Screenplay, Beda Docampo Feijoo, Juan Bautista Stagna Executive Producers, Karel Skop, Sabina Sigler; Associate Produc Jorge Sabate; Photography, Frantisek Uldrich; Assistant Directo Daniel Pires Mateus, Milos Kohout; Editor, Pablo Mari; Sound, J Luis Diaz, Carlos Abbate; Music, Jose Luis Castuneira De D Choreography, Miguel Angel Lumaldo, Boris Moravec; Costum Miguel Angel Lumaldo, Boris Moravec; Assistant Director, Ca Fijmay; Czechoslovakian-Argentine; Spanish with subtitles; Co Rated R; 105 minutes; October release

CAST

Nachman .... Sergio Re
Liba .... Barbara Mug
Smialek .... Victor La Pl
Baruj .... Oscar Ferri
Josef .... Gabriel Gi
Judith .... Paula Car
Szachna .... Bruno Stagn
Raquel .... Gabriela Tosc
Von Grotus .... Jan Po
Sikorski .... Karel Chro
David .... Filip R
Ermitano .... Frantisek Hu
Szoloch .... Jorge Sab
Ochendusko .... Sautopluk Pica
Sargento Ruso .... Karel Sek
Oficial Ruso .... Bohuslav Ka
Colaboracionista .... Pavel Van
Fotografo .... Jaroslav Va
Mujer Sikorski .... Edita Dindel
Hija de Von Grotus .... Jana Ludvicr
Otra Hija de Von Grotus .... Adala Ludvicr
Daniel .... Gabriel Ludvicr
and Carlos De Mateis, Pedro Loeb, Laura Valle, Thomas Voth, Kraus, Vit Pesina, Ivan Padobski

Left Center: Gabriel Rovito, Oscar Ferrigno

A CRY IN THE DARK

(WARNER BROS.) Producer, Verity Lambert; Director, Fred Schepisi; Screenplay, Robert Caswell, Fred Schepisi; Based on *"Evil Angels"* by John Bryson; Executive Producers, Menahem Golan, Yoram Globus; Line Producer, Roy Stevens; Photography, Ian Baker; Editor, Jill Bilcock; Music, Bruce Smeaton; Designer, Wendy Dickson, George Liddle; Costumes, Bruce Finlayson; Casting, Rhonda Schepisi, Forcast; Production Executive, Rony Yakov; Production Manager, Carol Hughes; Assistant Director, Steve Andrews; Video Director, Tony Leach; Art Directors, Dale Duguid, Brian Edmonds; Sound, Gary Wilkins; Production Coordinator, Sue Jarvis; Music Performance, Joe Chindamo, Loose Change; A Cannon Entertainment/Golan-Globus Production In Association with Cinema Verity Limited; Australian; Dolby Stereo; Eastmancolor; Panavision; Rated PG-13; 121 minutes; November release

CAST

Lindy .... Meryl Streep
Michael .... Sam Neill
Aidan 6 Years .... Dale Reeves
Aidan 8 Years .... David Hoflin
Aidan 11 Years .... Jason Reason
Reagan 4 Years .... Michael Wetter
Reagan 6 Years .... Kane Barton
Reagan 9 Years .... Trent Roberts
Azaria .... Lauren Shepherd, Bethany Ann Prickett, Alison O'Connell, Aliza Dason
Kahlia New Born .... Jane Coker
Kahlia 18 Months .... Rae-Leigh Henson
Kahlia 4 Years .... Nicolette Minster
Cliff Murchison .... Brian James
Avis Murchison .... Dorothy Alison
Barritt .... Maurie Fields
Macknay .... Peter Hosking
O'Loughlin .... Matthew Barker
Peter Dean .... Bruce Kilpatrick
Justice Muirhead .... Charles Tingwell
Barker .... Bruce Myles
Phillips .... Neil Fitzpatrick
Sturgess .... Dennis Miller
Tipple .... Lewis Fitz-Gerald
Kirkham .... Brendan Higgins
Cavanagh .... Ian Swan
Pauling .... Robert Wallace

Left Center: Meryl Streep, Sam Neill
Above: Meryl Streep, Neil Fitzpatrick
Top: Sam Neill, Meryl Streep
© *Cannon/Warner Brothers*

Dale Reeves, Meryl Streep

Sam Neill, Meryl Streep

BUSTER

(HEMDALE) Producer, Norma Heyman; Director, David Gre Screenplay, Colin Shindler; Executive Producers, John Daly, De Gibson; Association Producer, Redmond Morris; Photography, T Imi; Designer, Simon Holland; Music, Anne Dudley; Costum Evangeline Harrison; Editor, Lesley Walker; Camera, Tony Wh Sound, Ken Weston; Assistant Director, Michael Zimbrich; Cast Debbie McWilliams; Production Manager, Richard Hellman; Art rector, Clinton Cavers; Production Coordinator, Caroline Hill; Sou Colin Coder; Stunts, Mark McBride; *"Two Hearts (One Mind)"* Lamont Dozier & Phil Collins, and songs by various artists; Co Dolby Stereo; Rated R; 93 minutes; November release

CAST

Buster .... Phil Col
June .... Julie Wal
Bruce .... Larry La
Franny .... Stephanie Lawre
Nicky .... Ellen Bea
Harry .... Michael Attw
Ronnie .... Ralph Bro
George .... Christopher Elli
Mrs. Rothery .... Sheila Hanc
Inspector Mitchell .... Martin Ja
Sergeant Chalmers .... Clive W
Sir James McDowell .... Anthony Qua
Poyser .... Michael By
Justice Parry .... Harold Innoc
Fairclough .... Rupert Vansit
Jimmy .... John Benf
Walter .... John Barr
Linda .... Carole Col
Susan .... Amy Shinc
David .... David Shinc
Vicar .... Graham Li
Sally .... Pauline Li
Mandy .... Jessica Gr
Maria .... Evangelina S
and Tony Collins, Jonathan McKenna, Vincenzo Nicoli, Timo Davies, Roger McKern, David Arlen, Frank Ellis, Bill Rourke, Lowe, Christopher Gray, Alan Cowan, James Donnelly, Stewart H wood, Jean Ainslie, John Patrick, Francisco Morales, Martin Lasa Rodolpho De Alexandra, Sergio Calderon, Yolanda Vazquez, Alv Carcano

Left: Michael Attwell, Larry Lamb, Phil Collins, Ralph Brown Top: Julie Walters Phil Collins © *Hemdale*

DISTANT THUNDER

(PARAMOUNT) Producer, Robert Schaffel; Director, Rick Rosenthal; Screenplay, Robert Stitzel; Story, Robert Stitzel, Deedee Wehle; Photography, Ralf Bode; Editor, Dennis Virkler; Consultant, Robert Cowan; Music, Maurice Jarre; Casting, Lynn Stalmaster; Executive Producer, Richard L. O'Connor; Production Manager, Warren Carr; Assistant Director, David W. Rose; Art Director, Mark S. Freeborn; Costumes, Tish Monaghan; Set Decorator, Rose Marie McSherry; Sound, Larry Sutton; Production Coordinator, Tammy S. Oates; Stunts, Chuck Waters, Everett Creach; Special Effects, William H. Orr; *"Distant Thunder"* by Bill Thumm & R. D. Fairbairn/ Performance, Keith Bennett, *"Once We Get Started"* by Michael Watson & Johnny Elkins/Performance, Nadirah Ali, and songs by other artists; Canadian-U.S.; Dolby Stereo; Technicolor; Rated R; 114 minutes; November release

CAST

Mark Lambert .... John Lithgow
Jack Lambert .... Ralph Macchio
Char .... Kerrie Keane
Harvey Nitz .... Reb Brown
Barbara Lambert .... Janet Margolin
Larry .... Denis Arndt
Moss .... Jamey Sheridan
Louis .... Tom Bower
Andy .... John Kelly
Coach Swabey .... Michael Currie
Jane .... Hilary Strang
Holly .... Robyn Stevan
Sheriff .... David Longworth
Billy Watson .... Gordon Currie
Principal .... Walter Marsh
Buddy .... Allan Lysell
Jeanette .... Denalda Williams

© *Paramount Pictures/Jack Rowand*

Kerrie Keane, John Lithgow

WOMEN ON THE VERGE OF A NERVOUS BREAKDOWN

(ORION CLASSICS) Executive Producer, Agustin Almodovar; Director/Screenplay, Pedro Almodovar; Photography, Jose Luis Alcaine; Editor, Jose Salcedo; Sound, Guilles Ortion; Costumes, Jose M. De Cossio; Music, Bernardo Bonezzi; Set Decorator, Felix Murcia; Production Manager, Ester Garcia; Associate Producer, Antonio Llorens; An El Deseo, S.A./Laurenfilm Production; Spain; Spanish with subtitles; Color; Rated R; 92 minutes; November release

CAST

Pepa Marcos .... Carmen Maura
Carlos .... Antonio Banderas
Lucia .... Julieta Serrano
Candela .... Maria Barranco
Marisa .... Rossy De Palma
Paulina Morales .... Kiti Manver
Lucia's Father .... Yayo Calvo
Cristina .... Leles Leon
Ivan .... Fernando Guillen
German .... Juan Lombardero
Ana .... Ana Leza
Ambite .... Ambite
Lucia's Mother .... Mary Gonzalez
Paulina's Secretary .... Lupe Barrado
Priest .... Gabriel Latorre
TV New Anchorwoman .... Francisca Caballero
Real Estate Agent .... Agustin Almodovar
Pharmacist .... Carmen Espada
Doctor .... Gregorio Ross
and Guillermo Montesinos, Chus Lampreave, Angel De Andres Lopez, Jose Antonio Navarro, Joaquin Climent, Chema Gil

Carmen Maura, Maria Barranco, Antonio Banderas
Above: Carmen Maura, also Top and Below with Rossy De Palma

Top Right: Antonio Banderas, Carmen Maura
Below: Julieta Serrano
© Orion Pictures

TESTIMONY

(EUROPEAN CLASSICS) Producer/Director/Designer/Editor/Co-Screenplay, Tony Palmer; Photography, Nic Knowland; Screenplay, David Rudkin; Costumes, John Hibbs; Art Directors, Paul Templeman, Chris Bradley; Sound, John Lundsten, Alan Dykes; Assistant Directors, Andrew Montgomery, Chris Hall; Production Manager, Gladys Pearce; Associate Producer, Maureen Murray; Executive Producers, Michael Kustow, Grahame Jennings, Michael Henry; Music Performances, Yuzuko Horigome, Howard Shelley, Margaret Fingerhut; Vocals, John Shirley-Quirk, Felicity Palmer; Conductor, Rudolf Barshai; An Isolde Films Production, in association with The Mandemar Group, ORF, NOS, DR, SVT, HRK for Channel Four; British; Color/Black & White; Panavision; Not rated; 157 minutes; November release

CAST

Dimitri Shostakovich .... Ben Kingsley
Nina Shostakovich .... Sherry Baines
Galya .... Magdalen Asquith
Maxim .... Mark Asquith
Stalin .... Terence Rigby
Tukhachevsky .... Ronald Pickup
Zhdanov .... John Shrapnel
Brutus .... Robert Reynolds
Gargolovsky .... Vernon Dobtcheff
Stalin's Secretary .... Colin Hurst
Stalin's Mother .... Joyce Grundy
Young Stalin .... Mark Thrippleton
The English Humanist .... Liza Goddard
Glazunov .... Peter Woodthorpe
Meyerhold .... Robert Stephens
Khatchaturyan .... William Squire
The Film Editor .... Murray Melvin
The Journalist .... Robert Urquhart
Vanya .... Christopher Bramwell
H.G. Wells .... Brook Williams
Madam Lupinskaya .... Marita Phillips
Carnival Fat Man .... Frank Carson
Carnival Thin Man .... Chris Barrie
The Nun .... Mitzi Mueller
Tsvetayeva .... Tracey Spence
Akhmatova .... Dorota Rae
and Bronco McLoughlin, Val Elliot, Julian Stanley, Van Martin, Curly Carter, Jane Cox, Ed Bishop, Nicholas Fry, Rowena Parr, Igor Gridneff, Rosemary Chamney, David Sharpe, Peter Faulkner, The Panda Jazz, Rodney Litchfield & Chris d'Bray

© *European Classics*

WE THINK THE WORLD OF YOU

(CINECOM) Producer, Tomasso Jandelli; Director, Colin Gregg Screenplay, Hugh Stoddart; Co-Producer, Paul Cowan; Editor, Pete Delfgou; Costumes, Doreen Watkinson; Designer, Jamie Leonard; Ar Director, Chris Edwards; Photography, Mike Garfath; Assistant Direc tor, Gary White; Casting, Simone Reynolds; Sound, Tony Dawe British; Color; Rated PG; 94 minutes; December release

CAST

Frank .... Alan Bate
Johnny .... Gary Oldma
Megan .... Frances Barbe
Millie .... Liz Smit
Tom .... Max Wa
Rita .... Kerry Wis
Boy .... Danny McDonal
Judge .... Edward Jewesbur
Miss Sweeting .... Pat Kee
Butcher .... Nick Stringe
Bill .... David Swi
Bill's Wife .... Paula Jacob
Residents Asso. Lady .... Barbara Hick
Post Girl .... Nicola Wrigh
R.S.P.C.A. Inspector .... Ian Hasting
Mrs. Grant .... Barbara Nev
Meier Man .... David Treven
Stall Holder .... Steward Hardwoo
Woman at Party .... Sheila Ballantin

Above: Gary Oldman, Alan Bates

Gary Oldman, Frances Barber, Liz Smith, Ryan Batt, Max Wall, Alan Bates
© *Cinecom*

THE HOUSE OF BERNARDA ALBA (La Casa De Bernarda Alba)

ARAISO PRODUCIONES) Director, Mario Camus; Screenplay, ario Camus, Antonio Larreta; Based on the play by Fecerico Garcia rca; Photography, Fernando Arribas; Editor, Jose M. Biurrun; Art rector, Rafael Palmero; Spanish; Spanish with subtitles; Not rated; 6 minutes; December release

CAST

rnarda .... Irene Gutierrez Caba
lela .... Ana Belen
ncia .... Florinda Chico
igustias .... Enriqueta Carballeira
artirio .... Vicky Pena
agdalena .... Aurora Pastor
nelia .... Mercedes Lezcano

"The House of Bernarda Alba"
© *Paraiso Productiones*

A FORGOTTEN TUNE FOR THE FLUTE

(FRIES ENTERTAINMENT) Director, Eldar Ryazanov; Screenplay, Emil Braginsky, Eldar Ryazanov; Photography, Vadim Alisov; Art Director, Alexander Borisov; Music, Andrei Petrov; Russia; Russian with subtitles; Not rated; 118 minutes; December release

CAST

Leonid .... Leonid Filatov
Lida .... Tatyana Dogileva
Leonid's Wife .... Irina Kupchenko

Left: Elena Fadeeva, Leonid Filatov
© *Fries Entertainment*

Tatyana Dogileva Right: Elena Fadeeva, Vladislav Stzijenov, Leonid Filatov

GENESIS

NTERNATIONAL FILM CIRCUIT) Executive Producer, Marie iscale Osterrieth; Director/Screenplay, Mrinal Sen; Co-Producers, arabee Films (France), Mrinal Den PLRT Productions (India), Les lms de la Dreve (Belgium), Cactus Film (Switzerland); Photography, arlo Varini; Sound, Henri Morelle, Frank Struys; Music, Ravi Shanır; Editor, Elizabeth Waelchli; Art Director, Nitish Roy; India; Hindi ith subtitles; Not rated; 108 minutes; December release

CAST

ne Woman .... Shabana Azmi
ne Farmer .... Naseeruddin Shah
ne Weaver .... Om Puri
ne Trader .... M. K. Raina

"Genesis"

Alex Winter, Philip Anglim, Eric Stoltz, Alice Krige Top: Philip Anglim, Laura Dern, Alice Krige, Eric Stoltz

HAUNTED SUMMER

(CANNON GROUP) Producer, Martin Poll; Director, Ivan Pass Screenplay, Lewis John Carlino; Based on the novel by Anne Edwar Executive Producers, Menahem Golan, Yoram Globus; Photograph Guiseppe Rotunno; Designer, Stephen Grimes; Music, Christoph Young; Editor, Cesare D'Amico; Associate Producers, John Thom son, Mario Cotone; Costumes, Gabriella Pescucci; Casting, Jose V laverde; Production Manager, Attilio Viti; Assistant Directors, Car Quintero, Mauro Sacripanti; Production Executive, Rony Yacc Stunts/Fencing, Franco Fantasia; Sound, Drew Kunin; Art Direct Francesco Chianese; Effects Makeup, Manlio Rocchetti; Spec Effects, Ditta Corridori, Gino De Rossi; *"Mon Coeur Se Recommand Vous"* by Orlando di Lasso/Vocal, Julie Pritikin/Guitar, Gregg Nest British; Ultra-Stereo; Rated R; 115 minutes; December release

CAST

Percy Shelley .... Eric Sto
Lord Byron .... Philip Angl
Mary Godwin .... Alice Kri
Claire Clairmont .... Laura De
John Polidori .... Alex Win
Berger .... Giusto Lo Pipe
Rushton .... Don Hods
Fletcher .... Terry Richar
Maurice .... Peter Berli
Elise .... Alise McLa

THE DRESSMAKER

(EURO-AMERICAN FILMS) Producer, Ronald Shedlo; Director, Jim O'Brien; Executive Producer/Screenplay, John McGrath; Associate Producer, Steve Clark-Hall; Production Coordinator, Gail Samuelson; Assistant Director, Gary White; Casting, Priscilla John, Mary Colquhoun; Photography, Mick Coulter; Designer, Chris Townsend; Sound, Sandy MacRae; Music, George Fenton; Editor, William Diver; Costumes, Judy Moorcroft; Stunts, Jim Dowdall; British; Color; Not rated; 92 minutes; December release

CAST

Nellie .... Joan Plowright
Margo .... Billie Whitelaw
Rita .... Jane Horrocks
Jack .... Peter Postlethwaite
Wesley .... Tim Ransom
Mrs. Manders .... Rosemary Martin
Val .... Pippa Hinchley
Mr. Manders .... Tony Haygarth
Mr. Barnes .... Bert Parnaby
Shop Assistant .... Margi Clarke
Sgt. Zawadski .... Sam Douglas
Chuck .... Michael James-Reed

Billie Whitelaw, Jane Horrocks, Joan Plowright
Above: Jane Horrocks, Tim Ransom

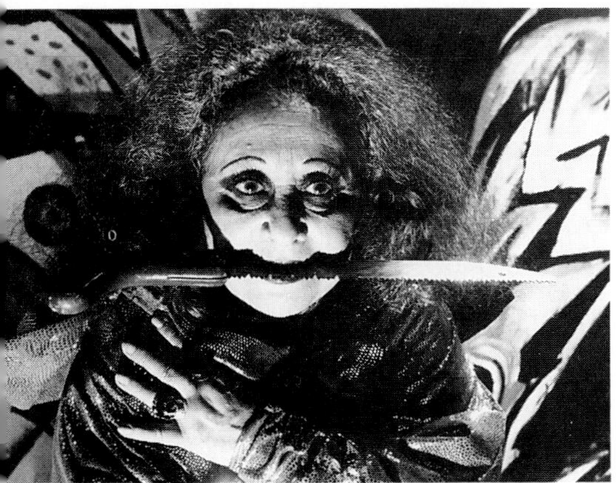

Lotte Huber in "Anita: Dances of Vice"
© *First Run Features*

Kate Vernon, Gregg Henry in "The Last of Philip Banter" © *Tesauro/Cinevista*

IGGLES ADVENTURES IN TIME (New Century/Vista) Produc-s, Pom Oliver, Kent Walwin; Director, John Hough; Executive roducer, Adrian Scrope; Co-Executive Producer, Paul Barnes-Taylor; creenplay, John Groves, Kent Walwin; Based on characters created by apt. W. E. Johns; Photography, Ernest Vincze; Editor, Richard Tre-or; Music, Stanislas; Sound, Peter Pardoe, Paul LeMare; Production esigner, Terry Pritchard; Costumes, Jim Acheson; Associate Pro-ucer, Peter James; Assistant Director/Co-Associate Producer, John 'Connor; Stunt Coordinator, Gerry Crampton; A Compact Yellowbill resentation in association with Tambarle Productions; British; Dolby tereo; Technicolor; Rated PG; 108 minutes; January release. CAST: eil Dickson (Biggles), Alex Hyde-White (Jim Ferguson), Fiona lutchinson (Debbie), Peter Cushing (Col. Raymond), Marcus Gilbert Von Stalheim), William Hootkins (Chuck), Michael Siberry (Algy), aniel Flynn (Ginger), James Saxon (Bertie), Francesca Gonshaw Marie), Alan Polonsky (Bill)

HE HORSE THIEF (Xian Film Studio) Producer, Wu Tianming; irector, Tian Zhuangzhuang; Screenplay, Zhang Rui; Music, Qu iaosong; Photography, Hou Yong, Zhao Fei; Chinese; Color; Not ated; 88 minutes; January release. CAST: Tseshang Rigzin, Dan Jiji, ayang Jmco, Gaoba, Daiba, Drashi

NITA: DANCES OF VICE (First Run Features) Producer/ irector, Rosa von Praunheim; Screenplay, Rosa von Praunheim, H. impach; Photography, Elfi Mikesch; Editors, Mike Shepherd, Rosa on Praunheim; Music, Konrad Elfers, Rainer Rubbert, Alen Marks, d Lieber; Production Companies, Road Movies, ZDF; Germany; erman with English subtitles; Not rated; 85 minutes; January release. AST: Lotti Huber (Anita Berber), Ina Blum, Mikael Honesseau

IAMMAME (Pacific Film Archives) Producers, Arcanal/ inematheque de la Danse, Maison de la Culture de Grenoble and heatre de la Ville de Paris; Director, Raul Ruiz; Screenplay, Jean-laude Gallotta, Raul Ruiz; Photography, Jacques Bouquin; Editor, lartine Bouquin; Music, Henry Torque, Serge Houppin; Production esigner, Raul Ruiz; Choreographer, Jean-Claude Gallotta; Chilean; olor; Not rated; 65 minutes; January release. CAST: Eric Alfieri, lathilde Altaraz, Muriel Boulay, Christophe Delachau, Jean-Claude allotta, Pascal Gravat, Priscilla Newell, Viviane Serry, Robert Sey-ied

HE TREE WE HURT (Greek Film Center) Producer/Director/ creenplay, Dimos Avdeliodis; Editor, Costas Foundas; Music, De-etris Papademetriou; Costumes, Maria Avdeliodis; Photography, hilipos Koutsaftis; Greek; Color; Not rated; 75 minutes; January elease. CAST: Yannis Avdeliodis (Boy/Narrator), Nikos Mioteris Runny-Nose Vangelis), Marina Delivoria (Narrator's mother), Takis goris (Man at head of funeral procession), Dimos Avdeliodis (Mad eaman)

IELO (European Classics) Producer, Marin Karmitz; Director/ creenplay, Alain Resnais; From a Play by Henry Bernstein; Photogra-hy, Charlie Van Damme, Gilbert Duhalde; Editors, Albert Jurgenson, ean-Pierre Besnard; Music, Philippe-Gerard; Art Director, Jacques aulnier; Production Companies, MK2 Productions, Films A2; French ith English subtitles; Not rated; 112 minutes; January release. CAST: abine Azema (Romaine Belcroix), Fanny Ardant (Christiane Leves-ue), Pierre Arditi (Pierre Belcroix), Andre Dussollier (Marcel Blanc), acques Dacqmine (Dr. Remy), Hubert Gignoux (Priest), Catherine rditi (Yvonne)

THE LAST OF PHILIP BANTER (Cinevista) Producer/Director, Herve Hachuel; Screenplay, Alvaro de la Huerta; Adaptation, Herve Hachuel, Alvaro de la Huerta; from a novel by John Franklin; Executive Producers, Clifford W. Lord, Jr., Alvaro de la Huerta; Photography, Ricardo Chara; Assistant Director, Miguel A. Gil; Art Director, Jose Maria Taplador; Sound, Chris Munro; Editor, Eduardo Biurrun; a co-production of Tesauro, S. A. and Banter, A. G.; Spanish; Dolby Stereo; Eastmancolor; Rated R; 105 minutes; January release. CAST: Scott Paulin (Philip Banter), Irene Miracle (Elizabeth Banter), Gregg Henry (Robert Prescott), Kate Vernon (Brent Holliday), Jose Luiz Gomez (Dr. Monasterio), Tony Curtis (Charles Foster), Patty Shepard (Alicia), Fernando Telletxea "Fama" (Enrique), Lola Bayo (Carmen), Maria Jose Sarsa (Banter's Secretary), Juana (Gypsy), Margarita Calahorra (Woman in Metro), Pepe Yepes (Drunk in bar), Douglas Tantallon (Vagabond), Adriano Dominguez (Consierge), Oscar San Juan (Foster's Chauffeur), Jose Maria Sastus (Maitre D'), Edison Tabare, Alfredo Belinchon, Javier Pimentael (Male Nurses), Lopez Gomez Molero (Taxi Driver)

THE LONE RUNNER (TransWorld) Producer, Maurizio Maggi; Director, Roger (Ruggero) Deodato; Screenplay, Chris Trainor, Steven Luotto; Photography, Robert Bennet (Robert Forges Davanzati), Editor, Eugene Miller (Eugenio Alabiso); Music, Charles Cooper (Carlo Maria Cordio); Art Director, Bob Glaser; Sound, Carl Schaefer; Special Effects, Burt Spiegel; Associate Producer, Peter Graf (Romeo Assonitis); Assistant Director, Jerry Vaughan; an Ovidio Assonitis production; Italian; Technicolor; Rated PG; 89 minutes; January release. CAST: Miles O'Keeffe (Garrett, the Lone Runner), Savina Gersak (Analisa Summerking), Michael J. Aronin (Emerick), John Steiner (Skorm), Hal Yamanouchi (Nimbus), Donald Hodson (Mr. Summerking), Ronald Lacey (Misha)

ANGUISH (Spectrafilm) Producer, Pepon Coromina; Director/ Screenplay, Bigas Luna; Photography, Josep Maria Civit; Editor, Tom Sabin; Music, J. M. Pagan; Casting/Costumes, Consol Tura; Set Decorator, Felipe de Paco; Makeup, Matilde Fabregat; Special Effects, Paco Teres; Associate Producers, Xavier Visa, George Coromina; Samba P. C. and Luna Films; Spanish; Agfa Color; J-D-C Widescreen; Rated R; 89 minutes; January release. CAST: Zelda Rubinstein (Alice), Michael Lerner (John), Talia Paul (Patty), Clara Pastor (Linda), Angel Jove (Killer), Isabel Garcia Lorca

Zelda Rubinstein, Michael Lerner in "Anguish" © *Spectrafilm*

"Higher Education"
© *Cinema Group Pictures*

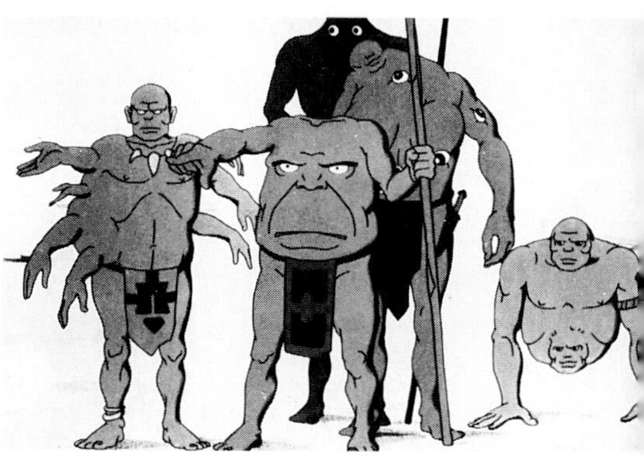

"Light Years"
© *Miramax Films*

THE MISFIT BRIGADE, formerly *Wheels of Terror* (Trans World) Producers, Just Betzer, Benni Korzen. Director, Gordon Hessler; Screenplay, Nelson Gidding; Based on the novel by Sven Hassel; Photography, George Nikolic; Editor, Bob Gordon; Music, Ole Hoyer; Production Designer, Vladislav Lasic; Line Producers, Benni Korzen, Milos Antic; British; Dolby Stereo; Eastmancolor; Rated R; 101 minutes; January release. CAST: David Carradine (Col. von Weisshagen), D. W. Moffett (Capt. von Barring), Keith Szarabajka ("Old Man"), Bruce Davison (Porta), Jay O. Sanders (Tiny), David Patrick Kelly (The Legionaire), Slavko Stimac (Sven), Andrija Maricic (Stege), Boris Komnenic (Bauer), Bane Vidakovic (Muller), Oliver Reed (The General), Irena Prosen (The Madam), Svetlana, Gordana Les, Lidija Pletl, Annie Korzen

HIGHER EDUCATION (Palisades Entertainment) Producer, Peter Simpson; Director, John Sheppard; Co-Producers, Ilana Frank, Ray Sager; Screenplay, John Sheppard, Dan Nathanson; Executive Producers, Peter Simpson, Peter Haley; Photography, Benton Spencer; Editor, Stephan Fanfara, Nick Rotundo; Music, Paul Zaza; Art Director, Andrew Deskin; Casting, Media Casting/Lucinda Sill; Assistant Directors, Roman Buchok, Frank Siracusa; Sound, Rick Cadger, Wayne Griffin; Stunt Coordinator, Dwayne Mclean; Canadian; Color; Rated R; 92 minutes; January release. CAST: Kevin Hicks (Andy Cooper), Isabelle Mejias (Carrie Hanson), Lori Hallier (Nicole Hubert), Stephen Black (Dean Roberts), Richard Monette (Robert Bley), Jennifer Inch (Gladys/Glitter), Emmanuel Mark (Droid), Sharolyn Sparrow (Helen Dobish), Alan Rose (Older Man/Doctor), Mae Lobban (Mom), Chick Roberts (Dad), Michael Copeman (Bus Driver), Bunty Webb (Woman on bus), John Mitchell (Student 1), Barbara Shearer (Girl 1), Michael Fielding (Crew Member), Lois Tucci, John Palubski, David Palmer, Alvin Jones, Doug Dyson (Bar Band)

THY KINGDOM COME . . . THY WILL BE DONE (Roxie Films) Executive Producers, Roger James, David Fanning; Producer, Written & Directed by Antony Thomas; Executive Producers, Roger James, David Faning; Photography, Curtis Clark; Editor, MacDonald Brown; A Central Independent Television production for Viewpoint '87 with WGBH for *"Frontline"*; U.K./U.S.; Documentary; Color; 107 minutes; Not rated; January release

LIGHT YEARS (Miramax) American Version: Producer, Bob Weinstein; Director/Screenplay, Rene Laloux; Screenplay Adaptation, Isaac Asimov; American Version Director, Harvey Weinstein; American Version Associate Producer, Susan Slonaker; Music, Jack Maeby, Bob Jewett, Gabriel Yared; Technical Director, Peter Fernandez; Editor Simon Nuchtern; Sound, Jim Klein; Sound Effects, Dennis Fierman Original Screenplay Translation, Cheryl Miller Houser; Animated France; Dubbed in English; Color; 86 minutes; Rated PG; January release. VOICE CAST: Glenn Close (Ambisextra), Earl Hammond (Blaminhor), Sheila McCarthy (Spokeswoman), John Shea (Sylvain) Alexander Marshall (Apod), Paul Shaffer (Optilow), Earl Hyman (Maxum), Teller (Maxum), Penn Jillette (Octum), Dennis Predovic Bridget Fonda, Chip Bolcik, Sheila McCarthy (The Heads), David Johansen (Shayol), Jennifer Grey (Airelle), Terrence Mann (The Collective Voice), Chip Bolcik, Alexander Marshal, Kevin O'Rourke, Ray Owens, Dennis Predovic (Men of Metal), Christopher Plummer (Metamorphis), Jill Haworth (Announcer), Bridget Fonda (Historian) Charles Busch (Gemnen)

LAND OF PROMISE (Tinc Productions) Director/Screenplay, Andrezj Wajda; Based on the book by Wladyslaw Reymonti; Photography, Witold Sobocinski, Edward Klosinski, Waclaw Dybowski; Music, Wojiech Kilar; Art Director, Tadeusz Kosarewicz; Polish, 1975 Eastman Color; Not rated; 165 minutes; February release. CAST: Daniel Olbrychski (Karol), Wojiech Pszoniak (Moryc), Andrej Seweryn (Maks), Anna Nehrehecka (Anka)

LOS AMBICIOSOS, aka *Fever Mounts at El Pao* (Azteca Films) Producer, Raymond Borderie; Director, Luis Buñuel; Screenplay, Luis Buñuel, Luis Alcoriza, Luis Sapin; Photography, Gabriel Figueroa; Editor, Rafael Ceballos; Music, Paul Misrachi; a Cinematografia Filmex S.A. Films Borderie production; Spanish, 1959; Not rated; 97 minutes; February release. CAST: Maria Félix (Inés Vargas), Gérard Philipe (Ramon Vasquez), Jean Servais (Alejandro Gual), Victor Junco (Indarte), Roberto Canedo (Colonel Olivares), Andres Soler (Carlos Barreiro), Domingo Soler (Juan Cárdenas), Luis Aceves Castaneda (López)

THE GOLD DIGGERS (Women Make Movies) Producers, Nita Amy, Donna Grey; Director, Sally Potter; Screenplay, Lindsay Cooper, Rose English, Sally Potter; Assistant Director, Deborah Kingsland; Sound, Diana Ruston, Melanie Chait; Art Director/Costumes, Rose English; Photography, Babette Mangolte; Music, Lindsay Cooper; A British Film Institute Production in association with Channel Four Television; British; black and white; Not rated; 90 minutes; February release. CAST: Julie Christie (Ruby), Colette Laffont (Celeste), Hilary Westlake (Ruby's Mother), David Gale (Expert), Tom Osborn (Expert's Assistant), Jacky Lansley (Tap Dancer), George Yiasoumi (Stage Manager), Trevor Stuart (Man on stage), Keith James (Officer Supervisor), Siobhan Davies, Juliet Fisher, Maedee Dupres (Dancers in dream), Marilyn Mazur (Drummer), George Born, Lol Coxhill, Dave Holland (Musicians in ballroom), Kassandra Colson (Welder), Vigdis Hrefna Palsdottir, Maria Petursdottir Ridgewell, Lucy Bennett (Young Ruby), Phil Minton, Craig Givens, Steve Godstone, Doug Bather, Fergus Early, Dennis Greenwood, Sheba

WHOOPS APOCALYPSE (MGM) Producer, Brian Eastman; Director, Tom Bussmann; Screenplay, Andrew Marshall, David Renwick; Production Supervisor, Christabel Albery; Casting, Mary Selway; Editor, Peter Boyle; Designer, Tony Noble; Photography, Ron

Colette Laffont, Julie Christie in "The Gold Diggers" © *BFI*

Alison Doody, Pierce Brosnan in "Taffin" © *MGM*

Ronald Allen (C) in "Supergrass" © *Hemsdale*

obson; Music, Patrick Gowers; Costumes, Liz Waller; British: Color; ated R: 89 minutes; February release. CAST: Loretta Swit (President arbara Adams), Peter Cook (Sir Mortimer Chris), Michel Richards ,acrobat), Rik Mayall (Specialist Catering Commander), Ian Richard- n (Rear Admiral Bendish), Alexei Sayle (Himself), Herbert Lom Gen. Mosquera), Joanne Pearce (Princess Wendy), Murry Hamilton, lifton James, Ian McNeice, Christopher Malcolm, Richard Wilson, ichard Pearson, Daniel Benzali, Shane Rimmer

N A GLASS CAGE (Cinevista) Producer, Teresa Enrich; Director/ creenplay, Agustin Villaronga; Photography, Jaume Peracaula; Mu- c, Javier Navaretto; Editor, Raul Roman; Art Director, Case Candini; TEM Productores Asociados production; Spanish; Not rated; Color; 12 minutes; February release. CAST: Gunter Meisner (Klaus), David ust (Angelo), Marisa Paredes (Griselda), Gisela Echevarria (Rena), nma Colomer (Maid), Josue Gausch, Alberto Manzano, Ricart Car- elero, David Cuspinet

AFFIN (MGM) Producer, Peter Shaw; Director, Francis Megahy; creenplay, David Ambrose; Based on the novel by Lyndon Mallet; xecutive Producer, Allan Scott; Associate Producer, John Davis; roduction Designer, William Alexander; Photography, Peter Beeson; ditor, Peter Tanner; Music, Stanley Myers, Hans Zimmer; Casting, os and John Hubbard; a United British Artists/Rafford Films/MGM/ A production; British; Technicolor; Rated R; 96 minutes; February lease. CAST: Pierce Brosnan (Mark Taffin), Ray McAnally)'Rourke), Alison Doody (Charlotte), Jeremy Child (Martin), Jim artley (Conway), Alan Stanford (Sprawley), Patrick Bergam (Mo), erald McSorley (Ed), Ronan Wilmont (The Deacon)

RYSTALSTONE (TMS Pictures) Producer, John Williams; Di- ctor/Screenplay, Antonio Pelaez; Co-Producer, Britt Lomond; Exec- ive Producer, Jose Carredano; Associate Producer, Jorge Gonzalez; hotography, John Stephens; Editor, Arnold Baker; Production De- gner, George Costello; Art Director, Maria Caso; Music, Fernando ribe; Casting, Eleanor Cooke, Pedro Sopena; Costumes, Julia San- iez; Production Manager, Francisco Ariza; Sound, Charles L. King I; a CCC production; British-Spanish; Color; Rated PG; 103 minutes; ebruary release. CAST: Frank Grimes (Capitan), Kamlesh Gupta 'ablo), Laura Jane Goodwin (Maria), Edward Kelsey (Hook), Sydney romley (Old man), Patricia Conti (Filomena), Helen Ryan (Aunt), erence Bayler (Policeman), Ann Way (Housekeeper), Brigit Forsyth sabel), Ruth Kettlewell (Dolores), Mario De Barros (Caballero de Alba), Lewis Gordon (Antique dealer), Ricardo Palacios (Fruit vendor), Fernando Villena (Priest), Luis Bar Boo, Alejandro Pavon, Joaquin Lopez Perez, Ignacio Carreno, Paloma Cela

THE SUPERGRASS (Hemdale) Producer, Elaine Taylor; Director, Peter Richardson; Screenplay, Peter Richardson, Pete Richens; Executive Producer, Michael White; Photography, John Metcalfe; Editor, Geoff Hogg; Sound, John Hayes; Art Director, Niki Wateridge; Costumes, Frances Haggett; Music, Keith Tippett & Working Week Big Band; Songs by various artists; British; Color; Rated R; 93 minutes; February release. CAST: Adrian Edmondson (Dennis), Jennifer Saunders (Lesley), Peter Richardson (Harvey), Dawn French (Andrea), Keith Allen (Wong), Nigel Planer (Gunter), Robbie Coltrane (Troy), Danny Peacock (Jim Jarvis), Ronald Allen (Robertson), Alexei Sayle (Perryman), Michael Elphick (Collins), Patrick Durkin (Franks), Marika Rivera (Landlady), Rita Treisman (Mrs. Carter), Neil Cunningham (Waiter), Michael White (Mr. Harding), David Beard (Disc jockey), Zoe Clark (Tamsyn), Joanna Crickmay (Jane), Kim Pappas (Receptionist)

SLUGS, THE MOVIE (New World) Producers, Jose A. Escriva, Francesca De Laurentiis, J. P. Simon; Director, J. P. Simon; Screenplay, Ron Gantman; Based on the novel by Shaun Hutson; Executive Producer, George Ferrer; Editor, Richard Rabjohn; Photography, Julio Bragado; Special Effects Supervisor, Emilio Ruiz; Special Make-up Effects, Carlo De Marchis; Music, Tim Souster; Production Supervisor, Larry Ann Evans; Assistant Director, Vito Hughes; Art Director, Gonzalo Gonzalo; Costumes, Maria Escriva; a Dister production; Spanish; Metrocolor; Rated R; 89 minutes; February release. CAST: Michael Garfield (Mike Brady), Kim Terry (Kim Brady), Phillip Machale (Don Palmer), Alicia Moro (Maureen Watson), Santiago Alvarez (John Foley), Concha Cuetos (Maria Palmer), John Battaglia (Sheriff Reese), Emilio Linder (David Watson), Kris Mann (Bobby Talbot), Kari Rose (Donna Moss), Manuel De Blas (Mayor Eaton), Andy Alsup (Officer Dobbs), Frank Brana (Frank Phillips), Stan Schwartz (Ron Bell), Juan Majan (Harold Morris), Lucia Prado (Jean Morris), Patty Shepard (Sue Channing), Miguel De Grandy (Mr. Riggs), Tammy Reger (Pam), Glen Greenberg (Danny Palmer), Jay R. Ingerson (Ricky Palmer), Harriet L. Stark (Mrs. Fortune), Tony Gold (Dino), Nazareno Natale (Chef), Carla M. Fox (Julie), Isabel Prinz, Laura Notario, Daniel L. Jones, Kristin L. Kilian, Edward Trathen, Erik Swanson, Karen Landberg, Anibal Blas, Laramie G. Evans, Nevada Killips, Larry Bornheimer, Wally Frazer

Pierce Brosnan, Ronan Wilmot in "Taffin" © *MGM*

Kris Mann, Kari Rose in "Slugs" © *New World*

Anat Waxman, Ika Zohar in "I Don't Give a Damn" © ***Trans World Entertainment***

Cristiana Lavigne (on cross) in "Subway to the Stars" © ***FilmDallas Pictures***

I DON'T GIVE A DAMN (Trans World Entertainment) Producers, Yair Pradelski, Israel Ringel; Director, Shmuel Imberman; Screenplay, Hana Peled; From the novel by Dahn Ben Amotz; Photography, Nissim Leon Nitcho; Editor, Atara Horenshtein; Music, Benni Nagari; Designer, Shlomo Tzafrir; Color; Israeli; Rated R; 90 minutes; February release. CAST: Ika Sohar (Rafi), Anat Waxman (Nira), Leora Grossman (Maya), Shmuel Vilogeni (Eli), Shlomo Tarshish (Amnon), DuDu Ben-Ze'ev (Yigal)

LE CAVIAR ROUGE (Galaxy International) Director, Robert Hossein; Screenplay, Frederic Dard, Robert Hossein, based on their novel; Music, Claude-Michel Schoenberg, Jean-Claude Petit; Panpipes, Gheorghe Zamfir; Photography, Edmond Richard; Production Manager, Georges Casati; Sound, Jean Labussiere; Editor, Sophie Bhaud; Art Director, Jacques D'Ovidio; Executive Producer, Yves Peyrot; A French-Swiss Co-production; Slotint S.A.—Television Suisse Romande (S.S.R.)/Philip Dussart S.A.R.L.; Color; Rated PG; 92 minutes; March release. CAST: Robert Hossein (Alex), Candice Patou (Nora), Ivan Desny (Yuri), Maurice Aufair (Sibenthal), Constantin Kotlarow (Vaska), Igor de Savitch (Barrioff), Peter Semler (Gator), Matthieu Chardet (Taxi Driver), Alex Freihart (Solkovitch), Pierre Hossein (Video Technician) Alexandre Koumpan (Video Assistant), Jacques Michel (Assistant #5), Nathalie Nerval (Woman Technician), Dimitri Rafalsky (Boris), Paul-Michel Toscano (Petia), Nathalie Nerval, Helene Valier (Women Technicians), Claude Goy, Yannek Sidlow, Antoine Soka (Assistants), Ledin Vaclav (Misha), Franco Franco, Andre Papandreou, Georges Wojcik (Drivers), Joelle Legoultre (Ilya), Bastien Hibon (Alex-child), Julianna Samarine (Alex's Mother), Caroline Tissot (Photographer)

AUSTERIA (AFRA Film Enterprises) Director, Jerzy Kawalerowicz; Screenplay, Jerzy Kawalerowicz, Tadeusz Konwicki, Julian Stryjkowski; Based on the novel by Julian Stryjkowski; Music, Leopold Kozlowski; Photography, Zygmunt Samosiuk; Editor, Wieslawa Otocka; A Film Polski production; Polish; Color; Not rated; 109 minutes; March release. CAST: Franciszek Pieczka (Tag), Wojciech Pszoniak (Shamiz), Jan Szurmiej (Cantor), Ewa Domanska (Kasia), Liliana Glabczynska (Yevdokha), Golda Tencer (Blanca), Marek Wilk (Bum), Wojciech Standello (Tzaddiq), Szymon Szurmiej (Wilf)

SUBWAY TO THE STARS (Filmdallas) Producer, Rodolfo Brandao; Director, Carlos Diegues; Screenplay, Carlos Diegues, Carlos Lombardi; Photography, Edgar Moura; Editors, Gilberto Santeiro, Dominique Boischot; Music, Gilberto Gil; Sound, Jorge Saldanha; Art Director, Lia Renha; production manager, Rene Bittencourt; Assistar Director, Juarez Precioso; Sound Editor, Hercilia Gardillo; Costumes Viviane Sampeio; Sound, William Flageollet; Georges Reinhart, Car los Henrique Braga, Skylight & Elipse; A French-Brazilian Cc Production; Chrysalide Films (Paris)/CDK Producoes (Rio de Janeiro) with the participation of Canal Plus; Color; Rated R; 103 minutes March release. CAST: Guilherme Fontes (Vinicius), Milton Goncalve (Freitas), Taumaturgo Ferreira (Dream), Ana Beatriz Wiltgen (Eu nice), Ze Trindade (Father), Miriam Pires (Mother), Tania Bosco (Bel), Flavio Santiago (Photographer), Betty Prado (Woman), Paula (Man), Christiana Lavigne (Saint), Ezquiel Neves (Producer), Ioland Cardoso (Grandmother), Marcos Palmeira (Jacare), Dinorah Brilhant (Mother), Jorge Fino (Giant), Ronney Vilela (Freitas' Assistant), Ott Machado (Uncle), Fausto Fawcett (Poet), Jose Wilker (Professor) Betty Faria (Camila), Daniel Filho (Journalist), Cazuza (Singer)

A JUMPIN' NIGHT IN THE GARDEN OF EDEN (First Ru Features) Producer/Director, Michael Goldman; Associate Producer Anne O. Craig; Photography, Boyd Estus; Sound, Colin Macnab, Joh Dildine; Documentary; English & Yiddish with subtitles; Documer tary; Color; Not Rated; 80 minutes; March release. CAST: Henr Sapoznik, Hankus Netsky, Kapelye and the Klezmer Conservator Band

TRAFFIC JAM (Capstone Film Co.) Producer, Silvio Clementelli no; Director, Luigi Comencini; Screenplay, Luigi Comencini, Rugger Maccari, Bernardino Zapponi; Photography, Ennio Guarnieri; Editor Nino Baragli; Music, Fiorenzo Carpi; Art Director, Mario Chiari Italian-French-Spanish-West German; Color; Not rated; 116 minutes March release. CAST: Annie Girardot, Fernando Rey, Miou Miou Gérard Depardieu, Ugo Tognazzi, Marcello Mastroianni, Stefania Sar drelli, Alberto Sordi, Orazio Orlando, Gianni Cavina, Harry Baer Angela Molina, Ciccio Ingrassia, Patrick Dewaere

HIGH SEASON (Hemdale) Producer, Clare Downs; Director, Clar Peploe; Screenplay, Clare Peploe, Mark Peploe; Co-Producer Raymond Day; Designer, Andrew McAlpine; Photography, Chri Menges; Music, Jason Osborn; Executive Producer, Michael White Editor, Gabriella Cristianti; Costumes, Louise Stjernsward; Associat Producer, Mary Clow; British; Color; Rated R; 104 minutes; Marc release. CAST: Jacqueline Bissett (Katherine), James Fox (Patrick) Irene Pappas (Penelope), Paris Tselios (Yanni), Sebastian Shaw (Bas Sharp), Kenneth Branagh (Rick), Lesley Manville (Carol), Ruby Bake (Chloe), Robert Stephens (Konstantinis)

Candice Patou, Robert Hossein in "Le Caviar Rouge" © ***Galaxy International***

Jacqueline Bissett, James Fox in "High Season" © ***Hemsdale***

Germain Houde, Lorne Brass, Gilles Maheu in "Night Zoo" © ***FilmDallas Pictures***

Tyler Butterworth, Vanessa Redgrave, Jonathan Pryce in "Consuming Passions" © ***Samuel Goldwyn Co.***

GHT ZOO (Filmdallas) Producers, Roger Frappier, Pierre Gen-n; Director/Screenplay, Jean-Claude Lauzon; Music, Jean Corri-u; Associate Producer, Louise Gendron; Line Producer, Suzanne ssault; Assistant Directors, Alain Lino Chartrand, Ginette Guillard; otography, Guy Dufaux; Art Director, Jean-Baptiste Tard; Cos-nes, Andree Morin; Sets, Michele Forest; Sound, Marcel Pothier, on Benoit; Editor, Michel Arcand; Set Designer, Raymond Larose; ecial Effects, Jean-Marc Cyr; Lyrics, Jean-Pierre Bonin, Daniel De aime; Casting, Lise Abastado, Sophie-Andree Blondin, Jean-ymond Chales, Nicolas Zavaglia; Canadian; Color; Not rated; 115 nutes; March release. CAST: Gilles Maheu (Marcel), Roger Le Bel bert), Corrado Mastropasqua (Tony), Lorne Brass (George), Ger-in House (Charlie), Jerry Snell (American), Lynne Adams (Julie), na-Maria Giannoti (Angelica), Nereo Lorenzi (Pepe), Walter Mas-(Mr. Chagnon), Dominique De Donato (Gino), Nicolas Clarizio, cent Ierfino, Amulette Garneau, Luc Proulx, Jean-Pierre Saulnier, n-Pierre Bergeron, Dominique Michel, Denys Arcand, Paolo Giura-Luigi Napolitano, Pierre Wiper, Serge Nadeau, Sophie Andree ondin, Julie Sicotte, Manon Girard, Anne-Marie Champagne, lene Mourez, Bertrand Bineau, Roger Lemyre, Andre Nickell, chel Barsalou, Khanh Hua, Fernando Cichi, Francois Caron, Jac-s Pelletier, Rex the Elephant

OUND THE WORLD IN 80 WAYS (Alive Films) Producers, vid Elfick, Steve Knapman; Director, Stephen MacLean; Screen-y, Stephen MacLean, Paul Leadon; Photography, Louis Irving; duction Designer, Lissa Coote; Costumes, Clarrissa Patterson; Edi-Marc Van Buuren; Production Manager, Catherine Phillips apman; Assistant Directors, Ian Page, Henry Osborne, Elizabeth vell; Sound, Paul Brincat; Make-up, Violette Fontaine; Stunt Coor-ator, Bob Hicks; Choreographer, Meryl Tankard; Music, Chris al; presented by Palm Beach Entertainment; Australian; Colorfilm; rated; 90 minutes; March release. CAST: Philip Quast (Wally vis), Allan Penney (Roly Davis), Diana Davidson (Mavis Davis), ly Dingwall (Eddie Davis), Gosia Dobrowolska (Nurse Ophelia k), Rob Steele (Alec Moffatt), Judith Fisher (Lotte Boyle), Jane rkey (Miserable Midge), John Howard (Doctor Proctor), Frank yd (Mr. Tinkle), Catherine Michalak (Mrs. Tinkle), Micki Gardner, en Simons, Elizabeth Burton (Geisha girls), Ric Carter (Financier), k Allan (Queensland mailman), Nell Schofield (Scottish Scrooge), arin Fairfax (Checkout chick), Carol Lopez (Chikita), Deni Gordon ikita's friend), Roy Hawkins (Elvis impersonator), Tony Ho inese chef), Robert James Rewi (Hawaiian bellboy), Meryl Tank-, Grant Dale, Harry Morris, Robert Wilkie (Dancers), Ralph, Sherry gs)

OM THE POLE TO THE EQUATOR (Museum of Modern Art) ducers/Directors, Yervant Gianikian, Angela Ricci; Music, Keith ich, Charles Anderson; a co-production of ZDF-TV; West German; rated; 96 minutes; April release. A documentary using archival tage by Italian cinematographer Luca Comerio.

NSUMING PASSIONS (Samuel Goldwyn) Producer, William tlidge; Director, Giles Foster; Screenplay, Paul D. Zimmerman, drew Davies, based on the play *"Secrets,"* by Michael Palin and ry Jones; Production Manager, Patricia Carr; Production Coordina-Carol Regan; Assistant Directors, Roger Simons, Mark Goddard, Peter Heslop; Photography, Roger Pratt; Camera, David Worley; Designer, Peter Lamont; Art Director, Terry Ackland-Snow; Set Decorator, Michael Ford; Editor, John Grover; Sound, Tony Dawe; Costumes, Barbara Kidd; Special Effects, Ian Wingrove, Terry Reed; British; Technicolor; Rated R; 98 minutes; April release. CAST: Vanessa Redgrave (Mrs. Garza), Jonathan Pryce (Farris), Tyler Butterworth (Ian Littleton), Freddie Jones (Graham Chumley), Sammi Davis (Felicity), Prunella Scales (Ethel), Thora Hird (Mrs. Gordon), William Rushton (Big Man), John Wells (Dr. Forrester), Timothy Wert (Dr. Rees), Mary Healey (Mrs. Eggleston), Andrew Sachs (Jason), Bryan Pringle (Gateman), Susan Field, Vicky Ireland, Julie (Women on TV), Adam Stocker (Trevor), Wincey Willis (Presenter), Linda Lusardi (French Beauth), Gerard Dimiglio (Frenchman), Preston Lockwood (Josiah), Angus Barnett (Josiah's son), Dick Brannick (Butcher), Deddie Davies (Mrs. Coot), Archie Pool (Rastafarian), Julian Ronnie (Waiter), Leonard Trolley (Mayor), Robert Bridges (Wooster), Patrick Newell (Lester), Joanna Dickens, Geraldine Griffith Griffiths, Helen Pearson, David Neville, Jamie Moore, Paddy Ward, Jo Warne, Donald Pelmear, Marc Boyle, Paul Dalton

I HATE ACTORS! (Galaxy International) Producer, Jean Nainchrik; Director/Adaptation, Gerard Krawczyk; Based on the novel by Ben Hecht; English Subtitles, Allan Wenger; Associate Producer, Alain Poire; Music, Roland Vincent; Production Manager, Guy Azzi; Photography, Michel Cenet; Art Director, Jacques Dugied; Editor, Marie-Josephe Yoyotte; Sound, Pierre Befve; Costumes, Rosine Lan; a coproduction of Septembre productions-Gaumont-Films A2; French; Color; Rated PG; 91 minutes; April release. CAST: Jean Poiret (Orlando Higgens), Michel Blanc (Mr. Albert), Bernard Blier (J. B. Cobb), Patrick Floersheim (Dan Korman), Michel Galabru (Laurence Bison), Pauline Lafont (Elvina Bliss), Dominique Lavanant (Miss Davis), Sophie Duez (Bertha Fancher), Guy Marchand (Lt. Egelhofer), Wojtek Pszoniak (Hercule Potnik), Jean-Francois Stevenin (Chester Devlin), Patrick Braoude (Fineman), Jezabel Capri (Caroma), Claude Chabrol (Lieberman), Jean-Paul Comart (Lieberman), Alex Descas (Allan), Vernon Dobtcheff (Kesselberger), Yan Epstein (Dennis Wilde), Benoit Ferreux, Marcel Gotlib (Assistants), Herve Hiolle (Cruikshank), Jean-Paul Lilienfeld (Blue), Roger Lumont (Walter Sloggins), Bernard Marcellin (Egelhofer's aide), Mike Marshall (John Paul Jones), Alexandre Mnouchkine (Samuel Zupelman), Claire Nadeau (Miss Wondershake), Andre Oumansky (Harry Hochstader), Lionel Rocheman (Peritz), Yan Roussel (Zupelman's lawyer), Michel Such (Sgt. Tittero), Allan Wenger (Bogart)

Pauline Lafont, Jean Poiret in "I Hate Actors!" © ***Galaxy International***

Jon Blake, Peter Phelps in "The Lighthorsemen" © *Cinecom*

Yvonne DeCarlo, Rod Steiger in "American Gothic" © *Vidmark*

THE POINTSMAN (Vestron) Producer/Director, Jos Stelling; Screenplay, George Brugmans, Hans De Wolf, Jos Stelling; Photography, Frans Bromet, Theo Van De Sande, Paul Van Den Bos, Goert Giltaij; Sound, Bert Flantua; Editor, Rimko Haanstra; Music, Michel Mulders; Dutch; Dutch with subtitles; Rated R; 95 minutes; April release. CAST: Jim Van Der Woude (Pointsman), Stephane Excoffier (Woman), John Kraaykamp (Engineer), Josse De Pauw (Postman), Ton Van Dort (Engineer's Assistant)

THE LIGHTHORSEMEN (Cinecom) Producers, Ian Jones, Simon Wincer; Director, Simon Wincer; Executive Producer, Tony Ginnane; Screenplay, Ian Jones; Music, Mario Millo; Editor, Adrian Carr; Designer, Hides; Photography, Dean Semler; Production Supervisor, Phillip Corr; Assistant Director, Bob Donaldson; Stunts, Grant Page; Special Effects, Steve Courtley; Costumes, David Rowe; Makeup, Felicity Schoeffel; Sound, Peter Burgess, Craig Carter, Livia Ruzic, James Currie; Australian; Color; Panavision; Rated PG; 110 minutes; April release. CAST: Peter Phelps (Dave), Nick Waters (Lighthorse Sgt.), John Larking (Station Master), Shane Briant (Reichert), Ralph Cotterill (VonKressenstein), Bill Kerr (Chauvel), Grant Piro (Charlie), Tony Bonner (Bourchier), Serge Lazareff (Rankin), Gary Sweet (Frank), John Walton (Tas), Tim McKenzie (Chiller), Jon Blake (Scotty), Patrick Frost (Sgt. Ted Seager), Adrian Wright (Lawson), Sigrid Thornton (Anne), Anne Scott-Pendlebury (Sister), Brenton Whittle (Padre), Anthony Andrews (Meinertzhagen), Anthony Hawkins (Allenby), Gerard Kennedy (Ismet Bey), Jon Sidney (Grant), Graham Dow (Hodgson), James Wright (Fitzgerald), Gary Stalker (Corp. Nobby), Scott Bradley (Lt. Frank Burton), Peter Browne (Arch)

STORM (Cannon) Producer/Director/Screenplay, David Winning; Editor, Bill Campbell; Photography, Tim Hollings; Music, Amin Bhatia; Associate Producer/Assistant Director, Michael Kevis; Casting, Larry Parish; Sound, Per Asplund, Kelly Zombor; Stunt Coordinator, Vic Trickett; a Groundstar Pictures Inc. production; Canadian; Color; Rated PG-13; 81 minutes; April release. CAST: David Palfy (Lowell), Stan Kane (Jim), Tom Schioler (Booker), Harry Freedman (Burt), Lawrence Elion (Stanley), Stacy Christensen (Cobi), Tibi (Lisa), Sean O'Byrne (Danny), James Hutchison (Hostage), Derek Coulthard (Farmer)

John Savage, Kara Glover in "Caribe" © *Miramax*

EMPIRE STATE (Vidmark) Producer, Norma Heyman; Direct Ron Peck; Screenplay, Ron Peck, Mark Ayres; Executive Produc Mark Ayres; Photography, Tony Imi; Editor, Chris Kelly; Mus various artists; Production Designer, Adrian Smith; Sound, K Weston; Costumes, William Pierce; Casting, Sheila Trezise; a Te Pictures production; British; Eastmancolor; Rated R; 104 minut April release. CAST: Cathryn Harrison (Marion), Jason Hogans (Pete), Elizabeth Hickling (Cheryl), Jamie Foreman (Danny), Em Bolton (Susan), Ian Sears (Paul), Martin Landau (Chuck), Lor Cranitch (Richard), Ray McAnally (Frank), Lee Drysdale (Rent-b

SHATTERED DREAMS (New Yorker) Producers, Victor Sch feld, Jennifer Millstone; Director/Screenplay, Victor Schonfeld; P tography, Peter Greenhalgh, Amnon Solomon, Dani Schneuer, Zach iah Raz, Yossi Wein, Yaacov Saporta, Jimmy Dibling; Music, A Rudich, Shlomo Bar, Shalom Hanoch; A Schonfeld production with assistance of Central TV in association with Channel 4; Documenta British; Color; Not rated; 165 minutes; May release.

WHITE OF THE EYE (Palisades Entertainment) Producers, C sian Elwes, Brad Wyman; Director, Donald Cammell; Screenpl China Cammell, Donald Cammell; Based on the Book "*Mrs. White*" Margaret Tracy; Associate Producers, Sue Baden Powell, Vicki T Photography, Larry McConkey; Designer, Phillip Thomas; Edit Terry Rawlings; Music, Nick Mason, Rick Fenn; Production Manag Sue Baden Powell; Production Coordinator, Aaron Warner; Assist Director, Andrew Z. Davis; Sound, Bruce Litecky; Dialogue Direct China Cammell; Set Decorator, Richard Rutowski; Costumes, Mer Greene; Special Effects, Thomas Ford; Stunts, Dan Bradley; "*T Grand Tour*" by Moras Wilson, Carmel Taylor, George Richey/Voc David Keith, and songs by various other artists; Dolby Stereo; Rated 111 minutes; May release. CAST: David Keith (Paul White), Ca Moriarty (Joan White), Alan Rosenberg (Mike Desantos), Art Ev (Mendoza), Michael Green (Phil Ross), Danielle Smith (Danie White), Alberta Watson (Anne Mason), William G. Schilling (Har Gideon), David Chow (Fred Hoy), Marc Hayashi (Stu), Mimi Lie (Liz Manchester), Pamela Seamon (Caryanne), Bob Zache (Lu Herman), Danko Gurovich (Arnold White), China Cammell (Ru Hoy), Jim Wirries (Grunveldt), Kate Waring (Joyce Patell), F Allison (TV Newsman), Clyde Pitfarkin (Hairdresser)

AMERICAN GOTHIC (Vidmark) Producers, John Quested, Ch Harrop; Director, John Hough; Executive Producers, George Walk Mike Manley, Ray Homer; Screenplay, John Hough, Terry Le Photography, Harvey Harrison; Editor, John Victor Smith; Line P ducer, Terry Lens; Presented by Brent Walker in association w Pinetalk Ltd.; A Manor Ground production; British; Color; Rated R; minutes; May release. CAST: Rod Steiger (Pa), Yvonne De Ca (Ma), Sarah Torgov (Cynthia), Michael J. Pollard, Fiona Hutchins William Hootkins

CARIBE (Miramax) Producer, Nicolas Stiliadis; Director, Mich Kennedy; Executive Producer, Syd Cappe; Screenplay, Paul Donov Photography, Ludek Boner; Editors, Stan Cole, Michael McMah Art Director, Bronwen Hughes; Casting, Adriana Grampa-Mich Special Effects, Brock Jolliffe; Production Manager, Paco Alvar Assistant Director, Roman Buchok; Production Coordinator, Phy Brown; Sound, Chiam Gilad; Stunts, T. J. Scott; Canadian; Agfa Col Rated R; 89 minutes; May release. CAST: John Savage (Jeff Richa son), Kara Glover (Helen Williams), Stephen McHattie (Whitehal Paul Koslo (Mercenary), Maury Chaykin (Capt. Burdoch), Sam M kin (Roy Forbes), Zack Nesis (Tommy Goff), T. J. Scott (Ston Johnny Goar (Willy), Lennox Penill (Foley), Sean Houck (Guard)

Stephen Shellen, Henry Thomas in "Murder One" © *Miramax*

Nicholas Picard, Christian Bale in "Land of Faraway" © *Miramax*

URDER ONE (Miramax) Producer, Nicolas Stiliadis; Director, aeme Campbell; Screenplay, Fleming B. "Tex" Fuller; Executive oducer, Syd Cappe; Associate Producer, George Flak; Photography, dek Bogner; Editor, Michael McMahon; Production Manager, Paco varez; Assistant Director, John Bradshaw; Sound, Chiam Gilad; ts, Theresa Buckley; Special Effects, Brock Jolliffe; Production oordinator, Alice O'Neil; Stunts, The Stunt Team; Music, Mychael anna; Designer, Bora Bulajic; Canadian; Color; Rated R; 90 minutes; ay release. CAST: Henry Thomas (Billy Isaacs), James Wilder (Carl aacs), Stephen Shellen (Wayne Coleman), Errol Slue (George ungee)

IE RECORD (Royal Star Prods.) Director/Screenplay, Daniel elfer; Photography, Kay Gauditz; Editor, Peter R. Adam; Music, The ance; Co-producted by the Academy of Film and Television Munich d Cactus Film Zurich, with the assistance of the Berlin Film Fund, avarian Television Munich, Swiss Television Zurich and Cinéfilm rich; German-Swiss; Black & White; Not rated; 92 minutes; May lease. CAST: Uwe Ochsenknecht (Rico Moreno), Laszlo I. Kisch anana), Catarina Raacke (Bigi), Kurt Raab (P. K. Wütrich)

HE TALE OF RUBY ROSE (Hemdale) Producers, Bryce Menzies, ndrew Wiseman; Director/Screenplay, Roger Scholes; Associate Producer, Ian Pringle; Photography, Steve Mason; Sound, Rob Cutcher; ssistant Director, James Legge; Editors, Ken Sallows, Roger Scholes; ustralian; Color; Rated PG; 102 minutes; May release. CAST: Melita risic (Ruby Rose), Chris Haywood (Henry Rose), Rod Zuanic em), Martyn Sanderson (Bennett), Sheila Florance (Grandma), eila Kennelly (Cook), John McKelvey (Tasker), Wilkie Collins ad), Nell Dobson (Mrs. Bennett)

KY PIRATES (International Film Marketing) Producers, John mond, Michael Hirst; Director, Colin Eggleston; Music, Brian May; reenplay/Story, John Lamond; Photography, Garry Wapshott; Degner, Kristian Fredrickson; Color; Rated PG-13; 86 minutes; May lease. CAST: John Hargreaves (Harris), Meredith Phillips (Melanie), ax Phipps (Savage), Bill Hunter (O'Reilly), Simon Chilves (Rev. itchell), Alex Scott (Gen. Hackett), David Parker (Hayes), Adrian right (Valentine), Peter Cummins (Col. Brien), Tommy Dysart (Baran), Wayne Cull (Logan), Alex Menglett (Sullivan), Nigel Bradshaw pencer), Chris Gregory (Appleton), John Murphy (Gus), Victor zan (Sir Manning Benson), Clive Hearne (Capt. Fisher), Bill Fozz entry), Hayes Gordon (Narrator)

GLASS FULL OF SNOW (SACIS) Producer, VE.Ga Produzioni/ AI Channel 1; Director, Florestano Vancini; Screenplay, Massimo lisatti, Florestano Vancini; Based on the novel by Nerino Rossi; otography, Aldo Di Marcantonio; Art Director, Elio Balletti; Cosmes, Luciani Calosso; Presented by Cinema Italia-Roberto Rosselli-Italian; Color; Not rated; 145 minutes; May release. CAST: Massi-Ghini (Venanzio), Anna Teresa Rossini (Mariena), Marne Maitland ullo), Anna Lelio (Argia), Antonio Piazza (Medea)

KING OPERA BLUES (Gordon's Films) Director/Co-Producer, ui Hark; Executive Producer, Claudie Chung; Screenplay, To Kwok ai; Photography, Poon Hung Seng; Music, James Wong; Editor, vid Wu; Costumes, Ng Po Ling; A Cinema City production; Canese; Not rated; Color; 98 minutes; May release. CAST: Lin Ching ia, Cherie Chung, Sally Yeh, Mark Cheng

JANAIKA (Kino International) Producers, Shoichi Ozawa, Jiri moda, Shigemi Sugisaki; Director/Story, Shohei Imamura; Screeny, Shohei Imamura, Ken Miyamoto; Photography, Masahisa meda; A Shochiku Films presentation; Japanese, 1981; Not rated; 1 minutes; May release. CAST: Shigeru Izumiya (Genji), Kaori Momoi (Ine), Ken Ogata (Furukawa), Masao Kusakari (Itoman), Shigeru Tsuyuguchi (Kinzo), Minori Terada (Ijuin), Yohei Koono (Hara)

LAND OF FARAWAY, aka *Mio in the Land of Faraway* (Miramax) Producer, Ingemark Ejve; Director, Vladimir Grammatikov; Screenplay, William Aldridge; From the book *"Mio, My Son"* by Astrid Lindgren; Photography, Alexander Antipenko, Kjeli Vassdal; Music, Anders Eljas, Benny Andersson; Designer, Konstantin Zagorsky; Costumes, Jevgenia Chervonskaya; Visual Effects, Derek Meddings; Sound, Bengt Lothner; Editor, Darek Hodor; Executive Producers, Klas Olofsson, Terje Kristiansen; Associate Producers, William Aldridge, Goran Lindstrom; Song *"Mio, My Mio"* by Benny Andersson, Bjorn Ulvaeus, performed by Gemini; from Nordisk Tonefilm International Gorky Film Studio in association with Norway Film Development Co., Swedish Film Institute and V/O Sovinfilm; Swedish-Soviet-Norwegian; Dolby Stereo; Technicolor; Rated PG; 104 minutes; May release. CAST: Timothy Bottoms (King), Susannah York (Weaver Woman), Christopher Lee (Kato), Nicholas Pickard (Mio), Christian Bale (Jum-Jum), Sverre Anker Ousdal (Sword Maker), Igor Isulovitch (Eno), Gunilla Nyroos (Aunt Edna), Linn Stokke (Mrs. Lundin), Stig Engstrom (Benke's Father), Geoffrey Staines (The Spirit)

WHITE ELEPHANT: THE BATTLE OF THE AFRICAN GHOSTS (Troma) Producer/Director, Werner Grusch; Screenplay, Werner Grusch, Ashley Pharoah; Photography, Tom D. Hurwitz; Music, Handel, African Brothers, Franco, Tabu Ley; Editor, Thomas Schwaim; Sound, Diana Ruston; A Worldoc Production; British; Color; Rated R; 99 minutes; May release. CAST: Peter Firth (Peter Davidson), Abi Adatsi, Kwabena Holm, Owusu Akyeaw, Sarfo Opoku, Toni Darko, Nana Abiri, Otchere Darko, Charles Annan, Klevor Abo, Samuel Amoah, Peter Sarpong, Nana Seowg, Ejissu Jasantua

THAT'S MY BABY (Troma) Producer, Edie Yolles; Director/Screenplay, Edie Yolles, John Bradshaw; Photography, W. W. Reeve; Editor, Stephen Withrow; Music, Eric N. Robertson; A Gemini Film production; Canadian; Color; Rated PG-13; 98 minutes; May release. CAST: Timothy Weber (Louis), Sonja Smits (Suzanne), Joann McIntyre (Sugar), Lenore Zann (Sally), Derek McGrath (Bob Morgan)

Melita Jurisic, Sheila Florance in "The Tale of Ruby Rose" © *Hemdale*

BEETHOVEN'S NEPHEW (New World) Producer, Orfilm/Marita Coustet; Director, Paul Morrissey; Co-Producer, Orfilm-Almaro-C.B.L.; Screenplay, Mathieu Carriere, Paul Morrissey; From a novel by Luigi Magnani; Art Director, Mario Garbuglia; Set Decorators, Nino Borghi, Joseph Chevalier; Photography, Hanus Polak; Costumes, Claudia Bobsin; Sound, Phillipe Lemenuel; Production Manager, Harry Nap; Editor, Albert Jurgenson, Michele Lauliac; Music, Beethoven; Color; Rated R; 103 minutes; June release. CAST: Wolfgang Reichmann (Beethoven), Dietmar Prinz (Karl van Beethoven), Jane Birkin (Johanna van Beethoven), Nathalie Baye (Leonore), Mathieu Carriere (Archduke Rodolphe), Ulrich Berr (Anton Schindler), Erna Korhel (Marie), Pieter Daniel (Karl Holz), Elena Rostropovitch (Countess Erdody), Walter Schupfer (Michael), Hellmuth Hron (Schoolmaster), David Cameron (Judge), Hubert Kramar (Johann van Beethoven)

HAIL HAZANA (Stillman International) Producer, José Samano; Director, José Maria Gutierrez; Screenplay, José Samano, José Maria Gutierrez; Based on the novel "El Infierno y la Brisa" by José Maria Vaz de Soto; Photography, Magi Torruella; Editor, Rosa Salgado; Spanish, 1978; Color; Not rated; 97 minutes; June release. CAST: Fernando Fernán-Gomez (Father Prefect), Héctor Alterio (Headmaster), José Sacristán, Gabriel Llopart, Luis Ciges, Enrique San Francisco

DARK NIGHT (Horizons Prods.) Producer, Hsu Li-Hwa; Executive Producer, Lo Wai; Director/Screenplay, Fred Tan; Based on the novel by Sue Li-Eng; Photography, Yang Wei-Han; Editor, Chen Po-Wen; Music, Peter Chang; Art Director/Costumes, Yu Wei-Yen; a Goodyear Movie Co. production; Chinese; Color; Not rated; 115 minutes; June release. CAST: Sue Ming-Ming (Li Ling), Hsu Ming (Yeh Yeun), Chang Kuo-Chu (Hwong Cheng-teh), Emily Y. Chang (Mrs. Niu)

IT COULDN'T HAPPEN HERE (Liberty Films) Producer/Director/Screenplay, Jack Bond; Executive Producer, Martin Haxby; Story, Jack Bond, James Dillon; Photography, Simon Archer; Editor, Rodney Holland; Art Director, James Dillon; Costumes, Leah Archer; Sound, Paul Le Mare; Assistant Directors, Peter Price, Roger Pomphrey; British; Rank color; Not rated; 90 minutes; June release. CAST: Neil Tennant, Chris Lowe (The Pet Shop Boys), Joss Ackland, Neil Dickson, Gareth Hunt, Barbara Windsor

GOING UNDERCOVER aka *Yellow Pages* (Miramax) Producer, Jefferson Colegate-Stone; Director/Screenplay, James Kenelm Clarke; Photography, John Coquillon; Executive Producers, Paul Jordan, Barry Plumley; Production Manager, Gerhard Pedesen; Production Coordinators, Rita Grant-Miller, Vicki Manning; Associate Producer, John Schofield; Co-Producer, Shaun Redmayne; Costumes, Moss Mabry; Editor, Paul Davis; Assistant Director, Andy Armstrong; Music, Alan Hawkshaw; British; Dolby Stereo; Rated PG-13; 88 minutes; June release. CAST: Chris Lemmon (Henry Brilliant), Jean Simmons (Maxine De La Hunt), Lea Thompson (Marigold De La Hunt), Mills Watson (Billy O'Shea), Viveca Lindfors (Mrs. Bellinger), Nancy Cartwright (Stephanie), Joe Michael Terry (Gary), Jewel Shepard (Peaches), Marilyn Child (Charlene Brilliant), Joyce O'Neal (Mrs. Van Eiko), Lynda Weismeier (Beach Girl), Lindy Nisbet (Waitress), Randy Polk (Roadie Spectrum), John E. Bristol (Roadie Hawk), Tracy Shakespeare (Pia), Jeffrey Orman (Handsome Young Man), Paul Leveque (Blond Headed Guy Transvestite)

MURPHY'S FAULT (Triax Entertainment Group) Producers, Chris Davis, Lionel A. Ephraim; Director/Screenplay, Robert J. Smawley; Photography, Rod Stewart; Editor, Simon Grimley; Executive Producers, David Barrett, on L. Parker; British; Color; Rated PG-13; 96 minutes; June release. CAST: Patrick Dollaghan (David Wayne), Anne Curry (Samantha), Stack Pierce

THE LOVE SUICIDES AT SONEZAKI (Film Forum/Michael Jeck) Producer/Director, Midori Kurisaki; Photography, Kazuo Miyagawa; Japan; Japanese with subtitles; Not rated; 88 minutes; July release

GOD DOES NOT BELIEVE IN US ANYMORE (Roxie Releasing) Producer, Kurt Kodal; Director, Axel Corti; Screenplay, Georg Stefan Troller; Photography, Wolfgang Treu; Editors, Ulrike Pahl, Helga Wagner; Sound, Herbert Koller; Produced for ORF, ZDF and SRG; Austrian; Black & White; Not rated; 110 minutes; July release. CAST: Johannes Silberschneider (Ferry Tobler), Armin Mueller-Stahl (Gandhi), Barbara Petritsch (Alena), Fritz Mulier (Mehlig), George Corten (Kron), Eric Schildkraut (Dr. Fein)

FAMILY VIEWING (Cinephile) Director/Screenplay, Atom Egoyan; Photography, Robert Macdonald, Peter Mettler; Music, Michael Danna; Editors, Atom Egoyan, Bruce Macdonald; Sound, Ross Redfern, Steven Munro; Designer, Ian Greig; an Ego Film Arts production with the participation of the Ontario Film Development Corp., The Canada Council and the Ontario Arts Council; Canadian;

Nathalie Baye, Dietmar Prinz in "Beethoven's Nephew" © *FilmDallas*

Color; Not rated; 86 minutes; July release. CAST: David Hembl (Stan), Aidan Tierney (Van), Gabrielle Rose (Sandra), Arsin Khanhian (Aline), Selma Keklikian (Armen), Jeanne Sabourin (Alin Mother), Rose Sarkisyan (Van's Mother), Vasag Baghboudari (Young Van), David Mackay, Hrant Alianak, John Shafer, Garfi Andrews, Edwin Stephenson, Aino Pirskansen

BLOOD RELATIONS (Miramax) Producer, Nicolas Stilliadis; I rector, Graeme Campbell; Screenplay, Stephen Saylor; Executive P ducers, Syd Cappe, George Flak; Photography, Rhett Morita; Edit Michael McMahon; An SC Entertainment production; Canadian; col Rated R; 90 minutes; July release. CAST: Jan Rubes (Dr. Andr Wells), Lydie Dernier (Marie DeSette), Kevin Hicks (Thomas Well Lynne Adams (Sharon Hamilton), Sam Malkin (Yuri), Stephen Say (Jack Kaplan), Carrie Leigh (Diane Morgan), Ray Walston (Char MacLeod)

SANTA FE (Roxie Releasing) Producer, Matthias Barl; Direct Axel Corti; Screenplay, Axel Corti, Georg Stefan Troller; Photog phy, Gernot Roll; Editors, Claudia Rieneck, Tamara Euller; Produc for Thalia Films with ORF, ZDF and SRG; Austrian; Black & Whi Not rated; 110 minutes; July release. CAST: Johannes Silberschnei (Ferry Tobler), Gabriel Barylli (Freddy "Alfred" Wolff), Ernst St kovsky (Feldheim "Johnny Field"), Gideon Singer (Popper Shapir Peter Luhr (Dr. Treuman), Doris Buchrucker (Lissa), Dagmar Schw (Frau Marmorek)

A FLAME IN MY HEART (Une Flamme dans mon coeur) (Ro Releasing) Producer, Paulo Branco; Director, Alain Tanner; Scenar Myriam Mezieres; Adaptation/Dialogue, Alain Tanner; Photograph Acacio de Almeida; Sound, Joaquim Pinto, Christian Argentino, H san El Geretly; Editor, Laurent Uhler; Casting, Jacqueline Duc, Pi rick Horde; Music, J. S. Bach/Performance, Neill Gotkovsky; Fran Switzerland, 1987; Color; Not rated; 112 minutes; July release. CAS Myriam Mezieres (Mercedes), Aziz Kabouche (Johnny), Benoit F gent (Pierre), Biana (Friend), Jean-Yves Berthelot (Partner), An Marcon (Etienne), Anne Rucki (Pianist), Jean-Gabriel Nordma (Metteur en scene)

LATE SUMMER BLUES (Kino International) Producers, Ilan D Vries, Renen Schorr, Doron Nesher; Director/Story, Renen Sch Screenplay/Additional Songs/Staging, Doron Nesher; Executive P

Lea Thompson, Chris Lemmon in "Going Undercover" © *Miramax*

cer, Ilan De-Vries; Photography, Eitan Harris; Editor, Shlomo azan; Music, Rafi Kadishzon; Produced with the assistance of Beit-/i & the Israel Fund for the Promotion of Quality Films; Israel; Color; ebrew with subtitles; Not rated; 101 minutes; August release. CAST: or Zweigenbom (Arileh), Yoav Tsafir (Mossi), Shahar Segal (Mar-), Omri Doley (Tsvillich), Noa Goldberg (Naomi), Vered Cohen hosh), Sharon Bar-Ziv (Kobi), Edna Fliedel (Principal), Moshe avazelet (Shimon Shoval), Miki Kam (Secretary), Maci Nesher (Stri-vsky), Ariela Robinovitz (Hava Carmeli), Amit Gazit (Col. Arbel), ava Chaplin (Doctor), Ada Ben-Nachum (Mrs. Shoval), Amitz Golan eargent), Ofra Ben-Yitzhak (Mother), Yossi Rozenbaum (Father), osh Geler (Major Yedida), Yehonadav Perlman (Brother), Yoram bel (Radio Announcer), Shiri Freibach, Ami Shavit, Chanoch Reim, arsha Obsisher, Amir Roshiani, Guy Zwoung, Danny Cohen, Ilan oldberg, David Danino, Katia Zimbris, Amalia Leizerovitz, Rafi onhardi, Eli Marcus, Israel Tauber, Shosh Meimon, Shavit Rabnit-y, Charlie Buzaglo, Sari Lichi

HE BIG BLUE (Weintraub Entertainment Group/Columbia) oducer, Patrice Ledoux; Director/Story, Luc Besson; Screenplay, ıc Besson, Robert Garland, Marilyn Goldin, Jacques Mayol, Marc rrier; Production, Gaumont; Assistant Directors, Jerome Chalou, ann Michel, Patrick Halpine, Gary Marcus; Casting, Nathalie Cher-, Lissa Pillu, Celestia Fox, Pat Orseth; Photography, Carlo Varini; oduction Managers, Bernard Grenet, Marc Maurette, Patrick Millet, dith Lyn Brown; Editor, Olivier Mauffroy; Sound, Pierre Befve; esigner, Dan Weil; Special Effects, Alain Guille; Set Decorators, trick Barthelemy, Carol Nast; Line Producer, Monty Diamond; Pro-ction Coordinator, Dale Pierce Johnson; France; In English; Dolby ereo; Color; Cinemascope; Rated PG; 119 minutes; August release. AST: Rosanna Arquette (Joanna), Jean-Marc Barr (Jacques Mayol), an Reno (Enzo Molinari), Paul Shenar (Dr. Laurence), Sergio Castel-to (Novelli), Jean Bouise (Uncle Louis), Marc Duret (Roberto), iffin Dunne (Duffy), Andreas Voutsinas (Priest), Valentina Vargas onita), Kimberley Beck (Sally), Patrick Fontana (Alfredo), Alessan-a Vazzoler (Mamma), Geoffroy Carey (Supervisor), Bruce Guerre-erthelot (Young Jacques), Gregory Forstner (Young Enzo), Claude esson (Jacques' Father), Marika Gevaudan (Angelica), Jan Rouiller loireuter), Peter Semler (Frank), Jacques Levy (Doctor), Tredessa alton (Carol)

HE MAN WHO MISTOOK HIS WIFE FOR A HAT (Films for e Humanities) Producer, Debra Hauer; Director, Christopher Raw-nce; Based on a story by Oliver Sacks; Photography, Christopher orphet; Editor, Howard Sharp; Music, Michael Nyman; Libretto, hristopher Rawlence; Sound, Greg Bailey; Designer, Jock Scott; An A production for Channel 4/Jane Balfour Films (London); British; lor; Not rated; 75 minutes; August release. CAST: Emile Belcourt he Neurologist), Frederick Westcott (Dr. P), Patricia Hooper (Mrs.), Oliver Sacks, John Tighe

TARLIGHT HOTEL (Republic Pictures) Producers, Finola wyer, Larry Parr; Director, Sam Pillsbury; Screenplay, Grant Hinden iller, based on his novel *"The Dream Monger"*; Photography, War-k Attewell; Editor, Mike Horton; Designer, Mike Becroft; Cos-mes, Barbara Darragh; Sound, Mike Westgate; Assistant Director, hris Graves; A Challenge Film Corp. presentation in association with e New Zealand Film Commission; Color; Rated PG; 93 minutes; ugust release. CAST: Peter Phelps (Patrick), Greer Robson (Kate), arshall Napier (Detective Wallace), The Wizard (Spooner), Alice aser (Aunt), Patrick Smyth (Uncle), Bruce Phillips (Dave Marshall), onogh Rees (Helen), Timothy Lee (Maxwell), Peter Dennet (Des), eresa Bonney (Melissa), Elrich Hooper (Principal), John Watson (Mr. urtis), Mervyn Glue (Skip)

ODY BEAT aka *Dance Academy* (Vidmark Entertainment) Pro-icers, Jef Richard, Aldo U. Passalacqua; Executive Producers, Guido e Angelis, Maurizio De Angelis, Giuseppe Giacchi; Director/ reenplay, Ted Mather; Story, Ted Mather, Guido De Angelis; Pho-graphy, Dennis Peters; Editor, Rebecca Ross; Music, Guido & aurizio De Angelis; Sound, Michael Moore; Choreographer, Dennon awles, Saymber Rawles; Assistant Directors, Sanford Hampton, aurizio Casa; Songs by various artists; an RAI-1/Together Prods. Intl. roduction; Italian; Color; Dolby Stereo; Rated PG; 96 minutes; Sep-mber release. CAST: Tony Dean Fields (Moon), Galyn Görg (Jana), ott Grossman (Tommy), Eliska Krupka (Patrizia), Steve La Chance ince), Paula Nichols (Paula), Julie Newmar (Miss McKenzie), Serge odnunsky, Michelle Rudy, Read Scot, Virgil Frye, Leonora Leal, atricia Zanetti, Timothy Brown

CHINESE GHOST STORY (Gordon's Films) Producer, Claudie hung; Director, Ching Siu Tung; Screenplay, Yuen Kai Chi; Execu-ve Producer, Tsui Hark; Photography, Poon Hang Seng, Sander Lee, om Lau, Wong Wing Hang; Music, Romeo Diaz, James Wong; ostumes, Chan Ku Fong; A Cinema City presentation; Cantonese; olor; Not rated; 98 minutes; September release. CAST: Leslie Cheung ing Choi Sin), Wong Tsu Hsien (Lit Siu Seen), Wo Ma (Yin Chek sia)

Jean-Marc Barr in "Big Blue"
© *Weintraub/Columbia*

DEATH OF A PRESIDENT (Amerpol) Director, Jerzy Kawalerowicz; Screenplay, Jerzy Kawalerowicz, Boleslaw Michalek; Photography, Witold Sobocinski, Jerzy Lukaszewicz; A Film Polski presentation; Polish, 1977; Color; Not rated; 144 minutes; September release. CAST: Zdzislaw Mrozewski (Narutowicz), Marek Walczewski (Niewiadomski), Czeslaw Byszewski (Nowak)

DOC'S KINGDOM (Filmagem) Executive Producers, Dominique Vignet, Paulo Branco; Director/Screenplay, Robert Kramer; Photography, Robert Machover; Editors, Sandrine Cavafian, Christine Aya; Music, Barre Phillips; Sound, Olivier Schwob; A Garance, Filmagem production; French; Color; Not rated; 90 minutes; September release: CAST: Paul McIsaac (Doc), Vincent Gallo (Jimmy), Ruy Furtado (Senor Ruy), Cesar Monteiro (Cesar), Roslyn Payne (Rozzie)

DOLLY, LOTTE AND MARIA (First Run Features) Producer/ Director, Rosa von Praunheim; Photography, Jeff Preiss; Editors, Mike Shepard, Rosa von Praunheim; Sound, Mike Shepard; Collaboration, Claudia Steinberg; In association with NDR-TV; West German; Documentary; Color; Not rated; 60 minutes; September release. With: Dolly Haas, Lotte Goslar, Maria Piscator

THE LOVE CHILD (British Film Institute) Producer, Angela Topping; Director, Robert Smith; Screenplay, Gordon Hann; Photography, Thaddeus O'Sullivan; Editor/Sound, John Davies; Designer, Caroline Hanania; Assistant Director, Andy Powell; Costumes, Katharine Naylor; A British Film Institute-Channel 4 presentation of a Frontroom Film; British; Color; Not rated; 102 minutes; September release. CAST: Sheila Hancock (Edith), Peter Capaldi (Dillon), Percy Herbert (Maurice), Lesley Sharp (Bernadette), Alexei Sayle (The Voices), Arthur Hewlett (Stan), Cleo Sylvestre (Celia), Stephen Lind (Colin), Ajay Kumar (Majid), Andrew Seear (Tony), Kevin (Cliff), Robert Blythe (Elvis), Cathy Murphy (Linda), Stephen Frost, Steven O'Donnell (Policemen)

NANOU (Umbrella Films) Producers, Simon Perry, Patrick Sandrin; Director/Screenplay, Conny Templeman; Photography, Martin Fuhrer; Music, John Kean; Assistant Director, Charles Lusseyran; Designer, Andrew Mollo; A co-production of Arion productions; British-French; MGM Color; Not rated; 110 minutes; September release. CAST: Imogen Stubbs (Nanou), Jean-Philippe Ecoffey (Luc), Christophe Lidon (Jacques), Daniel Day-Lewis (Max), Valentine Pelca, Roger Ibanez

Dolly Haas, Maria Piscator, Lotte Goslar
in "Dolly, Lotte and Maria" © *First Run Features*

Theresa Russell, Gary Oldman in "Track 29" © *Island Pictures*

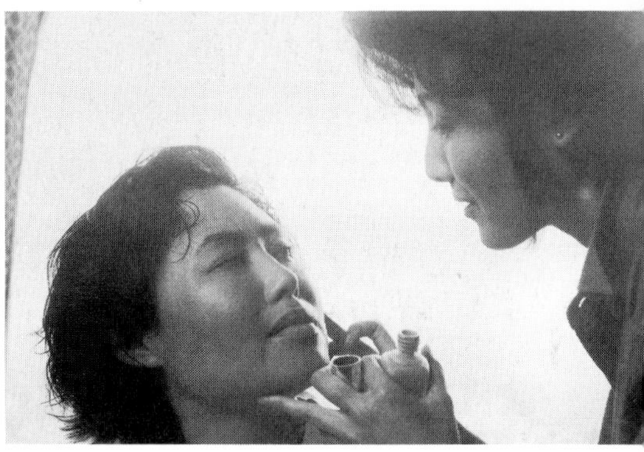

Sigin Gaowa, Josephine Koo in "Homecoming" © *J. T. Productions*

INTO THE FIRE, formerly *The Legend of Wolf Lodge* (Moviestore Entertainment) Producer, Nicolas Stiliadis; Director, Graeme Campbell; Executive Producer, Syd Cappe; Screenplay, Jesse Ballard; Music, Andy Thompson; Editor, Harvey Zlatarits; Casting, Adriana Grampa-Michel; Photography, Rhett Morita; Production Manager, Colin Brunton; Assistant Director, Brian Dennis; Set Decorator, Gina Hamilton; Special Effects, Ted Ross; Stunts, Marco Bianco; An SC Entertainment Corporation production; *"One More Kiss Dear"* by Vangelis & John Anderson/Performance, Andy Thompson & Sandy Singers, and songs by other artists; AGFA Color; Rated R; 92 minutes; Canadian; September release. CAST: Susan Anspach (Rosalind Winfield), Art Hindle (Dirk Winfield), Olivia D'Abo (Liette), Lee Montgomery (Wade Burnett), Maureen McRae (Vivian), Steve Pernie (Policeman), John Dondertman (Jimmy), Alice O'Neil (Mother), Bill Norman (Father), "Chubby" (Jackson)

TRACK 29 (Island Pictures) Producer, Rick McCallum; Director, Nicolas Roeg; Screenplay, Dennis Potter; Executive Producers, George Harrison, Denis O'Brien; Music, Stanley Myers; Photography, Alex Thomson; Designer, Shuna Harwood; Sound, David Stephenson; Casting, Joe D'Agosta, Mark Fincannon; Production Coordinator, Clare St. John; Art Directors, Curtis Schnell, Francine Mercandante; Set Decorator, Doug Mowat; Assistant Director, Bruce Moriarty; British; Color; Rated R; 90 minutes; September release. CAST: Theresa Russell (Linda Henry), Gary Oldman (Martin), Christopher Lloyd (Henry), Colleen Camp (Arlanda), Sandra Bernhard (Nurse Stein), Seymour Cassel (Dr. Bernard Fairmont), Leon Rippy (Trucker), Vance Colvig (Ennis), Jerry Rushing (Redneck), Tommy Hull (Counterman), J. Michael Hunter (Waiter), Steve Boles (Barman), Michael Lague (Customer), Richard K. Olsen (Delegate), Kathryn Tomlinson (Receptionist), Ted Barrow (Old Man)

THE BOXER AND DEATH (Pepper-Prince Co.) Director, Peter Solan; Screenplay, Jozef Hen, Tibor Vichta, Peter Solan; Based on the novel by Jozef Hen; Photography, Tibor Biath; Producer, Studio Hranych Filmov, Brastislava; Czech-German, 1962; Not rated; 107 minutes; October release. CAST: Stefan Kvietik (Kominek), Manfred Krug (Kraft), Valentina Thielova (Helga), Jozef Kondrat (Venzlak), Edwin Marian (Willi)

CALLING THE SHOTS (World Artists) Producers/Directors/Screenplay, Janis Cole, Holly Dale; Photography, John Walker, Sandi Sissel, Judy Irola; Editor, Janis Cole; Sound, Aerlyn Weissman, Alan Barker; Music, Lauri Conger; a Women in Cinema production; Canadian; Color; Not rated; 118 minutes; October release. A documentary on women filmmakers with Lizzie Borden, Jeanne Moreau, Susan Seidelman, Sandy Wilson, Claudia Weill, Martha Coolidge, Randa Haines, Ann Hui, Mai Zetterling, Karen Arthur, Donna Deitch, Joan Tewkesbury, Margarethe von Trotta, Joan Micklin Silver, Agnes Varda, Amy Heckerling, Lee Grant, Lea Pool

SEVEN WOMEN, SEVEN SINS (ASA Communications) Producers, Brigitte Kramer, Maya Constantine, Maxi Cohen; Director, Helke Sander, Bette Gordon, Maxi Cohen, Chantal Akerman, Valie Export, Laurence Gavronn, Ulrike Ottinger; Screenplay, Directors and Doerte Haak; Photography, Nurif Aviv, Frank Prinzi, Luc Benhamou, Joel Gold, Edgar Osterberger, Ulrike Ottinger, Martin Schafer; a ZDF Television production; W. German-French-U.S.-Austrian-Belgia Color; Not rated; 120 minutes; October release. CAST: Evelyne Dic Gariela Herz, Delphine Seyrig, Kate Valk, Roberta Wallach, Susan Widl, Irm Hermann

HOMECOMING (J.T. Productions) Producers, Ian Fok, Xia Men Yim Ho; Director, Yim Ho; Photography, Poon Hang-Sang; Scree play, Kong Liang; Music, Kitaro; Editor, Kin Kin; Chinese; Color; N rated; 96 minutes; October release. CAST: Siqin Gaowa (Ah Zhen Josephine Koo (Shan Shan), Xie Weixiang (Tsong), Zhou Yu (Zhong), Zhang Jugao (Tiao)

THE MAN WITH THREE COFFINS (New Yorker) Producer, Le Myung-Won; Director Lee, Chang-Ho; Screenplay, Lee, Jue-H Based on his novel *"A Wanderer Never Sleeps Even on the Road* Photography, Park, Seung-Bae; Music, Lee, Chong-Ku; Sound, Kir Byung-Soo; Executive Producer, Lee, Eun-Su; Korea, 1987; Kore with subtitles; Color; 104 minutes; October release. CAST: Kir Myung-Kon (Yang, Soon-suk), Lee, Bo-Hee (Yang's Wife), Wo Ok-Joo (Nurse/Ms. Choi/Prostitute/Shaman)

KENNY, aka *The Kid Brother* (Aska Film Distribution) Produce Kiyoshi Fujiimoto; Executive Producers, Matsuo Takashani, Mako Yamashina; Co-Producer, Hirohiko Sueyoshi; Director/Screenpla Claude Gagnon; Photography, Yudai Kato; Editor, Andre Corrivea Music, Francois Dompierre; Sound, Russell Fager; Designer, B Bilowit; Assistant Director, Eduardo Rossoff; A Kinema Amerik Yoshimura/Gagnon-Toho co-production; Canadian-Japanese; Fujic lor; Rated PG-13; 95 minutes; November release. CAST: Ken Easterday (Kenny), Caitlin Clarke (Sharon), Liane Curtis (Shar Kay), Zack Grenier (Jesse), Jesse Easterday Jr. (Eddy), Tom Red (Billy), Alain St. Alix (Philippe), John Carpenter (Grandfather)

OBSESSED (New Star Entertainment) Producers, Robin Spr Jamie Brown; Director, Robin Spry; Screenplay, Douglas Bowi Story, Douglas Bowie, Robin Spry; Suggested by the book *"Hit an Run"* by Tom Alderman; Photography, Ron Stannett; Editor, Dia Ilnicki; Music, Jean-Alain Roussel; Designer, Claude Paré; Assista Director, Mireille Goulet; Casting, Vera Miller; A Telescene Film production; Canadian; Color; Rated PG-13; 103 minutes; Novemb release. CAST: Kerrie Keane (Dinah Middleton), Daniel Pilon (M Middleton), Saul Rubinek (Owen Hughes), Lynne Griffin (Kar Hughes), Mireille Deyglun (Françoise Boyer), Ken Pogue (Det. Sg

Lee Bo-Hee in "Man with 3 Coffins"
© *New Yorker Films*

Alida Valli, Fosco Giachetti in "We the Living" © *Angelika Films*

Peter O'Toole, Beverly D'Angelo in "High Spirits" © *Tri-Star Pictures*

llivan), Vlasta Vrana (Phil Grande), Colleen Dewhurst (Judge), Alan ricke (Conrad Vaughan), Leif Anderson (Alex Middleton), Jacob erney (David Hughes), Mathew Mahay (Tony), Jeremy Spry (Scott)

ELLO ACTORS STUDIO (The Actors Studio) Producer, Anouk rault; Director, Annie Tresgot; Photography, Michel Brault, Serge iguere, Peter Reniers, Chris H. Leplus; Editor, Variety Mosznyski; usic, Luc Perini; A Copra production & Nanouk Films co-production; ocumentary; French; Color; Not rated; 165 minutes; November re-ase. With: Ellen Burstyn, Cheryl Crawford, Lee Grant, Elia Kazan, arvey Keitel, Norman Mailer, Joseph Mankiewicz, Vivian Nathan, ul Newman, Arthur Penn, Sydney Pollack, Maureen Stapleton, Rod eiger, Eli Wallach, Gene Wilder

IOLENCE AT NOON (Kino International) formerly *Daytime ssailant;* Producer, Masayuki Nakajima; Director, Nagisa Oshima; reenplay, Samu Tamura, from the novel by Taijun Takeoa; Photogra-y, Yasuhiro Yoshioka; Music, Hikari Hayashi; Japanese, 1966; ack and white; Not rated; 100 minutes; November release. CAST: ei Sato, Sanae Kawaguchi, Akiko Koyama, Rokuhiro Toura

'E THE LIVING (Angelika Films) Director, Goffredo Alessandrini; reenplay, Anton Giulio Majano; Based on the novel by Ayn Rand; daptation, Corrado Alvaro, Orio Vergani; Photography, Giuseppe aracciolo; Editor, Eraldo Da Roma; Music, Renzo Rossellini; Art irector, Andrea Beloborodoff, Giorgio Abkhasi, Amieto Bonetti; A calera Films production; Italy, 1942; Italian with subtitles; Not rated; 70 minutes; November release. CAST: Alida Valli (Kira), Rossano rzzi (Leo), Fosco Giachetti (Andrei), Giovanni Grasso (Tishenko), milio Cigoli (Pavel)

IGH SPIRITS (Tri-Star) Producers, Stephen Woolley, David aunders; Director/Screenplay, Neil Jordan; Executive Producers, ark Damon, Moshe Diamant, Eduard Sarlui; Co-Producers, Nik owell, Selwyn Roberts; Photography, Alex Thompson; Designer, nton Furst; Editor, Michael Bradsell; Music, George Fenton; Visual fects, Derek Meddings; Associate Producer, Jon Turtle; Casting, net Hirshenson, Jane Jenkins, Susie Figgis; Costumes, Emma Por-ous; Sound, David John; Production Supervisor, Hugh Harlow; Pro-uction Coordinator, Joyce Turner; Assistant Director, Patrick layton; Art Directors, Les Tomkins, Nigel Phelps, Alan Tomkins; Set ecorator, Barbara Drake; Special Effects, Bob Simmonds; Production oordinator, Susan Ford; Stunts, Martin Grace; Choreographer, Micha Bergese; Orchestration, Songs by various artists; British-U.S.; Dolby Stereo; Rank Color; Rated PG-13; 97 minutes; November release. CAST: Daryl Hannah (Mary Plunkett), Peter O'Toole (Peter Plunkett), Steve Guttenberg (Jack), Beverly D'Angelo (Sharon), Jennifer Tilly (Miranda), Peter Gallagher (Brother Tony), Liam Neeson (Martin Brogan), Martin Ferrero (Malcolm), Ray McAnally (Plunkett Senior), Connie Booth (Marge), Donal McCann (Eamon), Liz Smith (Mrs. Plunkett), Mary Coughlan (Katie), Tom Hickey (Sampson), Tony Rohr (Christy), Hilary Reynolds (Patricia), Isolde Cazelet (Julia), Little John (Gateman), Krista Hornish (Wendy), Matthew Wright (Woody), Paul O'Sullivan (Graham), Aimee Delamain (Great Granny Plunkett), Ruby Buchanan (Great Aunt Nan), Preston Lockwood (Great Uncle Peter)

IRON EAGLE II (Tri-Star) Producers, Jacob Kotzky, Sharon Harel, John Kemeny; Director, Sidney J. Furie; Screenplay, Kevin Elders, Sidney J. Furie; Executive Producer, Andras Hamori; Photography, Alain Dostie; Editor, Rit Wallis; Music, Amin Bhatia; Associate Producer, Stephanie Reichel, Asher Cat; Casting, Clare Walker; Production Manager, Doron Mizrachi; Assistant Director, Michael Zenon; Production Executive, Robert Misiorowski; Art Director, Ariel Roshko; Visual Consultant, Robb Wilson King; Costumes, Sylvie Krasker; Set Decorator, Giora Porter; Special Effects, George Erschbamer; Production Coordinators, Linda Nadler, Edna Rosen; Sound, David Lis; Stunts, Terry Leonard; An Alliance Entertainment production, in association with Harkot Prods; Canadian-Israeli; Songs by various artists; Soundtrack on Epic Records; Ultra-Stereo; Bellevue Pathe Color; Rated PG; 105 minutes; November release. CAST: Louis Gossett, Jr. (Chappy), Mark Humphrey (Copper), Stuart Margolin (Stillmore), Alan Scarfe (Vardovsky), Sharon H. Brandon (Valeri), Maury Chaykin (Downs), Colm Feore (Yuri), Clark Johnson (Graves), Jason Blicker (Hickman), Jesse Collins (Bush), Mark Ivanir (Balyonev), Uri Gavriel (Koshkin), Neil Munro (Strappman), Douglas Sheldon (Dmitriev), Azaria Ropoport (Stepanov), Nicolas Colicos (M. P. Connors), Gary Reineke (Bowers), Michael J. Reynolds (Secretary), Jery Hyman (Commanding Officer), Janine Manatis (Reporter)

AMERIKA, TERRA INCOGNITA (Coralie Films Intl.) Producers, Morelba Pacheco, G. Radonski; Director/Screenplay, Diego Risquez; Photography, Andres Agusti; Editor, Leonardo Henriquez; Music, Alejandro Blanco Uribe; a Cuakamaya Prods. film; Venezuelan; Not rated; 90 minutes; December release. CAST: Alberto Martin, Maria Luisa Mosquera, John Phelps, Luis Mariano Trujillo, Amapola Risquez, Nelson Varela, Boris Izaguirre, Blanca Baldo

Daryl Hannah, Steve Guttenberg in "High Spirits" © *Tri-Star Pictures*

Mark Humphrey in "Iron Eagle 2" © *Tri-Star Pictures*

Padraig O'Loingsigh, Gabriel Byrne in "The Courier" © *Vestron Pictures*

"Life Is a Dream" © *International Film Exchange*

THE COURIER (Vestron) Producer, Hilary McLoughlin; Director/ Screenplay, Frank Deasy; Director, Joe Lee; Co-Producer, Stephen Woolley; Executive Producers, Neil Jordan, Nik Powell, John Hambley; Production Manager, Mary Alleguen; Assistant Director, Martin O'Malley; Sound, Pat Hayes; Costumes, Consolata Boyle; Casting, Susie Figgis; Editor, Annette D'Alton; Designer, Dave Wilson; Special Effects, Gerry Johnston; Stunts, Dominick Hewitt; A Euston Films and Palace Production of a City Vision Film; Irish; Color; Rated R; 85 minutes; December release. CAST: Padraig O'Loingsigh (Mark), Cait O'Riordan (Colette), Gabriel Byrne (Val), Ian Bannen (McGuigan), Patrick Bergin (Christy), Andrew Connelly (Danny), Michelle Houlden (Sharon), Mary Ryan (Carol), Dave Duffy (Dunne), Stuart Dunne (Tony), Martin Dunne (Alfie), Joe Savino, Caroline Rothwell, Mary Elizabeth Burke Kennedy, Mick Egan, Mark Flanagan, Anne Enright, Liz Bono, Lucy Vigne-Welsh, Owen Hyland, Kevin Doyle, Albert Fahy, Alec Doran, Aidan Murphy, Aisling Cronin, Tony Coleman, Seay Ledwidge

HELLBOUND: HELLRAISER II (New World) Producer, Christopher Figg, Director, Rony Randel; Screenplay, Peter Atkins; Executive Producers, Christopher Webster, Clive Barker; Associate Producer, David Barron; Photography, Robin Vidgeon; Editor, Richard Marden; Music, Christopher Young; Designer, Mike Buchanan; Assistant Director, Andy Armstrong; Production Coordinator, Gillian Bates; Art Director, Andrew Harris; Casting, Doreen Jones; Sound, John Midgley; Makeup Effects, Geoff Portass, Bob Keen; Special Effects, Graham Longhurst; Flying Effects, Bob Harman; Orchestrator, Christopher Young; Stunts, Bronco McLoughlin; Dolby Stereo; In Association with Cinemarque; British; Color; Rated R; 97 minutes; December release. CAST: Clare Higgins (Julia), Ashley Laurence (Kristy), Kenneth Cranham (Channard), Imogen Boorman (Tiffany), Sean Chapman (Frank), William Hope (Kyle), Doug Bradley (Pinhead), Barbie Wilde (Cenobite), Simon Bamford (Butterball), Nicholas Vince (Chatterer), Oliver Smith (Browning), Angus McInnes (Ronson), Deborah Joel ("Skinless" Julia), James Tillitt (Cortez), Bradley Lavelle (Kucich), Edwin Craig (Patient), Ron Travis, Oliver Parker (Workmen), Catherine Chevalier (Mother)

A HUNGARIAN FAIRY TALE (M.D. Wax/Courier Films) Director, Gyula Gazdag; Screenplay, Gyula Gazdag, Miklos Gyorffy; Photography, Elemer Ragalyi; Editor, Julia Sivo; Sound, Gyorgy Fek; a Mafilm-Objektiv Studio Budapest Production; Hungarian; Eastmancolor, black & white; Not rated; 97 minutes; December release. CAST: David Vermes (Andris), Mária Varga (Maria), Frantisek Husal (Orbán), Ezster Csákány (The Girl), Szilvia Tóth, Judit Pógany, Géz Balkay, Gábor Reviczky

KAMILLA AND THE THIEF (Penelope Film) Producer Photography, Odd Hynnekleiv; Director/Screenplay, Grete Salomonsen; Based on the novel by Kari Vinje; Editors, Howard Lanning Geraldine Creed; Music, Ragnar Bjerkreim, Benny Borg; Sound, Fre Sharp, Kristine Bjorvatn; Costumes, Magda Stallamo, Ann Rasmussen; Norwegian-British; color; Not rated; 94 minutes; December release. CAST: Veronica Flaat (Kamilla), Dennis Storhöi (Sebastian) Agnete Haaland (Sofia), Kaare Kroppan (Joakim Jensen), Morte Harket (Christoffer), Helge Nygaard, Maria Del Mar Del Castillo Normann Liene, Alf Nordvang, Trine Liene, Brith Munthe, Björ Furuborg, Gwynn Overland

LIFE IS A DREAM ***(Memoire Des Apparences)*** **(International Film Circuit)** Director, Raul Ruiz; Producer, La maison de La Culture d Havre, Institut National de la Communication Audiovisuelle; Screenplay, Raul Ruiz, after the play with extracts from Pedro de la Barca' play *"Life is a Dream,"* translated by Jean-Louis Schefer; Photography Jacques Bouquin; Sound, Jean-Claude Brisson; Music, Jorge Arriagade; Editors, Martine Bouquin, Rodolpho Wedeles; Art Director Christian Olivares; France, 1986; Color; Not rated; 100 minutes; December release. CAST: Sylvain Thirolle, Roch Leibovici, Benedict Sire, Jean-Bernard Guillard, Jean-Pierre Agazar, Alain Halle, Jean Francois Lapalus, Alain Rimoux

THE MAGIC TOYSHOP (Roxie Releasing) Producer, Steve Morrison; Director, David Wheatley; Screenplay, Angela Carter, from he novel; Photography, Ken Morgan; Editor, Anthony Ham; Music, Bi Connor; Sound, Nick Steer; Production Designer, Stephen Finerer Costumes, Hilary Buckley; British; color; Not Rated; 104 minutes December release. CAST: Tom Bell, Patricia Kerrigan, Caroline Milmoe, Kilian McKenna, Lorcan Granitch, Marlene Sidaway, Garet Bushill, Georgina Hulme, Marguerite Porter, Lloyd Newson

RETRACING STEPS: AMERICAN DANCE SINCE POSTMODERNISM (Michael Blackwood Productions) Director/Producer Michael Blackwood; Writer/Consultant, Sally Banes; Photography Mead Hunt; Editor, Julie Sloane; Documentary; West German-U.S. Color; Not rated; 89 minutes; December release. WITH: Stephen Petronio, Molissa Fenley, Diane Martel, Wendy Perron, Blondell Cummings, Jim Self, Johanna Boyce, Bill T. Jones, Arnie Zane

Kenneth Cranham, Clare Higgins in "Hellbound" © *New World Pictures*

Caroline Milmoe in "Magic Toyshop" © *Roxie*

Huub Stapel, Monique van de Ven in "Amsterdamned" © *Vestron Pictures*

David Eberts, Faye Dunaway in "Burning Secret" © *Vestron*

MSTERDAMNED (Vestron) Producers, Laurens Geels, Dick aas; Director/Screenplay/Music, Dick Maas; Executive Producer, urens Geels; Designer, Dick Schillermans; Photography, Marc Felrlaan; Editor, Hans Van Dongen; Assistant Director, Myrna Van lst; Casting, Dorna X. Van Rouveroy; Sound, Georges Bossaers, Ad oest; Art Director, Peter Jansen; Stunts, Dickey Beers; Special fects, Martin Gutteridge; Makeup/Special Effects, Karin Van Dijk; ostumes, Yan Tax; Production Supervisor, Wim Lehnhausen; Proiction Manager, Yvonne C. Belonje; A First Floor Features Proction; Dutch; Color; Rated R; 113 minutes; December release. AST: Huub Stapel (Eric), Monique Van De Ven (Laura), Serge-Henri alcke (Vermeer), Hidde Maas (Ruysdael), Wim Zomer (John), Tanke Hartsuiker (Potter), Tatum Dagelet (Anneke), Edwin Bakker Villy), Lou Landre (Chef), Pieter Lutz (Skipper), Barbara Martijn rostitute), Door Van Boeckel (Maniac), Simone Ettekoven (Salvanist), Jan De Koning (Tinus), Koos Van Der Knapp, Pieter Loef, ul Van Soest, Jules Croiset, Helmert Woudenberg, G. H. Van Essen, rt Luppes, Lettie Oosthoek, Jaap Stobbe, Hans Dagelet, Bert Haana, Louise Ruys, Inge Ipenburg, Roelant Radier, Leontien Tuyters, on Duyns, Hans Beijer, Freark Smink, Myra De Vries, Jan Van jndthoven

URNING SECRET (Vestron) Producers, Norma Heyman, erhard Junkersdorf, Carol Lynn Greene; Director/Screenplay, Anew Birkin; Executive Producers, William J. Quigley, MJ Peckos; upervising Producer, Ron Carr; Music, Hans Zimmer; Photography, nest Day; Editor, Paul Green; Designer, Bernd Lepel; Costumes, arbara Baum, Monica Jacobs; Assistant Directors, Ron Carr, Vladiir Michalek; Production Managers, Wolfram Kohtz, Jan Kadlec, omas Gabriss; Sound, Chris Price; Art Director, Karel Vacek; Cast-g, Bridget Gilbert, Miroslav Vostiar; An N.F.H. Ltd. and C.L.G. ms Production in Association with B.A. Production; British; Dolby ereo; Rated PG; 107 minutes; December release. CAST: David oerts (Edmund), Faye Dunaway (Sonya), Klaus Maria Brandauer aron), Ian Richardson (Father), John Nettleton (Dr. Weiss), Martin bernigg (Concierge), Vaclav Stekl (Assistant Concierge), Vladimir ospisil (Hotel Manager), Dr. Karel Karas-Kratochvil (Doorman), Ivo iedrle (Sanatorium Manager), Jarmila Derkova (Frau Isambard), sef Kubicek (Station Master), Veronika Jenikova, Roman Hajek Kissing Couple), V. Kalendova (Tuchman Maid), Rebecca Wright Hotel Maid)

IERRA LEONE (Futura Filmverlag) Producers, Uwe Schrader, ylvia Koller; Executive Producer, Reneé Gundelach; Director/ creenplay, Uwe Schrader; Photography/Editor, Klaus Müller-Laue; Music by various artists; Sound, Günther Knon; a Filmverlag der Autoren presentation of a Uwe Schrader Filmprouktion/Bayerische Rundfunk production; West German; color; Not rated; 92 minutes; December release. CAST: Christian Redl (Fred), Ann-Gisel Glass (Alma), Rita Russek (Vera), Constanze Engelbrecht (Rita), Andras Fricsay, Gottfried Breitfuss, Hans Eckart-Echkart, Nikolaus Dutsch, Peter Gavajda, Janette Rauch, Mehmet Bademsoy

VICIOUS (SVS Films) Producers, David Hannay, Charles Hannah; Director, Karl Zwicky; Screenplay, Paul J. Hogan, Karl Zwicky; Executive Producer, Tom Broadbridge; Line Producer, Lynn Barker; Photography, John Stokes; Editor, Roy Mason; Music, Robert Scott, John Sleith; Sound, David Glasser; Stunt Coordinator, Bernie Ledger; Special Makeup Effects, Deryck De Neise; Assistant Director, Bob Howard; a Premiere Film Marketing Ltd. presentation, in association with Medusa Communications Ltd., of a David Hannay production; Australian; Atlab color; Not rated; 88 minutes; December release. CAST: Tambly Lord (Damon Kennedy), Craig Pearce (Terry), Tiffiny Dowe (Sondra Price), John Godden (Felix), Kelly Dingwall (Benny), Leather (Claire), Joanna Lockwood (Diane Kennedy), Frank McNamara (Gerry), Ralph Cotterill (Professor)

WATCHERS (Universal) Producers, Damian Lee, David Mitchell; Director, Jon Hess; Screenplay, Bill Freed, Damian Lee; Executive Producer, Roger Corman; Co-Producer, Mary Eilts; Based on the Novel *"Watchers"* by Dean R. Koontz; Photography, Curtis Petersen; Editors, Bill Freda, Carolle Alain; Music, Rick Fields, Joel Goldsmith; Production Manager, George Grieve; Assistant Director, Lee Knippelberg; Production Executives, Carl Borack, Robert Misiorowski; Casting, Trish Robinson; Designer, Richard Wilcox; Art Director, Tom Duquette; Set Decorator, Marti Wright; Costumes, Monique Stranan; Sound, Frank Griffiths; Special Effects, Rory Culter, Scott Stofer, Ron Craig; Concorde and Centaur Films, Inc. present A Rose & Ruby Production in Association with Canadian Entertainment Investors No. 2 and Company Ltd. Partnership; Canadian; Filmhouse Color; Rated R; 92 minutes; December release. CAST: Michael Ironside (Lem), Christopher Carey (TV Newscaster), Lala (Tracey), Corey Haim (Travis), Dale Wilson (Bill Keeshan), Blu Mankuma (Cliff), Colleen Winton (Deputy Porter), Duncan Fraser (Sheriff Gaines), Barbara Williams (Nora), Norman Browning (Hockney), Tong Lung (Teacher), Graeme Campbell, Dan O'Dowd, Lou Bollo, Jason Priestley, Matt Hill, Andrew Markey, Ghislaine Crawford, Justine Crawford, Keith Wardlow, Don S. Davis, Freda Perry, William Samples, Suzanne Ristic, Frank C. Turner, Boyd MacConnachie, Phillip Wong, Sandy the Dog

David Eberts, Klaus Maria Brandauer in "Burning Secret" © *Vestron*

Lala, Corey Haim, Barbara Williams in "Watchers" © *Universal*

Karen Allen

Eddie Albert

Suzy Amis

Woody Allen

Eve Arden

Ed Begley,

BIOGRAPHICAL DATA

(Name, real name, place and date of birth, school attended)

AAMES, WILLIE (William Upton): 1961.
ABBOTT, DIAHNNE: NYC, 1945.
ABBOTT, JOHN: London, June 5, 1905.
ABRAHAM, F. MURRAY: Pittsburgh, PA, Oct. 24, 1939. UTx.
ADAMS, BROOKE: NYC, 1949. Dalton.
ADAMS, DON: NYC, Apr. 13, 1926.
ADAMS, EDIE (Elizabeth Edith Enke): Kingston, PA, Apr. 16, 1929. Juilliard, Columbia.
ADAMS, JULIE (Betty May): Waterloo, Iowa, Oct. 17, 1928. Little Rock Jr. College.
ADAMS, MAUD (Maud Wikstrom): Lulea, Sweden, Feb. 12, 1945.
ADDY, WESLEY: Omaha, NB, Aug. 4, 1913. UCLA.
ADJANI, ISABELLE: Germany, June 27, 1955.
ADRIAN, IRIS (Iris Adrian Hostetter): Los Angeles, May 29, 1913.
AGAR, JOHN: Chicago, Jan. 31, 1921.
AGUTTER, JENNY: Taunton, Eng, Dec. 20, 1952.
AIELLO, DANNY: June 20, 1935, NYC.
AIMEE, ANOUK (Dreyfus): Paris, Apr. 27, 1934. Bauer-Therond.
AKERS, KAREN: NYC, Oct. 13, 1945, Hunter Col.
AKINS, CLAUDE: Nelson, GA, May 25, 1936. Northwestern U.
ALBERGHETTI, ANNA MARIA: Pesaro, Italy, May 15, 1936.
ALBERT, EDDIE (Eddie Albert Heimberger): Rock Island, IL, Apr. 22, 1908. U. of Minn.
ALBERT, EDWARD: Los Angeles, Feb. 20, 1951. UCLA.
ALBRIGHT, LOLA: Akron, OH, July 20, 1925.
ALDA, ALAN: NYC, Jan. 28, 1936. Fordham.
ALDERSON, BROOKE: Dallas, Tx.
ALEJANDRO, MIGUEL: NYC, Feb. 21, 1958.
ALEXANDER, ERIKA: 1970, Philadelphia, Pa.
ALEXANDER, JANE (Quigley): Boston, MA, Oct. 28, 1939. Sarah Lawrence.
ALLEN, BYRON: 1962 Los Angeles, Ca.
ALLEN, DEBBIE: (Deborah) Jan. 16, 1950, Houston, Tx.; HowardU.
ALLEN, JOAN: Rochelle, IL, Aug. 20, 1956, EastIllU.
ALLEN, KAREN: Carrollton, IL. Oct. 5, 1951. UMd.
ALLEN, NANCY: NYC June 24, 1950.
ALLEN, REX: Wilcox, AZ, Dec. 31, 1922.
ALLEN, STEVE: New York City, Dec. 26, 1921.
ALLEN, WOODY (Allen Stewart Konigsberg): Brooklyn, Dec. 1, 1935.
ALLYSON, JUNE (Ella Geisman): Westchester, NY, Oct. 7, 1917.
ALONSO, MARIA CONCHITA: Cuba 1957.
ALT, CAROL: Dec. 1, 1960, Queens, NY. HofstraU.
ALVARADO, TRINI: NYC, 1967.
AMECHE, DON (Dominic Amichi): Kenosha, WI, May 31, 1908.
AMES, ED: Boston July 9, 1929.
AMES, LEON (Leon Wycoff): Portland, IN, Jan. 20, 1903.
AMIS, SUZY: Oklahoma City, Ok., Jan. 5, 1958. Actors Studio.
AMOS, JOHN: Newark, NJ, Dec. 27, 1940. Colo. U.

ANDERSON, JUDITH: Adelaide, Australia, Feb. 10, 1898.
ANDERSON, KEVIN: Illinois, Jan. 13, 1960.
ANDERSON, LONI: St. Paul, Mn., Aug. 5, 1946.
ANDERSON, LYNN: Grand Forkes, ND; Sept. 26, 1947. UCLA.
ANDERSON, MELODY: Canada 1955, Carlton U.
ANDERSON, MICHAEL, JR.: London, Eng., 1943.
ANDERSON, RICHARD DEAN: Minneapolis, Mn, 1951.
ANDERSSON, BIBI: Stockholm, Nov. 11, 1935. Royal Dramatic Sch.
ANDES, KEITH: Ocean City, NJ, July 12, 1920. Temple U., Oxford.
ANDRESS, URSULA: Switz., Mar. 19, 1936.
ANDREWS, ANTHONY: London, 1948.
ANDREWS, DANA: Collins, MS, Jan. 1, 1909. Sam Houston Col.
ANDREWS, HARRY: Tonbridge, Kent, Eng., Nov. 10, 1911.
ANDREWS, JULIE (Julia Elizabeth Wells): Surrey, Eng., Oct. 1, 1935.
ANNABELLA (Suzanne Georgette Charpentier): Paris, France, July 14, 1912/1909.
ANN-MARGRET (Olsson): Valsjobyn, Sweden, Apr. 28, 1941. Northwestern U.
ANSARA, MICHAEL: Lowell, MA, Apr. 15, 1922. Pasadena Playhouse.
ANTHONY, LYSETTE: London, 1963.
ANTHONY, TONY: Clarksburg, WV, Oct. 16, 1937. Carnegie Tech.
ANTON, SUSAN: Yucaipa, CA. Oct. 12, 1950. Bernardino Col.
ANTONELLI, LAURA: Pola, Italy.
ARANHA, RAY: Miami, Fl, May 1, 1939. FlaA&M, AADA.
ARCHER, ANNE: Los Angeles, Aug. 25, 1947.
ARCHER, JOHN (Ralph Bowman): Osceola, NB, May 8, 1915. USC.
ARDEN, EVE (Eunice Quedens): Mill Valley, CA, Apr. 30, 1912.
ARKIN, ALAN: NYC, Mar. 26, 1934. LACC.
ARNAZ, DESI, JR.: Los Angeles, Jan. 19, 1953.
ARNAZ, LUCIE: Hollywood, July 17, 1951.
ARNESS, JAMES (Aurness): Minneapolis, MN, May 26, 1923. Beloit College.
ARQUETTE, ROSANNA: NYC, Aug. 10, 1959.
ARTHUR, BEATRICE (Frankel): NYC, May 13, 1924. New School.
ARTHUR, JEAN: NYC, Oct. 17, 1905.
ASHCROFT, PEGGY: London, Eng., Dec. 22, 1907.
ASHLEY, ELIZABETH (Elizabeth Ann Cole): Ocala, FL, Aug. 30, 1939.
ASNER, EDWARD: Kansas City, KS, Nov. 15, 1929.
ASSANTE, ARMAND: NYC, Oct. 4, 1949. AADA.
ASTIN, JOHN: Baltimore, MD, Mar. 30, 1930. U. Minn.
ASTIN, MacKENZIE: 1973, Los Angeles.
ASTIN, SEAN: 1971, Los Angeles.
ASTIN, PATTY DUKE: (see Patty Duke)
ATHERTON, WILLIAM: Orange, CT, July 30, 1947. Carnegie Tech.
ATKINS, CHRISTOPHER: Rye, NY, Feb. 21, 1961.
ATTENBOROUGH, RICHARD: Cambridge, Eng., Aug. 29, 1923. RADA.
AUBERJONOIS, RENE: NYC, June 1, 1940. Carnegie Tech.
AUDRAN, STEPHANE: Versailles, Fr., 1933.
AUGER, CLAUDINE: Paris, Apr. 26, 1942. Dramatic Cons.
AULIN, EWA: Stockholm, Sweden, Feb. 14, 1950.
AUMONT, JEAN PIERRE: Paris, Jan. 5, 1909.

AUTRY, GENE: Tioga, TX, Sept. 29, 1907.
AVALON, FRANKIE (Francis Thomas Avallone): Philadelphia, Sept. 18, 1940.
AYKROYD, DAN: Ottawa, Can., July 1, 1952.
AYRES, LEW: Minneapolis, MN, Dec. 28, 1908.
AZNAVOUR, CHARLES (Varenagh Aznourian): Paris, May 22, 1924.

BACALL, LAUREN (Betty Perske): NYC, Sept. 16, 1924. AADA.
BACH, BARBARA: Aug. 27, 1946.
BACKER, BRIAN: NYC, Dec. 5, 1956. Neighborhood Playhouse.
BACKUS, JIM: Cleveland, Ohio, Feb. 25, 1913. AADA.
BACON, KEVIN: Philadelphia, PA., July 8, 1958.
BAILEY, PEARL: Newport News, VA, March 29, 1918.
BAIN, BARBARA: Chicago, Sept. 13, 1934. U. ILL.
BAIO, SCOTT: Brooklyn, NY, Sept. 22, 1961.
BAKER, BLANCHE: NYC, Dec. 20, 1956.
BAKER, CARROLL: Johnstown, PA, May 28, 1931. St. Petersburg Jr. College.
BAKER, DIANE: Hollywood, CA, Feb. 25, 1938. USC.
BAKER, JOE DON: Groesbeck, TX, Feb. 12, 1936.
BAKER, KATHY WHITTON: Midland, TX., June 8, 1950. UCBerkley.
BALABAN, ROBERT (Bob); Chicago, Aug. 16, 1945. Colgate.
BALDWIN, ADAM: Chicago, Feb. 27, 1962.
BALDWIN, ALEC: Massapequa, NY, Apr. 3, 1958. NYU.
BALE, CHRISTIAN: 1974, Bournemouth, Eng.
BALIN, INA: Brooklyn, Nov. 12, 1937. NYU.
BALL, LUCILLE: Celaron, NY, Aug. 6, 1910. Chatauqua Musical Inst.
BALLARD, KAYE: Cleveland, OH, Nov. 20, 1926.
BALSAM, MARTIN: NYC, Nov. 4, 1919. Actors Studio.
BANCROFT, ANNE (Anna Maria Italiano): Bronx, NY, Sept. 17, 1931. AADA.
BANES, LISA: Chagrin Falls, Oh, July 9, 1955, Juilliard.
BANNEN, IAN: Airdrie, Scot., June 29, 1928.
BARANSKI, CHRISTINE: Buffalo, NY, May 2, 1952, Juilliard.
BARBEAU, ADRIENNE: Sacramento, CA. June 11, 1945. Foothill Col.
BARDOT, BRIGITTE: Paris, Sept. 28, 1934.
BARKIN, ELLEN: Bronx, NY, 1959. Hunter Col.
BARNES, BINNIE (Gitelle Enoyce Barnes): London, Mar. 25, 1906
BARNES, C. B. (Christopher): 1973, Portland, Me.
BARR, JEAN-MARC: San Diego, CA, Sept. 1960.
BARRAULT, JEAN-LOUIS: Vesinet, France, Sept. 8, 1910.
BARRAULT, MARIE-CHRISTINE: Paris, 1946.
BARRETT, MAJEL (Hudec): Columbus, OH, Feb. 23. Western Reserve U.
BARRON, KEITH: Mexborough, Eng., Aug. 8, 1936. Sheffield Playhouse.
BARRY, GENE (Eugene Klass): NYC, June 14, 1921.
BARRY, NEILL: NYC, Nov. 29, 1965.
BARRYMORE, DEBORAH: London, London Acad.
BARRYMORE, DREW: Los Angeles, Feb. 22, 1975.
BARRYMORE, JOHN BLYTH: Beverly Hills, CA, June 4, 1932. St. John's Military Academy.
BARTHOLOMEW, FREDDIE: London, Mar. 28, 1924.
BARYSHNIKOV, MIKHAIL: Riga, Latvia, Jan. 27, 1948.
BASINGER, KIM: Athens, GA., Dec. 8, 1953. Neighborhood Playhouse.
BATEMAN, JASON: 1968 Los Angeles
BATEMAN, JUSTINE: Rye, NY, Feb. 19, 1966.
BATES, ALAN: Allestree, Derbyshire, Eng., Feb. 17, 1934. RADA.
BATES, JEANNE: San Francisco, CA., May 21. RADA.
BAUER, STEVEN: (Steven Rocky Echevarria): Havana, Cuba, Dec. 2, 1956. UMiami.
BAXTER, KEITH: South Wales, Apr. 29, 1933. RADA.
BEAL, JOHN (J. Alexander Bliedung): Joplin, MO, Aug. 13, 1909. PA. U.
BEART, EMMANUELLE: 1965, Gassin, France.
BEATTY, NED: Louisville, KY. July 6, 1937.
BEATTY, ROBERT: Hamilton, Ont., Can., Oct. 19, 1909. U. of Toronto.
BEATTY, WARREN: Richmond, VA, March 30, 1937.
BECK, MICHAEL: Horseshoe Lake, AR, 1948.
BEDELIA, BONNIE: NYC, Mar. 25, 1952. Hunter Col.
BEDI, KABIR: India, 1945.
BEERY, NOAH, JR.: NYC, Aug. 10, 1916. Harvard Military Academy.
BEGLEY, ED, JR.: NYC, Sept. 16, 1949.
BELAFONTE, HARRY: NYC, Mar. 1, 1927.
BELASCO, LEON: Odessa, Russia, Oct. 11, 1902.
BEL GEDDES, BARBARA: NYC, Oct. 31, 1922.
BELL, TOM: Liverpool, Eng., 1932.
BELLAMY, RALPH: Chicago, June 17, 1904.
BELLER, KATHLEEN: NYC, 1957.
BELLWOOD, PAMELA (King): Scarsdale, NY June 26.
BELMONDO, JEAN PAUL: Paris, Apr. 9, 1933.
BELUSHI, JAMES: Chicago, May 15, 1954.
BENEDICT, DIRK (Niewoehner): White Sulphur Springs, MT. March 1, 1945. Whitman Col.
BENJAMIN, RICHARD: NYC, May 22, 1938. Northwestern U.
BENNENT, DAVID: Lausanne, Sept. 9, 1966.
BENNETT, BRUCE (Herman Brix): Tacoma, WA, May 19, 1909. U. Wash.
BENNETT, JILL: Penang, Malay, Dec. 24, 1931.
BENNETT, JOAN: Palisades, NJ, Feb. 27, 1910. St. Margaret's School.
BENSON, ROBBY: Dallas, TX, Jan 21, 1957.
BERENGER, TOM: Chicago, May 31, 1950, UMo.
BERENSON, MARISSA: NYC, Feb. 15, 1947.
BERGEN, CANDICE: Los Angeles, May 9, 1946. U. PA.
BERGEN, POLLY: Knoxville, TN, July 14, 1930. Compton Jr. College.
BERGER, HELMUT: Salzburg, Aus., 1942.
BERGER, SENTA: Vienna, May 13, 1941. Vienna Sch. of Acting.
BERGER, WILLIAM: Austria, Jan. 20, 1928. Columbia.
BERGERAC, JACQUES: Biarritz, France, May 26, 1927. Paris U.
BERLE, MILTON (Berlinger): NYC, July 12, 1908.
BERLIN, JEANNIE: Los Angeles, Nov. 1, 1949.
BERLINGER, WARREN: Brooklyn, Aug. 31, 1937. Columbia.
BERNHARD, SANDRA: June 6, 1955, Flint, Mi.
BERNSEN, CORBIN: Los Angeles, Sept. 7, 1954, UCLA.
BERRI, CLAUDE (Langmann): Paris, July 1, 1934.
BERRIDGE, ELIZABETH: Westchester, NY, May 2, 1962. Strasberg Inst.
BERTINELLI, VALERIE: Wilmington, DE, Apr. 23, 1960.
BERTO, JULIET: Grenoble, France, Jan. 1947.
BEST, JAMES: Corydon, IN, July 26, 1926.
BETTGER, LYLE: Philadelphia, Feb. 13, 1915. AADA.
BEYMER, RICHARD: Avoca, IA, Feb. 21, 1939.
BIEHN, MICHAEL: Ala. 1957.
BIKEL, THEODORE: Vienna, May 2, 1924. RADA.
BIRNEY, DAVID: Washington, DC, Apr. 23, 1939. Dartmouth, UCLA.
BIRNEY, REED: Alexandria, VA., Sept. 11, 1954. Boston U.
BISHOP, JOEY (Joseph Abraham Gottlieb): Bronx, NY, Feb. 3, 1918.
BISHOP, JULIE (formerly Jacqueline Wells): Denver, CO, Aug. 30, 1917. Westlake School.
BISSET, JACQUELINE: Waybridge, Eng., Sept. 13, 1944.
BIXBY, BILL: San Francisco, Jan. 22, 1934. U. CAL.
BLACK, KAREN (Ziegler): Park Ridge, IL, July 1, 1942. Northwestern.
BLADES, RUBEN: Panama 1948, Harvard.
BLAINE, VIVIAN (Vivian Stapleton): Newark, NJ, Nov. 21, 1923.
BLAIR, BETSY (Betsy Boger): NYC, Dec. 11, 1923.
BLAIR, JANET (Martha Jane Lafferty): Blair, PA, Apr. 23, 1921.
BLAIR, LINDA: Westport, CT, Jan. 22, 1959.
BLAKE, AMANDA (Beverly Louise Neill): Buffalo, NY, Feb. 20, 1921.
BLAKE, ROBERT (Michael Gubitosi): Nutley, NJ, Sept. 18, 1933.
BLAKELY, SUSAN: Frankfurt, Germany 1950. U. TEX.
BLAKLEY, RONEE: Stanley, ID, 1946. Stanford U.
BLOOM, CLAIRE: London, Feb. 15, 1931. Badminton School.

Albert Brooks

Coral Browne

Kirk Cameron

Joanna Cassidy

Dennis Christopher

Rae Daw Chong

BLYTH, ANN: Mt. Kisco, NY, Aug. 16, 1928. New Wayburn Dramatic School.
BOCHNER, HART: Toronto, 1956. U. San Diego.
BOGARDE, DIRK: London, Mar. 28, 1918. Glasgow & Univ. College.
BOHRINGER, RICHARD: 1942 Paris
BOLKAN, FLORINDA (Florinda Soares Bulcao): Ceara, Brazil, Feb. 15, 1941.
BOND, DEREK: Glasgow, Scot., Jan. 26, 1920. Askes School.
BONET, LISA: Nov. 16, 1967, San Francisco
BONO, SONNY (Salvatore): Detroit, MI, Feb. 16, 1935.
BOONE, PAT: Jacksonville, FL, June 1, 1934. Columbia U.
BOOTH, SHIRLEY (Thelma Ford): NYC, Aug. 30, 1907.
BORGNINE, ERNEST (Borgnino): Hamden, CT, Jan. 24, 1918. Randall School.
BOSCO, PHILIP: Jersey City, NJ, Sept. 26, 1930, CatholicU.
BOSTWICK, BARRY: San Mateo, CA., Feb. 24, 1945. NYU.
BOTTOMS, JOSEPH: Santa Barbara, CA, Aug. 30, 1954.
BOTTOMS, TIMOTHY: Santa Barbara, CA, Aug. 30, 1951.
BOULTING, INGRID: Transvaal, So. Africa, 1947.
BOVEE, LESLIE: Bend, OR, 1952.
BOWIE, DAVID: (David Robert Jones) Brixton, South London, Eng. Jan. 8, 1947.
BOWKER, JUDI: Shawford, Eng., Apr. 6, 1954.
BOXLEITNER, BRUCE: Elgin, IL., May 12, 1950.
BOYLE, PETER: Philadelphia, PA, Oct. 18, 1933. LaSalle Col.
BRACKEN, EDDIE: NYC, Feb. 7, 1920. Professional Children's School.
BRADLEY, BRIAN: Philadelphia, UFla.
BRAEDEN, ERIC: (Hans Gudegast): Braeden, Germany.
BRAGA, SONIA: Maringa, Brazil, 1951.
BRAND, NEVILLE: Kewanee, IL, Aug. 13, 1920.
BRANDO, JOCELYN: San Francisco, Nov. 18, 1919. Lake Forest College, AADA.
BRANDO, MARLON: Omaha, NB, Apr. 3, 1924. New School.
BRANDON, CLARK: NYC 1959.
BRANDON, HENRY: Berlin, Ger., June 18, 1912. Stanford.
BRANDON, MICHAEL (Feldman): Brooklyn, NY.
BRANTLEY, BETSY: Rutherfordton, NC, 1955. London Central Sch. of Drama.
BRAZZI, ROSSANO: Bologna, Italy, Sept. 18, 1916. U. Florence.
BRENNAN, EILEEN: Los Angeles, CA., Sept. 3, 1935. AADA.
BRIALY, JEAN-CLAUDE: Aumale, Algeria, 1933. Strasbourg Cons.
BRIAN, DAVID: NYC, Aug. 5, 1914. CCNY.
BRIDGES, BEAU: Los Angeles, Dec. 9, 1941. UCLA.
BRIDGES, JEFF: Los Angeles, Dec. 4, 1949.
BRIDGES, LLOYD: San Leandro, CA, Jan. 15, 1913.
BRIMLEY, WILFORD: Salt Lake City, UT, Sept. 27, 1934.
BRINKLEY, CHRISTIE: Malibu, CA., Feb. 2, 1954.
BRISEBOIS, DANIELLE: Brooklyn, June 28, 1969.
BRITT, MAY (Maybritt Wilkins): Sweden, Mar. 22, 1936.
BRITTANY, MORGAN: (Suzanne Caputo): Los Angeles, 1950.
BRITTON, TONY: Birmingham, Eng., June 9, 1924.
BRODERICK, MATTHEW: NYC, Mar. 21, 1963.
BRODIE, STEVE (Johnny Stevens): Eldorado, KS, Nov. 25, 1919.
BROLIN, JAMES: Los Angeles, July 18, 1940. UCLA.
BROMFIELD, JOHN (Farron Bromfield): South Bend, IN, June 11, 1922. St. Mary's College.
BRONSON, CHARLES (Buchinsky): Ehrenfield, PA, Nov. 3, 1920.
BROOKES, JACQUELINE: Montclair, NJ, July 24, 1930, RADA.
BROOKS, ALBERT (Einstein): Los Angeles, July 22, 1947.
BROOKS, MEL (Melvyn Kaminski): Brooklyn, June 28, 1926.
BROSNAN, PIERCE: County Meath, Ireland, May 16, 1952.
BROWN, BLAIR: Washington, DC, 1948; Pine Manor.
BROWN, BRYAN: Panania, Aust., 1947.
BROWN, GARY (Christian Brando): Hollywood, Ca., 1958.
BROWN, GEORG STANFORD: Havana, Cuba, June 24, 1943. AMDA.
BROWN, JAMES: Desdemona, TX, Mar. 22, 1920. Baylor U.
BROWN, JIM: St. Simons Island, NY, Feb. 17, 1935. Syracuse U.
BROWNE, CORAL: Melbourne, Aust., July 23, 1913.
BROWNE, LESLIE: NYC, 1958.
BUCHHOLZ, HORST: Berlin, Ger., Dec. 4, 1933. Ludwig Dramatic School.
BUCKLEY, BETTY: Big Spring, Tx., July 3, 1947. TxCU.
BUETEL, JACK: Dallas, TX, Sept. 5, 1917.
BUJOLD, GENEVIEVE: Montreal, Can., July 1, 1942.
BURGHOFF, GARY: May 24, 1943 Bristol, Ct.
BURGI, RICHARD: July 30, 1958, Montclair, NJ
BURKE, DELTA: Orlando, FL, July 30, 1956, LAMDA.
BURKE, PAUL: New Orleans, July 21, 1926. Pasadena Playhouse.
BURNETT, CAROL: San Antonio, TX, Apr. 26, 1933. UCLA.
BURNS, CATHERINE: NYC, Sept. 25, 1945. AADA.
BURNS, GEORGE (Nathan Birnbaum): NYC, Jan. 20, 1896.
BURR, RAYMOND: New Westminster, B.C., Can., May 21, 1917. Stanford, U. CAL., Columbia.
BURSTYN, ELLEN (Edna Rae Gillooly): Detroit, MI, Dec. 7, 1932.
BURTON, LeVAR: Los Angeles, CA. Feb. 16, 1958. UCLA.
BUSEY, GARY: Goose Creek, Tx, June 29, 1944.
BUSKER, RICKY: 1974 Rockford, Il.
BUTTONS, RED (Aaron Chwatt): NYC, Feb. 5, 1919.
BUZZI, RUTH: Wequetequock, RI, July 24, 1936. Pasadena Playhouse.
BYGRAVES, MAX: London, Oct. 16, 1922. St. Joseph's School.
BYRNE, GABRIEL: Dublin, Ireland, 1950.
BYRNES, EDD: NYC, July 30, 1933. Haaren High.
CAAN, JAMES: Bronx, NY, Mar. 26, 1939.
CAESAR, SID: Yonkers, NY, Sept. 8, 1922.
CAGE, NICOLAS: Long Beach, CA. 1964.
CAINE, MICHAEL (Maurice Michelwhite): London, Mar. 14, 1933.
CAINE, SHAKIRA (Baksh): Guyana, Feb. 23, 1947. Indian Trust Col.
CALHOUN, RORY (Francis Timothy Durgin): Los Angeles, Aug. 8, 1922.
CALLAN, MICHAEL (Martin Calinieff): Philadelphia, Nov. 22, 1935.
CALVERT, PHYLLIS: London, Feb. 18, 1917. Margaret Morris School.
CALVET, CORRINE (Corrine Dibos): Paris, Apr. 30, 1925. U. Paris.
CAMERON, KIRK: Panorama City, CA, 1970.
CAMP, COLLEEN: San Francisco, 1953.
CAMPBELL, BILL: Chicago 1960.
CAMPBELL, GLEN: Delight, AR, Apr. 22, 1935.
CAMPBELL, TISHA: 1969 Newark, NJ
CANALE, GIANNA MARIA: Reggio Calabria, Italy, Sept. 12.
CANDY, JOHN: Oct. 11, 1950, Toronto, CAN.

CANNON, DYAN (Samille Diane Friesen): Tacoma, WA, Jan. 4, 1937.
CANTU, DOLORES: 1957, San Antonio, TX.
CAPERS, VIRGINIA: Sumter, SC, 1925. Juilliard.
CAPSHAW, KATE: Ft. Worth, TX. 1953. UMo.
CAPUCINE (Germaine Lefebvre): Toulon, France, Jan. 6, 1935.
CARA, IRENE: NYC, Mar. 18, 1958.
CARDINALE, CLAUDIA: Tunis, N. Africa, Apr. 15, 1939. College Paul Cambon.
CAREY, HARRY, JR.: Saugus, CA, May 16, 1921. Black Fox Military Academy.
CAREY, MACDONALD: Sioux City, IA, Mar. 15, 1913. U. of Wisc., U. Iowa.
CAREY, PHILIP: Hackensack, NJ, July 15, 1925. U. Miami.
CARMEN, JULIE: Mt. Vernon, NY, Apr. 4, 1954.
CARMICHAEL, IAN: Hull, Eng., June 18, 1920. Scarborough Col.
CARNE, JUDY (Joyce Botterill): Northampton, Eng., 1939. Bush-Davis Theatre School.
CARNEY, ART: Mt. Vernon, NY, Nov. 4, 1918.
CARON, LESLIE: Paris, July 1, 1931. Nat'l Conservatory, Paris.
CARPENTER, CARLETON: Bennington, VT, July 10, 1926. Northwestern.
CARR, VIKKI (Florence Cardona): July 19, 1942. San Fernando Col.
CARRADINE, DAVID: Hollywood, Dec. 8, 1936. San Francisco State.
CARRADINE, KEITH: San Mateo, CA, Aug. 8, 1950. Colo. State U.
CARRADINE, ROBERT: San Mateo, CA, Mar. 24, 1954.
CARREL, DANY: Tourane, Indochina, Sept. 20, 1936. Marseilles Cons.
CARRIERE, MATHIEU: West Germany 1950.
CARROLL, DIAHANN (Johnson): NYC, July 17, 1935. NYU.
CARROLL, PAT: Shreveport, LA, May 5, 1927. Catholic U.
CARSON, JOHN DAVID: 1951, Calif. Valley Col.
CARSON, JOHNNY: Corning, IA, Oct. 23, 1925. U. of Neb.
CARSTEN, PETER (Ransenthaler): Weissenberg, Bavaria, Apr. 30, 1929. Munich Akademie.
CARTER, NELL: Birmingham, AL., Sept. 13, 1948.
CASH, ROSALIND: Atlantic City, NJ, Dec. 31, 1938. CCNY.
CASON, BARBARA: Memphis, TN, Nov. 15, 1933. U. Iowa.
CASS, PEGGY (Mary Margaret): Boston, May 21, 1925.
CASSAVETES, JOHN: NYC, Dec. 9, 1929. Colgate College, AADA.
CASSAVETES, NICK: NYC 1959, Syracuse U, AADA.
CASSEL, JEAN-PIERRE: Paris, Oct. 27, 1932.
CASSIDY, DAVID: NYC, Apr. 12, 1950.
CASSIDY, JOANNA: Camden, NJ, 1944. Syracuse U.
CASSIDY, PATRICK: Los Angeles, CA, Jan. 4, 1961.
CASSIDY, SHAUN: Los Angeles, CA., Sept. 27, 1958.
CASTELLANO, RICHARD: Bronx, NY, Sept. 3, 1934.
CATTRALL, KIM: England, Aug. 21, 1956, AADA.
CAULFIELD, JOAN: Orange, NJ, June 1, 1922. Columbia U.
CAULFIELD, MAXWELL: Glasgow, Scot., Nov. 23, 1959.
CAVANI, LILIANA: Bologna, Italy, Jan. 12, 1937. U. Bologna.
CHAKIRIS, GEORGE: Norwood, OH, Sept. 16, 1933.
CHAMBERLAIN, RICHARD: Beverly Hills, CA, March 31, 1935. Pomona.
CHAMPION, MARGE: Los Angeles, Sept. 2, 1923.
CHANNING, CAROL: Seattle, Wa., Jan. 31, 1921. Bennington.
CHANNING, STOCKARD (Susan Stockard): NYC, Feb. 13, 1944. Radcliffe.
CHAPIN, MILES: NYC, Dec. 6, 1954. HB Studio.
CHAPLIN, GERALDINE: Santa Monica, CA, July 31, 1944. Royal Ballet.
CHAPLIN, SYDNEY: Los Angeles, Mar. 31, 1926. Lawrenceville.
CHARISSE, CYD (Tula Ellice Finklea): Amarillo, TX, Mar. 3, 1922. Hollywood Professional School.
CHASE, CHEVY (Cornelius Crane Chase): NYC, Oct. 8, 1943.
CHAVES, RICHARD: Jacksonville, FL, Oct. 9, 1951, Occidental Col.
CHEN, JOAN: 1961 Shanghai, Cal-State.
CHER (Cherilyn Sarkirian) May 20, 1946, El Centro, CA.
CHIARI, WALTER: Verona, Italy, 1930.
CHONG, RAE DAWN: Vancouver, Can., 1962.
CHRISTIAN, LINDA (Blanca Rosa Welter): Tampico, Mex., Nov. 13, 1923.
CHRISTIE, JULIE: Chukua, Assam, India, Apr. 14, 1941.
CHRISTOPHER, DENNIS (Carrelli): Philadelphia, PA, Dec. 2, 1955. Temple U.
CHRISTOPHER, JORDAN: Youngstown, OH, Oct. 23, 1940. Kent State.
CILENTO, DIANE: Queensland, Australia, Oct. 5, 1933. AADA.
CLAPTON, ERIC: London, Mar. 30, 1945.
CLARK, DANE: NYC, Feb. 18, 1915. Cornell, Johns Hopkins U.
CLARK, DICK: Mt. Vernon, NY, Nov. 30, 1929. Syracuse U.
CLARK, MAE: Philadelphia, Aug. 16, 1910.
CLARK, PETULA: Epsom, England, Nov. 15, 1932.
CLARK, SUSAN: Sarnid, Ont., Can., Mar. 8, 1940. RADA.
CLAY, ANDREW: Brooklyn, 1958, Kingsborough Col.
CLAYBURGH, JILL: NYC, Apr. 30, 1944. Sarah Lawrence.
CLERY, CORRINNE: Italy, 1950.
CLOONEY, ROSEMARY: Maysville, KY, May 23, 1928.
CLOSE, GLENN: Greenwich, CT., Mar. 19, 1947. William & Mary Col.
COBURN, JAMES: Laurel, NB, Aug. 31, 1928. LACC.
COCA, IMOGENE: Philadelphia, Nov. 18, 1908.
CODY, KATHLEEN: Bronx, NY, Oct. 30, 1953.
COLBERT, CLAUDETTE (Lily Chauchoin): Paris, Sept. 15, 1903. Art Students League.
COLE, GEORGE: London, Apr. 22, 1925.
COLEMAN, GARY: Zion, IL., Feb. 8, 1968.
COLEMAN, JACK: 1958. Easton, PA., Duke U.
COLLETT, CHRISTOPHER: NYC, Mar. 13, 1968. Strasberg Inst.
COLLINS, JOAN: London, May 21, 1933. Francis Holland School.
COLLINS, KATE: 1959.
COLLINS, STEPHEN: Des Moines, IA, Oct. 1, 1947. Amherst.
COLON, MIRIAM: Ponce, PR., 1945. UPR.
COMER, ANJANETTE: Dawson, TX, Aug. 7, 1942. Baylor, Tex. U.
CONANT, OLIVER: NYC, Nov. 15, 1955. Dalton.
CONAWAY, JEFF: NYC, Oct. 5, 1950. NYC.
CONDE, RITA (Elizabeth Eleanor): Cuba.
CONNERY, SEAN: Edinburgh, Scot., Aug. 25, 1930.
CONNERY, JASON: London 1962.
CONNORS, CHUCK (Kevin Joseph Connors): Brooklyn, Apr. 10, 1921. Seton Hall College.
CONNORS, MIKE (Krekor Ohanian): Fresno, CA, Aug. 15, 1925. UCLA.
CONRAD, WILLIAM: Louisville, KY, Sept. 27, 1920.
CONROY, KEVIN: 1956 Westport, Ct. Juilliard
CONVERSE, FRANK: St. Louis, MO, May 22, 1938. Carnegie Tech.
CONVY, BERT: St. Louis, MO, July 23, 1935. UCLA.
CONWAY, KEVIN: NYC, May 29, 1942.
CONWAY, TIM (Thomas Daniel): Willoughby, OH, Dec. 15, 1933. Bowling Green State.
COOK, ELISHA, JR.: San Francisco, Dec. 26, 1907. St. Albans.
COOPER, BEN: Hartford, CT, Sept. 30, 1932. Columbia U.
COOPER, CHRISTOPHER: July 9, 1951, Kansas City, Mo. UMo.
COOPER, JACKIE: Los Angeles, Sept. 15, 1921.
COPELAND, JOAN: NYC, June 1, 1922. Brooklyn Col. RADA.
CORBETT, GRETCHEN: Portland, OR, Aug. 13, 1947. Carnegie Tech.
CORBY, ELLEN (Hansen): Racine, WI, June 13, 1913.
CORCORAN, DONNA: Quincy, MA, Sept. 29, 1942.
CORD, ALEX (Viespi): Floral Park, NY, Aug. 3, 1931. NYU, Actors Studio.
CORDAY, MARA (Marilyn Watts): Santa Monica, CA, Jan. 3, 1932.
COREY, JEFF: NYC, Aug. 10, 1914. Fagin School.
CORLAN, ANTHONY: Cork City, Ire., May 9, 1947. Birmingham School of Dramatic Arts.
CORLEY, AL: Missouri, 1956. Actors Studio.
CORNTHWAITE, ROBERT: St. Helens, OR. Apr. 28, 1917. USC.
CORRI, ADRIENNE: Glasgow, Scot., Nov. 13, 1933. RADA.
CORT, BUD (Walter Edward Cox): New Rochelle, NY, Mar. 29, 1950.
CORTESA, VALENTINA: Milan, Italy, Jan. 1, 1925.
COSBY, BILL: Philadelphia, July 12, 1937. Temple U.
COSTER, NICOLAS: London, Dec. 3, 1934. Neighborhood Playhouse.
COSTNER, KEVIN: 1954, Compton, Ca., CalStaU.

Ronny Cox

Denise Crosby

Jon Cryer

Catherine Deneuve

Ted Danson

Jane Eilbe

COTTEN, JOSEPH: Petersburg, VA, May 13, 1905.
COURTENAY, TOM: Hull, Eng., Feb. 25, 1937. RADA.
COURTLAND, JEROME: Knoxville, TN, Dec. 27, 1926.
COYOTE, PETER (Cohon): 1942.
COX, COURTNEY: 1964, Birmingham, Al.
CRAIG, MICHAEL: India, Jan. 27, 1929.
CRAIN, JEANNE: Barstow, CA, May 25, 1925.
CREMER, BRUNO: Paris, 1929.
CRENNA, RICHARD: Los Angeles, Nov. 30, 1926. USC.
CRISTAL, LINDA (Victoria Moya): Buenos Aires, Feb. 25, 1934.
CRONYN, HUME (Blake): July 18, 1911 Ontario, Can.
CROSBY, DENISE: Hollywood, CA, 1958.
CROSBY, HARRY: Los Angeles, CA, Aug. 8, 1958.
CROSBY, KATHRYN GRANT: (see Kathryn Grant)
CROSBY, MARY FRANCES: Calif., Sept. 14, 1959.
CROSS, BEN: London, 1948. RADA.
CROSS, MURPHY (Mary Jane): Laurelton, MD, June 22, 1950.
CROUSE, LINDSAY ANN: NYC, May 12, 1948. Radcliffe.
CROWLEY, PAT: Olyphant, PA, Sept. 17, 1932.
CRUISE, TOM (T. C. Mapother IV): July 3, 1962, Syracuse, NY.
CRYER, JON: NYC, Apr. 16, 1965, RADA.
CRYSTAL, BILLY: Long Beach, NY, Mar. 14, 1947, Marshall U.
CULLUM, JOHN: Knoxville, TN, Mar. 2, 1930. U. Tenn.
CULLUM, JOHN DAVID: Mar. 1, 1966, NYC
CULP, ROBERT: Oakland, CA., Aug. 16, 1930. U. Wash.
CUMMINGS, CONSTANCE: Seattle, WA, May 15, 1910.
CUMMINGS, QUINN: Hollywood, Aug. 13, 1967.
CUMMINGS, ROBERT: Joplin, MO, June 9, 1910. Carnegie Tech.
CUMMINS, PEGGY: Prestatyn, N. Wales, Dec. 18, 1926. Alexandra School.
CURTIN, JANE: Cambridge, MA; Sept. 6, 1947.
CURTIS, JAMIE LEE: Los Angeles, CA., Nov. 21, 1958.
CURTIS, KEENE: Salt Lake City, UT, Feb. 15, 1925. U. Utah.
CURTIS, TONY (Bernard Schwartz): NYC, June 3, 1924.
CUSACK, CYRIL: Durban, S. Africa, Nov. 26, 1910. Univ. Col.
CUSACK, JOAN: Chicago, 1962.
CUSHING, PETER: Kenley, Surrey, Eng., May 26, 1913.

DAFOE, WILLEM: Appleton, Wi. 1955.
DAHL, ARLENE: Minneapolis, Aug. 11, 1928. U. Minn.
DALLESANDRO, JOE: Pensacola, FL, Dec. 31, 1948.
DALTON, TIMOTHY: Wales, Mar. 21, 1946, RADA.
DALTREY, ROGER: London, Mar. 1, 1945.
DALY, TYNE: Feb. 21, 1947, Madison, Wi. AMDA.
DAMONE, VIC (Vito Farinola): Brooklyn, June 12, 1928.
DANCE, CHARLES: Plymouth, Eng., 1946.
D'ANGELO, BEVERLY: Columbus, OH., Nov. 15, 1953.
DANGERFIELD, RODNEY (Jacob Cohen): Babylon, NY, Nov. 22, 1921.
DANIELS, JEFF: Georgia, 1955. EastMichState.
DANIELS, WILLIAM: Bklyn, Mar. 31, 1927. Northwestern.
DANNER, BLYTHE: Philadelphia, PA. Feb. 3, 1944, Bard Col.
DANO, ROYAL: NYC, Nov. 16, 1922. NYU.
DANSON, TED: Flagstaff, AZ, Dec. 29, 1947. Stanford, Carnegie Tech.
DANTE, MICHAEL (Ralph Vitti): Stamford, CT, 1935. U. Miami.
DANTON, RAY: NYC, Sept. 19, 1931. Carnegie Tech.
DANZA, TONY: Brooklyn, NY., Apr. 21, 1951. UDubuque.
DARBY, KIM: (Deborah Zerby): North Hollywood, CA, July 8, 1948.
DARCEL, DENISE (Denise Billecard): Paris, Sept. 8, 1925. U. Dijon.
DARREN, JAMES: Philadelphia, June 8, 1936. Stella Adler School.
DARRIEUX, DANIELLE: Bordeaux, France, May 1, 1917. Lycee LaTour.
DAVIDSON, JOHN: Pittsburgh, Dec. 13, 1941. Denison U.
DAVIS, BETTE: Lowell, MA, Apr. 5, 1908. John Murray Anderson Dramatic School.
DAVIS, BRAD: Fla., Nov. 6, 1949. AADA.
DAVIS, CLIFRON: Oct. 4, 1945, Chicago, OakwoodCol.
DAVIS, GEENA: Wareham, MA, 1958.
DAVIS, MAC: Lubbock, TX, Jan. 21, 1942.
DAVIS, NANCY (Anne Frances Robbins): NYC July 6, 1921, Smith Col.
DAVIS, OSSIE: Cogdell, GA, Dec. 18, 1917. Howard U.
DAVIS, SAMMY, JR.: NYC, Dec. 8, 1925.
DAVIS, SKEETER (Mary Frances Penick): Dry Ridge, KY. Dec. 30, 1931.

DAY, DORIS (Doris Kappelhoff); Cincinnati, Apr. 3, 1924.
DAY, LARAINE (Johnson): Roosevelt, UT, Oct. 13, 1917.
DAY LEWIS, DANIEL: 1958, London, Bristol Old Vic.
DAYAN, ASSEF: Israel, 1945. U. Jerusalem.
DEAKINS, LUCY: NYC 1971.
DEAN, JIMMY: Plainview, TX, Aug. 10, 1928.
DeCAMP, ROSEMARY: Nov. 14, 1913, Prescott, Az.
DeCARLO, YVONNE (Peggy Yvonne Middleton): Vancouver, B.C., Can., Sept. 1, 1922. Vancouver School of Drama.
DEE, FRANCES: Los Angeles, Nov. 26, 1907. Chicago U.
DEE, JOEY (Joseph Di Nicola): Passaic, NJ, June 11, 1940. Patterson State College.
DEE, RUBY: Cleveland, OH, Oct. 27, 1924. Hunter Col.
DEE, SANDRA (Alexandra Zuck): Bayonne, NJ, Apr. 23, 1942.
DeFORE, DON: Cedar Rapids, IA, Aug. 25, 1917. U. Iowa.
DeHAVEN, GLORIA: Los Angeles, July 23, 1923.
DeHAVILLAND, OLIVIA: Tokyo, Japan, July 1, 1916. Notre Dame Convent School.
DELAIR, SUZY: Paris, Dec. 31, 1916.
DELPY, JULIE: Paris, 1970.
DELON, ALAIN: Sceaux, Fr., Nov. 8, 1935.
DELORME, DANIELE: Paris, Oct. 9, 1927. Sorbonne.
DeLUISE, DOM: Brooklyn, Aug. 1, 1933. Tufts Col.
DeLUISE, PETER: 1967, Hollywood, Ca.
DEMPSEY, PATRICK: 1966, Maine
DEMONGEOT, MYLENE: Nice, France, Sept. 29, 1938.
DeMORNAY, REBECCA: Los Angeles, Ca., 1962. Strasberg Inst.
DeMUNN, JEFFREY: Buffalo, NY, Apr. 25, 1947. Union Col.
DENEUVE, CATHERINE: Paris, Oct. 22, 1943.
DeNIRO, ROBERT: NYC, Aug. 17, 1943, Stella Adler.
DENISON, MICHAEL: Doncaster, York, Eng., Nov. 1, 1915. Oxford.
DENNEHY, BRIAN: 1938, Bridgeport, Ct., Columbia.
DENNER, CHARLES: Tarnow, Poland, May 29, 1926.
DENNIS, SANDY: Hastings, NB, Apr. 27, 1937. Actors Studio.
DEPARDIEU, GERARD: Chateauroux, Fr., Dec. 27, 1948.
DEREK, BO (Mary Cathleen Collins): Long Beach, CA, Nov. 20, 1956.
DEREK, JOHN: Hollywood, Aug. 12, 1926.

DERN, BRUCE: Chicago, June 4, 1936. U PA.
DERN, LAURA: California, 1966.
DeSALVO, ANNE: Philadelphia, PA., Apr. 3.
DEVINE, COLLEEN: San Gabriel, CA, June 22, 1960.
DeVITO, DANNY: Nov. 17, 1944. Asbury Park, NJ.
DEWHURST, COLLEEN: Montreal June 3, 1926. Lawrence U.
DEXTER, ANTHONY (Walter Reinhold Alfred Fleischmann): Talmadge, NB, Jan. 19, 1919. U. Iowa.
DEY, SUSAN: Pekin, Il, Dec. 10, 1953.
DeYOUNG, CLIFF: Los Angeles, CA, Feb. 12, 1945. Cal State.
DHIEGH, KHIGH: New Jersey, 1910.
DIAMOND, NEIL: NYC, Jan. 24, 1941. NYU.
DICKINSON, ANGIE: Kulm, ND, Sept. 30, 1932. Glendale College.
DIETRICH, MARLENE (Maria Magdalene von Losch): Berlin, Ger., Dec. 27, 1901. Berlin Music Academy.
DILLER, PHYLLIS (Driver): Lima, OH, July 17, 1917. Bluffton College.
DILLMAN, BRADFORD: San Francisco, Apr. 14, 1930. Yale.
DILLON, KEVIN: Mamaroneck, NY, 1965.
DILLON, MATT: Larchmont, NY., Feb. 18, 1964. AADA.
DILLON, MELINDA: Hope, AR, Oct. 13, 1939. Goodman Theatre School.
DOBSON, TAMARA: Baltimore, MD, 1947. MD. Inst. of Art.
DOMERGUE, FAITH: New Orleans, June 16, 1925.
DONAHUE, TROY (Merle Johnson): NYC, Jan. 27, 1937. Columbia U.
DONAT, PETER: Nova Scotia, Jan. 20, 1928. Yale.
D'ONOFRIO, VINCENT: 1960, Brooklyn.
DOOHAN, JAMES: Vancouver, BC, Mar. 3, Neighborhood Playhouse.
DOOLEY, PAUL: Parkersburg, WV, Feb. 22, 1928. U. WV.
DOUGLAS, DONNA (Dorothy Bourgeois): Baton Rouge, LA, 1935.
DOUGLAS, KIRK (Issur Danielovitch): Amsterdam, NY, Dec. 9, 1916. St. Lawrence U.
DOUGLAS, MICHAEL: New Brunswick, NJ, Sept. 25, 1944. U. Cal.
DOUGLASS, ROBYN: Sendai, Japan; June 21, 1953. UCDavis.
DOURIF, BRAD: Huntington, WV, Mar. 18, 1950. Marshall U.
DOVE, BILLIE: NYC, May 14, 1904.
DOWN, LESLEY-ANN: London, Mar. 17, 1954.
DOWNEY, ROBERT, JR.: 1965 NYC
DRAKE, BETSY: Paris, Sept. 11, 1923.
DRAKE, CHARLES (Charles Rupert): NYC, Oct. 2, 1914. Nichols College.
DREW, ELLEN (formerly Terry Ray): Kansas City, MO, Nov. 23, 1915.
DREYFUSS, RICHARD: Brooklyn, NY, Oct. 19, 1947.
DRILLINGER, BRIAN: Brooklyn, NY, June 27, 1960, SUNY/Purchase.
DRU, JOANNE (Joanne LaCock): Logan, WV, Jan. 31, 1923. John Robert Powers School.
DUBBINS, DON: Brooklyn, NY, June 28.
DUFF, HOWARD: Bremerton, WA, Nov. 24, 1917.
DUFFY, PATRICK: Townsend, Mt, Mar. 17, 1949. U. Wash.
DUKAKIS, OLYMPIA: Massachusetts, June 20, 1931.
DUKE, PATTY (Anna Marie): NYC, Dec. 14, 1946.
DUKES, DAVID: San Francisco, June 6, 1945.
DULLEA, KEIR: Cleveland, NJ, May 30, 1936. SF State Col.
DUNAWAY, FAYE: Bascom, FL, Jan. 14, 1941, Fla. U.
DUNCAN, SANDY: Henderson, TX, Feb. 20, 1946. Len Morris Col.
DUNNE, GRIFFIN: NYC June 8, 1955, Neighborhood Playhouse.
DUNNE, IRENE: Louisville, KY, Dec. 20, 1898. Chicago College of Music.
DUNNOCK, MILDRED: Baltimore, Jan. 25, 1900. Johns Hopkins and Columbia U.
DUPEREY, ANNY: Paris, 1947.
DURBIN, DEANNA (Edna): Winnipeg, Can., Dec. 4, 1921.
DURNING, CHARLES: Highland Falls, NY, Feb. 28, 1933. NYU.
DUSSOLLIER, ANDRE: Annecy, France, Feb. 17, 1946.
DUVALL, ROBERT: San Diego, CA, Jan 5, 1930. Principia Col.
DUVALL, SHELLEY: Houston, TX, July 7, 1949.
DYSART, RICHARD: Brighton, ME, Mar. 30, 1929.
EASTON, ROBERT: Milwaukee, WI, Nov. 23, 1930. U. Texas.
EASTWOOD, CLINT: San Francisco, May 31, 1930. LACC.
EATON, SHIRLEY: London, 1937. Aida Foster School.
EBSEN, BUDDY (Christian, Jr.): Belleville, IL, Apr. 2, 1910. U. Fla.
ECKEMYR, AGNETA: Karlsborg, Swed., July 2. Actors Studio.
EDEN, BARBARA (Moorhead): Tucson, AZ, Aug. 23, 1934.
EDWARDS, ANTHONY: 1963, Santa Barbara, Ca. RADA
EDWARDS, VINCE: NYC, July 9, 1928. AADA.
EGGAR, SAMANTHA: London, Mar. 5, 1939.
EICHHORN, LISA: Reading, PA, Feb. 4, 1952. Queens Ont. U. RADA.
EILBER, JANET: Detroit, MI, July 27, 1951. Juilliard.
EKBERG, ANITA: Malmo, Sweden, Sept. 29, 1931.
EKLAND, BRITT: Stockholm, Swed. Oct. 6, 1942.
ELIZONDO, HECTOR: NYC, Dec. 22, 1936.
ELLIOTT, CHRIS: 1960, NYC
ELLIOTT, DENHOLM: London, May 31, 1922. Malvern College.
ELLIOTT, PATRICIA: Gunnison, Co, July 21, 1942, UCol.
ELLIOTT, SAM: Sacramento, CA, Aug. 9, 1944. U. Ore.
ELY, RON (Ronald Pierce): Hereford, TX, June 21, 1938.
ENGLISH, ALEX: 1954, USCar.
ENGLUND, ROBERT: June 6, 1949.
ERDMAN, RICHARD: Enid, OK, June 1, 1925.
ERICSON, JOHN: Dusseldorf, Ger., Sept. 25, 1926. AADA.
ESMOND, CARL: Vienna, June 14, 1906. U. Vienna.
ESTEVEZ, EMILIO: NYC, May 12, 1962.
ESPOSITO, GIANCARLO: Copenhagen, Den., Apr. 26, 1958.
ESTRADA, ERIK: NYC, Mar. 16, 1949.
EVANS, DALE (Francis Smith): Uvalde, TX, Oct. 31, 1912.
EVANS, GENE: Holbrook, AZ, July 11, 1922.
EVANS, LINDA (Evanstad): Hartford, CT., Nov. 18, 1942.
EVANS, MAURICE: Dorchester, Eng., June 3, 1901.
EVERETT, CHAD (Ray Cramton): South Bend, IN, June 11, 1936.
EVERETT, RUPERT: Norfolk, Eng., 1959.
EVIGAN, GREG: 1954, South Amboy, NJ
EWELL, TOM (Yewell Tompkins): Owensboro, KY, Apr. 29, 1909. U. Wisc.
FABARES, SHELLEY: Los Angeles, Jan. 19, 1944.
FABIAN (Fabian Forte): Philadelphia, Feb. 6, 1943.
FABRAY, NANETTE (Ruby Nanette Fabares): San Diego, Oct. 27, 1920.
FAIRBANKS, DOUGLAS JR.: NYC, Dec. 9, 1907. Collegiate School.
FAIRCHILD, MORGAN: (Patsy McClenny) Dallas, TX., Feb. 3, 1950. UCLA.
FALK, PETER: NYC, Sept. 16, 1927. New School.
FARENTINO, JAMES: Brooklyn, Feb. 24, 1938. AADA.
FARINA, SANDY (Sandra Feldman): Newark, NJ, 1955.
FARR, FELICIA: Westchester, NY, Oct. 4, 1932. Penn State Col.
FARRELL, CHARLES: Onset Bay, MA, Aug. 9, 1901. Boston U.
FARROW, MIA: Los Angeles, Feb. 9, 1945.
FAULKNER, GRAHAM: London, Sept. 26, 1947. Webber-Douglas.
FAWCETT, FARRAH: Corpus Christie, TX. Feb. 2, 1947. TexU.
FAYE, ALICE (Ann Leppert): NYC, May 5, 1912.
FEINSTEIN, ALAN: NYC, Sept. 8, 1941.
FELDMAN, COREY: Encino, CA, 1970.
FELDON, BARBARA (Hall): Pittsburgh, Mar. 12, 1941. Carnegie Tech.
FELDSHUH, TOVAH: NYC, Dec. 27, 1953, Sarah Lawrence Col.
FELLOWS, EDITH: Boston, May 20, 1923.
FERRELL, CONCHATA: Charleston, WV, Mar. 28, 1943. Marshall U.
FERRER, JOSE: Santurce, P.R., Jan. 8, 1909. Princeton U.
FERRER, MEL: Elberon, NJ, Aug. 25, 1917. Princeton U.
FERRIS, BARBARA: London, 1943.
FERZETTI, GABRIELE: Italy, 1927. Rome Acad. of Drama.
FIEDLER, JOHN: Plateville, Wi, Feb. 3, 1925.
FIELD, SALLY: Pasadena, CA, Nov. 6, 1946.
FIGUEROA, RUBEN: NYC 1958.
FINNEY, ALBERT: Salford, Lancashire, Eng., May 9, 1936. RADA.
FIORENTINO, LINDA: Philadelphia, Pa.
FIRTH, PETER: Bradford, Eng., Oct. 27, 1953.
FIRESTONE, ROCHELLE: Kansas City, MO., June 14, 1949. NYU.

Stephen Geoffreys

Carlin Glynn

Giancarlo Giannini

Dody Goodman

Ed Harris

Ellen Green

FISHER, CARRIE: Los Angeles, CA, Oct. 21, 1956. London Central School of Drama.

FISHER, EDDIE: Philadelphia, Aug. 10, 1928.

FITZGERALD, BRIAN: Philadelphia, Pa, 1960, West Chester U.

FITZGERALD, GERALDINE: Dublin, Ire., Nov. 24, 1914. Dublin Art School.

FLANNERY, SUSAN: Jersey City, NJ, July 31, 1943.

FLEMING, RHONDA (Marilyn Louis): Los Angeles, Aug. 10, 1922.

FLEMYNG, ROBERT: Liverpool, Eng., Jan. 3, 1912. Haileybury Col.

FLETCHER, LOUISE: Birmingham, AL, July 1934.

FOCH, NINA: Leyden, Holland, Apr. 20, 1924.

FOLDI, ERZSEBET: Queens, NY, 1967.

FOLLOWS, MEGAN: 1967, Toronto, Ca.

FONDA, JANE: NYC, Dec. 21, 1937. Vassar.

FONDA, PETER: NYC, Feb. 23, 1939. U. Omaha.

FONTAINE, JOAN: Tokyo, Japan, Oct. 22, 1917.

FOOTE, HALLIE: NYC 1953. UNH.

FORD, GLENN (Gwyllyn Samuel Newton Ford): Quebec, Can., May 1, 1916.

FORD, HARRISON: Chicago, IL, July 13, 1942. Ripon Col.

FOREST, MARK (Lou Degni): Brooklyn, Jan. 1933.

FORREST, STEVE: Huntsville, TX, Sept. 29, 1924. UCLA.

FORSLUND, CONNIE: San Diego, CA, June 19, 1950, NYU.

FORSTER, ROBERT (Foster, Jr.): Rochester, NY, July 13, 1941. Rochester U.

FORSYTHE, JOHN (Freund): Penn's Grove, NJ, Jan. 29, 1918.

FOSTER, JODIE (Ariane Munker): Bronx, NY, Nov. 19, 1962. Yale.

FOX, EDWARD: London, 1937, RADA.

FOX, JAMES: London, May 19, 1939.

FOX, MICHAEL J.: Vancouver, BC, June 9, 1961.

FOXWORTH, ROBERT: Houston, TX, Nov. 1, 1941. Carnegie Tech.

FOXX, REDD: St. Louis, MO, Dec. 9, 1922.

FRAKES, JOHNATHAN: 1952, Bethlehem, Pa. Harvard

FRANCIOSA, ANTHONY (Papaleo): NYC, Oct. 25, 1928.

FRANCIS, ANNE: Ossining, NY, Sept. 16, 1932.

FRANCIS, ARLENE (Arlene Kazanjian): Boston, Oct. 20, 1908. Finch School.

FRANCIS, CONNIE (Constance Franconero): Newark, NJ, Dec. 12, 1938.

FRANCISCUS, JAMES: Clayton, MO, Jan. 31, 1934. Yale.

FRANCKS, DON: Vancouver, Can., Feb. 28, 1932.

FRANK, JEFFREY: Jackson Heights, NY, 1965.

FRANKLIN, PAMELA: Tokyo, Feb. 4, 1950.

FRANZ, ARTHUR: Perth Amboy, NJ, Feb. 29, 1920. Blue Ridge College.

FRAZIER, SHEILA: NYC, Nov. 13, 1948.

FREEMAN, AL, JR.: San Antonio, TX, 1934. CCLA.

FREEMAN, MONA: Baltimore, MD, June 9, 1926.

FREEMAN, MORGAN: Memphis, Tn, June 1, 1937, LACC.

FREWER, MATT: Washington, DC, 1957, Old Vic.

FULLER, PENNY: Durham, NC, 1940. Northwestern U.

FURNEAUX, YVONNE: Lille, France, 1928. Oxford U.

FYODOROVA, VICTORIA: Russia 1946.

GABLE, JOHN CLARK: Mar. 20, 1961, Los Angeles. Santa Monica Col.

GABOR, EVA: Budapest, Hungary, Feb. 11, 1920.

GABOR, ZSA ZSA (Sari Gabor): Budapest, Hungary, Feb. 6, 1918.

GAINES, BOYD: Atlanta, GA., May 11, 1953. Juilliard.

GALLAGHER, PETER: Armonk, NY, Aug. 19, 1955, Tufts U.

GALLIGAN, ZACH: NYC, 1963. ColumbiaU.

GAM, RITA: Pittsburgh, PA, Apr. 2, 1928.

GARBER, VICTOR: Montreal, Can., Mar. 16, 1949.

GARBO, GRETA (Greta Gustafson): Stockholm, Sweden, Sept. 18, 1905.

GARCIA, ANDY: 1948, Havana, Cuba. FlaIntlU.

GARDENIA, VINCENT: Naples, Italy, Jan. 7, 1922.

GARDNER, AVA: Smithfield, NC, Dec. 24, 1922. Atlantic Christian College.

GARFIELD, ALLEN: Newark, NJ, Nov. 22, 1939. Actors Studio.

GARLAND, BEVERLY: Santa Cruz, CA, Oct. 17, 1930. Glendale Col.

GARNER, JAMES (James Baumgarner): Norman, OK, Apr. 7, 1928. Okla. U.

GARR, TERI: Lakewood, OH, 1952.

GARRETT, BETTY: St. Joseph, MO, May 23, 1919. Annie Wright Seminary.

GARRISON, SEAN: NYC, Oct. 19, 1937.

GARSON, GREER: Ireland, Sept. 29, 1906.

GASSMAN, VITTORIO: Genoa, Italy, Sept. 1, 1922. Rome Academy of Dramatic Art.

GAVIN, JOHN: Los Angeles, Apr. 8, 1935. Stanford U.

GAYLORD, MITCH: Van Nuys, CA, 1961, UCLA.

GAYNOR, MITZI (Francesca Marlene Von Gerber): Chicago, Sept. 4, 1930.

GAZZARA, BEN: NYC, Aug. 28, 1930. Actors Studio.

GEARY, ANTHONY: Coalsville, Utah, May 29, 1947.

GEDRICK, JASON: 1965, Chicago, Drake U.

GEESON, JUDY: Arundel, Eng., Sept. 10, 1948. Corona.

GEOFFREYS, STEPHEN: Cincinnati, Oh., Nov. 22, 1964. NYU.

GEORGE, BOY (George O'Dowd): London 1962.

GEORGE, SUSAN: West London, Eng. July 26, 1950.

GERARD, GIL: Little Rock, AR, Jan. 23, 1940.

GERE, RICHARD: Philadelphia, PA, Aug. 29, 1949. U. Mass.

GERROLL, DANIEL: London, Oct. 16, 1951. Central.

GETTY, ESTELLE: NYC, July 25, 1923, New School.

GHOLSON, JULIE: Birmingham, AL, June 4, 1958.

GHOSTLEY, ALICE: Eve, MO, Aug. 14, 1926. Okla U.

GIAN, JOE: North Miami Beach, Fl. 1962.

GIANNINI, CHERYL: Monessen, PA., June 15.

GIANNINI, GIANCARLO: Spezia, Italy, Aug. 1, 1942. Rome Acad. of Drama.

GIBB, CYNTHIA: 1965

GIBSON, MEL: Oneonta, NY., Jan. 3, 1951. NIDA.

GIELGUD, JOHN: London, Apr. 14, 1904. RADA.

GILBERT, MELISSA: May 8, 1964, Los Angeles, CA.

GILES, NANCY: NYC, July 17, 1960, Oberlin Col.

GILFORD, JACK: NYC, July 25, 1907.

GILLIS, ANNE (Alma O'Connor): Little Rock, AR, Feb. 12, 1927.

GINTY, ROBERT: NYC, Nov. 14, 1948, Yale.

GIRARDOT, ANNIE: Paris, Oct. 25, 1931.

GIROLAMI, STEFANIA: Rome, Italy, 1963.

GISH, LILLIAN: Springfield, OH, Oct. 14, 1896.

GLASER, PAUL MICHAEL: Boston, MA, Mar. 25, 1943. Boston U.
GLASS, RON: Evansville, IN, July 10, 1945.
GLEASON, JOANNA: Winnipeg, Can, June 2, 1950, UCLA.
GLENN, SCOTT: Pittsburgh, PA, Jan. 26, 1942; William and Mary Col.
GLOVER, CRISPIN: 1964 NYC
GLOVER, DANNY: San Francisco, Ca., July 22, 1947, SFStateCol.
GLOVER, JOHN: Kingston, NY, Aug. 7, 1944.
GLYNN,CARLIN: Cleveland, Oh, Feb. 19, 1940, Actors Studio.
GODDARD, PAULETTE (Levy): Great Neck, NY, June 3, 1911.
GODUNOV, ALEKSANDR: Sakhalin, USSR, Nov. 28, 1949.
GOLDBERG, WHOOPI (Caryn Johnson): NYC, Nov. 13, 1949.
GOLDBLUM, JEFF: Pittsburgh, PA, Oct. 22, 1952. Neighborhood Playhouse.
GOLDEN, ANNIE: NYC, 1952.
GOLDSTEIN, JENETTE: Beverley Hills, CA, 1960.
GONZALEZ, CORDELIA: Aug. 11, 1958, San Juan, PR. UPR.
GONZALES-GONZALEZ, PEDRO: Aguilares, TX, Dec. 21, 1926.
GOODMAN, DODY: Columbus, OH, Oct. 28, 1915.
GORDON, GALE (Aldrich): NYC, Feb. 2, 1906.
GORDON, KEITH: NYC, Feb. 3, 1961.
GORING, MARIUS: Newport Isle of Wight, 1912. Cambridge, Old Vic.
GORMAN, CLIFF: Jamaica, NY, Oct. 13, 1936. NYU.
GORSHIN, FRANK: Apr. 5, 1933.
GORTNER, MARJOE: Long Beach, CA, 1944.
GOSSETT, LOUIS: Brooklyn, May 27, 1936. NYU.
GOULD, ELLIOTT (Goldstein): Brooklyn, Aug. 29, 1938. Columbia U.
GOULD, HAROLD: Schenectady, NY, Dec. 10, 1923. Cornell.
GOULET, ROBERT: Lawrence, MA, Nov. 26, 1933. Edmonton.
GRAF, DAVID: Lancaster, OH, Apr. 16, 1950. OhStateU.
GRAF, TODD: NYC, Oct. 22, 1959, SUNY/Purchase.
GRANGER, FARLEY: San Jose, CA, July 1, 1925.
GRANGER, STEWART (James Stewart): London, May 6, 1913. Webber-Douglas School of Acting.
GRANT, DAVID MARSHALL: Westport, CT, June 21, 1955. Yale.
GRANT, KATHRYN (Olive Grandstaff): Houston, TX, Nov. 25, 1933. UCLA.
GRANT, LEE: NYC, Oct. 31, 1930. Juilliard.
GRAVES, PETER (Aurness): Minneapolis, Mar. 18, 1926. U. Minn.
GRAY, CHARLES: Bournemouth, Eng., 1928.
GRAY, COLEEN (Doris Jensen): Staplehurst, NB, Oct. 23, 1922. Hamline U.
GRAY, LINDA: Santa Monica, CA; Sept. 12, 1940.
GRAYSON, KATHRYN (Zelma Hedrick): Winston-Salem, NC, Feb. 9, 1922.
GREEN, KERRI: Fort Lee, NJ, 1967. Vassar.
GREENE, ELLEN: NYC, Feb. 22, 1950. Ryder Col.
GREER, JANE: Washington, DC, Sept. 9, 1924.
GREER, MICHAEL: Galesburg, IL, Apr. 20, 1943.
GREGORY, MARK: Rome, Italy. 1965.
GREY, JENNIFER: NYC 1960.
GREY, JOEL (Katz): Cleveland, OH, Apr. 11, 1932.
GREY, VIRGINIA: Los Angeles, Mar. 22, 1917.
GRIEM, HELMUT: Hamburg, Ger. U. Hamburg.
GRIFFITH, ANDY: Mt. Airy, NC, June 1, 1926. UNC.
GRIFFITH, MELANIE: NYC, Aug. 9, 1957 Pierce Col.
GRIMES, GARY: San Francisco, June 2, 1955.
GRIMES, TAMMY: Lynn, MA, Jan. 30, 1934. Stephens Col.
GRIZZARD, GEORGE: Roanoke Rapids, NC, Apr. 1, 1928. UNC.
GRODIN, CHARLES: Pittsburgh, PA, Apr. 21, 1935.
GROH, DAVID: NYC, May 21, 1939. Brown U., LAMDA.
GUARDINO, HARRY: Brooklyn, Dec. 23, 1925. Haaren High.
GUILLAUME, ROBERT: Nov. 30, 1937, St. Louis, Mo. (Robert Williams).
GUINNESS, ALEX: London, Apr. 2, 1914. Pembroke Lodge School.
GUNN, MOSES: St. Louis, MO, Oct. 2, 1929. Tenn. State U.
GUTTENBERG, STEVE: Massapequa, NY, Aug. 24, 1958. UCLA.
GWILLIM, DAVID: Plymouth, Eng., Dec. 15, 1948. RADA.
HAAS, LUKAS: West Hollywood, CA, Apr. 16, 1976.
HACKETT, BUDDY (Leonard Hacker): Brooklyn, Aug. 31, 1924.
HACKMAN, GENE: San Bernardino, CA, Jan. 30, 1931.
HADDON, DALE: Montreal, CAN., May 26, 1949. Neighborhood Playhouse.
HAGERTY, JULIE: Cincinnati, OH, June 15, 1955. Juilliard.
HAGMAN, LARRY: (Hageman): Weatherford, TX., Sept. 21, 1931. Bard.
HAIM, COREY: Toronto, Can, 1972.
HALE, BARBARA: DeKalb, IL, Apr. 18, 1922. Chicago Academy of Fine Arts.
HALEY, JACKIE EARLE: Northridge, CA, 1963.
HALL, ALBERT: Boothton, AL, Nov. 10, 1937. Columbia.
HALL, ANTHONY MICHAEL: NYC, 1968.
HALL, KEVIN PETER: Pittsburgh, Pa, 1955. GeoWashU.
HAMILL, MARK: Oakland, CA, Sept. 25, 1952. LACC.
HAMILTON, CARRIE: Dec. 5, 1963, NYC.
HAMILTON, GEORGE: Memphis, TN, Aug. 12, 1939. Hackley.
HAMLIN, HARRY: Pasadena, CA, Oct. 30, 1951. Yale.
HAMPSHIRE, SUSAN: London, May 12, 1941.
HAN, MAGGIE: Providence, RI, 1959.
HANKS, TOM: Oakland, CA., 1956. CalStateU.
HANNAH, DARYL: Chicago, IL., 1960, UCLA.
HANNAH, PAGE: Chicago, IL., 1964.
HARDIN, TY (Orison Whipple Hungerford II): NYC, June 1, 1930.
HAREWOOD, DORIAN: Dayton, OH, Aug. 6. U. Cinn.
HARMON, MARK: Los Angeles, CA, Sept. 2, 1951; UCLA.
HARPER, TESS: Mammoth Spring, Ark., 1952. SWMoState.
HARPER, VALERIE: Suffern, NY, Aug. 22, 1940.
HARRELSON, WOODY: Lebanon, OH, 1962.
HARRINGTON, PAT: NYC, Aug. 13, 1929. Fordham U.
HARRIS, BARBARA (Sandra Markowitz): Evanston, IL, July 25, 1935.
HARRIS, ED: Tenafly, NJ, Nov. 28, 1950. Columbia.
HARRIS, JULIE: Grosse Point, MI, Dec. 2, 1925. Yale Drama School.
HARRIS, MEL (Mary Ellen): 1957 North Brunswick, NJ, Columbia.
HARRIS, RICHARD: Limerick, Ire., Oct. 1, 1930. London Acad.
HARRIS, ROSEMARY: Ashby, Eng., Sept. 19, 1930. RADA.
HARRISON, GEORGE: Liverpool, England, Feb. 25, 1943.
HARRISON, GREG: Catalina Island, CA, May 31, 1950; Actors Studio.
HARRISON, NOEL: London, Jan. 29, 1936.
HARRISON, REX: Huyton, Cheshire, Eng., Mar. 5, 1908.
HARROLD, KATHRYN: Tazewell, VA. 1950. Mills Col.
HART, ROXANNE: Trenton, NJ, 1952, Princeton.
HARTLEY, MARIETTE: NYC, June 21, 1941.
HARTMAN, DAVID: Pawtucket, RI, May 19, 1935. Duke U.
HASSETT, MARILYN: Los Angeles, CA, 1949.
HAUER, RUTGER: Amsterdam, Hol. Jan. 23, 1944.
HAVER, JUNE: Rock Island, IL, June 10, 1926.
HAVOC, JUNE (Hovick): Nov. 8, 1916, Seattle, Wa.
HAWN, GOLDIE: Washington, DC, Nov. 21, 1945.
HAYDEN, LINDA: Stanmore, Eng. Aida Foster School.
HAYES, HELEN: (Helen Brown): Washington, DC, Oct. 10, 1900. Sacred Heart Convent.
HAYS, ROBERT: Bethesda, MD., July 24, 1947, SD State Col.
HEADLY, GLENNE: New London, Ct, Mar. 13, 1955. AmCol.
HEALD, ANTHONY: New Rochelle, NY, Aug. 25, 1944, MiStateU.
HEARD, JOHN: Washington, DC, Mar. 7, 1946. Clark U.
HEATHERTON, JOEY: NYC, Sept. 14, 1944.
HECKART, EILEEN: Columbus, OH, Mar. 29, 1919. Ohio State U.
HEDISON, DAVID: Providence, RI, May 20, 1929. Brown U.
HEGYES, ROBERT: NJ, May 7, 1951.
HEMINGWAY, MARIEL: Nov. 22, 1961.
HEMMINGS, DAVID: Guilford, Eng. Nov. 18, 1938.
HENDERSON, FLORENCE: Feb. 14, 1934.
HENDERSON, MARCIA: Andover, MA, July 22, 1932. AADA.
HENDRY, GLORIA: Jacksonville, FL. 1949.

Holly Hunter

Richard Kiley

Sally Kellerman

Aron Kincaid

Sally Kirkland

Page Johnso

HENNER, MARILU: Chicago, IL. Apr. 4, 1952.
HENREID, PAUL: Trieste, Jan. 10, 1908.
HENRY, BUCK (Zuckerman): NYC, 1931. Dartmouth.
HENRY, JUSTIN: Rye, NY, 1971.
HEPBURN, AUDREY: Brussels, Belgium, May 4, 1929.
HEPBURN, KATHARINE: Hartford, CT, Nov. 8, 1907. Bryn Mawr.
HERMAN, PEE-WEE (Paul Reubenfeld): 1952.
HERRMANN, EDWARD: Washington, DC, July 21, 1943. Bucknell, LAMDA.
HERSHEY, BARBARA: (Herzstein): Hollywood, CA, Feb. 5, 1948.
HESTON, CHARLTON: Evanston, IL, Oct. 4, 1922. Northwestern U.
HEWITT, MARTIN: Claremont, CA, 1960; AADA.
HEYWOOD, ANNE (Violet Pretty): Birmingham, Eng., Dec. 11, 1932.
HICKEY, WILLIAM: Brooklyn, NY, 1928.
HICKMAN, DARRYL: Hollywood, CA, July 28, 1933. Loyola U.
HICKMAN, DWAYNE: Los Angeles, May 18, 1934. Loyola U.
HIGGINS, MICHAEL: Brooklyn, NY, Jan. 20, 1926, AmThWing.
HILL, ARTHUR: Saskatchewan, CAN., Aug. 1, 1922. U. Brit. Col.
HILL, STEVEN: Seattle, WA, Feb. 24, 1922. U. Wash.
HILL, TERENCE (Mario Girotti): Venice, Italy, Mar. 29, 1941. U. Rome.
HILLER, WENDY: Bramhall, Cheshire, Eng., Aug. 15, 1912. Winceby House School.
HILLERMAN, JOHN: Denison, TX, Dec. 20, 1932.
HILLIARD, HARRIET: (See Harriet Hilliard Nelson)
HINGLE, PAT: Denver, CO, July 19, 1923. Tex. U.
HIRSCH, JUDD: NYC, Mar. 15, 1935. AADA.
HOBEL, MARA: NYC, June 18, 1971.
HODGE, PATRICIA: Lincolnshire, Eng., 1946. LAMDA.
HOFFMAN, DUSTIN: Los Angeles, Aug. 8, 1937. Pasadena Playhouse.
HOGAN, PAUL: Australia, 1939.
HOLBROOK, HAL (Harold): Cleveland, OH, Feb. 17, 1925. Denison.
HOLLIMAN, EARL: Tennesas Swamp, Delhi, LA, Sept. 11, 1928. UCLA.
HOLM, CELESTE: NYC, Apr. 29, 1919.
HOMEIER, SKIP (George Vincent Homeier): Chicago, Oct. 5, 1930. UCLA.
HOOKS, ROBERT: Washington, DC, Apr. 18, 1937. Temple.
HOPE, BOB (Leslie Townes Hope): London, May 26, 1903.
HOPPER, DENNIS: Dodge City, KS, May 17, 1936.
HORNADAY, JEFFREY: San Jose, Ca., 1956.
HORNE, LENA: Brooklyn, June 30, 1917.
HORSLEY, LEE: May 15, 1955.
HORTON, ROBERT: Los Angeles, July 29, 1924. UCLA.
HOSKINS, BOB: Bury St. Edmunds, Eng., Oct. 26, 1942.
HOUGHTON, KATHARINE: Hartford, CT, Mar. 10, 1945. Sarah Lawrence.
HOUSER, JERRY: Los Angeles, July 14, 1952. Valley Jr. Col.
HOUSTON, DONALD: Tonypandy, Wales, 1924.
HOVEY, TIM: Los Angeles, June 19, 1945.
HOWARD, ARLISS: 1955, Independence, Mo. Columbia Col.
HOWARD, KEN: El Centro, CA, Mar. 28, 1944. Yale.
HOWARD, RON: Duncan, OK, Mar. 1, 1954. USC.
HOWARD, RONALD: Norwood, Eng., Apr. 7, 1918. Jesus College.
HOWELL, C. THOMAS: 1967.
HOWELLS, URSULA: London, Sept. 17, 1922.
HOWES, SALLY ANN: London, July 20, 1930.
HOWLAND, BETH: May 28, 1941, Boston, Ma.
HUBLEY, WHIP (Grant): 1957.
HUDDLESSON, DAVID: Vinton, VA, Sept. 17, 1930.
HUDDLESTON, MICHAEL: Roanoke, VA., AADA.
HUGHES, BARNARD: Bedford Hills, NY, July 16, 1915. Manhattan Col.
HUGHES, KATHLEEN (Betty von Gerkan): Hollywood, CA, Nov. 14, 1928. UCLA.
HULCE, TOM: Plymouth, MI, Dec. 6, 1953. N.C.Sch. of Arts.
HUNNICUT, GAYLE: Ft. Worth, TX, Feb. 6, 1943. UCLA.
HUNT, LINDA: Morristown, NJ, Apr. 2, 1945. Goodman Theatre.
HUNT, MARSHA: Chicago, Oct. 17, 1917.
HUNTER, HOLLY: Atlanta, Ga, Mar. 20, 1958, Carnegie-Mellon.
HUNTER, KIM (Janet Cole): Detroit, Nov. 12, 1922.
HUNTER, TAB (Arthur Gelien) NYC, July 11, 1931.
HUPPERT, ISABELLE: Paris, Fr., Mar. 16, 1955.
HURT, JOHN: Jan. 22, 1940. Lincolnshire, Eng.
HURT, MARY BETH (Supinger): Sept. 26, 1948, Marshalltown, Ia. NYU
HURT, WILLIAM: Washington, D.C., Mar. 20, 1950. Tufts, Juilliard.
HUSSEY, RUTH: Providence, RI, Oct. 30, 1917. U. Mich.
HUTTON, BETTY (Betty Thornberg): Battle Creek, MI, Feb. 26, 1921.
HUTTON, LAUREN (Mary): Charleston, SC, Nov. 17, 1943. Newcomb Col.
HUTTON, ROBERT (Winne): Kingston, NY, June 11, 1920. Blair Academy.
HUTTON, TIMOTHY: Malibu, CA, Aug. 16, 1960.
HYDE-WHITE, WILFRID: Gloucestershire, Eng., May 13, 1903. RADA.
HYER, MARTHA: Fort Worth, TX, Aug. 10, 1924. Northwestern U.
IGLESIAS, JULIO: Madrid, Spain, Sept. 23, 1943.
INGELS, MARTY: Brooklyn, NY, Mar. 9, 1936.
IRELAND, JOHN: Vancouver, B.C., CAN., Jan. 30, 1914.
IRONS, JEREMY: Cowes, Eng. Sept. 19, 1948. Old Vic.
IVANEK, ZELJKO: Lujubljana, Yugo., Aug. 15, 1957. Yale, LAMDA.
IVES, BURL: Hunt Township, IL, June 14, 1909. Charleston ILL. Teachers College.
IVEY, JUDITH: El Paso, Tx, Sept. 4, 1951.
JACKSON, ANNE: Alleghany, PA, Sept. 3, 1926. Neighborhood Playhouse.
JACKSON, GLENDA: Hoylake, Cheshire, Eng., May 9, 1936. RADA.
JACKSON, KATE: Birmingham, AL. Oct. 29, 1948. AADA.
JACKSON, MICHAEL: Gary, Ind., Aug. 29, 1958.
JACOBI, DEREK: Leytonstone, London, Eng. Oct. 22, 1938. Cambridge.
JACOBI, LOU: Toronto, CAN., Dec. 28, 1913.
JACOBS, LAWRENCE-HILTON: Virgin Islands, 1954.
JACOBY, SCOTT: Chicago, Nov. 19, 1956.
JAECKEL, RICHARD: Long Beach, NY, Oct. 10, 1926.
JAGGER, DEAN: Lima, OH, Nov. 7, 1903. Wabash College.
JAGGER, MICK: Dartford, Kent, Eng. July 26, 1943.

JAMES, CLIFTON: NYC, May 29, 1921. Ore. U.
JAMES, JOHN (Anderson): Apr. 18, 1956, New Canaan, Ct., AADA.
JARMAN, CLAUDE, JR.: Nashville, TN, Sept. 27, 1934.
JASON, RICK: NYC, May 21, 1926. AADA.
JEAN, GLORIA (Gloria Jean Schoonover): Buffalo, NY, Apr. 14, 1927.
JEFFREYS, ANNE (Carmichael): Goldsboro, NC, Jan. 26, 1923. Anderson College.
JEFFRIES, LIONEL: London, 1927, RADA.
JERGENS, ADELE: Brooklyn, Nov. 26, 1922.
JETT, ROGER (Baker): Cumberland, MD., Oct. 2, 1946. AADA.
JILLIAN, ANN (Nauseda): Massachusetts, Jan. 29, 1951.
JOHN, ELTON: (Reginald Dwight) Middlesex, Eng., Mar. 25, 1947. RAM.
JOHNS, GLYNIS: Durban, S. Africa, Oct. 5, 1923.
JOHNSON, BEN: Pawhuska, Ok, June 13, 1918.
JOHNSON, DON: Galena, Mo., Dec. 15, 1950. UKan.
JOHNSON, PAGE: Welch, WV, Aug. 25, 1930. Ithaca.
JOHNSON, RAFER: Hillsboro, TX, Aug. 18, 1935. UCLA.
JOHNSON, RICHARD: Essex, Eng., 1927. RADA.
JOHNSON, ROBIN: Brooklyn, NY: May 29, 1964.
JOHNSON, VAN: Newport, RI, Aug. 28, 1916.
JONES, CHRISTOPHER: Jackson, TN, Aug. 18, 1941. Actors Studio.
JONES, DEAN: Morgan County, AL, Jan. 25, 1936. Actors Studio.
JONES, JACK: Bel-Air, CA, Jan. 14, 1938.
JONES, JAMES EARL: Arkabutla, MS, Jan. 17, 1931. U. Mich.
JONES, JENNIFER (Phyllis Isley): Tulsa, OK, Mar. 2, 1919. AADA.
JONES, SAM J.: Chicago, IL, 1954.
JONES, SHIRLEY: Smithton, PA, March 31, 1934.
JONES, TOM (Thomas Jones Woodward): Pontypridd, Wales, June 7, 1940.
JONES, TOMMY LEE: San Saba, TX, Sept. 15, 1946. Harvard.
JORDAN, RICHARD: NYC, July 19, 1938. Harvard.
JOURDAN, LOUIS: Marseilles, France, June 18, 1920.
JOY, ROBERT: Montreal, Can, Aug. 17, 1951, Oxford.
JULIA, RAUL: San Juan, PR, Mar. 9, 1940. U PR.
JURADO, KATY (Maria Christina Jurado Garcia): Guadalajara, Mex., Jan. 16, 1927.
KAHN, MADELINE: Boston, MA, Sept. 29, 1942. Hofstra U.
KANE, CAROL: Cleveland, OH, June 18, 1952.
KAPLAN, JONATHAN: Paris, Nov. 25, 1947. NYU.
KAPLAN, MARVIN: Brooklyn, Jan. 24, 1924.
KAPOOR, SHASHI: Bombay 1940.
KAPRISKY, VALERIE: Paris, 1963.
KATT, WILLIAM: Los Angeles, CA, Feb. 16, 1955.
KAUFMANN, CHRISTINE: Lansdorf, Graz, Austria, Jan. 11, 1945.
KAVNER, JULIE: Burbank, CA, Sept. 7, 1951, UCLA.
KAYE, STUBBY: NYC, Nov. 11, 1918.
KAZAN, LAINIE (Levine): May 15, 1942, Brooklyn
KEACH, STACY: Savannah, GA, June 2, 1941. U. Cal., Yale.
KEATON, DIANE (Hall): Los Angeles, CA, Jan. 5, 1946. Neighborhood Playhouse.
KEATON, MICHAEL: Coraopolis, Pa., 1951. KentStateU.
KEATS, STEVEN: Bronx, NY, 1945.
KEDROVA, LILA: Leningrad, 1918.
KEEL, HOWARD (Harold Leek): Gillespie, IL, Apr. 13, 1919.
KEELER, RUBY (Ethel): Halifax, N.S., Aug. 25, 1909.
KEITH, BRIAN: Bayonne, NJ, Nov. 15, 1921.
KEITH, DAVID: Knoxville, Tn., May 8, 1954. UTN.
KELLER, MARTHE: Basel, Switz., 1945. Munich Stanislavsky Sch.
KELLERMAN, SALLY: Long Beach, CA, June 2, 1938. Actors Studio West.
KELLEY, DeFOREST: Atlanta, GA, Jan. 20, 1920.
KELLY, GENE: Pittsburgh, Aug. 23, 1912. U. Pittsburgh.
KELLY, JACK: Astoria, NY, Sept. 16, 1927. UCLA.
KELLY, NANCY: Lowell, MA, Mar. 25, 1921. Bentley School.
KEMP, JEREMY: (Wacker) Chesterfield, Eng., Feb. 3, 1935, Central Sch.
KENNEDY, ARTHUR: Worcester, MA, Feb. 17, 1914. Carnegie Tech.
KENNEDY, GEORGE: NYC, Feb. 18, 1925.
KENNEDY, LEON ISAAC: Cleveland, OH., 1949.
KERR, DEBORAH: Helensburg, Scot., Sept. 30, 1921. Smale Ballet School.
KERR, JOHN: NYC, Nov. 15, 1931. Harvard, Columbia.
KEYES, EVELYN: Nov. 20, 1917, Port Arthur, Tx.
KHAMBATTA, PERSIS: Bombay, Oct. 2, 1950.
KIDDER, MARGOT: Yellow Knife, CAN., Oct. 17, 1948. UBC.
KIER, UDO: Germany, Oct. 14, 1944.
KILEY, RICHARD: Chicago, Mar. 31, 1922. Loyola.
KILMER, VAL: 1960, Juilliard.
KINCAID, ARON (Norman Neale Williams III): Los Angeles, June 15, 1943. UCLA.
KING, ALAN (Irwin Kniberg): Brooklyn, Dec. 26, 1927.
KING, PERRY: Alliance, OH, Apr. 30, 1948. Yale.
KINGSLEY, BEN (Krishna Bhanji): Snaiton, Yorkshire, Eng., Dec. 31, 1943.
KINSKI, CLAUS: (Claus Gunther Nakszynski) Sopot, Poland, 1926.
KINSKI, NASTASSJA: Germany, Jan. 24, 1960.
KIRKLAND, SALLY: 1943, NYC Actors Studio
KITT, EARTHA: North, SC, Jan. 26, 1928.
KLEMPERER, WERNER: Cologne, Mar. 22, 1920.
KLINE, KEVIN: St. Louis, Mo, Oct. 24, 1947, Juilliard.
KLUGMAN, JACK: Philadelphia, PA, Apr. 27, 1925. Carnegie Tech.
KNIGHT, MICHAEL: 1959, Princeton, NJ
KNIGHT, SHIRLEY: Goessel, KS, July 5, 1937. Wichita U.
KNOWLES, PATRIC (Reginald Lawrence Knowles): Horsforth, Eng., Nov. 11, 1911.
KNOX, ALEXANDER: Strathroy, Ont., CAN., Jan. 16, 1907.
KNOX, ELYSE: Hartford, CT, Dec. 14, 1917. Traphagen School.
KOENIG, WALTER: Chicago, IL, Sept. 14. UCLA.
KOHNER, SUSAN: Los Angeles, Nov. 11, 1936. U. Calif.
KORMAN, HARVEY: Chicago, IL, Feb. 15, 1927. Goodman.
KORVIN, CHARLES (Geza Korvin Karpathi): Czechoslovakia, Nov. 21. Sorbonne.
KOSLECK, MARTIN: Barkotzen, Ger., Mar. 24, 1907. Max Reinhardt School.
KOTTO, YAPHET: NYC, Nov. 15, 1937.
KRABBE, JEROEN: Holland 1944.
KREUGER, KURT: St. Moritz, Switz., July 23, 1917. U. London.
KRISTEL, SYLVIA: Amsterdam, Hol., Sept. 28, 1952.
KRISTOFFERSON, KRIS: Brownsville, TX, June 22, 1936, Pomona Col.
KRUGER, HARDY: Berlin Ger., April 12, 1928.
KULP, NANCY: Harrisburg, PA, Aug. 28, 1921.
KUNTSMANN, DORIS: Hamburg, 1944.
KWAN, NANCY: Hong Kong, May 19, 1939. Royal Ballet.
LaBELLE, PATTI: Philadelphia, Pa., May 24, 1944.
LACY, JERRY: Sioux City, IA, Mar. 27, 1936. LACC.
LADD, CHERYL: (Stoppelmoor): Huron, SD, July 12, 1951.
LADD, DIANE: (Ladnier): Meridian, MS, Nov. 29, 1932. Tulane U.
LaGRECA, PAUL: Bronx, NY, June 23, 1962. AADA.
LAHTI, CHRISTINE: Detroit, MI, Apr. 4, 1950; U. Mich.
LAMARR, HEDY (Hedwig Kiesler): Vienna, Sept. 11, 1913.
LAMAS, LORENZO: Los Angeles, Jan. 28, 1958.
LAMB, GIL: Minneapolis, June 14, 1906. U. Minn.
LAMBERT, CHRISTOPHER: NYC, 1958.
LAMOUR, DOROTHY (Mary Dorothy Slaton): New Orleans, LA.; Dec. 10, 1914. Spence School.
LANCASTER, BURT: NYC, Nov. 2, 1913. NYU.
LANDAU, MARTIN: Brooklyn, NY, June 20, 1931. Actors Studio.
LANDON, MICHAEL (Eugene Orowitz): Collingswood, NJ, Oct. 31, 1936. USC.
LANDRUM, TERI: Enid, OK., 1960.
LANE, ABBE: Brooklyn, Dec. 14, 1935.
LANE, DIANE: NYC, Jan. 1963.
LANGAN, GLENN: Denver, CO, July 8, 1917.
LANGE, HOPE: Redding Ridge, CT, Nov. 28, 1933. Reed Col.
LANGE, JESSICA: Cloquet, Mn, Apr. 20, 1949. U. Minn.
LANSBURY, ANGELA: London, Oct. 16, 1925. London Academy of Music.
LANGELLA, FRANK: Bayonne, NJ, Jan. 1, 1940, SyracuseU.
LANSING, ROBERT (Brown): San Diego, CA, June 5, 1929.

Piper Laurie

Ralph Macchio

Emily Lloyd

Stephen McHattie

Marsha Mason

Robert Mitchum

LaPLANTE, LAURA: Nov. 1, 1904, St. Louis, Mo.
LARROQUETTE, JOHN: Nov. 25, 1947, New Orleans, LA.
LASSER, LOUISE: Apr. 11, 1939, NYC. Brandeis U.
LAUPER, CYNTHIA: Astoria, Queens, NYC. June 20, 1953.
LAURE, CAROLE: Montreal, Can., 1951.
LAURIE, PIPER (Rosetta Jacobs): Detroit, MI, Jan. 22, 1932.
LAW, JOHN PHILLIP: Hollywood, Sept. 7, 1937. Neighborhood Playhouse, U. Hawaii.
LAWRENCE, BARBARA: Carnegie, OK, Feb. 24, 1930. UCLA.
LAWRENCE, CAROL (Laraia): Melrose Park, IL, Sept. 5, 1935.
LAWRENCE, VICKI: Inglewood, CA, Mar. 26, 1949.
LAWSON, LEIGH: Atherston, Eng., July 21, 1945. RADA.
LEACHMAN, CLORIS: Des Moines, IA, Apr. 30, 1930. Northwestern U.
LEAUD, JEAN-PIERRE: Paris, 1944.
LEDERER, FRANCIS: Karlin, Prague, Czech., Nov. 6, 1906.
LEE, BRANDON: Feb. 1, 1965. EmersonCol.
LEE, CHRISTOPHER: London, May 27, 1922. Wellington College.
LEE, PEGGY (Norma Delores Egstrom): Jamestown, ND, May 26, 1920.
LEE, MARK: Australia, 1958.
LEE, MICHELE (Dusiak): Los Angeles, June 24, 1942. LACC.
LEIBMAN, RON: NYC, Oct. 11, 1937. Ohio Wesleyan.
LEIGH, JANET (Jeanette Helen Morrison): Merced, CA, July 6, 1926. College of Pacific.
LEMMON, JACK: Boston, Feb. 8, 1925. Harvard.
LENO, JAY: Apr. 28, 1950, New Rochelle, NY. Emerson Col.
LENZ, RICK: Springfield, IL, Nov. 21, 1939. U. Mich.
LEONARD, SHELDON (Bershad): NYC, Feb. 22, 1907, Syracuse U.
LEROY, PHILIPPE: Paris, Oct. 15, 1930. U. Paris.
LESLIE, BETHEL: NYC, Aug. 3, 1929. Brearley School.
LESLIE, JOAN (Joan Brodell): Detroit, Jan. 26, 1925. St. Benedict's.
LESTER, MARK: Oxford, Eng., July 11, 1958.
LEVELS, CALVIN: Cleveland, OH., Sept. 30, 1954. CCC.
LEVIN, RACHEL: 1954, NYC. Goddard Col.
LEWIS, CHARLOTTE: London, 1968.
LEWIS, DANIEL DAY: London, 1958, Bristol Old Vic.
LEWIS, EMMANUEL: Brooklyn, NY, March 9, 1971.
LEWIS, JERRY: Newark, NJ, Mar. 16, 1926.
LIGON, TOM: New Orleans, LA, Sept. 10, 1945.
LILLIE, BEATRICE: Toronto, Can., May 29, 1898.
LINCOLN, ABBEY (Anna Marie Woolridge): Chicago, Aug. 6, 1930.
LINDFORS, VIVECA: Uppsala, Sweden, Dec. 29, 1920. Stockholm Royal Dramatic School.
LINN-BAKER, MARK: St. Louis, Mo, June 17, 1954, Yale.
LIOTTA, RAY: 1955, Newark, NJ. UMiami.
LISI, VIRNA: Rome, Nov. 8, 1937.
LITHGOW, JOHN: Rochester, NY, Oct. 19, 1945. Harvard.
LITTLE, CLEAVON: Chickasha, OK, June 1, 1939. San Diego State.
LLOYD, EMILY: 1970, London.
LOCKE, SONDRA: Shelbyville, TN, May, 28, 1947.
LOCKHART, JUNE: NYC, June 25, 1925. Westlake School.
LOCKWOOD, GARY: Van Nuys, CA, Feb. 21, 1937.
LOCKWOOD, MARGARET: Karachi, Pakistan, Sept. 15, 1916. RADA.
LOGGIA, ROBERT: Staten Island, NY., Jan. 3, 1930. UMo.
LOLLOBRIGIDA, GINA: Subiaco, Italy, July 4, 1927. Rome Academy of Fine Arts.
LOM, HERBERT: Prague, Czechoslovakia, Jan 9, 1917. Prague U.
LOMEZ, CELINE: Montreal, Can., 1953.
LONDON, JULIE (Julie Peck): Santa Rosa, CA, Sept. 26, 1926.
LONE, JOHN: 1952, Hong Kong. AADA
LONG, SHELLEY: Ft. Wayne, IN, Aug. 23, 1949. Northwestern U.
LONOW, MARK: Brooklyn, NY.
LOPEZ, PERRY: NYC, July 22, 1931. NYU.
LORD, JACK (John Joseph Ryan): NYC, Dec. 30, 1928. NYU.
LOREN, SOPHIA (Sofia Scicolone): Rome, Italy, Sept. 20, 1934.
LOUISE, TINA (Blacker): NYC, Feb. 11, 1934, Miami U.
LOWE, CHAD: NYC, Jan, 15, 1968.
LOWE, ROB: Ohio, 1964.
LOWITSCH, KLAUS: Berlin, Apr. 8, 1936. Vienna Academy.
LOY, MYRNA (Myrna Williams): Helena, MT, Aug. 2, 1905. Westlake School.
LUCAS, LISA: Arizona, 1961.
LULU: Glasglow, Scot., 1948.
LUNA, BARBARA: NYC, Mar. 2, 1939.
LUND, JOHN: Rochester, NY, Feb. 6, 1913.
LUNDGREN, DOLPH: Stockholm, Sw., 1959. Royal Inst.
LUPINO, IDA: London, Feb. 4, 1916. RADA.
LuPONE, PATTI: Northport, NY, Apr. 21, 1949, Juilliard.
LYDON, JAMES: Harrington Park, NJ, May 30, 1923.
LYNLEY, CAROL (Jones): NYC, Feb. 13, 1942.
LYNN, JEFFREY: Auburn, MA, 1909. Bates College.
LYON, SUE: Davenport, IA, July 10, 1946.
LYONS, ROBERT F.: Albany, NY. AADA.
MacARTHUR, JAMES: Los Angeles, Dec. 8, 1937. Harvard.
MACCHIO, RALPH: Huntington, NY., Nov. 4, 1961.
MacGINNIS, NIALL: Dublin, Ire., Mar. 29, 1913. Dublin U.
MacGRAW, ALI: NYC, Apr. 1, 1938. Wellesley.
MacLAINE, SHIRLEY (Beatty): Richmond, VA, Apr. 24, 1934.
MacLEOD, GAVIN: Mt. Kisco, NY, Feb. 28, 1931.
MacMAHON, ALINE: McKeesport, PA, May 3, 1899. Barnard College.
MacMURRAY, FRED: Kankakee, IL, Aug. 30, 1908. Carroll Col.
MACNAUGHTON, ROBERT: NYC, Dec. 19, 1966.
MACNEE, PATRICK: London, Feb. 1922.
MacNICOL, PETER: Dallas, TX, Apr. 10, UMN.
MADISON, GUY (Robert Moseley): Bakersfield, CA, Jan. 19, 1922. Bakersfield Jr. College.
MADONNA (Madonna Louise Veronica Cicone): Aug. 16, 1958, Bay City, MI. UMi.
MAHARIS, GEORGE: Astoria, NY, Sept. 1, 1928. Actors Studio.
MAHONEY, JOCK (Jacques O'Mahoney): Chicago, Feb. 7, 1919. U. of Iowa.
MAHONEY, JOHN: Manchester, Eng., June 20, 1940, WUIll.
MAILER, KATE: 1962, NYC
MAJORS, LEE: Wyandotte, MI, Apr. 23, 1940. E. Ky. State Col.
MAKEPEACE, CHRIS: Toronto, Can., 1964.
MALDEN, KARL. (Mladen Sekulovich): Gary, IN, Mar. 22, 1914.
MALET, PIERRE: St. Tropez, Fr., 1955.
MALKOVICH, JOHN: Christopher, IL, Dec. 9, 1953, IllStateU.
MALLE, JADE: 1974, France.
MALONE, DOROTHY: Chicago, Jan. 30, 1925. S. Methodist U.
MANN, KURT: Roslyn, NY, July 18, 1947.
MANOFF, DINAH: NYC, Jan. 25, 1958. CalArts.
MANTEGNA, JOE: Chicago, IL, Nov. 13, 1947, Goodman Theatre.
MANZ, LINDA: NYC, 1961.
MARAIS, JEAN: Cherbourg, France, Dec. 11, 1913. St. Germain.

MARGOLIN, JANET: NYC, July 25, 1943. Walden School.
MARIN, JACQUES: Paris, Sept. 9, 1919. Conservatoire National.
MARINARO, ED: NYC, 1951. Cornell.
MARSHALL, BRENDA (Ardis Anderson Gaines): Isle of Negros, P.I., Sept. 29, 1915. Texas State College.
MARSHALL, E. G.: Owatonna, MN, June 18, 1910. U. Minn.
MARSHALL, KEN: NYC, 1953. Juilliard.
MARSHALL, PENNY: Bronx, NY, Oct. 15, 1942. U. N. Mex.
MARSHALL, WILLIAM: Gary, IN, Aug. 19, 1924. NYU.
MARTIN, DEAN (Dino Crocetti): Steubenville, OH, June 17, 1917.
MARTIN, GEORGE N.: NYC, Aug. 15, 1929.
MARTIN, MARY: Weatherford, TX, Dec. 1, 1914. Ward-Belmont School.
MARTIN, STEVE: Waco, TX, 1945. UCLA.
MARTIN, TONY (Alfred Norris): Oakland, CA, Dec. 25, 1913. St. Mary's College.
MASON, MARSHA: St. Louis, MO, Apr. 3, 1942. Webster Col.
MASON, PAMELA (Pamela Kellino): Westgate, Eng., Mar. 10, 1918.
MASSEN, OSA: Copenhagen, Den., Jan. 13, 1916.
MASSEY, DANIEL: London, Oct. 10, 1933. Eton and King's Col.
MASTERS, BEN: Corvallis, Or, May 6, 1947, UOr.
MASTERSON, MARY STUART: NYC, 1967, NYU.
MASTERSON, PETER: Angleton, TX, June 1, 1934. Rice U.
MASTRANTONIO, MARY ELIZABETH: Chicago, Il., Nov. 17, 1958. UIll.
MASTROIANNI, MARCELLO: Fontana Liri, Italy, Sept. 28, 1924.
MATHESON, TIM: Glendale, CA, Dec. 31, 1947. CalState.
MATHIS, JOHNNY: San Francisco, Ca., Sept. 30, 1935. SanFranStateCol.
MATLIN, MARLEE: Morton Grove, IL., Aug. 24, 1965.
MATTHAU, WALTER (Matuschanskayasky): NYC, Oct. 1, 1920.
MATTHEWS, BRIAN: Philadelphia, PA, Jan. 24, 1953. St. Olaf.
MATURE, VICTOR: Louisville, KY, Jan. 29, 1915.
MAY, ELAINE (Berlin): Philadelphia, Apr. 21, 1932.
MAYEHOFF, EDDIE: Baltimore, July 7. Yale.
MAYO, VIRGINIA (Virginia Clara Jones): St. Louis, MO, Nov. 30, 1920.
McCALLUM, DAVID: Scotland, Sept. 19, 1933. Chapman Col.
McCAMBRIDGE, MERCEDES: Jolliet, IL, Mar. 17, 1918. Mundelein College.
McCARTHY, ANDREW: NYC, 1963, NYU.
McCARTHY, KEVIN: Seattle, WA, Feb. 15, 1914. Minn. U.
MC CARTNEY, PAUL: Liverpool, England, June 18,1942.
McCLANAHAN, RUE: Healdton, OK, Feb. 21, 1935.
McCLORY, SEAN: Dublin, Ire., Mar. 8, 1924. U. Galway.
McCLURE, DOUG: Glendale, CA, May 11, 1935. UCLA.
McCOWEN, ALEC: Tunbridge Wells, Eng., May 26, 1925. RADA.
McCRARY, DARIUS: 1976, Walnut, Ca.
McCREA, JOEL: Los Angeles, Nov. 5, 1905. Pomona College.
McDERMOTT, DYLAN: 1962, NYC. Neighborhood Playhouse
McDOWALL, RODDY: London, Sept. 17, 1928. St. Joseph's.
McDOWELL, MALCOLM (Taylor): Leeds, Eng., June 19, 1943. LAMDA.
McENERY, PETER: Walsall, Eng., Feb. 21, 1940.
McFARLAND, SPANKY: Dallas, TX, Oct. 2, 1926.
McGAVIN, DARREN: Spokane, WA, May 7, 1922. College of Pacific.
McGILLIS, KELLY: Newport Beach, CA, July 9, 1957. Juilliard.
McGOVERN, ELIZABETH: Evanston, IL, July 18, 1961. Juilliard.
McGOVERN, MAUREEN: Youngstown, OH, July 27, 1949.
McGREGOR, JEFF: 1957, Chicago. UMn.
McGUIRE, BIFF: New Haven, CT. Oct. 25, 1926. Mass. State Col.
McGUIRE, DOROTHY: Omaha, NE, June 14, 1918.
McHATTIE, STEPHEN: Antigonish, NS, Feb. 3. AcadiaU, AADA.
McKAY, GARDNER: NYC, June 10, 1932. Cornell.
McKEE, LONETTE: Detroit, MI, 1954.
McKELLEN, IAN: Burnley, Eng., May 25, 1939.
McKENNA, VIRGINIA: London, June 7, 1931.
McKEON, DOUG: New Jersey, 1966.
McKUEN, ROD: Oakland, CA, Apr. 29, 1933.
McLERIE, ALLYN ANN: Grand Mere, Can., Dec. 1, 1926.
McNAIR, BARBARA: Chicago, Mar. 4, 1939. UCLA.
McNALLY, STEPHEN (Horace McNally): NYC, July 29, 1913. Fordham U.
McNICHOL, KRISTY: Los Angeles, CA, Sept. 11, 1962.
McQUEEN, ARMELIA: North Carolina, Jan. 6, 1952. Bklyn Consv.
McQUEEN, BUTTERFLY: Tampa, FL, Jan. 8, 1911. UCLA.
McQUEEN, CHAD: Los Angeles, CA, 1961. Actors Studio.
MEADOWS, AUDREY: Wuchang, China, 1924. St. Margaret's.
MEADOWS, JAYNE (formerly, Jayne Cotter): Wuchang, China, Sept. 27, 1920. St. Margaret's.
MEARA, ANNE: Brooklyn, NY, Sept. 20, 1929.
MEDWIN, MICHAEL: London, 1925. Instut Fischer.
MEISNER, GUNTER: Bremen, Ger., Apr. 18, 1926. Municipal Drama School.
MEKKA, EDDIE: Worcester, MA, 1932. Boston Cons.
MELATO, MARIANGELA: Milan, Italy, 1941. Milan Theatre Acad.
MELL, MARISA: Vienna, Austria, Feb. 25, 1939.
MERCADO, HECTOR JAIME: NYC, 1949. HB Studio.
MERCOURI, MELINA: Athens, Greece, Oct. 18, 1915.
MEREDITH, BURGESS: Cleveland, OH, Nov. 16, 1908. Amherst.
MEREDITH, LEE (Judi Lee Sauls): Oct., 1947. AADA.
MERRILL, DINA (Nedinia Hutton): NYC, Dec. 9, 1925. AADA.
MERRILL, GARY: Hartford, CT, Aug. 2, 1915. Bowdoin, Trinity.
METZLER, JIM: Oneonda, NY. Dartmouth Col.
MICHELL, KEITH: Adelaide, Aus., Dec. 1, 1926.
MIDLER, BETTE: Honolulu, HI., Dec. 1, 1945.
MIFUNE, TOSHIRO: Tsingtao, China, Apr. 1, 1920.
MILANO, ALYSSA: Brooklyn, NY, 1975.
MILES, JOANNA: Nice, France, Mar. 6, 1940.
MILES, SARAH: Ingatestone, Eng., Dec. 31, 1941. RADA.
MILES, SYLVIA: NYC, Sept. 9, 1932. Actors Studio.
MILES, VERA (Ralston): Boise City, OK, Aug. 23, 1929. UCLA.
MILFORD, PENELOPE: Winnetka, IL.
MILLER, ANN (Lucille Ann Collier): Chireno, TX, Apr. 12, 1919. Lawler Professional School.
MILLER, BARRY: Los Angeles, Ca., Feb. 6, 1958
MILLER, JASON: Long Island City, NY, Apr. 22, 1939. Catholic U.
MILLER, LINDA: NYC, Sept. 16, 1942. Catholic U.
MILLER, REBECCA: 1962, Roxbury, Ct. Yale.
MILLS, HAYLEY: London, Apr. 18, 1946. Elmhurst School.
MILLS, JOHN: Suffolk, Eng., Feb. 22, 1908.
MILNER, MARTIN: Detroit, MI, Dec. 28, 1931.
MIMIEUX, YVETTE: Los Angeles, Jan. 8, 1941. Hollywood High.
MINNELLI, LIZA: Los Angeles, Mar. 12, 1946.
MIOU-MIOU: Paris, Feb. 22, 1950.
MITCHELL, CAMERON (Mizell): Dallastown, PA, Nov. 4, 1918. N.Y. Theatre School.
MITCHELL, JAMES: Sacramento, CA, Feb. 29, 1920. LACC.
MITCHUM, JAMES: Los Angeles, CA, May 8, 1941.
MITCHUM, ROBERT: Bridgeport, CT, Aug. 6, 1917.
MODINE, MATTHEW: 1960, Utah
MOLINA, ALFRED: 1954, London. Guildhall
MONTALBAN, RICARDO: Mexico City, Nov. 25, 1920.
MONTAND, YVES (Yves Montand Livi): Mansummano, Tuscany, Oct. 13, 1921.
MONTGOMERY, BELINDA: Winnipeg, Can., July 23, 1950.
MONTGOMERY, ELIZABETH: Los Angeles, Apr. 15, 1933. AADA.
MONTGOMERY, GEORGE (George Letz): Brady, MT, Aug. 29, 1916. U. Mont.
MOOR, BILL: Toledo, OH, July 13, 1931. Northwestern.
MOORE, CONSTANCE: Sioux City, IA, Jan. 18, 1919.
MOORE, DEMI (Guines): Roswell, NMx, Nov. 11, 1962.
MOORE, DICK: Los Angeles, Sept. 12, 1925.
MOORE, DUDLEY: Apr. 19, 1935, Dagenham, Essex, Eng.
MOORE, FRANK: Bay-de-Verde, Newfoundland, 1946.
MOORE, KIERON: County Cork, Ire., 1925. St. Mary's College.
MOORE, MARY TYLER: Brooklyn, Dec. 29, 1936.
MOORE, ROGER: London, Oct. 14, 1927. RADA.

Judd Nelson

Dolly Parton

Don Nute

Michelle Phillips

Michael Pare

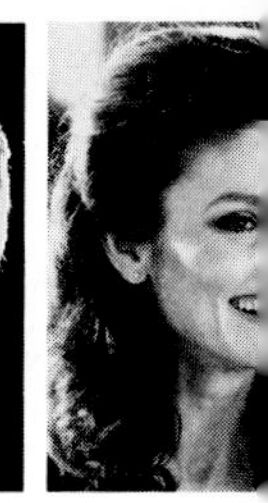
Paula Prenti

MOORE, TERRY (Helen Koford): Los Angeles, Jan. 7, 1929.
MORALES, ESAI: Brooklyn, 1963.
MOREAU, JEANNE: Paris, Jan. 23, 1928.
MORENO, RITA (Rosita Alverio): Humacao, P.R., Dec. 11, 1931.
MORGAN, DENNIS (Stanley Morner): Prentice, WI, Dec. 10, 1910. Carroll College.
MORGAN, HARRY (HENRY) (Harry Bratsburg): Detroit, Apr. 10, 1915. U. Chicago.
MORGAN, MICHELE (Simone Roussel): Paris, Feb. 29, 1920. Paris Dramatic School.
MORIARTY, CATHY: Bronx, NY, 1961.
MORIARTY, MICHAEL: Detroit, MI, Apr. 5, 1941. Dartmouth.
MORISON, PATRICIA: NYC, 1915.
MORITA, NORIYUKU "PAT": June 28, 1933, Isleton, Ca.
MORLEY, ROBERT: Wiltshire, Eng., May 26, 1908. RADA.
MORRIS, ANITA: Durham, NC, 1932.
MORRIS, GREG: Cleveland, OH, Sept. 27, 1934. Ohio State.
MORRIS, HOWARD: NYC, Sept. 4, 1919. NYU.
MORSE, DAVID: Hamilton, MA, 1953.
MORSE, ROBERT: Newton, MA, May 18, 1931.
MORTON, JOE: NYC, Oct. 18, 1947, HofstraU.
MOSS, ARNOLD: NYC, Jan. 28, 1910. CCNY.
MOUCHET, CATHERINE: Paris, 1959, Ntl. Consv.
MOYA, EDDY: El Paso, TX, Apr. 11, 1963. LACC.
MULHERN, MATT: Philadelphia, PA, July 21, 1960. Rutgers Univ.
MULL, MARTIN: N. Ridgefield, Oh., Aug. 18, 1941. RISch. of Design.
MULLIGAN, RICHARD: NYC, Nov. 13, 1932.
MURPHY, EDDIE: Brooklyn, NY, Apr. 3, 1961.
MURPHY, GEORGE: New Haven, CT, July 4, 1902. Yale.
MURPHY, MICHAEL: Los Angeles, CA, May 5, 1938, UAz.
MURRAY, BILL: Evanston, IL, Sept. 21, 1950. Regis Col.
MURRAY, DON: Hollywood, July 31, 1929. AADA.
MUSANTE, TONY: Bridgeport, CT, June 30, 1936. Oberlin Col.
NABORS, JIM: Sylacauga, GA, June 12, 1932.
NADER, GEORGE: Pasadena, CA, Oct. 19, 1921. Occidental College.
NADER, MICHAEL: Los Angeles, CA, 1945.
NAMATH, JOE: Beaver Falls, Pa, May 31, 1943. UAla.
NATWICK, MILDRED: Baltimore, June 19, 1908. Bryn Mawr.
NAUGHTON, DAVID: 1955
NAUGHTON, JAMES: Middletown, CT, Dec. 6, 1945. Yale.
NAVIN, JOHN P., JR.: Philadelphia, PA, 1968.
NEAL, PATRICIA: Packard, KY, Jan. 20, 1926. Northwestern U.
NEESON, LIAM: Ballymena, Northern Ireland, 1952.
NEFF, HILDEGARDE (Hildegard Knef): Ulm, Ger., Dec. 28, 1925. Berlin Art Academy.
NELL, NATHALIE: Paris, Oct. 1950.
NELLIGAN, KATE: London, Ont., Can., Mar. 16, 1951. U Toronto.
NELSON, BARRY (Robert Nielsen): Oakland, CA, Apr. 16, 1920.
NELSON, DAVID: NYC, Oct. 24, 1936. USC.
NELSON, GENE (Gene Berg): Seattle, WA, Mar. 24, 1920.
NELSON, HARRIET HILLIARD (Peggy Lou Snyder): Des Moines, IA, July 18, 1914.
NELSON, JUDD: Maine, 1959, Haverford Col.
NELSON, LORI (Dixie Kay Nelson): Santa Fe, NM, Aug. 15, 1933.
NELSON, WILLIE: Texas, Apr. 30, 1933.
NETTLETON, LOIS: Oak Park, IL. Actors Studio.
NEWHART, BOB: Chicago, IL, Sept. 5, 1929. Loyola U.
NEWLEY, ANTHONY: Hackney, London, Sept. 21, 1931.
NEWMAN, BARRY: Boston, MA, Mar. 26, 1938. Brandeis U.
NEWMAN, PAUL: Cleveland, OH, Jan. 26, 1925. Yale.
NEWMAR, JULIE (Newmeyer): Los Angeles, Aug. 16, 1935.
NEWTON-JOHN, OLIVIA: Cambridge, Eng., Sept. 26, 1948.
NGUYEN, DUSTIN: 1962, Saigon.
NICHOLAS, PAUL: London, 1945.
NICHOLS, MIKE (Michael Igor Peschkowsky): Berlin, Nov. 6, 1931. U. Chicago.
NICHOLSON, JACK: Neptune, NJ, Apr. 22, 1937.
NICKERSON, DENISE: NYC, 1959.
NICOL, ALEX: Ossining, NY, Jan. 20, 1919. Actors Studio.
NIELSEN, BRIGITTE: 1963, Denmark.
NIELSEN, LESLIE: Regina, Saskatchewan, Can., Feb. 11, 1926. Neighborhood Playhouse.
NIMOY, LEONARD: Boston, MA, Mar. 26, 1931. Boston Col., Antioch Col.
NIXON, CYNTHIA: NYC, Apr. 9, 1966. Columbia U.
NOBLE, JAMES: Dallas, TX, Mar. 5, 1922, SMU.
NOLAN, KATHLEEN: St. Louis, MO, Sept. 27, 1933. Neighborhood Playhouse.
NOLTE, NICK: Omaha, NE, Feb. 8, 1940. Pasadena City Col.
NORRIS, CHRISTOPHER: NYC, Oct. 7, 1943. Lincoln Square Acad.
NORRIS, CHUCK (Carlos Ray): Ryan, OK, 1939.
NORTH, HEATHER: Pasadena, CA, Dec. 13, 1950. Actors Workshop.
NORTH, SHEREE (Dawn Bethel): Los Angeles, Jan. 17, 1933. Hollywood High.
NORTON, KEN: Aug. 9, 1945.
NOURI, MICHAEL: Washington, DC, Dec. 9, 1945.
NOVAK, KIM (Marilyn Novak): Chicago, Feb. 18, 1933. LACC.
NUREYEV, RUDOLF: Russia, Mar. 17, 1938.
NUTE, DON: Connellsville, PA, Mar. 13, Denver U.
NUYEN, FRANCE (Vannga): Marseilles, France, July 31, 1939. Beaux Arts School.
O'BRIAN, HUGH (Hugh J. Krampe): Rochester, NY, Apr. 19, 1928. Cincinnati U.
O'BRIEN, CLAY: Ray, AZ, May 6, 1961.
O'BRIEN, MARGARET (Angela Maxine O'Brien): Los Angeles, Jan. 15, 1937.
O'CONNOR, CARROLL: Bronx, NY, Aug. 2, 1925. Dublin National Univ.
O'CONNOR, DONALD: Chicago, Aug. 28, 1925.
O'CONNOR, GLYNNIS: NYC, Nov. 19, 1956. NYSU.
O'CONNOR, KEVIN: Honolulu, HI, May 7, 1938, U. Hi.
O'DAY, DAWN: aka Anne Shirley (see).
O'HANLON, GEORGE: Brooklyn, NY, Nov. 23, 1917.
O'HARA, MAUREEN (Maureen FitzSimons): Dublin, Ire., Aug. 17, 1920. Abbey School.
O'HERLIHY, DAN: Wexford, Ire., May 1, 1919. National U.
O'KEEFE, MICHAEL: Paulland, NJ, Apr. 24, 1955, NYU, AADA.
OLDMAN, GARY: 1959, New Gross, South London, Eng.
OLIVIER, LAURENCE: Dorking, Eng., May 22, 1907. Oxford.
OLMOS, EDWARD JAMES: Feb. 24, 1947, Los Angeles, CA. CSLA.
O'LOUGHLIN, GERALD S.: NYC, Dec. 23, 1921. U. Rochester.
OLSON, NANCY: Milwaukee, WI, July 14, 1928. UCLA.
O'NEAL, GRIFFIN: Los Angeles, 1965.

O'NEAL, PATRICK: Ocala, FL, Sept. 26, 1927. U. Fla.
O'NEAL, RON: Utica, NY, Sept. 1, 1937. Ohio State.
O'NEAL, RYAN: Los Angeles, Apr. 20, 1941.
O'NEAL, TATUM: Los Angeles, Nov. 5, 1963.
O'NEIL, TRICIA: Shreveport, LA, Mar. 11, 1945. Baylor U.
O'NEILL, JENNIFER: Rio de Janeiro, Feb. 20, 1949. Neighborhood Playhouse.
O'SULLIVAN, MAUREEN: Byle, Ire., May 17, 1911. Sacred Heart Convent.
O'TOOLE, ANNETTE (Toole): Houston, TX, Apr. 1, 1952. UCLA.
O'TOOLE, PETER: Connemara, Ire., Aug. 2, 1932. RADA.
PACINO, AL: NYC, Apr. 25, 1940.
PAGE, TONY (Anthony Vitiello): Bronx, NY, 1940.
PAGET, DEBRA (Debralee Griffin): Denver, Aug. 19, 1933.
PAIGE, JANIS (Donna Mae Jaden): Tacoma, WA, Sept. 16, 1922.
PALANCE, JACK (Walter Palanuik): Lattimer, PA, Feb. 18, 1920. UNC.
PALMER, BETSY: East Chicago, IN, Nov. 1, 1929. DePaul U.
PALMER, GREGG (Palmer Lee): San Francisco, Jan. 25, 1927. U. Utah.
PAMPANINI, SILVANA: Rome, Sept. 25, 1925.
PANEBIANCO, RICHARD: 1971 NYC
PANTALIANO, JOEY: Hoboken, NJ. 1952.
PAPAS, IRENE: Chiliomodion, Greece, Mar. 9, 1929.
PARE, MICHAEL: Brooklyn, NY, 1959.
PARKER, ELEANOR: Cedarville, OH, June 26, 1922. Pasadena Playhouse.
PARKER, FESS: Fort Worth, TX, Aug. 16, 1927. USC.
PARKER, JAMESON: Baltimore, MD, Nov. 18, 1947. Beloit Col.
PARKER, JEAN (Mae Green): Deer Lodge, MT, Aug. 11, 1912.
PARKER, RAY, JR.: 1957, Detroit
PARKER, SUZY (Cecelia Parker): San Antonio, TX, Oct. 28, 1933.
PARKER, WILLARD (Worster Van Eps): NYC, Feb. 5, 1912.
PARKINS, BARBARA: Vancouver, Can., May 22, 1943.
PARSONS, ESTELLE: Lynn, MA, Nov. 20, 1927. Boston U.
PARTON, DOLLY: Sevierville, TN, Jan. 19, 1946.
PATINKIN, MANDY: Chicago, IL, Nov. 30, 1952. Juilliard.
PATRIC, JASON: 1966, NYC
PATRICK, DENNIS: Philadelphia, Mar. 14, 1918.
PATTERSON, LEE: Vancouver, Can., Mar. 31, 1929. Ontario Col.
PATTON, WILL: Charleston, SC, June 14, 1954.
PAVAN, MARISA (Marisa Pierangeli): Cagliari, Sardinia, June 19, 1932. Torquado Tasso College.
PAYNE, JOHN: Roanoke, Va., March 23, 1912.
PEACH, MARY: Durban, S. Africa, 1934.
PEARL, MINNIE (Sarah Cannon): Centerville, TN, Oct. 25, 1912.
PEARSON, BEATRICE: Denison, TX, July 27, 1920.
PECK, GREGORY: La Jolla, CA, Apr. 5, 1916. U. Calif.
PELIKAN, LISA: Paris, July 12. Juilliard.
PENHALL, BRUCE: Balboa, CA, 1958.
PENN, SEAN: Burbank, Ca., Aug. 17, 1960.
PENNY, JOE: London, 1957.
PEPPARD, GEORGE: Detroit, Oct. 1, 1928. Carnegie Tech.
PEREZ, JOSE: NYC 1940.
PERKINS, ANTHONY: NYC, Apr. 14, 1932. Rollins College.
PERKINS, ELIZABETH: Queens, NY, Nov. 18, 1960. Goodman School.
PERLMAN, RON: Apr. 13, 1950 in NYC. UMn.
PERREAU, GIGI (Ghislaine): Los Angeles, Feb. 6, 1941.
PERRINE, VALERIE: Galveston, TX, Sept. 3, 1944. U. Ariz.
PESCOW, DONNA: Brooklyn, NY, 1954.
PETERS, BERNADETTE (Lazzara): Jamaica, NY, Feb. 28, 1948.
PETERS, BROCK: NYC, July 2, 1927. CCNY.
PETERS, JEAN (Elizabeth): Canton, OH, Oct. 15, 1926. Ohio State U.
PETERS, MICHAEL: Brooklyn, NY, 1948.
PETERSON, CASSANDRA: Colorado Springs, CO, 1951.
PETTET, JOANNA: London, Nov. 16, 1944. Neighborhood Playhouse.
PFEIFFER, MICHELLE: Santa Ana, CA, 1957.
PHILLIPS, LOU DIAMOND: 1962, Phillipines, UTx.
PHILLIPS, MacKENZIE: Alexandria, VA, Nov. 10, 1959.
PHILLIPS, MICHELLE (Holly Gilliam): NJ, June 4, 1944.
PHOENIX, RAINBOW: 1973
PHOENIX, RIVER: Madras, Ore., 1970.
PICARDO, ROBERT: Philadelphia, PA, Oct. 27, 1953. Yale.
PICERNI, PAUL: NYC, Dec. 1, 1922. Loyola U.
PINCHOT, BRONSON: NYC May 20, 1959, Yale.
PINE, PHILLIP: Hanford, CA, July 16, 1925. Actors' Lab.
PISCOPO, JOE: Passaic, NJ. June 17, 1951.
PISIER, MARIE-FRANCE: Vietnam, May 10, 1944. U. Paris.
PITILLO, MARIA: 1965, Mahwah, NJ.
PLACE, MARY KAY: Port Arthur, TX, Sept., 1947. U. Tulsa.
PLAYTEN, ALICE: NYC, Aug. 28, 1947. NYU.
PLEASENCE, DONALD: Workshop, Eng., Oct. 5, 1919. Sheffield School.
PLESHETTE, SUZANNE: NYC, Jan. 31, 1937. Syracuse U.
PLOWRIGHT, JOAN: Scunthorpe, Brigg, Lincolnshire, Eng., Oct. 28, 1929. Old Vic.
PLUMB, EVE: Burbank, Ca, Apr. 29, 1958.
PLUMMER, AMANDA: NYC, Mar. 23, 1957. Middlebury Col.
PLUMMER, CHRISTOPHER: Toronto, Can., Dec. 13, 1927.
PODESTA, ROSSANA: Tripoli, June 20, 1934.
POITIER, SIDNEY: Miami, FL, Feb. 27, 1924.
POLITO, LINA: Naples, Italy, Aug. 11, 1954.
POLLAN, TRACY: 1962, NYC
POLLARD, MICHAEL J.: Pacific, NJ, May 30, 1939.
PORTER, ERIC: London, Apr. 8, 1928. Wimbledon Col.
POWELL, JANE (Suzanne Burce): Portland, OR, Apr. 1, 1928.
POWELL, ROBERT: Salford, Eng., June 1, 1944. Manchester U.
POWER, TARYN: Los Angeles, CA, 1954.
POWER, TYRONE IV: Los Angeles, CA, Jan. 1959.
POWERS, MALA (Mary Ellen): San Francisco, Dec. 29, 1921. UCLA.
POWERS, STEFANIE (Federkiewicz): Hollywood, CA, Oct. 12, 1942.
PRENTISS, PAULA (Paula Ragusa): San Antonio, TX, Mar. 4, 1939. Northwestern U.
PRESLE, MICHELINE (Micheline Chassagne): Paris, Aug. 22, 1922. Rouleau Drama School.
PRESNELL, HARVE: Modesto, CA, Sept. 14, 1933. USC.
PRESTON, WILLIAM: Columbia, Pa., Aug. 26, 1921. PaStateU.
PRICE, LONNY: NYC, Mar. 9, 1959, Juilliard.
PRICE, VINCENT: St. Louis, May 27, 1911. Yale.
PRIMUS, BARRY: NYC, Feb. 16, 1938. CCNY.
PRINCE (P. Rogers Nelson): Minneapolis, MN, June 7, 1958.
PRINCE, WILLIAM: Nicholas, NY, Jan. 26, 1913. Cornell U.
PRINCIPAL, VICTORIA: Fukuoka, Japan, Mar. 3, 1945. Dade Jr. Col.
PROCHNOW, JURGEN: Germany, 1941.
PROVAL, DAVID: Brooklyn, NY, 1943.
PROVINE, DOROTHY: Deadwood, SD, Jan. 20, 1937. U. Wash.
PROWSE, JULIET: Bombay, India, Sept. 25, 1936.
PRYCE, JONATHAN: Wales, UK, June 1, 1947, RADA.
PRYOR, RICHARD: Peoria, IL, Dec. 1, 1940.
PULLMAN, BILL: Delhi, NY, 1954, SUNY/Oneonta, UMass.
PURCELL, LEE: Cherry Point, NC, June 15, 1947. Stephens.
PURDOM, EDMUND: Welwyn Garden City, Eng., Dec. 19, 1924. St. Ignatius College.
PYLE, DENVER: Bethune, CO, May 11, 1920.
QUAID, DENNIS: Houston, TX, Apr. 9, 1954.
QUAID, RANDY: Houston, TX, 1950, UHouston.
QUAYLE, ANTHONY: Lancashire, Eng., Sept. 7, 1913. Old Vic School.
QUINE, RICHARD: Detroit, MI, Nov. 12, 1920.
QUINLAN, KATHLEEN: Mill Valley, CA, Nov. 19, 1954.
QUINN, AIDAN: Chicago, IL, Mar. 8, 1959.
QUINN, ANTHONY: Chihuahua, Mex., Apr. 21, 1915.
RADNER, GILDA: Detroit, MI, June 28, 1946.
RAFFERTY, FRANCES: Sioux City, IA, June 16, 1922. UCLA.
RAFFIN, DEBORAH: Los Angeles, Mar. 13, 1953. Valley Col.
RAINER, LUISE: Vienna, Aust., Jan. 12, 1910.
RALSTON, VERA: (Vera Helena Hruba) Prague, Czech., July 12, 1919.

Mickey Rooney

Theresa Russell

Roy Scheider

Ally Sheedy

Ray Sharkey

Ione Skye

RAMPLING, CHARLOTTE: Surmer, Eng., Feb. 5, 1946. U. Madrid.
RAMSEY, LOGAN: Long Beach, CA, Mar. 21, 1921. St. Joseph.
RANDALL, TONY (Leonard Rosenberg): Tulsa, OK, Feb. 26, 1920. Northwestern U.
RANDELL, RON: Sydney, Australia, Oct. 8, 1920. St. Mary's Col.
RASHAD, PHYLICIA (Ayers-Allen): Houston, Tx. June 17, 1948.
RASULALA, THALMUS (Jack Crowder): Miami, FL, Nov. 15, 1939. U. Redlands.
RAY, ALDO (Aldo DeRe): Pen Argyl, PA, Sept. 25, 1926. UCLA.
RAYE, MARTHA (Margie Yvonne Reed): Butte, MT, Aug. 27, 1916.
RAYMOND, GENE (Raymond Guion): NYC, Aug. 13, 1908.
REAGAN, RONALD: Tampico, IL, Feb. 6, 1911. Eureka College.
REASON, REX: Berlin, Ger., Nov. 30, 1928. Pasadena Playhouse.
REDDY, HELEN: Australia, Oct. 25, 1942.
REDFORD, ROBERT: Santa Monica, CA, Aug. 18, 1937. AADA.
REDGRAVE, CORIN: London, July 16, 1939.
REDGRAVE, LYNN: London, Mar. 8, 1943.
REDGRAVE, VANESSA: London, Jan. 30, 1937.
REDMAN, JOYCE: County Mayo, Ire., 1919. RADA.
REED, OLIVER: Wimbledon, Eng., Feb. 13, 1938.
REED, PAMELA: Tacoma, WA, Apr. 2, 1949.
REED, REX: Ft. Worth, TX, Oct. 2, 1939. LSU.
REEMS, HARRY (Herbert Streicher): Bronx, NY, 1947. U. Pittsburgh.
REEVE, CHRISTOPHER: NJ, Sept. 25, 1952. Cornell, Juilliard.
REEVES, KEANU: 1965.
REEVES, STEVE: Glasgow, MT, Jan. 21, 1926.
REGEHR, DUNCAN: Lethbridge, Can., 1954.
REID, ELLIOTT: NYC, Jan. 16, 1920.
REID, KATE: London, Nov. 4, 1930.
REINER, CARL: NYC, Mar. 20, 1922. Georgetown.
REINER, ROB: NYC, Mar. 6, 1945. UCLA.
REINHOLD, JUDGE (Edward Ernest, Jr.): Wilmington, DE, 1957. NCSchool of Arts.
REINKING, ANN: Seattle, WA, Nov. 10, 1949.
REISER, PAUL: NYC, Mar. 30, 1957.
REMAR, JAMES: Boston, Ma., Dec. 31, 1953. Neighborhood Playhouse.
REMICK, LEE: Quincy, MA. Dec. 14, 1935. Barnard College.
RETTIG, TOMMY: Jackson Heights, NY, Dec. 10, 1941.
REVILL, CLIVE: Wellington, NZ, Apr. 18, 1930.
REY, ANTONIA: Havana, Cuba, Oct. 12, 1927.
REY, FERNANDO: La Coruna, Spain, Sept. 20, 1917.
REYNOLDS, BURT: Waycross, GA, Feb. 11, 1935. Fla. State U.
REYNOLDS, DEBBIE (Mary Frances Reynolds): El Paso, TX, Apr. 1, 1932.
REYNOLDS, MARJORIE: Buhl, ID, Aug. 12, 1921.
RHOADES, BARBARA: Poughkeepsie, NY, 1947.
RICHARDS, JEFF (Richard Mansfield Taylor): Portland, OR, Nov. 1. USC.
RICHARDSON, LEE: Chicago, Sept. 11, 1926.
RICHARDSON, NATASHA: 1964, London
RICKLES, DON: NYC, May 8, 1926. AADA.
RIEGERT, PETER: NYC, Apr. 11, 1947. U Buffalo.
RIGG, DIANA: Doncaster, Eng., July 20, 1938. RADA.
RINGWALD, MOLLY: Rosewood, CA, Feb. 14, 1968.
RITTER, JOHN: Burbank, CA, Sept. 17, 1948. U.S. Cal.
RIVERS, JOAN (Molinsky): Brooklyn, NY, June 8, 1933.
ROBARDS, JASON: Chicago, July 26, 1922. AADA.
ROBERTS, ERIC: Biloxi, MS, Apr. 18, 1956. RADA.
ROBERTS, RALPH: Salisbury, NC, Aug. 17, 1922. UNC.
ROBERTS, TANYA (Leigh): NYC, 1955.
ROBERTS, TONY: NYC, Oct. 22, 1939. Northwestern U.
ROBERTSON, CLIFF: La Jolla, CA, Sept. 9, 1925. Antioch Col.
ROBERTSON, DALE: Oklahoma City, July 14, 1923.
ROBINSON, CHRIS: Nov. 5, 1938, West Palm Beach, FL. LACC.
ROBINSON, JAY: NYC, Apr. 14, 1930.
ROBINSON, ROGER: Seattle, WA, May 2, 1941. USC.
ROCHEFORT, JEAN: Paris, 1930.
ROCK-SAVAGE, STEVEN: Melville, LA, Dec. 14, 1958. LSU.
ROGERS, CHARLES "BUDDY": Olathe, KS, Aug. 13, 1904. U. Kan.
ROGERS, GINGER (Virginia Katherine McMath): Independence, MO, July 16, 1911.
ROGERS, MIMI: Coral Gables, FL, 1956
ROGERS, ROY (Leonard Slye): Cincinnati, Nov. 5, 1912.
ROGERS, WAYNE: Birmingham, AL, Apr. 7, 1933. Princeton.
ROLAND, GILBERT (Luis Antonio Damaso De Alonso): Juarez, Mex., Dec. 11, 1905.
ROLLINS, HOWARD E., JR.: 1951, Baltimore, MD.
ROMAN, RUTH: Boston, Dec. 23, 1922. Bishop Lee Dramatic School.
ROMANCE, VIVIANE (Pauline Ronacher Ortmanns): Vienna, Aust. 1912.
ROME, SIDNE: Akron, OH. Carnegie-Mellon.
ROMERO, CESAR: NYC, Feb. 15, 1907. Collegiate School.
RONSTADT, LINDA: Tucson, AZ, July 15, 1946.
ROONEY, MICKEY (Joe Yule, Jr.): Brooklyn, Sept. 23, 1920.
ROSE, REVA: Chicago, IL, July 30, 1940. Goodman.
ROSS, DIANA: Detroit, MI, Mar. 26, 1944.
ROSS, JUSTIN: Brooklyn, NY, Dec. 15, 1954.
ROSS, KATHARINE: Hollywood, Jan. 29, 1943. Santa Rosa Col.
ROSSELLINI, ISABELLA: Rome, June 18, 1952.
ROUNDTREE, RICHARD: New Rochelle, NY, Sept. 7, 1942. Southern Ill.
ROURKE, MICKEY: Miami, FL, 1950.
ROWE, NICHOLAS: London, Nov. 22, 1966. Eton.
ROWLANDS, GENA: Cambria, WI, June 19, 1934.
RUBIN, ANDREW: New Bedford, MA, June 22, 1946. AADA.
RUBINSTEIN, JOHN: Los Angeles, Ca, Dec. 8, 1946, UCLA.
RUBINSTEIN, ZELDA: Pittsburg, Pa.
RUCKER, BO: Tampa, Fl, Aug. 17, 1948.
RUDD, PAUL: Boston, MA, May 15, 1940.
RULE, JANICE: Cincinnati, OH, Aug. 15, 1931.
RUPERT, MICHAEL: Denver, CO, Oct. 23, 1951. Pasadena Playhouse.
RUSH, BARBARA: Denver, CO, Jan. 4, 1929. U. Calif.
RUSSELL, JANE: Bemidji, MI, June 21, 1921. Max Reinhardt School.
RUSSELL, JOHN: Los Angeles, Jan. 3, 1921. U. Calif.
RUSSELL, KURT: Springfield, MA, Mar. 17, 1951.
RUSSELL, THERESA: San Diego, CA, Mar. 20, 1957.
RUSSO, JAMES: NYC, Apr. 23, 1953.
RUTHERFORD, ANN: Toronto, Can., Nov. 2, 1917.

RUYMEN, AYN: Brooklyn, July 18, 1947. HB Studio.
RYAN, MEG: 1962, NYC NYU
RYAN, TIM (Meineslschmidt): 1958, Staten Island, NY. Rutgers U.
RYDER, WINONA: Winona, MN, Oct. 1971.
SACCHI, ROBERT: Bronx, NY, 1941. NYU.
SAINT, EVA MARIE: Newark, NJ, July 4, 1924. Bowling Green State U.
ST. JACQUES, RAYMOND (James Arthur Johnson):CT.
ST. JAMES, SUSAN (Suzie Jane Miller): Los Angeles, Aug. 14, 1946. Conn. Col.
ST. JOHN, BETTA: Hawthorne, CA, Nov. 26, 1929.
ST. JOHN, JILL (Jill Oppenheim): Los Angeles, Aug. 19, 1940.
SALA, JOHN: Los Angeles, CA., Oct. 5, 1962.
SALDANA, THERESA: Brooklyn, NY, 1955.
SALINGER, MATT: New Hampshire, 1960. Princeton, Columbia.
SALMI, ALBERT: Coney Island, NY, 1925. Actors Studio.
SALT, JENNIFER: Los Angeles, Sept. 4, 1944. Sarah Lawrence Col.
SANDS, TOMMY: Chicago, Aug. 27, 1937.
SAN JUAN, OLGA: NYC, Mar. 16, 1927.
SARANDON, CHRIS: Beckley, WV, July 24, 1942. U. WVa., Catholic U.
SARANDON, SUSAN (Tomalin): NYC, Oct. 4, 1946. Catholic U.
SARGENT, RICHARD (Richard Cox): Carmel, CA, 1933. Stanford.
SARRAZIN, MICHAEL: Quebec City, Can., May 22, 1940.
SAVAGE, JOHN (Youngs): Long Island, NY, Aug. 25, 1949. AADA.
SAVALAS, TELLY (Aristotle): Garden City, NY, Jan. 21, 1925. Columbia.
SAVIOLA, CAMILLE: Bronx, NY, July 16, 1950.
SAVOY, TERESA ANN: London, July 18, 1955.
SAXON, JOHN (Carmen Orrico): Brooklyn, Aug. 5, 1935.
SBARGE, RAPHAEL: NYC, Feb. 12, 1964.
SCALIA, JACK: Brooklyn, NY, 1951.
SCARPELLI, GLEN: Staten Island, NY, July 1966.
SCARWID, DIANA: Savannah, GA. AADA, Pace U.
SCHEIDER, ROY: Orange, NJ, Nov. 10, 1932. Franklin-Marshall.
SCHEINE, RAYNOR: Emporia, Va., Nov. 10th. VaCommonwealthU.
SCHELL, MARIA: Vienna, Jan. 15, 1926.
SCHELL, MAXIMILIAN: Vienna, Dec. 8, 1930.
SCHLATTER, CHARLIE: 1967, NYC, Ithaca Col.
SCHNEIDER, MARIA: Paris, Mar. 27, 1952.
SCHRODER, RICKY: Staten Island, NY, Apr. 13, 1970.
SCHWARZENEGGER, ARNOLD: Austria, July 30, 1947.
SCHYGULLA, HANNA: Katlowitz, Poland. 1943.
SCOFIELD, PAUL: Hurstpierpoint, Eng., Jan. 21, 1922. London Mask Theatre School.
SCOLARI, PETER: Sept. 12, 1956. Scarsdale, NY, NYCC.
SCOTT, DEBRALEE: Elizabeth, NJ, Apr. 2.
SCOTT, GEORGE C.: Wise, VA, Oct. 18, 1927. U. Mo.
SCOTT, GORDON (Gordon M. Werschkul): Portland, OR, Aug. 3, 1927. Oregon U.
SCOTT, LIZABETH (Emma Matso): Scranton, Pa., Sept. 29, 1922.
SCOTT, MARTHA: Jamesport, MO, Sept. 22, 1914. U. Mich.
SCOTT-TAYLOR, JONATHAN: Brazil, 1962.
SEAGAL, STEVE: 1951.
SEAGULL, BARBARA HERSHEY see Hershey, Barbara
SEARS, HEATHER: London, Sept. 28, 1935.
SECOMBE, HARRY: Swansea, Wales, Sept. 8, 1921.
SEGAL, GEORGE: NYC, Feb. 13, 1934. Columbia.
SELLARS, ELIZABETH: Glasgow, Scot., May 6, 1923.
SELLECK, TOM: Detroit, MI, Jan. 29, 1945. USCal.
SELWART, TONIO: Watenberg, Ger., June 9, 1906. Munich U.
SERNAS, JACQUES: Lithuania, July 30, 1925.
SERRAULT, MICHEL: Brunoy, France, 1928, Paris Consv.
SETH, ROSHAN: New Delhi, India, 1942.
SEYLER, ATHENE (Athene Hannen): London, May 31, 1889.
SEYMOUR, JANE (Joyce Frankenberg): Hillingdon, Eng., Feb. 15, 1951.
SEYRIG, DELPHINE: Beirut, 1932.
SHANDLING, GARRY: Tucson, Az, 1950, UAz.
SHARIF, OMAR (Michel Shalhoub): Alexandria, Egypt, Apr. 10, 1932. Victoria Col.
SHARKEY, RAY: Brooklyn, NY, 1952. HB Studio.
SHATNER, WILLIAM: Montreal, Can., Mar. 22, 1931. McGill U.
SHAVER, HELEN: St. Thomas, Ontario, Can., 1951.
SHAW, SEBASTIAN: Holt, Eng., May 29, 1905. Gresham School.
SHAW, STAN: Chicago, IL, 1952.
SHEA, JOHN V.: North Conway, NH, Apr. 14, 1949. Bates, Yale.
SHEARER, MOIRA: Dunfermline, Scot., Jan. 17, 1926. London Theatre School.
SHEEDY, ALLY: NYC, June 13, 1962. USC.
SHEEN, CHARLIE (Carlos Irwin Estevez): Santa Monica, CA, Sept. 3, 1965.
SHEEN, MARTIN (Ramon Estevez): Dayton, OH, Aug. 3, 1940.
SHEFFIELD, JOHN: Pasadena, CA, Apr. 11, 1931. UCLA.
SHEPARD, SAM (Rogers): Ft. Sheridan, IL, Nov. 5, 1943.
SHEPHERD, CYBILL: Memphis, TN, Feb. 18, 1950. Hunter, NYU.
SHIELDS, BROOKE: NYC, May 31, 1965.
SHIRE, TALIA: Lake Success, NY, Apr. 25, 1946, Yale.
SHIRLEY, ANNE (Dawn Evelyn Paris): Apr. 17, 1918 NYC.
SHORE, DINAH (Frances Rose Shore): Winchester, TN, Mar. 1, 1917. Vanderbilt U.
SHORT, MARTIN: Toronto, Can, Mar. 26, 1950, McMasterU.
SHOWALTER, MAX (formerly Casey Adams): Caldwell, KS, June 2, 1917. Pasadena Playhouse.
SHUE, ELIZABETH: 1964, South Orange, NJ. Harvard
SHULL, RICHARD B.: Evanston, Il, Feb. 24, 1929.
SIDNEY, SYLVIA: NYC, Aug. 8, 1910. Theatre Guild School.
SILVER, RON: NYC, July 2, 1946. SUNY.
SILVERMAN, JONATHAN: Los Angeles, Ca, Aug. 5, 1966, USCal.
SIMMONS, JEAN: London, Jan. 31, 1929. Aida Foster School.
SIMON, SIMONE: Marseilles, France, Apr. 23, 1910.
SIMPSON, O. J. (Orenthal James): San Francisco, CA, July 9, 1947. UCLA.
SINATRA, FRANK: Hoboken, NJ, Dec. 12, 1915.
SINCLAIR, JOHN (Gianluigi Loffredo): Rome, Italy, 1946.
SINDEN, DONALD: Plymouth, Eng., Oct. 9, 1923. Webber-Douglas.
SINGER, LORI: NYC, May 6, 1962, Corpus Christi, TX. Juilliard.
SKALA, LILIA: Vienna. U. Dresden.
SKELTON, RED (Richard): Vincennes, IN, July 18, 1910.
SKERRITT, TOM: Detroit, MI, Aug. 25, 1933. Wayne State U.
SKYE, IONE (Leitch):1971, Hollywood, Ca.
SLATER, CHRISTIAN: Aug. 18, 1969, NYC.
SLATER, HELEN: NYC, Dec. 15, 1965.
SMIRNOFF, YAKOV (Yakov Pokhis): Odessa, USSR.
SMITH, ALEXIS: Penticton, Can., June 8, 1921. LACC.
SMITH, CHARLES MARTIN: Los Angeles, CA, 1954. CalState U.
SMITH, JACLYN: Houston, TX, Oct. 26, 1947.
SMITH, JOHN (Robert E. Van Orden): Los Angeles, Mar. 6, 1931. UCLA.
SMITH, KURTWOOD: San Francisco, CA, 1942.
SMITH, LEWIS: Chattanooga, Tn, 1958. Actors Studio.
SMITH, LOIS: Topeka, KS, Nov. 3, 1930. U. Wash.
SMITH, MAGGIE: Ilford, Eng., Dec. 28, 1934.
SMITH, ROGER: South Gate, CA, Dec. 18, 1932. U. Ariz.
SMITHERS, WILLIAM: Richmond, VA, July 10, 1927. Catholic U.
SMITS, JIMMY: 1956, Brooklyn, NY. Cornell U
SNODGRESS, CARRIE: Chicago, Oct. 27, 1946. UNI.
SOFONOVA, ELENA: 1956, Russia
SOLOMON, BRUCE: NYC, 1944. U. Miami, Wayne State U.
SOMERS, SUZANNE (Mahoney): San Bruno, CA, Oct. 16, 1946. Lone Mt. Col.
SOMMER, ELKE (Schletz): Berlin, Nov. 5, 1940.
SOMMER, JOSEF: Greifswald, Germany, June 26, 1934.
SORDI, ALBERTO: Rome, Italy, June 15, 1919.
SORVINO, PAUL: NYC, 1939. AMDA.
SOTHERN, ANN (Harriet Lake): Valley City, ND, Jan. 22, 1907. Washington U.

Stella Stevens

Sting

Elaine Stritch

Rip Torn

Rachel Ward

John Travolta

SOUL, DAVID: Aug. 28, 1943.
SPACEK, SISSY: Quitman, TX, Dec. 25, 1949. Actors Studio.
SPANO, VINCENT: Brooklyn, NY, Oct. 18, 1962.
SPENSER, JEREMY: Ceylon, 1937.
SPINER, BRENT: Houston, Tx.
SPRINGER, GARY: NYC, July 29, 1954. Hunter Col.
SPRINGFIELD, RICK (Richard Springthorpe): Sydney, Aust. Aug. 23, 1949.
STACK, ROBERT: Los Angeles, Jan. 13, 1919. USC.
STADLEN, LEWIS J.: Brooklyn, Mar. 7, 1947. Neighborhood Playhouse.
STAFFORD, NANCY: Ft. Lauderdale, FL.
STALLONE, FRANK: NYC, July 30, 1950.
STALLONE, SYLVESTER: NYC, July 6, 1946. U. Miami.
STAMP, TERENCE: London, July 23, 1939.
STANDER, LIONEL: NYC, Jan. 11, 1908. UNC.
STANG, ARNOLD: Chelsea, MA, Sept. 28, 1925.
STANLEY, KIM (Patricia Reid): Tularosa, NM, Feb. 11, 1925. U. Tex.
STANWYCK, BARBARA (Ruby Stevens): Brooklyn, July 16, 1907.
STAPLETON, JEAN: NYC, Jan. 19, 1923.
STAPLETON, MAUREEN: Troy, NY, June 21, 1925.
STARR, RINGO (Richard Starkey): Liverpool, England, July 7, 1940.
STEEL, ANTHONY: London, May 21, 1920. Cambridge.
STEELE, TOMMY: London, Dec. 17, 1936.
STEENBURGEN, MARY: Newport, AR, 1953. Neighborhood Playhouse.
STEIGER, ROD: Westhampton, NY, Apr. 14, 1925.
STERLING, JAN (Jane Sterling Adriance): NYC, Apr. 3, 1923. Fay Compton School.
STERLING, ROBERT (William Sterling Hart): Newcastle, PA, Nov. 13, 1917. U. Pittsburgh.
STERN, DANIEL: Bethesda, MD, 1957.
STERNHAGEN, FRANCES: Washington, DC, Jan. 13, 1932.
STEVENS, ANDREW: Memphis, TN, June 10, 1955.
STEVENS, CONNIE (Concetta Ann Ingolia): Brooklyn, Aug. 8, 1938. Hollywood Professional School.
STEVENS, FISHER: Chicago, IL, Nov. 27, 1963. NYU.
STEVENS, KAYE (Catherine): Pittsburgh, July 21, 1933.
STEVENS, MARK (Richard): Cleveland, OH, Dec. 13, 1920.
STEVENS, SHADOE (Terry Ingstad): 1947.
STEVENS, STELLA (Estelle Eggleston): Hot Coffee, MS, Oct. 1, 1936.
STEVENSON, PARKER: CT, June 4, 1953, Princeton.
STEWART, ALEXANDRIA: Montreal, Can., June 10, 1939. Louvre.
STEWART, ELAINE: Montclair, NJ, May 31, 1929.
STEWART, JAMES: Indiana, PA, May 20, 1908. Princeton.
STEWART, MARTHA (Martha Haworth): Bardwell, KY, Oct. 7, 1922.
STILLER, JERRY: NYC, June 8, 1931.
STIMSON, SARA: Helotes, TX, 1973.
STING (Gordon Matthew Sumner): Wallsend, Eng., Oct. 2, 1951.
STOCKWELL, DEAN: Hollywood, Mar. 5, 1935.
STOCKWELL, JOHN: Galveston, Texas, March 25, 1961. Harvard.
STOLER, SHIRLEY: Brooklyn, NY, Mar. 30, 1929.
STOLTZ, ERIC: California, 1961, USC.
STORM, GALE (Josephine Cottle): Bloomington, TX, Apr. 5, 1922.
STRAIGHT, BEATRICE: Old Westbury, NY, Aug. 2, 1916. Dartington Hall.
STRASBERG, SUSAN: NYC, May 22, 1938.
STRASSMAN, MARCIA: New Jersey, 1949.
STRAUSS, PETER: NYC, Feb. 20, 1947.
STREEP, MERYL (Mary Louise): Summit, NJ, June 22, 1949., Vassar, Yale.
STREISAND, BARBRA: Brooklyn, Apr. 24, 1942.
STRITCH, ELAINE: Detroit, MI, Feb. 2, 1925. Drama Workshop.
STRODE, WOODY: Los Angeles, 1914.
STROUD, DON: Hawaii, 1937.
STRUTHERS, SALLY: Portland, OR, July 28, 1948. Pasadena Playhouse.
SULLIVAN, BARRY (Patrick Barry): NYC, Aug. 29, 1912. NYU.
SUMMER, DONNA (LaDonna Gaines): Boston, MA, Dec. 31, 1948.
SUTHERLAND, DONALD: St. John, New Brunswick, Can., July 17, 1934. U. Toronto.
SUTHERLAND, KIEFER: 1967, Los Angeles, Ca.
SVENSON, BO: Goteborg, Swed., Feb. 13, 1941. UCLA.
SWAYZE, PATRICK: 1952, Houston, Tx.
SWEENEY, DANIEL BERNARD: 1961, Shoreham, NY
SWINBURNE, NORA: Bath, Eng., July 24, 1902. RADA.
SWIT, LORETTA: Passaic, NJ, Nov. 4. 1937. AADA.
SYLVESTER, WILLIAM: Oakland, CA, Jan. 31, 1922. RADA.
SYMONDS, ROBERT: Bistow, AK, Dec. 1, 1926, TexU.
SYMS, SYLVIA: London, June 1, 1934. Convent School.
SZARABAJKA, KEITH: Oak Park, IL, Dec. 2, 1952, UChicago.
T, MR. (Lawrence Tero): Chicago, May 21, 1952.
TABORI, KRISTOFFER (Siegel): Los Angeles, Aug. 4, 1952.
TAKEI, GEORGE: Los Angeles, CA, Apr. 20. UCLA.
TALBOT, LYLE (Lysle Hollywood): Pittsburgh, Feb. 8, 1904.
TALBOT, NITA: NYC, Aug. 8, 1930. Irvine Studio School.
TAMBLYN, RUSS: Los Angeles, Dec. 30, 1934.
TANDY, JESSICA: London, June 7, 1909. Dame Owens' School.
TAYLOR, DON: Freeport, PA, Dec. 13, 1920. Penn State U.
TAYLOR, ELIZABETH: London, Feb. 27, 1932. Byron House School.
TAYLOR, ROD (Robert): Sydney, Aust., Jan. 11, 1929.
TAYLOR-YOUNG, LEIGH: Wash., DC, Jan. 25, 1945. Northwestern.
TEAGUE, ANTHONY SKOOTER: Jacksboro, TX, Jan. 4, 1940.
TEAGUE, MARSHALL: Newport, Tn.
TEEFY, MAUREEN: Minneapolis, MN, 1954; Juilliard.
TEMPLE, SHIRLEY: Santa Monica, CA, Apr. 23, 1927.
TERRY-THOMAS (Thomas Terry Hoar Stevens): Finchley, London, July 14, 1911. Ardingly College.
TERZIEFF, LAURENT: Paris, June 25, 1935.
TEWES, LAUREN: 1954, Pennsylvania
THACKER, RUSS: Washington, DC, June 23, 1946, Montgomery Col.
THAXTER, PHYLLIS: Portland, ME, Nov. 20, 1921. St. Genevieve.
THELEN, JODI: St. Cloud, MN., 1963.
THOMAS, DANNY (Amos Jacobs): Deerfield, MI, Jan. 6, 1914.
THOMAS, MARLO (Margaret): Detroit, Nov. 21, 1938. USC.
THOMAS, PHILIP MICHAEL: Columbus, OH, May 26, 1949. Oakwood Col.
THOMAS, RICHARD: NYC, June 13, 1951. Columbia.

THOMPSON, JACK (John Payne): Sydney, Aus., 1940. U. Brisbane.
THOMPSON, MARSHALL: Peoria, IL, Nov. 27, 1925. Occidental.
THOMPSON, REX: NYC, Dec. 14, 1942.
THOMPSON, SADA: Des Moines, IA, Sept. 27, 1929. Carnegie Tech.
THOMSON, GORDON: Ottawa, Can., 1945.
THORSON, LINDA: June 18, 1947, Toronto, Can. RADA
THULIN, INGRID: Solleftea, Sweden, Jan. 27, 1929. Royal Drama Theatre.
TICOTIN, RACHEL: Bronx, NY, 1958.
TIERNEY, GENE: Brooklyn, Nov. 20, 1920. Miss Farmer's School.
TIERNEY, LAWRENCE: Brooklyn, Mar. 15, 1919. Manhattan College.
TIFFIN, PAMELA (Wonso): Oklahoma City, Oct. 13, 1942.
TILLY, MEG: Texada, Can., 1960.
TODD, ANN: Hartford, Eng., Jan. 24, 1909.
TODD, RICHARD: Dublin, Ire., June 11, 1919. Shrewsbury School.
TOGNAZZI, UGO: Cremona, Italy, 1922.
TOLO, MARILU: Rome, Italy, 1944.
TOMEI, MARISA: Brooklyn, NY, Dec. 4, 1964, NYU.
TOMLIN, LILY: Detroit, MI, Sept. 1, 1939. Wayne State U.
TOOMEY, REGIS: Aug. 13, 1902, Pittsburgh, Pa.
TOPOL (Chaim Topol): Tel-Aviv, Israel, Sept. 9, 1935.
TORN, RIP: Temple, TX, Feb. 6, 1931. U. Tex.
TORRES, LIZ: NYC, 1947. NYU.
TOTTER, AUDREY: Joliet, IL, Dec. 20, 1918.
TOWSEND, ROBERT: Chicago, 1966.
TRAVERS, BILL: Newcastle-on-Tyne, Engl, Jan. 3, 1922.
TRAVIS, RICHARD (William Justice): Carlsbad, NM, Apr. 17, 1913.
TRAVOLTA, JOEY: Englewood, NJ, 1952.
TRAVOLTA, JOHN: Englewood, NJ, Feb. 18, 1954.
TREMAYNE, LES: London, Apr. 16, 1913. Northwestern, Columbia, UCLA.
TREVOR, CLAIRE (Wemlinger): NYC, March 8, 1909.
TRINTIGNANT, JEAN-LOUIS: Pont-St. Esprit, France, Dec. 11, 1930. Dullin-Balachova Drama School.
TRYON, TOM: Hartford, CT, Jan. 14, 1926. Yale.
TSOPEI, CORINNA: Athens, Greece, June 21, 1944.
TUBB, BARRY: 1963, Snyder, Tx., AmConsv.Th.
TUNE, TOMMY: Wichita Falls, TX, Feb. 28, 1939.
TURNER, KATHLEEN: Springfield, MO, June 19, 1954. UMd.
TURNER, LANA (Julia Jean Mildred Frances Turner): Wallace, ID, Feb. 8, 1921.
TURNER, TINA: (Anna Mae Bullock) Nutbush, Tn, Nov. 26, 1938.
TURTURRO, John: Brooklyn, NY, Feb. 28, 1957, Yale.
TUSHINGHAM, RITA: Liverpool, Eng., 1940.
TUTIN, DOROTHY: London, Apr. 8, 1930.
TWIGGY (Lesley Hornby): London, Sept. 19, 1949.
TWOMEY, ANNE: Boston, Ma, June 7, 1951, Temple U.
TYLER, BEVERLY (Beverly Jean Saul): Scranton, PA, July 5, 1928.
TYRRELL, SUSAN: San Francisco, 1946.
TYSON, CATHY: Liverpool, Eng., 1966, RoyalShakeCo.
TYSON, CICELY: NYC, Dec. 19, 1933, NYU.
UGGAMS, LESLIE: NYC, May 25, 1943, Juilliard.
ULLMANN, LIV: Tokyo, Dec. 10, 1938. Webber-Douglas Acad.
UNDERWOOD, BLAIR: 1964, Tacoma, Wa. Carnegie-MellonU
USTINOV, PETER: London, Apr. 16, 1921. Westminster School.
VACCARO, BRENDA: Brooklyn, Nov. 18, 1939. Neighborhood Playhouse.
VALANDREY, CHARLOTTE: (Anne-Charlotte Pascal) Paris, 1968.
VALLI, ALIDA: Pola, Italy, May 31, 1921. Rome Academy of Drama.
VALLONE, RAF: Riogio, Italy, Feb. 17, 1916. Turin U.
VAN ARK, JOAN: June 16, 1943, NYC. Yale.
VAN CLEEF, LEE: Somerville, NJ, Jan. 9, 1925.
VAN DE VEN, MONIQUE: Holland, 1957.
VAN DEVERE, TRISH (Patricia Dressel): Englewood Cliffs, NJ, Mar. 9, 1945. Ohio Wesleyan.
VAN DOREN, MAMIE (Joan Lucile Olander): Rowena, SD, Feb. 6, 1933.
VAN DYKE, DICK: West Plains, MO, Dec. 13, 1925.
VAN FLEET, JO: Oakland, CA, Dec. 30, 1919.
VAN DAMME, JEAN CLAUDE: 1961, Belgium.
VANITY (Denise Mathews): 1963, Niagra, Ont., Can.
VAN PATTEN, DICK: NYC, Dec. 9, 1928.
VAN PATTEN, JOYCE: NYC, Mar. 9, 1934.
VAN PEEBLES, MARIO: 1958, NYC, ColumbiaU
VANCE, COURTNEY B.: Detroit, MI, Mar. 12, 1960.
VARNEY, JIM: Lexington, KY, 1950.
VARSI, DIANE: Feb. 23, 1938, San Francisco, Ca.
VAUGHN, ROBERT: NYC, Nov. 22, 1932. USC.
VEGA, ISELA: Mexico, 1940.
VENNERA, CHICK: Herkimer, NY, Mar. 27, 1952. Pasadena Playhouse.
VENORA, DIANE: Hartford, Ct., 1952. Juilliard.
VENUTA, BENAY: San Francisco, Jan. 27, 1911.
VERDON, GWEN: Culver City, CA, Jan. 13, 1925.
VEREEN, BEN: Miami, FL, Oct. 10, 1946.
VICTOR, JAMES (Lincoln Rafael Peralta Diaz): Santiago, D.R., July 27, 1939. Haaren HS/NYC.
VILLECHAIZE, HERVE: Paris, Apr. 23, 1943.
VINCENT, JAN-MICHAEL: Denver, CO, July 15, 1944. Ventura.
VIOLET, ULTRA (Isabelle Collin-Dufresne): Grenoble, France.
VITALE, MILLY: Rome, Italy, July 16, 1938. Lycee Chateaubriand.
VOHS, JOAN: St. Albans, NY, July 30, 1931.
VOIGHT, JON: Yonkers, NY, Dec. 29, 1938. Catholic U.
VOLONTE, GIAN MARIA: Milan, Italy, Apr. 9, 1933.
VON DOHLEN, LENNY: Augusta, Ga., Dec. 22, 1958, UTex.
VON SYDOW, MAX: Lund, Swed., July 10, 1929. Royal Drama Theatre.
WAGNER, LINDSAY: Los Angeles, June 22, 1949.
WAGNER, ROBERT: Detroit, Feb. 10, 1930.
WAHL, KEN: Chicago, IL, 1957.
WAITE, GENEVIEVE: South Africa, 1949.
WAITS, TOM: 1949.
WALKEN, CHRISTOPHER: Astoria, NY, Mar. 31, 1943. Hofstra.
WALKER, CLINT: Hartfold, IL, May 30, 1927. USC.
WALKER, NANCY (Ann Myrtle Swoyer): Philadelphia, May 10, 1921.
WALLACH, ELI: Brooklyn, Dec. 7, 1915. CCNY, U. Tex.
WALLACH, ROBERTA: NYC, Aug. 2, 1955.
WALLIS, SHANI: London, Apr. 5, 1941.
WALSH, M. EMMET: Ogdensburg, NY, Mar. 22, 1935, Clarkson Col., AADA.
WALSTON, RAY: New Orleans, Nov. 22, 1917. Cleveland Playhouse.
WALTER, JESSICA: Brooklyn, NY, Jan. 31, 1940. Neighborhood Playhouse.
WALTERS, JULIE: 1950, London
WALTON, EMMA: London, Nov. 1962, Brown U.
WANAMAKER, SAM: Chicago, June 14, 1919. Drake.
WARD, BURT (Gervis): Los Angeles, July 6, 1945.
WARD, FRED: San Diego, Ca.
WARD, RACHEL: London, 1957.
WARD, SIMON: London, Oct. 19, 1941.
WARDEN, JACK: Newark, NJ, Sept. 18, 1920.
WARNER, DAVID: Manchester, Eng., 1941. RADA.
WARREN, JENNIFER: NYC, Aug. 12, 1941. U. Wisc.
WARREN, LESLEY ANN: NYC, Aug. 16, 1946.
WARREN, MICHAEL: South Bend, IN, Mar. 5, 1946. UCLA.
WARRICK, RUTH: St. Joseph, MO, June 29, 1915. U. Mo.
WASHINGTON, DENZEL: Mt. Vernon, NY, Dec. 28, 1954. Fordham.
WASSON, CRAIG: Ontario, OR, Mar. 15, 1954. UOre.
WATERSTON, SAM: Cambridge, MA, Nov. 15, 1940. Yale.
WATLING, JACK: London, Jan. 13, 1923. Italia Conti School.
WATSON, DOUGLASS: Jackson, GA, Feb. 24, 1921. UNC.
WAYANS, KEENEN IVORY: NYC, 1958. Tuskegee Inst.
WAYNE, DAVID (Wayne McKeehan): Travers City, MI, Jan. 30, 1914. Western Michigan State U.

Ann Wedgeworth

Wil Wheaton

Tuesday Weld

Gene Wilder

Alfre Woodard

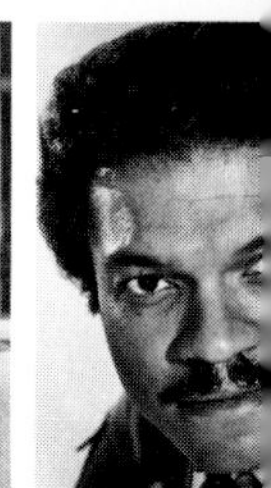
Billy D[...] Willia[...]

WAYNE, PATRICK: Los Angeles, July 15, 1939. Loyola.
WEATHERS, CARL: New Orleans, LA, 1948. Long Beach CC.
WEAVER, DENNIS: Joplin, MO, June 4, 1924. U. Okla.
WEAVER, FRITZ: Pittsburgh, PA, Jan. 19, 1926.
WEAVER, MARJORIE: Crossville, TN, Mar. 2, 1913. Indiana U.
WEAVER, SIGOURNEY (Susan): NYC, Oct. 8, 1949. Stanford, Yale.
WEBBER, ROBERT: Santa Ana, CA, Sept. 14, 1925. Compton Jr. Col.
WEDGEWORTH, ANN: Abilene, TX, Jan. 21, 1935. U. Tex.
WELCH, RAQUEL (Tejada): Chicago, Sept. 5, 1940.
WELD, TUESDAY (Susan): NYC, Aug. 27, 1943. Hollywood Professional School.
WELDON, JOAN: San Francisco, Aug. 5, 1933. San Francisco Conservatory.
WELLER, PETER: Stevens Point, Ws., June 24, 1947. AmThWing.
WELLES, GWEN: NYC, Mar. 4.
WESLEY, BILLY: July 1966, NYC.
WESTON, JACK (Morris Weinstein): Cleveland, OH, Aug. 21, 1915.
WHEATON, WIL: Burbank, CA; Jul. 29, 1972.
WHITAKER, JOHNNY: Van Nuys, CA, Dec. 13, 1959.
WHITE, BETTY: Oak Park, IL, Jan. 17, 1922.
WHITE, CAROL: London, Apr. 1, 1944.
WHITE, CHARLES: Perth Amboy, NJ, Aug. 29, 1920. Rutgers U.
WHITE, JESSE: Buffalo, NY, Jan. 3, 1919.
WHITE, VANNA: Feb. 18, 1957, North Myrtle Beach, SC
WHITMAN, STUART: San Francisco, Feb. 1, 1929. CCLA
WHITMORE, JAMES: White Plains, NY, Oct. 1, 1921. Yale.
WHITNEY, GRACE LEE: Detroit, MI, Apr. 1, 1930.
WHITTON, MARGARET: Philadelphia, PA., Nov. 30.
WIDDOES, KATHLEEN: Wilmington, DE, Mar. 21, 1939.
WIDMARK, RICHARD: Sunrise, MN, Dec. 26, 1914. Lake Forest.
WIEST, DIANNE: Kansas City, MO, Mar. 28, 1948, UMd.
WILBY, JAMES: 1958, Burma
WILCOX, COLIN: Highlands, NC, Feb. 4, 1937. U. Tenn.
WILDE, CORNEL: NYC, Oct. 13, 1915. CCNY, Columbia.
WILDER, GENE (Jerome Silberman): Milwaukee, Ws., June 11, 1935. UIowa.
WILLIAMS, BILLY DEE: NYC, Apr. 6, 1937.
WILLIAMS, CINDY: Van Nuys, CA, Aug. 22, 1947. LACC.
WILLIAMS, CLARENCE III: NYC, Aug. 21, 1939.
WILLIAMS, DICK A.: Chicago, IL, Aug. 9, 1938.
WILLIAMS, ESTHER: Los Angeles, Aug. 8, 1921.
WILLIAMS, JOBETH: 1953. Houston, Tx. BrownU.
WILLIAMS, ROBIN: Chicago, IL, July 21, 1952. Juilliard.
WILLIAMS, TREAT (Richard): Rowayton, CT. Dec. 1, 1951.
WILLIAMSON, FRED: Gary, IN, Mar. 5, 1938. Northwestern.
WILLIAMSON, NICOL: Hamilton, Scot; Sept. 14, 1938.
WILLIS, BRUCE: Penns Grove, NJ, Mar. 19, 1955.
WILLISON, WALTER: Monterey Park, CA., June 24, 1947.
WILSON, DEMOND: NYC, Oct. 13, 1946. Hunter Col.
WILSON, ELIZABETH: Grand Rapids, Apr. 4, 1925.
WILSON, FLIP (Clerow Wilson): Jersey City, NJ, Dec. 8, 1933.
WILSON, LAMBERT: Paris, 1959.
WILSON, NANCY: Chillicothe, OH, Feb. 20, 1937.
WILSON, SCOTT: Atlanta, GA, 1942.
WINCOTT, JEFF: 1957, Toronto, Canada.
WINDE, BEATRICE: Chicago, Jan. 6.
WINDOM, WILLIAM: NYC, Sept. 28, 1923. Williams Col.
WINDSOR, MARIE (Emily Marie Bertelson): Marysvale, UT, Dec. 11, 1924. Brigham Young U.
WINFIELD, PAUL: Los Angeles, May 22, 1940. UCLA.
WINFREY, OPRAH: Kosciusko, Ms., Jan. 29, 1954. TnStateU.
WINGER, DEBRA: Cleveland, OH, May 17, 1955. Cal State.
WINKLER, HENRY: NYC, Oct. 30, 1945. Yale.
WINN, KITTY: Wash., D.C., 1944. Boston U.
WINTERS, JONATHAN: Dayton, OH, Nov. 11, 1925. Kenyon Col.
WINTERS, ROLAND: Boston, Nov. 22, 1904.
WINTERS, SHELLEY (Shirley Schrift): St. Louis, Aug. 18, 1922. Wayne U.
WITHERS, GOOGIE: Karachi, India, Mar. 12, 1917. Italia Conti.
WITHERS, JANE: Atlanta, GA, Apr. 12, 1926.
WONG, RUSSELL: 1963, Troy, NY. Santa Monica Col.
WOODARD, ALFRE: Nov. 8 in Tulsa, Ok. Boston U.
WOODLAWN, HOLLY (Harold Ajzenberg): Juana Diaz, PR, 1947.
WOODS, JAMES: Vernal, UT, Apr. 18, 1947. MIT.
WOODWARD, EDWARD: June 1, 1930, Croyden, Surrey, Eng.
WOODWARD, JOANNE: Thomasville, GA, Feb. 27, 1930. Neighborhood Playhouse.
WOOLAND, NORMAN: Dusseldorf, Ger., Mar. 16, 1910. Edward VI School.
WOPAT, TOM: Lodi, WI, Sept. 9, 1951, UWis.
WORONOV, MARY: Brooklyn, Dec. 8, 1946. Cornell.
WORTH, IRENE: (Hattie Abrams) June 23, 1916, Neb. UCLA.
WRAY, FAY: Alberta, Can., Sept. 15, 1907.
WRIGHT, AMY: Chicago, Apr. 15, 1950.
WRIGHT, MAX: Detroit, MI, Aug. 2, 1943, WayneStateU.
WRIGHT, ROBIN: 1966, Texas.
WRIGHT, TERESA: NYC, Oct. 27, 1918.
WYATT, JANE: Campgaw, NJ, Aug. 10, 1911. Barnard College.
WYMAN, JANE (Sarah Jane Fulks): St. Joseph, MO, Jan. 4, 1914.
WYMORE, PATRICE: Miltonvale, KS, Dec. 17, 1926.
WYNN, MAY (Donna Lee Hickey): NYC, Jan. 8, 1930.
WYNTER, DANA (Dagmar): London, June 8, 1927. Rhodes U.
YORK, DICK: Fort Wayne, IN, Sept. 4, 1928. De Paul U.
YORK, MICHAEL: Fulmer, Eng., Mar. 27, 1942. Oxford.
YORK, SUSANNAH: London, Jan. 9, 1941. RADA.
YOUNG, ALAN (Angus): North Shield, Eng., Nov. 19, 1919.
YOUNG, BURT: Queens, NY, Apr. 30, 1940.
YOUNG, LORETTA (Gretchen): Salt Lake City, Jan. 6, 1912. Immaculate Heart College.
YOUNG, ROBERT: Chicago, Feb. 22, 1907.
YOUNG, SEAN: 1960, Louisville, Ky. Interlochen.
ZACHARIAS, ANN: Stockholm, Sw., 1956.
ZADORA, PIA: Hoboken, NJ. 1954.
ZAPPA, DWEEZIL: 1970, Hollywood, Ca.
ZETTERLING, MAI: Sweden, May 27, 1925. Ordtuery Theatre School.
ZIMBALIST, EFREM, JR.: NYC, Nov. 30, 1918. Yale.
ZUNIGA, DAPHNE: 1963, Berkeley, Ca. UCLA

OBITUARIES

AWRENCE W. BUTLER, 80, who won 5 Academy Awards for chnical achievements beginning with *The Thief of Bagdad* in 1940, ıd as recently as 1975, died of a heart attack when his pickup truck ·ashed October 19, 1988 in San Diego, CA. He was head of the ·ecial-effects department at Columbia Pictures in the 1940's, and his lms include *The Caine Mutiny, The Devil at 4 O'Clock,* and *'arooned.* No reported survivors.

VILLIAM J. CAGNEY, 82, New York-born film producer, actor, ·other and manager of the late James Cagney, died January 3, 1988 of a eart attack in Newport Beach, CA. After an early career as an actor in ome 10 films, including *Palooka,* he went on to produce such films as *ohnny Come Lately, Blood on the Sun, Kiss Tomorrow Goodbye, A ion in the Streets, The Time of Your Life* (featuring James Cagney and is sister Jeanne), and he was associate producer of *Yankee Doodle andy* and *Captains of the Clouds.* He is survived by a daughter and two ons.

VILSON CAMP, 74, screen actor, died March 12, 1988 in Tarzana, A. After an early career as a grip, he segued to an acting career in such lms as *Night of the Comet, Armed and Dangerous, Choose Me, Walk ike a Man, Valley Girl* (which featured his daughter, actress Colleen 'amp), and *Fatal Beauty.* He is survived by his wife, daughter and two ons.

OLIVE CAREY (Olive Golden) 92, actress and widow of Western ar Harry Carey, died March 13, 1988 in Carpenteria, CA. She made er screen debut in 1913 in D. W. Griffith's *The Sorrowful Shore* (with er future husband), followed by *The Soul Herder, Trader Horn, Rogue 'op, The Cobweb, The Searchers* (in which she played the mother of er own son, actor Harry Carey Jr.), *Two Rode Together, The Alamo, 'illars of the Sky, Night Passage, Gunfight at the O.K. Corral, Run of ıe Arrow,* and *Billy the Kid VS. Dracula.* She is survived by her son, aughter, sister, six grandchildren and seven great-grandchildren.

LUCIEN BALLARD, 84, Oklahoma-born cinematographer, died October 1, 1988 of injuries from a traffic accident in Rancho Mirage, 'A. He worked on more than 100 films during his 50 year career, ıcluding *Crime and Punishment, Band of Angels, The Wild Bunch, rue Grit, The Lodger* (among 5 films he photographed starring Merle Oberon, his wife from 1945–49), *The Caretakers* (1963 Academy Award nomination), many of the Three Stooges comedies, *Inferno* (in ·D), and *Rabbit Test,* before he retired in 1978. He is survived by a rother, two sons, six grandchildren and one great-grandchild.

ALLARD BERKELEY, 83, British-born screen, stage, and TV ctor, died January 19, 1988 in London. His films include *Chinese 'ungalow, In Which We Serve, See How They Run, East Meets West, he Outsider, They Made Me a Fugitive, The Wildcats, The Long Dark 'all,* and *Star!.* He is survived by his wife, a son and two daughters.

DeWITT BODEEN, 79, Fresno, CA-born screenwriter, and play-wright, died March 12, 1988 of bronchial pneumonia in Woodland Hills, CA. His screenplays include *Cat People, The Curse of the Cat 'eople, Seventh Victim,* and he also wrote or co-wrote *Yellow Canary, 'he Enchanted Cottage, Night Song, I Remember Mama, Mrs. Mike, 'he Girl from the Kremlin, Twelve to the Moon,* and *Billy Budd.* His ooks include *Ladies of the Footlights, Romances of Emma, The Films f Cecil B. DeMille, Chevalier: The Life and Films of Maurice Cheva-er,* and *13 Castle Walk.* The one time member of the executive board f the Writers Guild of America is survived by a sister and brother.

JOHN CARRADINE (Richmond Reed Caradine), 82, New York ·ity-born character actor of screen, stage, and TV who appeared in over 20 films in a career that spanned a half-century, and was the patriarch f an acting family, died November 27, 1988 of natural causes in Milan, aly. He played roles as disparate as Hamlet and Dracula, and his vast lm credits include *Tol'able David* (1930), *Bright Lights, The Sign of ıe Cross, The Invisible Man, Cleopatra, The Crusades, The Black Cat, 'ride of Frankenstein, Les Miserables, Cardinal Richelieu, Dimples, A Message to Garcia, Under Two Flags, The Prisoner of Shark Island, Ramona, Anything Goes, The Garden of Allah, Mary of Scotland, Daniel Boone, Winterset, The Hurricane, Captains Courageous, Of Human Hearts, Four Men and a Prayer, Alexander's Ragtime Band, Kidnapped, Submarine Patrol, Jesse James, Drums Along the Mohawk, The Hound of the Baskervilles, Stagecoach, Captain Fury, Five Came Back, The Grapes of Wrath* (as Preacher Casey), *Chad Hanna, The Return of Jesse James, Brigham Young—Frontiersman, Western Union, Blood and Sand, Son of Fury, Bluebeard, The Invisible Man's Revenge, The Mummy's Ghost, Adventures of Mark Twain, Fallen Angel, House of Frankenstein, House of Dracula, Johnny Guitar, The Kentuckian, Around the World in 80 Days, The Ten Commandments, The Court Jester, The Unearthly, The Story of Man-ind, The Last Hurrah, The Adventures of Huckelberry Finn, Tarzan the Magnificent, The Patsy, Boxcar Bertha* and *The McMasters* (with son David), *Myra Breckinridge, Hex* (with son Keith), *The Last Ty-coon, The Howling, House of the Long Shadows, Ice Pirates, Peggy Sue Got Married,* and *The Coven,* among others. He is survived by his five sons, actors David, Robert, Keith, Bruce, and Christopher (an architect), and several grandchildren.

EDWARD CHODOROV, 84, New York City-born screenwriter, playwright, and film producer, died October 9, 1988 after a brief illness at his home in New York City. Among the some 50 films he wrote or produced were *The Story of Louis Pasteur, The Hucksters, Road House, Craig's Wife,* and *Kind Lady.* He was blacklisted after refusing to assist the House Un-American Activities Committee in 1953, and later that same year his most successful play, *Oh, Men! Oh, Women!* opened to great success on Broadway. He is survived by his wife, two children, his brother, and two grandchildren.

WILD BILL CODY (Frederick Garfield Penniman), 75, character actor born on the Onondago Indian reservation in Syracuse who portrayed both cowboys and Indians in films in the 1930's and '40's, died October 25, 1988 in Evansville, Indiana. He made his last film, *Alien Outlaw,* in 1985. No further information provided.

BILLY CURTIS, 79, actor in more than 50 films, died of a heart attack November 9, 1988 in Dayton, Nevada. The 4ft.-2in. actor began in vaudeville, partnered with his sister Mary, and went on to appear in such films as *Terror of Tiny Town* (1938), *The Wizard of Oz, Hellzapoppin', Pygmy Island, Two Tickets to Broadway, The Incredible Shrinking Man, High Plains Drifter,* and *Eating Raoul.* Survived by his wife, three sons, a daughter and six grandchildren.

ALLAN CUTHBERTSON, 67, Australian-born screen actor, died February 8, 1988 in London. His more than 40 films include *The Guns of Navarone, Tunes of Glory, Term of Trial, Law and Disorder, The Informers, Seventh Dawn, Room at the Top, Life at the Top, Court Martial, Killers of the Kilimanjaro, The Brain, Rocket to the Moon, Performance, The Adventurers, Captain Nemo and the Underground Underwater City, One More Time, Nightmare Rally, Hopscotch, The Sea Wolves, The Mirror Crack'd,* and *Invitation to the Wedding.* He is survived by his wife and an adopted son.

HAZEL DAWN (Hazel LaTout), 98, Utah-born silent-screen star and celebrated singer and actress on Broadway in the early 1900's who was known as "The Pink Lady," died August 28, 1988 at the home of her daughter in Manhattan. She starred on Broadway in shows including the original *Ziefgfeld Follies* and in early silent films of the Famous Players, including *My Lady Incog.* and *Devotion.* She married Charles Gruwell, a Montana mining engineer in 1927 and gave up her career, making a brief comeback after his death in the film *Margie* in 1946. She is survived by her daughter, her son, and five grandsons.

DENNIS DAY (Eugene Denis McNulty), 71, Bronx-born Irish tenor and actor on screen, stage, TV, and radio, best known as Jack Benny's comic foil on his radio and TV shows, died June 22, 1988 after a long illness at his California home. His 25 year association with Benny [beginning in 1939] was one of the longest in broadcasting, and he appeared with other members of the Benny troupe in *Buck Benny Rides Again* in 1940, and in other films including *Music in Manhattan, The Girl Next Door,* and *I'll Get By.* He is survived by his wife, a brother, and 10 children.

PRISCILLA DEAN, 91, New York-born screen silent film actress, died December 27, 1987 in Las Vegas as a result of a fall the previous September. She began her film career at age 14 and went on to become a leading actress in such films as *The Gray Ghost, The Virgin of Stamboul, Under Two Flags, Outside the Law, Reputation, Conflict, Wild Honey, The Flame of Life, The White Tiger, Drifting, Storm Daughter, The Siren of Seville, A Cafe in Cairo, The Crimson Runner, West of Broadway, The Speeding Venus, Forbidden Waters, The Danger Girl, Birds of Prey, The Dice Woman, Jewels of Desire,* and *Behind the Stone Walls* (1932). Divorced from actor Wheeler Oakman and the widow of Gen. Leslie Arnold, there are no survivors.

GABRIEL DELL, 68, Brooklyn-born screen, stage, and TV actor, who first gained prominence as one of the original "Dead End Kids" on Broadway and in films, died July 3, 1988 of leukemia at his home in North Hollywood, CA. He acted in numerous films with the "Dead End Kids," also known as "The Bowery Boys" and "The Eastside Kids," and his many film credits include *Angels With Dirty Faces, Crime School, Little Tough Guy, They Made Me a Criminal, Angels Wash Their Faces, You're Not So Tough, Give Us Wings, Hell's Kitchen, Dress Parade, Hit the Road, Mob Town, Mr. Wise Guy, Let's Get Tough!, Tough As They Come, Smart Alecks, Neath Brooklyn Bridge, Kid Dynamite, Mug Town, Keep 'Em Slugging, Bowery Champs, Block Busters, Mr. Hex, Spook Busters, Hard-Boiled Mahoney, Bowery Buckaroos, Angel's Alley, Jinx Money, Fighting Fools, Angels in Disguise, Master Minds, Blonde Dynamite, Blues Busters, Triple Trouble, Framed, Earthquake, The Escape Artist,* and *The Manchu Eagle Murder Caper Mystery* for which he also co-wrote the screenplay. He is survived by two sons, actors Gabriel Jr. and Michael, and a sister.

John Carradine

Hazel Dawn

Dennis Day

Gabriel Dell

Divine

Jeff Donnell

AMAPOLA DEL VANDO, 78, Spanish-born screen, stage, and TV actress, died February 25, 1988 in Lake View Terrace, CA. She appeared in more than 50 films, including *Viva Villa, Snows of Kilimanjaro, Maracaibo, Flying Down to Rio, The Golden Hawk, Cowboy, The Burning Hills, The Appaloosa,* and *Justine,* among others. She is survived by her husband, producer Bill Gohl, and daughter.

I. A. L. DIAMOND (Itek Dommnici), 67, Rumania-born screenwriter, best known as associate producer and longtime collaborator of director Billy Wilder, died April 21, 1988 of cancer at his Beverly Hills home. His screenplays include *Murder in the Blue Room, Never Say Goodbye, Two Guys from Milwaukee, Always Together, Two Guys from Texas, It's a Great Feeling, The Girl from Jones Beach, Let's Make It Legal, Monkey Business, Something for the Birds, That Certain Feeling, Merry Andrew,* and *Cactus Flower,* and he collaborated with Wilder to write *Love in the Afternoon, Some Like It Hot, One Two Three, The Fortune Cookie, Irma La Douce, Kiss Me Stupid, The Private Life of Sherlock Holmes, The Front Page, Fedora, Avanti, Buddy, Buddy,* and *The Apartment,* which won them the Best Screenplay Academy Award as well as Oscars for Best Picture and Best Director. He is survived by his wife, Barbara Bently Diamond, his son, screenwriter Paul Diamond, his daughter Ann, and a grandson.

DIVINE (Harris Glenn Milstead), 42, Baltimore-born actor and singer of screen and stage, who rose to prominence with his comic-transvestite roles in such films as *Pink Flamingos* and *Female Trouble,* died March 7 in his room at the Regency Plaza Hotel in Los Angeles, while in town filming an episode of the TV series *Married with Children,* of natural causes due to an enlarged heart. The 300 pound-actor also starred in such films as *Roman Candles, Eat Your Makeup, Mondo Trasho, Multiple Maniacs,* and the mainstream *Lust in the Dust, Trouble in Mind,* and *Hairspray.* He is survived by his parents.

JEFF DONNELL, (Jean Marie Donnell) 66, Maine-born film and TV actress who played George Gobel's wife on the 1950's TV series *The George Gobel Show,* died April 11, 1988 of an apparent heart attack at her Hollywood, CA home. She appeared in more than 50 films, including *My Sister Eileen, What's Buzzin' Cousin?, A Night to Remember, Three is a Family, Over 21, Power of the Whistler, Cowboy Blues, Tars and Spars, The Unknown, Mr. District Attorney, Easy Living, In a Lonely Place, The Fuller Brush Girl, Walk Softly Stranger, Skirts Ahoy!, The First Time, Because You're Mine, The Blue Gardenia, The Magnificent Roughnecks, Sweet Smell of Success, My Man Godfrey, Gidget Goes Hawaiian, Gidget Goes to Rome, The Iron Maiden, The Comic, Tora!Tora!Tora!, The Thief of Damascus,* and *Stand Up and Be Counted.* She was most recently familiar to TV audiences as Stella Fields on ABC's *General Hospital.* She is survived by a son and daughter.

WARDE DONOVAN (Warde Donovan Tatum), 72, screen, stage, and TV actor, died April 16 in Los Angeles. His films include *The Slowest Gun in the West, The Private Navy of Sgt. O'Farrell, Gus, No Deposit, No Return, The Treasure of Macumbe, Hot Lead Cold Feet, MacArthur, The Apple Dumpling Gang, Herbie Goes Bananas,* and *The Devil and Max Devlin.* He is survived by his wife, actress-comedienne Phyllis Diller, two sons and one grandson.

ANDREW DUGGAN, 64, Indiana-born film and TV actor, known to television audiences for his starring roles in *Bourbon Street Beat, Lancer,* and *Room for One More,* died May 15, 1988 of throat cancer at his Los Angeles home. His film appearances include *Seven Days in May, Allied Dolphin, The Secret War of Harry Frigg, Patterns, The Chapman Report, In Like Flint, Three Brave Men, Merrill's Marauders,* and *Doctor Detroit.* He is survived by his wife, a son, two daughters, and a brother and sister.

FLORENCE ELDRIDGE (Florence McKechnie), 87, Brooklyn-born screen and stage actress who appeared with her husband, Frederic March, in films including *Another Part of the Forest* and on Broadway in plays including her most memorable role as Mary Tyrone in the original production of *Long Day's Journey Into Night,* died of natural causes August 1, 1988 in Santa Barbara, CA. She began her film career in 1928 in such films as *The Studio Murder Mystery* (opposite March) *Charming Sinners, The Greene Murder Case, The Divorcee, The Matrimonial Bed, Dangerously Yours, The Story of Temple Drake, A Modern Hero,* and from 1935 on only in films with her husband including *Les Miserables Mary of Scotland, An Act of Murder, Christopher Columbus,* and *Inherit the Wind* (1960). In 1978, three years after her husband's death, she appeared in the telefilm *First You Cry.* She is survived by her daughter, and four grandchildren.

MORGAN FARLEY, 90, Mamaroneck, NY-born screen, stage, and TV actor who was a prominent figure on Broadway in the 1920's and 30's, died of natural causes October 11, 1988 in San Pedro, CA. He appeared in such films as *Gentleman's Agreement, Macbeth, Flamingo Road, Goodbye My Fancy, Julius Caesar, High Noon, Jivaro, Hello Dolly!, Sextette, Soylent Green, At Long Last Love, Scorpio, Heaven Can Wait,* and *Dreamer.* Survived by a nephew and two nieces.

VIRGINIA FARMER, 90, screen and stage actress who founded the LA chapter of the Federal Theater Project in the 1930's, died May 19, 1988 in Long Beach, CA. Her films include *This Gun for Hire, Lady in the Dark, To Each His Own, Another Part of the Forest, Cyrano De Bergerac* and *The Men.* Her labeling as an unfriendly witness by the House Un-American Activities Committee impeded her career, and she later taught at the LA Actors Studio. No reported survivors.

PARKER W. FENNELLY, 96, Maine-born actor and playwright best known for playing Titus Moody on radio's *Allen's Alley* in the 1940's, and as spokesman for Pepperidge Farm products on radio and TV until 1977, died January 22, 1988 at his Peekskill, New York, home after a brief illness. His films include *The Whistle at Eaton Falls, The Trouble with Harry, It Happened to Jane, Angel In My Pocket, The Russians are Coming,* and *How to Frame a Figg.* No reported survivors.

MICHAEL FESSIER, 83, screenwriter for films and TV and author of short stories and novels, died of heart failure September 19, 1988 in Northridge, CA. His some 25 films include *You'll Never Get Rich, You Were Never Lovelier, Women are Trouble, Speed, Angels Wash Their Faces, It All Came True, Fired Wife, Greenwich Village, That Night With You, Slave Girl, The Woman They Almost Lynched,* and *Red Garters.* He is survived by his wife, former actress Lilian Bond, a son writer Michael Jr., a daughter, and five grandchildren.

BRAMWELL FLETCHER, 84, Yorkshire-born screen, stage, and TV actor best known for his performances in plays by George Bernard Shaw, died June 22, 1988 in Westmoreland, NH. He appeared is such films as *The Mummy* and *Svengali.* He is survived by his wife, a daughter and two sons.

GEORGE FOLSEY, 90, cinematographer who received 13 Academy Award nominations over a career that spanned 50 years, died November 1, 1988 in Santa Monica, CA. after a stroke and long illness. Best known for his collaborations with directors Vincent Minelli, George Cukor, Frank Capra, Ernst Lubitsch, Rouben Mamoulian and Busby Berkeley, his films include *Animal Crackers, State of the Union, Meet Me in St. Louis,* and his Oscar nominated work on such films as *Seven Brides for Seven Brothers* and *The Balcony.* In 1976 he made a brief comeback to film special footage of Fred Astaire and Gene Kelly for *That's Entertainment Part II.* He is survived by his wife of 61 years Angele, a son and two grandchildren.

ROSS FORD, 65, screen and TV actor, best remembered as Johnny Boone Jr. on the 50's TV series *Meet Millie,* died June 22, 1988 of cardiac arrest in Hollywood. He appeared in such films as *Sign of the Ram, He's a Cockeyed Wonder, The Adventures of Mark Twain, The Fuller Brush Man,* and *Jungle Patrol.* Survived by his wife, a son and daughter.

ındrew
Duggan

Florence
Eldridge

Bramwell
Fletcher

Leonard
Frey

Gert
Frobe

Lee
Goodman

OROTHY ADAMS FOULGER, 88, North Dakota-born screen ctress, died March 16, 1988 in Woodland Hills, CA. She appeared in ome 40 films, including *Shepherd of the Hills, Bedtime Story, So roudly We Hail, Laura, Since You Went Away, Fallen Angel, The Best ears of Our Lives, Miss Susie Slagle's, The Foxes of Harrow, Down to he Sea in Ships, Carrie, The Man in the Gray Flannel Suit, Johnny oncho, These Wilder Years, Gunman's Walk, The Big Country, From he Terrace,* and *The Good Guys and the Bad Guys*. Survived by two aughters, a sister, and three grandchildren.

IELVIN FRANK, 75, Chicago-born, writer, director, and producer, vho collaborated with Norman Frank for 38 years to create such iemorable films as *Mr. Blanding Builds His Dream House, White hristmas,* and the musical *Li'l Abner* on both stage and screen, died of omplications from open-heart surgery on October 13, 1988 in Los ıngeles. His more than 38 films include, *My Favorite Blonde, Thank 'our Lucky Stars, The Reformer and the Redhead, Road to Utopia, trictly Dishonorable, Above and Beyond, Callaway Went Thataway, he Court Jester, Knock on Wood, The Facts of Life, Strange Bedfel- ows,* and *The Road to Hong Kong*. He is survived by his second wife, a aughter, two sons and three grandchildren.

EONARD FREY, 49, Brooklyn-born screen, stage, and TV actor, vho received a 1971 Academy Award nomination for his portrayal of Motel in *Fiddler on the Roof,* died August 24, 1988 of AIDS in New 'ork. He first gained prominence off Broadway in *Boys in the Band* and ecreated his role of Harold in the 1970 film version. He also appeared ı such films as *The Magic Christian, Up the Academy, Tattoo,* and *'here the Buffalo Roam*. He is survived by a brother and a nephew.

ERT FROBE, 75, West German screen, stage, and TV actor, best nown for his portrayal of the title role of the villainous *Goldfinger,* ied of a heart attack September 4, 1988 in Munich. His many film redits include *Berliner Ballade* (1948 debut), *Those Magnificent Men ı Their Flying Machines, It Happened in Broad Daylight, Mr. Arka- 'in, The Girl Rosemarie, Her Crime Was Love, Special Delivery, Duel f Death, Prisoner of the Volga, The Crook and the Cross, Sing the Voods, The Longest Day, The Green Archer, The 1,000 Eyes of Dr. Iabuse, Three Penny Opera, Backfire, Greed in the Sun, Enough 'ope, A High Wind in Jamaica, Is Paris Burning?, Crook's Honor, 'riple Cross, Rocket to the Moon, Chitty Chitty Bang Bang, Monte 'arlo Or Bust, I Killed Rasputin, The Man Without a Face, Ten Little ndians, Invitation to Murder, The Twist, Cassandra Crossing, The 'erpent's Egg, Bloodline, Death of Freedom, The Umbrella Curse,* and *'he Holy Warrior*. He is survived by his fifth wife and two sons from revious marriages, Utz and Andreas.

HERIDAN GIBNEY, 84, New York City-born screenwriter, play- vright, and producer, who won two 1936 Academy Awards for his riginal story and screenplay for *The Story of Louis Pasteur,* died April 1, 1988 of cancer in Missoula, Montana. He wrote or collaborated on uch films as *I Am a Fugitive from a Chain Gang, The World Changes, merica Kneels, The House on 56th Street, Green Pastures, Anthony dverse, Letters of Introduction, Disputed Passage, Cheers for Miss 'ishop, Once Upon a Honeymoon, Our Hearts Were Young and Gay* which he also produced), *The Locket,* and *Everything But the Truth*. He erved as president of the Screen Writers Guild from 1930–41 and 957–48. Survived by his wife, two daughters, and grandchildren.

UGAR GEISE (Tanya Geise), 71, Chicago-born screen and stage ctress, dancer and popular cabaret performer of the 1940's, died October 30, 1988 in Hollywood after a brief illness. She appeared in uch films as *42nd Street, Sing Baby Sing, Swing Time, A Day at the 'aces, Shall We Dance, Collegiate, You're a Sweetheart, College 'wing, For Me and My Gal, A Lady Takes a Chance, The Crowded Sky,* nd *Advance to the Rear*. Survived by her husband, daughter and randdaughter.

LEE GOODMAN, 64, actor and nightclub comedian, died February 6, 1988 of complications from tuberculosis at his Manhattan home. After early successes in nightclubs with his longtime partner, James Kirkwood, he segued to Broadway and appeared in films including *Imitation of Life, Bachelor in Paradise,* and *The Music Man*. He is survived by a sister.

CHRISTOPHER GORE, 45, screenwriter, playwright, and lyricist, who won an Academy Award nomination for his screenplay for *Fame,* died May 18, 1988 of cancer in Santa Monica, CA. He is survived by his mother and three brothers.

ETHEL GRANDIN, 94, silent screen star whose career dated back farther than any other surviving performer, died September 28, 1988 in Woodland Hills, CA. She starred in such silent films as *Traffic in Souls, The Crimson Stain Mystery, Beyond Price, Garments of Truth, The Hunch, A Tailor-Made Man,* and with her own company, in partnership with her husband, cinematographer-director Ray Smallwood, in *The Adopted Daughter, The Burglar and the Mouse,* and *His Doll Wife,* before retiring in 1922. Her husband died in 1964.

CHARLES HAWTREY (George Hartree), 73, London-born screen, stage, and TV actor and legit producer, who appeared in 23 of the British *Carry On* film comedies beginning with *Carry On Sergeant* in 1958, died October 27, 1988 in Walmer, near London. His more than 50 other films include *Canterbury Tale, Passport To Pimlico, The Goose Steps Out, You're Only Young Twice, Brandy for the Parson, The Galloping Major, Who Done It?, Where's That Fire?, Good Morning Boys, The Terrornauts, Zeta One,* and *The Ghost of St. Michael's*. He is survived by his brother.

COLIN HIGGINS, 47, New Caledonia-born screenwriter and director, best known for his screenplay for the cult classic *Harold and Maude,* died August 5, 1988 of AIDS at his Los Angeles home. He also wrote *Silver Streak* and wrote and directed *Fould Play, 9 to 5, The Best Little Whorehouse in Texas* (co-author), and co-wrote and co-produced the ABC-TV miniseries *Out on a Limb*. He is survived by his parents and five brothers.

ANTHONY HOLLAND, 60, Brooklyn-born screen, stage, and TV actor, who had been suffering from AIDS for some time, committed suicide on July 9, 1988 in his Manhattan apartment. His films include *The Out-of-Towners, Oh, God!, Bye Bye Braverman, The Anderson Tapes, Klute, Lucky Lady, The Tempest, Popi, Hammersmith Is Out, Hearts of the West, Wise Guys,* and *All That Jazz*. Survived by his mother, a brother and a sister.

JOHN HOUSEMAN, 86, Bucharest-born, screen actor and producer, legit producer and director, opera director, TV producer, playwright, academic and autobiographer, who achieved fame and a 1974 Academy Award at age 71 for his role as Professor Kingsfield in *The Paper Chase,* which he recreated in the subsequent TV series, died of spinal cancer at his home in Malibu, CA. on October 31, 1988 (the 50th anniversary of the notorious Mercury Theatre of the Air broadcast of *The War of the Worlds* which he coproduced with Orson Welles) He produced such films as *Letter From an Unknown Woman, They Live By Night, Julius Caesar, On Dangerous Ground, The Cobweb, Executive Suite, Lust for Life, The Blue Dahlia, All Fall Down, Two Weeks in Another Town, In the Cool of the Day, This Property Is Condemned,* he was an uncredited collaborator on the *Citizen Kane* screenplay, and his films garnered 20 Academy Award nominations and won 7 Oscars, 5 of them for *The Bad and the Beautiful*. He also acted in such films as *Too Much Johnson* (Welles unfinished 1938 film), *Ill Met By Moonlight, Seven Days in May, Three Days of the Condor, St. Ives, The Cheap Detective, Old Boyfriends, The Fog, Ghost Story, Bright Lights Big City, Another Woman, Scrooged,* and *The Naked Gun*. His many honors include three Emmy Awards. He published three volumes of autobiography: "*Run-Through*" (1972), "*Front and Center*" (1979), and "*Final Dress*" (1983). He is survived by his wife and two sons.

Ethel Grandin

Colin Higgins

Bonita Granville

Anthony Holland

John Houseman

Trevor Howard

TREVOR HOWARD, 71, English-born screen, stage and TV actor, died January 7, 1988 in a hospital near London with his wife, actress Helen Cherry, at his side, after a brief illness. He gave memorable performances in some 80 films, including *The Way Ahead* (1944 debut), *Brief Encounter, I See a Dark Stranger, The Passionate Friends, They Made Me a Fugitive, Run for the Sun, Around the World in 80 Days, The Key* (British Film Academy Best Actor Award), *The Roots of Heaven, Sons and Lovers* (Academy Award nomination), *Mutiny on the Bounty, The Lion, Father Goose, Operation Crossbow, Von Ryan's Express, The Poppy Is Also a Flower, The Liquidator, Triple Cross, The Long Duel, Battle of Britain, Twinky, The Night Visitor, Kidnapped, Mary Queen of Scots, Pope Joan, Ludwig, A Doll's House, 11 Harrowhouse, Conduct Unbecoming, Aces High, Hennessy, The Bawdy Adventures of Tom Jones, The Passover Plot, The Last Remake of Beau Geste, Meteor, Superman, Hurricane, Light Years Away, The Sea Wolves, Windwalker, Gandhi, The Missionary, Sword of the Valiant, Foreign Body,* and *The Unholy,* to name just a few. He is survived by his wife of 44 years, actress Helen Cherry.

HOWARD JEFFREY, 53, Philadelphia-born choreographer, dancer, and producer of films and TV, died November 2, 1988 of AIDS in Los Angeles. He began his career as assistant to Jerome Robbins', on Broadway and for the film *West Side Story,* was Herbert Ross' assistant for *Inside Daisy Clover, Doctor Doolittle, Funny Girl,* and *Funny Lady,* Gene Kelly's assistant on *Hello, Dolly!,* and he choreographed *On a Clear Day You Can See Forever.* His producing credits include *The Seven Percent Solution, The Turning Point, Nijinsky, Divine Madness, Jinxed, Looker, To Be Or Not To Be,* and *Protocol.* He is survived by his mother and brother.

ERROL JOHN, 64, Trinidad-born screen, stage and TV actor and playwright, died July 10, 1988 in London. He acted in such films as *The African Queen, The Nun's Story, The Sins of Rachel Cade, Assault on a Queen,* and *Guns at Batasi,* and he is the author of plays including *Moon on a Rainbow Shawl.* Survived by his wife, two children and two grandchildren.

DUANE JONES, 51, Pennsylvania-born screen, stage, and TV actor and director, best known for his leading role in the cult classic *Night of the Living Dead,* died July 22, 1988 of a cardiopulmonary arrest in Mineola, NY. His other films include *Rise, Ganja and Hess, Beat Street,* and *Vampires* (1986). Survived by his mother, sister and brother.

JIM JORDAN, 91, screen, stage and radio actor, who is best remembered as Fibber McGee on screen and, for more than 20 years, on radio's *Fibber McGee and Molly,* died April 1, 1988 in Los Angeles, after being in a coma with a blood clot on his brain caused by a fall at his home a week earlier. Like the residents of 79 Wistful Vista Place in the series, the stars were married in real life, and Jim and Marian Jordan developed the characters during their early careers in vaudeville. He is survived by his second wife, Gretchen Stewart, and a son and daughter from his marriage to Marian, who died of cancer in 1961.

ROY KINNEAR, 54, British screen, stage, and TV actor, died of a heart attack September 20, 1988 in Madrid after falling from a horse during the filming of *The Last Return of the Three Musketeers,* in which he was reprising his role of Planchet, which he created in *The Three Musketeers* in 1974. His other films include *Help!, How I Won the War, A Funny Thing Happened on the Way to the Forum,* and *A Man for All Seasons* (1988). He is survived by his wife and three children.

HENRY KOSTER, 83, Berlin-born screenwriter, and director of such films as *Harvey, The Bishop's Wife, My Cousin Rachel, The Robe,* and *A Man Called Peter,* died September 21, 1988 in Camarillo, CA after a long illness. His some 40 films also include *Three Smart Girls, 100 Men and a Girl, First Love, Spring Parade, It Started With Eve, The Rage of Paris, Between Us Girls, Music for Millions, The Unfinished Dance, The Luck of the Irish, Come to the Stable, The Inspector General, Wabash Avenue, My Blue Heaven, No Highway in the Sky, Mr. Belvedere Rings the Bell, Stars and Stripes Forever, O'Henry's Full House, Good Morning Miss Dove, D-Day, The Power and the Prize, The Naked Maja, Flower Drum Song, Mr. Hobbs Takes a Vacation, Take Her She's Mine, Dear Brigitte,* and *The Singing Nun* (1966). He is survived by his wife, former actress, Peggy Moran, and two sons including assistant director Robert J. Koster.

MILTON KRASNER, 84, Philadelphia-born cinematographer who won a 1954 Academy Award for *Three Coins in the Fountain,* died of heart failure July 16, 1988 in Woodland Hills, CA. He lensed some 170 films, including *Golden Harvest* (1933), *You Can't Cheat an Honest Man, The Bank Dick, Buck Privates, Arabian Nights* (Oscar nominated), *The Ghost of Frankenstein, Pardon My Sarong, The Woman in the Window, Scarlet Street, The Dark Mirror, The Farmer's Daughter, The Egg and I, A Double Life, All About Eve* (Oscar nominated), *No Way Out, Monkey Business, O'Henry's Full House, Dream Wife, Desiree, The Seven Year Itch, Bus Stop, 23 Paces to Baker Street, An Affair to Remember* (Oscar nominated), *Boy on a Dolphin, Kiss Them for Me, A Certain Smile, Bells Are Ringing, Four Horsemen of the Apocalypse, Two Weeks in Another Town, The Courtship of Eddie's Father, Goodbye Charlie, The Sandpiper, King of Kings, How the West Was Won, Sweet Bird of Youth, Love With the Proper Stranger, The Singing Nun, Hurry Sundown, The St. Valentine's Day Massacre, The Sterile Cukoo, Beneath the Planet of the Apes,* and *Zachariah.* He is survived by a son, granddaughter and two brothers.

MILTON ROBERT KRIMS, 84, New York City-born screenwriter, novelist, former actor, and film editor and critic for Holiday magazine and the Saturday Evening Post from 1972–75, died of bronchopneumonia in Woodland Hills, CA. He had suffered from Parkinson's disease for many years. His more than 25 screenplays include *Dude Ranch* (1934, from his novel), *Speed, The Great O'Malley, Green Light, Secrets of an Actress, The Sisters, Confessions of a Nazi Spy, A Dispatch from Reuters, The Lady with Red Hair, The Iron Curtain, Prince of Foxes, One Minute to Zero, Crossed Swords, Tennessee's Partner,* and *Mohawk.* Survived by his wife, a daughter, stepson, two grandchildren, a sister and brother.

ERIC LARSON, 83, Utah-born veteran animator who during his 50 year career worked on all the Disney full-length animated films from *Snow White . . .* in 1933 to *The Great Mouse Detective* in 1986, and of the artists Walt Disney nicknamed his "nine old men," died October 25, 1988 at his home in La Canada-Flintridge, a suburb of Los Angeles. He is survived by two brothers.

ROBERT LIVINGSTON, 83, Illinois-born screen stage, and TV actor, best known as Stoney Brooke in Republic Pictures 29-film series *The Three Mesquiteers* in the 1930's, died March 7, 1988 of emphysema at his home in Tarzana, CA. He appeared in more than 100 movies between 1926 and 1975, including such films as *The Collegians* series, the *Lone Ranger* series (as the Lone Ranger), *The Band Plays On, West Point of the Air, Baby Face Harrington, Three Godfathers, The Bold Caballero, Come On Cowboys!, Renfrew of the Royal Mounted, Arson Racket Squad, Ladies in Distress, The Kansas Terrors, Pistol Packin' Mama, Beneath Western Skies, Storm Over Lisbon, Brazil, Steppin' in Society, Don't Fence Me In, Dakota, Valley of the Zombies, Daredevils of the Clouds, The Feathered Serpent, Mule Train, Night Train to Galveston, Once Upon a Horse, Girls for Rent, The Naughty Stewardesses,* and *Blazing Stewardesses.* In 1987 he received the Golden Boot Award for cowboy actors from the Motion Picture & Television Fund. He is survived by a son with the late Margaret Roach, daughter of Hal Roach.

PAUL FRANCIS (JIMMY) LLOYD, 69, Iowa-born screen and TV actor who made more than 250 films, died August 26, 1988 in Medford, Oregon. His films include *Calamity Jane, It's a Great Life, The Gallant Journey, Down to Earth, Snafu, Let's Go Steady,* and *Together Again.* He is survived by his wife, two sons, two daughters and a sister.

ane
nes

Roy
Kinnear

Bob
Livingston

Joshua
Logan

Ralph
Meeker

Kim
Milford

SHUA LOGAN, 79, Texas-born screen and stage director, pro-
·er, author, died July 12, 1988 at his New York home. He had been ill several years with supranuclear palsy. His list of Broadway suc-
ses includes *Annie Get Your Gun, Mister Roberts, South Pacific*, and Pulitzer Prize winning *Picnic*, and his film credits began in 1938 h *I Met My Love Again* (co-director), followed by *Picnic* (1955 :ar nomination), *Bus Stop, Sayonara* (Oscar-nominated), *South cific, Tall Story, Fanny, Ensign Pulver, Camelot*, and *Paint Your gon*. He suffered for many years from manic depression, which he ntioned in his autobiographies "*Josh, My Up and Down, In and Out* ?" (1976) and "*Movie Stars, Real People and Me*" (1978). He is vived by his wife, former actress Nedda Harrigan, a son, a daughter a stepson.

EDERICK LOWE, 86, Berlin-born composer who, with lyricist author Alan Jay Lerner, formed one of the most legendary part-
ships in the history of the American musical theatre, and col-
orated on musical plays and films including their masterpiece *My ir Lady*, died of cardiac arrest on February 14, 1988 in Palm Springs, . He will be remembered for his outstanding musical scores for the ge and screen versions of *Brigadoon, Paint Your Wagon, Gigi* (1959 ademy Award for Best Picture), *Paint Your Wagon, Camelot*, and ir final collaboration, *Little Prince*, written expressly for the screen 974. There are no survivors.

ARGERIE BONNER LOWRY, 83, Michigan-born silent screen ress, author, and widow of novelist Malcolm Lowry, died Septem-
28, 1988 in Los Angeles after being in ill health since suffering a ke several years ago. She appeared in such films as *Reno* (1923 ut), *Rapid Fire Romance, Riding Romance, A Made-To-Order ro, The Trail of Courage, The Four-Footed Ranger, Paying the ce* (with her sister Priscilla in 1927), *Daughters of Today, The cient Highway, Broadway Lady, High and Handsome, Secret Or-
s, Poor Girls*, and *Sinner's Parade*. Unable to make the transition to nd pictures, she wrote radio scripts and worked on animated films Walt Disney, wrote two novels, "*The Shapes That Creep*" and "*The st Twist of the Night*, and also published an unfilmed screenplay for *ider in the Night* written in collaboration with her husband. She is vived by her sister.

YTON LUMMIS, 84, New Jersey-born screen, stage, radio and actor with more than 50 films and 400 TV shows to his credit, died e 23, 1988 in Santa Monica, CA. He was seen in such films as *Ruby ntry, Androcles and the Lion, Prince of Players, My Sister Eileen, e Cobweb, The Court-Martial of Billy Mitchell, Compulsion, The d Seed, Julius Caesar, All I Desire, How to Marry a Millionaire, The oilers, A Man Called Peter, 20,000 Leagues Under the Sea, High iety, The Glenn Miller Story, The Wrong Man, Spartacus, From ll to Texas*, and *Elmer Gantry*. He is survived by his son.

LPH MEEKER, 67, Minneapolis-born screen, stage and TV actor o first achieved stardom on Broadway in the 1953 Pulitzer Prize-
nning play *Picnic*, died of a heart attack in Woodland Hills, CA. His cess on Broadway led to a career in films including *Teresa* (1951 ut), *Glory Alley, Four in a Jeep, Shadow in the Sky, Glory Alley, nebody Loves Me, Jeopardy, Code Two, Kiss Me Deadly* (as Mike mmer), *Big House USA, Desert Sands, A Woman's Devotion, Ada, ll of Noise, Gentle Giant, The Detective, The Devil's Eight, I Walk Line, The Happiness Cage, Love Comes Quietly, Brannigan, John-
Firecloud, The Alpha Incident, The Food of the Gods, Winter Kills, ths of Glory, Run of the Arrow, The Dirty Dozen, The St. Valentine's y Massacre, The Anderson Tapes*, and *My Boys are Good Boys*.

M MILFORD, 37, screen and stage actor and singer-composer, d June 16, 1988 of heart failure in Chicago, where he had undergone rt surgery several weeks earlier. He appeared in such films as *rvette Summer* and *Escape*. He is survived by his mother, brother and) sisters.

ELI MINTZ, 83, Polish-born screen, stage, and TV actor, best known as Uncle David in the stage, screen and TV versions of *The Goldbergs*, died of pneumonia June 8, 1988 in New Jersey. His film appearances include *Murder Inc.* and *The Proud Rebel*. He is survived by his wife, two daughters, and four grandchildren.

COLLEEN MOORE, 85, Michigan-born silent screen star, who commanded one of the highest salaries of her era and, at the peak of her career, inspired a fashion craze with her short skirts and Dutch Boy bob, died January 25, 1988 after a long illness at her ranch home in Templeton, CA. She made her screen debut at age 14, and appeared in some 100 films, between 1917 and 1934 including *Flaming Youth, The Perfect Flapper, Flirting With Love, So Big, Sally, Twinkletoes, Naughty But Nice, Her Wild Oat, Irene, Lilac Time, The Power and the Glory* (her personal favorite), *Smiling* and *Smiling Irish Eyes*, to name just a few. She also wrote four books, including her autobiography, "Silent Star." She is survived by her husband, Paul Maginot, a daughter, a son, and five grandchildren.

MARY MORRIS, 72, British screen, stage and TV actress, died October 14, 1988 in Aigle, Switzerland of unreported causes. Her films include *Prison Without Bars, Pimpernel Smith, Major Barbara, High Treason, Train of Events, Thief of Bagdad, The Man from Morocco, Undercover*, and *The Spy in Black*.

KEN MURRAY, 85, Manhattan-born actor, comedian, producer, director, author, and vaudevillian, who captured the golden age of Hollywood for over 38 years in 16mm home movies which he later edited into the 1979 film anthology *Ken Murray's Shooting Stars*, died October 12, 1988 in Burbank, CA. His film career began in *Half-Marriage* in 1929, and he also appeared in such films as *Leatherneck-ing, Ladies of the Jury, Crooner, Disgraced, From Headquarters, You're a Sweetheart, A Night at Earl Carroll's, Juke Box Jenny, The Marshall's Daughter, The Man Who Shot Liberty Valance, Son of Flubber, Follow Me Boys!*, and *The Power* (1968). He received a special Academy Award in 1947 for "novel and entertaining use of the medium" fantasy *Bill & Coo* which starred a cast of rigorously trained birds. His show *Ken Murray's Blackouts* set a record for the longest-running show in the history of Los Angeles, playing from 1942–49, and his CBS TV series *The Ken Murray Show* which he produced, directed and starred in was one of the top rated programs on the air from 1950 to '53. He wrote books including "*Life On a Pogo Stick*," "*The Body Merchant*," and the 1971 bestseller "*The Golden Days of San Simeon*." He is survived by his wife, son, two daughters and grandchildren.

ALAN NAPIER (Alan Napier-Clavering), 85, England-born screen, stage, and TV actor, best remembered for his role as Alfred Pennyworth the butler on the 1966–68 *Batman* TV series, died August 8, 1988 of natural causes in Santa Monica, CA. His more than 50 films include *Loyalties, The Four Just Men, The Invisible Man Returns, The House of the Seven Gables, Random Harvest, The Song of Bernadette, Cat People, Ministry of Fear, Thirty Seconds Over Tokyo, Joan of Arc, Appointment in Berlin, Lassie Come Home, Lost Angel, Hangover Square, The Hairy Ape, The Uninvited, Three Strangers, Forever Amber, House of Horrors, Sinbad the Sailor, Master Minds, Johnny Belinda, The Strange Door, Julius Caesar, The Court Jester, Young Bess, Desiree, Journey to the Center of the Earth, The Sword in the Stone, Marnie, My Fair Lady, Signpost to Murder*, and *The Paper Chase*. He is survived by a daughter, stepdaughter and three grandchildren.

CHRISTINE NORDEN (Mary Lydia Thornton), 63, British-born screen and stage singer, dancer, and actress, a protege of Sir Alexander Korda considered Britain's first postwar sex symbol, died September 21, 1988 of a chest infection in suburban London. She appeared in such films as *Night Beat*, (1947 debut), *Mine Own Executioner, Reluctant Heroes, Idol of Paris, The Interrupted Journey, Black Widow, An Ideal Husband, Saints and Sinners, A Yank Comes Back, A Case for PC 49*, and *Little Shop of Horrors* (1986). She is survived by her husband, a son, and a sister.

Eli Mintz

Greta Nissen

Ken Murray

Eva Novak

Alan Napier

Heathe O'Rour

GRETA NISSEN (Grethe Ruzt-Nissen), 82, Oslo-born leading lady of silent films, early talkies, and Broadway, died May 15, 1988 of Parkinson's disease in Montecito, CA. She appeared in such silent films as *Lost—a Wife, The King on Main Street, The Popular Sin, Blonde or Brunette, The Wanderer, The Lucky Lady, The Lady of the Harem, The Love Thief, Fazil, The Butter and Egg Man,* and the original version of *Hell's Angels,* in which she was replaced by a then-unknown Jean Harlow, when Howard Hughes decided to reshoot with sound, because her English was still poor. After studying English and virtually eliminating her accent, she made her first talkie, *Women of All Nations* (which required her to use a heavy Swedish accent!), followed by *Transatlantic, Ambassador Bill, Good Sport, The Silent Witness, Rackety Rax, The Unwritten Law, The Circus Queen Murder, Melody Cruise, Best of Enemies, Life in the Raw, Hired Wife, Luck of a Sailor, Spy 77* (aka *On Secret Service*), *Red Wagon,* and *Danger in Paris,* before retiring in 1937. No reported survivors.

EVA NOVAK, 90, St. Louis-born, screen and TV actress who began her career as one of Mack Sennett's Beathing Beauties, died of pneumonia April 17, 1988 in Woodland Hills, CA. Known for doing her own stunts, she was Tom Mix's leading lady in 10 films, including *Sky High* and *Trailin',* and also appeared in such films as *The Wild Seed, She Wore a Yellow Ribbon, Fort Apache, Stagecoach,* and *The Bells of St. Mary's.* She is survived by her sister, actress Jane Novak, two daughters, and 10 grandchildren.

VIRGIL OLIVER Jr., 72, actor who played bullies "Butch" and "Tuffy" in the *Our Gang* movie shorts of 1925, earning $7.50 a day until he outgrew the role, died June 8, 1988 in Baton Rouge, LA. No survivors reported.

HEATHER O'ROURKE, 12, a child star on screen and TV from the age of 5, died during emergency surgery for complications from a congenital disorder February 1, 1988 at Children's Hospital in San Diego, CA. She appeared in *Poltergeist, Poltergeist II* (in which she coined the now familiar tag line: "They're baaack!"), and *Poltergeist III.* She is survived by her parents.

PAUL OSBORN, 86, Indiana-born screenwriter and playwright, died May 13, 1988 in Manhattan. He wrote films including *The Young in Heart, Cry Havoc, Madame Curie, The Yearling, Portrait of Jennie, East of Eden, Sayonara, South Pacific,* and *Wild River.* His many plays include *On Borrowed Time, The World of Suzie Wong,* and *Morning's at Seven,* which earned him a 1980 Tony Award for best Broadway revival. He is survived by his wife, a daughter, and a grandaughter.

EMERIC PRESSBURGER, 85, Hungarian-born screenwriter, producer, director, and Academy Award winner who collaborated with his longtime partner Michael Powell to make such acclaimed films as *The Red Shoes* (Oscar nominated.) and *Tales of Hoffman,* died February 5, 1988 of bronchial pneumonia at a nursing home in Saxstead, England. After early films including *Abschied* (1930), *La Vie Parisienne, The Challenge, Contraband, 49th Parellel* aka *The Invaders* (1941 Academy Award for Best Original Story/Best Screenplay nomination), *One of Our Aircraft is Missing* (Oscar nominated and his first collaboration with Powell), *The Silver Fleet, Colonel Blimp, The Volunteer, A Canterbury Tale, I Know Where I'm Going, A Matter of Life and Death, Black Narcissus, The End of the River, The Small Back Room, Gone to Earth, The Elusive Pimpernel, Oh Rosalinda!,* and *The Battle of the River Plate* (aka *Pursuit of the Graf Spee*), and *The Boy Who Turned Yellow* (1972). He wrote, produced, and directed *Twice Upon a Time* and *Miracle in Soho,* and published two novels, *Killing a Mouse on Sunday* (filmed as *Behold a Pale Horse* in 1964) and *The Glass Pearls.* In 1983 he was invited to become one of the first Fellows of the British Film Institute, along with Powell. He is survived by his daughter and two grandsons.

KURT RAAB, 46, Czechoslovakia-born screen actor, screenwriter, art director and director, best known for his roles in many films by Rainer Werner Fassbinder, died of AIDS June 28, 1988 in Hambu He acted in some 14 Fassbinder films including *Why Does Herr R. R Amok?* (1969), *Love is Colder Than Death, The American Soldier, T Merchant of Four Season, Eight Hours Don't Make a Day, Jail Ba World on a String, Martha, Fox and His Friends, Fear of Fear* (also director), and *Bolwieser (The Stationmaster's Wife),* and in such oth films as *The Tenderness of Wolves* (also screenplay), *The Brutalizati of Franz Blum, Group Portrait with Lady, The Magic Mountain, Ang Harvest, Out of Order, Boarding School, Adolf and Marlene, Una Lock and Key, The Fall, Belcanto, How Do I Make It in the Movie Why the UFOs Steal Our Lettuce, Angel of Iron, Council of Lov Transit Dreams, Flies in the Light, Parker,* and he wrote and direct *The Island of the Bloody Plantation.* No reported survivors.

ELLA RAINES, 67, Washington-born screen and TV actress, leadi lady in such films as *Phantom Lady, Hail the Conquering Hero,* a *The Suspect,* died of throat cancer May 30, 1988 in Los Angeles. H some 20 films also include *Cry Havoc, Corvette K-255, The Stran Affair of Uncle Harry, Time Out of Mind, Tall in the Saddle, The We Brute Force, The Senator Was Indiscreet, Enter Arsene Lupin, T Runaround, White Tie and Tail, The Walking Hills, Impact, A Dange ous Profession, Singing Guns, The Second Face, Fighting Coa Guard, Ride the Man Down, A Man in the Road,* and she starred in 1953–54 NBC-TV series *Janet Dean-Registered Nurse.* Two daughte and a grandaughter survive.

ANNE RAMSEY, 59, Nebraska-born screen and stage actress w climaxed her 37 year career by achieving stardom and a 1988 Acader Award nomination for her performance as Momma in *Throw Mom From the Train,* died August 11, 1988 of throat cancer in Los Angele Her other films include her screen debut opposite her husband, Log Ramsey, in *The Sporting Club* (1971), as well as *Up the Sandbox, F Pete's Sake, The New Centurions, Goin' South, The Black Marb National Lampoon's Class Reunion, The Goonies, Weeds, Any Whi Way You Can, Scrooged, Dr. Hackenstein, Homer and Eddie,* a *Good Ole Boy.* In addition to her husband, she is survived by her fath a brother and sister.

ADELA ROGERS ST. JOHNS, 94, Los Angeles-born journali author, screenwriter, and Hollywood chronicler, known as "Moth Confessor of Hollywood" and "the world's greatest girl reporter" in 1920's and 30's, died in Arroyo Grande, CA. Considered by her pe to be "a tough, hard newspaper woman, one of the guys . . . a figu from the old roaring days of Hearst journalism, which no longer live She began reporting in 1913, and her filmed novels include *The S Rocket, A Free Soul,* and *The Single Standard.* She wrote the stories such films as *The Great Man's Lady, Government Girl, That Brenn Girl, Smart Woman,* and *The Girl Who Had Everything.* Her bestselle include *Final Verdict* (about her father, criminal attorney Earl Roger *Tell No Man, The Honeycomb* (her 1969 autobiography), *How to Wr a Short Story, Affirmative Prayer in Action, Some Are Born Gre Love, Laughter and Tears—My Hollywood,* and *No Goodbyes.* She w awarded the Medal of Freedom by President Nixon in 1970. She survived by a daughter, son Mac, former journalist and current busine agent for Intl. Publicists Guild Local 818, son Richard, a producer, a 10 grandchildren.

BILLIE RHODES, 93, San Francisco-born stage, vaudeville a silent-screen star, died March 12, 1988 in Los Angeles. She made h screen debut in 1913 in *Perils of the Sea,* followed by some 200 fil including *Almost a King, And the Best Man Won, Their Friend t Burglar, Father's Helping Hand, A Seminary Scandal, Some Nurs Beware of Blondes, The Lion and the Lamb, Girl of My Dreams, T Love Call, His Pajama Girl, The Star Reporter, Leave It To Gerry* a *Fires of Youth.* To name a few. In recent years she had teamed w ragtime pianist Galen Wilkes, with whom she performed as recently two weeks before her death. No reported survivors.

'lla
aines

Billie
Rhodes

Irene
Rich

Renato
Salvatori

Victoria
Shaw

Mona
Washbourne

.ENE RICH, 96, Buffalo-born silent-film star and radio star of *Dear* *hn* in the 1930's, died April 22, 1988 of heart failure at her home in pe Ranch, CA. Her most notable films include *Lady Windermere's n, Craig's Wife, Jes' Call Me Jim, They Had to See Paris, That rtain Age, The Lady in Question, Fort Apache,* and *Joan of Arc.* She survived by two daughters, and two grandsons.

EORGE ROSE, 68, British-born actor of screen and stage, was led May 5, 1988 by four men, including his adopted son and the ung man's biological father, near his vacation home in the Dominican public. One of the most beloved actors on the Broadway stage, where earned two Tony Awards and three other Tony Award nominations, appeared in more than 30 films, beginning with *The Pickwick Papers* 952), and including *A Night to Remember, Hawaii,* and *The Pirates of nzance.* There are no survivors.

AL ROSSON, 93, New York City-born cinamatographer who ceived an honorary Academy Award in 1936 for pioneering tech-color work on *The Garden of Allah,* and was Oscar nominated for *om Town, Thirty Seconds Over Tokyo, The Asphalt Jungle,* and *The d Seed,* died of natural causes September 6, 1988 at his home in Palm ach, FL. His first film was *David Harum* in 1915, and his many edits include *Abie's Irish Rose, Treasure Island, Captains urageous, The Wizard of Oz, The Squaw Man, Gentlemen Prefer ondes, Tarzan the Ape Man, Duel in the Sun, My Brother Talks to orses, On the Town, Singin' in the Rain, The Asphalt Jungle, The Red dge of Courage, Pete Kelly's Blues, The Actress, A Star is Born, El rado* (1967), and several films with Jean Harlow, who became his fe (for eight months) in 1933, including *Red Dust, Bombshell, d-Headed Woman,* and *Hold Your Man.* No reported survivors.

ENATO SALVATORI, 55, Italian-born character actor in some 70 ms, died March 27, 1988 in Rome of cirrhosis of the liver. He peared in such films as *Three Girls from Rome, The Three Corsairs, blic Opinion, Jolanda, Daughter of the Black Corsair, Poor But autiful, Grandmother Sabella, Poor Millionaires, One Night in me, Big Deal on Madonna Street, Fiasco in Milan, Marisa the Flirt, ngerous Wives, The Professor, Two Women, Day of the Lion, The ortest Day, Una Bella Grinta (Reckless), Of Flesh and Blood, sorder, Harem, Three Nights of Love, Z, Burn, The Burglars, State Siege, The Light at the Edge of the World, A Brief Vacation, Face of a y, The Last Woman, Illustrious Corpses, Ernesto, Rendezvous With yous Death, Twilight Travelers, Lost Objects, La Luna, Tragedy of a diculous Man, Louisiana* (1985), and he acted with his wife, Annie rardot, in *Rocco and His Brothers, Le Gitan (The Gypsy), The ganizer, Smog,* and *The Suspect.* He is survived by his daughter, tress Giulia Salvatori (who made her screen debut opposite Giradot in *Vie Continue*), and a son.

ICTORIA SHAW (Jeanette Elphic) 53, Australian-born screen tress, died August 17, 1988 near Sydney after a battle with asthma. er films include *Cattle Station, The Eddy Duchin Story, Edge of ernity, The Crimson Kimono, I Aim at the Stars, To Trap a Spy, varez Kelly,* and *Westworld.* Formerly married to actor Roger Smith, e is survived by two sons, a daughter, her mother, three sisters and a other.

UCKER SMITH, 52, Philadelphia-born actor-singer-dancer on reen, stage, and TV, best known for his memorable performance of *'ool"* in the Academy Award-winning *West Side Story,* died Decem-r 22, 1988 of cancer in Los Angeles. He moved from Broadway to the g screen and appeared in *Hearts of the West, How To Succeed in isiness Without Really Trying, To Be or Not To Be, Harry and Walter o to New York, At Long Last Love,* and others. He is survived by three sters.

BRAHAM SOFAER, 91, English-born actor of screen, stage and V, died of congestive heart failure January 21, 1988 in Woodland lls, CA. He appeared in such films as *Dreyfus, The Wandering Jew, embrandt, The Voice in the Night, Christopher Columbus, Quo Vadis, Pandora and the Flying Dutchman, His Majesty O'Keefe, The Naked Jungle, Elephant Walk, Bhowani Junction, The First Texan, The Sad Sack, Taras Bulba, Captain Sinbad, Twice-Told Tales, The Greatest Story Ever Told, Journey to the Center of Time, Che, King of Kings, Justine,* and *Chisum.* He is survived by his wife, a son, four daughters, and seven grandchildren.

MILTON SPERLING, 76, New York City-born screenwriter and producer who received a 1955 Academy Award nomination for *The Court-Martial of Billy Mitchell,* died August 26, 1988 after a long illness at his Beverly Hills home. His other films include *Sing Baby Sing, Sun Valley Serenade, South of St. Louis, The Enforcer, Marjorie Morningstar, The Bramble Bush,* and *Captain Apache.* Survived by his wife of 23 years, three daughters, a son and nine grandchildren.

PAOLO STOPPA, 81, one of Italy's foremost screen and stage actors, died May 1, 1988 of complications from leukemia in Rome. His many film appearances include *Becket, Rocco and His Brothers, Behold a Pale Horse,* and *Once Upon a Time in the West.* No reported survivors.

MONA WASHBOURNE, 84, England-born screen and stage actress, died November 15, 1988 in London of unreported causes. Her many screen credits include *Billy Liar, Night Must Fall, My Fair Lady, Maytime in Mayfair, To Dorothy a Son, The Collector, The Bluebird, The Winslow Boy, If . . ., O Lucky Man, What Became of Jack and Jill?, Fragment of Fear, Cast a Dark Shadow, A Cry from the Streets, Count Your Blessings, Mrs. Brown You've Got a Lovely Daughter, The Third Day, Brides of Dracula, The Good Companions, Doctor in the House, Child's Play, The Bed Sitting Room, The Games, Romeo and Juliet,* (1971), and *The Blue Bird.* No survivors reported.

KENNETH WILLIAMS, 62, British-born screen, stage, TV, and radio actor, died of undisclosed causes March 15, 1988 at his London home. He starred in 22 of the farcical British *Carry On* movies, including *Carry on Sergeant, Carry on Camping,* and *Carry on Cleopatra.* No reported survivors.

LOIS WILSON, 93, Alabama-born screen, stage, and TV actress whose best known roles were Molly Wingate in *The Covered Wagon* (1923) and Daisy Buchanan in *The Great Gatsby* (1926), died of pneumonia March 3, 1988 in Reno, Nev. She made her screen debut in 1915 in *The Dumb Girl of Portici,* and subsequently appeared in more than 100 films during the next 33 years, opposite such leading men as Rudolph Valentino and John Gilbert. She retired from films in 1941 except for a brief film comeback in *The Girl From Jones Beach* in 1949 and appeared on Broadway and TV. No reported survivors.

BONITA GRANVILLE WRATHER, 65, Manhattan born screen and TV actress, producer, philanthropist, and longtime executive of the Wrather Corporation, founded by her late husband, Jack Wrather, died of cancer October 11, 1988 in Santa Monica, CA. She appeared in more than 50 films including *Westward Passage* (her debut at age 7), *These Three,* (for which she received a 1936 Oscar nomination), *Ah, Wilderness The Plough and the Stars, Maid of Salem, Quality Street, Now Voyager, Hitler's Children, Calvacade, The Guilty,* and the *Nancy Drew* series. She retired from the screen in 1947 to marry Wrather, appearing occasionally in teleplays plays, and became associate producer of the *Lassie* TV series, and subsequently the film *The Magic of Lassie.* She was the chairman of the American Film Institute. For her work on *Lassie* and her work in behalf of environmental conservation, she received a Boy Scouts of America National Award and a National 4-H Congress Conservation Award. She is survived by two daughters, a son and nine grandchildren.

MARTIN WYLDECK, 74, British character actor on screen, stage, and TV, died in 1988 in London. Film credits include *Night Must Fall* (1964 remake), *That Kind of Girl, The Return of Mr. Moto, Robbery, The Oblong Box, The Bushbaby, A Touch of the Other, Cool It Carol, Die Screaming Marianne, The Four Dimensions of Greta, Tiffany Jones, Universal Soldier, The Shadow Line,* and *Exchange and Divide.* Survived by his wife, a son and two daughters.

INDEX